Poor
but
Proud

The University of
Alabama Press

Tuscaloosa and
London

Wayne
Flynt

Poor but Proud

Alabama's Poor Whites

Manufactured in the United States of America

Publication of this book was made possible,
in part, by a grant from the Auburn University
Humanities Fund.

Library of Congress Cataloging-in-Publication Data

Flynt, J. Wayne, 1940–
  Poor but proud.

  Bibliography: p.
  Includes index.
    1. Rural development—Alabama.   2. Rural poor—
Alabama.   3. Alabama—Rural conditions.   1. Title.
HN79.A133C64   1989   305.5′69′09761   88-20859
ISBN 0-8173-0424-X (alk. paper)
British Library Cataloguing-in-Publication Data available.

TO ANCESTORS REMEMBERED

Julius Homer and Annie Phoebe Flynt

Felix Maxwell and Shirley Belle Moore

Lou Allen and Mae House

Harris Washington and Julia Ann Smith

CONTENTS

PART FOUR   DISRUPTION AND INTEGRATION

PREFACE

The most fundamental question concerning Alabama's poor whites is also the hardest to answer: how does one define them? Although poor whites were often powerless, that was not always the case. In the antebellum years an alliance of yeomen and poor whites controlled a substantial share of political power, perhaps greater than that of planters. In later years, various organizations of poor whites, sometimes allied with blacks, wielded power through labor unions and political factions. Certainly "poor" does not refer to culture, for their culture sustained a remarkable sense of pride and dignity. Through religious and musical expressions, crafts, and lore, poor people created a subculture that had meaning to them, that survived various homogenizing influences, and one that they often considered superior to the culture of their economic "betters." All generalizations contain exceptions, and some poor whites consistently stood outside the state's political, social, and cultural institutions. To the extent that "poor white trash" had any meaning at all, it described a small residue of people who may be distinguished not only from middle and upper class whites but from impoverished poor whites as well. Refusing to pursue whatever meager opportunities came their way, they were satisfied with a subsistence existence consisting of a bit of corn and whiskey, freedom to hunt and fish whenever they chose, the most casual kind of living arrangements with the opposite sex, little effort at child rearing, and no institutional involvement in churches, political parties, farmers' organizations, or schools. Illiterate and transient, they moved through Alabama's history like a shadow, leaving little if any impression. But most poor whites occasionally made their mark on church rolls, census lists, union membership, or voting records. Striving, not accomplishment, often became their legacy.

Although degenerate poor whites appear only infrequently in the historical record, they dominate the fictional accounts of the white bottom class. From the southwestern humorists to Harper Lee, poor whites appear as an object of satire and scorn, characterized by shiftlessness, racism, violence, and demagoguery. Perhaps every society feels compelled to rationalize to itself the presence of so many poor people. What better way than to depict them as receiving what they deserve, suffering the consequences of their own failure of will. Blacks could be summarily dismissed; theirs was a racial failure, an inadequacy decreed by birth. But how could one explain more than half Alabama's Caucasian population living in substandard housing and earning a salary inadequate for proper clothing and health? How could one explain extensive child labor and widespread landlessness? And what prevented such people from recognizing the commonality of their grievances with those of poor blacks? Why did racial caste loom so much larger than economic class?

I have chosen to address these questions more in thematic than chronological fashion. Obviously events of epochal proportions swept across the South, affecting every layer of society. The Civil War and the Great Depression of the 1930s come to mind. But for the most part, those events which punctuate the human experience and provide it chronological structure—political administrations, economic cycles, technological innovations—changed their lives without substantially improving them. Certainly that was true in the short term, though sometimes the delayed effects were more helpful. For that reason I have described poor white experiences in four major patterns.

The first two chapters trace the rural origins of poverty, the first migrations to industrial jobs, and the cataclysmic and disruptive effect of the Civil War on once-prosperous yeomen and planters as well as poor whites.

The second set of chapters treats poverty by occupation. Poor whites were absorbed from their marginal existence on the fringe of the antebellum economy into important places in the tenant, timber, textile, mining, and iron-making systems. These chapters span the years from 1865 to the 1930s, years during which the South remained essentially an isolated regional labor market.

The third set of chapters examines the poor across occupational lines. Though differing in many ways from occupation to occupation, they were remarkably alike in society, culture, and political powerlessness. If focus on occupation tends to fracture the poor white experience, attention to the social and cultural patterns tends to unify it.

The final two chapters examine the painful process of economic and social integration. Well-intentioned liberals set in motion during the 1930s enormously disruptive forces. These forced millions off the land in a process that was probably both inevitable and in the long run beneficial. But the short-term consequences of the collapse of the regional southern economy and the integration of southerners into a national market for unskilled labor brought interregional migration, severance from kin and neighbors, shock to institutions such as churches, and great personal anguish.

Within these four broad patterns the organizing principle for this study will be social and economic. From the antebellum years until the Second World War, membership in certain occupational groups generally qualified one for the designation "poor white." So pervasive was the assumption about "nigger work" jobs that some whites avoided those occupations because of the stigma attached; but most were only too glad to obtain any work with a cash income however small.

Farming, the first category, is elemental and also the key to all the others. Farmers without land—whether called farm laborers, tenants, or sharecroppers—stood at the bottom of the economic ladder. Even as late as the 1930s, New Deal agencies reached them last, offered them least, and deserted them first.

So desperate was agricultural poverty that landless farmers sought almost any source of alternate employment. Although industrial jobs held brighter prospects in the long run, the wage system improved their lot only marginally over the short term. Alabama's poorly developed economy offered few choices at any rate, none of them good. Birmingham's steel industry probably afforded the best opportunities, though many of the early steelworkers might argue that point. Beneath them came miners (mainly of coal, but also iron ore and even gold), textile workers, timber and sawmill operatives. Together these occupations regularly accounted for a substantial majority of Alabama's gainfully employed manufacturing and industrial employees. All were low wage and labor intensive.

Obviously not every sharecropper, textile worker, or sawmill operative was poor. Occasionally a young married man would sharecrop his father's land as a temporary stage between youthful dependence and middle class yeomanry. Some highly skilled industrial workers earned good salaries. But miners and mill workers usually earned less than a dollar a day until well into the twentieth century, and sharecroppers far less than that. Workers missed shifts because of sickness, and few industries operated every day. Textile mills shut down because of drought that dried up the streams that powered them or when cotton supplies ran short. Heavy rains kept lumber workers out of forests. Gas buildups forced miners from their dark corridors. So most industrial workers usually earned between two and three hundred dollars annually regardless of their daily rate.

Their low economic status, lack of educational opportunity, and increasing self-consciousness divided Alabamians along class lines. Even religious groups organized around economic interests. Only race proved a cement strong enough to bind whites together. Caste counted for most; but when society accepted the principle of white superiority, whites could then divide into relatively distinct classes.

Although economics and occupations provide the structure for this study, they do not tell the entire story. In fact they do not even reveal the most interesting parts. The arresting segment of the historical drama is the human dimension. So my task is twofold: to present the abstractions, categories, and generalizations; then to introduce the people whose lives provide sinew and flesh to the dry bones. My goal is not to provide a book about abstract theories of history or a sociological and economic statement about ideology and class, as important as these may be. I prefer to tell the story of a people, how they arrived at their low status, how they coped, retained their dignity, and made sense out of their world.

It is my hope that those who read may understand that this story is no work of fiction from another land. It is the story of my ancestors and those of most white Alabamians now living in the relative affluence of the last years of the twentieth century. And it is written to help us all remember where we came from and the price others paid for our journey.

One assumes many debts when striving for so long on so elusive a topic. Auburn University provided a generous research grant and another to help with preparation of the manuscript. The Auburn Humanities Development Fund provided a generous publication subvention. I am particularly grateful to Vice President for Research Paul Parks for this assistance. Librarians and archivists, the unsung heroes and heroines of most books, played no small role in this one. At one time or another they have mailed me notes left on desks, provided a place for me after they locked up, lent me portable microfilm readers, missed buses while searching for hidden documents, and helped me locate inexpensive boardinghouses. I only wish I could acknowledge each by name. That failing, I commend them by institution and earnestly hope that some special providence will smile on them and give them long lives and appropriate salaries: the Auburn University library, whose staff was unfailing in service; the special collections staffs at Samford University, The University of Alabama, and the Southern History Collection at the University of North Carolina; the staffs of the Alabama Department of Archives and History in Montgomery, the Library of Congress, the National Archives, and the Franklin D. Roosevelt Library in Hyde Park, New York. And no author ever had a better editor than Beverly Denbow or publisher than Malcolm M. MacDonald.

A special note about Mrs. Samuel Snyder and Mrs. Florence Frost, who took in a stranger and made him welcome. Their "boardinghouses" in Washington and Hyde Park were more like homes than boarding-houses, and their hospitality more that of hostess than landlady.

I owe an even larger debt to a great many proud and now often prosperous people who talked with great candor about their lives. We often touched painful subjects, and I noticed how selective memory is, often editing out the worst episodes and remembering the good times. I was also taught to be wary of oral sources, as I am wary of written records, to approach every historical claim with a critical eye and ear. But even when oral sources exaggerated or distorted the past, they provided a drama lost to written records, a notion of how it really was to be alive then and share the anger or the sense of hopelessness—or maintain dogged determination. Especially to all of those people I am indebted, for they became the teachers and I the student.

PART ONE

Origins

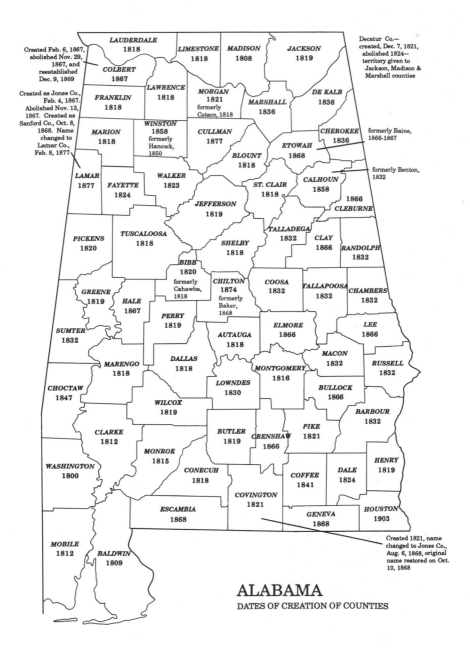

Created Feb. 6, 1867, abolished Nov. 29, 1867, and reestablished Dec. 9, 1869

Created as Jones Co., Feb. 4, 1867. Abolished Nov. 13, 1867. Created as Sanford Co., Oct. 8, 1868. Name changed to Lamar Co., Feb. 8, 1877

Decatur Co.— created, Dec. 7, 1821, abolished 1824— territory given to Jackson, Madison & Marshall counties

LAUDERDALE 1818

COLBERT 1867

LIMESTONE 1818

MADISON 1808

JACKSON 1819

LAWRENCE 1818

FRANKLIN 1818

MORGAN 1821 formerly Cotaco, 1818

MARSHALL 1836

DE KALB 1836

MARION 1818

WINSTON 1858 formerly Hancock, 1850

CULLMAN 1877

CHEROKEE 1836

formerly Baine, 1866-1867

ETOWAH 1868

LAMAR 1877

FAYETTE 1824

WALKER 1823

BLOUNT 1818

ST. CLAIR 1818

CALHOUN 1858

formerly Benton, 1832

JEFFERSON 1819

1866 CLEBURNE

PICKENS 1820

TUSCALOOSA 1818

SHELBY 1818

TALLADEGA 1832

CLAY 1866

RANDOLPH 1832

BIBB 1820 formerly Cahawba, 1818

CHILTON 1874 formerly Baker, 1868

COOSA 1832

TALLAPOOSA 1832

CHAMBERS 1832

GREENE 1819

HALE 1867

PERRY 1819

ELMORE 1866

LEE 1866

SUMTER 1832

AUTAUGA 1818

MACON 1832

RUSSELL 1832

MARENGO 1818

DALLAS 1818

MONTGOMERY 1816

CHOCTAW 1847

LOWNDES 1830

BULLOCK 1866

WILCOX 1819

BARBOUR 1832

CLARKE 1812

BUTLER 1819

CRENSHAW 1866

PIKE 1821

MONROE 1815

WASHINGTON 1800

CONECUH 1818

COFFEE 1841

DALE 1824

HENRY 1819

COVINGTON 1821

ESCAMBIA 1868

GENEVA 1868

HOUSTON 1903

MOBILE 1812

BALDWIN 1809

Created 1821, name changed to Jones Co., Aug. 6, 1868, original name restored on Oct. 10, 1868

ALABAMA
DATES OF CREATION OF COUNTIES

"Unknown and Forgotten Ancestors"

The Agricultural Origins of Poverty

The forces that drove men and women to the Alabama frontier were not unlike the ones that brought them to America in the first place. They wanted land, a better living, and more freedom. A certain internal selection process occurred when people pulled up stakes and headed for a new home. They were unwilling to accept existing conditions; they were optimistic that the next place would be better than the last; they had confidence in their own ability to cope with unforeseen circumstances. But the key to all their expectations was land.

Perhaps it was the distant memory of serfdom in Europe or the more recent struggle for land in Virginia or the Carolinas that drove pioneers westward. Or perhaps the soil seemed so abundant, the continent so vast, that settlers simply treated it without respect, exhausting its fertility, then moving on south or west. Whatever the source, the ownership of land seemed a magical elixir that promised to cure what ailed them.

For those who came early, Alabama was a generous earth mother. Her huge forests yielded to ax and plow, her fertile river bottoms brought forth harvests fit for any person. If great fortunes were rare in the early days, settlers were patient and could wait. Their primitive cabins and educational illiteracy belied their dreams, but gradually they carved out good farms, some large enough to be called plantations, most small enough to provide labor for only one family.

The form of agriculture and the social system which supported it dictated that the large units would be worked with slaves and provide most of the cash crops that made possible the South's distinctive society. The yeoman fitted nicely into the system also, providing food crops for nearby towns and some plantations, abundant livestock, and a modest quantity of cotton.

The planters, though looming large in romance and fiction, were a relatively small class in actual number. Far more numerous were the thriving yeomen who forged an alternative set of institutions and substantially exceeded the planters in political power. By 1850, 37,000 pupils attended 1,300 public schools, a total that was probably 40 percent of the state's white school-age population. Their Methodist and Baptist churches, profiting from the emotional revivals that swept the South, might embarrass the more educated and affluent but suited the yeomen's needs quite well. Jeffersonian in their beliefs that the best life was the one closest to the land, they did not share the occasional civic enthusiasm expressed over creation of a new textile mill. Independent and proud, they expressed their egalitarianism in support of the national Democracy and local Jacksonian candidates. They might aspire to be planters themselves someday, but in the meantime they gloried in the designation "common man" and were prouder to be identified with the poor who were struggling for justice and fair treatment, whatever that meant politically, than to be counted among effete, affluent, and affected planters.

There existed in the same region with yeomen and planters yet another group. Legendary for their fecundity and their excesses both of religion and of iniquity, poor whites were a poorly defined class in antebellum Alabama. Population growth was spectacular, bringing landless whites by the tens of thousands. Their numbers increased 1,230 percent in the teens, 122 percent in the 1820s, 76 percent in the 1830s, 27 percent in the 1840s, and 23 percent in the 1850s.[1] Although prosperous immigrants came, many more needed only a small container to transport all their earthly possessions.

Most of these landless folk lacked money with which to purchase land and simply "squatted" where they pleased. As Indian lands were opened for settlement, pioneers pushed into the hollows and hillsides, not bothering to wait for the obligatory federal land surveys that preceded land sales. "Squatters" were a recognized breed in American settlement, pushing always in advance of settlement and illegally occupying land. Upon finding an appealing tract of land, they would establish their claim by girdling a few trees and laying the first logs for a cabin. Later they sought to legalize their claims through "preemption," the notion that preferential right to a plot belonged to the person who first settled it. In that way violations of land laws subsequently could be legally recognized.

Several barriers prevented easy access to federal land. The minimum price of $1.25 an acre and the smallest unit of sale (varying over time from 160 acres to 80 or 40 acres) required more money than most squatters possessed. Furthermore, they had to compete with land speculators, who often purchased newly surveyed land as it was offered, then increased the price before reselling it to squatters. This practice generated bitter animosity between prosperous speculators and poor squatters.

Complicating the issue was regional conflict between the settled Northeast, which feared the loss of cheap labor, and the newly opened lands of the South and Northwest. Missouri Senator Thomas Hart Benton emerged as the major spokesman for land-hungry squatters. His scheme was simple. Because good land sold first at public auction, it should bring a higher price. Poor land that remained unsold should be offered at a reduced rate. Benton introduced a "graduation bill" in 1824, but Congress refused to pass it. The bill was immensely popular in Alabama and Mississippi, the two leading public domain states in the South. Each contained vast tracts of unsurveyed federal land.[2] Grateful Alabama legislators named an east Alabama Piedmont county for Benton.

No extensive Alabama tracts were surveyed and offered for sale until 1818, and federal troops tried first to prevent squatters, then later to remove them. They were even ordered to burn the cabins of any who refused to leave; but all such policies were to no avail.[3] By the early spring of 1816 some 10,000 squatters were illegally occupying Creek Indian lands. After that date an avalanche of poor settlers poured into the state. Food became scarce and starvation threatened. In 1816 flour sold for twenty dollars a barrel and corn for four dollars a bushel. In some locales food could not be obtained at any price. Thomas Freeman observed: "Provisions are so scarce in that country that a large portion of the present Intruders will be compelled to abandon their Improvements, and seek existence in the older settlements to prevent starvation, yet there are hundreds of families arriving daily."[4]

Freeman underestimated the fierce determination of the poor. When the land office at St. Stephens auctioned parcels in 1815, groups of squatters formed a condemnation committee and threatened outsiders who came to bid. Immigrants who came later feared large debts if they purchased their tracts from speculators, so they intimidated land speculators into not bidding at federal land auctions.[5]

Such tactics failed more often than they succeeded. When land sales were held at Huntsville in 1809, only one-third of the squatters were able to purchase the land they had cleared.[6] And even those who made a down payment were not guaranteed land. The economic depression of 1819–20 caused many settlers to forfeit their lands because they could not make their loan payments. Alabama settlers relinquished more land than pioneers in any other states (in fact three times as much land as in other states combined).[7] Congressional relief helped, but the specter of land hard to obtain and easy to lose bequeathed a bitter legacy.

The question of public land remained a major issue through most of the antebellum period. As late as 1835 Alabama had by far the largest quantity of unsold federal land (22 million acres). Surveying increased rapidly after that date and land sales reduced the total: 1.9 million acres were sold in 1836, 382,000 in 1837, and 151,000 in 1838. By 1850 only 23,677 acres of the state's 32 million remained unsurveyed.[8]

The acquisition of land, which dominated the thoughts of most early settlers, also established the broad contours of Alabama politics. From the first settlement patterns in the Tennessee Valley, divisions arose between planters with mainly Georgia connections and small farmers generally of Tennessee origins. The key to election was at first mainly rhetorical: to convince the plain folk of one's genuine claim to be a common man in a state with universal manhood suffrage.[9] But as politicians sought substantive issues on which to launch careers, they early fixed on the issue of land. Their position on land—the extinction of Indian claims, preemption rights for squatters, reduction of land prices and minimum acres per purchase, the graduation of land prices according to the quality of soil—became the litmus test of their Jacksonian rhetoric.

Expressed in class terms, resentment of the rich and fear of corporate wealth became important themes in antebellum Alabama history. Democrats sought to identify Whigs with "commercial elements" who warred against farmers. The public issue became "the supremacy of the rich over the poor," despite the fact that Alabama Whiggery seldom espoused elitist views. Within the legislature this ideological class dispute took the form of poorer elements favoring reduced taxes and biennial sessions of the legislature while opposing aid for internal improvements or state charters for banks or railroads. Common whites also opposed expansion of women's rights, prohibition, or increased expenditures for education and mental health. Their tax policy was to levy the highest rates on slaves, with land a lesser source of tax revenue. Secondary taxes should be levied on the ostentatious symbols of wealth: gold watches, private libraries, race horses, and the like. Thanks to the legislative successes of common whites, the wealthiest one-third of Alabama's population paid two-thirds of the taxes. Despite their influence on tax legislation, the single consistent thread running through the tapestry of common white ideology was opposition to laws that would concentrate more power in government. They justifiably believed that strong government was more likely to respond to the special interests of planters.[10]

Insofar as land and public policy were debated, poor whites and yeomen shared a common outlook. The economic mobility of the Alabama frontier was so great, the social structure so fluid, that this year's squatter could easily become next year's landowning yeoman. Yeomen and poor whites worshiped in the same churches, crafted the same white-oak baskets, told the same tales, plucked the same dulcimer or banjo tunes, danced the same jigs, and fought the same politicians.

However limited their formal educations might be, poor whites had a profound understanding of their own self-interest. They also had a fierce class consciousness that even casual observers noticed. Antebellum travelers commented on the frequency with which they observed ostracism based on a reversal of social status: most Alabamians disdained wealth and education. Political candidates might win an election to the state legislature or even a congressional seat by portraying themselves as common men and arguing that "a rich man cannot sympathize with the poor."[11]

Successful politicians had to advocate and practice social equality, and the appropriate expression of their belief was easy access to land. By the 1820s, the state of Alabama was a firm and consistent advocate of liberalized land policy. In 1826 the Alabama legislature petitioned Congress to peg the price of land to its true value and recommended that the minimum purchase be reduced to forty acres and the price to twenty-five cents an acre. Concerned legislators also asked for a preemption act affording squatters first right to purchase their land.

Such efforts obtained some satisfactory results. An 1830 preemption act legalized squatters' rights to their claims and helped early settlers in the Tennessee Valley legally record their homesteads.[12] Seven years later Alabama's general assembly petitioned Congress to reduce the minimum purchasable tract to twenty acres. Such portions were too small for plantations, but legislators believed that "many poor persons" would settle "in the hollows, and on the small creeks in the mountainous parts of the country" and could "obtain homes for their families, and contribute something to the prosperity and convenience of the country, by the breeding of cattle, sheep, and hogs."[13]

By 1845 the U.S. commissioner of public lands had received so many petitions from state legislatures and private individuals that he joined the chorus for easier settlement. Western emigration was occurring so rapidly as to outpace federal surveys. Opening forty-acre tracts to preemption would help those "whose scanty means prevent them from entering a larger quantity." Squatters would become yeomen with an interest in the soil, not "mere tenants at will to either private individuals [speculators] or the government."[14]

The time was ripe for a bold initiative and it came from an appropriate source. The cosponsors of the first homestead bill to be introduced into Congress were Felix Grundy McConnell of Alabama and Andrew John-

son of Tennessee. McConnell was a native Tennessean who had migrated to Talladega in the Appalachian foothills. Although limited in
education he had taught himself law. But his physique suited him better
for physical labor. Standing six feet tall and weighing two hundred
pounds, he was an imposing figure as he roamed his mountain district
selling and fixing saddles. He boasted of his working class origins and
identified with laboring people. Once while traveling he met a poor
family whose only horse had died. Springtime planting was impossible
and calamity awaited them. McConnell dismounted, presented his horse
to the indigent farmer, hoisted his saddle onto his shoulder, and set out
for town fifteen miles away. Such folklore did his political career no
harm among the deprived folk who inhabited mountainous portions of
Talladega, Cherokee, Benton, Randolph, Tallapoosa, and Chambers
counties. He was elected to the legislature in 1838 and to Congress in
1843, carrying the hilly areas and losing the flatlands. He was reelected
in 1845 as an Independent Democrat despite the claims of his Democrat
opponent that McConnell indulged "too freely in social class."[15]

Even McConnell's vices were typical of the class he represented. He
drank too much and embarrassed sophisticated Washington with his
backcountry manners. During a concert by a renowned violinist,
McConnell interrupted the "exquisite performance" with an egalitarian
shout: "None of your highfalutin, but give us Hail Columbia, and bear
hard on the treble."[16]

In 1846 McConnell joined Congressman Andrew Johnson in introducing a bill to give "every white man 160 acres of ground, provided
he would work it." The cosponsors argued that unoccupied land belonged to the laboring poor who had a right to a "homestead." So as to
leave no doubt about the intent of the sponsors, Johnson even proposed
that homesteaders be required to swear an oath of poverty that would
be notarized by three witnesses. The bill did not pass Congress. Eastern
congressmen opposed it, as did southern representatives from plantation
districts. Major support came from northeastern workingmen's assem-
blies and southern congressmen representing those who lived in mountain regions and on the poor soil of the pine belt.[17]

Two of McConnell's congressional friends shared his concern for the
welfare of Alabama's poor whites. Williamson Robert Winfield Cobb
resembled his fiery Alabama colleague in many particulars: like Mc-
Connell, he was a native Tennessean limited in education. He also
became a skilled and modestly successful craftsman, peddling and repairing clocks in Madison County. And he represented a mountain district in east Alabama to the north of McConnell's. After his election to
the state legislature in 1844, he left no doubts as to where his sympathies
lay. He introduced a bill in the legislature to exempt plates, cups, sau-

cers, a coffee pot, and furniture from forced sale when a poor family could not pay its debts. Following a brief stint in the legislature he offered for Congress in 1847, running for the seat from the northeastern corner of the state. His was a mountain district of small farmers with the highest rate of illiteracy in Alabama, and his campaign was directed at that constituency. He rattled tinware and crockery for attention and entertained his audiences with songs that he composed for the occasion. His most successful number was entitled "The Homestead Bill" and its opening lyric stirred strong emotions among the poor: "Uncle Sam is rich enough to give us all a farm." Verses were sufficiently lengthy to cover all the possessions a poor man might crave, from land and mules to furniture. Should the folksy lyric not identify him completely with the "common man," he also campaigned while chewing onions and corn bread. Planter opponents and urban newspapers sputtered with rage; Cobb was "very popular with the lowly and unlearned, whose devotion was singularly ardent and defied reason." But an exasperated opponent admitted in 1853 that Cobb would continue to win because of the prejudice "of those who can't or don't read, against any lawyer, townsman or states rights man—each of whom is regarded as a suspicious character."[18]

Such condescension only stirred greater emotion among Cobb's rustic followers. In 1847 he carried every county but one against a planter opponent. And six years later he demolished the planter candidate extraordinaire, Clement Claiborne Clay, by branding him a States Rights Disunionist. Like most of his isolated followers, Cobb had no particular stake in the slave system and was deeply and nationalistically committed to the Union. During the stormy days of 1861 he opposed secession and refused to depart Congress on the day his colleagues withdrew. As hostility to secession increased with every Confederate defeat, his constituents elected him in 1864 to the Confederate Congress, from which he was afterwards expelled for treason.[19]

Across the state in northwest Alabama, McConnell and Cobb found a kindred spirit. William Russell Smith's congressional district also consisted of hill counties. Smith championed the homestead bill from a Jeffersonian belief in the supremacy of farms to cities. Free land would allow cities to disgorge "their cellars and their garrets of a starving, haggard and useless population." Nor was the millennium for city dwellers only. Any of the numerous and landless sons of poor farmers could "rise up and go forth to take possession of his estate, not only [as] a freeman, but a landlord."[20] To Smith, McConnell, and Cobb, as to Jefferson and Andrew Jackson, landownership would alleviate poverty and ensure democracy. The proper role of government was to provide equal opportunity and then leave the citizen alone.

On this much planter, yeoman, and poor white might agree, though there was plenty of room for arguments on specifics. Behind the handsome ideological facade of independence and equality, however, lurked a landscape full of snares. Shrewd, articulate planters not only contested land policies with self-proclaimed messiahs of impoverished hill people, but they also argued over state-chartered banks, internal improvements, railroads, and fencing laws. Despite their general suspicion of commercial development, Whig planters were much more likely to favor state support of railroad development than were legislators who represented poor white constituencies. Transportation by canal, river, or rail was important to planters who relied on a credit-and-cash economy and who produced cotton for national and international markets. Although backwoods farmers occasionally sold livestock and small amounts of surplus crops, their market was local and their economy basically trade and barter.

Reliant as they were on supplementing subsistence farming by hunting, fishing, and livestock grazing, yeomen and poor whites evolved a looser definition of property rights than planters. As late as 1850 only 4.4 million acres of Alabama's total acreage (32 million) consisted of improved farmland producing crops.[21] Unimproved land might be privately owned but it was neither cleared nor fenced. Yeomen and poor whites believed in the common right to use unimproved land for fishing, hunting, and grazing, and they bitterly resisted the increasing effort of Alabama planters and agricultural reformers to fence land. The fencing movement that began in the late antebellum years encountered determined opposition from poor farmers throughout the nineteenth century.[22]

Because all whites could agree essentially on the significance of equality, independence, and white supremacy, the full implications of class conflict were not realized in antebellum Alabama. Direct, exploitive labor relations usually involved whites supervising blacks and only infrequently whites supervising other whites. Spatial separation also helped; most poor whites lived in the hills of north Alabama, along the eastern border with Georgia, or in the southeastern Wiregrass. But by the 1850s the social and economic implications of their differences were already obvious. Planters strove to restrict democracy in state government and to divert attention from economic issues. Concern for independence eclipsed anxiety about equality. The greatest threat to freedom increasingly seemed to emanate from abolitionists and Yankee reformers rather than from Black Belt planters.[23] By biding their time, planters discovered that national events favored them. And the successes of the poor and their Jacksonian spokesmen, augmented by the incredible prosperity wrought by cotton, altered Alabama's political landscape. Poor whites acquired land, diligent yeomen became planters, and small planters forged baronish empires. The primacy of land slowly gave way to the preeminence of slavery.

Revolutions of rising expectations do not occur exclusively in exotic non-Western nations. Such a phenomenon swept Alabama in the last decade of the antebellum era. The major expansion of cotton acreage during the 1850s occurred precisely in those regions with the largest concentrations of yeomen farmers and poor whites. Some small farmers in the north Alabama hills, the southeastern Wiregrass, and the southern piney woods were converting from subsistence farming and livestock raising to a cash crop. Cotton income allowed them to purchase amenities important to their upward mobility. By 1860 approximately 80 percent of Alabama's yeomen farmers owned the land they tilled.[24]

But prosperity did not result in greater political power because towns and industry grew apace, and if anything, state government became more malleable to Alabama's economic elite. Nor did the disparity in wealth drive wedges between whites on the critical issue of slavery. The Southern Rights candidate in 1860, John C. Breckinridge, ran strongest in the north Alabama hill counties and in the Wiregrass.[25] Planters succeeded in rallying their less-prosperous fellows because the prevailing economic system seemed to be more open and inclusive than earlier, the possibility of upward mobility appeared greater, and because they identified their cause with the two ideologies that mattered most to aspiring yeomen and poor whites: liberty and equality.

This description of Alabama life in the 1850s is like a snapshot of a vast panorama, true insofar as it depicts its subject but wholly inadequate in detail. Were one to enlarge segments of the photograph, striking variations would appear that confound the general impressions. Although some yeomen prospered, others disappeared altogether from the census table as they moved west in search of better land. Other yeomen died in the decade, and their lands were divided among sons into small and often unprofitable units.

Even greater complexity appears when one probes the most fundamental unit of southern political life, individual counties. Dallas County was in many ways the quintessential Black Belt county. Located in the center of the state just west of Montgomery, its rich black soil supported large numbers of plantations and slaves. Selma, its major town, was a center of social and cultural life near enough to the state capital at Montgomery to exercise enormous political influence. Although often thought of as a two-class society of opulent planters and slaves, Dallas contained numbers of indigent whites scattered through the county. During the 1850s Dallas experienced a high degree of white mobility based on class. Although several factors influenced who left and who stayed, the most consistent and dramatic variable was wealth. The wealthiest whites were the most likely to remain, whereas 8 percent of the tenants, overseers, and agricultural day laborers left the county during the decade. Small yeomen and the rural poor could not successfully compete against planters. And perhaps their proximity to planters and their scattered settlement made them less socially secure and confident. At least in the mountain areas and Wiregrass, their concentration allowed their own institutions to flourish and afforded them political power. As a consequence of migration, the number of farms in Dallas declined by 20 percent during the 1850s. Although other poor whites came to replace those who left, "Dallas was a society increasingly polarized in the 1850s along class, social, and ethnic lines between its stable and wealthy slaveholders in the countryside and its poorer newcomers clustered in Selma and divorced from the courses of traditional landed wealth."[26]

In some regards white society in the mountain counties was more cohesive and the folk culture more enduring than in the celebrated Black Belt. Before the 1850s the counties located between the Tennessee Valley and the central Alabama plantation district grew corn and other subsistence crops. Most crops were consumed locally. A few were sold to nearby plantations or towns. To be sure, few hill people could match the opulent Greek revival mansions of Demopolis or the expansive fields of cotton so radiant under the September sun. But the hill counties also lacked the economic peaks and valleys of Dallas, the extremes of wealth that frustrated poor whites by their very proximity to such affluence. Word might penetrate the remote hollows about the incredible riches to be had further south, but no examples existed within their circumscribed world. For the most part yeoman and poor white differed only marginally in education, culture, and even prosperity.

Census records reveal how widespread was the wealth of the late antebellum world. Although few enjoyed riches, many possessed adequate resources to furnish all their needs and most of their wants. In Winston County, a north Alabama mountain domain consisting almost entirely of whites, virtually all families possessed a small patch of land and a little furniture and livestock. Although the average value of both real estate and personal property was slight, the predominant occupations in the 1860 census were "Farmer," "Mechanic," "Preacher," "Carpenter," and for women "Seamstress" or "Domestic" (meaning farmer's wife). Some "Farm Laborers" lived in Winston, but all except three of them were relatives (usually sons) of the family with whom they resided. The three propertyless males apparently not related to the families for whom they worked were young (ages twenty-three, nineteen, and seventeen), and could hope that they too would soon join Winston's yeomanry.[27]

If Winston was the most extreme example of isolated and rural pure white democracy, and Dallas the prototype of the Black Belt plantation county, Calhoun was a fine example of a mixed economy. Created in 1832, it was originally named Benton in honor of the Missouri senator. The western portion of the county bordering the Coosa River was a land of hills and hollows, as was the eastern portion along the Georgia boundary that contained dense forests and the Appalachian mountains. Between them, however, were fertile bottomland and broad valleys well suited to agriculture.

One of the pioneers who entered this promising new world was Smith Lipscomb. He brought his family from Spartanburg, South Carolina, fourteen years after Benton County was formed. The family left South Carolina two days after Christmas in 1845 and arrived near Alexandria in the center of the county on January 16, 1846. Smith was forty-two, his wife Sally two years his junior. Life was not easy in their new home. Neither they nor the children adjusted easily to the weather, and they complained constantly of poor health. With the help of neighbors they erected two stables and a house twenty-two feet long by twenty-four feet wide; then they added an outside kitchen that was sixteen feet square. At first they squatted on seven acres because they did not have money enough to buy land. A road ran fifty yards from their cabin door and a stream with fish meandered across the valley a hundred yards beyond the road. Behind the stream a small mountain rose from the valley. Like most squatters they had a little education but not enough to allow them "to put on airs." And like many of their companions, they were ambivalent about the sacrifices they had made in uprooting their family and leaving relatives in South Carolina: "It will be better for the rising generation if not for ourselves but I think it will be the best for us all that live any length of time."

One compensation was the beauty of their homestead: "Benton is a mountainous country but ther is a heep of good levil land to tend in it. There is mayapple and buckeye all over the woods." Smith Lipscomb did complain that everything was so "unhandy": it was five miles to one of his fields, and "we have to tote water four hundred yards." As much as he sought his own land and house, the exertion to obtain them was enormous and enervating during planting and harvesting seasons; he departed for the fields at dawn and did not return before eight in the evening.[28]

But his efforts were not in vain. His crops were good and his livestock flourished. In 1852 he harvested 15,805 pounds of cotton from one field and 1,373 pounds from another patch, a total of more than thirty-three bales. His industrious wife Sally supplemented their income as a seamstress. In 1851 she sold a shirt for 75¢, a pair of pantaloons for 25¢, three pairs of pants for a total of $2.62, and three pairs of socks at 37¢ a pair.[29]

By 1860 Lipscomb had transformed his family from landless poor whites into prosperous yeomen. For the Lipscombs, poverty had been a temporary state in a transient and highly mobile world. Although landless and indigent when they arrived, the security of their South Carolina relatives and the prospects of their new home caused their pioneering to pose little real peril. Their condition differed little from their neighbors', and Smith soon became clerk of the Hebron Baptist Church and a respected member of the community. His credit was good with his neighbors, and he frequently purchased coffee and sugar that way. Except for such luxuries, his farm was largely self-sufficient.

In this regard Lipscomb was typical of Benton's yeomanry, and Benton's agriculture was representative of the diversified pattern of most yeoman and poor white farms. By 1840 wheat had become the most important money crop in the county, its production ranking second only to one other Alabama county. Twenty years later it led all counties, producing 103,000 bushels. Indian corn was the second most valuable crop (655,000 bushels in 1860). In 1840 Benton farmers grew 30,000 pounds of tobacco, though this crop fell to only 4,700 pounds in 1860. Irish and sweet potatoes flourished, and the county contained 5,000 mules and 16,000 cattle in 1860. Farmers produced 109,000 pounds of butter, though their cotton yield ranked them no higher than twenty-seventh among the state's counties. Farms tended to be small: there were only 16 of 500 to 1,000 acres and 367 of 100 to 500; there were 521 of 50 to 100 acres and 632 of 20 to 50.[30] Land was no longer the primary concern of citizens, a fact symbolized by the change of the county's name. By 1858 Thomas H. Benton was considered a traitor to the South because of his waffling on the slave question. With the ascendancy of slavery as the compelling issue among all classes of whites, the county was renamed in honor of secessionist Senator John C. Calhoun.

Unfortunately Smith Lipscomb's family saga, though typical, was not exclusive. Buried beneath such happy tributes to the American Dream was a large class of poor whites who did not fare so well. The causes of their persistent poverty were complex. Many came late, after the best land had already been settled. A few were recently arrived European immigrants. Others were products of a new industrial world developing in Alabama during the 1850s. By 1860 Calhoun County ranked first among the state's iron-producing counties. Benton County Iron Works on the banks of Cane Creek six miles from where its waters flowed into the Coosa River was the largest furnace in Alabama.

In 1860 Calhoun contained 4,343 slaves, 28 free blacks, and 17,169 whites. Hundreds of those whites were listed in the 1860 census as owning nothing, neither real estate nor personal property. Even among property owners, wealth was distributed thinly; 59 percent owned less than five hundred dollars' worth. As in Dallas County, many of the poor lived in rapidly growing villages, including Alexandria, Oxford, Jacksonville, and White Plains. In such communities could be found thirteen dry-goods clerks who owned no property; other propertyless residents included seven painters, seven blacksmiths, one plasterer, one bricklayer, three shoemakers, seven carpenters, seven mechanics, two hatters, one tanner, and five laborers in the iron furnace. Out in the rural areas lived isolated people who were unable to obtain land: one hunter, one basket maker, a fifty-nine-year-old male "gardener" from Germany, and a thirty-year-old female "washer woman" with an eleven-year-old daughter.

Far more numerous were the rural farm laborers, listed under various headings, depending on the whim of the census taker: "Day Laborer," "Farm Laborer," "Laborer," "Hireling," "Farm Hand," and "Ditcher." Most persons so listed in 1860 were relatives of a landowner, living in his house, and would soon become landowners themselves, either through the division of land when parents died or by purchase; 242 farm laborers in Calhoun County had the same family names as the person with whom they lived and for whom they worked. However, 120 whites with different family names lived with families for whom they performed farm labor. All but one of them were males. Several were married, but the overwhelming majority were single. A sample of the ages of 31 provided an average of 23.5 years. Only 1 man was more than 40. For most of them landlessness was a temporary state, or at least so they thought. Like Smith Lipscomb, they harbored great expectations for the future. They were white, male, young, strong, and had no cause to worry over their temporary indigence.

Others were not so certain about the future. They were numbered among the 179 heads of families in Calhoun who were farm laborers. They owned minimal personal property (usually a bit of furniture or a few head of livestock) but no land. Typically their families were large, their ages older, their personal estates small, and their prospects bleak. A sample of 20 families revealed a dramatically different profile from their younger colleagues without families. The average age of the 20 male heads of family was 31.15. Although they did possess a personal estate, it averaged only seventy-five dollars. From these meager resources, they had to provide on the average for a wife and four children (only 1 of the 20 was a widower and only 4 were childless). None of them owned any real estate. Many of their older offspring had already continued the cycle of rural poverty and were listed in the census as day laborers.

At the bottom of Calhoun's agricultural ladder were 60 families whose heads were farm laborers but who owned neither real estate nor personal property. Their ages and offspring differed little from their more numerous fellow sufferers who had small personal estates. A typical family was that of Wilson Hunnicutt, age 44. Hunnicutt had a wife and five children; two of his sons were listed as farmhands.

Combining these with the earlier figures produces a conservative estimate of more than 1,900 landless whites, or slightly more than 11 percent of the total 1860 white population of the county.[31] Most of these people owned neither personal property nor real estate. The minority who held any personal estate valued it at less than $150. The total might be considerably higher because many men listed as "Farmers" in the 1860 census have no entry under either real estate or personal estate. This estimate is lower than a recent study of Russell County that estimates white tenancy rates of 16 percent or more in 1860.[32]

Far removed from the balanced agriculture of Calhoun County was the Wiregrass region of southeastern Alabama. The long nutritious grass that furnished the region its name grew on the floor of extensive pine forests, providing abundant fodder for foraging livestock. Its sandy soil, though ideal for pine trees and wire grass, was not well suited to agriculture. Settlers grew corn and other food crops for local consumption but little cotton. Called variously the piney woods (for its trees), the pine barrens (for its sparse population), or cow country (for its heavy economic dependence on livestock grazing), the region encompassed four southeastern Alabama counties in 1860 (Henry, Dale, Coffee, and Covington). Like their north Alabama counterparts, the counties contained people of Anglo-American origin, of Jeffersonian and Jacksonian political persuasion, overwhelmingly Primitive or Missionary Baptist in religion, and subsistence farmers in occupation. Though not as renowned for family feuds and violence as mountain people, physical conflict seems to have been just as pervasive. The same frontier conditions, the slow development of stabilizing institutions such as schools, churches, and towns, and extensive consumption of whiskey all contributed to this atmosphere. Although violence was a way of life in the Wiregrass, animosities were usually directed to people of the same race, sex, and even family rather than toward blacks or other social or economic groups. Slaves constituted only 19.63 percent of the population of the four counties, which totaled only 43,207. Less than 15 percent of the white families owned any slaves. A surprisingly large percentage of the heads of families were female, suggesting both some impermanence in family structure and perhaps an unusually high death rate. One sample of 1,128 heads of families found 77 percent female heads, a phenomenally high statistic.[33] The rate of illiteracy was high, slightly more than 20 percent, but many illiterates owned land. Among illiterates, 15 persons owned property worth $2,100 to $3,000; 28, $1,100 to $2,000; 36, $600 to $100; 126, $1 to $500; and only 6 owned no property at all.[34]

Settlers carved small farms out of the vast pine thickets and allowed cattle and hogs to forage in the open forests. Occasionally they would round up the livestock and drive them to markets in Tallahassee, Mobile, or elsewhere. They infrequently sold corn and other produce from their subsistence farms to plantations in adjacent Black Belt counties in order to earn cash.

The class structure was no simpler than in the Black Belt or the hill country. At the top of the pyramid was a small group of relatively wealthy farmers, herdsmen, and merchants. A prosperous middle class consisted of basically the same groups. Next and most numerous was a Wiregrass yeomanry with incomes of $150 to $700; at the bottom was the same propertyless group that existed in Calhoun County, made up of farm laborers and renters. Their incomes consisted of less than $100. Although the extent of this class has not been computed for the Alabama Wiregrass, a careful study of the same region just across the Chattahoochee River in Georgia puts the lowest poor white class at 15 percent of the population, with the yeomanry constituting nearly 40 percent, the middle class 30 percent, and the wealthiest group only 15 percent.[35] Inasmuch as the Alabama Wiregrass was settled later and was slightly more unstable, it is likely that the level of indigence was higher; it certainly was no lower. This rate is also consistent with the percentage of propertyless heads of family in Calhoun and Russell counties to the north (estimated at 11 and 16 percent).

Although both poverty and prosperity are relative, Wiregrass counties were substantially poorer than Calhoun, as demonstrated by a number of agricultural categories: production of food crops and cotton, size and value of farms, and family income. In the category of livestock, however, the averages were nearly equal, reflecting the tremendous importance of herding to the economy of southeastern Alabama. Indeed, livestock totals for the four-county Wiregrass region demonstrate widespread distribution of wealth and the substantial strength of the yeomanry: 9,000 horses and mules, 47,000 cattle, 4,300 oxen, 112,000 swine, and 20,000 sheep. Some apparently landless farmers in both Calhoun and south-eastern Alabama undoubtedly possessed considerable livestock, although there is no evidence to suggest that such ownership was extensive enough to remove most of them from the poor white class.[36]

Covington County, one of the four Wiregrass counties, offers a more detailed look at lower class mobility. The first land was placed on sale there about 1825 at $1.25 per acre. Sales were slow. The poor soil and thick pine forests dissuaded settlers who could move farther north and purchase premium Black Belt soil for the same price. Many pioneers who entered the county between 1820 and 1854 were illegal squatters; in 1850 only 28,160 acres, or about 3.7 percent of the county's total, had been purchased. Most of this land was located in the fertile river bottoms. Then in April 1854 a change in federal policy launched a boom. Land prices were placed on a sliding scale from 12.5¢ to $1.25 an acre. In October 1854 alone, more land was sold in Covington than during all of 1853. Between 1854 and 1860, 47,000 acres of federal land were sold in the county, most for the lower range of prices, either 12.5¢ or 25¢ per acre. The county's population increased by 60 percent within five years after 1854 as landless immigrants poured in from Georgia and South Carolina. Many of these newcomers continued to squat on public land, moving when necessary to avoid prosecution. Even with this boom, abundant tracts of land remained unsold in 1860. Private sales, railroad land grants, and gifts to the state amounted to fewer than 300,000 acres; the federal government still owned 470,000 acres on the eve of the Civil War. In 1860 Covington was a predominantly white, small farmer democracy. It contained 5,631 whites, 817 slaves, and 81 free blacks.[37]

Thus economic and political fortunes varied from county to county and from agrarian/rural to industrial/urban sections; but there were many consistent elements. Landownership was central to economic well-being and mobility. And such ownership was neither particularly difficult nor extraordinary. Rigid class patterns did not develop, partly because acquisition of land was either a reality or a widely anticipated future expectation, and partly because personal relations between whites were seldom directly exploitive. Spatial separation often isolated whites of different classes, and primitive transportation and communication further insulated them from contact with each other. Politically, poor whites and yeomen gave as good as they got, electing congressmen and legislators who represented their interests, influenced both federal and state land policy, and placed the burden of taxes primarily on those best able to pay. By 1820 only Maryland, Kentucky, and Alabama permitted all white adult males to vote. In only Georgia, Louisiana, and Alabama could voters elect the powerful members of the county court that governed counties.

The Urban and Industrial Origins of Poverty

Although rural poverty was the most common form of deprivation in antebellum Alabama, those who left the land to seek better opportunities found little satisfaction. In towns such as Selma, Montgomery, and Mobile, workers discovered that factories could be as inhospitable as barren land. Planters who feared the corrupting influence of poor whites pouring into urban centers began to create isolated mill towns that would provide jobs for impoverished whites, avoid the threat posed by urban mobs, and not incidentally turn a handsome profit for the owners.

Alabama's industrial expansion, especially during the decades of the 1840s and 1850s, was impressive. Though backward by northern standards, the state enlarged its manufacturing force until it employed 10.5 percent of the state's white males by 1860. Most of the industrial growth was in railroading or in traditional manufacturing closely associated with agriculture. The largest manufacturing industry consisted of gristmills; the second largest was sawmilling. Urban jobs provided work for artisans of every sort: mechanics, teamsters, stevedores, boatmen, seamstresses, domestics, and a host of others.

The most spectacular manufacturing growth occurred in the textile industry, which by 1860 was Alabama's second largest industrial employer. Textile employment doubled in the 1850s to 1,312 operatives who earned nearly $200,000 in wages, or an average of $150 annually. Although such a salary might seem impressive compared to the rural poverty they had left behind, it barely was adequate for survival. It also was the lowest average annual salary of the twelve manufacturing occupations listed in the 1860 census (the highest average, $344, was paid to Alabama's fifty-four coal miners).[38]

Historians have made much of the 1880s' New South crusade for textile mills when industrialists and planters camouflaged their self-interest with lofty preachments about saving impoverished poor whites from squalor, indigence, and the temptations of urban life. But such rhetoric preceded the New South campaign in Alabama by a generation. In November 1851 the *Alabama Beacon* deplored the destitution that drove urban white workers begging from house to house, "roving, worthless creatures," prowling, sleeping where they could, setting fires and committing outrages.[39] Half a decade earlier Alabama Chief Justice Henry W. Collier had advised the establishment of mills to prevent poor whites from remaining "an incubus on the bosom" of society. He recommended cotton mills as containing nothing "prejudicial to health . . . , nothing in tending a loom to harden a lady's hand . . . , nothing to cause the rouge upon the cheek to fade, although the skin may become bleached by remaining so much in the shade."[40] Collier's suggestion that women would constitute much of the labor force in the new mills was prophetic. Four years later, Collier, then governor of Alabama, warned planters that unemployed whites might well blame their ill fortune on slavery, and he urged planters to patronize mills that provided jobs to poor whites. Such strategy not only served the purpose of social order but also their economic self-interest: wage-earning whites became consumers of local mechanical services and food products.[41]

Other planters were not so certain about Collier's advice, and the 1850s produced a spirited debate. Some proslavery writers denounced industry and warned against the abuse of workers or their concentration in cities. Such practices would hasten the rise of a southern proletariat class that would disrupt orderly society. Alabama author-planter Daniel R. Hundley mistakenly rejoiced in 1860 that poor whites remained "wholly rural; hence, the South will ever remain secure against any species of agrarianism, since such mob violence always originates in towns and cities, wherein are herded together an unthinking rabble."[42]

Some measure of paternalism was no doubt present in the thinking of many planters who launched the cotton mill crusade. To them, mill work was the salvation of the health and morals of indigent whites. The editor of Montgomery's *Tri-Weekly Flag and Advertiser* asserted in 1848 that 50,000 poor and idle Alabama whites were available for employment.[43]

The most articulate spokesman for this view was planter-industrialist Daniel Pratt. He feared the corrupting influence of cities and the rise of class consciousness. His solution to both was to locate his cotton mill in a small factory village where it could utilize local cotton, farm products, and idle, needy whites. Pratt established his first cotton mill in 1846, employing 160 men, women, and children. He preferred families, though he did hire single girls and children. One operative at the mill remembered that the laborers were "brought up from the piney woods, many of them with no sort of training of any kind of labor; and in learning many mistakes and blunders were made."[44] Unable to obtain land, they sought work wherever they could find it.

Altruism and fair treatment were Pratt's defense against the rise of class conflict. In 1850 Pratt paid 73 women an average of nine dollars and 63 men an average of sixteen dollars per month. He furnished sixty-five cottages of uniform size at low rent, a day care center, and school for the children of workers. A deeply religious man of New Hampshire upbringing, Pratt prohibited the sale of liquor, required children to attend Sunday school, financed local churches, and sought to nurture habits of diligence and thrift. A local historian who also worked in the mill praised Pratt's humanitarianism toward mill hands who "were of the poorest class. . . . withal ignorant people from obscure parts of the country . . . having never enjoyed any religious privilege."[45]

The establishment of Pratt's facility is a watershed in the rise of antebellum mills in Alabama. From the construction of the first mill in the Tennessee Valley in 1818, most entrepreneurs had favored slave labor as cheaper and more contented than white. White mechanics demanded high wages and many poor whites had an aversion to manual labor, which they associated with slavery. Slaves continued to be used in some mills through the 1850s, denying whites manufacturing opportunities for a better life. Such practice contained the potential to unite white workers and nonslaveholding farmers into an antislavery, antiplanter coalition, but the possibility did not become a reality. There were never sufficient industrial workers to matter, and rural whites, aspiring to become planters themselves, worried little about the plight of mill workers. Furthermore, poor white industrial workers were generally docile and caused little trouble. Mills offered them new experiences and tremendous opportunities, as well as sources for resentment.

Inspired by Pratt's efforts, many tried to match his success. Civic leaders in Mobile, distressed by a tide of immigrants washed in on every boat, established the Dog River Mill with forty French girls as the work force. Many poor Irish immigrants obtained jobs there, as did some native-born poor whites.

Elsewhere the labor force varied. A new mill in Autaugaville began in 1850 with male workers aged fifteen to twenty-five; but by the end of 1851 a majority of the eighty-one operatives were females. The planter-owner of the Tallassee Factory opened his mill in 1845 with a half white–half slave labor force, but he converted to all white (forty women, thirty-one men) by 1850. The Fish Pond Factory on Elkhatchie Creek in Tallapoosa County was the sole source of employment for the area's poor whites, and its wages (in 1850 ten men earned an average of six dollars per month, twelve women, five dollars), though well below the Alabama average, were high by community standards. The mill on Socapatoy Creek in Coosa County resembled Pratt's in the social control of workers' lives; the owner prohibited liquor sales and provided a company Sunday school, church, and school.

The economic depression of the 1840s also strained the social fabric in the Tennessee Valley. An entrepreneur in the river town of Florence reasoned that poor whites who remained in the woods "from whence we obtained them" produced nothing. Mill work enabled them to "live more comfortable, and by constant employment, enables them to make much more useful and better citizens." By establishing a mill, day school, Sunday school, and church, he hoped "to benefit them, while we benefit ourselves."[46]

Racial animosity doomed most biracial mill efforts, although Scottsville Mill in Tuscaloosa efficiently and profitably employed an integrated labor force. The key to this success probably was an unusually high wage scale for whites, who were paid an average of fifteen dollars per month for males and ten dollars for females. Even this experiment floundered by 1860 when the mill force had become all white. Daniel Pratt went in the other direction, switching to a mixed labor force in the 1850s. His decision resulted from the failure of many poor whites to perform adequately because of poor health and morals. He discovered that the lethargy and insobriety of piney woods whites were difficult to eradicate by education and moral discipline. Poor whites moved frequently, disrupting his labor force and his job training. Males also had other employment options in sawmills, gristmills, or as mechanics, forcing textile mills to rely more heavily on women and children as operatives or turn to black males.

Mobility sometimes resulted from a rejection of mill discipline, but it also might be a form of protest against bad conditions or low pay. The Dog River Mill in Mobile sent a labor recruiter to persuade Pratt's operatives to move. Shadrach Mims, Pratt's labor agent, wrote Col. Price Williams, owner of the Dog River Mill, bitterly protesting the raid. He chided Williams's agent for promising inflated salaries. Focusing on one family that moved, Mims revealed a great deal about the background of his operatives.

The Butler family had gone to work for Pratt in 1852. According to Mims, Butler was "poor an afficted [sic]." No one in his large family had ever heard preaching. Only Butler's wife could read or write. Through the benevolent influence of Prattville's church, all family members had become Christians. Some of the children had learned to read. Mims had personally spent thirty dollars on the family, and when they departed for Mobile they neither repaid him nor paid sixty dollars in debts that they owed. Although Mims's letter did no good, Butler apparently proved no more permanent at the Dog River Mill than he had for Pratt. The 1855 and 1860 state and federal censuses revealed no family named Butler working at the Dog River facility.[47]

Such mobility should not have been surprising in a society where manual labor was associated with slavery and where the initial choice to become a mill worker was often an act of economic desperation. Nor did workers view their conditions with the equanimity of Daniel Pratt. One of his workers for fifteen years wrote wearily of his experience: "I have about paid my expenses and no more." He had performed the hardest work of his life and wrecked his health.[48]

Ambivalence about industrial jobs was well grounded. The state's industrialists paid relatively high wages and cared well for operatives

compared to other southern states. By 1860 some operatives had accumulated extensive personal property. But most were better represented by Pratt's operative who had nothing to show for fifteen years
except broken health and bitter memories. When the water wheel broke
at the Tallassee mill in 1861, one local woman grieved because "It will
turn so many of the poor people out of employment, when they can
scarcely live at best now."[49] While mills were returning annual profits
of 25 percent, workers barely survived.[50] And owners who pledged to
save the impoverished poor whites in the 1840s unnecessarily feared
insurrection by an aroused white working class by 1860.

Just as the textile industry was the largest one employing poor whites,
Mobile was the most important city where they lived and labored. The
city gained population faster than any other American metropolis during
the 1830s and experienced another spurt in the 1850s due primarily to
the arrival of large numbers of immigrants. By 1860, Mobile contained
60 percent of Alabama's urban population and 24 percent of its foreign-
born. Of the whites living in Mobile County, 63 percent (nearly 6,000)
owned neither land nor personal property. Of these indigents, the largest
number were artisans and industrial workers.[51] In the city, the level of
indigency was even higher: 64.1 percent for white males, 76.1 percent
for white females.

Exploitation of child and female labor, often thought to date from a
later time, already existed in antebellum Mobile. Some 353 white children aged twelve to seventeen worked as bricklayers, clerks, painters,
dressmakers, and in other occupations in 1860. Many of them lived in
households headed by single women. Both the Catholic and Protestant
orphanages in the city allowed their older charges to be farmed out to
artisans and textile factories so that "habits of industry" could be "in-
culcated on their minds."

Women formed a large portion of the city's bottom class. Obviously,
antebellum white women who remained unmarried or who were widowed, deserted, or divorced faced grave economic hardships. By 1850,
8 percent of Mobile's industrial labor force was female. They labored
primarily in the millinery, clothing, confectionary, furniture, brick, and
lumber industries. By 1860 they constituted only 10 percent of the work
force but were disproportionately represented in the textile mill on Dog
River and as domestics. Immigrant Irishwomen dominated work in the
port city's hotels and private homes and as washerwomen, driving both
black and native-born poor white women into other jobs or out of the
labor market.[52]

Complicating the problem of poverty was the large infusion of immigrants. During the 1850s the number of French-born in the population increased by 72.6 percent to 538, the number of Germans by

148.7 percent to 1,276, the total of Irish by 64.6 percent to 3,307. By 1860 immigrant labor constituted 62 percent of all free labor in the city, squeezing out both blacks and native-born whites.

Mobile citizens early acknowledged the presence of the poor and tried various remedies for their poverty. In 1854 a local pastor wrote a series of newspaper columns entitled "Life-Gatherings Among the Poor." Whether their indigence resulted from their own sins or the unjust circumstances of society, he was unsure. But that they were numerous was obvious to anyone who bothered to look.

During the city's 1855 commercial stagnation, many artisans had no work, and the rector of St. John's Episcopal Church reported that fifty working-class families in the vicinity of the church relied entirely on charity for food, clothing, and fuel. In such straits, the editor of the *Mobile Advertiser* found no theological lessons whatsoever: "No one can doubt that this want is directly traceable to circumstances over which the sufferers have no control."

The city responded to such exigencies in different ways. To prevent vagrancy and begging, municipal authorities enacted laws fining or jailing transients who could not earn a livelihood. The city did provide modest aid in the form of free medical care for indigents funded from an annual poll tax of one dollar per adult white male. Most white indigents were treated at the City Hospital, which was completed in the 1830s. The city also contributed to the Female Benevolent Society, which provided for "the most unfortunate and helpless" widows. The society used municipal funds to construct "Widows Row," a housing district that furnished shelter to sixteen indigent and dependent women.

Special crises led to extraordinary efforts to befriend the poor. During the 1837 yellow fever epidemic that decimated the poor districts, civic leaders founded the Samaritan Society to dispense aid to the ill and destitute. Two years later during a visitation of malaria, twelve men organized another association for the indigent. Unaware of the irony of the name insofar as it applied to the poor, they called their group the Can't Get Away Club.

Private religious charities were also active. Catholics, Protestants, and Jews established benevolent societies to help the poor of their respective faiths. Episcopal women also formed the Protestant Episcopal Church Employment Society, which obtained sewing jobs for poor women.

Rather than provide free public schools to educate the offspring of the poor, city officials subsidized indigents who attended private schools. In the late 1830s the extent of indigence became so great that it seemed a greater economy to establish a Free Department at Barton Academy; in 1839 the free school for indigents accounted for 150 of the academy's 350 pupils. Denominational schools enrolled other poor white children.

Even with tax-subsidized private schools, 42 percent of Mobile's white school-age children attended no school at all in 1851. One newspaper noted: "No workingman can afford to send his children to school in Mobile." The result was a campaign for public education that would be free and would attract both indigents and the upper class so as not to stigmatize the poor. Leadership of the public school crusade came from well-educated middle class men, many of them born in the North, who hoped to stabilize and protect Mobile's social order. Citizens endorsed the concept in an 1852 referendum, and county politicians persuaded the state legislature to establish a statewide public school system in 1854. The 1855 legislature provided school funding through license fees and property taxes. By 1860 one-fourth of Mobile's school-age white children attended public schools, and they represented a cross section of economic classes.

In Mobile as elsewhere in the state the poor experienced gradations of poverty. For those at the very bottom of the lower class there was the poorhouse. Created by the county government, the almshouse accepted the poor who were diseased, mentally ill, elderly, friendless, or without relatives. Because of the general resentment against the dole or direct relief, inmates of the house were supposed to work toward self-sufficiency and raise their own food. That seldom occurred. In 1860 eighteen paupers including two elderly blind lived at the house. Nine of them were immigrants, eight from Ireland.[53]

The Separate World of Poor Whites

Economic marginality translated into social and cultural isolation. Because the poor played no central role in the economy, most planters and yeomen simply ignored them. Where the impoverished posed a social menace, as they did in towns, civic leaders provided minimal services to keep them tranquil if not content. Poor whites responded by forging their own social and cultural systems, sometimes closely related to those of planters and yeomen, sometimes quite dissimilar.

In some ways Mobile's approach to the problem of poverty was duplicated throughout the state. Alabama's approach to poor relief, indeed the entire nation's philosophy, was modeled on the English Poor Law of 1601, which had established workhouses to care for the able-bodied poor. The Territory Law of 1799 had provided for appointment of overseers of the poor in every township. In 1803 the Mississippi Territory (which included the present state of Alabama) charged counties with responsibility for support of paupers. Early Alabama constitution makers did not give the matter high priority, however. Reflecting a frontier individualism that charged every person with his or her own welfare, they made no mention of supporting paupers in the state's first constitution nor in the 1861 constitutional revision.[54] The result was a haphazard pattern. Some towns such as Mobile were influenced by religious and humanitarian leaders and established almshouses to care for the poor; other towns were too busy to care. Counties followed the same mixed pattern.

As in Mobile, many farsighted Alabamians perceived illiteracy to be the critical element in perpetuating white poverty. Travelers through the state were appalled at the extent of the problem. One reported in 1840 not less than 22,000 white illiterates above the age of twenty, a figure he believed too low.[55] That same year Cherokee County in the northeast corner of the state contained 8,773 persons; 1,001 were whites above the age of twenty who could neither read nor write. There were two common schools in the county that enrolled only thirty-two pupils.[56] Statewide the number of illiterates over twenty climbed from 33,757 in 1850 to 37,605 in 1860, though the proportion of the electorate that was illiterate declined slightly from 14 to 12 percent.[57]

As in Mobile, the solution lay in public schools; but an effective statewide system of public education was decades away. Still, the state was not as bereft of schools as some casual travelers believed. By 1850 there were already 1,323 schools with 1,630 teachers and 37,237 pupils, which represented an estimated 40 percent of the school-age white population. Four years later the legislature passed the Public School Act and the number of public schools climbed to 1,900.[58]

Neither the presence of public schools nor their absence meant quite as much as a modern observer might think. Many prosperous yeomen and not a few planters obtained wealth and influence without benefit of *McGuffey's Reader*. Alabamians often expressed disdain for education, trusting in rearing, riding, and riches more than reading, writing, and arithmetic. Nor did the presence of a school guarantee appreciation for the finer things of life. A young schoolteacher newly arrived in Butler County in 1860 described teaching there as " 'a very unpleasant occupation': I do not know where we wil go to yet but we wil not be apt to stay in butler, I think it is a very good country for farming but ther is no society nor nothing elce her the people is more like hogs an dogs than they are like folks . . . I will try to stay heare this year without saying much."[59]

The fluid and unstable life of the Alabama frontier played havoc with poor white family life. Although divorce was rare, desertion or cohabitation was not unusual, judging by the large number of single female heads of families found in census reports. The unsettled conditions also took a high toll on life, leaving many widows and widowers with large families to tend. Travelers exaggerated the extent of filth, clay eating, and drunkenness, but such degradation did occur.

Although it was the South's most persistent taboo, even interracial unions were not unknown. Alabama did not restrict interracial marriages until 1852 and did not penalize the couple even then. Slightly more than half (51 percent) of the state's interracial marriages involved a black male and a white female, and all the whites involved were either yeomen or poor whites. Most of these interracial unions occurred in sparsely settled rural areas of north Alabama, especially in the hill counties of Pickens, Fayette, Marion, Limestone, Morgan, and Lawrence. In these counties there were few Negroes and large numbers of poor whites.[60]

Such deviations in family life were exceptions. Both personal preference and social convention restricted poor white family life to accepted norms. Most families demonstrated remarkable stability and the same problems and tensions common to all classes: high fertility rates, frightful levels of infant mortality, ostracism of community reprobates, careful attention to the religious and moral training of children, and affection for outdoor activities such as hunting and fishing, which also supplemented diets.

There remains an additional important element in class identification.[61] A distinctive culture can separate people as dramatically as gradations in wealth or ownership of land. Often the poor attended different churches, practiced a different kind of medicine, believed different superstitions, and established a different literary tradition. Whereas planters and yeomen relied on the written word, poor whites were more likely to transmit culture through long-remembered folk tales and songs. The informal and oral transmission of folk culture counted for more than formal education.

Class was a product both of self-perception and of broader cultural understanding. Or, put a different way, yeomen and upper class people distinguished poor whites by attributing to them a different and inferior culture: such people were illiterate, boorish, immoral, bizarre, unreliable, and lazy. Poor whites also believed they were different, although they assigned an alternate set of values to the differentness: they were practical, democratic, down-to-earth, hospitable, common people, outdoorsmen, independent, witty, fun-loving, not materialistic or hypocritical. They believed themselves more religious than the upper class to whom they assigned distinctive sins of affluence: horse racing, gambling, cheating, unethical business practices, materialism, excessive drinking, and idleness.

Whereas the modern student of folkways may find poor white culture a colorful kaleidoscope of beautiful patterns, antebellum contemporaries found no such attractions. Although few if any poor whites ever read their accounts, the haughty condescension of travelers and prosperous fellow citizens must have been expressed in a thousand demeaning ways: in offhanded insults, averted eyes, quick street crossings when approaching a poor white family in town, and shrill family councils upon the discovery that a planter's son intended to marry a girl of little means or education.

Even religion was not beyond class connotations. Although disputes over theology and decorum were not exclusively related to class, many Christians of lowly estate identified riches with corruption and poverty with godliness. No sooner had Alabamians established their first territorial capital at St. Stephens, on the banks of the Tombigbee River, than an itinerant preacher troubled their ease in Zion. Feeling rather proud of the sophistication and prosperity of their community, townspeople did not welcome the religious provocateur. But he persisted in his emotional and condemnatory preaching, ignoring a ban against such activities passed by the town leaders expressly to silence him. Finally fed up, citizens set him adrift on the river. As he floated downstream, he looked back toward town and shouted one last defiant word: "St. Stephens be damned. I came unto you and you received me not. I now confine this den of iniquity to the snakes, bats and owls."

Not all early ministers challenged polite society. Many in fact perceived themselves as the agents of salvation and culture among a primitive and wicked people. An early Methodist leader depicted Washington County settlers as "grossly worldly and extremely wicked" who "could no more be impressed with the obligations and benefits of the Christian religion than could the beasts of the forest in which they lived." A Presbyterian reported from the Tennessee Valley in the 1820s that "no part of our country is more destitute of spiritual instruction."

Religion was far more this-worldly than many observers have realized. Because they were an agrarian people reliant upon natural forces over which they exercised no control, Alabamians, like ancient Hebrews, relied upon primary causes to restrain the rains or to empty the clouds, to stay the winds or make fertile their crops. One impetuous Methodist layman, Billy Grizzard, came right to the point in an 1830s prayer for relief from a prolonged drought: "Good Lord, send us a root-soaker and a gully-washer."

The religion might be fundamental but it was also reasonable. According to one piece of religious folklore, a poor north Alabama mountain family believed that its precious oxen team could be properly managed only through frequent bursts of profanity. When a protracted camp meeting began in a nearby hollow, the entire family was saved except one boy. Neighbors anxiously pressed upon him the urgency of salvation until finally he put religion into its limited human context: "Dad went down there and got religion; Mom she went down there and got religion; John went down there and got religion. If I went, who'd drive the oxen?"

Within the broadly shared common religious faith of Alabamians, differences existed based largely on class. One persistent element of southern religious folklore sought to explain the variations in denominations: a Methodist was a Baptist who wore shoes; a Presbyterian was a Methodist with a bank account; an Episcopalian was a Presbyterian who lived off his investments. Though obviously an oversimplification, it is true that Methodists and Baptists enjoyed a near monopoly among Alabama plain folk, partly because Presbyterians and Episcopalians worried too much about an educated and theologically trained clergy. Bivocational Methodist and Baptist preachers worked their fields during the week and proclaimed the gospel to whoever would listen on Sunday.

Often intradenominational squabbles contained elements of class conflict. The Cumberland Presbyterian faction appealed to yeomen and poor whites in the hill country. Although Primitive or antimissionary Baptists possessed strength statewide, their strongest areas also contained the highest concentrations of yeomen and poor whites. Conversely, the missionary Baptist stronghold was the Black Belt. By 1837, twelve of Alabama's twenty-one Baptist associations were divided over the issues of missions, education, and the creation of Bible and temperance societies, with the missionary faction in favor and the Primitives opposed. The rapid spread of Alexander Campbell's movement in north Alabama during the 1830s further complicated matters, with the Disciples of Christ gaining adherents in the same hill counties where Primitive Baptists thrived. Primitive Baptists placed little value in educated, salaried ministers, opposed denominational colleges and mission programs for blacks, and often considered low country missionaries and denominational leaders haughty and arrogant.[62]

Educated parsons of prosperous Black Belt churches were not the only ones who believed that poor whites were products of a different and inferior social order. Antebellum travelers and humorists left a misinformed legacy that did not flatter Alabama's bottom class. In fact, by 1860 every stereotype of poor whites was already familiar to the reader of antebellum literature. Writers described them as filthy, lazy, profane, drunken, sallow complexioned, clay eaters, mentally slow, racist, democratic, witty, individualistic, hunters and fishermen, and prolific at reproducing their own kind.

Traveling east from Montgomery into Creek Indian territory during January 1835, Englishman George W. Featherstonhaugh described "miserable-looking cabins without fences" and one particularly "filthy

cabin where a villainous-looking white man sold tobacco and whiskey."
Three other "brutal-looking whites" were enjoying the antics of a tall
Indian who was drunk and "stark naked"; they were trying to persuade
him to jump into a nearby stream.[63] Maj. Caleb Swan described whites
living in the Creek Territory during the 1830s as fugitives, horse thieves,
gamblers, and drunks, "the most abandoned wretches that can be found;
there is scarcely a crime that some of them have not been guilty of."[64]
English geologist Sir Charles Lyell described a "cracker" family moving
west from Alabama on a steamboat, the mother smoking a pipe. He
described girls of nine imitating their elders by smoking paper cigars
and a mother who, after suckling an infant, gave it some tobacco to
chew.[65]

Frederick Law Olmsted crossed north Alabama in the summer of
1860 and left an account of what he saw. Most of the dwellings he
passed were rude log cabins "unwholesomely crowded" with children.
Invited to share a meal with a prosperous farmer, he recorded his host's
description of a white farm laborer who was a "bad, lazy man," often
found lounging in the fields or abusing Negroes: "He was about the
meanest white man I ever see; he was a heap meaner'n niggers. I reckon
niggers would come somewhere between white folks and such as he."

Continuing his journey, Olmsted saw white women, half-naked for
comfort in the boiling June sun, digging for iron ore on a hillside. A
man applied a pick to the vein while the women and children shoveled
the ore and piled it on kilns of timber where it was fired and then carried
to a forge. The women and children of eight or ten years who carried
lumps of ore worked as hard as the man. Their employer described the
family as "powerful poor, common, no account people" who lived "over
the hill" and "come right nigh starvin' thar" before he gave them work.
They had moved into an old cabin. He praised the woman whom he had
known since childhood as an industrious bright person, but he considered her husband "no account."

Olmsted's talkative host described a hunter named John Brown who
lived with his large family in a cabin on the mountain. He pretended to
plant a corn patch but never made a crop. When neighboring farmers
sought him out to help with their harvests, he rejected their offers,
saying that "he'd be damned if he was going to work." To feed his family
he hunted deer and turkey and, according to community suspicions,
stole corn, hogs, and cattle. His children were scrawny half-starved
wretches and his wife had begged work and corn the previous summer.
One sympathetic farmer sent her into his cotton fields to pick beside
his slaves. There she labored for two days, taking her pay in corn, which
her little boy carried to the mill to be ground. When Olmsted inquired
if there were many such vagabonds in north Alabama, his host assured:

"Yes, a great many on the mountain, and they make a heap of trouble. There is a law by which they might be taken up [if it could be proved that they had no visible means of support] and made to work to support their families; but the law is never used."[66]

Although Olmsted mistakenly lumped together poor whites and yeomen into a single class, his detailed descriptions clearly differentiate and provide rare insights into the way independent farmers viewed their indigent neighbors. During a journey on the Alabama River to Mobile four years earlier, Olmsted had observed the complexity of the relationship between poor whites and blacks. Noticing that Irishmen did the most dangerous work, such as loading cotton bales, the visitor was told that "niggers are worth too much to be risked here; if the Paddies are knocked overboard, or get their backs broke, nobody loses anything." Fashionable passengers rode on the upper deck, while poor whites and Negroes were confined to the lower.

Once in Mobile in 1856, Olmsted noted that most of the servants at the Battle House Hotel were Irish. He also observed a white man—"a native, country fellow"—nailing up a fence with two Negro laborers under the supervision of a slave carpenter who bossed the team. Although Olmsted had seen Negroes directing Irish labor, he had never before seen a slave boss a native born white man.[67]

Other travelers recorded fragments that help reconstruct the lives of the bottom class. Describing poor whites as men whose only worldly possessions consisted of a wife, a dog, and a gun, they emphasized the affection of the class for the outdoors, for hunting, fishing, and a simple life. Though some were trapped by such an existence, many chose it over a life of exertion and tension.

Many travelers commented on the poor whites' commitment to democracy. Sir Charles Lyell recounted an election in Clarke County where the common man's candidate emphasized the education and success of his opponent as grounds for disqualification: "A rich man can not sympathize with the poor." Lyell recorded another instance of a candidate who traveled long distances on foot, though he owned a horse. In Mobile he heard of a legislator deserted by many farmer supporters because his daughter came to a ball in a dress with flounces in the latest Parisian style. Lyell also contrasted his comfortable lodgings in the city with the "humblest class of 'crackers,' or some low, illiterate German or Irish emigrants, the wife sitting with a piper in her mouth, doing no work and reading no books."[68]

Not all depictions of poor whites were so negative or serious. In fact, Alabama's poor whites became the subject of one of the richest veins of American literature, "old southwestern humor." The typical southwestern humorist was a professional—lawyer or newspaperman usually—well educated, well traveled, and intensely political. As prosperous men typically committed to the aristocratic ideals of the Whig Party, they capitalized on poor white vernacular to belittle and lampoon the supposed ignorance and backwardness of the common people who constituted the backbone of Jacksonian democracy. Although they depicted poor whites as illiterate, shiftless, and malaria-ridden, they also portrayed them as witty survivors who were in no way pathetic.[69] And from these writers, many of them Alabamians, emerged America's most truly distinctive literary tradition.

The best purveyor of the genre in Alabama was Johnson J. Hooper, who settled near the tiny village of LaFayette in the hills of east-central Alabama. He later moved to Dadeville where in 1840 he became a census enumerator, a job that put him in contact with thousands of poor whites within a nine-hundred-square-mile area of Tallapoosa County. Poor whites resented his meddling and threats to their independence and believed that his tedious lists would become the basis for a tax. Because the enumerator counted even their livestock and poultry, they called him the "chicken man."[70] One of Hooper's most famous tales recounted "the old she savage" widow Judy Tompkins and her four children "all between five and a hundred years old" who threatened to cut off President Martin Van Buren's head for sending census takers to meddle in her affairs and tax the poor people so that the president could eat "his vittils out'n gold spoons."[71]

Hooper's central character, Simon Suggs, combined elements of both yeoman and poor white. Born the son of a Primitive Baptist preacher, he grew up devoted to vices such as gambling, racing plow horses, and staging rooster fights. He earned a meager living as a hog drover for farmers. His ethical maxim was simple: "It is good to be shifty in a new country." And shifty he was, stealing money at a protracted revival or manipulating himself into leadership of the Tallapoosa Militia. But Hooper recognized the complex levels of poor white society and created an antagonist for Suggs, a "durned, little, dirt-eatin' deer-face," who was even poorer. Harassed constantly by his diminutive adversary, whom he called "Yellow-legs" for his clay eating and sallow complexion, Hooper finally relented: "I oughtent to git aggravated at him, no how. He's a poor signifiken runt, that's got the mark of the huckle-bery ponds on his legs, yit, whar the water come to when he was a-gatherin 'em, in his raisin' in Northkurliny."[72]

A story concerning a fishing trip up the Tallapoosa River afforded an opportunity for more extensive description of the subsistence life of poor whites. Amid the hollows along the river lived a people "half agricultural, half piscatorial—a sinewy, yellow-headed, whiskey-loving set." Those

south of the river lived in "Possum Trot," those north in "Turpentine."
Mainly the lazy and shiftless people fished and told stories. Jim Edwards,
who resided in a cabin along the river, lived on catfish:

> Don't do nothin' but ketch 'em. Some of the boys says he's got slimy
> all over, like a cat . . . ; all I know is, we ketcht one in the seine,
> that weighed over forty pounds. Thar was a moccasin tuk out of it
> longer than my arm. And nobody wouldn't have it, but Jim. As we
> was goin' home, Jim a totin' the fish, ses I—Jim, you ain't a gwine
> to eat that cat surely! Ses he—'pshaw! that moccasin warn't noth-
> ing'; I noticed it good, and it warn't rotten a bit. Ses I—Jim, enny
> man that'll eat that cat, would eat a bullfrog. And with that, he
> knocked me down and like to a killed me.[73]

Despite their popularity as a source of frontier humor, poor whites
attracted the attention of few serious Alabama writers, who were more
eager to describe the grandeurs of plantation life. One exception was
Daniel R. Hundley, an Alabama planter who described the South's social
classes on the eve of the Civil War. Unlike Olmsted, he correctly depicted a complicated class structure. He devoted chapters in descending
order of importance to "The Southern Gentleman," "The Middle Class,"
"The Southern Yeoman," "The Southern Bully," "Poor White Trash,"
and "The Negro Slaves." His description of the "class of lazy vagabonds
known as Poor Whites" is the best evidence of how complete class
identification had become by 1860, at least from the standpoint of the
planter.

Hundley even gave poor whites a separate genetic heritage, maintaining that they had descended from paupers, convicts, and indentured
servants. They were the result of bad blood, not hostile environment.
Living unto themselves, they built their log cabins among the sterile
hills or in the "dismal solitude of the burr-oak or pine barrens," as far
away as possible from the simple but sturdy yeoman and the prosperous
planter. But the "squatters," "crackers," "sandhillers," "Rag Tag Bob-
Tail," "People in the Barrens," or just plain "Poor White Trash" lived
close to each other, nurturing a small patch of corn, pumpkins, and
vegetables.

Hundley related the story of an overseer who persuaded a sandhiller
to come down to the nearest alluvial soil being cultivated by a planter.
As soon as the

> juvenile Bobtail reached the open country, his eyes began to dilate,
> and his whole manner and expression indicated bewilderment and
> uneasiness. "Bedadsezed!" exclaimed he at last, "if this yere

ked'ntry haint got nary sign ov er tree! How in thunder duz folks live down yere? By G-o-r-y! this beats all that Uncle Snipes tells about Carlina. Tell yer what. I'm goin' ter make tracks fur dad's— yer heer my horn toot!"

Though ignorant and degraded, rural poor whites did not go hungry. They hunted, fished, grew corn, and obtained luxuries by selling the venison they killed. Their barter economy provided a better living, Hundley believed, than that of European peasants or New York mechanics. Physically, they were "lank, lean, angular, and boney, with flaming red, or flaxen, or sandy, or carroty-colored hair, sallow complexions, awkward manners, and a natural stupidity or dullness of intellect that almost surpasses belief." Women were even more intolerable than men, "owing chiefly to their disgusting habit of snuff-dipping and even sometimes pipe-smoking." Their sparse possessions consisted principally of a spinning wheel, the family rifle, a pack of hunting dogs, and chickens.

Poor whites were prolific, filling their cabins with "dirty, squalling, white-headed little brats" known as "Tow-Heads." Most of them also pursued "idle habits" such as hunting, gander-pulling, marble and card playing, and drunkenness: "All they seem to care for, is to live from hand to mouth; to get drunk, provided they can do so without having to trudge too far after their liquor . . . ; to vote at elections; to eat and sleep; to lounge in the sunshine and to bask in the warmth of a roaring wood fire." They elected ignorant demagogues to represent them, supported slavery because of their "downright envy and hatred of the black man," believed in silly superstitions, and worshiped in Primitive Baptist "Hard Shell" churches whose parsons were "in the main of the Order of the Whang Doodle."[74]

Hundley's sketch of Alabama's bottom class was not a pretty picture. But there is no reason to assume that it differed markedly from the way other planters viewed the bottom class. The tastes of planter and poor white differed in politicians, in domicile, land policy, religion, architecture, sport, and just about everything else.

Although we know a great deal about what travelers, planters, and even yeomen thought of them, we know little about how poor whites viewed themselves. Yet their choices of politicians, residence, occupations, and churches strongly suggest that they saw themselves as a distinct group, sharing much in common with their yeomen neighbors, but with many distinctions and grievances also.

Historian Minnie Boyd, commenting on Alabama society during the 1850s, noted the destitution and outrages of poor whites; but she warned also that the bottom class retained its self-respect, that the term "po' white" was responsible "for much devious thinking."

How they lived we can only guess, because moths and rust . . . corrupt the records and relics of the poor, and their homes are as transient as the tenants. They deeded no property, kept no books and made no wills. What they thought or felt we do not know, because they were inarticulate, leaving no literary remains. They are unsung, unknown and forgotten ancestors.[75]

"A Poor
Man's Fight"

On the eve of the Civil War, Alabama's population was overwhelmingly a small farmer democracy despite all the images of stately plantation houses and opulent owners. Approximately 85 percent of the white residents owned property, with rates varying from county to county and region to region. That was the good news, the saga of the American Dream fulfilled. More troubling was the reality that even after the enormous agricultural prosperity of the 1850s and the steady growth of industry, some 15 percent of the state's white residents owned no land and fewer than $150 in property. Virtually every decade from the Civil War to the Great Depression brought increases in farm tenancy and industrial indigence. No other cycle in American history resulted in so sustained and extensive downward mobility for so numerous a population. How could such a process occur in a land of such abundant natural resources? The first step in the downward cycle was the Civil War. The war and defeat disrupted economic patterns, removed many productive males and even more work animals, fostered bitter class grievances, and greatly expanded indigence because of new labor arrangements. Reconstruction years also introduced most of the strategies by which both state and federal governments would seek to deal with poverty during the following century.

The war began amid great enthusiasm. Calhoun County, the northernmost county favoring secession, furnished many Confederate volunteers. For Smith Lipscomb, support of secession confirmed his long pilgrimage from landlessness to respectability. By 1861 he owned large acreage and some slaves. The story of his family had been one of steady upward mobility. But the war proved a watershed that broke the continuity of his life. It propelled his family on a path that would bring some of his children and grandchildren full circle back to the poverty of the family's first years in Alabama. His son Joshua, in whom he had placed so many hopes, died in Confederate service during 1861. His wife Sally died shortly after the conflict ended. His brother-in-law moved to Lamar County, Texas, in search of better opportunities. The stable society he had once known disintegrated. The daughter of one of his relatives bore two children by a black father. Smith Lipscomb begged his sister to deny the rumor; she not only confirmed it but added that there were "no hopes of her stopping" the scandalous affair. Although Lipscomb converted one of his newly manumitted slaves to the status of tenant farmer, his financial fortunes declined. The family complained bitterly about high property taxes, though Lipscomb's personal property was valued at only $56. When he could not repay a $200 note to Gadsden lawyers, they threatened to sue him. Another debt of $75 was two years past due in 1880. That same year Bowling and Company dunned him for $8 of interest owed since the fall of 1879. Green and Whatley Dry Goods at Alexandria demanded repayment of $7.30. By 1880 the Smith Lipscomb family was well on its way down the agricultural ladder.[1]

The great surge of nationalism that swept across Calhoun County and the South in 1860–61 carried away many of the differences that had divided white southerners. Class conflict had not been pronounced in antebellum Alabama. Too many factors mitigated against the potential conflicts between planter, yeoman, and poor white: the nonaristocratic origins of many planters, kinship networks that crossed class lines, social egalitarianism, the political power exercised by common whites, the availability of land, common folkways, and the ideology of white supremacy. The rapid economic growth of the 1850s tended to confirm the high expectations of yeomen and poor whites that it was only a matter of time until they also prospered. Although there were obvious exceptions, most white Alabamians of all classes favored secession. Every county but one in the southeastern Wiregrass elected secession delegates to the 1860 convention. Before the Confederate government resorted to the draft, 18 percent of the whites in Henry County volunteered for the army. Two other Wiregrass counties, Coffee and Covington, produced rates of 19 and 17 percent. The hill counties opposed secession, but the issue was often closely contested, with cooperationists and Unionists winning by the narrowest of margins. And once the decision was made, 11 percent of the whites in Calhoun and 10 percent in Jackson County volunteered to fight. Percentages in the twelve Black Belt counties were not much different, ranging from 9 to 16 percent.[2]

But the hardy bloom of patriotism soon wilted under the searing heat of war. Even the initial vote on secession pitted common whites in the hill counties against more prosperous whites in the plantation belt. Secessionist majorities in Black Belt counties such as Macon, Montgomery, Perry, Marengo, Sumter, Wilcox, and Lowndes numbered between 90 and 100 percent. But in the hill counties with the highest concentrations of poor whites and the fewest slaves—Limestone, Morgan, and Winston counties—between 90 and 100 percent favored cooperation and continued union; in Franklin, Marion, Fayette, Walker, Lawrence, Madison, Marshall, and DeKalb, cooperationists won between 70 and 90 percent of the votes. Statewide, the secessionists elected fifty-four delegates to the convention, cooperationists and Unionists forty-six. The popular vote was equally close, 35,693 to 28,181, with no historical records from one strong Unionist county. Obviously, class was not the sole issue in the secession crisis. Wiregrass counties voted overwhelmingly for secession.[3] But their enthusiasm for the Confederacy would dissipate quickly.

Once secession was accomplished, whites rallied to the cause regardless of their initial misgivings. Despite a rich folklore about Unionist sympathizers in the hill country, only 2,578 Alabamians actually fought in the Union army. Conversely, by the end of 1864, many poor white counties had furnished more soldiers to the Confederate army than their number of votes. Some 17 percent of Alabama's entire white population was by that time in military service. As a result, women and children were left behind to plow, plant, and harvest. As the optimistic days of autumn gave way to winter and spring without sign of victory, soldiers began to fret about their families. Most of them had planted crops and even begun to harvest before enlistment in 1861. So the real crisis came in the spring and summer of 1862. To make matters worse, many counties suffered severe drought during the second summer of the war. Twenty counties did not produce enough corn for their own populations, including three from the Wiregrass and eleven from the hill country. In Coosa County the corn crop declined by 150,000 bushels in 1862.[4]

Pitiful letters began to collect on the desk of Governor John Gill Shorter. A resident of Guntersville in the northeastern hill country informed Shorter of the failure of the county's wheat crop, told of "poor women and children crying for bread," and warned of starvation to come. The probate judge in Lawrence County described the plight of some seventy Winston County poor white families whose male heads had enlisted in Lawrence County Confederate units. The soldiers from Lawrence and Winston counties were "mostly very poor men, which multiplys our lists of indigent familys to such a large number that we cannot assist Winston Co. any longer." The supply of salt was nearly exhausted in both counties. Illiterate wives of Confederate soldiers in Henry County persuaded a male community leader to write the governor on their behalf, complaining that relief to the destitute in their Wiregrass county for the entire year was less than their counterparts received in prosperous Barbour County each month. The wife of Marion Rudd, who had been in the Confederate army for twelve months, had received only twelve bushels of corn and thirty pounds of meat. She had been promised $85, then $40, but "the fact is she don't git anything," and she was living on charity. She had already lost two sons in Confederate service and inquired how she could draw the salary due them before their deaths. From nearby Coffee County a writer reminded the governor that his area was filled with "very poor people" who had trouble living even under "the most favorable circumstances"; but current conditions made it impossible for them. Poor husbands had been conscripted into the Confederate army and only the charity of neighbors sustained their families.[5]

The sources of such indigence were complex. Many of these people had lived close to the precipice even in the best of times. With the oldest males removed by military service, those left behind could not carve a living from the land. Wartime inflation eroded wages. In 1860 Alabama's farm laborers earned an average of $12.41 per month plus board. By 1862 that figure was less than a living wage. By 1864 wages had risen to $18 a month, but two bushels of corn might cost as much as $13. Privates in the Confederate army, the rank held by most poor whites, earned only $11 a month, less even than a farm laborer.[6] Weather was a continual problem. The drought of 1862 was followed by a similar one in the southeastern Wiregrass in 1863 and in north Alabama during 1864.[7]

Despite natural calamities, enough corn was produced to feed the population if the distribution had been equitable. Crops in central Alabama and the Black Belt were good throughout the war. But poor transportation made it hard to distribute corn to those who most needed it. Southeastern Alabama had no railroads and none connected food surplus counties in central Alabama to needy north Alabama. Such wagon roads as existed were impassable during parts of the year. Profiteering by farmers and distributors drove the price to extortionist levels. A bushel of corn in Mobile sold for $1 in 1862, $3 in 1863, and $7 in 1865. Prices in north Alabama were even higher.[8] Salt sold for $2 a sack in 1861 and for $80 a year later. When revenues failed to meet needs, the Alabama legislature levied a tax-in-kind of one-tenth of a family's crop. These taxes, designed to be used to help the poor, fell heaviest on the whites who could least afford them.

Federal occupation and guerilla fighting in the Tennessee Valley were additional sources of suffering, forcing families to become refugees or live in danger of their lives. Marauding Confederate cavalry and home guards inflicted even more havoc than the federals, invading the hill and Wiregrass counties looking for deserters, pillaging and looting as they went.[9]

As disaffection grew, Governor Shorter and the legislature groped for ways to help. Taxes on wealthier citizens climbed steadily and the proceeds provided a system of welfare and relief. In most southern states the war resulted in a notable shift of the tax burden toward the wealthiest citizens as a means of reducing poor white disaffection.[10] Alabama enacted a special 25 percent levy on all taxable property in order to provide aid to "indigent families of absent volunteers." At first the aid was distributed in the county where the tax was levied. The sums made available varied from $4 per family in poor white counties such as Winston and Blount to $66 per family in the Black Belt's Dallas County, which had much wealth and few indigents. Such inequities increased the belief of many poor whites that they were not treated fairly. Governor Shorter summoned a special session of the legislature in October 1862 to provide additional assistance. The result was a special appropriation of $2 million for indigent families of soldiers that was administered at uniform rates across the state. Subsequent state appropriations in August and December 1863 provided an additional $4 million. The state also provided salt and drugs to the indigent. In all, the state appropriated nearly $12 million for the poor, but the destitution continued.

Administration was the responsibility of probate judges, agents appointed by them, or some other county official. The money appropriated never equaled the need, and many poor whites charged officials with unfairness, inefficiency, and corruption.

One result of these efforts was lengthy lists of indigents. One such list for Blount County in January 1862 filled forty-three pages. According to one estimate, from the latter months of 1862 until the end of the war, at least one-quarter of the white population was supported by state or county doles. In Barbour County during 1864, 280 families received half their supplies from the state or county, and 649 families were completely destitute. In Washington County three-fourths were indigents; in Coosa County one-half; in Randolph County 1,600 soldiers' families were destitute. The city of Mobile contained 7,020 impoverished families. Although the rate of indigence varied, median averages were 7 percent in 1862, 34 percent in 1863, and 39 percent in 1864. In the latter year more than 35,000 families with nearly 130,000 people were indigent. Despite increasing aid, the number of poor people increased from 1 in 10 families in 1862 to 3 in 10 a year later. And the highest concentrations of destitution were in the Wiregrass and hill counties.[11]

Well-to-do Alabamians appreciated the sacrifices of the poor. Whether from a sense of self-preservation or genuine concern, they helped wherever they could. Mobile citizens organized a relief society that distributed food from a free market. By mid-1861 it was supplying 1,800 persons daily. Montgomery established in April 1861 the Soldiers' Fund

Committee, which received and distributed donations for the indigent. Selma began a similar organization. A few such charitable societies appeared in counties, notably in Calhoun, but the rural areas generally went begging in the most literal sense of that word.

Private acts of charity occurred across the state. A Talladega County merchant gave a pair of shoes to all soldiers' wives in his beat who did not own slaves. A company in east-central Alabama distributed cotton and woolen thread to poor whites in Randolph County. Talented performers sponsored benefit concerts for the poor wives of sailors. Churches contributed food and clothing. The mistress of one plantation employed a poor woman whose husband was in service; she also carried thread to rural women, paying them to weave for her in exchange for syrup, sugar, and produce.[12]

Despite such initiatives both by the state and by private citizens, deprivation continued. The best evidence of the deepening crisis was the 1864 appearance of the "corn women." They mainly came to Black Belt counties, sometimes in groups of ten or twenty, carrying several sacks apiece. Boats and trains traversing the impoverished regions furnished transportation. The women scoured the country for corn, begging or stealing as the occasion demanded. Some were in desperate need; others were opportunistic imposters. Although most prosperous farmers and planters contributed to all rather than turn any genuinely needy woman away, resentment grew. One Black Belt citizen reflected a patrician's view of corn women as an 1860s version of welfare cheaters:

"They soon become perfect nuisances. When you objected to giving they abused you; they no longer brought papers [identifying them as indigent families of soldiers]; when we had no corn to spare we gave them money, which they said they would rather have. . . . I saw a party of them on a steamboat counting their money. They had hundreds of dollars and a quantity of corn. . . . I was afterward told by a railroad official that their husbands and fathers met them at the depot and either sold the corn or took it to the stills and made it into whiskey. They hated the army and all in it and despised the negro, who returned the compliment with interest. The very sight of a corn woman made them and the overseer angry."[13]

Some suspicious planters wrote Governor Thomas H. Watts in 1864, inquiring if the "corn women" really deserved aid.[14] It was never easy for prosperous people to distinguish between deserving and undeserving poor.

The Reverend Francis M. Grace—a Methodist minister, farmer, schoolteacher, and newspaper editor from Jefferson County—left a more sympathetic description of the corn women. In 1865 he became an agent to procure homes for the orphans of deceased Confederate soldiers. Learning of a number of destitute families at Irondale, where the Confederacy had established an iron works, he visited the community only to find the cottages nearly deserted. The women had left for the Worthington plantation on Village Creek where the overseer offered corn for sale at two dollars a bushel. The women had crossed the mountain with sacks to demand corn for themselves and their children. The overseer had refused to give them the grain, and Mr. Grace met them at the foot of the mountain, the woman in the lead hastily concealing a pistol from his view as they approached. When the minister asked about their mission, they told him they had received no provisions. They had intended to take the corn by force if necessary, but the overseer had stood them off with a shotgun. Mr. Grace then produced money that had been given by south Alabama planters and gave five dollars to each woman, telling them to return to the plantation and purchase what they needed.[15]

Mr. Grace also forcibly resettled orphans. On occasion he had to take the Jefferson County sheriff with him because neighbors refused to give up the children. In April 1865 he transported a wagon load of orphans south over the protests of those who had been caring for them. Discovering his charges had "scabies," popularly called "the itch," Mr. Grace stopped in Greensboro to allow a woman to administer a treatment of sulphur and lard. By the end of the month the children were cured, but Mr. Grace had no money to pay the widow who had cared for them. Despite the end of the war, the emancipation of their slaves, and the economic dislocation that followed, local planters paid the woman in meat and corn and agreed to raise the impoverished children.[16]

Obviously efforts by the corn women did not solve the crisis. In 1863 29 of Alabama's 52 counties had one-third or more of their families on indigent lists. Some of the county rates were staggering. Among Wiregrass counties, Henry's was 37 percent, Covington's 48 percent; in north Alabama, rates were 45 percent in Randolph, 35 percent in Calhoun, 36 percent in Cherokee and Winston, and 25 percent in Jackson. Although rates were lower in the Black Belt, suffering among whites had increased alarmingly even there: in Montgomery County 20 percent of all white families received relief, in Lowndes 21 percent, in Dallas 10 percent.[17]

The worst suffering was in the cities where poor whites produced no food for home consumption. Bread riots swept Mobile in April and again in September 1863. Mobs led by destitute soldiers' wives raided provision stores on Whitehall and Dauphin streets, then paraded through town carrying banners that proclaimed "Bread or Blood." Secessionists denounced the perpetrators. Troy's *Southern Advertiser* condemned the rioters in language that reflected class differences: "The class composing the mobs are of the lowest—prostitutes, plug uglies, fresh from Baltimore, and those who have always been a nuisance to the community." The editor denied that they were starving or even hungry. They were merely robbers who were "too trifling to obtain [food] honestly."[18] Other citizens were not so sure this was a true description. A member of the legislature from southeastern Alabama wrote Governor Watts of the widespread hunger, then warned that unless counties with surpluses shared their food "the cry will be here, give us bread or give us blood."[19]

Nor was the anarchy confined to Mobile. Some poor Confederate families in Winston County accused Probate Judge T. P. Curtis, who was charged with food distribution, with being a Unionist who channeled state provisions to the families of men serving in the Union army. A band of men seized the judge, forced his wife to surrender the key to the jail where salt and food were stored, confiscated the provisions, and killed their hostage.[20]

Conditions worsened in 1864. Desperate letters again poured into the governor's office. Col. J. L. Sheffield of the Forty-eighth Alabama Regiment wrote Governor Watts in April that families of Confederate soldiers living in north Alabama were starving: "I find hundreds of them entirely destitute of everything upon which to live, not even bread. Nor is it to be had in the county. Something should be done else they are bound to suffer. All they ask is bread."[21] One soldier's wife begged for cotton cards or yarn to make clothing for her family: "Shall we their familys suffer the searching rays of heat or the winter blast in rags and nakedness for lack of implements to work with? We are poor our all is in servis."[22]

Other crises also plagued the people. Fighting in northeastern Alabama intensified in 1863 as a federal corps wheeled through Cherokee County. Sarah R. Espy, a widow trying to tend a large plantation, entrusted her account to her diary. After an army of federals encamped on her land, there was "not a living thing on the place except a few chickens. God help us, for we have almost nothing. Of our abundant crop of corn, not an ear remains except that which is scattered on the ground." Neighbors who were skipped by the marauding armies refused to share their food with the unfortunates. Confederate sympathizers killed a local Unionist. Invasion was followed by summer drought. Then on July 28, Espy's best mule died, leaving her with only one mule to operate the plantation. A few miles away at Pollard's Bend two Union soldiers raided the Thornton farm, shot their hog, kicked over their beegum, and carried off chickens tied to their saddles.[23] Poorer families suffered more; their children picked wild berries while their mothers boiled potato vines to ward off starvation.

By the end of 1864 the number of counties with at least one-third indigent white families had risen to thirty-five and the state's total reached 130,000, 37 percent of all families in the state.[24]

Although many factors led to Confederate collapse, one of the most important was the blanket of poverty and suffering settling over the South's civilian population. Confederate soldiers began to desert en masse. Their reasons were complex, but they stated them most frequently in a stark motto rooted in class grievances: it was a "rich man's war but a poor man's fight." Despite all the attempts at ameliorating the suffering of poor whites, class grievances abounded. From the outset of the war, Confederate officials had exempted from the draft one white male for each twenty slaves on a plantation. The object was innocent: to maintain control of slaves and production. But many poor whites and yeomen viewed it as a privilege of the rich who could then hire a substitute and escape the fighting. And their belief had some basis in fact, for Alabama's governors' papers are filled with requests for exemptions by middle and upper class whites. Although the Alabama legislature dramatically increased taxes on the rich so that in fact it was both a rich man's war and a rich man's fight, the taxes-in-kind hit the poor farmer hardest. Though he possessed little property and no money, he was forced to pay a substantial portion of his crops in taxes.[25]

Many other factors also caused desertions. Early volunteers believed the war would end quickly and despaired as it dragged on for years. Others left when Confederate officials arbitrarily extended their terms beyond the initial enlistment of twelve months. They realized what more-prosperous officials ignored: their families were destitute and could not survive another year without a harvest.

As the war continued, the suffering of Confederate soldiers became intolerable. The state of Alabama could not clothe, shoe, or feed its troops, and poor white soldiers could not provide for themselves. During one battle 50 men of the Twentieth Alabama Regiment entered combat without shoes. The Fifty-ninth Alabama contained 180 shoeless men in January 1864, and another 100 wore nothing but strips of leather that covered parts of their feet. Their pay was frequently in arrears. Meanwhile, back at home taxes-in-kind were levied against their families and impressment agents sometimes confiscated the necessities of life. In Tuscaloosa County impressment officers took the last milk cow from a family that had no meat. From another they took a horse and every cow. From a third they confiscated twenty-three of twenty-eight head of cattle.[26] Profiteering and inflation made it impossible to purchase salt and other essentials.

Starving wives begged their husbands to come home in letters barely literate or written for them by educated neighbors. Many such letters never reached their destinations. They were intercepted and sent to the headquarters of Gen. Robert E. Lee and other commanders. But Confederate leaders realized the source of their trouble. In September 1863 the *Democratic Watchman* summarized the problem for north Alabama: "What brings home half the deserters? It is the cries of mothers, sisters, wives, and daughters."[27]

In July 1863 the Confederate general in charge of conscription in Alabama, Mississippi, and Tennessee estimated that 8,000 to 10,000 deserters and Union conscripts were hidden in the hills of north Alabama. The state's official "Deserter Book" contained 7,994 names on November 30, 1864. One judge in the Wiregrass reported 2,000 deserters in his region alone. They plundered large sections of Covington County, and the state representative, a Unionist sympathizer, assisted the federals and finally fled to their garrison in Pensacola. Of the 90,000 Alabamians who served in the Confederate army, between 9,000 and 15,000 deserted.[28]

Most of them found refuge in the hills or Wiregrass. They came from counties with the fewest blacks, the lowest taxes, and the poorest whites. Although the disaffection followed sectional lines, the underlying cause was economic.[29] As one poor white wrote, rich men "think all you are fit for is to stop bullets for them, your betters, who call you poor white trash."[30]

Many poor whites expressed their resentment in guerilla warfare against affluent Confederate sympathizers. As a consequence, murder, random violence, robbery, and looting plunged some counties into anarchy. Confederate recruiters were bushwhacked; poorly disciplined Confederate home guards and cavalry retaliated with bloody raids. One Confederate officer who captured thirty Union sympathizers in north Alabama described them as "the most miserable, ignorant, poor, ragged devils I ever saw."[31] Even allowing for literary license, his description fits the class origins of whatever sedition existed among poor whites.

But most poor whites did not so much favor the Union as they simply wished the war over. And their principal weapon was the ballot, not the musket. They formed three semipolitical, secret peace societies, one in Covington, Coffee, and Henry counties in the Wiregrass, and two others in the hill counties of Randolph, Calhoun, Blount, Winston, and Walker. Most members came from the poorest class.[32] They demonstrated amazing political sophistication, reversing their historic Democratic voting patterns in order to convince the state's leaders that they meant business.

Alabama politicians had long used racial appeals to unite the white classes. Civil War Governor John Gill Shorter, an ardent planter-secessionist from Barbour County, had warned yeomen and poor whites in 1852 that if slaves were freed, planters would be rich enough to leave the land

and follow other occupations; but poor whites would be left behind, reduced to degrading servitude. In the 1861 gubernatorial election, Shorter represented the Democratic secessionists of the Black Belt. Thomas H. Watts, a lifelong Whig from Montgomery, spoke for the more cautious and conservative planters and merchants. Although north Alabamians initially preferred a third candidate, when they were forced to choose between Shorter and Watts, they voted for Shorter out of long-standing loyalty to the Democratic party. Paradoxically, Shorter, a secessionist, received his strongest support from the antisecessionist hill counties.

During Shorter's term the conscription act, taxes-in-kind, and increasing hunger created opposition to his administration. He was forced to dispatch cavalry to Randolph and other counties to put down armed resistance. Poor whites interpreted his appointment of "deputy clerks" and "deputy sheriffs" as a strategy to help his rich friends avoid the draft. By 1863 discontent with Shorter had merged with disillusionment over secession, shortages, inflation, and profiteering to give Watts an excellent chance at the governorship.

Watts ran a shrewd campaign, attacking Shorter's record and arguing that poor whites could not cure meat for lack of salt or make garments for want of cloth. In the August 1863 general election, Watts defeated Shorter by a margin of three to one. He carried all but four counties in north Alabama, a dramatic reversal from two years earlier. Many poor whites viewed him as the peace candidate despite his earlier advocacy of secession. The legislature elected with him consisted mainly of new men, many of them favoring peace. Poor whites and yeomen had virtually abandoned party politics in favor of ending the war.[33] As governor, Watts took more interest in the poor. In a public appeal during April 1864, he described the suffering of the wives and children of soldiers from Marshall County, adding that the people of south Alabama had permitted soldiers' families "to perish whilst we have plenty and to spare." If people could not give corn, he urged them to sell the corn "at peace prices for these poor women and children."[34]

The Union army managed to accomplish in 1865 what many Alabama poor whites had elected Watts to do: end the war. But the first months of peace were a continuation of starvation and anarchy. Wilson's Raiders swept through central Alabama in April 1865, disrupting transportation, spreading confusion, and interrupting planting at a critical time. Bad weather crippled crops in parts of the state. When W. B. Cooper, a prominent conservative Democrat, returned to his Jacksonville home in Calhoun County, he was besieged by women pouring into town, some having walked several miles from rural homes. All wanted to know how they could obtain bread. More than fifty people urgently asked the same question. Cooper wrote Governor Lewis E. Parsons: "I pledge you my word, I've never heard such a cry for bread in my life. And it is impossible to get relief up here. The provisions are not here and if they were there is no money here to buy with." He closed with the same earnest plea the hungry had directed toward him: "If any thing can be done, for God's sake do it quickly. This is no panic but real great hunger that punishes the people."[35]

Similar cries went up across the state. A Bibb County official reported in November 1865 nearly 600 indigent families containing 2,270 people. Conecuh County listed 728 destitute women and children on January 1, 1866. Tuscaloosa County contained 700 such families with 2,800 people. Louis Wyeth reported from Guntersville in Marshall County that 3 persons had already starved to death and 3,000 more were destitute. One widow with 7 children had not eaten for a week. In Baldwin County on the Gulf of Mexico, many families were begging food and only 5 persons in the county were able to provide it. Benjamin F. Porter wrote from Greenville: "This very moment my wife is dividing our small store with a dozen ragged children who will want again tomorrow."[36] So desperate were the people of Jackson County for salt to cure meat that 4 men drove two wagons all the way to Salt Springs in Virginia in the fall of 1865. The round trip took them seven weeks.[37]

Cherokee County suffered perhaps more than any other in the state. Foraging armies containing tens of thousands had spent nearly two weeks there in 1864. Drought destroyed most corn crops that year and again in 1865. Thirty prominent men drafted a petition to Governor Parsons in August 1865, explaining that even once-prosperous farmers were destitute.[38] The following March, citizens held a public meeting at Centre where they drafted a resolution begging again for help. The audience contained few poor whites, who were then able to receive aid from the Freedmen's Bureau. This was a new class of poor, men who had recently been prosperous citizens. Now "we have no money, we have no cotton, we have no credit." Before, the only destitution known in Cherokee had been among the "old, infirm, decrepit, soldiers' wives, widows, their children and orphans; not so now, nearly all of all classes are in the same category." These were proud people who never before had asked for help; now all was "gloom and wretchedness and woe." But this appeal maintained class distinctions that separated them from poor whites: "The provisions made by the U.S. Government through the Freedmen's Bureau will relieve the indigent who have no re-sources—present or perspective [*sic*], but the destitute laboring classes, *who are the meritorious sufferers,* are not provided for, and *their loss* will be disastrous to the state."[39] The petition urged the state to sell $500,000 in bonds to aid the "worthy" needy.

Another public meeting in September 1866 was less specific about the source of assistance. The people who attended requested that federal Maj. Gen. Wager Swayne, Governor Parsons, and the railroads help destitute families to leave Cherokee County. One beat contained twenty-three families with 147 members who were utterly destitute, without land or corn; eight of these families desired to emigrate to Texas, eight to Arkansas, five to Tennessee, and two to Mississippi. By late October many of these families had moved west.[40]

After surveying the white mountain counties, the *Athens Post* concluded that they had "been reduced to a state of suffering which from all accounts, equals, in ghastliness of features, the horrid scene of the Irish famine years; and amid the gloomy shades of those Alabama mountains the sickening wail of perishing people is hourly heard crying for bread."[41]

Many of those desperate in 1866 soon recovered their prosperity. For others the calamity was the beginning of a long decline into poverty. Many small farmers could not pay the taxes on their lands, which were then sold at public auctions to cover taxes of fewer than $10. One farmer lost a quarter section because he could not pay 37.5¢. Entire issues of the *Union Springs Times* in Bullock County were given over to advertisements for land being sold for nonpayment. In March 1870, seventy thousand acres of land were advertised for the cost of back taxes.[42]

Nor was such trauma confined to economics. The entire structure of poor white society groaned beneath the burden. The family structure, already shaken by the war, was further disrupted by the threat of equality for blacks, who now competed with whites for the lowest-paying jobs. Paternalistic planters temporarily lost social control of both blacks and poor whites; the result was often violence and terrorism, as poor whites sought to restrict and control freedmen.

Whether accurate or not, planters and other prominent Alabamians blamed poor whites for Reconstruction-era violence against freedmen. Generally, northern public opinion and federal officials serving in the state accepted such charges at face value. An official of the Selma, Rome, and Dalton Railroad complained to Alabama's Republican governor that although the "better class" of Calhoun County whites favored the northern-financed road, "the ignorant short sighted and those blind to the interests of the country" engaged in violence, terrorism, and lynching. Community leaders blamed the "lower classes" for the trouble. But when the culprits were actually apprehended and brought to trial, they included small farmers, landowners, and a Baptist preacher.[43]

Family disruption took many forms. In 1870 William Bowling, a twenty-one-year-old laborer, lived in Colbert County in the Tennessee Valley. He owned $400 in personal property but no land. His wife Susan was twenty-two years old. In order to meet expenses, they shared their house with four white laborers, Charles Bell, aged twenty-six, Solomon Miller, eighteen, James Henry, nineteen, and Samuel Cook, seventeen. All had migrated to the valley after the war.[44]

At the opposite extreme from interracial violence, though perhaps related to it psychologically, was miscegenation. Interracial sex was not unknown in antebellum Alabama. But the disruption of family structure during the war created the sort of problems that so appalled Smith Lipscomb's relatives. Tacitly condoned or ignored in the antebellum years, interracial sex was publicly condemned by virtually all whites after emancipation. Before the Civil War, white males of marriageable age outnumbered white females by about 2,000. War reversed the ratio. By 1870, some 10,000 Alabama white women of marriageable age had no partner. Scarcity of white men and agricultural conditions that demanded male assistance no doubt explain both the increasing frequency of interracial sex and the angry reaction of poor whites against blacks, who now became sexual as well as economic rivals.

In 1867 two white women were arrested for living with black men. A year later Thornton Ellis, a freedman, and Susan Bishop, a white woman, were indicted for living together in adultery. In May 1867, a white woman was arrested for killing the mulatto baby she had borne.[45] Mollie Wright wrote a cousin local gossip in March 1867:

> Another scandal has come to light on the other side of Smith's Hill. You know Mary Martin. Old Mrs. Hill died last fall which left Mary alone and she would not go anywhere though several tried to get her but she would not go and last week it was found out that she had taken up with a negro. The negro disappeared suddenly. Some think he run off but the negroes say he has been killed and hid away. No one knows but the negroes are hostile and are making heavy threats. I don't know how it will end. I have almost wished that my girls were all boys. A mother can't be too particular with girls.[46]

Illegitimacy among poor whites also troubled communities. Sarah Espy, a widow and Cherokee County planter, was summoned one night in March 1866 to help deliver an illegitimate son to a "Mrs. B": "She is an ignorant, weak-minded woman, but, she knew better than that. Has a large circle of relatives who deplore her fall."[47]

Another consequence of deepening poverty was migration. Rates of migration are associated to some degree with how well one is satisfied with his or her circumstances. Prosperous people did not move as frequently as poor people. Unfortunately, exact patterns are impossible to follow. Many poor whites migrated to other states; others only crossed county lines. To complicate matters, the Alabama legislature created thirteen new counties in the postwar years, altering the boundaries of all but seventeen of the state's fifty-two counties. County analysis of individual families is thus extremely difficult.[48]

Despite the problem of identifying them specifically, tens of thousands of Alabama poor whites left their lands in the 1860s and 1870s. Between 10 and 15 percent of the entire white population of Alabama migrated out of state, an exodus exceeded only in South Carolina. The total probably exceeded fifty thousand, with a third of them heading for Texas. Many white farm laborers along the Georgia and Florida boundaries crossed into those states. All classes participated, but many migrants were new recruits into the lower class. Poor whites increasingly saw Alabama as a state of lost opportunities. Their dreams of joining the planter class clashed with the reality that landownership was actually contracting because of foreclosures and forced tax sales. Despite dozens of pleas between 1865 and 1867 to the legislature urging passage of a law to prevent foreclosure of agricultural land, more and more acres fell under the control of large planters, new industrialists, or insurance and mortgage companies.[49] As a consequence, many people simply gave up and moved west.

J. D. P. Wilkinson experienced both downward mobility and out-migration. Before the war he had been a businessman and planter in Pleasant Ridge in Greene County. During the war he sank into debt. Despite the patience of both creditors and friends after 1865, he lost both his spouse and his confidence. After his wife left him, his daughter Annie taught school to supply necessities. In 1870 he moved to Little Rock, Arkansas, where he sold insurance. Failing that, he located in Memphis, Tennessee, where he worked in a bootery until he lost that job also. He drifted into the country, where he became a wage laborer, but he even failed at that. After living on the charity of a generous railroad conductor in Bowling Green, Kentucky, he tried selling newspapers and insurance. Finally demoralized and incapable of coping, he found his way into a benevolent Shaker community in South Union, Kentucky, in 1874. The Shakers finally found a menial job he could perform, "pasting papers."[50]

Internal migration within the state between 1860 and 1870 redistributed population. Many poor whites left the mountains and Wiregrass in search of jobs in the Black Belt, where they crowded into towns such as Demopolis, Marion, Montgomery, and Selma. Finding no work and competing with freedmen, they drifted north into the mineral belt around the newly founded industrial town of Birmingham. Gradually the expansion of railroads, coal mining, and the steel industry absorbed some of the surplus population and stabilized the region. The contact of poor whites from isolated regions with newly emancipated blacks in the Black Belt probably accounted for some Reconstruction-era violence, though not as much as planters claimed.[51]

The Homestead Act offered poor whites some initial hope. Having long sought such legislation, they quickly filed claims. Between 1867 and 1874, some eight thousand whites, most from the mountains and Piedmont, took out applications with the federal land offices at Huntsville and Montgomery. Despite rapid land sales in the 1850s, vast acreage in Alabama still belonged to the federal government. In mountainous Cleburne County, formed in 1866 from part of Calhoun, public lands numbered more than 21,000 acres as late as 1893. In Covington County at the other end of the state, only 12 percent of the land was owned by individuals in 1871; 25 percent was owned by railroad companies, and 60 percent was still owned by the federal government. Unfortunately, such land was also typical of the remaining federal domain available for homesteaders. Most of the land in Cleburne was so mountainous it later became part of the Talladega National Forest. And the land in Covington was remote from streams and useful mainly for growing pine trees. As a consequence, only a few hundred families actually secured title to their homestead.[52]

With the dream of landownership either a failure or a spur to migration elsewhere, those who were landless and remained in Alabama faced difficult decisions. Almost inevitably the months just after the war forced them to seek help beyond their own resources.

Unable to ignore the massive extent of white poverty, Alabama's more affluent citizens and state and federal officials tried a variety of remedies. In fact, most of the strategies perfected in later years were tried in the 1860s: charity, federal programs, state-funded institutions, and the creation of new jobs.

Public-spirited citizens traveled to more-prosperous states to solicit gifts of food and clothing. Louis Wyeth of Guntersville traveled north to Nashville, Louisville, and Cincinnati, appealing to ministers and civic leaders for help. Large public rallies in all three cities listened to Wyeth's appeals, then pledged 3,000 bushels in Nashville and even more in the other two towns. A group of New Yorkers who heard Alabama Governor Lewis E. Parsons describe the destitution in his state called a public meeting at Cooper Institute to provide aid. Baltimore women organized the Ladies Southern Relief Association, which sent $3,000 for use in Randolph, Chambers, and other east-central Alabama counties. The women of Hannibal, Missouri, sent $630.[53]

Such aid was a mere raindrop in a vast sea of misery. Systematic help came from a less-predictable source. Congress created the Bureau of Refugees, Freedmen and Abandoned Lands in March 1865 to assist newly emancipated blacks. General Swayne organized the Alabama bureau that July and began to distribute food and rations to the needy. Most Alabamians think of the Freedmen's Bureau as a radical social agency aimed at suppressing whites and enabling blacks to improve themselves. Both reputations are greatly exaggerated. The bureau launched no revolution in race relations, and it helped far more of Alabama's poor whites than blacks.

Gen. O. O. Howard, who headed the bureau, had no funds at his disposal, but he could issue food and clothing to "destitute freedmen and refugees." Howard interpreted "refugees" broadly to include virtually any indigent whites. Officials in Alabama quickly provided many candidates. General Sewall described white widows and orphans living in pine-bough shelters on the outskirts of Talladega in the winter of 1865–66. Although he could not document a case of actual white starvation (which he did find among freedmen), he witnessed women and children walking long distances to beg food.

The bureau began distributing rations in Alabama during the summer of 1865, with the quantity increasing steadily after that, particularly in the mountain counties. Fall crop failures worsened conditions, forcing the legislature to appoint a Committee on Destitution to gather data. The house committee subsequently reported that 130,000 whites were destitute. In December, the legislature established the Office of Commissioner for the Destitute to distribute supplies provided by both the state and the Freedmen's Bureau. Governor Robert M. Patton appointed Marcus H. Cruikshank to the job and the legislature appropriated $500,000 for distribution. Unfortunately, the new agency did not begin operations until the new year, so the bureau remained the chief source of relief for the remainder of 1865.

When Cruikshank began to function, he supplied General Swayne with a monthly estimate of the number of destitute in each county without a bureau agent. He also compiled lists of indigents from reports of the local probate judges. Swayne added estimates of county bureau agents in order to arrive at a statewide total. Rations were dispensed from depots in Mobile, Montgomery, Selma, Greenville, Demopolis, Talladega, Tuscaloosa, and Huntsville. Because the state lacked funds for transportation, it authorized individual counties to issue bonds for the purpose. Typically, supplies were shipped by rail from one of the depots to a county seat, where either Freedmen's Bureau officials or the probate judge presided over distribution. Agents kept a list of names of recipients, listing the race, age, and sex of each.

Rations were usually issued for a month at a time and tended to follow a seasonal cycle. Winter and spring brought the greatest need; as garden vegetables matured, distribution declined in the summer and fall.[54]

Cruikshank's instructions stipulated that supplies be distributed only to the destitute and without regard to color. But he maintained an age-old American inclination to distinguish between the needy who were deemed worthy of help and those who were not. As Cruikshank phrased it, assistance should not encourage "idleness by feeding those who by the use of proper industry might support themselves."[55]

The distribution in the hill counties was heavy. In the early spring of 1866 the Huntsville depot provided 5,000 rations daily with most going to Lauderdale (664), Cherokee (626), Blount (563), and Jackson (426) counties. Less accessible counties such as Winston did not fare so well (158 rations daily). Urban areas also received considerable help, with Mobile furnishing 22,080 rations to 1,206 persons during June 1866.[56]

Aid was discontinued in October 1866 except to those who were confined to hospitals or to orphans. The principal reason was not lack of need but widespread abuses within the administration and distribution of supplies. In fact, the destitution remained so great that President Andrew Johnson exempted Alabama from the order ending the program and authorized $40,000 for corn and bacon to be distributed in the state for three additional months.

At no time in the tenure of the Freedmen's Bureau in Alabama did black aid recipients outnumber white. From November 1865 to October 1866, the ratio of poor white aid recipients to black was 2.3 to 1. In February 1866, the ratio reached 4 times as many white recipients as black.[57] Only whites without need or those with selective memories could curse the Freedmen's Bureau as a worthless agency that created only mischief in the proud commonwealth of Alabama.

For those beyond the pale of family or bureau, a sadder fate awaited. The lowest of the low, indigents physically or mentally incapable of taking care of themselves, had no alternative but the poorhouse. The new Reconstruction legislature installed in 1868 sought to aid the poor of all races. Dominated by white scalawags and carpetbaggers, but containing a large minority of blacks as well, it showed unusual concern for the poor. Legislators increased appropriations for public schools, health, and other state services. The new 1868 Reconstruction constitution drafted by them required the general assembly "to make adequate provisions in each county for the maintenance of the poor." Unfortunately, the law provided no guidelines on keeping records or operating procedures, and the legislature did nothing more than establish county poorhouses. Even that cursory interest ended when a new white Democratic legislature in 1875 transferred this chore to individual counties.

Counties developed two patterns for operating the facilities, which were designated as either "poorhouses," "almshouses," or simply "county homes." Some employed a superintendent for a stipulated salary; others contracted the services to an individual for a fixed sum. Both systems led to corruption and wretched care for indigents, especially as facilities became antiquated and supervision lax.[58]

Bullock County in southeastern Alabama operated a typical poorhouse. So extensive was the poverty in Bullock when the legislature established the county in 1866 that the first act of the county commissioners was to create committees to assist the poor. The committees selected a location for the poorhouse and instructed the probate judge to provide county warrants of up to ten dollars per indigent until the house was completed. Most of the county's three hundred indigents drew between three and five dollars per month. In May 1867 the local tax assessor appropriated half of the state's increased taxes for the relief of indigents and for the county jail.[59]

A final strategy for absorbing the growing number of poor whites was to attract new industrial jobs for them. As reports of destitution poured into Montgomery during 1866, Governor Robert Patton recommended industry as the solution. One of his correspondents in Cherokee County caught the governor's spirit. Amid sickness, drought, and deprivation, S. K. McSpadden agreed to discuss industrialization with the few capitalists who lived in Cherokee. When conditions stabilized, McSpadden enthused, "I have no doubt but the tributaries of the gentle Coosa— The Chatooga and Little Rivers . . . , will be dotted with factory buildings, whilst their sparkling waters will mingle their glad notes with the music of the spindle and loom and the joyous laugh of the youthful operatives."[60]

Soon the governor won equally exuberant converts. The number of manufacturing establishments in the state increased from 1,459 in 1860 to 2,070 in 1880 and 2,977 by 1890. The capital invested barely regained the 1860 figure by 1880 ($9,098,181 invested in 1860, $9,668,008 in 1880), but it more than quadrupled during the next decade. The value of Alabama's manufactured products increased only from $10,588,566 to $13,565,504 in 1880; but stimulated by the Birmingham mineral district, it exploded to $51,226,605 in 1890.[61] Although the progress was scattered and irregular (for instance, Bullock County contained twenty industries employing only 150 men in 1890) during the 1880s, industry did absorb tens of thousands of poor whites into new industrial jobs. But the jobs were in extractive industries such as iron and steel, coal mining, timber, and textiles. Once the timber was cut or the coal extracted, jobs played out and the land was as poor as before. At least on the land poor whites could hunt and fish, vary the cycle of their lives, and eat fresh vegetables and fruits in season. In the industrial towns they performed monotonous, dangerous jobs, lived in cramped neighborhoods, and did not necessarily improve their lot very much. In 1870 the largest number of Mobile whites without any personal wealth were artisans and industrial laborers.[62]

But for most of the newly poor, attachment to the land bound them in a web too tight to break. They remained on farms and sought to cope as best they could. Sarah A. E. Bynerson was such a person. She was a widow living near Robinson Springs, where she languished in the summer of 1866, hopeless and fearful of starvation. She owned some notes from better times that she had turned over to a lawyer to collect. If she received any money, she intended to purchase several mules, a hundred bushels of corn, and two bales of hay. But thus far she had been unable to collect anything. She had rented land belonging to a Captain Long and had become a tenant farmer, working in the fields beside four black freedmen. Although she begged the state relief committee for a loan of mules, corn, and hay, she received only daily rations barely sufficient to sustain her existence. Her plea for help was as universal as it was futile: "If some relief is not given . . . I do not know what is to become of me."[63]

PART TWO

Occupations

THREE

"Looking for Something Better"

Alabama's Farm Tenants

Wealthy Holley made a poor living in Geneva County, Alabama, in the summer of 1880. She was a white sharecropper. A female head of family, she parented seven children, including five sons aged fourteen, twelve, seven, six, and five, and two daughters, aged ten and one. Whether unmarried or widowed was information the census left discreetly unknown. But it does supply some of the details of her life. She farmed four acres. The value of farm products sold, consumed, or on hand during the previous year amounted to only fifteen dollars. She possessed no horses, mules, cows, or oxen, but she did own five swine. Her only crop consisted of ten bushels of corn.[1]

Although not exactly the quintessential white Alabamian, Wealthy Holley was no stranger either. As the maelstrom of war subsided, Alabama's plain folk resumed the business of making a living. But times were hard and new economic structures were evolving.

One such structure was farm tenancy. The cycle of a tenant's life became as regular as the seasons. The appearance of spring brought the need for a mule to plow the earth and for seed to plant. The owner of the land provided these essentials for a fixed rent or a share of the crop. The optimism of planting time turned to the anxiety of summer, when the searing heat could wilt plants and people, when too much rain could rot cotton, when there were never enough hands to hoe weeds from the rows, when not even the open passageway of a dogtrot cabin or its flimsy construction provided enough ventilation for comfort. Then came fall and the back-breaking labor of pulling the puffy wad from the boll, fingers cut and split by burrs, back aching with fatigue, no sundown or thunderstorm unwelcome that promised an end to the day's toil. "Settling up" time followed, with the occasional good years outweighed by the bad ones. Winter arrived with growing debts at the nearest crossroads store, debts that almost always equaled or exceeded the cropper's share of what was left in the fall. And so it went, year after year, decade after decade.

Establishing a tenant farm meant contracting with a landlord. The simplest and most favorable arrangement for a tenant was fixed rent (also called "standing rent" or "cash tenancy"), wherein the tenant paid the landowner a stipulated sum for a year's rent. Share-cash tenants paid part of their rent in cash and part in shares of crops or livestock. Share tenants furnished their own equipment and work animals; as a consequence they usually paid one-third of their grain and one-fourth of their cotton for rent (hence the term "farming on thirds and fourths"). At the bottom of the tenancy system and most pervasive in Alabama was the sharecropper. Under this arrangement, the landowner normally furnished land, housing, fuel, working stock, livestock feed, farm implements, and seed. The cropper provided the labor and fed and clothed his family. If the cropper used fertilizer, the landlord often chose the brand and deducted the cost from the final output before the crop was divided. When the cotton crop was harvested, owner and cropper shared equally (hence the term "farming on halves"). The contract, as frequently oral as it was written, specified the amount of land to be planted in each major crop, the amount of capital to be supplied by the landowner, the proportion both cropper and owner were to receive, the term of the lease (usually one year), and a provision that the cropper would follow the landlord's direction concerning management of the farm.

The fact that contracts were often verbal gave rise to disputes and misunderstandings. The state of Alabama required no written contracts as late as 1940. Either party could terminate a tenancy agreement by giving ten days' notice in writing. As a result, most tenants had no idea how much debt they had incurred. Owners carried over debts from year to year, meaning that if the tenant stayed on the same land, each year often began in debt.

Because of primitive technology, cotton cultivation was a labor-intensive form of farming. Consequently, farms were small. Children were a valuable economic resource because they extended the productivity of the family. But even large families could farm at most forty acres, and farms that large were rare among white tenants.

Alabama had the dubious distinction of being one of the leading tenancy states. As early as 1880 only 53.2 percent of the state's farmers were owners and managers whereas 45.8 percent were cash or share tenants. By 1910 Alabama's rate of tenancy had reached 60.2 percent and by 1930, 64.7 percent, a rate surpassed only by four neighboring states. Sharecroppers, who occupied the bottom rung of the agricultural ladder, numbered 69,780, or 26.5 percent of Alabama farmers in 1910. Of all white farmers, 42.6 percent were tenants in 1910, 46.6 percent by 1930.[2] And the number of white sharecroppers increased between 1910 and 1920 from 36,665 to 51,209, despite high cotton prices during the First World War. As blacks deserted the land for jobs in the North, whites constituted an ever-expanding majority of tenants. Among the state's sharecroppers in 1930, whites outnumbered blacks 37,562 to 27,572. In other categories of tenants, whites held a narrower edge, 50,983 to 50,303.[3]

The Origins of Tenancy

In a world where landownership was the persistent ideal, and one extensively if not universally realized in antebellum Alabama, why did so many whites find themselves landless? The origins of tenancy are shrouded in obscurity and confused by partisan ideological debates. Historians have blamed everything from the wartime destruction of livestock to manipulation of economic resources by exploitive planters and merchants. Most explanations have one thing in common. They try to reduce an enormously complicated institution to a set of simple propositions.

Specific sources of tenancy date from prewar years as well as from the experiences of the Civil War and Reconstruction. As with most historical crises that seem to arise suddenly and without continuity with the past, the roots of white tenancy cling to deeper soil. For decades many white farmers had barely survived. Existing on the fringe of plantation society, they had been left behind by their harder-working, healthier, and luckier fellow yeomen. Squatting illegally on federal land, or eking out a subsistence existence on ten or twelve acres, or hunting and trapping in some Appalachian hollow, they were incidental to Alabama's commercial antebellum economy. Occasionally they played a larger role as miners, textile mill operatives, or farm laborers, but even in those expanded roles they were marginal to the state's prewar economy. What is often forgotten is how many poor whites inhabited Alabama in 1860.[4]

To be sure, antebellum tenancy patterns differed somewhat from those that followed the war. Most notably, tenancy before the war was almost exclusively white. Partly for that reason, antebellum tenants retained more control over their daily lives, what they would plant, and how they would live. Their preference for food crops over cotton, the

likelihood that they would own their own stock animals and farm implements, and the economic mobility they often demonstrated, all related
them closely to yeomen whose culture and social norms they usually
shared. Thus the postwar tenancy patterns, at least for many poor
whites, were more likely changes in rigidity, supervision, and economic
integration into commercial agriculture, not dramatic changes in their
lives. Of course the lessening of economic mobility, the increasing reliance on cotton, and the increasing class rigidity wrought their own
damage. But all this was not some strange new world remote from their
previous experiences.

The extent of white tenancy and the integration of tenants into Alabama's cotton economy were the changes that broke continuity with
the previous era. Many white tenants were newcomers to tenancy without prewar connections. The growing number of whites absorbed into
the system demands an explanation from postwar circumstances. And
the possibilities are extensive. Wartime destruction reduced many yeoman farmers to insolvency. Although relatively little fighting occurred
in Alabama, groups of marauders, stragglers, draft dodgers, Confederate
recruiters, outlaws, and guerrillas wreaked havoc on small farmers and
planters alike. They stole, "confiscated," and slaughtered livestock,
helped themselves to food crops, and generally spread devastation wherever they went. Occasionally, armies numbering thousands retreated or
advanced across Alabama, creating the sort of chaos already described
in Cherokee County. When marauding armies slaughtered chickens,
pigs, and cattle, or stripped cornfields, it made little difference to many
farmers what color uniforms the soldiers wore. The practical consequences were the same even if the farmers were sympathetic to the
boys in gray. After the war ended, no chicken or pig was safe from
hungry people of both races without regard to the niceties of proper
ownership. Poor people stole in order to eat. As a consequence of wartime
foraging and Reconstruction thievery, the value of Alabama livestock
declined from $43 million in 1860 to $26 million in 1870. The value of
animals slaughtered dropped 60 percent. A society that in 1840 could
feed itself and produce an estimated surplus of 100,000 hogs for export,
in 1880 fell 1.5 million hogs short of meeting its own needs.[5]

During the antebellum era, southern yeomen had shown a marked
preference for hog and cattle raising over careful cultivation of food
crops. They realized considerable economic benefits from the sale of
livestock, a factor not easily translated into economic terms. But clearly
the extensive losses of livestock among herders and yeoman farmers
created an economic crisis that propelled many of them into tenancy.
Postwar efforts by planters to fence in livestock and thus deny herders

the open range to which they were accustomed further eroded the position of Alabama's "plain folk."[6]

Reconstruction policies did little to solve the enduring problems of poor people of either race. By denying blacks their own land, federal policy made inevitable some form of tenancy for most blacks. But white yeomen owned land that Reconstruction policies made it difficult for them to retain. Although some of these policies should have won their support—free public schools, expansion of railroads, and the establishment of charitable institutions—the taxes to support such reforms created white opposition. The major taxes during antebellum days had been on slaves and luxuries, thus largely exempting yeomen. But Reconstruction legislators utilized taxes on property to make up for revenue lost when slaves were emancipated. Land taxes produced two-thirds of state revenues during a decade when state expenditures climbed sharply. Alabama taxed at a rate of 2 mills in 1860 and at a rate of 7.5 mills in 1870. Despite the sharp decline in the value of farms recorded in the 1870 census (obviously a decline partly due to chaotic economic conditions and partly to undervaluing of property in order to avoid Reconstruction taxes), the tax on farmland multiplied almost 2.5 times. The average Reconstruction-era tax was twice the 1860 level and represented 1 percent or more of the total cash income of farmers, a figure 50 percent higher than in 1860. Such taxes help explain not only the bitter opposition of yeoman farmers to Reconstruction but also their worsening economic condition. Of course this harm can be overestimated, because when white Democrats regained control of government in the 1870s, they immediately reduced taxes to near 1860 levels.[7]

The acts of God seemed as capricious as those of man. Cotton rust and cotton caterpillars ruined crops for several years during the 1870s. So bad were crops in Bullock County that the *Union Springs Herald* editorialized in 1880: "this section is in the worst financial shape since 1873." As a consequence, sharecropping increased rapidly among both whites and blacks.[8] Drought burned up crops in many hill counties. During the summer of 1871 Cherokee County received no measurable rain for seven weeks. One farmer wrote relatives: "I never saw crops suffer so bad in [my] life."[9] A farmer in Choctaw County raised a splendid crop of cotton and corn, all of which he lost to floods in 1892.[10] Prosperous large farmers could usually survive such calamities. Marginal yeomen often could not. The consequence for them was reduced incomes, increased mortgages, ultimate foreclosure, and descent into tenancy.

Added to natural disasters were personal tragedies. Alcoholism, poor health, shiftlessness, or the sudden death of a head of family could plunge independent yeoman farmers into tenancy. Mrs. L. A. House married a small farmer in December 1899. Together they bought a farm in Shelby County. But before they could pay off the farm, her husband developed mouth cancer. Medical bills accumulated. With a wife and five children to support, he finally sold the farm to a neighbor before he died: "We signed the deeds to it. There wasn't a thing left in it for us, not a dollar." After her husband died, Mrs. House rented a farm for a hundred dollars. Her brother came to help her and the oldest children worked the fields, though their efforts proved futile and she eventually left the tenant farm for mill work. Nancy Nolan experienced a similar fate. When her husband died, leaving her with three children, the oldest a nine-year-old son, she began to tenant farm a patch of Dale County land. She managed to survive for five years as a tenant before giving up and moving into Eufaula, where she found work in a textile mill.[11]

Regional, national, and even international market conditions deepened the crisis. Even though the number of cotton bales increased, the rate of growth in per capita crop production fell in each of the last three decades of the nineteenth century. World demand for cotton declined from an annual growth rate of 5 percent between 1820 and 1860 to 1.3 percent between 1866 and 1895.[12]

Declining demand for American cotton complicated other tendencies within the labor market. The abundance of cheap labor caused planters to neglect technology. But how could labor be utilized most efficiently?

At first planters tried the wage system. But both currency and credit were scarce, making it difficult to pay cash wages. In addition, farm labor was unreliable at critical times when cotton had to be harvested quickly or left in the fields to rot. Sharecropping was the perfect solution. From the planter's view, it provided a more reliable labor force. From the cropper's view, it afforded a contractual system that increased self-esteem and reduced the level of direct supervision and control over his or her life.

The South's isolated regional labor market further embedded the tenancy system. Alabama developed more industrial jobs than most southern states, but rural people never had enough alternatives to farming. Although highly mobile, poor whites did not migrate to other regions. Because they possessed no real job skills, tenancy was often the only recourse if they lost their own land.

The South also experienced the highest birth rates in the United States in the years following the Civil War. The population consistently grew faster than the demand for cotton or the number of available jobs in industry.

The solution to this dilemma was the expansion of cotton production into the Piedmont, Wiregrass, and hill country. Although the rate of growth slowed from the peak years of the 1850s, cotton demand grew at an estimated rate of 2.7 percent between 1880 and 1900. As a consequence, many yeoman farmers converted their small acreage from subsistence food crops to commercial cotton production.

Several important developments made this expansion necessary. With Reconstruction tax rates on land climbing sharply, farmers needed cash to pay taxes. Paying off personal debts also demanded currency. Cotton was the only reliable source of income. Even when prices were low, cotton would always bring some cash payment. Furthermore, cotton produced more value per acre than any alternative use of the land.

Another development fostering the expansion of cotton was the availability of fertilizers. As production reached the poorer soils of the Wiregrass, Piedmont, and hill country, fertilizers became imperative. Fortunately the international price of guano declined in the last decades of the century, making expansion onto poorer soils feasible.

The final factor encouraging this movement was railroad construction. Postwar northern and foreign capital investment made it possible to expand significantly the South's railroad system. As lines reached formerly inaccessible regions, farmers no longer had to rely on rivers to get their crops to market. Now farmers in mountain valleys or rolling hills far from navigable rivers could ship their crops from rail junctions in newly developing towns.

The Louisville and Nashville Railroad played a major role in opening north Alabama to cotton production. The L&N took over the South and North line, which had reached as far as Birmingham by 1865, and extended it north to Nashville. As coal camps sprang up in the Warrior Basin, the railroad extended like a web across north Alabama. The L&N also passed through the Wiregrass on its way to Pensacola and gradually spawned trunk lines to serve timber camps within that region.

The Selma, Rome, and Dalton line had reached the Anniston area in western Calhoun County by 1861. In subsequent years and under northern control, the railroad traversed Calhoun County and crossed into northwestern Georgia. Altogether, the railroad mileage in the state increased from 1,843 miles in 1880 to 5,226 in 1910. Much of the new cotton production occurred in counties penetrated by railroad lines, which thereby afforded farmers reliable transportation.

The towns spawned by these lines and the growing importance of furnishing merchants who extended farmers credit also dramatically affected the lives of yeomen. Social strain between country and townspeople quickly developed, and farmers increasingly blamed their troubles on greedy merchants and their urban allies who controlled both economic and political institutions.[13]

The problem of obtaining credit became critical. In 1869 the entire state contained only two national banks.[14] As a consequence credit generally came from one of two sources. In the plantation counties, planters usually furnished credit to black tenants. In the hill and Wiregrass counties, merchants provided white tenants the same service.

Obtaining credit became a simple process at the outset. A planter or merchant lent money during the months when a tenant had nothing to sell except a bit of firewood. To secure the loan, a lien was taken against the tenant's share of the crop and any personal property (horses and mules were most common). Should the tenant be unable to pay the debt at "settling up time" in the fall when the cotton crop was sold, whoever lent the money could take the tenant's livestock or share of the cotton crop in payment. Such practices often allowed planters and merchants to end a crop year with three-thirds of the cotton crop rather than the one-fourth, one-third, or one-half provided by sharecropping agreements.

The crop-lien system entered Alabama law in 1866 when the state legislature allowed whoever provided land, tools, or livestock to a farmer to take a lien on the crop as a guarantee of repayment. Merchants and landlords received the same rights to collect from their debtors. As the lien system spread, the tenant signed a crop lien at the first of a season and did business with the merchant until the crop was harvested. The person providing the credit often dictated the amount of acreage to be devoted to cotton and demanded that the tenant buy goods at the creditor's store, gin the crop at the creditor's gin, and store it in the creditor's warehouse.

In time, conflicts arose between planters and merchants over who had first claim to a crop in cases where the tenant owed one for land, livestock, equipment, and fertilizer, and another for clothes, food, and provisions. An 1871 Alabama law made the landowner's lien superior to any other debt. The law effectively restricted merchants primarily to the white hill counties, where they became the primary sources of credit. Planters dominated the credit system in the Black Belt. Political warfare swirled around this issue for decades. Planters supported agrarian radicals who demanded the abolition of the crop-lien system in the hill counties, though they refused to countenance tampering with it in the plantation counties.[15] Agrarian reformers used the issue effectively in the hill counties to mobilize opposition to merchants who increasingly became the largest hill county landowners. They also harnessed the issue of agricultural credit to the service of political and agricultural reform movements, including the Grange, the Greenback-Labor party, the Farmers' Alliance, and the Populist party.

The *Southern Plantation*, an Alabama farm journal that in 1874 became the official organ of the state Grange, waged war on the crop lien.

The editor of the paper, William C. Stubbs, who was a professor of chemistry at Auburn University (then called Alabama Agricultural and Mechanical College), blamed the crop lien for bankrupting Alabama's small farmers. The lecturer for the Alabama Grange, George Johnston, often attacked the lien and blamed it for the state's agricultural woes. He alleged that merchants utilized the lien to force farmers to trade with the merchants and use their gins and warehouses. Some of the journal's correspondents wrote Stubbs that their dilemma was more complex. They had rather deal with a "shylock" than be unable to obtain credit to plant at all.[16]

Despite an altered name, the *Farm Journal*, and a new publisher, planter-lawyer William H. Chambers, the paper continued its assault on the crop lien. The system degraded labor by allowing blacks who owned no stock, property, or tools to compete with whites as tenant farmers. These white farmers had to compete against blacks with the same landlords, who sought the lowest possible terms regardless of their effect on the land. Chambers did chide debtors for blaming merchants for their fate, claiming that debtors should assume responsibility for their own plight.[17]

Hiram Hawkins, master of the Alabama Grange, recalled years later that merchants in the 1870s charged as much as fifty cents on the dollar for the credit they supplied. They generally limited the loans to five months, thus earning 10 percent per month. Small farmers became "tenants upon their land, paying rentals in the shape of interest."[18] Soon they would become tenants upon another person's land.

At a 1901 hearing on conditions of agriculture in Alabama, Pitt Dillingham, a black man who served as principal of the Calhoun Colored School in Calhoun County, testified that the crop-lien system oppressed both races: "The small white farmers are in the same boat with the colored farmers, so far as the crop-mortgage and the credit-price system go, and their effects on land and people."[19] Unfortunately this recognition did not result in effective biracial cooperation.

In addition to credit, small farmers and tenants struggled with landowners over fencing laws. Antebellum yeoman farmers had maintained large numbers of swine, cattle, and sheep that had been allowed to roam freely in the forests. The only legal requirement was that the livestock be branded. In the 1880s and 1890s the Alabama legislature responded to the demands of landowners that those who owned livestock must fence them in. Small farmers, many of them descendants of Celtic ancestors who had a long open-range tradition of "the commons" (land that was used by all), viewed such legislation as a violation of custom and a threat to their livelihood. Such laws did make it harder for small farmers to maintain their independence and helped drive them into tenancy, particularly in the Wiregrass region where poor soil had encouraged a large population of herders.

Proposed laws to "prohibit stock from running at large," to "regulate the enclosure of stock," or "to prohibit the owner . . . from allowing any . . . animal to go at large off the premises of such owner" stirred class divisions among whites. One proposed law made it clear that the intent was to protect "lands and plantations from depredations by stock."[20] Alabama farm journals, edited by planters or other advocates of landowning interests, favored fencing laws in order both to protect crops and to improve stock breeds.[21]

John Horry Dent, a prominent planter who owned properties in both Georgia and Alabama, played a major role in the political battles to fence land during the 1880s. During one closely divided election he predicted that "all the negroes and whites who own no land, and by right and justice should not . . . vote . . . will vote for fencing [of crops not animals]." "It is simply a question of labor and capital." In later years sheep raisers in Washington County opposed fencing laws. Landless farmers and small farmers in Wilcox County supported continuation of the open range against breeders of "improved stock." In Montgomery and Greene counties, landowning farmers desired to fence the range over the opposition of small farmers and tenants. Sometimes the state legislature mandated fencing, but other times it merely empowered a county to conduct a referendum on the issue. These elections usually pitted large landowners against tenant and small farmers. Although there were exceptions, Alabama political campaigns reveal a strong correlation between counties with high levels of white poverty, open-range or antifencing sentiment, and populistic political insurgency.[22]

Small farmers and tenants also cooperated in other protests. They opposed oppressive railroad freight rates, exorbitant charges for cotton bagging, and other abuses by trusts and "Wall Street." As a consequence, full-fledged political insurgency raged in the hill country and Wiregrass among white tenants and small farmers who feared correctly that they were slipping closer to tyranny with every passing year.

Whatever the source of the tenancy or the conflicts generated by it, the economic decline of Alabama's white yeomanry was precipitous. Measured statistically it was reflected in declining production despite the opening of new land to agriculture. Corn production stood at more than thirty-three million bushels in 1860 compared to twenty-five million in 1880. Not until 1900 did production edge slightly above the prewar figure. The number of cotton bales declined from 990,000 in 1860 to 700,000 in 1880. The prewar figures were not exceeded until 1900. The value of livestock in 1900 remained well below the figure for 1860.[23]

These impersonal statistics spelled doom for many small white farmers. Farmers in Clarke County, which is located in southwest Alabama's pine belt between the Alabama and Tombigbee rivers, produced only one-third as much cotton in 1870 as in 1860. Pea, bean, potato, and corn production all fell well below 1860 output. Even allowing for the inaccuracies of the 1870 U.S. census, the crisis can be corroborated from other sources. During the 1860s, 150 of Clarke's 901 farms failed and 174,000 acres of farmland went out of production. One county historian described the predominant emotion as an "apparent hopelessness for working up again in life." Tenancy had become well established by 1880, and sharecropping increasingly replaced fixed annual rent between 1880 and 1890. By the later year, only 56 percent of Clarke's farms were cultivated by owners; 17 percent of the farmland was rented to tenants, and 27 percent was rented for shares of the crops.[24]

Farm income in Bullock County, well to the east of Clarke, followed the same pattern. In 1880 the total value of farms in the county was $1.6 million. Ten years later their total worth had fallen to $1.1 million. The future held little hope for the county's 628 white illiterates.[25]

Small farmers simply did not have enough capital for profitable farming. Their existing resources did not provide most of them a decent diet, clothes, health care, or education. Progress through diversification was largely meaningless because they already produced a substantial portion of the food they consumed.[26] Perishable crops could not be stored and transported profitably. And there was little if any local market for their food crops. Most of their neighbors produced the same products or had no money with which to buy them.

Planters viewed tenancy as a logical response to market conditions.[27] They had work to do and tens of thousands of freedmen and poor whites needed work. In 1872 Charles Carter Langdon of Mobile began publishing a journal he called the *Rural Alabamian*, which was devoted to "progressive agriculture and improved industry." He ran several articles supporting sharecropping as the best remedy for Alabama's labor shortage. In addition to receiving half the crop, Langdon claimed that croppers used a free cottage, received free wood for fuel and buildings, and could keep swine, milk cows, and cattle, as well as hunt on the owner's land. Correspondents to the official state Grange newspaper, the *Southern Plantation*, also praised the system. According to one farmer, sharecropping resulted in better crops because the landowner and laborer worked toward common goals.[28]

White tenants reacted more negatively. For them, tenancy represented a decline in status even if sometimes it brought an improvement in income. As they became producers of cotton crops with relatively high cash value, their income might actually rise over the subsistence farming that had characterized their prewar experience. But landowners subjected them to close supervision and were more likely to dictate how much of the land must be planted in cotton rather than food crops.

Black and white tenants had more in common than they had differences in their economic arrangements, but whites were more aware of their caste status as whites than their class status as tenants. White notions of equality and justice rested on their assumption of black subordination. No matter how low their economic conditions or squalid their lives, they believed that any white person was better than any black. And to some degree white Alabama society recognized their claims. Most Alabamians extended more respect to landless whites than they did even to landowning blacks.

The racial differences between tenants also owed much to political divisions. Blacks overwhelmingly favored the Republican party. Yet the centers of white tenancy and poverty—north and east Alabama hill counties and the southeastern Wiregrass—were the strongest centers of the antebellum Democratic party.

Although Alabama's white landowners extended to all whites some status based on racial solidarity, they often preferred black tenants to farm their land. They believed that blacks were more easily satisfied and gave less trouble. Whites made more demands, insisted on higher status, and wanted larger gardens, better houses, and less supervision. They moved more frequently and were more likely to challenge a landlord's authority or bookkeeping. White tenants were more likely to have their own livestock and tools, had more education, produced more, and earned higher incomes.[29]

The racial composition of tenancy tended to follow geographical boundaries in Alabama. Blacks constituted the overwhelming majority of tenants across the plantation belt of central Alabama that stretched from Barbour and Macon counties across Montgomery to Lowndes, Dallas, Wilcox, Greene, Sumter, and to the Tombigbee River. They also constituted the majority in some traditional plantation areas of the Tennessee River Valley. But across most of northern, eastern, and southeastern Alabama, white tenancy predominated.

Tenancy Patterns in Ten Alabama Counties

To dramatize the plight of white Alabama sharecroppers, one need only examine their lives closely. An examination of 372 heads of families in ten Alabama counties reveals a great deal about them.[30] The ten counties include Winston in northwestern Alabama; Jackson in the northeastern corner; Cherokee, which borders Georgia in the northeast; four contiguous counties in northeastern Alabama—Calhoun, Cleburne, Randolph, and Clay; and three contiguous counties in southeastern Alabama—Covington, Crenshaw, and Geneva. The seven in north Alabama are all Appalachian hill counties; the three in the south are all flat Wiregrass counties. All ten were overwhelmingly white: in the 1880 census they contained 109,110 whites and only 21,152 blacks. They were not historically cotton counties, but produced a variety of products. For instance, the first census after Cleburne became a county in 1866 revealed that farmers had 5,641 cattle, 3,871 sheep, 10,659 hogs, 960 horses, and 524 mules. They produced only 873 bales of cotton in 1870, but 10,997 pounds of tobacco, 6,496 pounds of wool, 9,999 gallons of sorghum molasses, 17,547 bushels of potatoes, 186,763 bushels of corn, and 35,739 bushels of wheat.[31] The ten counties were among the poorest in one of America's most impoverished states. In 1920, Alabama's per capita income ranked forty-fourth among the forty-eight states. By 1935 the state had dropped to forty-sixth. In 1929 three of the six poorest counties were Clay, Cleburne, and Winston. Cleburne's per capita income of $156 was the lowest in the state, but none of the other nine counties did much better.[32]

The seven north Alabama counties demonstrated the characteristic patterns of Appalachian development. Large areas were so remote and isolated as to make any economic activity other than subsistence agriculture difficult if not impossible. As late as 1893 Cleburne County contained 21,740 acres of public land, most of it mountainous that would later be incorporated into the Talladega National Forest.[33] Winston also contained vast stretches of high mountains and deep canyons that later became the heart of the Bankhead National Forest. Although some commercial agriculture thrived along river bottoms and in broad valleys, much of these seven counties consisted of subsistence farms that produced corn and livestock.

The three Wiregrass counties provide quite a different pattern. Named for the tall grass that grew on the floor of tall yellow pine forests, the region had soil that was not well suited to cotton. So settlement patterns favored small farmers who kept herds of cattle and swine and flocks of sheep. They sold these both in nearby urban markets and in adjacent plantation counties. The farmers and herdsmen tended to be self-sufficient yeomen who were proud of their independence.

Politically, the ten counties were predominantly Jacksonian Democratic, though remote Winston County boasted a strong Republican allegiance, largely due to its opposition to secession and to wartime depredations conducted by Confederate officials. But on substantive issues, most of the small white farmers and tenants thought alike. On the issue of fencing, for instance, seven of the ten counties in 1880 maintained the open range; only Crenshaw, Randolph, and Calhoun had laws regulating stockmen.[34]

But perhaps the most notable similarity in the ten counties was the rapid increase in white farm tenancy between 1880 and 1940. By 1900 the ten counties contained 9,586 white tenant farmers. Ten years later the same counties contained 13,609. By 1920 the figure stood at 15,524. As late as 1940 the counties listed 15,031 white tenants. In that year rates of tenancy ranged from a low of 38.4 percent in Winston to a high of 66.6 in Geneva. And of the 16,999 tenant farmers in the ten counties, 88.4 percent were white.[35]

A profile of 365 white sharecroppers in 1880 reveals that most were young, male, and unrelated to the person whose land they farmed. Nearly half, 42.5 percent, were younger than thirty. Another 27.9 percent were under forty. Only 14 of the 365 whose ages were known were in their sixties, only 4 in their seventies, only 1 in his eighties.

Nor was sharecropping purely a male experience. Within five of the ten counties checked for the sex of white heads of families, 10 of 239 sharecroppers (4.2 percent) were female. The average age of forty-seven was a good deal older than for males, perhaps indicating that many were widows.

Not all sharecroppers were necessarily poor either. Many were young men, newly married, who were beginning farming on a relative's farm. Although some croppers may have lived on land owned by a relative with a different last name, and thus made it impossible to track family relationships, many young white croppers lived on a tenant farm immediately adjacent to someone with the same last name. Of seven counties checked for such coincidence, forty-seven sharecroppers (20.6 percent of the total) were listed next to a landowning farmer with the same last name. Of these forty-seven, thirty-two were in their teens or twenties. Sons-in-law with different last names no doubt increased this total. For most of them tenancy was merely a temporary passage from adolescence to adulthood. Many would wind up as landowners either by purchase or inheritance.

Even with the multitude of children sired by rural whites, most sharecroppers could tend a farm no larger than forty acres, and few in the sample were that large. The average was slightly more than twenty-one acres. The range between counties was minimal, from a low average of nearly eighteen acres in Jackson County to a high of a little more than thirty in Cherokee.

Neither the worth of the farm nor its products was large. Census enumerators valued the land, fences, and buildings at an average of $303, but even this modest figure was inflated by the estimates of three farms. They listed the value of the remaining 220 farms at an average of $284. The value of all farm products sold, consumed, or on hand in 1879 amounted to an average of $191.

The renowned antebellum yeoman with his large herds of livestock bore little resemblance to the white postbellum cropper, though here and there a tenant maintained the heritage. In the traditional herding county of Geneva in the Wiregrass, Hezakiah Hendrix, who share-cropped his father's land, kept 90 sheep. In nearby Covington County, M. Y. Bullock tended 150. The largest cattle herd, with 31, belonged to Epharim Ward, who also sharecropped his father's land in Geneva County. One sharecropper in Winston County tended 50 swine and one in Jackson County owned 75. M. Y. Bullock of Covington County led the poultry producers with 136. But such individual cases are clearly exceptions.

Most sharecroppers tended some livestock: 335 of 372 listed cows, cattle, or oxen; 295 of 372 kept swine; 300 of 372 tended poultry. But the totals were small. Of the 295 sharecroppers who owned swine, 83 (28.1 percent) had 1 or 2. Of the 335 who had cattle or oxen, 88 (26.3 percent) had only 1 or 2 head. Even more desperate were the 10 percent who owned no cows, cattle, or oxen, or those who owned no swine or poultry (19.3 and 20.6 percent respectively).

At the bottom of the sharecropping structure were those who owned no work animals. They had to provide as much as half their cotton to the owner who furnished them land, house, and draft animals. Although an ox occasionally performed such labor, most farmers relied on horses and mules. The death of such an animal was often an occasion for genuine mourning because it plunged the sharecropper's family into an even lower status within the complex tenancy system. Of the 372 share-croppers, 115 (30.9 percent) owned neither horse nor mule. And 181 others (48.7 percent) owned only one work animal.

Such animals pulled plows that broke the ground for a variety of crops. Cotton was most important because it was the only reliable cash crop. Other crops could be eaten, fed to livestock, or processed and used. But only cotton regularly and predictably could be transformed into cash. Although farmers increasingly grew cotton and many merchant-planter landlords required that a specified amount of land be planted in cotton, white sharecroppers apparently were allowed some freedom to grow what they wanted. Large numbers produced sweet potatoes, though few grew Irish potatoes. Almost all sharecroppers (365 of 372) grew corn. In fact the 372 sharecroppers devoted nearly twice as many acres to corn than to cotton. More than a third in seven counties grew wheat. Nor did they necessarily do without fresh fruit. In eight of the counties, 11 percent kept apple trees (in fact an astounding average of 44.31 trees per sharecropper, indicating almost certainly that some marketed fruit commercially) and 12.8 percent had peach trees (with an even larger average of 55.14 trees each).

But cotton was still king even of the sharecropper's modest domain. Of the 372 families examined, 282 produced a total of 650 bales of cotton, an average of 2.3 bales per farmer. Within nine of the counties studied, it took an average of 3.35 acres to produce 1 bale of cotton. In 1879 cotton sold for an average of 10¢ a pound, one of only two years between 1876 and 1900 when it reached that high. A commercial bale weighed about five hundred pounds, so the 282 white croppers averaged $115, which they then either divided in half (if the owner-merchant provided animals and tools) or gave one-fourth to the landowner if they provided animals and implements. Assuming that the average cropper used 3.35 acres to produce a bale, he grew 149 pounds of cotton on each acre. At the inflated price of 10¢ a pound, he made $14.90 an acre before dividing, or $7.45 after "settling up" on halves. It was pitifully little for a season's back-breaking labor. And only twice in twenty-five years did the price reach 10¢ a pound. It might sink as low as 5¢, as in the 1890s.[36] In the 1879 crop year, the average sharecropper earned a cash income, after dividing his crop, of between $87 (for those sharing one-fourth with the landlord) and $58 (for those dividing the crop equally). The average black sharecropper in 1880 earned an estimated annual income of $60, so whites could take no other pride than in the color of their skin.[37]

The source of supply for the expanding number of sharecroppers is not hard to discover. Within these same ten counties, small landowning farmers, their farms heavily mortgaged, were hanging on to the land by their finger tips. A random sample of twenty-five landowning heads of families in Winston and Geneva counties revealed that they were often doing worse than the sharecroppers. They farmed smaller plots (13.5 acres vs. 21.4), and their farms were less valuable ($202.96 compared to $302.85). The value of their products ($94.25) was less than half that of the sharecroppers ($190.87). They did possess twice as many cattle, sheep, and swine on average, but they produced less corn. Apparently many of the small farmers did not view cotton as any quick fix to their problems. In Geneva County, for instance, the poor soil of landowners produced only one bale per 4.1 acres, well below the average for share-croppers statewide (though considerably better than their cropper neighbors in the county who planted an average of 7.1 acres in cotton in order to produce one bale). Geneva County small farmers averaged only 1.18 bales. Even though they could keep the entire $59 that their crop brought them in 1879, landowners had only $2 more cash than the average sharecropper realized from his share of the crop during the same year. And the typical Geneva County sharecropper actually produced more cotton (1.59 bales to 1.18) than the small farmer. Because the small farmers obviously raised livestock for sale, their cash income was undoubtedly higher than the croppers', but not by much. In Winston County a total of 124 farm owners produced crops in 1879 worth $75 or less (compared to the county's 111 white sharecroppers whose products had an average value of $126.06). Many sharecroppers farmed better land than small landowners. Because they worked for leading planters and merchants who controlled the best lands in the county, they often produced more products.

Analyzed in this way, one understands clearly where the cascading stream of tenants originated. Many of the small landowners of the 1880 census would appear as sharecroppers in 1890 and after. This reality, probably as clear to them as to us, also explains the increasing political radicalism that led them into the Populist party and to other forms of insurgency in a desperate attempt to alter the fate that they saw only too clearly in the plight of their sharecropper neighbors.

One question remains, and it is perhaps hardest of all to answer. What connection did 1880 white sharecroppers have to antebellum agriculture? Of the 372 sharecroppers, only a few aged thirty-eight or older could be traced to the 1860 census when they would have been at least eighteen years old. But 22 of them appeared in both the 1860 and 1880 lists. For most of these, the American Dream of landownership and a better life had been reversed during the intervening two decades. They had descended the ladder of success, though few of them had ever climbed very high in the beginning. In 1860, Wilson Ayers had owned $600 in real estate and another $300 in personal property. Alexander McKinsey (listed as McKinzie in the 1860 census) owned $1,500 in real estate and $700 in personal property. John J. Moody owned $1,500 and $1,300. Jacob G. Barrow's farm was valued at $700, but his personal property totaled a prosperous $6,570. The Reverend Solomon F. Moody was a Methodist minister in 1860 with a modest $400 in real estate and $373 in personal property. James Parker farmed, with values of $800 and $1,813, as did Hiram Cagle with $400 and $300. David Manasco was more prosperous than most Winston County farmers, with real estate and personal property valued at $700 each. Squire L. Pittman was a moderately prosperous farmer in the same county with a total of $1,000 in land and property. All of these fell into sharecropping by 1880 from a much higher status.

Others descended from a less august financial ancestry. In 1860 William Boyd was the illiterate eldest son of seven children living on his father's farm. Henry Mitchum, the eldest of ten children, worked as a farm laborer on his father's Randolph County farm. Henry Austin of

Jackson County was an illiterate farmer who owned no real estate, though he did list $110 in personal property. William J. Adderholt worked as a carpenter without real estate or personal property, though his father was a large and prosperous Calhoun County farmer. Jackson A. Andrews and John L. Scott, both of Calhoun County, listed no property in 1860. Absolem Garrison lived with his father but listed $600 in real estate. Robert M. Ingle lived on his mother's small Winston County farm but listed no property. Judged by this sample, about half of the 1880 sharecroppers seem to have been little better off in 1860, though a number of them lived with more successful parents.

When agricultural productivity is included in the equation, the 1860 farmers seem to have tumbled dramatically downward. Of the twenty-two farmers located in 1860, fourteen appeared in the agricultural census of that year. Their average farm value of $815.38 was considerably higher than the 1880 average of $389. They also farmed more acres in 1860 (38.61 compared to 30.40). They owned more horses and mules (1.78 horses, 0.28 mules in 1860; .90 horses, 0.31 mules in 1880), swine (20.78 in 1860, 11.13 in 1880), and cattle/oxen (18.35 to 6.13). They produced a great deal more corn (287.14 bushels to 69.25) and wheat (33.16 to none). And defying the notion that sharecroppers declined because of forced reliance on cotton production, they actually produced more cotton in 1860 than in 1880 (ten of fourteen produced an average of 2.5 bales in 1860; three of twenty-two listed an average of 1.6 bales twenty years later). The intervening years of war, Reconstruction, and chaos obviously took their toll on Alabama's sturdy yeomen.

The Human Dimension of Tenancy

As important as such statistics may be, they obscure the personal dimensions of rural poverty. Tenants rarely pondered the intricacies or the origins of the tenancy system. The individual reality of lives suspended between hope and despair, the perspective on the world gained walking barefoot through a field following the hind quarter of a mule—these vantage points afford a different view of the experience, how they became tenants, acquired land and credit, broke land and cultivated it, and coped with their plight.

The descent into tenancy was intensely personal. Every tenant told a different story. Homer Flynt came from a small plantation family near High Falls, Georgia. He ran away from home in 1884 after his mother died. The sixteen-year-old went to the Joppa community in north Alabama to live with his sister. But she lived only a few months after he arrived, so he took a job at a foundry near Morrisville. Nearly illiterate, he married Annie Phoebe Owens but did not get along well with her family. So he left foundry work early in the twentieth century and joined the ranks of Calhoun County's sharecroppers.[38]

Mary Wigley's family lived on Sand Mountain, a high plateau in northeast Alabama renowned for its all-white population of fiercely proud independent farmers. Her father farmed but derived most of his income from a country store he operated. He furnished credit for the community's farmers who patronized his store because it served also as a post office. As a community leader, Wigley helped bring Rural Free Delivery to Sand Mountain, but when the system began many farmers no longer visited his store. The years of 1903–04 were drought years on Sand Mountain, and many farmers were unable to pay their debts. Wigley was deeply in debt himself to a railroad furnishing merchant who demanded payment. So Wigley began to walk the country roads of Sand Mountain trying to collect debts owed him. Tensions mounted. The family found a pile of charred splinters underneath their porch, evidence of an attempt to burn their house. Wigley sold his daughter's pet cow, despite her tearful pleas on behalf of the animal. Her mother explained that the cow must be sold to help pay debts or the family would lose its land and store. Mary decided to ask God for money to save their home:

> How I felt when I finally decided to pray the all-important prayer for money to pay the debts is one of the most distinct memories of my life. It was almost dark when I slipped out alone in the side yard at the chimney-end of the house. There on my knees, with my eyes tightly closed, I poured out my heart to God. I pleaded that he save me from being like a little orphan girl with no home. I told Him I did not want one penny for myself—just enough to pay the debts— and would He please put the money for the debts in the empty ash can nearby.
>
> With my eyes still tightly closed and with my face buried in my hands, I waited and kept waiting. I was afraid to go look in the can. When I finally did and found it empty, I remember thinking to myself and probably said out loud, "Just about as I expected." That was the first and last time I ever asked God to grant a petition in keeping with a fantastic fairy tale of a miraculous Santa Claus.[39]

No salvation came, whether from human or divine sources. The Wigley family spent a last moneyless Christmas in their home, then moved to a tenant farm at the end of a dirt road. Mary assumed her work of spreading a mixture of rotted manure and pine straw on cotton rows from a twenty-five-pound lard can. Exhausted and filthy, she nonetheless converted quickly from the daughter of a prosperous and influential country merchant to a sharecropper's daughter. The merchant often depicted as villain in the drama of poverty had become one of its victims. Or as one Calhoun County landowner wrote, "the tenant skins the land, and the landlord skins the tenant . . . and he who can skins the landlord. It is the dynamics of poverty."[40]

Carlie H. Crocker was born in Bibb County in 1908. Her father died when she was five, so she went to live with her grandparents. She married when she was seventeen, "just a child." The newlyweds had three dollars between them. Her husband worked at a sawmill for two dollars a day. But sometime in the late 1920s, he lost his job and they became sharecroppers, farming on halves.[41]

Carl Forrester of Houston County began farming on halves in 1927 and farmed thirty acres with a mule for two seasons before he married in December 1928. All his family managed to provide them was two mattresses and ten turkey eggs, although his father did cosign a note so Carl could borrow fifty dollars. With that the couple bought a small wood-burning stove, two iron bedsteads with springs, and a kitchen cabinet. An uncle made them a table and a bench out of poplar. They rented a farm on halves and set the turkey eggs under a hen. Weeks later she hatched nine small turkeys and raised them like her own until cockleburs came up in the garden. The young turkeys ate the cockleburs and every one of them died. It was not an auspicious beginning for the new tenant family.[42]

Human relations were as complicated as economic ones. Although many tenants remembered their creditors with scorn, others believed they were treated fairly. Mary Wigley's family experienced both on Sand Mountain.

Major Brothers at Lebanon, Alabama, furnished supplies to the Wigleys. Mr. Major charged 25 percent interest for six months' credit, a customary rate on the mountain. He treated Mr. Wigley kindly and with respect. In fact, they became close personal friends, a friendship that lasted as long as they both lived. When young Mary began teaching school, she replaced the merchant by financing her father's crop.

In later years, Mary Wigley attended Auburn University and became one of the first Home Demonstration agents in north Alabama. As part of her duties, she helped obtain members for the Farm Bureau. A major impetus of the bureau's drive in that section of the state was to reduce high-interest farm credit and make farmers self-supporting. As she recruited names on petitions, she learned to avoid banks and credit merchants who were "local financial czars." The head of a major automobile dealership first signed her petition, then removed his name because "this thing is going to split the Baptist Church." The manager of a wholesale grocery company first hunted her down to sign the petition, then searched for her again in order to remove his name when his largest customer, a credit merchant, threatened to change suppliers.[43]

If the landlord did the furnishing, he might provide it in credit from a store he operated on the plantation. Or he might pay a monthly stipend and allow the tenant to purchase goods wherever he could. Kathleen Knight's family left northwest Alabama in the 1920s to sharecrop in the Mississippi Delta. Although they were a relatively stable family in Alabama, their status quickly declined in the Delta. One landlord operated a store for his tenants. Another advanced twenty dollars a month, beginning in March and continuing through August. When the family harvested its cotton, it "settled up" debts with the landlord. He let them keep the money from sale of the cotton seed to buy food until they could pay their bills: "It was usually a rat race, I guess you would call it, because you just pay up and go back [into debt], and they would furnish you again." The family never signed a written agreement; all its dealings were based upon oral understandings.[44] As with so many other sharecroppers, when the landlord settled with them, he usually had virtually all their crop.

William D. Nixon ran a store that furnished his tenants at Merrellton in Calhoun County. As a landowner and merchant he viewed his relationship differently. In 1911 the Nixons rented land to twenty-one tenant families, sixteen of them white and five black. The white tenants made between twenty-five and two hundred dollars that year after paying debts. Nixon considered 1911 a "good year for both tenants and landlords." But by 1921 cotton prices had fallen precipitously, and Nixon lost two hundred dollars furnishing one sharecropper who moved away without paying his bills.[45]

Not all years were bad, nor was cotton the only source of income. Many croppers supplemented their meager earnings by selling firewood from forests, fruits from orchards, or eggs, sorghum molasses, or fresh pork. White sharecroppers often maintained sufficient latitude over the allocation of land to allow older children to raise a small garden, the proceeds of which they could use however they wished. Children could also "hire out" to other farmers for cash wages when they finished chores or harvests on their own farms. Homer Flynt's children received their own garden plots, hired out, and also made money by selling blackberries to a country store for the munificent sum of one penny per quart.[46]

When times were bad, sharecroppers might go months with little or no money. Lillie Mae Flynt Beason remembered a visit by an itinerant photographer who proposed to take a family portrait. Her father, mother, and all the children pooled their resources and managed just enough: "It's odd how little money [you had]; why it would just be months that you wouldn't . . . see a penny." But when times were good, as in 1918 when the family sold its cotton for forty cents a pound, euphoria prevailed.

> Oh we had a shed out in the cotton—in the middle of this big field . . . to put the cotton . . . under. . . . We'd stand under that shed and sing what we wanted. And Ora [her sister] and I wanted white shoes in the summertime. You see, you had laced up shoes, you didn't have slippers, with little buckles and things. And we agreed that . . . whatever happened . . . we'd just be in a good mood if we said "white shoes" to each other. If we see one getting mad, we'd say "white shoes" and then make 'em happy again. . . . We got the white shoes that year; that's the first time in the summer we had shoes. You see, you went barefooted except in the wintertime. And, we got these white shoes, and we kept 'em polished. Oh, how we did polish those shoes. . . . We never had had that kind of money before.[47]

The monopoly of the country merchant was occasionally interrupted by the "rolling store." Sometimes operated by a Jewish peddler who added an exotic dimension to rural life, the rolling store was a wagon or truck modified as a mobile store. It roamed backcountry dirt roads, offering cloth, needles, thread, and a variety of other sundries and foodstuffs. Best of all the peddler would usually exchange his wares for barter. He would lay out his goods for inspection, then trade them for eggs, chickens, turkey, meat from the smokehouse, or fresh fruit from the orchards. These he would trade at other farms that had less livestock and poultry for fresh berries, honey, or molasses.[48]

With money in hand or credit secured, the tenant could begin the arduous and back-breaking labor of planting and raising his crops. The task began with plowing.

Horses and mules represented significant investments of scarce resources, so many tenants had none, a fundamental issue that determined whether a sharecropper farmed on halves or thirds and fourths. For those who had no stock animals, life was more difficult. Kathleen Knight's father had to get up earlier than mule-owning tenants because he had to walk to his landowner's barn to get the mule. At dinnertime he walked the mule back from the fields to the barn to feed it. For the Flynt family, acquisition of a mule coincided with their best cotton crop and a substantial increase in status. During one prosperous year of the First World War, the Flynts obtained their largest farm (forty acres), bought a mule, sold their cotton for an unprecedented forty cents a pound, and transferred from farming on halves to farming on thirds and fourths.[49]

Mules represented such an advance in status that the animal's welfare counted for nearly as much as a family member's. Carlie Crocker remembered a young mule her family bought that grew up with the children. A railroad track crossed their tenant farm, and the mule got out of his fence one day and raced down the track oblivious to the shouts of family members. A railroad trestle over a creek stopped him a quarter-mile away, where one of many sharecropper dramas unfolded:

And it was time for the little old doodle bug . . . passenger train to come. And I looked and seen it a comin' and I started cryin' cause I knowed that if the mule got killed we didn't have money to buy another one. And the train seen the mule and it rolled up to the other side of the trestle and started blowing the whistle. And here come the old mule back, with his ears throwed back, he was just diggin' 'em up. And . . . the boys headed him at the house and he just shook, he was scared nearly to death. But I cried; I knowed if the mule died we wouldn't have nothing to plow with.[50]

An industrious farmer with a good mule and a six- or seven-inch steel-beam plow could break an acre of land a day. So it took weeks to prepare the ground for spring planting. In fact many farmers quantified farms not by how many acres they had but by how many horses or mules it took to cultivate them (hence such phrases as "a one-horse farm" or a "two-mule place").[51]

Planting seeds was not a task to be taken lightly. Because so much of farming was governed by whim, fate, or God, depending on the cosmology of the tenant, nothing could be left to chance. Many a prayer for good harvests accompanied planting time. Most croppers planted by the signs. Frank Uptain planted corn on the day after a full moon or a first moon. He planted Irish potatoes when the "sign is in the feet" because the crop grew inside the ground. Other crops he planted in the "twin days." To protect his watermelon patch from crows, he tied a string on sticks around his patch and the birds would not go inside the string. Or he would lay a small rock on each melon and the birds would not peck them. The Uptains further insured crops with a traditional meal of hog jowls and black-eyed peas on New Year's Day. Mary Wigley's father prayed for cloud cover when a late frost in the spring threatened his cotton crop.[52]

But the prosperity of a tenant family could not be left to a capricious fate. Work was the key to their success and work they did. Homer Flynt and his oldest son began their day at 4:00 A.M., when they rose and fed the stock. Then they hitched the mule and at daylight were in the fields plowing. As soon as Claude, the oldest boy, reached age seven or eight, he began plowing. Annie Flynt taught the younger children how to hoe and adjusted the handles to fit their sizes. She carried the youngest baby to the fields and laid it on a pallet while she worked. If the family had a cooked meal at lunch during the heat of the day, she would leave the fields at 10:00 to begin cooking. The family would quit for lunch and a rest, then return when the day began to cool in the afternoon and work until dark. In the spring and fall, before the days became so hot and humid, they took a picnic basket and ate lunch in the fields. When the oldest daughter was large enough, she learned to sew on a machine before she could reach the floor treadle. So her older brother did the treadling while she guided the material through the needle.[53] Like the Flynts, Kathleen Knight began hoeing and picking cotton as a child: "I mean when you got big enough to pull a sack you was in the field; that was expected of you."[54]

Mary Wigley began to distribute guano and cotton seeds while a young girl. Calamity struck one season when her father broke his wrist. Relatives and friends came to his aid, taking over the plowing. Wigley learned to hoe with one hand and gained such skill that he decided to try plowing. With Mary on one handle and her father on the other, they tried to plow a furrow. As her confidence mounted Mary begged to try plowing by herself.

> Father was evidently tired of my begging and probably had mischief in his eyes as he surrendered his left plow handle with no argument.
>
> Before I knew it, the plow was almost out of the ground and I did what seemed right—I pressed down on both handles. Contrary to reason, that made the metal plow come out of the ground completely, and with the load suddenly lighter Old Beck [the mule] struck up a fast walk.
>
> Things were going wrong. I wanted to get the plow back in the ground and in my excitement yelled in a loud voice, "Wait!" This made the mule go faster. Father always said "gee" and "haw" softly to gentle Old Beck, and she could not understand my language. As I yelled louder and louder, she trotted across the field faster and faster until she reached the pasture fence.
>
> Father had followed his new plow girl part of the way but when I finally had a chance to look back, he was all bent over, slapping his knee with his good hand, laughing and hollooing.[55]

As this episode demonstrates, tenants tried as best they could to find happiness in their work. The Wigleys made corn shelling, hard and monotonous work normally, into a joyous family affair. Because they could not afford a corn sheller, they pushed back the furniture and spread a large sheet on the floor of their cabin in front of the fireplace. Mr. and Mrs. Wigley sat in chairs at opposite corners of the sheet. The children piled on the edges and all began shelling toward the middle. They alternated racing each other, eating hot deep-roasted ears of corn, and talking. Children laughed, joked, and "cut up," something normally forbidden by their stern father. They filled the stovebox with cobs to serve as winter fuel and shelled two bushels of corn to be milled into flour. The shelling was "neither work nor play but truly halfway between."[56]

The Wigleys' lack of a corn sheller was symbolic of the tenant farmer's paucity of equipment. In 1900 the average Alabama farmer owned only $39 in machinery and equipment, and tenants had far less than that. By comparison Nebraska farmers the same year averaged $205 in machinery and Iowa farmers $253.[57] Such equipment as walking cultivators, seed planters, and corn shellers, which could substantially reduce labor and improve efficiency, simply were not normally a part of the white sharecropper's world.

The decision about what to grow was perhaps the simplest decision a sharecropper faced: whoever owned the land usually made the decision. Although most landlords allowed corn for feeding livestock and for meal and flour, they directed that all other acreage be devoted to cotton. And few sharecroppers objected because cotton was their only cash crop, their only hope for prosperity and their own piece of land. As Carl Forrester put it, "if you missed a cotton crop, you didn't have no money."[58] Owners allowed croppers to plant peanuts between the rows of cotton, and usually they permitted a small garden.

But most tenants had one kind of trouble or another over cotton acreage. Homer Flynt thought the owner would not take a share of the crop from a tiny patch of cotton he gave his son to cultivate. He was wrong. Mary Wigley's father planted a large vegetable garden on his tenant farm. But when a new landlord bought the farm he informed Wigley that from then on he must plant all the fields in cotton and corn. The Wigleys did not take the news well: "This was a blow to freedom and pride, also to our way of subsistence farming. It drove home the fact that we were not on our own. We were mere tenants. It made us want all the more a home of our own. If we could not have that, the next best thing was to have an accomodating [sic] landlord."[59]

The Wigleys' landowner finally agreed to allow the family to pay "standing rent" of seventy-five dollars a year. The changed status was hard to maintain because of the 1907 depression. But the freedom was worth it. Mrs. Wigley could now have her beloved flowers because her husband saved the ends of the cultivated rows nearest the house for her. With no landlord to interfere and only a tinge of regret at the small amount of cotton lost, she grew China asters whose clusters of purple, pink, and white blossoms bent down the stalks that held them.[60]

In northwestern Alabama a landlord allowed Kathleen Knight's family a pasture for livestock and a garden for vegetables. But when they moved to the Mississippi Delta, the new landowner allowed no garden other than their yard or the spaces between cotton rows. Their farm had no pasture; if they kept a cow at all, they had to stake her on a ditch or canal bank or on a levee. They simply could not provide enough vegetables, so their family in northwestern Alabama sent what it could.[61]

Within the small space allocated to them, tenants cultivated carefully. Carlie Crocker remembered ordering seeds from the Hasting Seed Catalogue and cabbage plants from Texas. Favorite crops in addition to corn included sweet potatoes, peas, cane for syrup making, okra, and tomatoes.[62]

The preeminence of cotton was easy to understand. The per-acre value of cotton was about twice that of corn, the only other possible cash crop. Cotton tenants needed virtually no supervision, whereas crating, shipping, and marketing vegetables required constant attention and considerable skill. So production of food crops declined in relationship to cotton.[63]

This fact alone kept Alabama farmers basically inefficient, for while new technology revolutionized the planting and harvesting of grain crops, it had little impact on cotton. It took 102 hours of labor to produce an acre of cotton in 1895.[64] Thus a typical white Alabama sharecropper exchanged 102 hours of his family's time for $14.90 an acre in good years such as 1880, or about 14.6¢ per hour. During bad years such as 1895 their income averaged only $8.10 an acre, or 7.9¢ an hour.[65]

An insect finally did what generations of agricultural experts had failed to do: persuade Alabama farmers to diversify their crops. When the boll weevil finally reached Alabama in the teens on its pilgrimage from Mexico across the cotton belt, it ravaged crops. In 1921 the insect dropped the state's cotton yield by 32 percent from the previous year.[66] From the beginning of the invasion, tenant farmers suffered terribly, losing their sole predictable cash crop. Many a tenant shared E. J. Alexander's experience. In 1938 he rented thirty acres, but the boll weevil destroyed his cotton crop and a drought scorched his corn.[67] Although the boll weevil may have been considered a blessing in disguise by landowning farmers, tenants received few benefits. When farmers decided to quit raising cotton, they often diverted their fields into pasture for cattle. This reduced the need for labor, and the changing agricultural patterns displaced tens of thousands of tenants.[68] Without a cash crop, even the remote possibility of a banner year for cotton prices such as in 1918 or 1919 vanished, depriving the sharecropper of all hope.

The psychology of tenancy slowly changed. At first most whites became tenants while believing the status to be a short-term expedient, a first step toward landownership. As one Clay County farmer wrote: "Lurking at the heart of every ambitious young man . . . was the hope that within a few years he could save enough money from the sale of cotton to buy land and cease to be a tenant."[69] But something terrible happened on their journey toward the American Dream. They became frozen in time as tenancy stretched across years, then decades, and even generations. A comprehensive investigation by the Alabama Farm Tenancy Committee, published in 1944, concluded that the original expectation of tenants that renting was a step toward independent ownership "has been disproved in recent years, for it has been demonstrated that on the whole, second-generation tenants actually seem to have less prospects for advancement." The percentage of tenants over fifty-five years of age had increased for several decades, indicating that the possibility of landownership was actually less likely than before. A two-year study between 1934 and 1936 in an Appalachian foothill community reached the same conclusion. Most landowners had never been tenants. A rural sociologist at Auburn University studied several hundred Alabama sharecroppers and found that three-fourths of the farmers who began farming as croppers remained croppers. Less than one-tenth became owners.[70]

Hope slowly gave way to bone-weary despair. Ellen Alexander confided to an interviewer in the late 1930s: "I ain't old, just forty-two, but I feel pretty old. If I could have looked ahead I guess maybe I would have picked a different road."[71]

Perpetual poverty had many dimensions. In a tiny north Alabama hamlet intensely studied in the mid 1930s, landowners owned $915 in household goods, cash, livestock, and equipment. Tenants related to them owned $275. Unrelated tenants possessed $190 in personal property. White sharecroppers held property valued at $125. Only black sharecroppers whose goods equaled a mere $55 stood below them. The community's white sharecropper families earned an average income in 1935 of only $153. Although a barter economy flourished among cash renters and small landowners, only 30 percent of white sharecroppers had anything to barter.[72]

Individual sharecroppers retain specific images of poverty. Mary Wigley remembered months on short rations; worn clothes repeatedly mended; cornmeal mush used to extend bread supplies; meat limited to wild game and fish; vegetables consisting of wild greens gathered from the fields; drink substitutes derived from roasted grain, okra seed, and dry crusts; and medicines concocted from herbs, wild leaves, bark, and roots. Lillie Mae Flynt Beason described poverty on the Johnson farm near Oxford about 1907. Her family lived in a shack with only Negro neighbors. They carried water from a spring some distance away, and it was there also that Annie Flynt washed clothes. Their landowner brought her a doll and the family fruit for Christmas. The next Christmas at another farm was even worse. No kindly owner intruded on their poverty and only a fortuitous piece of good luck provided relief. With not a penny to buy presents, Annie and Homer grieved over their inability to provide anything at all for their children. But then Annie found a chicken nest with an amazing eighteen eggs. She traded the eggs for candy, apples, and oranges; that provided the only Christmas they had.[73] Jake Brown, a sharecropper in the Hog Mountain community, recalled: "I had every kind of patch there was on my overalls except a tatter patch."[74]

One positive by-product of poverty was self-reliance. The tenant became a jack-of-all-trades because no money was available to hire work done. Annie Flynt developed expert skills as a carver, making plates and goblets out of cedar. She split white oak to make cotton baskets and bottom chairs. She made the family's clothes and the children's toys. She sawed off sections of logs for wagon wheels and made a sled from wood slabs salvaged from a sawmill. The Forrester family made plow beams, ax, hammer, and hoe handles, and bottomed their chairs with cypress bark from a swamp. They made furniture out of poplar. Jake Brown learned to do his own blacksmithing and to rive cedar shingles.[75]

Another by-product of tenancy was transience. White tenants moved even more frequently than blacks, perhaps the best evidence of their discontent with their status. Moving was one possible act of rebellion, an assertion of their rights in the face of an economic system they could not master. In 1940 approximately 46,000 Alabama tenant families had occupied the farms on which they worked for fewer than fifteen months. The average move cost a tenant about fifty dollars and led to a folk saying that "three moves are equal to a fire" in damage to furniture and equipment. Moving also led to gullied fields and dilapidated buildings because short-term residents took care of neither land nor dwellings.[76] Debts left behind went unpaid and helped establish the reputation for tenants of unreliability.

Sharecroppers remember it as akin to a fever that struck. The Hamric family moved nearly every year. The longest they sharecropped on one farm was four years. As a daughter recalled her father: "Nobody wants to move but him but the fever'd strike him and we'd have to go." Lillie Mae Flynt Beason pegged the chronology of her life to the places where her family lived—the Hop Francis place, the Johnson place, and the Bell place—"We just moved every time there was a baby." Asked why she thought her father moved so frequently, she replied:

> Well, he was looking for something better. You know, he had a lot of pride. I think my dad had more pride than was really good for him. And he was always bettering himself. I can just see him now coming in and telling my mother that one time when we moved to Wellington . . . how . . . everything was just going to be rosy. He was gonna have this and this and this. He always bettered himself, he said, as he moved. I'm not so sure about it, but he said he did.[77]

Ellen Alexander moved constantly during her childhood because her carpenter father was always seeking work. So when she married a Perry County sharecropper she was prepared for a life of itinerancy. They had hoped "by each move to better their condition"; but they had not done so.[78]

Like poverty, moving provided a rich store of folklore. So mobile were white sharecroppers, went the saying, that all a farmer had to do to move was "whistle up the dog and spit in the fire." According to one story, a sharecropper's chickens became so accustomed to having their legs tied and being suspended on nails in the wagon when the family moved, that anytime the chickens saw a wagon being loaded, they would roll over and cross their legs.

Such transience made education difficult for children, a problem compounded by lack of shoes, clothes, and books. A small north Alabama community had built a high school about 1915. Of the seventy-five graduates in the following twenty years, sixty-six were children of landowners and only four belonged to sharecropper families (a ratio of one-half the owners' children and one-tenth the tenants'). During the mid 1930s, two-thirds of the owners' children were enrolled in high school compared to one-third of the croppers' children.[79]

Among white sharecropper families, obtaining education was neither easy nor a high priority. Parents withdrew children from school when cotton had to be picked in the fall. E. J. Alexander had a bit of education but not much. M. B. Truitt left school after the fifth grade to help his family work, and Jake Brown quit at age sixteen. Homer Flynt could not sign his name or read well.[80]

But for the Flynt children and many other offspring of sharecroppers, education represented a way of escaping abject poverty. Because the educational system was so backward, salaries so low, and the status of teachers so wretched, Alabama had great difficulty supplying teachers for its rural schools. At the most, a youngster needed only to complete high school, matriculate for a few months at a teacher's college, and pass a state examination in order to begin a professional career. Lillie Mae Flynt Beason chose this route out of poverty. After spending a year at Jacksonville State Teachers College she found employment as a rural teacher in Calhoun County. Mary Wigley followed a similar path, as did six of her brothers and sisters. She remembered:

If our educational system in Alabama had been more modern then, I do not know where I would be today. I was not held back by the stiff requirements of a graded school system. . . .

Poor as we were, I would have been blocked in my tracks by the modern teacher requirements. The time, the place, the customs, the likes, dislikes, hopes and aspirations of my friends—even the backward educational system, as it turned out—were collectively a boon to me.[81]

The quality of life for sharecroppers depended heavily on the house in which they lived. In 1940 the average value of a landowner's rural dwelling was $681 and of a tenant's about half that amount. A statewide survey of tenant housing that year characterized it as "dilapidated, unsightly . . . , usually of slip-shod construction with unscreened windows and leaky roofs." Only 1.4 percent had running water, only .07 percent a flush toilet, 11.6 percent a refrigerator, and 19.9 percent a radio.[82] A survey two years earlier in a north Alabama community found that 60 percent of the owners' homes had screened windows compared to 20 percent of the croppers' homes. The average owner's house had six rooms, the average tenant's fewer than four. So ashamed were tenants of their houses that housewives refused to join Home Demonstration clubs because they held meetings in the homes of members.[83] One Home Demonstration agent described rural housing in Shelby County. Only three of six houses had toilets and only two had more than three rooms. Pigpens and cow pens were located fewer than thirty feet from the houses.[84] As one piece of rural folklore put it: a sharecropper "could study astronomy through the roof and geology through the floor."

Styles of houses varied. The family of Kathleen Knight lived in a four-room shotgun house, so called because it had rooms one after another so that a shotgun fired into the front door would penetrate every room in the house. Dogtrot houses were more common, with two or four rooms connected by an open breezeway or "dogtrot." The Flynt children remembered how cold it was in the wintertime when they snuggled close to the fire to put on their sleepwear, then darted across the open breezeway and under the quilts in their unheated bedroom. Tenant farmer "Bull" Elliott and his wife lived with six children in two rooms and a "lean-to" shed. So ashamed was Mrs. Elliott of her situation that she avoided neighbors and seldom left her home.[85]

Such attitudes were not uncommon. Many white tenants had little self-esteem. Although some tenants won the respect of their neighbors, they virtually never became community leaders. And whether or not it was true, they often believed such people "looked down" on them. Kathleen Knight explained her family's experience in the Mississippi Delta: "Well . . . the sharecroppers was always more closer neighbors, of course. The landlords were, I guess you would say friendly, but they was just in a higher class than we were and so we just didn't feel as comfortable with them as we did with our common sharecropping neighbors." It seemed to her that the children of owners received the best roles in school plays: "And of course we didn't think much about it. We was use to taking second place."[86]

White sharecroppers tried desperately to preserve pride and self-respect, but it was no easy task. When Kathleen Knight's father decided to carry a load of cotton to the gin, the landlord told him to get down from the wagon and return to picking in the fields, that he would drive the wagon. Her father responded that he would take it, but the owner started to climb aboard the wagon. The proud sharecropper, marshaling all the courage he had, picked up a glass jar that he used to carry water and warned the owner that he would knock him off the wagon. He vowed that he was going to take his own cotton into town:

Well he let him carry it on, but I think that was the last time that he . . . made an effort . . . to carry his own cotton. He just give in I reckon. . . . It would affect you . . . if you wanted to rent another plantation. Well the way you did had a whole lot to do with where you could get it or not [at] a good rent. And they did a lot of moving around down there. I reckon they was just trying to find something better all the time—better house and better way of being treated.[87]

How people maintained pride in such circumstances may seem strange, but maintain it they did. Perhaps the Mississippi Delta with its huge plantations was a more highly structured society than the Alabama hill country, where even the most prosperous people were only marginally better off than their neighbors. Mary Wigley remembered that on Sand Mountain being poorer than one's acquaintances did not produce an inferiority complex. The Wigley children dated youngsters from the finest families. Elsewhere in the state such easy familiarity across class lines was not so common. In one north Alabama community, only four daughters and two sons of owners married tenants (and none married the offspring of sharecroppers).[88]

But sharecroppers protected family pride in other ways. When Lillie Mae Flynt's mother gave birth, a neighbor lady provided meals. As the eldest daughter, Lillie Mae stayed home from school to help with the new baby. The kindly neighbor offered to tutor her in her schoolwork as well as provide meals. At one tutoring session, the neighbor asked Lillie Mae to empty the family's slop jar, used at night in place of the outdoor toilet. The girl innocently explained the episode to her parents and her father exploded: "he would not [have them] making a servant out of me. And so he didn't let me go there and take lessons or anything anymore. It hurt his pride."[89]

Landlord relations spanned the range from openly exploitive to warmly helpful. As Kathleen Knight explained, owners "were good and they were bad. . . . But most of them had rather that you just let them handle the business part of it, and do what they said to do." Most tenants echoed her sentiments. M. B. Truitt praised his landlord outside Opelika as "a fine man, the best boss I ever worked for." He helped the Truitts buy presents for their children and encouraged Truitt to switch from sharecropper to standing renter. Charles Bell, a banker who owned the last farm worked by Homer Flynt, tried to work out a payment arrangement so he could buy the land. Their relationship was one of mutual respect. Orrie Robinson, a sharecropper near Talladega Springs, remembered that after he "settled up" with Shep Cooper, his landlord, "we ain't got a thing." But then he added: "I don't know what we'd do if it wasn't for Shep, so I don't 'grudge him nothing. He's let us have sump'um to eat when thay wasn't a penny he could hope to git." Not all landlords were so paternalistic. Mary Wigley remembered bad landlords as well as good ones. But even a greedy one who tried to force her father to grow fewer vegetables and more cotton finally relented. He realized that Wigley was too conscientious a tenant to lose and allowed him to shift from sharecropping to standing rent as a way to provide the stubborn tenant greater independence and freedom. Mitchell Garrett, himself the son of a landowning farmer in Clay County, remembered landlords who took "all [a white tenant's] movable property except his poor clothing and his scant furniture" for debts, then "set [him] adrift to repeat the performances somewhere else."[90] Like tenants, landlords came in all types, arrogant exploiters and fellow sufferers in the tragedy of southern sharecropping.

Whatever kindly thoughts tenants might express about their landlords, owners did not necessarily reciprocate. Most owners believed white tenants to be shiftless, lazy, and ignorant. Although Mitchell Garrett did not exempt his own class from blame, he considered "the worst offenders against . . . thrift" to be "the poor white families, who despite the restraints and warnings of their landlords usually contrived to consume more than they produced during the year." Many of the sharecroppers were lazy and sickly and never earned enough to pay their bills. Herman C. Nixon, son of a landlord and country store owner in

Calhoun County, believed that white sharecroppers could not manage money. He recalled one cropper who managed to acquire a single silver dollar. The man held up the dollar before a small group of customers in the Nixon store and told them: "That eagle means to let her fly, and that's what I does."[91]

For their many problems tenant farmers had little recourse. They turned to politics to protect themselves, allying with a series of political movements that included the Greenback-Labor party, the Farmers' Alliance, the Populist party, and the Farmers Union. But none triumphed, and their opponents found ingenuous ways to disfranchise them. Many tenants were too uneducated or hopeless to even attempt to vote. Others were disfranchised effectively by the poll tax. To pay the cumulative tax, especially if they had skipped several years, took a major portion of a year's income. So they simply gave up the vote, which had done them little good anyway. In one north Alabama community during the mid-1930s, 85 of 195 heads of family were qualified to vote. All were white and 68 percent were landowners; only 2 percent were tenants who were unrelated to owners. The largest barrier to voting in the community was the annual $1.50 poll tax, which often accumulated over the years until it totaled $30 or more in a community where the average white sharecropper earned only $153 in total income during 1935.[92] Homer Flynt took great personal interest in politics, joined the Farmers Union, carefully perused several newspapers after he learned to read, and boasted of his loyalty to the Democratic party. But he never registered to vote because he could not afford to pay back poll taxes.[93] So the avenue of redress open to most Americans was effectively denied tenant farmers by a political process designed to protect government from people who owned no land and little property. The strategy worked well. For three-quarters of a century, from 1865 until 1940, the tide of white tenancy rolled across Alabama with gathering force.

FOUR

"A Sight to Gratify Any Philanthropist"

Alabama's Textile Workers

As rural people sought better jobs, their journey usually led into town. Within the confines of small Alabama communities they often lived in a separate world. Uptown people became merchants, businessmen, professionals, salesmen, even skilled craftsmen. Across town and usually a set of railroad tracks existed another community dominated by a textile mill. Within its huge rectangular buildings, amid whirling machinery, choking lint, and unbearable heat, mill workers labored. Their location on the periphery of southern towns was as much symbolic as physical. They attended their own churches and schools, traded at their own commissary, and courted their own kind. Woe be to the uptown boy who dated a mill girl with respectable intentions, for he faced hostile interrogation at home and derision from peers of his own class. Athletic contests between uptown and mill schools gave a new meaning to the word "competition." And many communities sought to avoid unnecessary conflict by having uptown schools play other uptown schools and mill-town teams schedule similar opponents.

Such divisions were not inherent in southern life nor did they appear overnight. They were based on real differences in education, religious preferences, and economic backgrounds. They were also rooted in misperceptions, negative stereotypes, self-deception, and half-truths.

The Rise of Textile Mills

Although the textile industry played no dominant role in antebellum Alabama, it did become firmly established. By 1860 Alabama had fourteen mills with 35,700 spindles. The industry represented an investment of $1.3 million and employed 1,300 operatives. The years immediately following the Civil War brought little growth as sharecropping spread across the land and former Confederates struggled to make their peace both with their country and with its new industrial order. In 1878 Alabama contained only four mills more than it had in 1860, although the number of looms had increased by a third and the growth of spindles had exceeded even that pace.[1] Most of this modest growth had occurred in the Chattahoochee River Valley, which separated south Georgia from Alabama. The industry spread from the antebellum manufacturing center of Columbus across the river and up the valley to Langdale and River View in Alabama.

The New South crusade of the 1880s rapidly accelerated this growth. Although a few mills were scattered across the central and northern portions of the state, most were clustered in the Chattahoochee Valley, the Birmingham region, and Huntsville. By 1929 the number of mills had nearly doubled again to eighty-three. Depression crippled the industry and drove many mills out of business, but the number of units actually increased to eighty-five in 1942. The industry ranked first both in value of products manufactured between 1914 and 1930 and in number of employees.[2]

Although the state's ranking actually declined from 10 percent of all cotton mills in 1880 to only 8 percent in 1910, the number of employees steadily increased: 3,636 in 1890, 9,049 in 1900, 12,723 in 1910, 16,020 in 1920, 23,443 in 1925, and 55,000 in 1947.[3] Textile mills accounted for one-fifth of all Alabama manufacturing jobs before 1923 and for one-third by 1931. Even though the industry was hard hit by the depression, it declined less than any other. Only 4,300 workers had lost their jobs by 1935, and twenty-six plants were still operating in February of that year.[4]

Historians have sometimes exaggerated the role of northern capital in this industry, but it did play a major role in Alabama. In Huntsville, which became the second-ranking cotton mill town in the South, a mixture of local and northeastern funding established the industry. The first large weaving mill to locate there was Dallas Mills, incorporated in 1891. Funding came from local sources, Nashville, and New York investors. In 1894, 52 percent of the company's stockholders resided in Huntsville, but they owned only 16.7 percent of the common stock and 1.7 percent of the preferred. The 22 percent of the New York stockholders controlled 43 percent of the total stock. One sympathetic historian of the industry claims that most mills were owned by out-of-state interests.[5]

Whatever the source of ownership, the industry as a whole prospered. Dallas Mills in Huntsville increased its profits from $91,000 in 1900 to $205,000 in 1910, $358,000 in 1915, and $762,000 in 1920; after that, depression settled over the industry and reduced earnings to $39,700 in 1925 and only $6,600 in 1929. Locally owned Avondale Mills, headquartered in Birmingham, experienced its best year in 1917. That year the director charged off $109,000 in depreciation, deducted a 100 percent dividend on preferred stock of $611,900, and still reported gross earnings of $631,900.[6]

If much of the capital came from the North, virtually all labor was native-born. Most mill workers were rural poor whites, many of them former tenant farmers who gave up the uneven struggle on the land for the regularity of life and salary in a mill town. Of fifteen textile workers whose life histories were used, virtually every one came from a rural background.

Nor are the reasons for leaving the land hard to find. If a farm laborer made $34.12 per month, the average in 1928, his annual income would amount to $409.44. The same man's wage in a cotton mill in Alabama, the state with the lowest average full-time earnings of $13.42 per week, would total $697.84. And when the exodus to mill towns began in 1879, the wage for a farmhand in Tuscaloosa County was only $10 per month.[7]

The causes of the exodus varied. Julia Rhodes was born in 1903 on a farm in Tallapoosa County. But her father grew weary of the back-breaking labor and the parsimonious return, so he packed up his belongings and moved his family to Alexander City, where he put his two oldest daughters to work in a cotton mill.[8]

Nancy Nolan and Mrs. L. A. House also entered mill work out of necessity. As described earlier, the Nolan family of five lived on a tenant farm in Dale County when Mr. Nolan died. Mrs. Nolan and her son tried tenant farming for five years before finally giving up and moving into Eufaula, where Mrs. Nolan got a job at Cowikee Mill. Mrs. House experienced a similar fate, also discussed earlier. Following her husband's death, she farmed as a tenant for three years, aided by her brother and oldest son. She put the younger girls to work hoeing. Finally, about 1920, she gave up and moved her family into Sylacauga where she went to work at Avondale Mills.[9]

Hope for a better life attracted Sybil Chandler and Andrew McClain. Sybil Chandler was born into an Alabama tenant family but dreamed of becoming a nurse. Her rural county had such limited educational facilities that she could complete only the seventh grade. Unwilling to

Pell City Mill, November 1910. "Doffers in Pell City Cotton Mill."
—Lewis Hine. (Courtesy of Lewis Hine Photographic Collection, Library of Congress)

sacrifice her future, she moved to Birmingham and began working at Avondale Mills in 1924. As the eldest of seven children, she assumed responsibility for the entire family after her father's death, and her dream of becoming a nurse ended. Andrew McClain left a farm in order to earn nine dollars a week in a cotton mill. It seemed a fortune compared to life on a farm: "I've plowed a mule from sunup to sundown for fifty cents a day or take a bushel of corn if I couldn't get no money."[10]

Whatever inspired them, women constituted an ever-expanding portion of textile workers. In 1890, of 3,636 cotton and woolen textile workers, 3,262 were native-born whites (only 71 were first- or second-generation immigrants and 303 were blacks). Of all white workers, 1,525 were males and 1,808 were females. In the decade between 1885 and 1895, a sample of Alabama mills reveals that the number of male operatives increased 31 percent, the number of women 75 percent, the number of girls below the age of eighteen by 148 percent, and the boys under eighteen by 81 percent. By 1900 the cotton mill labor force had established a slight male preponderance, 4,804 to 4,255, and by 1910 the margin was 6,357 males to 5,569 females. But the differential existed solely among unskilled laborers. Among semiskilled workers in knitting and cotton mills, women led 5,102 to 4,912.[11]

This "family wage" system also brought children into the labor market. Because many adult males earned too little to support their families, children had to go to work as soon as they were able. By 1900, 25 percent of Alabama's mill workers were under the age of sixteen. In 1910 the industry employed 997 children between the ages of ten and thirteen out of a total mill force of 12,723.[12] Among fifteen mill workers whose life histories were studied, six began mill work at age sixteen or younger. The youngest began at age nine. And of those who moved into mill towns later in life, they allowed or were forced to permit their children to work. Nancy Nolan had to put her sons, the oldest only fourteen, to work in order to survive.[13] Although many textile workers at first moved back and forth between tenant farms and textile communities, mill work often became generational as the years passed.

Far from deploring child labor, many entrepreneurs celebrated it. Arguing that farm children had to work from their earliest days in order to provide a marginal living, they saw no reason why they should not work in cotton mills. When Saffold Berney published a handbook in 1892 designed to publicize and expand the state's industry, he devoted an entire section to the ease with which Alabama mills acquired labor. "Thousands upon thousands of young children and young women stand anxiously idle for want of opportunity," he mused. Then in a passage seldom matched for exaggeration, he rhapsodized child labor:

> It is astonishing how rapidly these little folks learn to "keep up an end," . . . to piece a yarn, . . . to spin, to reel, to warp, to weave, . . . to perform the multifarious duties which go to make up the daily routine of a well ordered mill.
>
> It is a sight to gratify any philantropist [sic], to see eighty or a hundred comfortably dressed, well fed, cheerful young people of both sexes engaged in their daily duties, bright, cheerful, good tempered, orderly, obedient young folks, as they pass rapidly among their exquisite machines, sometimes singing in concert, and content— the very people who have had all their lives long nothing to do!
>
> Strikes are unknown among these really worthy people, who fill their appropriate squares in the great chess board of life, dutifully and gladsomely, as good citizens, as much worthy of respect and consideration as the merchant princes of the land.[14]

As we shall see, the children seemed to have lost their singing voices somewhere along the way.

To Berney, the motive of businessmen in starting cotton mills was obvious. Managers were "men of humanity, of even pity for those whom the fate of life has doomed to lower fortunes than themselves."

Many journalists agreed with Berney's assessment. They praised mill owners whose investments would usher in an age of prosperity and whose unsullied paternalism would uplift the poor and improve the community. Huntsville's *Mercury Centennial* surveyed the town's cotton mills, then pronounced that

> the mill villages of this industrial community have done as much if not more than any other similar communities in any part of the world in uplift work. . . . Any man or woman, boy or girl (of proper age) can find employment, at good wages in buildings that are kept in a perfectly sanitary condition, heated and electrically lighted and at a character of work that is interesting and not laborious; where there is plenty of room at the top for those who are energetic, industrious and ambitious.[15]

Civic clubs, ministers, and chambers of commerce begged, entreated, and cajoled businessmen to build mills in their towns. B. B. Comer explained why he started Avondale Mills in Birmingham following successful careers in milling, wholesale trade, and banking: it was "a civic enterprise at the request of the Chamber of Commerce to help give employment to those badly in need of it in the young and struggling city of Birmingham."[16] Nor was such a declaration merely self-serving rhetoric. When a Dadeville businessman representing his town's civic club sought prosperity and progress for his community, he urged Donald Comer to locate a cotton mill in Dadeville: "Remember the whole town of Dadeville will be behind the building of a Mill."[17]

Paternalism did play a role in the industry. B. B. Comer often expressed concern for his workers, and his son Donald became legendary for his personal interest in operatives and for his philanthropies.

B. B. Comer came to believe that mill villages and cities corrupted workers. Acting on this belief, he bought or established mills in Bevelle, Eufaula, Pell City, Sylacauga, and Sycamore. He urged operatives to stay on their farms if they could and use mill work as a supplemental source of income. An active Methodist layman, he endowed his home church and sent money to poor preachers. His son Donald enlarged this philanthropy, providing college scholarships for mill children, expanding recreational opportunities, and serving as chairman of the Alabama Relief Administration during the 1930s.[18]

Such policies contributed to making Avondale Mills the largest and most prosperous mill operation in Alabama. By 1947, Avondale owned ten mills with more than seven thousand employees and consumed 20 percent of all the cotton grown in the state.[19] But B. B. Comer's mills were by no means models for the industry. He was the largest employer of child labor and his mill villages received harsh criticism from Progressive-era reformers.

Other mills ranged from the most exploitive to extremes of paternalistic uplift. The West Point Manufacturing Company instituted a diverse program of social welfare for its white labor. It supplemented county school funds in order to maintain a nine-month school term and made available free kindergartens and lyceum courses. Community halls were open three times a week for a variety of meetings, programs, and films. The company built swimming pools and bathhouses and provided life insurance to each employee.[20] But such extensive welfare commitments were an exception to the rule.

Living

Many a white tenant farmer fancied his salvation in a cotton mill town, with its row upon row of sturdy houses, its orderly dirt streets, angular commissary, trim rectangular church, all presided over by a towering gray mill. They did not compare long hours spent before cacophonous machinery to the life of better-paid industrial workers elsewhere. They compared such conditions to the arduous monotony of cotton picking or tobacco chopping, to the years when they saw scarcely a dollar between harvests. Hard as it was, Mrs. L. A. House insisted, it was "easier than digging."[21]

And it was more sociable too. Women and children often expressed delight at the variety of activities, the improved housing, and the proximity of neighbors. Churches offered additional services such as Sunday school and youth activities. Mill recreation programs sponsored baseball teams and community dances. By no means did every village appear drab and exploitive. Especially as villages became better organized and as the textile market expanded between 1900 and 1920, managers had to compete hard for a labor force. In 1902 cotton mill owners from Alabama, Mississippi, and Georgia met in Montgomery, Alabama, to try to resolve their labor problems. They were recruiting each other's laborers, even offering free transportation from one mill to another. One chief attraction was the quality of mill life.

If newly arrived folk disliked the mill village, they could and did move on to another village or back to the country. In fact, the shifting back and forth between farm and mill, or from textile work to sawmilling, was a frequent occurrence. This mobility postponed a sharp break with rural life and provided mill workers a firm sense of alternative opportunities, especially during the early years of industrialization. They planted gardens, kept hens, and maintained rural traditions, religious institutions, folk music, home remedies, and kinship ties. And when they became angry enough, they simply moved.[22]

The mill village itself was fairly standard. Susie R. O'Brien described Ellawhite Mill Village, located one mile east of Uniontown and owned by California Cotton Mill. The road to Uniontown ran north and south through the village, flanked by a commissary and filling station, church and school, all owned by the company. The school doubled as a community center, serving for dances, plays, Boy Scouts, and other entertainments. A swimming pool afforded summertime fun. Two smaller streets paralleled the main road, intersected periodically by short cross streets. The mill plant stood off to one side of a street; foremen and other company officials lived immediately across from the mill. A hundred or so houses stretched close together along the streets nearest the mill. Farther away stood another row of houses that looked less prosperous. On the southern outskirts of town a third section of housing sheltered unskilled workers. Not so thickly settled as the other two, this area contained dilapidated houses with bare yards. Their inhabitants were able to obtain work only a few days each week.[23]

Like Ellawhite Mill Village, most mill towns were constructed just outside the city limits of a larger town. As Mrs. O'Brien's description indicates, housing varied considerably from village to village and even within the same community. Dallas Mills in Huntsville began its village in 1900, and fifteen years later it contained 120 houses and seventy-four tenement buildings. By the time the company sold its houses to residents in the 1940s, the village had reached a peak of 380 houses. Merrimack Mill in the same town constructed 280 houses. Both companies charged a uniform rent of one dollar per room per month, an excellent bargain in the early twentieth century and one reason the mills were able to retain an ample supply of workers (Dallas Mills employed 1,200 and Merrimack about 750 in 1900).[24]

But even the best-built villages contained houses close together with privies between or behind. And as the community grew older or as profits declined, companies were not meticulous in maintaining the village. Workers who had gleefully moved into new houses from rundown rural dogtrots turned sour as years passed. Mobility patterns increased as workers sought better or cheaper housing. By 1912 a muckraking reporter for *Survey* magazine toured Avondale Mill Village in Birmingham and left an unflattering account. The community contained 130 dreary company houses mostly one story high. Built on a low flat of cinders broken by small patches of grass or small trees, the cubelike houses were often enshrouded by the mill's smoke, which left a residue on dingy walls. Spaces between rows, unpaved and without sidewalks, served as alleys and streets. Privies and barrels lined the alleys. Children played amid family coal piles and water hydrants. Residents had to haul water to their houses. Large families had even less privacy, the reporter observed, than did big-city tenement dwellers. A row of houses called "Hell's Half Acre" at one end of the community housed prostitutes. Three girls under the age of fourteen from these houses came before Birmingham courts on prostitution charges during a single year.[25]

In a sense their houses were windows into the workers' lives. When they first moved to mill town, they usually considered the houses decent and the rents fair. W. W. Jewell moved his new bride to West Point Pepperell Mill Village in 1930 and paid seventy-five cents a week rent, which included water and electricity. As Jewell remembered the house: "It was, back in those days, it was a fairly nice house. It wasn't no fancy nothing, it wasn't bad, if you know what I mean." Seventeen years later Pauline Brewer moved into the adjacent mill village at Opelika Manufacturing and rented a house for a dollar a week. Mrs. L. A. House came in from the country a widow and thought her house wonderful.[26]

Hard times closed mills and threatened villages as well. Operatives were usually allowed to continue in mill housing until called back to work; but protracted layoffs threatened the community. Porches rotted down and in some villages desperate workers ripped up wood floors to burn for fuel during the Great Depression.[27]

Some mills began selling houses to workers during the depression, though most delayed such action until the 1940s and 1950s. Those lucky enough to buy during the 1930s received bargains. Tom Alsobrook bought his house from the mill for ten dollars a month over eight years at 5 percent interest. As late as the 1950s, Opelika Manufacturing sold its four-room houses for five hundred dollars a room.[28] One of the first acts of the new owners was to individualize their homes, whether by adding porches or rooms, painting, or some other modification. The sterile sameness of the mill village gave way to a variety of shapes and colors, as if workers were determined to proclaim their new independence and better prospects through their houses.

Mill-village schools and churches tended to separate textile workers further from those who lived in adjacent communities. Although some villages relied on "uptown" schools that served the entire community, mill schools were more common, especially for elementary grades. Some owners supplemented county school funds to provide higher teacher salaries for schools that they owned.

Mill owners also built a "union church" available to all denominations on alternating Sundays. The church was constructed on company property, often tapped mill resources for heat, water, and electricity, and received a supplement for the pastor's salary. As denominations became stronger, they also grew more independent, preferring their own building and weekly services. This development was usually arranged through the largesse of the mill owner, who would likely donate additional land and money for a new church. At Mignon, the Avondale Mill village in Sylacauga, the Comers paid fifty or a hundred dollars a quarter to each church and ran heating pipes from the mill to the churches. Presumably the owners could have interfered with disruptive pastors too eager to identify with operatives or to encourage unionism. In reality such meddling was seldom necessary in a world where preachers were usually as hostile as management to unions. But incipient clashes were always present, as in an incident at Mignon when the Comers constructed a recreation building and employed a social director to organize dances. The pastor at Mignon Baptist Church, while denying that he intended either to endorse or oppose the dances, did ask his congregation a loaded question: "Can a man kneel down and pray and rise up to dance?" The rhetorical question caused quite a stir in the village. The mill owner asked one Sunday school teacher why he opposed dancing. And the new recreation director began attending services to determine what the preacher was saying about dancing and the new recreation program.[29] Although the entire affair seems ludicrous in retrospect, it does demonstrate how carefully mill owners monitored the everyday events in their villages.

The commissary served a practical function in mill villages. Although the physical isolation of the community from nearby towns was not great, long work shifts and lack of transportation made it difficult for mill people to shop in downtown stores, which were usually a mile or more away. So at one level the commissary was a convenience, a general merchandise store selling a variety of items needed by mill families. At a second level the store was a place where workers could buy on credit or with scrip advanced against their wages. Whether workers thought the commissaries overcharged varied from one community to another. Mrs. L. A. House remembered the company scrip, which Avondale workers called "goo-ga-loo." They could trade it for groceries and sundries at the Mignon commissary, a long rectangular building behind the village and a long walk from downtown Sylacauga. She did not recall the prices as being out of line, although she did buy groceries downtown. She purchased fresh meat, which had to be bought more frequently, at the commissary for scrip.[30]

Working

During the first decades of the twentieth century most textile workers spent nearly as many hours in the mill as in the village. In 1902 Huntsville's Dallas Mills began its 12.5-hour day shift at 5:45 in the morning and let off at 6:15 in the evening.[31] Such a workday was common throughout the state. Mrs. Sam Anderson, Mrs. Lee Snipes, and Mrs. L. A. House entered mills in Eufaula and Sylacauga between 1900 and 1920 and all worked a 12-hour shift, 6:00 to 6:00. Some worked all day Saturday, others only half a day. By the mid-1920s, Carter Priest began working a 10- or 11-hour day plus a half day on Saturday. North Carolina and Georgia had limited workers to a 60-hour week and South Carolina to 55 hours by 1926. But Massachusetts had set a 48-hour limit by that date, and Alabama still had no legal limit at all.[32] By the mid-1930s, when Tom Alsobrook, Andrew McClain, and Pauline Brewer went to work, federal pressure had resulted in a maximum 8-hour day in state mills.[33]

In addition to northern capital and long hours, the third ingredient in the rapid growth of the industry in Alabama was low wages. In 1885 women spinners working in the state's mills averaged $2.76 a week. Ten years later their weekly wages had declined to $2.38. Assuming a fifty-week year, the female operatives earned approximately $120 a year. By 1920 the annual cotton mill wage in Alabama had increased to $453. By 1928 full-time female textile workers averaged $11.88 per week for a fifty-five-hour week (a projected income of $594 over a fifty-week year). Alabama's textile operatives still trailed others in the region in 1930. They earned 26¢ an hour, compared to Georgia workers at 27, South Carolina mill employees at 28, and North Carolina operatives at 30. (During the July 1934 strike, Alabama workers demanded a thirty-hour week, a $12 minimum weekly wage, and termination of the stretch-out system by which the number of operatives was reduced and their work intensified.) When compared to nonsouthern salaries, the wage scale was even lower.[34] In 1924 Alabama's cotton textile workers earned about half of what Massachusetts operatives made. One student of regional textile wages warned in 1926: "The idea that the South 'is burying its Anglo-Saxons' under the weight of an oppressive industrial system finds plausibility in a single comparison of wages in the North and South."[35]

Individual life histories reveal a similar reality although with little apparent resentment. The reason low salaries entailed so little bitterness is simple. Alabama mill workers did not compare what they made to equivalent scales in Massachusetts. They compared earnings in their new jobs to income from tenant farms; and that comparison left them initially satisfied with their lot, grateful to their employers, and unwilling to join unions. Nine of fifteen textile workers interviewed between 1937 and 1984 remembered their starting salaries, itself a startling fact. Either the contrast with previous wages or some other coincidence etched the figure in their memories. And the figures contain a remarkable congruity. Three textile operatives who began work around 1900 earned

25¢ for a night shift and between 50 and 75¢ for a day. Workers who entered the mills in 1922 and 1924 recalled salaries of $2.50 a week and a sliding scale of 10¢ an hour for sweepers, 15¢ for processing cotton bales, and $26.4¢ for mill technicians, with total salaries ranging from $6 to $16 a week. Two female operatives who began in the 1930s started at $9 a week, as did another female who was uncertain what year she earned that salary. Although some complained that they could not feed their families on what they made, others believed they managed as well then as they did much later on larger salaries. W. W. Jewell, who began mill work for $11.55 a week in 1926, recalled that his house rent was only 75¢ a week, that prime steak cost 15 to 20¢ a pound, and bacon 2.5¢ a pound. But the life histories speak mainly of hard times, and the desperate and violent textile strikes of 1929 and 1934 did not result from happy workers content with their circumstances.[36]

Work inside the mill seems monotonous and oppressive in retrospect. Heat and humidity sapped workers' strength and cotton dust penetrated their lungs. Many urged their children to find employment elsewhere even though such options were slim indeed. But in their own accounts of their work, the dominant mood is neither bitterness nor despair. For many of them, the work was challenging and they took pride in it.

One source of their satisfaction was the amazing variety of work that went on in a cotton mill. Obviously technology changed the industry dramatically between 1865 and 1930. In the nineteenth century, mills depended heavily on water power and often shut down during floods or droughts. Machinery breakdowns idled workers. But during all periods mills provided a multitude of jobs. When a farmer came in from the country seeking a job, he spoke with the mill foreman who determined whether or not to hire him. Then he might go to work in one of a number of jobs. The lowest category was "sweeper," accounting for the handful of blacks who found mill employment. They swept up the factory floor, a never-ending chore in the early days of the industry.

Usually the mill backed to a railroad line and cars delivering 500-pound cotton bales disgorged their loads at a dock. All the bales were unloaded by hand, sometimes by black laborers. Then skilled graders evaluated the cotton in the yard by daylight to determine quality and to make sure the fiber was not damp or rotten. The cotton was weighed and sized. Unloading required a crew of forty-five to fifty men at Sylacauga's Avondale Mill during the 1920s. They handled and stacked each bale by hand. Then three men, called "openers," unwrapped the bale, picking and cleaning debris from the outside. An opening machine started the cleaning process. The fiber was then loaded into hoppers and transported by air suction into the mill to "pickers," who cleaned and rolled it into a "lap." They took it from this machine and put four laps onto another piece of equipment, which repeated the exercise. Then they repeated this process a third time. At Avondale, a crew of ten men operated the "picker room."

Then the fiber went through three processes: carding, spinning, and winding. In the carding room, workers combed and disentangled the fibers. Then came the drawing room. Large strands of cotton, as big as a finger, were attached to frames, eight at a time, to make one end of the drawing. The strands ran through the back and front of the frames. Then the fiber went to a "slubber" of flyframe, which had a number of ends and spindles and reduced the size. An "intermediate" pulled the cord down smaller than the slubber. This process ultimately reduced the strand from the size of a finger to one no larger than a match stem, and wrapped it on a bobbin about eighteen inches long and twenty-one inches around when full. Then a "doffer" in the weaving room loaded the bobbin on a loom, which wove the thread into a piece of cloth. Most doffers were men whose hands were large enough to handle easily several bobbins, though the fast pace required to remove and empty the bobbin and replace it with a full one while handling a number of looms often taxed the dexterity and patience of men and women alike. Spinning was mainly for women and children. A "fixer" or "loom fixer" was a general-purpose mechanic, almost always male, who repaired machinery and usually drew one of the highest salaries in the mill.[37]

Mill hands especially recalled the noise and dust. The machinery was literally deafening, leaving many operatives with impaired hearing. And the dust was so bad in the carding room that one worker remembered when cylinders were being cleaned that he could not see men on the other side of the machine. Some women claimed they started dipping snuff to clear their mouths of lint when they spat.[38] Brown lung was endemic as operatives breathed material that ultimately damaged their lungs. Air conditioning was introduced in the 1950s, but working with the fiber required a certain level of noise and humidity that guaranteed an unpleasant work place for those unaccustomed to it.

Despite the hazards, workers adjusted and often expressed great pride in the number of bobbins they could manage or the skill of their weaving. Carter Priest worked as a doffer at Opelika Manufacturing, but in his earlier days he had been a Golden Glove boxer: "I was one of about the fastest doffers ever worked at that mill down there, because I . . . used to be a professional boxer. And in that type of work you got to move your hands fast. I was—well, I have large hands. I can hold more bobbins than could hardly anyone else."[39]

Although some workers held their bosses accountable for their grievances, just as many respected paternalistic owners. Paternalism involved more than merely feigned concern for the welfare of workers. Operatives were not fools. They knew the difference between an owner or manager who genuinely cared about them and one whose main interest was keeping them out of unions.

Donald Comer affords the best contrast between the two types. Son of a former Alabama governor and founder of Avondale Mills, Donald succeeded his father as president of Alabama's largest textile empire. Always interested in civic improvement and the welfare of his employees, Donald Comer served ably as chairman of the state's relief effort during the 1930s. But the best testimony to his efforts came from workers in his mills. Four operatives at Cowikee Mill in Eufaula spanned the ownership of Comer's predecessor (Eufaula Cotton Mill) and then the era after the Comers purchased the mill in the early 1900s. Mrs. Lee Snipes began working in the mill as a small child, working a twelve-hour shift for subsistence wages. The only toilet had been a filthy outdoor privy. When Comer purchased the mill, conditions changed. He installed decent toilets, "five commodes, all cleaned every day." Workers in each department wore uniforms of different colors. Tom Alsobrook remembered the change as well. Comer had installed new machinery and modernized the plant. He sold houses to employees and lent children of mill workers money for college. Life was not easy for Alsobrook, but he liked Comer and working in the mill. Nancy Nolan agreed, especially praising Comer for allowing workers to buy their homes. Mrs. Champion echoed the sentiments of the other three. Despite her own illiteracy and her husband's alcoholism, she had made a living, bought her house, and loved Donald Comer and the mill. Mrs. Lee Snipes contrasted the two worlds that resulted from greed and paternalism: "It used to be we were just factory folk or 'lint heads.' Now we are 'mill operatives' and we hold our heads high. All work is honorable you know, and we are proud of ours." Then she added, "my work is such happiness."[40]

Mrs. L. A. House worked for Donald Comer in a different mill, Avondale at Sylacauga. But her experience was similar to that of the others. She recalled a particularly grueling day, running old cotton on a frame. Every time she tied a knot, the strand broke. She noticed that a man "dressed very ordinary, just cool and common" was talking to a friend of hers at a frame. When the stranger asked what was wrong with the yarn, she blurted out: "It's just rotten, only kind the Comers will buy." When the stranger laughed heartily and walked on, her friend, who had listened to the exchange in horror, informed her that the curious inquirer was Donald Comer. Mrs. House spent the rest of the day expecting to be called to the foreman's office and fired.[41]

The fear Mrs. House experienced that afternoon reflected the extent of control owners exercised over the lives of employees. Some like Comer laughed and went on their way. Others were vindictive and malicious, or at least were perceived that way by workers. Carter Priest was a mechanical whiz who invented a grinder, electric toothbrush, screwdriver, and landing gear valve, as well as a set of mechanical legs. Although his job at Opelika Manufacturing was as a doffer, he tinkered with equipment and informally became a skilled "fixer." He never earned the title or wage because "the boss man—if you didn't brownnose him—you never could get no where with him. And another thing I beat up one or two of the pets [the boss's favorite employees]." Asked how his bosses had treated him through the years, W. W. Jewell replied:

Well, it was just according to how the bossman felt when he come in. And if he felt good, well, everything went fine, but if he felt bad, I always said if his wife didn't give him none before he come to the mill, well he was hell to put up with that day. And other than that, I got along with pretty near every boss I ever had, except my brother-in-law.[42]

The difference between being "just factory folk or 'lint heads' " and being "mill operatives" seemed a sharp distinction in the experience of Mrs. Lee Snipes. But for many workers the larger community never let them forget they were "lint heads," no matter how many new commodes their mill had or what color uniforms they wore. The clash between "town people" and "mill people" found expression in a dozen ways: manners, education, dress, diet, child-rearing practices, religious expression, politics, and especially the cotton lint that seemed to cling tenaciously to clothes and hair.[43] Mrs. L. A. House believed that uptown people considered themselves superior to mill folk. Their children did not get along at ball games. On one occasion, while attending a parade with her grandson, she overheard boys mocking them as "cotton heads." Angered as much for her grandson's embarrassment as for the boys' bad manners, she turned to the thoughtless children and scolded sternly: "If it wasn't for the 'cotton heads' you wouldn't have nothing to eat in Sylacauga." Other children of operatives remembered no such incidents and cultivated close friends from among the offspring of mill bosses and uptown people.[44]

Middle class folk often recorded opinions more politely than the boys who taunted Mrs. House's grandson. A liberal-minded young journalist who grew up near the textile communities in Anniston, Talladega, and Sylacauga remembered the paternalism of owners and the uneasy fraternization of mill, town, and rural children. He did not describe the lives of mill workers entirely in somber terms, but neither did he nor his rural friends wish such a life for themselves:

> On the contrary, there was something abhorrent about them. We knew the shabby streets, or rather the rutty clay roads, where the factory people lived—two or three families of them in a house that looked forlorn and miserable with its rough unpainted boards and bare yard marked with lines the water had made after splashing from the roof. On Saturday afternoons we would see the mill people, off for a few hours from their work. Walking usually in single file, as if they were still following a narrow path over hills in the country, they could be seen going into town. Their shoulders and arms drooped with obvious weariness; soiled lint from the mills hung on their clothing and in their hair. . . . Now and then we would encounter them in some of the grocery stores. Mainly they seemed to buy snuff and stick candy, but the clerks never paid much attention to them one way or the other. They were just the cotton mill people. The clerks often asked them to wait while other customers were being attended to, and the cotton mill people never seemed to mind.[45]

Although Alabama textile workers often thought of themselves as different, they seldom developed a rigid sense of class consciousness. Numerous factors account for that. In a society with multiple boundaries, those associated with caste or race counted for more than class. At least all whites believed themselves superior to blacks, no matter how economic reality seemed to dispute their assumption. Of all poor white occupations, the textile industry was the one that most completely excluded blacks. In 1920 Alabama textile mills employed only 3,272 Negroes among more than 20,000 workers.[46] Whether because of the industry's growth in upland counties where whites vastly outnumbered blacks or because fierce racial prejudice would have denied owners an adequate white work force had they hired blacks, cotton mills became bastions for white plain folk. Textile workers responded favorably to the political and racial demagoguery of Tom Heflin and to the Democratic demagogues who harangued them with tales of black debauchery and imminent peril unless Negroes were kept in their place.[47] Mill hands both participated in and precipitated lynchings.

Other factors also help explain the uneasy truce between southern classes. Southern religion emphasized the common humanity of all white people and also held them aloof from too much association with this world's problems.

Merrimack Mill, Huntsville, November 1913. "Pinkie Durham, eight-year-old sweeper, and his sister Eliza. She began at eleven; not twelve according to school record. She recently had her leg broken in the mill. Boy run a doffing box into her. She has been working for one year in Merrimack Mfg. Co."—Lewis Hine. (Courtesy of Lewis Hine Photographic Collection, Library of Congress)

Organizing

As the years passed and relations were strained by economic depression and vigorous union drives, some workers became angry and discontented. Swirling in the center of this storm were low wages, poor working conditions, and the larger issue of generational hopelessness. As their children grew up and entered the mills, it became obvious to some mill workers that a cycle of illiteracy, poverty, and lack of opportunity had shackled them as completely to their looms as if the thread they wove encircled and bound them. Although many parents did not object to their children's working, for reasons that will be explored later, child labor contributed to the sense of estrangement common among mill workers.

A number of studies of child labor shook the foundations of Alabama's textile industry between 1900 and 1915. In 1901 English labor activist Irene M. Ashby-Macfayden investigated child labor on behalf of the American Federation of Labor. She visited more than half the state's forty-three cotton mills and found conditions appalling. Of 6,725 operatives in twenty-five mills, she estimated that 400 were children younger than twelve. Photographer–social reformer Lewis Hine photographed many of these children at their work, documenting in vivid black-and-white photographs what Ashby-Macfayden described.[48] Mrs. John Van Vorst obtained access to mills, thanks to a letter of introduction from a Birmingham textile owner. She was appalled to talk with one female stockholder who tried to convince her that child labor was "a necessary evil" in Alabama: "When you know more of these people, you'll see that they're just like animals. In the mill they have some chance of getting civilized. If we made laws restricting labor we should frighten away capitalists and wreck our very surest chances of progress and prosperity."[49]

Even allowing for reformist zeal and literary hyperbole, what Mrs. Van Vorst discovered in Alabama mills was unsettling. In Anniston she interviewed a family living in squalor without running water or electricity. The twelve-year-old daughter and ten-year-old son worked in the mill, the boy because his parents lied about his age. One doffer in the carding room of an Anniston mill said he was "goin' on twelve," and had worked at the mill for four years. He had never attended school and worked a daily twelve-hour shift for $2.40 per week. A seven-year-old worked as a sweeper for 20¢ a day. Although the manager argued that mountain people were "dwarfs," which explained the diminutive size of so many operatives, she asked a boy about a tiny companion and he explained: "He's 'most six. He's been here two years. He come in when he was 'most four. His little brother 'most four 's working here now."[50]

Everywhere she went the story was the same. Of 65 children aged seven to eleven originally enrolled in a third grade mill school class in Gadsden, 10 had quit school to work in the mill. At Alabama City she estimated that 75 percent of the 275 employees in the spinning room of a mill were below age twelve. Of 17 children she interviewed at a mill in Pell City, 2 were twelve and the others ranged from seven to eleven. Expecting an answer such as football or baseball, she asked one tiny mill worker what he liked best. He replied: "weaving." Of 350 school-aged children in the Pell City mill, only 80 or 90 attended school. Teachers despaired of the chronic absenteeism and the mobility of families.[51]

The *Survey* magazine dispatched reporters to Birmingham's Avondale Mills in 1911. The resulting article described a mill school in which grades one through three met in one room. The ages of students in the elementary class ranged from six to nineteen.[52]

Attempts to limit child labor by restricting the age at which children could begin work to twelve and the hours to sixty per week encountered fierce opposition. Although religious leaders and organized labor endorsed

Pell City, Alabama, Cotton Mill, November 1910. "Some of the spinners in Pell City Mill, grouped for me by the overseer. Mr. E. A. Thompson, Superintendent of the Mill, is also Mayor of Pell City."—Lewis Hine. (Courtesy of Lewis Hine Photographic Collection, Library of Congress)

the reforms, many mill owners bitterly protested. Thanks to the rigorous campaign led by Montgomery Episcopal priest Edgar Gardner Murphy, Alabama passed a law in 1907 that limited ages and hours and required compulsory schooling. However, an attempt to amend the law in 1911 to raise the age to fourteen was defeated, thanks mainly to spirited opposition from the cotton mill lobby. As late as 1923 even paternalistic Donald Comer lobbied against a federal child labor bill before Congress, arguing that it was unnecessary.[53]

Alabama's child labor inspector filed the first legal cases in 1912 against Lowe Manufacturing Company of Huntsville and Opelika Cotton Mill. Warrants charged the companies with failing to obtain affidavits from parents that stated the age of minors.[54]

As a result of child labor, illiteracy was widespread among mill workers. Among eleven subjects of oral histories, only one graduated from high school. Another began high school but was unable to finish. Three completed only grammar school. Two had fewer than six years of schooling, and two never attended at all. Of Mrs. Sam Anderson's four children, her daughter completed high school, but none of her sons did. One of Nancy Nolan's sons attended school long enough to learn to read and write; he taught what he could to the other children who had to work in the mill.[55]

Merrimack Mill in Huntsville joined Alabama's adult literacy drive in 1921. The mill sponsored a night school from 7:00 until 9:00 P.M. three nights a week. The state paid half the expenses and the mill the other half. Only illiterates aged sixteen or older could attend. Eleven teachers instructed more than one hundred students. But twice that many poor whites in the mill village were eligible.[56]

Labor organizers shrewdly used illiteracy, child labor, and the family wage system to try to unite Alabama textile workers. For the most part their efforts failed. The Knights of Labor launched a major drive to organize Alabama workers in the late 1880s. Most members attracted by the union were artisans, miners, and iron workers, but some were textile operatives. One mill in Cottondale, organized by the Knights in 1887, tolerated the union so long as members made no demands. But in 1888 a drunk foreman rode a horse into their meeting hall and cursed the members. The local took the man to court. During the court proceedings the Cottondale firm reduced wages. When the Knights protested, the company locked them out of their jobs until they agreed to sign contracts pledging to quit the union. The Knights' state assembly called for a boycott of goods manufactured at Cottondale, but it had no effect and the local was destroyed.[57] One historian of Alabama labor was able to find only a single minor textile strike before 1900.[58] It involved only ten employees and lasted one day. It was not an auspicious beginning for textile unionism.

The various organizing efforts in the early twentieth century fared little better. Complex factors explain the inability of national unions to organize state workers. Unlike coal miners who were concentrated in a handful of counties and engaged in similar work, textile workers were scattered in mills throughout the state and engaged in a variety of jobs.

The largest strike in American history, the 1934 textile strike, began in Alabama. Before it ended, 23,000 of the state's 35,000 mill workers walked off their jobs. They closed down twenty-eight of Alabama's forty mills. But the strike failed both in the state and throughout the nation. The failure signaled the end of effective organizing of the industry until the 1940s.[59]

Individual workers seldom expressed neutrality about textile unions. Nine of fifteen workers whose biographies were available expressed opinions about the union; five strongly supported it and four just as strongly opposed. For most of those who joined, the union represented better wages and working conditions plus a chance to be represented effectively with management. But the struggle to unionize was a long one. Virtually all the operatives had been nonunion until after the Second World War and in some cases until the 1970s. Two of the five knew workers who had been fired for union activities.[60] Carter Priest, who had wanted to be a mechanic but never could get support from the foreman, expressed the greatest bitterness. He had tried to organize several times:

> They should have been organized, every mill should be organized now I think. I know they should be because . . . mill workers . . . have a hard time. They was overloaded, they been overloaded for years. . . .
>
> Well, I got fired . . . two or three times on account of it . . . they's some of them . . . usually pimp on you, tell everything that happened. And lot of times they'd give you a hard time . . . , tried to get you beat up and everything else. But I am glad . . . the old mill is organized now; but if it hadn't been for colored people, I don't believe it'd be organized yet.
>
> But colored people stick together better than white people. I don't give a durn what you say about them, I know they'll stick. And I admire them for it. I'm glad they've got guts enough to organize, which a lot of white people has learned.[61]

Coal miners learned about racial solidarity early. But the nearly all-white textile industry paradoxically had to wait for black workers to unionize.

Many anti-union workers confirmed the effectiveness of company strategies to prevent organizing. They boasted that though their mills were unorganized, they earned slightly more than union members and without union dues or the threat of lost time in strikes. They reaped the benefits of unionism with none of its liabilities or responsibilities. Sometimes the reason given for opposing unions was loyalty to bosses in response to their paternalism.[62] Mrs. Lee Snipes, who had experienced both bad bosses and good, explained why she did not join the union: "We are proud to work for Mr. Donald Comer and there has never been a strike or any trouble in any of the mills. We would fight for him, not against him."[63] For Mrs. L. A. House the issue was simple. Donald Comer had given her an opportunity for a decent life far superior to what she had experienced as a young widow on a tenant farm. He gave her a job and a steady wage. She gave him loyalty and devotion in return.

Such was the mixture of anger and protest, loyalty and paternalism, benevolence and support, despair and resignation. Whatever else they believed about their work, few of them were willing to go back to the tenant farms from whence they came. But even fewer wanted their children to live as they had lived, covered with lint, soaking wet, deafened by noise, and steadily inhaling the material that would eventuate in brown lung.

"Dark as a Dungeon, Damp as a Dew"

Alabama's Coal Miners

The early settlers of north Alabama were easily misled by the solitary beauty of an Appalachian autumn. When trees exploded with color and cribs filled with corn, it was no wonder that so many travelers originally bound for richer land succumbed to the gentle seduction of the mountains. But if the casual wanderer spent a winter there, or tried to eke out a living on a farm or to forage for game up a hollow, the mountains seemed forbidding enough. Deep valleys and mountain ridges made transportation difficult. Infertile land except in river bottoms afforded hardy folk a poor living on small patches that produced corn, sweet potatoes, and wheat. Riches in these regions lay beneath the soil, not atop it.

The Warrior, Cahaba, and Coosa coalfields stretched across most of the northern third of the state. Early settlers began to mine coal almost as soon as Alabama became a state. Chunks of coal were gathered by hand from outcrops that broke the surface of hillsides or riverbanks. Or miners followed seams into drift mines as far as they could go, hauling the coal to the surface on carts pulled by horses or mules. Then they floated the coal by flatboat down one of Alabama's numerous rivers to Mobile for use there or for transport.

Antebellum coal production never reached significant levels. In 1860 only fifty-four miners made a living at the trade, and they earned an average annual wage of $344, making them the state's highest-paid industrial workers. Production amounted to 10,200 tons in 1860.

America's industrial revolution changed all that. Railroads penetrated the state's coalfields as they connected the new industrial city of Birmingham to Nashville, Chattanooga, and Montgomery. The demand for iron and steel, plus new technology for using coke as a fuel in iron

Birmingham-area coal mine, circa 1900. (Courtesy of Birmingham Public Library)

making, stimulated demand. Between 1875 and 1885 Alabama's production of coal soared from 67,200 to 2,492,000 tons. By 1900 production had reached nearly 8,400,000 tons and ten years later had doubled again. In 1910 Alabama ranked sixth among twenty-seven coal-producing states and second only to West Virginia among southern and border states. By 1919 the value of coal mined in Alabama was $37,300,000, an average of $2.08 per ton.[1]

Production increases required extensive changes in the labor force. Prewar miners often were well-paid entrepreneurs and were too few to constitute a distinct occupational group. But the New South experience brought a sharp departure from earlier patterns.

By 1919 more than two hundred coal mines operated in the state. Most were drift mines that meandered underground, following the coal seams. Although Jefferson and Walker counties contained most of the mines, others were scattered across eleven northern counties. In 1930, 16,000 of the state's 24,000 coal miners worked in Jefferson or Walker County.[2]

Growth in the labor force matched production figures. The number of coal miners increased from 11,751 in 1900 to 26,200 in 1920 before falling to 25,208 in 1929. Largely a young man's occupation, 56.5 percent of Alabama's miners in 1921 were between the ages of twenty and forty-five.[3]

Living

Many white miners were essentially bivocational, managing small dirt farms when the coal market was slack, and digging coal for cash income. Others relocated their families into bleak coal camps for periods but returned to farming when they tired of mining.[4] A Dr. Sharpe, one of the first physicians in war-ravaged Cherokee County, persuaded so many people from the area to move to the booming coal camp at Blossburg that the town named a street "Cherokee Row" in the 1890s.[5]

Adjustment to long shifts and cramped quarters did not come easily for rural people. Drunkenness and violence were common. Young un-married miners lived as hard as they worked. Saturday night afforded ample customers for Birmingham's saloons and brothels as miners crowded into town from outlying coal camps. In sections of the city bearing such colorful names as Scratch Ankle, Beer Mash, and Buz-zard's Roost, whiskey ran freely, violence was common, and decent women were as rare as virtuous men.

Coal miners moved as often as tenant farmers. In the years just before United States Steel bought Tennessee Coal, Iron, and Railroad Com-pany, TCI had to recruit 2,000 new men each year to maintain its 11,000-man labor force of miners and iron makers. In 1929 DeBardeleben Coal Corporation experienced an unusually low rate of labor turnover, only 20 percent, and New Castle Coal Company did even better, losing only 25 men. But Alabama Fuel and Iron Company, Montevallo Coal Com-pany, Woodward Iron Company, and TCI were more typical. Their rates varied from 40 percent to 180 percent. During 1921, 80 percent of the miners in seventeen mines quit their jobs. But even that figure was lower than the industry-wide total of 99.8 percent.[6]

Individual life histories confirm the transient nature of the occupation. Woodie Roberts went to work in 1934 in a wagon mine operated by his father and four brothers. After a year he moved to Felix Towney Coal Mine, where he worked for three years. From 1938 until 1942 he worked mainly at Dave Seger's Mine, but he mined coal elsewhere during in-tervals when that mine was closed. In 1940–41 he spent seven months in a Civilian Conservation Corps camp. In 1943 he left military service because of a disability and began working in his brother's mine. Alfred J. Renshaw experienced an even more extreme example of transience. He began mining coal in 1908 and continued for sixty-two years. He

TCI coal-mining camp near Birmingham. (Courtesy of Samford University Archives)

moved at least thirty-four times to work at different Alabama mines, not including a year's job as a fireman with the Southern Railroad, a year mining in Illinois, and two years in Harlan County, Kentucky.[7]

Once located in a coal town, rural whites discovered a world quite different from their previous experiences. The company owned everything: the land, houses, schools, churches, and commissary. After a particularly nasty strike in 1908, one of the largest coal companies put a clause into house leases that allowed the company to determine what persons would be permitted on company property. Miners, their families, or even visitors could be expelled upon the decision of the company. A deputy sheriff maintained law and order, but the company typically paid his salary. Among his responsibilities was to keep out "undesirable persons" of "sinister purpose." Coal operators explained to one reporter in 1911 that a labor organizer would fit this description.[8]

Houses ranged from hastily constructed one-room shacks to comfortable four-room houses. Charlie Cross remembered houses in the 1890s at TCI's Muscoda Camp just south of Birmingham:

> There were no homes. Not anything you could call a home. The place here was half a wilderness, a mining camp of the worst order. The company had put up about forty-two planked shotgun houses.

They charged you a dollar-and-a-half a room a month whether you lived in them or not. They simply took it off your pay. The houses were neither painted nor ceiled, just planks knocked together.[9]

Housing elsewhere was little better. At Coalburg in 1899 company houses rented for $2.10 per room or four rooms for $8.40 per month. One miner angrily described them as "not fit for barns, and the company will graciously allow its workers to repair the houses themselves, provided however, that they buy the lumber from the company at the rate of fourteen dollars per thousand feet." And as Charlie Cross remembered, miners had to pay rent in many camps whether or not they lived in company houses. Elmer Burton, who worked at Gamble Mines, confirmed this practice. His family lived on a farm in order to grow their own food, but his father paid $4 a month house rent to prevent being fired during slack times.[10]

Not every miner was so negative. Luther V. Smith lived for thirty years in a four-room company house at Gamble Mines in Walker County. The company kept it in good shape, and the house, lights, and water cost him only $8.25 per month.[11]

Apparently Alabama contained many coal communities such as the one Charlie Cross described. A thorough study published in the January 1912 issue of *Survey* magazine reported life in the mining camps of the Birmingham district. A transient mining population of six hundred lived at Sandusky, just outside the city; 80 percent of them were white. Because the community contained no public water supply, residents secured water from private wells. Filthy and neglected privies polluted the wells, causing a 1907 typhoid epidemic that took fifteen lives. Because so few owned homes, miners demonstrated no sense of community pride. The mining community of Palos contained four hundred people, a third of them white. Like most camps, the whites and blacks lived in different sections, with blacks nearer the summits of steep hills overlooking the mines. Whites preferred the lower slopes because, without a public water supply, inhabitants had to carry water up the hillsides. Adjacent farmers sold water for twenty-five cents a barrel; miners could obtain fifty gallons for what Birmingham citizens paid for one thousand gallons. Privies were filthy and had not been cleaned all summer. When the company cleaned them it charged twenty-five cents per month, a sum that also included the school tax during months when the school operated.[12]

A national survey taken ten years later was equally unflattering. Of 713 company-controlled coal-mining communities examined, only 1 in Alabama ranked among the highest 75; 3 scored in the lowest group. In 1922–23, 65.9 percent of all Alabama miners lived in company-owned dwellings. All of the 3,617 coal-camp houses were made of wood and only 21 contained inside plaster. Only 3.7 percent provided running water and none contained bathtubs or showers; none had flush toilets and less than half contained electricity or gas. The prevailing rent for Alabama's mining houses was between six and seven dollars per month.[13]

Those who came to live and work in coal towns did so in expectation of a better life, but their hopes were no more fulfilled in diet than in residence. Although the cash income of north Alabama farmers was low, they at least grew nourishing vegetables and fruits in season. In the coal camp, food constituted the largest expense and nutrition was inadequate. A government survey in the early 1920s estimated that a mining family of four spent slightly more than $472 a year on food, out of median annual earnings of $930 for full-time miners. Miners paid by the day earned median salaries of only $800 a year. But layoffs and other work stoppages meant that few miners actually earned such salaries. Food that met standard nutritional requirements would have cost such a family $724 a year, or nearly its entire income. When added to the second-largest expense, clothing, at an average cost of $167 annually, obviously miners earned too little to meet basic needs.[14] Of course, farm people retained a traditional rural preference for cheap foods that did not cost as much, such as molasses, meal, and pork. Lack of nutritious foods was as much a matter of choice as inadequate income. But poor diet worsened health problems caused by inadequate housing, sanitation, and water supplies.

Complicating life even more in coal towns was the company commissary. Although coal operators often depicted the store as a convenience for miners who might live miles from the closest town, the commissary actually was a major source of company profit, sometimes exceeding the profitability of coal itself. Mining lore celebrated the commissary in song lyrics: "You load sixteen tons and what do you get? Another day older and deeper in debt. Saint Peter don't you call me 'cause I can't go. I owe my soul to the company store." Ila Hendrix, widow of a coal miner at Alabama By-Product, remembered that the commissary operator didn't like women to order from a Sears and Roebuck catalog instead of buying at the commissary. John Gates, a miner in the Cahaba field near Helena, recalled that prices were so high that miners preferred to walk to Helena to trade on payday. The commissary did sell snuff at the regular price, so when forced to exchange company scrip for goods, he would trade it for snuff at the Paramount Commissary, then walk into Helena where he would swap cases of snuff for groceries. Sam Brakefield remembered a time at Gamble Mines when miners who did not buy at the company commissary were fired. Spies reported them when they bought elsewhere, or so he believed. Luther Smith confirmed the practice Brakefield described. Also employed at Gamble Mines, Smith recalled that "if you didn't trade at the store sooner or later you'd be contacted and [they would] want to know why you wasn't trading at the store and if you didn't trade at the store, why you didn't tote the company's money . . . , not for long." He believed that commissary prices were higher than "outside" but that quality was also better. A Czechoslovakian miner's wife at Brookside remembered that the company preferred that miners take their pay in scrip and spend it in the commissary.[15]

The United States Coal Commission confirmed miners' impressions about high commissary prices. Its survey in the early 1920s revealed that purchasing a year's supply of groceries from a company store cost a mining family 7 percent more than they would have paid for the same products at an independent store in the district. However, in many cases, this modest overcharge was less than the extra cost and trouble to a miner of traveling outside the coal camp to shop. The commission discovered that Alabama mining companies made the most vigorous effort to retain the miner's trade of any region it surveyed. Larger companies kept a record of the percentage of the miners' payroll that was spent at the commissary. Such records allowed the business to determine whether store sales kept pace with earning power. Commissaries also conducted local advertising and promotions. One camp store sponsored a pig race at 5:30 on sales day: "Catch the long, slim razorback greased pig and the pig is yours." Another commissary offered free barbeque on Saturday with each purchase of five dollars or more on Friday.[16]

One reason miners traded at commissaries was that many coal companies paid salaries in scrip. When a miner first wandered down from the hills into a coal camp looking for work, he usually had to labor three weeks before receiving his first paycheck. During that time expenses of "packing his bucket" for a hurried meal in the mine or for feeding his family and establishing them in a company house required an advance on his salary. The company was willing to advance him money in the form of company scrip or "clacker." Coins of various denominations, usually marked with the company symbol or imprint, could be used at the commissary either for full face value or for a small discount. But if independent stores accepted them at all, they discounted the scrip a substantial part of its total value. After miners received their first checks, they were paid either monthly or twice a month. Any illness or unexpected expense forced them to draw scrip against their salaries.

Sam Brakefield at Gamble Mines was paid once a month. In order to survive he drew clacker in the intervals between paydays. For such largesse the company charged a premium. It would advance only eighty cents of clacker for every dollar of wage, and the scrip was redeemable only at the commissary.[17]

The routine of coal-camp life varied substantially from the freer, if poorer, rural existence left behind. A "wildcat" whistle summoned miners from their slumber at five o'clock each morning. They called it a wildcat whistle because it sounded as shrill as a wildcat's squalling. Women scrambled to prepare breakfast for husbands and older boys, to pack their lard buckets with lunches, and to rouse reluctant younger children for school. Wisps of smoke drifted from chimneys as miners stoked coal-burning stoves to provide a bit of warmth against crisp north Alabama mornings. Despite their low pay and the abundance of coal, they had to buy their own coal from the company. Fringe benefits were not part of the world of an Alabama coal camp. The older males then hurried off for a seven o'clock shift.[18] When they emerged eight to twelve hours later, filthy on the outside from crawling through tiny passageways, with lungs to match from breathing dry coal dust, they headed for company showers.

Weekends interrupted the monotony of a workweek. Following their Saturday shifts, bachelor miners might head for Birmingham and a Saturday night of hell raising. More settled men stayed in the camps, where dances and baseball games were favorite pastimes. Every camp had its musicians, skilled with fiddle, banjo, and guitar, who would play for dances to earn a bit of cash and a lot of fame. Women often engaged in quilting and other practical crafts to divert their minds from the danger of the mines. On Sundays religious miners made their way to company-built churches, at first mainly Methodist and Baptist, but increasingly Nazarene, Church of God, or other pentecostal sects. Less religious miners took advantage of a morning to sleep.[19]

Payday was a special time. Many companies paid on the fifteenth and thirtieth of the month. One payday, described in detail during the 1930s, began as the afternoon shift emerged from the mines. Miners gathered at pay windows in two lines, one for blacks and another for whites. Most miners were in good spirits and there was little pushing or shoving. Miners who had already been paid assembled in small groups, swapping stories and jokes, eating crackers or drinking sodas. Bill collectors circulated through the crowds, looking for debtors who sought obscurity behind larger miners. Three or four black women sold barbeque while a company deputy with a gun on each hip eyed the proceedings with grim attention. A preacher and singer performed on the commissary porch, grateful for a captive audience that they might never see on a Sunday morning. Out in the crowd more secular matters vied for a miner's eye and ear. A white miner's wife observed Negro girls "switch-

"Dago Hill," up from Number Nine Slope, Wenonah, TCI village (so called because Italian miners lived in this area of the camp). (Courtesy of Samford University Archives)

ing this way and that" to attract the attention of Negro boys standing in line.[20]

Although such comments reflected the inevitable racial consciousness of a southern coal camp, relations were as harmonious as the times allowed. Dozens of interviews reveal two predominant attitudes among white miners. Blacks lived in a separate world both spatially and in spirit. Whites usually referred to the black section as "nigger hill," "Baptist Bottom," or some equally descriptive phrase. If large numbers of foreigners resided in the camp, they usually lived together in a third section. White miners believed that in the work place black miners were the same as whites. They earned the same wage, worked the same hours, ran the same risks, traded at the same commissary, and belonged to the same local union. However, blacks worshiped at different churches, attended their own dances, and were believed to be more superstitious.[21]

Foreign miners contributed a unique dimension to life in Alabama coal camps. Although they came from many countries, two distinct patterns emerged. Before 1900 most came from the United Kingdom. After that most originated in Italy or the Slavic countries. They came

Hog snoozes beneath steps to a duplex on "Dago Hill." (Courtesy of Samford University Archives)

because of energetic recruitment and because the steady expansion of coal production provided a constant need for more labor. Although they added an exotic dimension to some coal camps, they were swamped by the tidal wave of poor blacks and whites moving in from the poverty-stricken countryside. Unlike Pennsylvania, where native whites had greater opportunities and immigrants came to fill more dangerous jobs such as mining, native-born Alabamians flocked to coal camps. Among miners and quarrymen listed in the 1900 census, 8,735 were black, 5,984 were native-born whites, and 1,573 were foreign-born whites. Most of the immigrants came from Great Britain, especially from coal-mining areas of Wales and Scotland. Of those with parents born abroad, 1,112 came from Britain and only 171 from Italy. By 1930 foreign immigrants were more likely to come from southern and eastern Europe, but their numbers had declined. Of some 24,000 miners listed in that year, 12,742 were black, 10,843 were native-born whites, and only 371 were foreign-born whites. Although coal mining was the most racially integrated occupation in Alabama, it was the most sexually segregated. Of the state's miners in 1930, 23,956 were males and only 9 were females.[22]

One of the Italian miners, John Gioiello, was born in Torino, Italy, in

1898. Orphaned when a child, he became a farm laborer. In 1921 he left his native country bound for Alabama, where he had relatives. He began working a nine-hour shift for TCI in 1922 at the age of twenty-three and mined coal for twenty-nine years. Although he had attended elementary school in Italy, he spoke no English. Five or six Italian miners translated instructions for him.[23]

John Sokira experienced different circumstances. His father had been a shepherd in Czechoslovakia. The family came to Birmingham in 1900 and began mining coal at Brookside. Young John went to work beside his father when he was thirteen, although he knew boys as young as nine who mined. He earned fifty cents a ton but could mine fewer than five tons a day. The small shafts where he worked were often too narrow to stand, so he wielded his pick while balancing on his knees. Although his family spoke no English, they felt at home in a mining camp with some three hundred Slovakian miners. Those who had come earlier translated instructions for newcomers. Sokira married the daughter of a Slovak miner, had ten children, and attended a school while out on strikes.

Mining camps provided challenges to women. Mrs. John Sokira came to Brookside about 1901 from Czechoslovakia. She married her fellow Czech and learned to make his shirts and underclothes. The knees of his pants posed a special problem. Because he had to crawl on his hands and knees through the narrow mining shafts, he quickly wore out the knees of his pants. She tried sewing pads but they ripped off. She finally solved the problem by cutting out rubber knee covers from old car inner tubes. She had to wash his one suit and underclothes and dry them on the back of the stove during cold and overcast weather. Saturday was wash day so the clothes would dry on Sunday and be available for use on Monday morning. His long hours required two evening meals. She fed the children, then put his food aside so he could eat when his shift ended. The Sokiras also adjusted child rearing to their occupation. She became the primary parent because he usually left before sunup and returned after the younger children were asleep.[24]

Mrs. Jimmie Evans had a different set of problems. Her daughters insisted on marrying early and usually made poor choices. But of more concern to her was her husband's life. After she first married she would wake in the middle of the night and sneak down to the mine where women were considered bad luck. She denied the superstition and determined to be there when his night shift ended:

"You know, when you love a man you're always worryin' about him. Sometimes I guess them that don't love get by easier. Anyway, I'd wake up, and when I'd get to thinkin' about him, I'd get so lonesome

I wouldn't know which way to turn. Then I'd fix up some sand-wiches to give me an excuse for goin', and go down there to him. Oh, he'd scold me sometimes, but then he'd laugh and tell me I was the beatenest woman he ever saw."[25]

Working

G iven the wretched living conditions of many min-ing camps, why did so many come to live and work? The answer to that question was simple. Life in a coal camp was better than what they left behind. Rocky Appalachian farms provided little cash income. Sam Brakefield explained his reasons for leaving the land for Gamble Mines in 1887: "When I was a boy growing up, I talked my dad [into] letting me leave our hillside farm that was so poor we couldn't even raise enough for the cows and pigs to eat." Ellis Self began to mine because there were no other jobs when he quit school.[26]

For hill country farmers who remained bivocational, getting to work was no simple matter. Lester D. Williams walked 3 miles each way from his home at Maxine to the Powhatan Mine. Ellis Self walked 10 miles round trip to a TCI mine. Woodie Roberts lived 2 miles from Brilliant Coal Mines, where he worked, requiring a thirty- to forty-minute walk twice a day. Elmer Burton walked 2.5 miles from his Walker County farm to Gamble Mines until he bought a 1926 Chevrolet secondhand in 1929. John Gates walked 3 miles each way to work at Paramount Mine near Helena.[27]

Even double jobs provided only a marginal income. Elmer Burton remembered that his family remained on the farm because "you couldn't make a living in the mines." Sam Cash, who mined coal in a small mine four miles east of Mentone, explained: "I have been farming and mining ever since I can remember and I still don't know which one is the worse to make a living at."[28]

Lack of education often determined the occupation of the poor. They had no job skills nor the functional literacy to learn any. William T. Minor, born in Jefferson County in 1893, never attended school a single day. At first he did not go because his father did not make him. Then as the years passed he was too ashamed to attend with children less than half his size and age. One of eleven children of a poor dirt farmer, his illiteracy afforded him few options. Woodie Roberts finished the sixth grade before he dropped out at age thirteen and began working at a Ramseur Hollow mine in Marion County. Joseph Davis attended school only nine months. One of eight sons of a part-time Methodist preacher and blacksmith, Davis began digging coal at age twelve. Later he joined

Bessie Mine (Sloss-Sheffield Steel and Iron Company), December 1910. "Shorpy Higginbotham, a 'greaser' on the tipple at Bessie Mine, of the Sloss-Sheffield Steel and Iron Co. Said he was 14 years old, but it is doubtful. Carries two heavy pails of grease, and is often in danger of being run over by the coal cars."—Lewis Hine. (Courtesy of Lewis Hine Photographic Collection, Library of Congress)

other aspiring miners, hired a teacher, and learned to read well enough to pass the mine foreman's examination.[29]

Nor were such experiences uncommon. Of 7,966 Alabama miners listed in the 1890 census, 2,841 (35.7 percent) were illiterate. By 1920, slightly more than 14 percent of Alabama's 26,000 miners could neither read nor write. Although many of these miners were blacks, a substantial number were white.[30] Many rural parents saw no reason for schooling beyond a few years, and mine owners cared even less. The work, particularly in the early years of mining, required no reading or writing skills. A strong back and a weak mind sometimes constituted the ideal combination sought by owners. One employer, whom a journalist described as a man "without ideals and apparently without shame," explained that he prevented labor trouble by hiring no one who knew how to read. The only reason he ever hired a literate miner was because "there aren't enough illiterate" ones to go around.[31]

If mine owners were willing to hire young children, hill-country parents made little effort to stop them. They put little stock in education, and families needed the extra income. So as in textiles, the "family wage" became the rule. A single head of family could not earn enough to support everyone; therefore, boys entered the mine as soon as they were able. In many pits, a miner was given a car to fill no matter how old he was. A son working by his father meant an extra car to load.[32] The father could do most of the hard work, and his young son could help him load. As a result, mining was often an occupation passed along from one generation to the next.

According to the report of a United States Coal Commission in the mid-1920s, only 7.5 percent of Alabama coal miners descended from fathers who dug coal. In fact, that percentage of second-generation miners was the lowest of any leading coal state.[33] But my sample of twenty life histories included seven whose fathers were miners. The father of Woodie Roberts mined at Brilliant Coal Mines, and all six of his sons became miners, as did his one son-in-law. Woodie also married a coal miner's daughter. At one point in his career he and three brothers worked in the same mine with their father. Alfred Renshaw was a third-generation miner who went to work for his father, who supervised a Pratt Consolidated Company mine. William Warren grew up in the Piper-Coleanor Mine Camp and joined his father in the mine in 1933. Elmer Burton attended school at the Gamble Mines until old enough to work with his father, who needed income from the extra coal car he received when his son began to work. Bill McDaniel and John Sokira went to work beside their fathers. James H. Phillips also descended from a coal miner.[34] Most of the other miners came from families of small bivocational farmers whose lives offered no alternative to some form of industrial work. As farmer-carpenters, farmer-blacksmiths, or farmer-preachers, they earned barely enough to feed their families.

One myth surrounding poor whites was the belief that their irresponsibility allowed them freedom to frolic, lay out of school, and enjoy the abandon of prolonged childhood. Such notions had little basis in the reality of coal miners' lives. Elmer Burton began mining part-time at age eleven during school vacation. For Joseph Davis, William W. Sewell, Bill McDaniel, William Warren, Alfred Renshaw, and William Minor, passage from childhood to adult work occurred at age twelve. Minor's brother of nine began with the older boy of twelve. Woodie Roberts and John Sokira started at age thirteen, Sam Brakefield at fourteen, and Ellis Self at fifteen.[35] Thus eleven of the twenty miners entered the mines before their sixteenth year. For the industry statewide in 1920, 1,384 children between ages ten and seventeen mined coal.[36]

The work they performed varied from mine to mine. Until after 1900 most mine jobs were not specialized. A miner often learned to set timber, blast, haul coal cars, and maintain equipment, as well as any other job that needed doing. But gradually miners learned a special skill.

Most boys began in larger mines separating slate from coal either in the mine or at the face where they stood at the end of conveyor belts. Many of the mines were nonmechanized operations that employed fewer than ten miners. Miners called such activities by a variety of names to differentiate them from larger mines: "wagon" or "truck," "push" or "mule" mines. Typically they were too small for profitable commercial operations, so many were run by coal miners themselves. But their owners seldom became successful entrepreneurs. Usually they worked a small coal seam, often employing a crew consisting of sons, brothers, or other relatives. When the seam played out, they returned to work for a larger mine, as poor as when they left.[37]

Although a few Alabama mines contained a shaft where men descended straight down in an elevator, most mines sloped into mountains. As crews followed the seams deeper into hillsides, they sometimes had a long walk or crawl from the mine face to their work. Until the United Mine Workers organized the industry in the 1930s, miners were not paid portal-to-portal. Pay commenced when they arrived at the coal face and began loading coal into their car. And they were usually paid by the ton of coal, earning nothing for the blasting and slate. In some mines with a thick seam and high ceiling, the journey might be pleasant enough. But in others the passageway was full of mud and gray clay. Miners often emerged covered with mud from head to toe. At the Slicklizzard Mine in Walker County someone told a miner emerging from the face, "you're as slick as a lizard." The name stuck.[38]

Inside the mine men descended into a black world. To illuminate the darkness, miners relied at first upon kerosene oil lamps. The small metal containers, some three or four inches high, held the fuel. A spout somewhat longer contained a wick. A hook protruding from the back attached to a soft cloth cap. This arrangement freed the miner's hands for work. The oil sometimes produced so much smoke that miners had to load their car by touch because they could not see it. Shortly after the turn of the century, more sophisticated carbide lamps replaced the oil version. Carrying a variety of brand names—"Justrite," "Autolite," "Guy's Dropper"—and shapes, the principle was the same. Miners put water or saliva in a chamber in the top and carbide in another on the bottom. A metal arm on the top regulated the flow of water. When water reached the carbide, it created a gas emitted through a reflector on the face of the lamp. A device next to the orifice worked like a cigarette lighter. The result was a steady light more reliable than the flickering wick of the old kerosene version. Both had the liability of producing a flame, always dangerous in a coal mine where gas often collected. By the 1940s bat-

Birmingham-area coal miners, February 1937. Photo by Arthur Rothstein.
(Courtesy of Farm Security Administration Photographs, Library of
Congress)

tery-powered lamps and hard hats had replaced the more primitive
equipment. But many miners liked the carbide lamp better, claiming
that if a miner entered a chamber with "dead or tight air," the carbide
lamp would go out, thus warning the miner of danger.[39]

Along the passageways miners carved out "rooms," at first with picks
and later by blasting. Seams could be undercut, then broken or blasted
down. When blasting, miners bored holes with auger drills, pressing a
curved breastplate against their chest for leverage. Then they placed
blasting powder at the back of the hole and perhaps another charge
toward the front. They put a "squib" in the front of the hole, the predecessor of a fuse. They lit the squib and took off running because the
squib jumped quickly to the charge and set off the powder. The explosion blew down a chunk of coal, breaking it into odd-shaped pieces or
disintegrating it into dust. This they loaded aboard a car brought down
the passageway and into the rooms on rail. When the car was loaded,
mules pulled it to the face of the mine where the coal was weighed.

Miners often became attached to their mules, giving them affectionate
names (one celebrated song called them "Darling"). Alfred Renshaw
described the mules as smaller and smarter than farm mules. In small

mines, a three-mule team or "spike team" carried the cars up inclines. Sometimes miners used teams of as many as seven or eight mules. William W. Sewell began working as a mule driver at age thirteen, making eighteen cents a day. At sixteen he was promoted to boss driver, the head of mule teams, at a salary of twenty-two cents a day. He remembered that "the men didn't have the value that a mule had." A song popular among white miners contained a chorus describing the value of a miner's life: "Kill a mule, buy another, Kill a nigger, hire another."[40]

Ceilings posed a constant hazard. Huge, loose pieces of slate often fell, crushing miners. "Roof pots," or petrified tree stumps, were especially dangerous, causing many rock falls. To stabilize roofs, miners left columns of coal or brought in timbers and metal plates, which they affixed to the ceiling of a "room" for support.[41]

Few miners entered a pit without serious misgivings. Never far from their consciousness was the memory of some tragedy, a rock fall or explosion that cost the lives of relatives or friends. Even the most fatalistic miner, whose religion and culture convinced him that nothing could harm him until his "number was up," experienced gut-wrenching fear.

Seldom did a miner work long without some personal injury. In 1916 a rock fell on William Sewell, breaking his leg and hip. The company assumed no responsibility, leaving Sewell to rig a pulley for traction and homemade crutches for support. Sewell had another close call with death while working at Sayreton Number One mine when it exploded. Fortunately his shift was off, so he went down as a member of the rescue team instead of coming up as a corpse. John Gates was luckier; his only bodily testimony to years of mining consisted of blue facial scars, the result of mining injuries that had healed over coal dust. C. D. Patterson's brother died in a 1918 accident.[42]

Although less dramatic, the damage done by coal dust was more insidious and just as deadly in the long run. Many of Alabama's mines were "wet," containing seepage and moisture that made miners damp and uncomfortable but also reduced the amount of coal dust in the air. But in "dry" mines, the dust was choking, filling the nose and lung with a foul black soot. A miner could wash the filth off his skin but not from his lungs. If he worked in the mines long enough, he contracted black lung, technically called pneumoconiosis. Symptoms varied but included chest pains, difficulty in breathing, a deep, hacking cough, and dizziness. Herbert South, a bivocational miner and Methodist preacher, slept only three hours a night, and then only with his head raised and a fan blowing to help him breathe.[43]

Charlie Cross began mining as a boy of twelve in 1890 before state regulation of Alabama mines. During his long career he worked his way up to superintendent of a TCI ore mine. But he never forgot those early days: "There was no safety work of any kind. If a man was hurt, it was his look-out. . . . I've seen men go in there [hospital] and have an arm or leg cut off as a result of an accident with the company taking no responsibility at all."[44]

Mining was an inherently dangerous occupation, one of the most dangerous in the world. Between 1839 and 1927, 121,209 men died in American coal mines; 3,242 died in 1907 alone, 702 of them in the month of December. Many of these tragedies occurred in Alabama. Usually the pattern that followed an explosion was an investigation, some type of inadequate reform, company emphasis on safety, followed by another explosion and a new cycle. Each participant in the drama blamed the others, miners accusing owners, owners accusing workers, and both faulting state officials.

An 1890 explosion at Coalburg in Jefferson County killed eleven miners and created the impetus both for organization of the United Mine Workers of America and for Alabama's first attempt to regulate a business through legislative action. The Mine Inspection Act of 1890 provided for a mine inspector to visit once every three months every underground coal and iron mine employing twenty or more miners. The inspector could notify the owner in writing of any required changes that had to be made in a "reasonable time." If the owner procrastinated, the inspector could refer the matter to a probate judge for a hearing.

Although this law was designed to make the mines safer, miners complained that it did not go far enough. The *Alabama Sentinel*, official paper of the Knights of Labor, complained that the mine inspectors provided by the law could not possibly visit all the mines every three months. Laborers requested many changes to tighten and strengthen the law. Some miners charged collusion between owners and inspectors, alleging that owners knew when the state officials were coming and showed them only the safest parts of the mines.[45]

Whether such practices occurred or not, the new law did not eliminate disasters. The number of deaths in coal mines rose steadily as industrialists opened new pits to cope with industry's insatiable appetite for fuel. In 1893, the first year that the state recorded statistics, 17 died in Alabama coal mines; in 1899 the figure increased to 40; by 1904 fatalities numbered a record 185. Fatal accidents declined to 154 in 1907 and to 129 in 1909. Of the 1909 fatalities, most (70) resulted from rock or coal falls. The racial mix of fatalities varied, as did the number of convicts and free miners who were killed. In 1899 28 blacks, 5 of them convicts, and 12 whites (1 convict) died. In 1914, 65 white miners and 61 blacks died, leaving behind 42 widows and 64 orphans.[46]

The steady escalation of deaths caused the legislature to overhaul the state mine inspection law during the Progressive reform period after 1900. Under the new system, the governor appointed three inspectors to three-year terms, one of them to serve as the state's chief mining inspector. To qualify, a man had to have five years of experience as a miner but could not own a mine. Their duties consisted primarily of inspecting each coal mine every three months. The law also required standard scales for weighing coal, annual mine reports, minimum ventilation, emergency equipment, escapeways, maps of mines, timbers for support, and guidelines to prevent dangerous accumulation of gases. The law also prohibited women or boys younger than fourteen from working in Alabama mines.[47] The law was strengthened in 1911.

A more thorough discussion of the linkage between state politics and mine safety must wait for a broader context, but all reform efforts proved futile. Between 1918 and 1928 Alabama's accident and fatality rate remained higher than the American average. Alabama averaged one fatality per 185,663 tons of coal mined; the national rate was one fatality per 258,629 tons. Finally the safety program began to yield results in 1929 when Alabama's fatality rate dropped to one per 256,000 tons compared to a national average of one per 276,019. The years from 1930 to 1945 brought further improvements, though Alabama's coal mines remained the third most dangerous in America, trailing only those of Tennessee and Virginia.[48]

Although miners usually blamed their owners or supervisors for disasters, many companies upgraded safety practices. DeBardeleben Coal Corporation provided each employee with a book of safety rules in 1929. The first violation brought a warning, the second suspension, and the third discharge. Any miner coming to work drunk was discharged immediately. Fire bosses at Alabama Fuel and Iron Company mines searched men at shift changes for matches, pipes, cigarettes, or other smoking articles. They fined miners five dollars for each violation discovered at the mine face. If supervisors discovered a miner with a match inside the mine, they deducted five dollars from the salary of the fire boss. One miner blamed most rock falls on neglect and carelessness by fellow miners together with inadequate supervision by section foremen.[49]

Whoever was to blame, the human carnage was frightful. Many casualties resulted from spectacular explosions. In 1905 more than a hundred miners died in an explosion at Virginia City. Two years later the Yolande mine blew up.

Yolande Mining Camp in northeastern Tuscaloosa County, some thirty-five miles from Birmingham, was considered a model community. Owned by a physician who had been a Populist gubernatorial candidate, it was regarded as one of the safest mines in America. On Monday morning, December 16, a superintendent inspected the mine and praised its safety procedures. As he rode away on horseback, he heard a deafening explosion. The blast blew timber fragments three hundred feet from the mine face across a ravine. Rescuers were kept out of the mine by heat and a blackened ooze at the mouth. By noon, 14 badly burned survivors had crawled to the surface, leaving little hope that other miners 1,500 feet below might be alive. When rescuers reached their bodies, they found 57 victims, most of them single men in their twenties. Ironically, 2 of the victims were Matthew Stokes and his son Andrew. Stokes had left Irwin, Pennsylvania, with his wife and five younger children to work at Yolande, which paid above-average wages and had special safety equipment. The owner paid to send the bodies back to Pennsylvania. But only the widow and her surviving five children attended the funeral. Friends of the Stokeses were attending their own funeral for 239 miners killed four days earlier when the Darr Mine at Jacob's Creek blew up.[50]

Other explosions in 1908, 1909, and 1910 took hundreds of lives. In 1911 another "model mine," Banner, blew up. The explosion killed 132 miners, 123 of them convicts. The next year the Alabama legislature once again reformed the mine inspection law.

A decade and many "reforms" later, four trip cars broke loose on the tipple at Woodward Iron Company mine and raced down Number Three Slope. The slope had a thirty-degree pitch and was eight hundred feet long. The breakaway cars created huge clouds of dust and shredded a 3,300-volt cable that ran down the hillside. The arcs from the cable ignited the dust and streaks of flame shot out of the mine's mouth "like lightening bolts from some subterranean abyss." The fire incinerated the tipple and many of the men working near the face of the mine. Mine inspectors had recently pronounced the mine safe, but the 477 men working in the mine that day must have wondered at the report. Miraculously the explosion spared the ventilation system. But the closest phone was two miles away at the company office, delaying rescue teams. By the time they reached the casualties, 90 were dead.

The Overton Mine, owned by Charles DeBardeleben's Alabama Fuel and Iron Company, blew up two weeks before Christmas in 1925. Miners discovered gas in the mine during the morning shift. Later two miners turned up their carbide lamps to inspect timber supports, causing an explosion that tore through the mine and killed 53 men.[51]

The regularity with which disasters overwhelmed them and their helplessness in the face of such events deeply troubled coal miners. Many found solace in the fatalism of Appalachian religion. Others shielded themselves with folk magic and superstition. Dangerous occupations spawn a high level of superstition, and few jobs were riskier than coal mining. Sometimes folk beliefs were simple and traced their origin to poor white culture. For instance, miners believed that women were bad luck in a mine and often refused to enter one where a woman had been. Some beliefs were more complicated and bizarre. Most miners believed that rats moving about in a mine were a sign of disaster. They believed that rats sensed movements in rock and slate and sought to protect themselves by leaving an area that was about to cave in. Many a miner swore by the rats; and when the rats "went to moving," so did they.[52]

The danger inherent in their occupation was also a source of pride. Though they earned barely enough to live, coal miners coped with the danger that drove weaker spirits away from their dark and dangerous world. Sam Brakefield rejoiced that none of his eight children who survived to adulthood decided to become miners. But mining was so much a part of his life that he refused to quit even when work was sporadic, wages low, and danger ever-present. Bennie Amerson loved the mine, explaining simply: "It sort of gets a fellow when he follows it awhile."[53]

Too much can be made of such statements. Each disaster left its psychic casualties as well as physical cripples. For each miner who buried his fears in fatalism or superstition, another miner "took to walking." Transience rates, which hovered near 100 percent a year during the first three decades of the twentieth century, demonstrated conclusively that miners never entirely came to terms with their fears.

Of course other factors caused them to quit. Wages provided no more than a marginal existence at best. One of the jarring realities of these decades, one that seriously eroded faith in the American Dream that financial success resulted from diligent labor, was that a man could work hard amid danger and remain desperately poor. Although wages varied from one mine to another, the prevailing scale was fairly consistent. William Sewell began picking slate out of coal at age twelve in 1892 for eleven or twelve cents a day. The following year he became a mule driver, making eighteen cents. At sixteen, as a boss driver of teams, he earned twenty-two cents. Sam Brakefield at age fourteen went to work in 1887, digging coal from sunup to sundown for eighty cents. Joseph Davis began picking out slate at age twelve for seventy-five cents a day. Elmer Burton started mining at about the same age for less than a dollar.[54]

By the war years salaries were better. James Phillips's father began mining about 1914 or 1915 for 29¢ a ton. Most skilled miners could load between five and ten tons a day, earning a daily salary ranging from $2.50 to $5. Luther Smith started working a twelve-hour day at Gamble Mines in 1920 for $1.85. Ellis Self began mining in 1925 at age fifteen for $2 a day. The miners did recall a certain egalitarianism to their poverty: blacks, native-born whites, and immigrants all earned the same rate.[55]

Two additional factors complicated the low salaries. Demand for coal was both highly seasonal and cyclical. Because one major use for coal was home heating, demand increased in winter months and declined during other seasons. Industrial use followed national economic cycles, with highest demand during boom times. As a result, miners were frequently placed on one- or two-day weeks and were laid off during slack seasons. Such seasonal variation allowed many small farmers to pick up occasional work in the winter when employment increased, then devote their time to farming during the spring and summer. But men trying to earn their livelihood entirely by mining suffered from the periodic slumps.

Although the high rates of labor turnover make it clear that upward mobility was not the rule, some miners who remained with the same companies and developed their skills prospered at least temporarily. Sam Brakefield, who began his career earning 80¢ a day, had risen to foreman by 1903 and took home a straight salary of $75 a month. He saved his money and bought forty-six acres and a house. Joseph Davis, who began work for 75¢ a day, earned as much as $900 a month as a mine foreman during the 1920s. The Davises bought and paid for a house and even built five rental houses. The median annual wage paid in Alabama's fifty-three coal mines during 1921 was $930 to those paid by the ton and $800 to miners paid a daily wage. These figures were well below the national median for nonunion mines during that year ($1,420), but they were well above the wages of earlier years.[56]

But the capricious nature of the industry made prosperity ephemeral. After steady growth in the industry between 1900 and 1926, employment began to decline in 1927 and continued through the middle of the depression. The length of the workday was trimmed to retain as many miners as possible. In 1929 some 25,000 miners worked an average of 231 days a year and mined an average of 3.08 tons per man per day. By 1933 fewer than 20,000 miners worked an average of only 145 days per year. The average rose to 163 days in 1934, then fell again to 160 in 1935.[57]

The personal dimensions of this economic catastrophe were overwhelming. Mrs. John Sokira remembered one desperate depression year when her husband earned only $52 to support a family of twelve. Widow Ila Hendrix recalled that her husband had earned only $2.08 a day when he worked at all. She kept a garden, cows, and chickens to help the family survive. C. D. Patterson could obtain work only two days a week. When Joseph Davis lost his foreman's job in 1930, he could no longer pay the mortgage on his five rental houses. One by one he lost them and finally even the home he and his wife had so proudly built in better times. He tried farming but failed at that. The electric company shut off his electricity because he could not pay the bill. Nor could the family afford schoolbooks for their children. After three years of futile labor, Davis gave up farming, still owing more for his farm than he could obtain by selling it. Fortunately the coal industry was recovering, and he found work at Sayreton Mine, earning $3.80 a day. But he had to use kerosene lamps in his company house until his first paycheck. The children urged their parents to leave the house dark so their friends would not discover that they were too poor to afford electricity. But the Davises refused to be shamed by what they could not help. Davis's experience and hard work served him well for a time, and he soon increased his salary to $6 a day. Then disaster struck again. A doctor forced him to quit because of high blood pressure and failing health. Dera Davis became the breadwinner, obtaining a job with the Federal Emergency Relief Administration teaching miners to read and write.[58]

Organizing

Unionism operates at two levels. It functions distinctly within an occupation by responding to the unique problems that workers encounter in their lives and work. In this role it addresses specific worker grievances, helps shape a sense of occupational identity, and often separates one group of employees (skilled versus unskilled, male versus female, black versus white, miners versus textile workers) from another.

At a second level, labor organizations unite all workers in a statewide political effort that transcends specific grievances. Unions join in common causes such as workers' compensation or safety campaigns. This sort of effort requires reshaping political structures. I will discuss the second, political function in a separate chapter. But labor left its mark particularly on coal miners.

Of the many occupations pursued by Alabama's poor, only one created a firm sense of working-class solidarity. Coal miners not only learned to cooperate across racial lines, they also waged vigorous campaigns for more than fifty years to unionize their industry. And once organized permanently in the 1930s, they demonstrated a loyalty rarely found among southern workers.

Why coal miners more than other laborers should have followed such a pattern is a matter of speculation. Perhaps the danger associated with their jobs, which prompted intensive demands for better safety and health conditions, created a sense of urgency. Coal miners were also more concentrated than textile and sawmill workers. Though coal camps might be scattered across dozens of hollows in rugged hill country, the vast majority of Alabama's miners worked in two adjacent counties, Jefferson and Walker. Kinship patterns were strong among Appalachian people, who made up most of the white work force. Pay scales did not vary because of race or ethnic background, which perhaps encouraged cooperation and made it more difficult for coal companies to divide higher-paid white workers from poorer-paid blacks. Many miners also begat miners, creating an occupational link that spanned several generations and made upward mobility seem unlikely.

Working-class solidarity also resulted from specific middle class attitudes that often ridiculed or put down miners. William T. Minor remembered Dick Acuff, who managed the commissary at Clift Mine, as a man who "didn't associate much with the miners, was sort of to himself." Dera Bledsoe recalled that her father, a Birmingham justice of the peace, "looked down on the laboring class." When she informed him that she was dating a coal miner, he exploded: "Dera Bledsoe you haven't got one bit of marryin' sense in your head. . . . You know very well that miners are a bunch of ignorant, profane, crapshooters with no ambition."[59] From such comments did working-class consciousness derive.

The factor that often prevented workers from cooperating was race. White owners shrewdly exploited the racism inherent in southern society, using strikebreakers of one race to thwart strikes by workers of another. Mutual distrust and animosity usually took care of the rest.

This strategy worked better in other industries than it did in coal mining for several reasons. The racial balance in mining provided blacks an opportunity to protect themselves. By 1929 blacks made up 60 percent of the DeBardeleben Coal Corporation's miners, 65 percent at the New Castle and Montevallo Coal companies, 70 percent at the Alabama Fuel and Iron Company, 73 percent at TCI's mines, and 80 percent at the Woodward Iron Company.[60]

Another explanation may be the nature of mining itself. Work crews were integrated and many white miners gained a grudging respect for blacks who worked with them. They shared the same dangers, frustrations, and uncertainties. More than once black men saved the lives of white miners, and whites reciprocated. Both despised the use of convict labor, which displaced free miners and afforded an ample supply of strikebreakers. And both worked hard to organize unions and shut down mines during strikes. Although the races learned to work cooperatively over time, racial tension was never entirely absent, and in the early years it crippled organizing efforts.

Unionization followed an uneven pattern in the Alabama fields. Early efforts by the Knights of Labor and the United Mine Workers achieved mixed success. They both proved incapable of sustained progress, recruiting most of their members during periods of crisis that almost always resulted in a strike. Usually the union lost and the membership disintegrated. This cycle continued into the twentieth century. Union membership climbed and fell like a roller coaster, reaching 65 percent of the work force in 1902, falling to 16 percent in 1905, and to only 4 percent three years later. During the years between 1912 and 1915 it dropped below 1 percent before soaring to 26 percent in 1918, then dropping back to 2 percent in 1923. Of 25,809 Alabama coal miners, only 1,023 belonged to the UMW in January 1923. When William Mitch and William Dalrymple came to Birmingham in June 1933 to reorganize the Alabama district, only 225 miners belonged to two UMW locals. A month later, they had enrolled 18,000 in eighty-five locals in one of the most amazing union campaigns in state history.[61]

Although wages, safety, and working conditions afforded the major stimuli for organizing drives, the use of convict labor was often the focus of conflict. Convict labor actually affected all other issues by depressing wages, creating safety hazards, and providing a large labor reserve for use as strikebreakers. State laws aimed specifically at blacks in filling the convict rolls, though whites served in fewer numbers. Of 72 Jefferson County convicts killed in the Banner Mine explosion in April 1911, 30 percent had been sentenced to no more than twenty days for such offenses as carrying concealed weapons, gambling, vagrancy, or violating prohibition laws. Between 1907 and 1912 an average of 2,500 state and 700 county convicts were leased to private parties who paid the state for their services and provided for their upkeep. Slightly more than 80 percent were blacks, and the rest were poor whites. More than half the convicts worked in Birmingham-area coal mines. In 1912, 590 worked in TCI mines, 325 in Sloss-Sheffield Company mines, 170 for Pratt Consolidated Company, and 100 for Red Feather Coal Company.[62]

Those poor whites who descended into the system often disappeared as mysteriously as black convicts. J. A. Reynolds lived in the western Jefferson County town of Adamsville in 1916. Miners were out on strike during December and Reynolds sought to make Christmas money however he could. A man knocked on his door on the bitterly cold night of December 22 and asked to buy a pint of home-brew whiskey. Despite pleas from his wife Minnie not to sell the liquor, he took the money. As soon as he did, a deputy sheriff stepped out of the darkness and arrested him. The county set bond at three hundred dollars, which he was unable to pay. On February 21, 1917, he pleaded innocent. Brought to trial two days later in the circuit court, he was found innocent by the jury. But he never came home. The next news arrived four months later when his wife received word that he had been shot in the back and killed by a prison guard while trying to escape from Maxine Mine Number Five near the Praco community in Jefferson County. In 1983, Reynolds's son, who was only two months old when his father disappeared, began an investigation. He found no evidence that his father had been convicted of a crime. Explaining why his mother had not questioned authorities in 1916, he noted: "Back then you didn't ask no questions. . . . She had to take care of us. Momma didn't even know where they'd sent him."[63]

The mixture of coal mining, race, politics, and the convict-lease system made for an explosive brew. Miners tried to organize as early as 1876, but these meetings accomplished little. As one miner complained, "those that ran fastest got to the bosses first."[64] But some miners persisted, and by the autumn of 1877 they had organized several clubs in and around Birmingham. By mid-1878 nine Greenback-Labor clubs operated in Jefferson County with six others in formative stages. Although the first clubs contained only white miners, blacks soon began their own clubs and produced the most charismatic leader, a twenty-nine-year-old miner named Willis Johnson Thomas. The most active white club at Jefferson Mines financed Thomas's travels through the county as an organizer for the Greenbackers. His popularity was so great that predominantly white clubs invited him to speak, and his revivalistic fervor resulted in interracial meetings. The clubs began appointing biracial committees composed of two whites and two blacks to negotiate contracts and conduct biracial elections among members before striking or settling a work stoppage.[65] Such efforts may seem tame by later standards, but in a state less than a decade removed from Reconstruction, it was a daring racial experiment necessitated by hard times and economic desperation.

Wages were a major issue on the Greenback-Labor agenda, but the convict-lease system caused even greater consternation. It denied free miners their only economic leverage, an effective strike. The Eureka Mining Company at Helena first introduced convicts in June 1878 to break a strike. The company fired the strikers, ordered them off company property, and herded eighty-nine convicts into the mine. Greenback-Labor organizers used the threat of convict labor both to organize free miners and to galvanize their members into political action in order to elect sympathetic officials. But neither effort achieved notable success.[66]

Conditions deteriorated during the following decade. In July 1880, miners struck at Coketon because they had to pay the labor employed in pushing coal cars from the main slope. The company employed the Helena strategy, using one hundred convicts to break the strike. In May

1882, five hundred miners struck Pratt Mines. When the mine operator vowed to use convicts to continue operations, someone sent him a death threat. Undeterred, he followed the successful strategy employed earlier at Helena and Coketon. Other strikes at J. T. Pierce Company, Alabama Mining Company, Coalburg, and Warrior increased tensions and intensified owner determination to break the unions by using convicts. As a consequence, several hundred miners formed the Miners' Union and Anti-Convict League in July 1885.[67]

The Greenback-Labor party received help from the Knights of Labor, which entered the state in the late 1870s but was able to attract only a few hundred miners. Internal debates over excluding blacks from membership hurt the union, as did internal discord over whether to endorse strikes. The Knights' official policy was racial equality, but white miners often resisted interracial unions.[68] As the convict-lease issue began to infuriate miners, the Knights made better progress.

In 1888 ten companies bid for Alabama's state convicts. The newly arrived Tennessee Coal, Iron, and Railroad Company won a ten-year contract, but other companies shared the labor of county prisoners. By 1894 TCI worked 1,138 convicts at its Pratt Mines, and Sloss Company used 589 more at Coalburg. Use of convicts intensified the class strife. The Knights of Labor newspaper, the *Alabama Sentinel*, tried to win middle class allies by warning that convicts increased "wealth of a favored few to the disadvantage of all"; by robbing free labor of jobs, the system would bankrupt local merchants.[69]

William Sewell joined the Knights of Labor during these tumultuous days. He recalled union meetings held in the woods by candlelight with the union charter nailed to a tree. Sometimes company deputies stalked their meetings, shooting at them to break up the union. One cold December day Sewell and a nephew had to swim the Warrior River to escape.[70]

Miners made periodic attempts to unify their fragmented forces. In 1888 they founded the Alabama Miners Federation. But the most important consolidation occurred in 1890 when several unions merged to form the United Mine Workers. The fledgling union plunged into controversy immediately when it struck the Coalburg Mine, where eleven miners had just been killed. Although it received no recognition, the union did help create public pressure for passage of Alabama's first Mine Inspection Act that year.[71]

The UMW declined early in the 1890s but sprang back to life in 1893 with five thousand members. The union's recovery coincided with one of the nation's most severe depressions. As demand for coal dropped, companies reduced wages and laid off workers. Economic desperation forced more than eight thousand miners to walk off their jobs on April

14, 1894, in the largest strike in nineteenth-century Alabama history. The strike lasted for four months. Blacks played a major role in the work stoppage, cooperating with their white cohorts. At a massive rally of four thousand miners at Lake View Park in Birmingham, half the demonstrators were Negroes, some of whom carried banners proclaiming "United We Stand," "We, The Colored Miners of Alabama, Stand With Our White Brothers," and "Convicts Must Go." One prominent coal operator wrote that an "unexpected" feature of the strike was the "stubborness [sic] and unity" of Negro miners who seemed "as determined in their purpose as the white."[72]

The companies resorted to importing Negro strikebreakers because there were too few convicts to operate the mines, but most black miners remained true to the biracial alliance. Although at least one black striker became an informer, blaming the strike on Scottish miners, racial solidarity and the prominent role of blacks in organizing unions threatened Alabama's racial caste system and provided owners their most effective argument against the UMW.[73]

The 1894 strike set important patterns for subsequent conflicts. It was biracial and furnished middle class society evidence to charge the union with radicalism. Violence occurred often as frustrated miners used Winchesters and dynamite, the only tools that remained to them, to shut down mines worked by convicts and imported strikebreakers. The violence alienated whatever friendly middle class support might have existed and was used by the state's governor to justify sending troops into the mining district.

Although the UMW suffered a serious blow in the 1894 defeat, it remained the strongest union in Alabama and dominated the Alabama Federation of Labor from its creation in 1900. It played a major role in persuading the state to eliminate statewide leasing of convicts, although counties continued to lease prisoners until the late 1920s.

Its strikes largely account for the cyclical nature of membership. Curiously, UMW ranks increased during national economic crises such as 1893, 1907, and 1919, then declined sharply as the union lost strikes. In 1904, TCI fired several union leaders, causing miners to walk off their jobs. Despite the presence of Mary H. "Mother" Jones and Socialist presidential candidate Eugene V. Debs, who spoke in Birmingham on behalf of miners, the UMW lost the strike, many of its members, and some of its influence in the Alabama Federation of Labor. When the union finally ended its strike twenty-six months later, UMW membership had dropped from 11,000 to fewer than 4,000.[74]

Four years later in 1908, owners imposed a wage reduction of ten cents per ton, fired a number of union members, evicted them from company houses, and imported strikebreakers. The UMW strike in July resulted in widespread violence. At first miners met trains carrying strikebreakers from the North and tried to persuade them to return home. But as companies placed armed guards on the trains, the situation turned ugly. On August 8, 150 striking miners ambushed a trainload of strikebreakers and special deputies at Blocton, killing 3 men and wounding 11. Officials arrested 13 black and 14 Slavic miners who were accused of the murders.[75]

Alabama Governor B. B. Comer sent one thousand national guardsmen to restore order. Many of the guardsmen were small farmers from the rural districts of south and central Alabama and they sided with the miners.[76] What made such sympathy unusual was the concerted effort of Alabama newspapers to depict the strike as a communistic effort at race mixing. The press, noting that a majority of UMW members were black, accused the union of advocating social equality for Negroes. A Birmingham paper reported that a black preacher had addressed a meeting at Dora that was attended by white women and children. Black miners had been treated as equals, even advising whites on moral and social issues. White miners sought to recruit blacks for the UMW by advocating social equality. A Negro had even put his arm around a white speaker. "Dolly Dalrymple," the woman's editor of the *Birmingham Age-Herald*, wrote that the strike was destroying the fine relationship between white women and their black "mammies." To some degree the charges were true. Tent camps contained miners of both races. A black miner served as UMW vice-president of District 20, and three blacks served on the eight-member executive committee. Exploitation of the racial issue contributed to breaking the strike. At a public meeting held in Birmingham, some speakers proposed lynching the strike leaders after the Blocton ambush. And one letter from the southern part of the state warned that if "Fairley [the union leader] and his black co-conspirators had invaded southern Alabama and perpetrated the same damnable deeds he has inflicted on the people of Jefferson County, nothing further would be needed but the coroner."[77] The national guard, on Governor Comer's orders, took down the strikers' tents, leaving them without shelter and hastening the end of the strike.

Many miners deserted the UMW after the unsuccessful strikes in 1904 and 1908. From 65 percent of the state's miners under union contract in 1902, the total fell to 5 percent in 1909, a total of fewer than seven hundred members. And 75 percent of these members were blacks, as whites left the biracial union in large numbers.[78]

Companies hastened the decline of unionism by both carrot and stick policies. Enlightened businessmen such as TCI's president, George Gordon Crawford, instituted an extensive plan of welfare capitalism. Crawford's medical and social reforms became models for the entire industry and eroded miner interest in unionism. Other mining companies took a different approach. They hired deputy sheriffs to patrol their camps. Although theoretically agents of county law enforcement, these deputies were in fact paid by a coal company and regarded themselves as company employees. One reporter, preparing a story on Birmingham for a national magazine in 1911, was stopped twice by deputies as he strolled through coal camps with his Kodak camera. Explaining that he was "hired to keep people he didn't know off the property," one deputy ordered him to leave. Both deputies explained their function as primarily to prevent labor agents from trying to employ miners or labor union organizers from entering company property.[79] Yet another strategy was "blacklisting," whereby the company circulated a list of "troublemakers" to other mines so they could act cooperatively to deny employment to strike leaders. William Sewell was blacklisted as a consequence of his union activities and was unable to obtain a mining job until 1911, when a lieutenant from his Spanish-American War unit became a superintendent at the Sayreton Mine and made Sewell an independent contractor to mine coal for the company.[80]

Both the First World War and a more sympathetic Democratic administration in Washington emboldened Alabama miners in 1917. A UMW drive increased membership to 26 percent of the mining force and a short strike resulted in a 10 percent wage increase. But the UMW failed to win union recognition. Woodrow Wilson appointed a Bituminous Coal Commission, which recommended both wage increases and collective bargaining, but operators refused to yield. The commission discovered that in the bituminous coal industry the value of coal had increased by 130.4 percent between 1902 and 1918 while the wage rate per ton for miners had gone up only 68.6 percent.

Labor conflict continued after the war. Amid charges of wartime profiteering by companies, 15,000 of Alabama's 26,000 miners struck in 1919. Months later, in July 1920, another strike occurred that was characterized by racial imbalance: 76 percent of the striking miners were black. Tension between black and white miners demonstrated that despite occupational cooperation, racism remained a formidable barrier among miners. In 1918 an Alabama UMW official requested that George Pollock and G. H. Edmonds, two union organizers, be reassigned elsewhere. He had hoped they would be helpful in organizing black miners but had concluded that they did not "understand conditions in the South. . . . Edmonds is making many statements to the colored people which may have a tendency to inflame or prejudice the white people in the district or will lead the people outside the organization to say that the United Mine Workers of America are advocating social equality."

In the 1920 strike, newspapers once again attacked northern organizers for allowing blacks to speak from the same platforms as whites. Operators claimed that their chief opposition to recognizing the UMW was its practice of social equality. Justifying the governor's decision to summon the national guard, one company official denounced the "large number of foreign Negro and white agitators, whose presence and inflammatory addresses have occasioned the disturbance." Union opponents quoted part of the UMW oath in which members pledged "never to discriminate against a fellow worker on account of creed, color, or nationality."[81]

By September 1920, twelve thousand miners had left their jobs. Violence increased during the summer, and in mid-September miners and deputies fought a pitched battle near Patton in Walker County. A general manager of the Corona Coal Company and a deputy sheriff were killed and three deputies suffered serious wounds in an attack on houses where miners had taken refuge. Governor Thomas Kilby sent seven companies of the state guard, but the violence continued. The publisher of a pro-union paper was brutally beaten. A local UMW president, Adrian Northcutt, who was also a Nazarene preacher, was killed by one of the militiamen. Northcutt's son-in-law, Will Baird, shot one of the soldiers who had killed his relative, then fled to a remote area near Natural Bridge in the northwest corner of the state. Baird surrendered after officials promised him a fair trial. Instead he was taken from a jail in Jasper and lynched, allegedly by militiamen, who then riddled his body with bullets.[82]

Unionists tried to refute the charges that the UMW advocated social equality. The *Labor Advocate* printed an editorial in October that declared:

> The fight is not social—rather an industrial fight. The Negro miner is entitled to the same wage and working conditions as white miners. The Negro miners are a fine set of men for the coal operators as long as they are willing to work for starvation wages without complaining, but when they . . . attempt to raise the standards of living for the white miner and his family as well as themselves, then the coal operators attempt to prejudice the case . . . by taking up the race question.[83]

Union leaders noted that during the strike nineteen operators had been indicted for profiteering. These owners paid two to three dollars a day less for labor than in other areas.[84]

All such arguments were in vain. TCI blacklisted a number of UMW members. Those miners who kept their jobs were, together with their families, required by guards to have written passes in order to leave the coal camps. Some companies constructed high board fences around the camps and posted armed guards at entrances. In one, deputies prevented farmers carrying provisions from entering the camp and closed the commissary to strikers. By January 1921, operators had evicted 2,000 miners and their families, who were forced to face a cold north Alabama winter sheltered only by war-surplus army tents. More than 40,000 people in the strike region depended on the UMW for relief, a burden that exhausted its meager resources. During the last week of the strike (February 16–22, 1920), the union claimed to have fed 47,000 people and housed 8,000 families.[85]

Many miners never forgot the ordeal. Bill McDaniel and his father left Alabama to mine in other states after they were blacklisted as union sympathizers; they did not return until 1935. William T. Minor joined the UMW in 1919 or 1920, participated in the strike, was fired and evicted from his house, and quit mining to work as a carpenter for nearly a decade.[86]

The UMW spent nearly two million dollars in unsuccessful efforts to organize Alabama miners during the 1920s. But when it called workers out in 1922, its strength had fallen to less than 2 percent of the work force. It could pay no strike benefits, and Bennie Amerson remembered receiving handouts of navy beans, side meat, potatoes, flour, and sugar, the amount varying with the size of families.[87]

Perhaps it is entirely appropriate that Alabama's white Appalachian coal miners, among the most individualistic folk in America, should have reacted so differently to labor unions. Some refused to join because of the black presence. Others forged a class solidarity with blacks born of common suffering and deprivation. They remember the union days with a mixture of pride and fierce loyalty. Elmer Burton first joined the UMW in the woods near Praco Mines where the miners slipped in one or two at a time for fear of being fired. William Sewell joined the Knights of Labor during the 1890s and remained a union man for the rest of his life. In 1931 Sayreton Mines tried to make him a foreman, but he would not leave the union to take the job.[88]

Others were not so sure. Luther V. Smith lived in a company house for thirty years in defiance of the transient life of most miners. He blamed radicals for most of the strikes during his career, and he did not believe they accomplished very much: "We hadn't never had nothing and we didn't know whether we wanted anything or not." During strikes, life "was rough as hell, and you just done the best you could." The best James Phillips's father could do during strikes was supply his family a diet of catfish from the Cahaba River, poke salad, and turnip greens. When her husband was on strike it just made life harder for Ila Hendrix, who clothed herself and her family with flour and feed sacks.[89]

Escape from rural poverty had brought many poor whites into a world filled with danger and violence. Life was hard in a world "dark as a dungeon and damp as a dew."

SIX

"A Man That's Lumbering as Long as Me Knows a Few Things"

Alabama's Timber Workers

Stretching from the Gulf of Mexico to the Tennessee River, an unbroken expanse of forest greeted Alabama's first settlers. Hardwoods predominated on the rugged hills to the north. Stately yellow pines covered the Wiregrass and sandy soil to the south. At first the forests represented only an impediment to farming, and trees were cut and burned. But during antebellum days planters established sawmills near Mobile where they could employ their slaves during the agricultural off-season. Logs floated down rivers made the city a major exporter of timber by the time of the Civil War.

America's industrial boom in the late nineteenth century transformed the Southeast into a major supplier of lumber. By the early decades of the twentieth century the region produced half the nation's lumber, mainly pine harvested from the tremendous expanse stretching from Jacksonville, Florida, to the Texas border. Until the 1920s lumber and timber products constituted the largest southern industry in terms both of employment and of value added, though in Alabama it was eclipsed by iron and steel making. As railroads reached the yellow pine belt, local entrepreneurs as well as northern and foreign businessmen bought huge tracts of land. Before the development of wood preservatives, wooden railroad ties quickly rotted and had to be replaced regularly. Of three thousand railroad ties per mile, two hundred had to be replaced each year. Pine was a soft wood easily adapted to all sorts of construction and found a ready market in the building industry.

The lumber and forest-products industries attracted poverty-stricken rural labor. Although the pine belt was slightly south of the center of black population, many blacks were attracted to the occupation. This attraction resulted less from racism than from such market forces as the availability of labor and the experience of workers. Lumbering afforded similar opportunities to poor whites. The counties containing most of the yellow pine forests—counties such as Covington, Conecuh, and Baldwin—also contained high concentrations of indigent whites.

The end of the Civil War left the region destitute and thousands of whites displaced. In Baldwin County the poor could not earn a decent living farming the unproductive soil.[1] Most of the population worked in turpentine mills, lumbering, or stock raising. Simeon Ward and his brother Moses abandoned their farms, left their younger children with relatives in the Pea Ridge community, and moved near Andalusia in Covington County. There they and their older sons found work in sawmills. The Wards tied the timber into rafts and floated them down the Conecuh River to Pensacola, a distance of a hundred miles by water that required four days to complete.[2]

Much of the timberland in Covington County could have belonged to Simeon and Moses Ward if only they had understood the process or possessed modest resources. In 1871 individuals owned only 12 percent of county land. Railroads owned another 25 percent and the state 2.5 percent; but the federal government held title to 60 percent. Between 1870 and 1920 unscrupulous timber companies used the homestead laws, often fraudulently, to gain control of the remaining public lands. Of 32,462,000 acres of public land available in Alabama in 1866, all but 4,638,000 had been sold or given away by 1876. Loggers clear-cut the timber, leaving the sandy soil virtually worthless. One could obtain it merely by paying overdue taxes.[3]

The technology of sawmilling changed slowly between 1880 and 1930. The era began as the age of the skilled axman who could cut a tree and hew the ends square with such skill that a casual observer could scarcely see the blade marks. One writer has called these expert axmen "the aristocrats of the laborers."[4] They notched a tree on the side in the direction they wished it to fall, then cut through on the opposite side.

By the early 1890s axes began to give way to crosscut saws. The new equipment made slow progress because sawdust choked the teeth and yellow pine resin collected to form a gummy layer. But lumbermen learned to use kerosene to clean the teeth, and manufacturers added raker teeth. The new edge consisted of a series of alternating saw and raker teeth arranged in various patterns for cutting different types of wood. Using a crosscut saw required less skill than that possessed by an expert axman but utilized the same strategy for felling a tree. Crews

These oxen are pulling a two-wheeled caralog, with pine logs attached to the bottom and dragging behind. The vehicle greatly simplified transporting timber. (Courtesy of Alabama State Archives)

used an ax to notch the tree on one side, then applied the crosscut saw to the other. They removed the branches, topped the tree, then cut the log into sections.

The next operation was transporting the logs to a stream bank or railroad line. At first oxen dragged the logs, but this method was ineffective except for short distances. Lumbermen tried wagons, but they were hard to load because of the weight and bulk of the logs. Finally they developed a cart called a "caralog," which had two wheels some seven to ten feet in diameter. They attached one end of the log to the axle and let the other end drag on the ground. An ox, mule, or horse could pull the cart distances of a mile or two. After 1900 a Mississippi operator developed an eight-wheel logging wagon. By 1904 five thousand of these vehicles were in use in the South and eleven of the largest Alabama lumber companies used them.

Power to operate a sawmill came from water at first. But by the 1880s steam engines had replaced water power and allowed log lifters to raise logs onto railroad cars. The McGiffert Log Loader, patented in 1908 in Minnesota, was a self-propelled machine with four legs that straddled a railroad track. It lifted the logs onto cars pulled by small steam loco-

*Extension of train track into the Wiregrass expanded jobs in the timber
industry. Narrow-gauge logging railroads such as this one met the caralogs
that dragged pine logs to rail junctions. (Courtesy T.E. Armitstead/Museum
of the City of Mobile Collection, University of South Alabama Photographic
Archives)*

motives over narrow-gauge track. As lumber crews moved farther away
from rivers, the railroads became as critical to the expansion of timber
production as they were to the expansion of cotton acreage.

Portable operations, often called "peckerwood sawmills," actually
went on the trains with crews. Steam engines ran them until an area
was cut; then the machinery was dismantled, loaded aboard the train,
and hauled to a new location. Here and there a larger mill town provided
permanent facilities. Scattered across the town were houses, schools,
churches, a commissary, and a work area. The mill pond first received
the logs, where they were stored until needed. Virgin pine floated on the
water, making the logs easier to handle and more resistant to insects.
The sawmills varied in complexity from small crude mills that cut lumber for local consumption to complex facilities capable of supplying a
million board feet daily. The circular saw, invented in the eighteenth
century, was used almost exclusively in Alabama by the 1880s. By World
War I, band saws began to replace the older types. In fact, the first band

saw installed south of the Ohio River was put into operation by the
Arantz Brothers at Decatur, Alabama, about 1906. Band saws had rows
of teeth that revolved beltlike around two large wheels. The teeth were
not as thick as those of a circular saw, made a finer cut, wasted less
wood, and cut faster.

Logs moved from the mill pond up a "jack ladder" or trough driven
by a powered chain. The chain pulled the logs up to a platform where
lumbermen secured them on a power-driven carriage that ran on tracks
back and forth past the saw. Then the lumber was seasoned either in
the open air or by heat in a kiln.

Although the head sawyer was a highly skilled professional, most of
the laborers had no particular skill. Strength was important, but most
rural people were accustomed to strenuous, back-breaking labor. Most
loggers were part-time farmers who either left home well before daylight
and returned after dark or followed the cuts, living in tents, shacks, or
even dormitory boxcars, returning to their families on Sundays.

Some lumber companies experimented with naval stores because they
owned vast pine reserves. Kaul Lumber Company managed more than
250,000 turpentine boxes in Coosa County alone in the early twentieth
century. But companies discovered that turpentining formed excess
resin and lowered the value of the trees. Because it was not profitable
for lumber companies, turpentining usually became a separate operation
dominated by black labor. Both the technology and the work routine
were substantially different, though naval stores still relied heavily on
seasonal laborers who farmed poor plots part of the year. By 1900 turpentine and resin workers numbered 3,716, and the value of their products ranked the industry ninth among Alabama manufacturers. By 1930
the total labor force had dropped to 2,947, of whom 2,087 were black
and 856 were native-born whites.[5]

By 1900, lumbering had also become a major state industry. The
manufacture of lumber provided salaries for 9,273 people employed in
1,111 establishments, making it the state's second-largest manufacturing industry behind iron and steel. The industry produced lumber valued
at $8.5 million, an increase of 51.2 percent from the preceding decade.
By 1910, employment in the industry had risen to 25,927, or 31.1 percent
of all persons employed in manufacturing. In terms of value added by
fabrication and size of work force, the industry had temporarily become
Alabama's largest.[6]

Despite fluctuations in demand, lumbering remained a major employer
of poor people of both races. In 1929, forest products accounted for
nearly half of Alabama's 2,848 manufacturing establishments. Most
mills were small. Planing mills employed an average of only 14, sawmills
and turpentine operations an average of 20 to 30. Despite this modest

unit size, rapid expansion of the industry in the first two decades of the century brought employment to 30,000 by 1920, 28.7 percent of all manufacturing workers. After a sag in the early 1920s, the figure returned to 30,000 in 1929 before dropping to half that total by 1931. The number of mills declined from 1,141 in 1929 to 274 in 1933 and accounted for a substantial part of Alabama's unemployment. A survey in 1935 located 73 closed mills that had employed 8,088 employees during better times. Most of the dismissals, 6,188, had occurred in southwestern Alabama.[7]

Although the depression added special stress, lumbering was never a stable occupation. Like coal mining, the work was seasonal with frequent periods of unemployment. Also like mining, the industry experienced rapid labor turnover, making it difficult for companies to maintain a regular work force.

Like turpentining, lumber's labor force was a mixture of white and black, though whites almost always held the supervisory and skilled positions. As with coal mining, it was also a male-only occupation. In 1890, 1,163 of the sawmill operatives were black, 1,615 were native-born whites, and only 34 were foreign born. By 1910 the ratios had changed a bit, with whites constituting 1,250 of the 2,226 semiskilled sawmill workers and 4,729 of the 10,140 sawmill laborers.[8]

Many lumbermen were woefully unprepared for other occupations. In 1890, 1,040 of some 2,800 sawmill workers could neither read nor write. Child labor was common. In 1910, 293 of the 12,366 sawmill workers were age ten to thirteen. Ten years later the number of such children working in sawmills had increased more than 600 percent, to 1,773.[9]

Some lumber and turpentine companies dealt with the problem of recruiting and retaining labor in ingenious ways. Throughout the South in the years following Reconstruction, white industrialists devised methods to replace slavery with other forms of economic and legal compulsion. As U.S. Attorney Erastus J. Parsons explained in 1908: "The tendency of the legislative enactments of this State since the Reconstruction period has been uniformly, to weave about the ignorant laborer . . . a system of laws intended to keep him absolutely dependent upon the will of the employer and the land owner."[10]

To accomplish this task required a sympathetic political system. Because most laborers caught in the web spun by peonage were black, it won easy approval by the Alabama legislature. An 1885 Alabama law provided that a laborer who signed a contract and received an advance in money, intending fraud, then left the job without repaying the money, should be punished as if he had stolen the funds.

Obviously proving intent to defraud was not easy for prosecutors, so the legislature tightened the law in a series of acts passed in 1901, 1903, and 1907. The 1901 Alabama Labor Law stated that a person who abandoned a labor contract without informing his new employer of his previous obligation committed a penal offense. The 1903 law eliminated the need to prove intent to defraud; the act of leaving a job without repaying a monetary advance was prima facie evidence of intent to defraud. In 1907 the legislature spelled out the punishment: a laborer could be fined double the damage to a total of three hundred dollars. And Alabama's rule of evidence prohibited testimony from a laborer indicted under the law, making conviction virtually inevitable.[11]

In the early twentieth century, Alabama furnished America's most dramatic examples of peonage. Many of the worst cases originated in sawmill and turpentine camps and involved itinerant black laborers. But the abuse spread widely enough to entrap poor whites as well. Word quickly spread among local poor whites who were leery of the system of advanced payments with ensuing legal entanglements. But newly arrived immigrants were not so lucky.

Unscrupulous labor agents in northern cities gladly recruited desperate immigrants for Alabama's pine forests. So infamous did the system become that Congress in 1908 appointed a special Immigration Commission to investigate peonage, which was discovered in a variety of southern industries: farming, lumbering, logging, turpentine gathering, and railroad, mining, and construction work.[12]

The most publicized case of peonage in Alabama involved the Jackson Lumber Company at Lockhart, a small south Alabama community near the Florida border. Wisconsin and Michigan capitalists organized the company in 1903 as one of the largest mills in the South, controlling 150,000 acres of pine lands. The company built a town complete with churches and schools for its white and black employees. The poor of both races found employment that significantly improved their lives. The company enjoyed an excellent reputation until July 1906. In that month five German immigrants appeared in Pensacola, Florida, and related a harrowing tale of cruelty. More than a hundred laborers, most of them Italian, Hungarian, Bulgarian, German, and Russian Jewish immigrants, had been held against their will in a heavily guarded labor camp. Recruited in New York when they had arrived in America, the immigrants had been promised good wages and fair treatment. Instead they had been poorly fed, beaten, and held against their will. As they described it, they had been treated "worse than dogs" and had become "white slaves."

In the ensuing trial of Jackson Lumber Company officials, some native-white workers as well as the immigrants testified that they were forced to work twelve hours a day in violation of their contract and at less than stipulated wages. One supervisor caught a runaway Hungarian turpentine worker and threatened to kill him. Some company officials were found guilty and sentenced to eighteen-month prison sentences and three-thousand-dollar fines. Although prominent Alabama politicians successfully petitioned for a reduction of the sentences, many decent Alabama citizens were outraged at the abuses of poor people working in the lumber and turpentine industries. Their reaction to the revelations of peonage played a substantial role in Alabama's modest Progressive movement for political reform during the first two decades of the twentieth century.[13]

The industries also used convict labor to supplement contract immigrants and Negro and poor white workers. A mill run by the Stollenworck family in Butler County used convicts in the early 1890s. The L. L. Moore Mill at River Falls and the Flowers and Flowers Lumber Company at Bolling followed the same pattern. In 1903 all the convicts working at Flowers and Flowers were white. During the years 1910 to 1914, an average of 300 state convicts worked in sawmills and another 175 in turpentine camps. Many more county convicts sentenced to less than two-year terms found their way into the same system.[14]

Even for salaried free labor, sawmill towns afforded a drab and desperate existence. The payroll for W. T. Smith Lumber Company in January 1897 listed wages by skill. They ranged from a high of two dollars a day for the foreman, to one dollar a day for common labor, and thirty-five cents a day for water boys. One W. T. Smith employee earned eighty cents a day wages and paid forty cents per day board. The company town contained forty-four houses in 1900 that were listed as "two dollar houses, one dollar houses, and fifty cent shacks." The commissary advanced cash, charged a high markup over prevailing retail prices elsewhere, and the company paid in checks redeemable in merchandise. One such check stipulated: "Good only in merchandise at store of W. T. Smith Lumber Co., Chapman, Alabama."[15]

Work in the village was as dangerous as life in the forests. Accidents occurred frequently, a result usually of falling trees, steam boiler explosions, or carelessness around saws. One W. T. Smith employee claimed that hardly a week passed that a man was not killed. Even managers admitted that accident rates were high. Kaul Lumber Company in Tuscaloosa kept accurate records back to 1913 when it employed between four hundred and five hundred loggers. In 1913 the company recorded 124 accidents and in 1914, 150 more. Before Alabama's workman compensation law was enacted in January 1920, the employer assumed little responsibility for the safety of workers. Although some companies assessed employees a dollar a month for medical services, a logger disabled by an injury was usually left to fare the best he could.[16]

Such conditions fostered unionism in other regions of the South. In fact, one of the nation's most radical unions, the Industrial Workers of the World, gained a foothold among loggers in the east Texas–Louisiana forests. But except for isolated incidents, timber workers proved hard to organize. The Knights of Labor made some progress in the late nineteenth century at Brewton. Organizers tried to unionize the Harold Mill, but the owner, a German immigrant, promised to close the mill if his employees walked off their jobs. They struck anyway and he was as good as his word, closing the mill and putting two hundred men out of work. The manager of Tuscaloosa's Kaul Lumber Company noticed that employees were holding meetings behind one of his mills. He hired an undercover Pinkerton detective to attend a meeting, and the detective reported that an employee was trying to organize a union. The manager fired the lumberman, though company machinists joined a union later. The president of Kaul allowed the more skilled and essential machinists to organize, but he warned them that he was "still going to damn well run the company." The Knights did strike the Bear Creek Lumber Mill at Excel in 1900 and organized two locals at the Alger-Sullivan Lumber Company at Foshee, Alabama, in May 1901. The union contract revealed how modest were the demands of Alabama's working class. The one-year contract pledged no strikes or boycotts during the life of the agreement in return for the following wages: ox drivers, $1.25 per day; log sawyers, $1.10 per day plus board; common labor, $1.25 per day or $1.00 plus board; with all wages to be paid in "U.S. money" rather than scrip.[17]

Specific life histories provide elaborate detail about life in a sawmill camp and explain why workers were often unhappy. George Carter lived in a shanty seven miles west of Talladega Springs in east-central Alabama when he was interviewed in the late 1930s. A big man, six feet three inches tall and weighing 220 pounds, he had the ideal physique for a logger, an occupation he had followed for forty-two years. He had begun cutting timber in the 1890s at age twenty, working with a cross-cut saw from "sunup to sundown" for fifty cents a day. As a "boss logger" in the 1930s he had increased his daily wages to two dollars. Although he was contracted to work an eight-hour day, "I could count on my ten fingers how many times I got out of the woods fore good dark." Although Carter possessed no rigid Marxist sense of class distinction, he did harbor a bitter resentment against his bosses, whom he accused of religious hyprocrisy and greedy injustice:

One time I went to him 'bout my pay, an' he put on a mouth that was as pore as a widder woman. He says "George, you know I'm yore friend; I'd pay you more if I could. But my sales is 'way down. If I'm go'nter keep eatin' myself, I can't pay my help no more. It'd bust me, an' then we'd all be out in th' cold." Well, I ain't been to him since that day. He thinks I'm a damned fool, but I ain't blind. A man that's been lumbering as long as me knows a few things. I can look at th' stock in his sheds an' know that he was lying' with a face as bare as a baby's rump. I know what I cut in th' woods, an' I know how much lumber it'll make.[18]

Cecil Spencer began cutting timber in 1908 at the age of fifteen. Although he descended from Clay County farmers and tried to raise crops himself in 1912 and 1913, he began lumbering because it paid better. At fifteen he earned seventy-five cents per day by working eleven-hour shifts six days a week. He began in Clay County, pushing a cart loaded with timber, then graduated to a crosscut saw. Accidents were frequent in the forest, as men were hit by falling limbs and trees. In the mill, whirling saws maimed men. Spencer once saw six injured men brought out of the woods at one time, and in 1926 he lost a hand to a saw. The racial mix in the Clay County mill where he worked contained more blacks than whites.

In 1911 he left for west Florida and a better job. Like many poor whites, kinship provided mobility. A brother had preceded him to Florida and helped him obtain work. Up to that time, Spencer, though nineteen years old, had never been more than twenty-five miles from his east Alabama home. When he got off the train in Appalachicola, he had so many self-doubts that he contemplated walking three hundred miles back to Clay County. Although his wages increased in Florida, he never earned more than a $1.10 a day. The mill used oxen and mules to drag the logs to a railroad line, which was extended daily to keep pace with the loggers.

Life in mill town was hard. The company tried to prohibit whiskey in the camp and promptly fired drunks, but brawls were common. Ritualized fights occurred at the picnic grounds where men who had differences would go to resolve disputes with their fists. As Spencer phrased it, "if you couldn't tote your opponent they'd walk over you." Racial relations were often tense.

The company ran the sawmill town. It paid workers in scrip redeemable at the commissary. It constructed a church and paid the utilities and half the preacher's salary of twenty-five dollars. Although an astute judge of events, Spencer was apolitical, having no time or inclination for voting.

By 1926 loggers had cut 92,000 acres of pine forests around Milton, Florida, and Spencer left for a sawmill job near Tuscaloosa, Alabama. There he followed his trade until he was too old to work.[19]

Isaac Johnson labored in the turpentine forest along the Tombigbee

Cajan children in Mobile County, early twentieth century. (Courtesy of Alabama State Archives)

River in Washington County. He followed the trade of his father, who had cut timber and gathered turpentine before him. His father had done well at the trade, earning enough from the virgin timber to buy a forty-acre farm. Isaac, forced to live off second-growth trees, was not so lucky. He lived in a three-room pine cabin in a community ironically named Happy Hill. His cabin had no window panes in the 1930s, and the turpentine business was as depressed as the national economy, earning him only fourteen cents a gallon. Sawmills where he had once worked to supplement his income had closed down. He claimed Cajan descent from Spanish and Indian ancestors, but local whites believed Cajans contained Negro blood and treated him accordingly. He married a white woman of higher station who taught him to read and write. But local whites considered it an interracial marriage and ostracized them. His wife finally found work teaching at the Cajan school, where sympathetic county school officials believed she served ably.[20] Perhaps only in the isolated poor white world of turpentining could such a couple hope to be left alone. No doubt many of their neighbors dismissed such social iconoclasm as just another example of the degeneracy of lumber and turpentine folk.

SEVEN

"Barefoot Man at the Gate"

Iron Workers
and Appalachian
Farmers

Although the vast majority of poor whites labored away their lives in four occupations—in farm tenancy, textile mills, coal mines, and in the sawmill/turpentine/lumber industry—others found alternative ways of surviving. And occupational categories are misleading because many poor people moved easily back and forth between occupations without significantly improving their lives.

Reuben Farr became one of the early leaders of the Steel Workers Organizing Committee in 1936. His unit, Fairfield Local 1013, was the initial one established in the South. Its members elected Farr the first president and a district director of the United Steel Workers of America in 1942, a position he held until his retirement in 1966. But little in Farr's early years suggested his later success.

The boll weevil destroyed Farr's cotton crop and chased him off his small Shelby County farm in 1918. He moved north to Jefferson County and went to work for TCI in the ore mines. When the mines shut down a few weeks later, he began to truck farm. When local economic conditions made it impossible to sell his produce in 1928, he returned to TCI as third helper at the Fairfield open-hearth furnace, shoveling dolomite and cleaning the area in front of the furnace. Bosses were capricious at TCI. Supervisors might give him a raise and then take it away. They might hire someone at a lower wage to take his job. When he tried to organize a local of the Amalgamated Association of Iron, Steel and Tin Workers, the company fired him. Employees mistrusted supervisors and barely survived on low wages: if workers complained, their bosses would say, "Don't come back, there's a barefoot man at the gate waiting to be hired."[1]

Iron and Steel Workers

Farr's odyssey from farm to mine to steel mill was not unusual. Unlike most southern states, where the only alternative to sharecropping was the cotton mill or sawmill, Alabama furnished many industrial opportunities. On the whole, jobs in iron and steel making and the subsidiary industries they spawned (iron pipe shops, stove foundries, rolling mills, bridge and railroad car plants) demanded skilled workers and paid correspondingly higher salaries. But the same industries hired unskilled employees at wages similar to other low-wage extractive industries.

Alabama had a small antebellum iron industry that swelled to significant size during the Civil War but fell upon hard times after 1865. In 1880 the state had only 352 iron- and steelworkers. Growth was steady after that, reaching 7,234 in 1900, 19,165 in 1919, and peaking at more than 25,000 in 1925.[2] The industry was concentrated in the Birmingham district, an area centered in the city and extending for a radius of some sixty miles through Tuscaloosa, Walker, Etowah, Calhoun, St. Clair, Shelby, and Bibb counties. Several cities, notably Anniston and Gadsden, developed substantial iron and steel facilities of their own.

Although the technology of iron and steel production changed rapidly between 1880 and 1930, the process remained a complex industrial operation. Birmingham's chief advantage was the presence of coal, iron ore, limestone, and dolomite all within five miles of the city. This proximity reduced transportation costs and allowed Birmingham companies to produce the cheapest pig iron in the nation. It even undersold English pig iron in England. A secondary advantage was cheap labor due to the large number of impoverished black and white farmers in the state.

Disadvantages existed too, preventing the industry from realizing its full potential. Although much blame has been attributed to northern control of the industry after 1907, this was a late development and not a critical problem. Far more worrisome were the head start enjoyed by the Pittsburgh area, the absence of a technological community in the South capable of producing sufficient engineers and innovative equipment, and the isolation of markets for both labor and iron. Because the South provided few local markets, 90 percent of Birmingham's iron was shipped north or abroad during the 1880s and 1890s. Undercapitali-

Birmingham steel (Courtesy of Photographic Archives, University of South Alabama)

zation, overexpansion, keen competition, and problems in obtaining skilled machinists, engineers, and mechanics forced frequent mergers and consolidations and disrupted the industry.[3]

Iron and steel making, like textile work, involved many different jobs that demanded widely varying skills. Production involved three separate phases. Miners had to dig iron ore from the Red Mountain veins and haul it to mills where it was graded and crushed. From adjacent fields they brought coal that was reduced to coke in beehive-shaped ovens by heating it for several days without air. The resultant coke was almost pure carbon with high heating value.

Then iron ore and limestone used for flux were placed in the top of a blast furnace and coke was loaded into the bottom. The sustained heat produced a liquid runoff from the bottom of the furnace that was drained into small sand chambers. As the molten ore cooled the compartments formed it into "pigs" that could be shipped, refired, and shaped depending on the use.

Henderson Steel Company produced the first Birmingham steel in 1888, but lack of capital and quality controls hobbled the industry. High phosphorous content limited production processes to the basic open hearth with the Bessemer converter used as an auxiliary. Pig iron from a group of blast furnaces was conveyed in twenty-five-ton ladles to a metal mixer. The mixer weighed charges of pig iron exactly, then poured it into another ladle that ran on an elevated track into large converters. Heat was applied to the converter to eliminate all silicon, manganese, and carbon or leave a portion of the carbon. The metal then went to the open-hearth furnaces in a ladle from which it was poured by means of an overhead electric crane. Here heat was added to cause a rapid evolution of gases and a violent "kick" or reaction that often sent frothy slag and metal blowing out around the doors and ports of the furnace and temporarily suspending pouring. After tests for carbon and phosphorous content, the molten ore was poured into a ladle. The slag accompanying the liquid overflowed through a spout that diverted it into special slag cars. An electric crane then conveyed the ladle to ingot molds where the ladle emptied its load to cool.[4]

Obviously such a complicated process required a mixture of many labor skills. Unskilled men dug ore and coal, tended beehive ovens, loaded coke, tended slag, cleaned furnaces and hearths. These jobs absorbed most of the blacks and poor whites drifting into Birmingham, Anniston, or Gadsden from rural areas plus immigrants newly arrived from Europe. Virtually all the common labor jobs recruited males only.

By the beginning of the First World War, steel ranked second in value of all Alabama industrial products, pig iron third, and coal fourth. These industries, together with electricity and cotton textiles, accounted for well over half of Alabama's industrial production. By the early 1920s the state's workers produced nearly 7.5 percent of America's pig iron and 3.25 percent of its steel ingots.[5]

Within the industry, labor conditions followed familiar patterns. During periods of short labor supply and high demand, wages kept pace with those in other parts of the country. And skilled workers always fared better than unskilled. But for those newly arrived tenant farmers pouring off the farms, life could be grim in an iron furnace or steel mill. In 1893 the Shelby Iron Company paid machinists and carpenters a rate ranging from 90¢ to $2.50 per day. But furnacemen and yard workers earned a maximum of $1.50 a day, and those who screened ore received $1.25. This might be a luxurious wage to a sharecropper, but it barely covered family expenses in an iron-mill community. Most ironworkers fell into the unskilled category during the late nineteenth century. James W. Sloss, a pioneer Birmingham iron maker, estimated in 1883 that fewer than 10 percent of his ironworkers were skilled. The industry also leased large numbers of state convicts for its mines, and one stove foundry won a state contract for seventy-five convicts.[6] Attitudes toward workers ranged from condescension to bitter condemnation. One TCI official described the labor force as "shiftless, thriftless, sloppy and dirty." An outside observer called Birmingham's industrial population "floating and of a very undesirable sort."[7]

Work at a furnace was monotonous and hard, hours were long and wages low. As late as 1912 Alabama's blast furnaces generally ran twelve-hour shifts seven days a week with a double shift on Sundays, so that every other Sunday a man worked twenty-four hours. Obviously, not every man worked every shift and hours varied somewhat depending on skill. Common labor tended to work ten-hour shifts, and Sunday work was usually just enough to keep the furnaces operating. Whereas Pittsburgh steelworkers labored about the same number of hours, common labor there earned 17.5¢ an hour. Jones-Laughlin's common labor in Lackawanna, Pennsylvania, earned 15¢ an hour. TCI in Birmingham paid a double rate of 13.5 and 15¢ an hour. The lower rate went to the "poorer grade of labor" without distinction to race.[8]

Many iron and steel companies housed workers in company towns surrounding the plants. Although some of these, such as Corey (Fairfield), were considered model industrial communities, others rivaled Avondale for squalor and filth. One northern writer called the Sloss-Sheffield village in downtown Birmingham "an abomination of desolation." The community contained a slag dump at its rear, blast furnaces and beehive coke ovens for a front view, railroad tracks in the street, and "indecently built toilets in the back yards." Houses went unpainted, fences were tumbling down, and occasionally a board was missing from a house. He attributed the problems to a preliminary period of capitalism when operators invested almost all their capital in plants and mines and had little remaining to spend on amenities for the labor force.[9]

It is true that most Birmingham-area iron and steel facilities were underfunded until U.S. Steel bought out TCI during the 1907 panic. Newly arrived ironworkers rebelled the same way they had back on tenant farms: they moved. Unaccustomed to the steady work, unable to quit their labor occasionally in order to fish or hunt, rural-minded men often came to view industrial labor as a short-term palliative. They would leave their farms for a few months' work at a steel mill, then move on to another industrial job or back to the land. Their patterns of life were still essentially rural, where labor might be back-breaking for a season. But once they had "laid crops by" in August, they had ample time for camp meeting revivals, visiting relatives, or just resting. After they picked cotton in the fall, the routine of their lives relaxed considerably until the following spring when crops needed planting. Although they had plenty of work to do tending livestock, making baskets, clothes, and quilts, mending equipment, or other chores, they controlled the pace of their lives.

In a steel mill they had to arrive at a predetermined time, work all

day, week after week, month after month. Instead of the variety of farm
chores, their jobs in the plant became routine. They began to lay out,
partly due to the poor health they brought from the country and partly
due to the boredom and tediousness of work.

The result was an inefficient and unpredictable work force. In 1883
James W. Sloss had to put 509 men on his payroll in order to assure his
iron furnace of the 269 laborers he needed. When U.S. Steel sent George
Crawford to manage its TCI facility in 1908, he encountered a number
of problems but none more perplexing than labor instability. The facility
had a phenomenal annual turnover rate of 400 percent. Native-born
white employees worked an average of only 20.5 days per month. Labor
turnover and absenteeism became his greatest challenge as president
of TCI, one he resolved by introducing the most extensive system of
welfare capitalism in southern industry. It was precisely by tackling the
problems of poor workers of both races and substantially improving their
lives that Crawford made TCI an immensely profitable operation. His
social workers, teachers, and physicians reduced labor turnover from
400 percent in 1912 to 145.3 percent in 1919 and 57.4 percent in 1923.
Crawford explained his policies as a mixture of paternalism and self-
interest: it was "good business as well as good ethics to treat employees
as human beings."[10] Few Alabama industrialists were so enlightened.

Appalachian Subsistence Farmers

Many of these new iron- and steelworkers drifted
into Birmingham from the hill country. Remote
from the blazing furnaces of Fairfield, thousands of Appalachian people
lived in poverty more debilitating than ironworkers experienced. Locked
into isolated hollows or remote mountains across the northern third of
the state, they survived on a limited diet and a mostly barter economy.
Technically, they often appeared in census records as landowners. But
the land they owned was so unproductive and transportation so primitive
that commercial crops such as cotton were difficult. They made a living
primarily by growing small patches of corn, which they utilized in a
variety of ways. Fed to hogs, it furnished what little fresh meat they
ate. Milled into flour, it provided corn bread, a staple item in their diet.
Distilled into whiskey, it contributed their only source of cash income.

Isolation resulted in restricted educational opportunities. A woman
who spent months during the 1920s walking and camping in north
Alabama remembered a man in one mountain community who asked
for her newspaper. He explained: "I'm the onliest one that kin read in

this settlement, and whin I gits holt of a paper I reads hit to all the neighbors. I cain't read writin' though." The community had a school-house but no students: "Whut with the boll weevil and the childern hevin' ter work and all the likely young folks gone down ter the mill, thar hain't nobody ter go noways."[11]

Education represented the way that mountain people could transform their lives. Obtaining teachers, however, was no simple task for moun-tain schools. Generally they attracted them in two ways. Either they retained their own young people or attracted teacher-missionaries who came under the auspices of denominational agencies. Their own chil-dren better understood and posed less threat to mountain culture. The teacher-missionaries often tried to alter mountain ways to reflect their own more sophisticated values. But both groups realized that grinding poverty was their chief enemy, the local people because they were so often a product of poor white Appalachian culture, the outlanders be-cause poverty was so shocking compared to their own backgrounds.

Industrial work was only one way out of poverty and was reserved largely for men. Women had to find another way. Lillie Mae Beason and Mary Wigley both became schoolteachers as a first step that would lead them away from the sharecroppers' world in which they grew up. Beason borrowed money from an uncle and attended Jacksonville State Teach-ers College for nine months before taking her first teaching job in a two-room school at Poplar Springs. When she began teaching, she was as poor as the impoverished children she taught. She had no new shoes or dresses to wear, nor a single penny with which to purchase them. So her mother raided the family supply of dried peas, and with the money from their sale bought material to make her several dresses and a pair of flat shoes. She boarded with families in the community near the school and walked long distances just as her children did. The five-month school term paid her a munificent sixty dollars per month, a sum that seemed princely in the early 1920s in Appalachia. Years later she com-pleted a baccalaureate degree at The University of Alabama.[12]

Mary Wigley began her teaching career with even less preparation than Beason. By the age of sixteen she was firmly convinced "that the best way to fight poverty was to study hard and get an education." But obtaining schooling for sharecroppers was no easy task. It involved com-promises that required some children to double up work loads so that others could study. For the Wigleys it meant moving to a less desirable tenant farm in Geraldine, a community reputed to have the best schools on Sand Mountain. It involved hours of studying a test brochure for the state teachers exam. But finally Wigley obtained her teaching job, though she had not finished high school. After years of teaching high school–age children on Sand Mountain, she returned for her own senior year. At age thirty she looked like "a conspicuous antique," but the embarrassment of attending class with teenagers was lessened by her fierce desire to obtain education as a means of escaping her family's poverty.[13]

John C. Campbell, who later became a renowned expert on Appalachia, began his career teaching school at Joppa on Sand Mountain. When Campbell arrived in 1895, the Joppa community contained a dozen houses, a few stores where the trade consisted mainly of barter, a church "minus everything that a church should have—even windows," and a school building. His school opened with 185 pupils ranging in age from five to twenty-five, the students "poorly clothed and not all too clean but by no means lacking in intelligence." He described desperately poor girls walking miles to school, clad only in light clothes even in wintertime, without shoes, their bodies shivering from the cold. One by one the girls dropped out, one because she had to cut and pile brush, another because she had to plow. One of his brightest pupils lived on nothing but cornmeal and was too poor to buy oil for a lamp. She studied at night by the light from a pine-knot fire. One of the major chores that the Campbell family assumed was gathering and distributing clothes, coats, and shoes. On one day alone Grace Campbell was interrupted six times by poor mountain people seeking clothing and shoes. The recipients of this largesse insisted on paying what they could in farm produce, for they accepted no charity. The mountain diet was as deficient as their closets, consisting mainly of dishes derived from corn supplemented with eggs. Filth and disease were endemic. Girls in particular believed that education did them little good. One mountain girl explained why she was leaving school by noting that the best-educated boys all left Sand Mountain. If she stayed in school and remained on the mountain, she would have to marry someone without education who would support her. "I'm wanting things I can't have," she explained; "I'd better be left in my ignorance."[14]

Although Campbell contributed much to the poor children of Joppa and vicinity, he also brought the cultural condescension so detested by mountain people. Speaking in the North to raise money for his work, he tried to transport his audience to Joppa where it could "see much to offend the aesthetic sense—women dipping snuff, children unkempt and dirty, men clad in tattered garments, and all chewing tobacco. We now begin to have a stronger sympathy for Peter, the select Jew, in his first feeling toward the despised Gentiles."[15] Despite the condescension, Campbell's description of Sand Mountain's poverty was real enough.

Nor was the poverty isolated. Just north of Sand Mountain, where the high plateau descended sharply into the Tennessee Valley, Jackson County contained many poor mountain people. In 1923 Augusta B. Martin founded a church/school/welfare center at Sauta Bottom in a valley between July and Gunters mountains. She chose the site some eight miles from the county seat of Scottsboro because it was by local consensus "the most heathenest place in these parts." The surrounding community contained eighty farm families of which eighteen owned their farms, thirty-one were tenants, and an equal number were day laborers. The eighty families in 1938 owned seven automobiles, five radios, and two telephones. When Miss Martin arrived she initially acquired a deserted tenant shack to house her work. Utilizing volunteer local labor she built a story-and-a-half log house.[16] Then she began her work, sponsored by the Episcopal Diocese of Alabama.

Her first visit was to a remote cabin in Coon Hollow. She found a mother and her children dressed in rags who survived on roasted green ears of corn and fish. Her fourteen-year-old son had a badly infected foot. The youngest child was so thin that her shoulder blades protruded, and all the children were badly malnourished. The mission began to offer shelter to abused and orphaned children as well as education, and soon it was thriving. The first session opened with fifty-six children between the ages of five and twenty-one. During the first few years the mission was inundated with sick, poorly clothed, malnourished mountain people. Miss Martin found a woman in a shack only weeks from the end of her pregnancy, sleeping on sacks stuffed with straw and lying on planks across an old bedstead. The bed had no sheets and only three thin quilts for protection against the cold winter. On another occasion a mother of six summoned her to help a family of five who had wandered to her door with a desperately ill baby:

"The scene I found is indelibly impressed on my memory. It was in a dismal shack with its walls dark from the smoke of torches that had in times past been stuck in its cracks. A mother, with her emaciated, dying baby held close to her breast was rocking back and forth in a straight chair and sobbing aloud. On two filthy beds and on quilts on the floor, eleven human beings were lying, making thirteen in the small room. The only light came from a small oil lamp with a hole in one side and without a chimney. The odor in the room was suffocating as both door and the only window were closed. I immediately opened these and sent for Dr. Boyd although the baby looked beyond human help.

"It lingered until three the next morning. All night long, I sat moistening the parched lips of the baby which had been placed on a dirty pillow . . . in a chair. When the end came, the mother was so exhausted she fell asleep in a few minutes after I persuaded her to lie down by her husband on one of the unspeakable beds.

"Then I prepared the baby for burial and sat, the only one awake, in this room with twelve people and the little corpse until daylight."

The baby was buried in an ecumenical service. Miss Martin persuaded a Primitive Baptist neighbor to read the burial service from the Episcopal Prayer Book. She then found a farm for the wandering family.[17]

Such incidents were a regular occurrence. Talking with a mother and three children sick with typhoid fever, Miss Martin discovered that the family did not possess a teaspoon, glass, lamp, or wash pan. They slept on planks laid across a bedstead with sacks of straw for a mattress. The only utensil from which they could take medicine was the bottom of a bottle, which they had adapted by tying a kerosene string around the neck, setting the string afire, and then breaking off the neck. She acquired an orphan family consisting of one girl and three boys when their parents died of pneumonia within three weeks of each other. The four children had wandered for days without food except for walnuts they gathered in the woods; they had slept in barns or cowsheds. A mountain neighbor finally offered them temporary shelter until Miss Martin could travel the fifteen miles by buggy and three additional miles by foot after the road ended. But her normal prescription of "soap, soup, and salvation" failed the four urchins. One took a mule and tried to find relatives and another stole money from her purse while she played the organ in church.[18]

Most of the poor were far too proud and independent to cause such trouble. They insisted on paying for clothes and shoes with chickens, eggs, or firewood. Determined to maintain their self-respect, many of them found a source of revenue in moonshine whiskey made from their corn crop. It was much easier for mountain people to convert their corn into liquor and transport it in jugs tied to a rope and thrown across a mule than to haul corn over narrow mountain trails. Furthermore, they could sell the condensed product for five to six times what they could earn from corn. They believed they had a perfect right to sell home brew and had little respect for laws infringing upon traditional practices.

Appalachian folk brought great ingenuity to their whiskey making. Cold running water was an absolute necessity, so stills were constructed close to streams. Inaccessibility was another requirement. Beyond these two considerations, nature often determined construction. Caves or abandoned coal mines served well. Sometimes moonshiners used a pit concealed by a log shed or even bent saplings. A ravine or gulley afforded protection, as did a laurel thicket. A dry still away from water could be serviced by pipe running underground to the nearest stream on higher ground. Constantly moving the still also helped protect it from revenue agents.

After finding a good location the next step was constructing the furnace. A rock platform above the firebox kept the bottom of the still from coming into contact with the fire. The sides of the furnace touched the still at only one point to prevent scorching. The flue was important for maximum draw. Every part had to fit correctly to prevent leaking. One practitioner used three thin sheets of copper for the still, cap, cap arm that ran to a jug, and condenser walls. After construction, shiners would feed hardwood logs of oak or hickory into the firebox.

The simplest and one of the best stills heated fermented mash in the copper still. Then a copper arm conveyed the steam from the still to a copper worm that was coiled tightly to get the maximum length into a minimum space. The steam condensed into liquid while in the worm. Often the worm was placed inside a water barrel where cold water could be constantly circulated. The alcohol then flowed out the worm through the bottom of the barrel where it was strained through hickory coals and into a container. A slop arm attached to the still drained off the spent beer into another container. Using such a rig a shiner could make two gallons of excellent whiskey per bushel of corn, or a final yield of twelve gallons after proofing. Less qualitative operations could yield three hundred gallons per run.[19]

Although whiskey could be viewed as one element in the social disintegration of Appalachian institutions, that view seriously distorted its economic importance. Nor is the "Snuffy Smith" cartoon stereotype very useful. In many ways the struggle between moonshiner and revenuer operated at two levels. Economically, it was a battle waged by Appalachian people to preserve one of the few sources of cash income. Culturally, it was an attempt to preserve mountain ways in the face of American modernization. Mountain people viewed federal regulation of homemade whiskey as an intrusion of national authority into local patterns of life. Except for the Federalist era and the War of 1812, the United States government had not imposed taxes on distilled liquor. Then during the Civil War the federal government had enacted legislation requiring all distillers of whatever size to purchase licenses and pay taxes on each gallon they produced. Although modified after the war, the taxes remained. But in mountainous north Alabama, where cotton grew poorly and primitive roads made transportation difficult, subsistence farmers ignored the law. The same rugged terrain that isolated them from modernity shielded them from inquiring revenue agents and afforded free-flowing streams for good water. For poor Appalachian farmers, whiskey making was not a luxury to be taxed but an economic necessity, a vital link in the independence and survival of mountain traditions. They believed that taxes were designed to benefit large commercial distillers by driving the little producers from the market.[20]

Deputy marshals, revenue agents, and federal commissioners enforced the laws, which won little respect from local people. Moonshiners unlucky enough to be caught stood trial in Birmingham or Huntsville because no local jury would convict them. Sentences ranged from a month to three years in prison and minimum fines of one hundred dollars.[21]

In order to compensate for lack of local support, federal agents offered to pay persons who were willing to provide information on moonshiners. Also the pay of deputy marshals depended on a fee system; the more stills they seized and arrests they made, the more fees they earned. As a consequence the justice system was corrupted at both the local and federal levels. A federal grand jury in Birmingham in September 1893 heard 440 cases, most involving moonshining. Jurors concluded that deputy marshals and commissioners, eager to augment their salaries, fabricated many of the cases. The jury, in fact, indicted three deputy marshals and an equal number of commissioners. All six were convicted after a subsequent investigation by a Justice Department examiner that revealed widespread local corruption in north Alabama.[22]

Illicit whiskey making sometimes created profound tensions in poor white society. In the east Alabama hill counties of Cleburne and Cherokee, violence became common in 1893. The violence, known as "whitecapping," stemmed from conflicts between moonshiners and informers. Although local moonshiners viewed the issue as solely economic, as a struggle between poor white Appalachian people and commercial distillers, the violence actually occurred among poor whites divided into whiskey makers and informers.[23]

Frank Uptain carried on the moonshining tradition a generation later. Born in 1907 in mountainous northwestern Alabama, he followed an interesting cycle of careers as tenant farmer, deputy sheriff, and moonshiner. As a Marion County deputy sheriff for four years, he worked primarily finding and destroying stills. But later in Walker County he sold whiskey that his brother made in their still. The still on Black Water Creek produced about twelve gallons a week. Jim Uptain, his brother, made whiskey for fifteen or twenty years and was caught twice, serving a year and a day in Kilby Prison. Whiskey making began in the springtime after hunting season and before planting began. It was an ideal time. Hunters who might stumble onto the still had left the woods. Trees had begun to sprout, affording cover. And the income came in handy at a time when farmers badly needed capital for seed, fertilizer, and equipment. Frank Uptain paid forty dollars for five gallons of corn whiskey in 1941 and sold it for five dollars a pint, making a profit that greatly exceeded what he could earn on a farm. The Walker County sheriff offered to leave him alone in return for a bribe of a hundred dollars a month. Uptain, an unusually feisty farmer, replied: "I ain't paying you no hundred dollars a month. If you know so much about my business you go ahead and catch me and I'll pay off." Shortly the sheriff and his deputies descended on the Uptains' farm. They woke Uptain, who had just returned from a night of coon hunting, and announced that they had a warrant to search his place for whiskey. He wished them good luck, announcing that he surely needed a drink badly. They searched house and barn, then reported that they could find neither whiskey nor home brew. "Yeah, I got plenty a both of it," Uptain announced, but "I got it where you guys can't find it. I can go to it in a few minutes, but you'uns cain't." Despite all the sheriff's efforts, he never found Uptain's storage area deep beneath his stove wood pile.[24]

Far to the south along the Coosa River in east-central Alabama, Charley Ryland made his living the same way. Ryland had once worked as a coal miner in north Alabama and West Virginia, but after a mining mishap that cost him an eye, he moved back to his birthplace on the banks of the Coosa River. An illiterate whose wife was dead and his seven children grown, Ryland fished trotlines and made whiskey. His cabin contained little furniture: a zinc water bucket, a washpan and bar of cheap soap, a dilapidated cot, an ancient quilt, wood-burning stove, table and bench. When visited by an interviewer in the late 1930s, his pantry contained a sack of cornmeal and a bag of coffee. He subsisted mainly on corn bread and on catfish taken from the river.[25]

Jim Lauderdale lived near Ryland in the Talladega Springs community. But he was not so lucky as Frank Uptain. Relying on whiskey making for his living, he was caught and sent to Kilby Prison. By the 1930s he was a lonely seventy-six-year-old man deserted by his wife, filthy, his shoes held together with twine and his trousers ragged and unkempt. Desperately poor, he had "settled down t' wait fer the ol' man" (death).[26]

Another neighbor, Orrie Robinson, followed the same occupation as Ryland and Lauderdale. Illiterate, he lived in a shack with his father, mother, and two sisters during the 1930s. He made whiskey from his limited corn crop and subsisted on fish and cornmeal. He had never seen a movie and no one in the family could read. When asked if he was hungry, he replied: "Hungry?—Hell I'm allus hungry."[27]

If Ryland, Lauderdale, and Robinson represent the degradation into which the poor could sink, they are by no means typical, even of those whose economic woes they shared. Miss Martin, who met so many of the poor in Jackson County, described their dominant characteristic as independence. The mountain poor were individualists, "proud and clannish," shrewd traders with a skill refined by deprivation.[28]

Adventurer Eleanor De La Vergne Risley discovered a great deal of tension between mountain people who had gone to work in nearby mills and their kin and neighbors who had stayed behind. Mary Wigley Harper recorded the same emotion. Her poor neighbors on Sand Mountain rejected work in mills and factories located in towns surrounding the mountain. Even though they themselves were poor, they were inclined to pity people who left the mountain for work in cotton mills or steel and rubber plants as "the area's poorest families." Harper attributed this reluctance to leave the mountain to self-esteem and independence.[29]

But poverty little respected the pride of Alabama's white poor. It took a heavy toll on their resilience and self-respect.

PART THREE

Society, Culture, and Politics

EIGHT

"We Ain't Low-Down"

Poor White Society

Inadequate incomes resulted in poor diet, health, and housing and put tremendous stress on families. Despite occasional breakdowns, the poor white family proved remarkably resilient. Poor whites maintained their social institutions with a tenacity that confounds the stereotype of "poor white trash."

Such perseverance was not easy. At every turn the family encountered formidable obstacles. Lack of income damned poor whites to a sparse and unhealthy diet. They seldom lacked something to fill their stomachs or for calories and carbohydrates. But their foods were woefully deficient in certain key ingredients.

A 1940 survey of how a typical sharecropper spent a dollar revealed the problem. Of the sixty-five cents spent on food, twenty-four went for flour, eleven for lard, ten for meat, five for coffee, two for molasses, and thirteen for incidentals.[1] The vegetables and fruits available to rural people did not adequately supplement this diet; and among mill hands and miners, even greater deficiencies existed.

Occasionally poor whites experienced real hunger. Mitchell Garrett, a farmer in Clay County, remembered a sharecropper family who exhausted their supply of bacon, sorghum, and cornmeal. Unable to obtain further credit from their landlord, the family subsisted for two or three weeks on sweet potatoes. The children were potbellied and sometimes ate the "dry, red clay daubing that chinked the crevices in the rock chimney which stood outside the end of the house. They crumbled off small chunks of the dry clay with their fingers and allowed it to melt in their mouths like fudge."[2]

Even had the family Garrett described not run out of bacon, sorghum, and cornmeal, members would have been in serious trouble. Such a diet was typical among Alabama's poor because it was both cheap and tasty. Sharecropper M. B. Truitt described a diet consisting mainly of turnip greens, peas, collards, biscuits or corn bread, fried white meat, and

Pike County, Alabama, May 1939. A ten-year-old child of George Crowley, a rural rehabilitation client, was suffering from a diet deficiency (probably rickets), which caused her bones to break easily. One leg had been broken five times. Photo by Marion Post Wolcott. (Courtesy of Farm Security Administration Photographs, Library of Congress)

syrup. James H. Phillips, a coal miner, remembered strikes when the family survived on poke salad, turnip greens, and catfish caught in the Cahaba River. The fare of sharecropper Kathleen Knight consisted mainly of dried beans, cornmeal and white meat, supplemented by dried fruits sent by relatives. Mary Wigley remembered that fresh meat "was always scarce with the poor on the [Sand] Mountain, especially if cotton was the main crop."[3]

Health

Pellagra had thrived for a century among people with such a diet. First diagnosed in America in 1902, the early symptoms were hard to identify. The skin reddened as if the patient suffered from sunburn or poison oak. Then the skin crusted and peeled, leaving a smooth, glossy layer of tissue underneath. Symmetrical lesions appeared on hands, arms, feet and ankles, often crowned by a butterfly-shaped design across the nose. If untreated, the disease spread to the digestive tract, where it produced a general listlessness and malaise. Diarrhea or constipation, weakness, and a burning sensation often accompanied other symptoms. In severe cases, the disease affected mental processes, causing melancholy, depression, confusion, hallucination, a sense of persecution, and occasionally even suicide. The disease was often chronic and seasonal, appearing after Christmas and worsening during the spring, then abating during the summer and fall. It could be fatal and was often referred to as the disease of the four d's: diarrhea, dermatitis, dementia, and death.[4]

Physicians attributed pellagra to a variety of sources, including spoiled corn, germs, and bad sanitation. But Dr. Joseph Goldberger, a Jewish immigrant working for the Public Health Service, correctly proclaimed in June 1914 that the disease resulted from a diet of meat, meal, and molasses. To prevent it he recommended fresh meat, milk, and eggs. Not all southern physicians accepted his diagnosis. Dr. J. F. Yarborough, who had established a pellagra hospital at Columbia, Alabama, attacked Goldberger's theory in 1916 and proposed drugs for primary treatment.

By 1916 Goldberger had concluded that pellagra, diet, and southern poverty were intertwined. The food southerners needed for good health was simply not available to people with low incomes. In rural districts of Alabama, physicians reported not only high incidence of pellagra, but actual hunger. Conditions were especially bad in textile communities where fresh vegetables and meat were scarce and workers made too little to purchase them. As Goldberger observed of mill workers: "I doubt if they are any worse off in Belgium. Some day this will be realized and something done to correct it." Among his sample of South Carolina mill workers, he found fifty-one cases per thousand people, with two-thirds of the cases among children aged two to fifteen. Although the disease was less often fatal than he first believed, it was also considerably more widespread. He found a perfect inverse correlation of income to pellagra. Families with incomes of less than six dollars per adult male for a fifteen-day period experienced a disease rate of forty-three per thousand. The rate dropped steadily with each increase in income until it reached three and one-half cases per thousand in families with incomes of fourteen dollars or more. The smaller the income the scarcer the supplies of fresh meat, green vegetables, fresh fruit, eggs, butter, cheese, milk, lard, sugar, and canned foods. The lower the income, the greater the reliance on salt pork and cornmeal. Pellagra was rooted in economics. It was a "hard time" disease almost unique to the poor.[5]

This revelation infuriated prominent Alabamians who protested that their citizens were neither starving nor particularly poor. But time proved Goldberger right and made hollow the proud rhetoric of the state's leaders. In 1916, the states of Alabama, South and North Carolina, Tennessee, and Texas reported seventy thousand cases of pellagra.

When cotton prices soared in 1917–18, the rate of pellagra declined sharply, only to turn up again as the agricultural depression of the 1920s settled over the South. In the early 1920s Goldberger discovered that brewer's yeast cured the disease quickest and most cheaply. When the 1927 Mississippi River floods drowned livestock and ruined gardens, the Public Health Service rushed in tons of yeast, which briefly arrested the disease. But rates soared between 1927 and 1929 with several Delta counties experiencing more than one thousand cases. By June 1928, pellagra deaths had returned to the high levels of 1915. Mortality rates from the disease jumped 58 percent between 1924 and 1928.[6]

By the 1930s the disease had begun to decline. Researchers at the University of Wisconsin traced pellagra to a deficiency of nicotinic acid, one of the B-complex vitamins. Home Demonstration agents encouraged home gardens, and landowners allowed sharecroppers to plant vegetables on land withdrawn from production in order to meet federal crop reductions. New dietary habits in the 1940s and the use of flour and bread enriched with synthetic vitamins also contributed to the solution of the problem.[7]

In his 1910 presidential address, the president of the Alabama Medical Association recognized that pellagra was a primary issue confronting the state's citizens.[8] His concern was not misplaced. Between 1914 and 1917, the number of pellagra cases reported in Alabama doubled to 1,604 with 1,073 deaths. The increase was particularly dramatic among children and in textile mill villages. Although twenty cotton mills had hired nurses to try to stem the tide, fifty others had none.[9]

Kathleen Knight's father contracted pellagra in the Mississippi Delta. His case worsened after the 1927 flood but improved when he began to take dried yeast three times a day. The family shipped dried fruit and even collard greens through the mail from north Alabama. But hard times caused his symptoms to reappear. When the New Deal began agricultural changes designed to reduce cotton acreage, his landlord allowed the family to plant corn and vegetables. But in 1934 or 1935 his physician advised him to move back to Alabama to cure his pellagra. The poverty of Orrie Robinson's family living alongside the Coosa River in Talladega County resulted in his sister's contracting pellagra.[10]

Like the rest of the southern states, Alabama made rapid progress against the disease during the 1930s. Dr. Tom D. Spies, who while growing up on a Texas farm had watched farm laborers die of pellagra, experimented with nicotinic acid to treat indigents at Hillman Hospital in Birmingham. At the House of Happiness in Jackson County, missionaries distributed a curious but effective combination of canned salmon and yeast. Home Demonstration agents from Auburn played a major role in dietary change. They emphasized foods rich in vitamins and nutritional value. The House of Happiness utilized Alma Bentley, the local Home Demonstration agent, to conduct cooking schools in rural areas of Jackson County. An agent in Shelby County plunged into the work, sending back to Auburn disparaging reports about what she found in rural households: half-cooked pork, overcooked cabbage, cobblers, hoecakes, and fermented syrup.[11]

Persuading people to eat more raw carrots, yeast, and canned salmon and less molasses, corn bread, and white meat was not entirely an exercise in economics. Long after Alabama's poor whites gained more land to plant fresh vegetables and sufficient cash to purchase nutritious foods, pellagra tenaciously held on, though in greatly reduced numbers. Gradually the state's poor found other foods that appealed to them, and the change in taste together with economic improvements cured one of the South's most enervating diseases.

Although pellagra was probably the most perplexing poor folks' disease, hookworm was the most widely debilitating. Hookworm resulted from two widespread deficiencies of rural life: lack of shoes and unsanitary outdoor toilets.

The hookworm usually entered its victim's body through the skin between the toes, causing an irritation that rural people in the nineteenth century called "ground itch." The bloodstream carried the parasite to the lungs, where it entered the alveoli. From there it continued its journey up the bronchial passage into the throat, where it was swallowed into the gastrointestinal tract. Fastened onto the lining of the small intestine, it feasted on the host's blood. The female could lay as many as ten thousand eggs a day, most of which exited the body with the victim's feces to begin the cycle again. The South's climate perfectly suited the hookworm, which thrived in warm, moist, sandy or loamy soils. The infestation usually resulted in too little loss of blood to produce external signs; but in extreme cases hookworm resulted in severe anemia, especially among poor people with inadequate diets. Blacks built up tolerance to the disease, which affected poor whites worst. Symptoms included anemia, pale skin, indigestion, weakness, shortness of breath, mental slowness, and muscle weakness. Because the disease often caused a slow gait, sallow complexion, and lack of energy, the public stereotyped poor whites in terms closely related to the symptoms of the disease: yellow skinned, shiftless, and lazy.[12]

Physicians long associated another dietary peculiarity of the South, clay eating, with hookworm, but recent research does not support this linkage. The propensity to eat certain clays, described by Mitchell Garrett among white sharecroppers in Clay County, was real enough. Poor whites and blacks did seek out and eat certain clays. In this practice they had companions on every continent as far back in history as 300

B.C., when Aristotle described the practice. It was historically most common among pregnant women because of its ability to reduce nausea. In some parts of Africa 30 to 50 percent of pregnant women consumed clay. Slaves brought the practice to America, where it became extensive among poor whites as well. Gradually the admonitions of physicians and the social stigma of upper and middle class opinion reduced the incidence among poor whites. However, the most recent research into geophagy, or the consumption of soils, indicates that certain sour-tasting clays may supply minerals otherwise deficient in local diets, fight nausea, indigestion, and diarrhea, and even counter ingested poisons. One expert believes that normal consumption of southern clay neither benefited nor harmed its users. Debate about the phenomenon continues, including recently at a 1986 symposium at the annual meeting of the American Association for the Advancement of Science.[13]

Charles W. Stiles was to hookworm what Joseph Goldberger was to pellagra: chief diagnostician and publicist. As chief of the Division of Zoology, Hygienic Laboratory, in Washington, D.C., Dr. Stiles operated from a position of considerable prominence and respect. In 1903 Stiles addressed the Medical Association of Alabama and delivered a blunt warning about hookworm. He announced that his findings indicated that hookworm occurred mainly in rural sections in sandy soil, that whites appeared to be more severely infected than blacks, and that symptoms were more severe in summer than in winter. He also linked the disease to pica, the technical name for a craving for inedible substances common among people suffering from iron-deficiency anemia. Stiles obviously communicated the urgency of his message. In 1910 the president of the association noted that hookworm was second only to tuberculosis as a menace to public health, infecting as many as 35 percent of those examined in Alabama. Hookworm was prevalent in at least sixty-three of the state's sixty-seven counties.[14]

Medical surveys confirmed the extent of infestation. Based on an intensive study of North Carolina, experts estimated in 1911 that as many as 7.5 million people in nine southern states might be victims of the disease. By the end of 1914 specialists had examined nearly 550,000 children between the ages of six and eighteen; 216,828 were found to be infected, 39 percent of the total. When elements of the Alabama National Guard were sent to the Mexican border just before the First World War, 60 percent were discovered to have hookworm. An additional survey by Stiles revealed the cause. Some 50 percent of the 250,680 homes inspected contained no privies of any sort. Only about 10,000 possessed outhouses that met Stiles's minimum standards.[15]

The physician interested northern philanthropists in the problem, resulting in the establishment of the Rockefeller Sanitary Commission for the Eradication of Hookworm Disease. The commission performed herculean duty in testing and treating hookworm patients. Public schools became the primary battleground where tens of thousands were tested and treated. But long after the commission closed its doors, declaring that "hookworm disease has almost disappeared from the United States," Stiles found in the 1930s a rate of infection varying from 26 to 49 percent.[16] Part of the problem was the low level of funding for public health that was typical of all southern states. Entrenched political elites kept taxes low, preventing adequate funding of public health programs for the poor who otherwise could not afford them. Paradoxically, the federal government and northern philanthropists did far more to aid poor Alabamians than their middle and upper class neighbors. In 1910 the state appropriated only $16,982 for all public health programs. By 1918 the figure had increased to $26,200. But $19,700 of that amount went for administrative salaries. That same year the Alabama legislature, obviously more concerned about sick livestock than sick people, appropriated $28,000 for the prevention of hog cholera, $25,000 for eradication of cattle ticks, and a total of $83,000 for disease prevention in animals.[17]

But even a legislature filled with statesmen, not a common occurrence in Alabama's political history, could not have solved the problem entirely. Like so many other problems associated with poverty, hookworm was as deeply rooted in culture as in economics. Proud Alabamians deeply resented the allegations that hookworm disease was epidemic in the state. Too proud to acknowledge the disease, they boasted of the state's virile manhood and fine physical specimens, neither of which greatly impressed the lowly hookworm. They resented the tests, which seemed demeaning. The only effective diagnosis involved inspection of the victim's feces. Independent, often shy poor whites, already the brunt of jokes about incest and clay eating, deeply resented this further intrusion into their privacy. And if the tests proved positive, it only emphasized their poverty, their inability to provide shoes for their children or outdoor toilets. In one remote mountain community whites refused to allow their children to be tested. So an ingenious community nurse offered the children bribes, one piece of stick candy for each feces specimen and another if they took their medicine. Children who scarcely tasted candy even at Christmas pressured their parents, who sometimes claimed that the nurse was trying to poison their children. But the nurse finally triumphed when she provided a picnic with ice cream for all children in the first three grades who upon reexamination were free of hookworm.[18]

But eradication, as Charles Stiles noted in 1933, was not the end of the problem. So long as poverty remained, so long as parents could not afford shoes or sanitary outdoor privies, the infection would recur. The real solution waited for economic well-being. The Flynt family had their first outdoor privy in 1919 when they moved to the Downing place at Shady Glen in Calhoun County. By then high cotton prices and education concerning public health combined to make sanitary toilets a reasonable possibility for them.[19]

Whatever the debilitating effects of hookworm, at least it took few lives. But it did so weaken its victims that they became ill with more dangerous diseases, such as pneumonia. Poorly constructed houses and inadequate clothing made pneumonia a deadly matter. The House of Happiness took in a family of four children orphaned when their parents died within three weeks of each other from the disease. Miss Martin, who managed the facility in Jackson County, called pneumonia "the scourge of Sauta Bottom."[20]

Typhoid fever also plagued poor whites in Jackson County. Like hookworm, typhoid resulted from unsanitary toilets that allowed the family's drinking water to become contaminated. The spatial arrangement of Alabama's farm buildings did not provide for health considerations. The haphazard arrangement of well, privy, and animal pens allowed animal or human wastes to drain into wells. One Home Demonstration agent in Shelby County reported in 1926 that of the six farmhouses she visited on a tour, only three had toilets and they had cow pens and pigpens only fifteen to twenty feet from the houses. About this same time a typhoid epidemic among white sharecroppers in north Alabama took 3 lives. In 1913 Alabama public health officials reported 565 deaths from typhoid fever.[21]

That same year 435 Alabamians died from malaria. Because so much of the housing for poor people lacked screened windows, malaria-carrying mosquitoes also posed a menace.[22] The work force at TCI coal camps and steel mills reported 8,000 cases of malaria in 1912. But thanks to vigorous measures by Dr. Lloyd Noland, employed by George Crawford to improve health and reduce absenteeism and labor turnover, malaria cases declined dramatically to only 370 in 1913.[23]

Tuberculosis posed the greatest threat to life of all diseases that afflicted the poor. The president of the state medical association called it Alabama's greatest health menace in 1910. In 1916, the state reported 2,898 cases of tuberculosis with 2,526 deaths, or a mortality rate of nearly 90 percent. Although the disease touched all classes, it was particularly virulent among the poor. The House of Happiness staff saw many cases among poor whites in Jackson County and could offer little help except cots so that the patients did not have to sleep with uninfected family members. The missionaries provided nourishing food and whatever medicine a doctor prescribed. Poor families could pay physicians as money became available. But unless some agency such as the House of Happiness provided medicine, they had no recourse. Finally in 1912, Jefferson County established a tuberculosis camp; but other counties lacked even this facility.[24]

A variety of additional diseases, too many to mention, plagued poor whites. Of 47,867 Alabama draftees examined by local draft boards in 1918, 11,498 were rejected because of disease or physical defects. Most were minor and preventable by proper hygiene, diet, and care. Although poor people could ignore many ailments, others demanded attention and almost always precipitated a family crisis. When Carlie Crocker's daughter contracted diphtheria she borrowed a car to carry the daughter to a physician. Unfortunately, the doctor did not look in her mouth because she started to cry, and two days later the child died. As a twelve-year-old boy, James H. Flynt contracted osteomyelitis when he stepped on a nail. When the disease began to kill the bone, the family was able to get a doctor to visit their home, paying over time with produce or precious cash. During the year he was out of school, family friends used their cars to drive him into nearby Anniston for treatment.[25]

Occupational diseases added to poor white miseries. Unfortunately two occupations that employed large numbers of poor whites, cotton textiles and coal mining, also contained substantial health risks. Breathing coal dust in dry mines caused black particles to adhere to the lungs. Textile mills provided a hazard in the form of brown lung, the result of breathing cotton particles that swirled and floated among the looms and spindles. The cacophonous noise also posed a serious threat to ear drums and many a mill worker retired with seriously impaired hearing.[26]

Without financial resources to purchase modern medical care or drugs, or too remote and isolated to reach them, poor people sought alternative remedies. Poor whites handed down from generation to generation a variety of herbs and remedies, borrowed from Indians and Africans or discovered by themselves, to cure what ailed them. Some had proven medicinal properties; many were mere superstitions without basis in fact. Frank Uptain claimed he could remove warts by paying a penny and taking them away. He could cure thrush by taking twigs from three different white oak trees, peeling the bark off, and running it through the baby's mouth while reciting a secret incantation. To stop bleeding he rubbed blood on a stick and pushed it into the ground, vowing that the bleeding would stop by the time the stick was buried. Lillie Mae Beason remembered her mother's applying onion poultices for flu and pneumonia and catnip tea for stomachache. Carlie Crocker recalled her mother's trying to cure chicken pox by putting the children under the chicken house door and letting the chickens fly out over them. Mrs. Sam Anderson explained that she dipped snuff because it would prevent hookworm. Orrie Robinson regretted that he had not killed the rattlesnake that bit his sister, thereby destroying some of the poison in her system. But at least he had known to cut open a hen and stick her hand inside to draw off the poison. Her arm had swelled to nearly double its normal size, but she had survived. So valuable were certain herbs, roots, and barks that Mary Wigley's brother made good spending money gathering them in the forests of Sand Mountain and selling them to be concocted into medicines.[27]

Although some of the cures sound worse than the ailments, they were not inferior to the level of rural medical care. Carter Priest's father was a farmer and country doctor outside Guntersville in northeast Alabama. He could and did set bones, but most of his additional arsenal of remedies consisted of herbs.[28] At least herbs and superstitions filled the void. Without money or transportation, poor people had no real alternative. The herbs and roots allowed them to do something even if it was not very much. They felt less helpless, more in control of their fate.

The next stage of health care, as financial resources became more accessible or old remedies were forgotten, consisted of cheap patent medicines. Their chief advantage was that the poor could obtain them without visiting a doctor who might conduct an embarrassing examination or charge more than they could pay. Ila Hendrix used two basic remedies for her children's troubles: castor oil on the inside and Vick's Salve on the outside. Annie Flynt used Black Draught and calomel as purgatives to treat malaria and diphtheria. William D. Nixon's country store at Merrellton in Calhoun County dispensed a variety of patent medicines to its mainly tenant clientele: "Dr. King's New Discovery" for "coughs, colds, and all throat and lung afflictions," "Dr. M. A. Simmons Liver Medicine," "Tutt's Pills," "Wine of Cardui," epsom salts, and "Vermifuge."

Turpentine and castor oil constituted one-third of all medicines found in one poor isolated community in north Alabama. Vick's Salve and Black Draught were the favorite patent medicines.[29]

Not until 1879 did the state provide for public health. In that year the legislature appropriated three thousand dollars to employ a state health officer. By 1883 eleven counties had employed county health officers, but their main concern was epidemic diseases, such as yellow fever, that threatened an entire community. The Medical Association of Alabama became the State Board of Health and each county society constituted a local branch.[30] Not until the twentieth century did these agencies devote much time, money, or effort to the unique health problems of the poor.

The most extensive attempt to provide medical care for workers actually came from a private corporation rather than from the state. George

Crawford created an effective system of health care for his employees at TCI. In fact, the system was the centerpiece in his company welfare system. TCI's medical division, directed by Dr. Lloyd Noland, employed thirty-five physicians in 1915 and had forty-six plus a dozen dentists by 1926. Employees could use physicians, dispensaries, or Lloyd Noland Hospital by participating in a voluntary payroll deduction of 75¢ per month ($1.25 by the 1930s). But the program was costly to the company. In 1916 it cost $213,000, of which employee fees covered only $130,000. TCI subsidized the difference of $83,500. By 1938 the company share still amounted to $43,500, and TCI began to phase out the program as public health care filled the vacuum.[31]

Most poor people found ways to obtain medical care and adequate food. But for the elderly sick without family to care for them, the orphaned, the mentally retarded, or the physically incapacitated and neglected, poverty held special horrors.

State programs of relief for the poor between Reconstruction and the First World War consisted of two parts. "Outdoor relief" provided a small monthly allowance to paupers who remained at home. "Indoor relief" amounted to Alabama's traditional state provision for the dispossessed indigent: domicile in a poorhouse or "almshouse." Of Alabama's sixty-seven counties, fifty-eight contained poorhouses in 1918. The counties usually leased the houses to private individuals who provided for inmates for a stipulated sum per person. The counties received bids, then granted a lease to the lowest bidder, not necessarily the best way to guarantee quality care. Typical appropriations per person during the 1870s and 1880s ranged from four to eight dollars a month. By the First World War the range had increased to between seven and twelve dollars. Infrequently did the keeper of a poorhouse receive a fixed salary. Because of the high risk of abuse inherent in such a lease system, county grand juries frequently inspected poorhouses, and the physicians who served as county health officers also conducted reviews. Once a county established a poorhouse it usually refused any other form of public relief. Although rural facilities housed between five and fifty paupers, Birmingham's house might care for hundreds.

No matter how frequent the inspections, abuses occurred. When the legislature finally got around to requiring annual state inspection, the first annual report in 1909 was unemotional, understated, and devastating:

> In many cases the Board of County Commissioners let the paupers out to the lowest bidder, and in the majority of instances these bids are very low and insufficient for the proper care and attention of these unfortunates. The majority of the paupers of our state are

either mentally unbalanced, or physically disabled, and it is necessary that they at all times have more or less attention, and with the low bid at which they are taken, it is impossible to give them this, hence they get very little attention, and in many cases actually suffer.

In many cases I am impressed with the idea that the alms houses are maintained for the purpose of having a place of banishment, so to speak, a quiet secluded spot to carry those unfortunates to die.[32]

A 1912 exposé on the Jefferson County almshouse at Ketona described conditions in greater detail. Because Hillman Hospital, the only public facility that accepted charity patients, did not take contagious and infectious cases, they went to Ketona. The so-called county pest house accepted smallpox cases; but often those incapable of obtaining care there because of crowding wound up at the almshouse. The building at Ketona was a rambling wooden structure, "a veritable tinder box." Rotten boards, creaking planks, and unpainted buildings demonstrated years of neglect. During the summer of 1911 the county appropriated one hundred dollars a month for medical care for seventy-one inmates. Of the seventy-one persons housed there, seven—including two white men and one white woman—had tuberculosis. Apparently their poverty or mental condition kept them out of the new Jefferson County anti-tuberculosis facility. None of the patients were confined to their beds and no one seemed responsible for their care. A jail included in the almshouse contained four "imbecile men and women who had committed the crime of being poor." The toilet consisted of a crude seat without either wooden frame or cover. Water used to flush it was turned on occasionally from the hall. A stench permeated the area. Bed covers were old and dirty and were thrown on the floor in a corner when not in use.[33]

In 1910 the 739 inhabitants of Alabama's almshouses were almost evenly divided between white and black.[34] Amazingly, a white society that tolerated virtually no race mixing except in brothels placed black and white indigents into the same facilities. Perhaps such an act reflected better than any other the prevailing apathy toward the welfare of poor whites.

By 1923 Alabama had fifty-five almshouses that cared for an average of nine hundred people. The state spent less per inmate than any other studied in a national survey that year, even less than poor sister states such as Mississippi, Kentucky, and Tennessee. Nationwide, care per inhabitant averaged $334.64; Alabama averaged $187.53 per inmate during 1923. The survey described Alabama's almshouses: "The buildings are usually one or more dilapidated frame shacks, inflammable, fireplaces, stoves, oil lamps, privies, well water, no sewerage, sanitary conditions filthy and dangerous."[35]

Another 1920s report described the almshouses as poorly managed, slovenly kept, and in deplorable physical condition. Few had adequate sanitary facilities or electricity. Unpainted buildings in rural areas, inaccessible except for rutted dirt roads, isolated poorhouses from the public. Bedridden patients suffered from neglect, and few inmates engaged in any constructive or healthy work.[36]

Alabama's almshouses began to disappear during the 1930s. Desire for more humane treatment contributed to their demise, as did public assistance provided by the 1935 Social Security Act. The Alabama Relief Administration, established in 1933, permitted public relief other than institutionalization and was a major step forward. The Alabama Department of Public Welfare, organized in August 1935, made care of the poor a state as well as a county responsibility, thus evening out care between affluent and poor counties. Between November 1935 and August 1936, thirty-one houses were closed. By February 1941, only nine were left, and by 1951 only two remained.[37]

Careful analysis of the inmates of such houses provides one of the best insights to life at the very bottom of Alabama society. In 1880 the Calhoun County poorhouse contained six white residents. Mary Howard and Jicy Burnett, ages forty and fifty-five, were listed as idiotic and illiterate. Cynthia Still, age sixty-five, could not read. Jefferson Wilkinson, a twenty-five-year-old male, was listed as idiotic. James L. Johnson, age thirty-six, crippled and bedridden, was listed as a pauper. Sylvanus Stokes, age eighty-seven, was an illiterate farm laborer. According to the young couple who managed the 120-acre Butler County poorhouse in Greenville from 1921 until 1936, most residents were whites. Many were mentally retarded or elderly. The saddest inmate was an elderly retarded white man, Dave Majors, who occasionally hitchhiked to visit relatives. During one such trip, a school bus passed and the children began to shout and call him names. He threw a rock at the bus, breaking a window. Terrified, he hurried to his relatives, where the superintendent of the almshouse found him hiding. He interceded with school officials to keep the old man out of trouble and to prevent a recurrence of the juvenile harassment.[38]

During 1885 the Jefferson County poorhouse admitted thirty-two blacks and forty-two whites. The reasons for admission of whites fell into seven categories: four were paupers, one was insane, three females were pregnant, three had syphilis, and seventeen were admitted because of illness; eleven were children admitted with a parent because no one was available to care for them; and one was an alcoholic. The social condition varied as well. Two women were prostitutes. One was the pregnant wife of a convict. Another was indigent with typhoid fever. The prognosis for the inmates was not good: nine ran away; one died; six were transferred, most to the insane hospital in Tuscaloosa; fourteen were discharged without indication of recovery; and five recovered their health. The pattern in subsequent years remained essentially the same. The great majority admitted to the poorhouse were paupers or sick. Many were children of patients with nowhere else to go. The total admitted and the numbers of whites increased dramatically: in 1888, of 222 admissions, 83 were white; in 1889, there were 288 admissions, 104 white; in 1890, of 337 admissions, 176 were white; in 1905, there were 369 admissions, 149 white; in 1906, of 443 admissions, 133 were white.[39]

The Mobile County poorhouse differed both in size and nationality of inmates. In 1890 nine of its thirteen white admittees were immigrants; six were born in Ireland and the other three in England, Scotland, and Sweden. In 1906, twenty-one of fifty-four indigents admitted were white. Of the twenty-one whites entering that year, seven died in the poorhouse, four were transferred to the insane asylum in Tuscaloosa, two were transferred to hospitals, and eight left of their own accord. In 1913 the number of admissions (fifty-four) and the ratio of whites (twenty-four) remained relatively stable.[40]

When the almshouses were phased out during the 1930s, information about departing inhabitants provided another profile. Of the total population of almshouses in 1935, 1,413 or 67.5 percent were white, about the same distribution as the state's population. Most (909) had living relatives, but of the 504 with none, 255 were whites. More than 61 percent were over the age of sixty-five. The state spent $14.65 per resident each month. Only twenty-three had completed high school; 42.3 percent had never attended school at all. The median education was first grade. Only nine had any income at all, and 62.1 percent had serious physical handicaps.[41]

It is no wonder that the word "almshouse" could inspire terror in poor whites. Ketona, site of Jefferson County's poorhouse, was a place avoided and seldom mentioned. The place name came to mean not a suburb in northeastern Birmingham, but a place where indigents disappeared into oblivion. Only the most calamitous set of circumstances—illiteracy, indigence, illness, and lack of family—brought one to such a destination.

Short-term illness could bring unfortunates to the poorhouse, but by 1900 charity hospitals had opened in some cities. Birmingham had two: Hillman, a public facility, and St. Vincent's, a Roman Catholic institution founded in 1901. St. Vincent's contained two charity wards, one to accommodate eighty-six whites, the other for twenty-two blacks. Overflow patients slept on cots in the halls. Some mining companies and railroads paid for beds for their workers, and the Brick Layers' Union supported one bed. The city appropriated money for five charity patients, but the wards usually contained ten or twelve. The charity wards for both races at Hillman and St. Vincent's usually overflowed.[42]

Lack of provision for the poor may be attributed partly to the low income of the state's entire population and its lack of economic resources. But the state legislature usually found money for what it considered important. In 1910 legislators appropriated $25,000 for public health care in Alabama. But it appropriated $500,000 for relief of needy Confederate veterans and their widows. The only eligibility requirement was that a veteran must not own property worth more than $2,000. In addition the state provided a Soldier's Home at Mountain Creek for indigent veterans and their wives or widows so they would not become wards of their families or inhabitants of an almshouse.[43] If any of the hundreds of thousands of destitute poor whites inhabiting the state read of that legislation, they must have marveled that people with nearly $2,000 in property required assistance from the state.

Housing

Diet, health, and housing were closely related and determined largely by the extent of poverty. The earliest folk housing in Alabama consisted of log structures similar to those found in southern Pennsylvania, Maryland, and Virginia. Dirt floors were common, as were log pens used as kitchens. As the frontier receded, a second stage of log houses appeared that included some common features regardless of design. They used foundation piers that raised the house floor from six inches to as much as two or three feet off the ground. Two square hewn sills extended across the longer sides of the house. Log floor joists hewn flat on top provided support. A gable roof with its ridge parallel to the sills covered the dwelling. A gable side chimney was attached to the center of an outside wall. Early basic houses consisted of four types: single-pen, double-pen, dogtrot, and saddlebag. The single-pen was an oblong-shaped house of about twenty-one feet in length. A frame addition created a double-pen. The dogtrot provided two oblong rooms often of different sizes, frequently with a loft over one or both and joined by a roof and open space or "dog run" between the two sections. It was characterized by its great width, often fifty or so feet. The saddlebag house was distinguished by a chimney located in the middle of the house rather than on the ends. Building materials varied. In most areas folk builders used hewn, notched logs, but in north Alabama fieldstones were piled up while clearing fields and were used for house construction.[44]

Windows lacked screens but had shutters to keep out inclement weather. Fireplaces provided heat, and nearby wells, springs, or creeks afforded water. A haphazard assortment of outbuildings—barns, smokehouses, chicken coops, and pigpens—surrounded the house. With luck, the front yard would contain an oak tree for shade. Meticulous housekeepers would sweep the hard-packed dirt yard with a straw broom.

Log cabins had a certain rustic charm, a connectedness to a celebrated pioneer past, that made some Alabamians nostalgic, though there is slight evidence that the people who lived in them ever eulogized the dwellings. Home Demonstration agent Mary Wigley formed a "log house club" on Sand Mountain; only log house dwellers could join. But the club died for lack of participation. One of the staff at the House of Happiness described Jackson County's log cabins:

> No other dwelling ever fit so well into the wooded coves and hills of our mountain country. There is a charm about the cabin that few other homes possess. . . . When spring plants, daffodils beside its grey walls, and peach blooms hide the dark hued cedars, there is a charm about it that few homes in any region have. They fit into their hillsides so well that often your eye is drawn to them only by the smoke from a broad chimney, or by a line of gaily colored quilts spread out to air and sun on the railings of the fence. The spinning wheel is usually on the porch where suspended from the rafters are pepper "burney" beans and ears of seed corn and the saddle hangs from a peg on the wall. Through the open door you can see the beds with their bright colored quilts and the large fireplace where a fire smolders, even in summer. The little straight-back chairs with their woven hickery [sic] bottoms give the home a quaint and old-time atmosphere, as charming as it is simple.[45]

As portable saw mills invaded formerly inaccessible coves, board houses replaced log cabins. And even the romantic observers in the House of Happiness recognized other kinds of folk housing: "dilapidated two room shack with lean-to kitchen" containing "one small window with a wooden shutter." When William Warren, a St. Clair County coal miner, married, he and his bride lived with his father until they could finish building a one-room shack just above the coal mine where he worked. Washington County turpentiner Isaac Johnson lived in a three-room pineboard cabin without window panes. Tenant farmer "Bull" Elliott, his wife, and six children inhabited two rooms and a lean-to near Lowndesboro. Henry Kelly lived in a pine shack near the Coosa River. Sharecropper Kathleen Knight disliked her family's simple four-room frame house in the Mississippi Delta, where the hard water made it difficult to wash clothes or hair, and the soil they called "gumbo" climbed up their shoes in a sticky goo when it rained. Compared to such lodging, even the simple housing of a coal camp or textile village was an improvement.[46]

One feature of the new industrial housing was the presence of persons other than the nuclear family. In one sample from Birmingham, a quarter of newlywed families had relatives living with them. Later as children were born, poor families augmented family income by taking in boarders or contributing relatives. W. W. Jewell's mother and father were able to stay in their mill-town house after they retired by feeding and sleeping boarders, a service the textile mill encouraged.[47]

Family Life

Taking in boarders was just one example of the multiple challenges posed by industrialization to the traditional family. As factories and mills pulled poor white families off the land, they increased pressures. Prostitution, alcohol abuse, and crime did not begin in towns and cities, but crowding thousands of people into cramped quarters and subjecting them to economic cycles that often threw them out of work certainly added to the problems. Montgomery Episcopal priest Edgar Gardner Murphy feared that "the industrial readjustment of a population moving from the conditions of agriculture to the conditions of manufacture must bear with severity upon every form and aspect of family life." Birmingham newspapers shared Mr. Murphy's concern and featured frequent articles deploring crime, prostitution, and drunkenness and extolling the virtues of stable family life. So great was middle class concern that Birmingham created a city welfare department to handle "the family problem."[48]

Most of this concern was unnecessary. The poor white family weathered industrialism and urbanization as well as it had rural poverty, which is not to say that all was well in the family. But at least the casualties were light, and poor white society proved amazingly resilient.

The family cycle began with the rearing of children. Most poor white families believed in strict discipline. Reinforced by religious teachings that frowned upon dancing, using alcoholic beverages, mixed bathing, movies, and gambling, most parents raised their children to obey their elders and to shun frivolity. June W. Odom grew up as an only child in a strict Church of Christ cotton mill family in Cordova. Her father did not permit her to dance or attend movies. As she explained simply, "I was raised rather strictly." Most of her friends were raised the same way, though she recalled that Methodist and Baptist neighbors were a bit more lenient than her parents. Obviously her early training had its effect. When she left Cordova for Birmingham, she became so homesick that she began commuting. Finally she settled permanently in Cordova.[49]

Odom's family had few opportunities for recreation other than church socials, which also formed the sole recreation of coal-mine widow Ila Hendrix. Late summer revivals and camp meetings afforded welcome relief from a summer's labor. Although other families also found social outlets in the church, rural congregations met infrequently and sponsored few social or educational programs. So the farm folk found other outlets. They fished and hunted, placing great stress on their prowess at each. They made white-oak fish baskets to catch catfish migrating up the banks of creeks swollen by spring rains, or strung trotlines across rivers. They maintained the antebellum folk tradition of marksmanship, describing how they "barked off" squirrels. Shooting the small animal scurrying about high in a tree was little challenge. So they prided themselves on hitting the bark or limb underneath, or shooting the creature through the eye so as to leave the meat and skin untouched.[50] Nor were hunting and fishing merely recreational. Game added precious protein to their diet.

Children especially looked forward to the holidays. Rural folk often made elaborate Halloween and Thanksgiving displays. Even when Christmas brought only a single orange, apple, or homemade toy, it was a time of closeness and joy for children if not always to their hard-pressed parents.[51]

The Odom family's aversion to dancing was not universal among poor whites. The House of Happiness sponsored a dance each Friday night that was attended by 150 Jackson County youth who danced to "Devil's Hiccup," "Hell After Yearlin'," "Who Bit the Tater," "Shoot the Buffalo," or "Alabama Gals." Carl Forrester remembered square dances that featured music by local fiddlers. A mountain fiddling contest and dance provided Yankee schoolteacher Carl Carmer one of his most vivid memories of Alabama folk culture.[52]

Lillie Mae Beason remembered how her mother preferred making toys or playing with her children to housework. She whittled toys and made wagons and sleds.[53]

In mining camps and mill villages, dances and movies supplemented the social life afforded by churches. Most communities also had a town baseball team in which everyone took pride. Sunday afternoons brought most of the community together to watch ball games between their team and nearby rivals.[54]

As battery-powered radios became available, some poor families invested precious economic resources in order to reduce their isolation. What later generations would take for granted seemed a miracle to hard-pressed Alabamians. In 1975 Carlie Crocker remembered vividly the event that half a century earlier had enriched the lives of her share-cropper family:

> Well, the first radio we ever got, my husband was still living and it was a battery radio. And we had to be so careful just to listen at it at certain times and it only cost about nineteen dollars and some-thin'. We paid three dollars down and about two dollars a month, and . . . our neighbors called us rich folks cause we'se the only [ones] in the community that had a radio and every Saturday night we'd have company to listen at the Grand Ole Opry; boxing come on . . . Joe Lewis, I believe it was Joe Lewis, somebody, I forgot who . . . but anyhow they'd come to hear the boxing match.[55]

Carl Forrester also managed to squeeze enough earnings from his sharecropping to buy his family a battery-powered radio during 1937 or 1938. As with Crocker, every detail remained vivid.[56]

Like most poor families, the Forresters tried to make work into a pleasant family gathering whenever possible. Several families would assemble before a wintertime fire to shell peanuts. While the men went to the woods to cut stove wood, women and children would shell peanuts. They made candy, using the family's store of homemade syrup. Children would have contests to see who could shell the most peanuts in an evening.[57]

But not all work could be made pleasant, and childhood ended early on tenant farms. Virtually all children who grew up on such a farm remembered hard labor in the fields as soon as they were able to wield a hoe or pick a cotton boll.[58]

Parents carried the same notions off the farm and into industrial towns. They needed the wages children brought in to supplement mea-ger adult wages. They saw no great value in education beyond functional literacy. And they believed that children should earn their own way in the world as soon as they could. As much as reformers in their own time and historians afterward blamed callous owners and heartless su-perintendents for child labor, the hard truth is that many poor whites were as much to blame as exploitive capitalists. Frequently sons of coal miners went to work with their fathers so they could claim a second truck on which to load coal. Even some men who moved up to foreman or managed tiny mines of their own urged their eleven- and twelve-year-old sons into the mine as soon as they were big enough.[59]

Early twentieth-century Alabama reformers who determined to elimi-nate child labor in the state's textile mills encountered fierce opposition from parents. Poor whites feared the loss of wages but also resented the way compulsory school attendance laws meddled with their children's lives. When Mrs. John Van Vorst conducted an intensive survey of north Alabama cotton mills, she found many examples. At an Alabama City mill a small girl explained why she did not attend school: "my momma don't want me to go." Parents of an eleven-year-old had encouraged their sons to work in the mills and had been able to save money to buy their own home. One parent had encouraged her eleven-year-old daughter to work in the mill to earn her own Christmas money. Several ten-year-olds worked in the mills because they disliked school and their parents allowed them to drop out. The widow of a sheriff sent her two children into the mills as soon as they were able to work because she had no other means of support. Mrs. Van Vorst interviewed a girl with a large bruise over her forehead where she said a boy had hit her with a rock. She refused to allow the injury to keep her from school because of fear that her stepmother would make her return to a job in the mill. Her parents believed that at age eleven she was old enough to earn her own way. Mrs. Van Vorst concluded that child labor thrived in Alabama because of the greed of manufacturers and the ignorance of parents.[60]

Child labor reformer Rev. Edgar Gardner Murphy agreed. Alabama had constructed an industrial system that appealed to "the greed of idle parents." When Mr. Murphy began his crusade to abolish child labor in Alabama by attacking the avarice of some northern-owned mills, the treasurer of Alabama City Mills, one of the worst offenders, sent him a copy of a letter to the superintendent of spinning that instructed him not to employ children under age twelve. But such a policy would cost much of his labor force because parents insisted that their children work to supplement family income. If the mill did not hire their children, parents would leave for other mills that would employ them.[61]

Much of this rebuttal can be dismissed as self-serving rationalization. Had the mills paid a decent wage, women and children could have remained home. Factories and mills incorporated the "family wage" into southern industrialization, then blamed parents for insisting that children must work. But much evidence demonstrates how little parents cared. When Irene M. Ashby-Macfayden drafted a bill to limit child labor, opponents presented a petition against the bill signed by seventeen operatives at Montgomery's Alabama Cordage Company. A clergyman from a Lanett mill church explained to Mr. Murphy that members of his flock "were distressed at the idea of a law which should prevent them and their children from earning their living in the cotton mill" and "entreated him with tears" to oppose the bill at public hearings.[62]

In the industrial city of Birmingham children of working-class parents were more likely to be employed than their mothers. Sending children to work early seems to have been at least partly an alternative to their mother's employment. Whether because many males believed their wives should not work or because the high birth rate required women to stay home with babies and small children, the fact remains that children were significant sources of income.[63]

Few children could work twelve-hour days in field or factory and still obtain an education. So children grew to adulthood unable to read or write. While Alabamians boasted about attracting new industry and jobs after 1880, they seldom emphasized their leadership in another category, illiteracy. In 1880, 25 percent of native-born whites aged ten and older were unable to write. By 1890 the rate had declined slightly to 18.84 percent (17.47 percent for white males, 20.19 for females), which was still the fourth-highest rate in the United States. At the turn of the century 103,570 Alabama whites aged ten years and older (14.8 percent) were illiterate. And the state's standing had slipped further; only South Carolina and Louisiana stood beneath Alabama. Despite intensive efforts during the next two decades, Alabama's white illiteracy rate remained at 6.4 percent in 1920. The state sponsored a careful study in 1914 that helped launch a major reform effort. Predictably, white illiteracy was least prevalent in the wealthy Black Belt and highest in the areas of greatest white poverty, the Wiregrass and mountainous north Alabama.[64]

Where schools existed in rural areas, they were often remote from sharecroppers' cabins. Tales told by children of walking miles to school were true. And when they arrived, the schools were taught by poorly paid teachers not much older than many of them and in some cases not much better educated. Of 4,570 rural Alabama schools for whites in 1913, 3,401 were one-teacher rural schools where grades one through twelve were taught by the same person. Only 277 of the state's public schools had three or more teachers.[65] In cities where decent schools existed and children could easily attend them, they cost too much. One Birmingham ironworker complained in 1883 that there were three grades in the school his child attended. The school charged $1.00 in grade one, $1.50 in grade two, and $2.00 in the third grade. A working man with five or six children could not afford to educate them, perhaps explaining why the illiteracy rate among whites was so high in 1890.[66]

Poor children thus entered adolescence with two substantial disadvantages. They were expected by society and often by their parents to begin earning their own living; and they had little education to prepare them for such a task. It is no wonder that children already working long hours and earning an income should have accelerated dating, courtship, and marriage. They had already given up many of the functions of childhood and assumed a number of adult roles. Assuming one more

Opelika Cotton Mill, October 1914. "Whistle blows noon, Opelika Cotton Mill . . . girl is Velma Smith, a tiny little spinner with a steady job all day. I found her at home crying bitterly because her father refused to let her have any money out of the pay envelope she brought home. Mother said: 'That haint no way to encourage children to work.' Mother, father, and several children work. Her mother admitted she worked here before 12 years old, and at Ellawhite Mill and one other city for about a year. Says they have no family record, but claims Velma is 12 now (which is doubtful)."—Lewis Hine. (Courtesy of Lewis Hine Photographic Collection, Library of Congress)

Old schoolhouse, Gum Springs District, Clay County, Alabama, built about 1892; one room, 20 by 30 feet. (Courtesy of Alabama State Archives)

responsibility that made them independent of their parents and satisfied sexual urges as well seemed logical enough.

Parents usually supervised females more closely than males. When foundry worker Homer Flynt, then in his 30s, began to court Annie Phoebe·Owens, who was ten years younger, the young couple had great difficulty finding privacy. Mr. Owens had eighteen children, ten by his first wife before her death and eight by his second. The children pestered them "till they didn't have a place to sit and talk." Because the couple was older, their courtship did not last long. But Annie had lived a sheltered life. After they borrowed a horse and buggy to drive to their wedding, Homer waited until they turned a bend in the road out of sight of the Owens clan, then reached over to kiss his fiancée. She "slapped him good and hard" to remind him of proper conduct until they were officially married.[67]

June Odom and her textile-worker girl friends experienced the same strict supervision. They were not allowed to date until they were sixteen or seventeen, although "there was a little slipping around." When they began to date, boys understood that they were supposed to leave at a specified time, "and it had to be completely moral and everything on the up and up." Her parents established an eleven o'clock curfew except for very special occasions, and she "never in my life gave my parents any trouble whatsoever about anything like that." On Saturday she would attend Cordova's single movie theater. Beyond that or an occasional trip to the swimming pool at nearby Jasper, dating consisted of hayrides, box suppers, or races.[68]

Textile worker W. W. Jewell, who had been quite wild in his early years, played the field, dating four other girls while courting his future wife. She pressured him to stop dating the others, and he proposed one rainy night at the Barnum and Ringling Brothers Circus. After she accepted, they dated another year and a half because she was so young. When Jewell went to get the marriage license, his fiancée's father found out and lied to courthouse officials that his fifteen-year-old daughter was too young to consent. Jewell, furious because his beloved was actually sixteen, picked her up the next Saturday and with a friend drove to Leesburg, Georgia, where they were married by a justice of the peace. "Her mother didn't like it a bit, but her daddy didn't say anything."[69]

L. A. House, a logger–textile loom fixer in Sylacauga, tried a different strategy with his daughters. A very strict father, he would admonish them as they left on dates: "Remember, your good name is all you have."[70]

Parental disapproval was a frequent occurrence, especially among parents of daughters. Often the dislike was rooted in a feeling that a boy was not good enough. Although the Owens family was not wealthy, they resented Homer Flynt because he was an outsider from Georgia and a foundry worker. As one of their grandchildren remembered: "You know the Owens always had an air . . . and we felt it all our lives, that they were just a little bit over and above and higher than we were and had a little more." When Dera Bledsoe began dating an uneducated coal miner who was much older and a widower with three children, her father was outraged. She was a schoolteacher, her father a justice of the peace, a prominent member of the Birmingham Chamber of Commerce, and influential in local politics. He judged all miners by the ones who had appeared in his court and "looked down on the laboring class." When he discovered that she was dating a miner he raged: "I won't stand idly by and let my daughter keep company with one of that crowd, let alone marry one of 'em. I forbid you even to see him again, and if he keeps on seeing you after what I've just said—well, I guess there's nothing left but to shoot him, and damned if I won't do it." The young couple married anyway.[71]

Although men often married in their twenties, girls usually married earlier. Among a selection of poor whites—three from sharecropper families, two from coal miners, and three with textile parents—the average age of marriage for the brides was fifteen compared to nineteen and a half for the grooms. Fairly typical was the family of Pauline Brewer, an Opelika textile worker who had three children. Alice married at thirteen, Sue at sixteen, Ricky at nearly twenty-one. As women recounted their ages, they often expressed a tinge of regret at the loss of childhood. Mrs. L. A. House, recalling her marriage at fourteen, reminisced: "Married real young. Been married all my life." Carlie Crocker, although the oldest of the eight in the sample when she married at seventeen, regretted her timing: "I'se seventeen years old; just a child. And I think we had three dollars in money."[72]

Middle class reformers attempted to change the structure of poor white families in a variety of ways, including compulsory education and the prohibition of child labor. But none of the reforms better revealed how extensive and personal their reforms were than efforts to reshape marriage patterns. The female staff of the House of Happiness attempted to dissuade mountain girls from early marriages. But even among the poor such unions were often considered calamitous, and many parents warned against them. A soulful ballad that circulated in Jackson County and later entered mainstream American culture proclaimed:

"Seven long years I've been married,
Wishing to live an old maid.
My husband is drinking and gambling.
I'd ruther be in my grave.

Chorus
"Beautiful, beautiful brown eyes,
Beautiful, beautiful brown eyes,
Beautiful, beautiful brown eyes,
I'll never love blue eyes again.

"Get up early in the morning
Working and toiling all day,
Supper to cook in the evening
And dishes to clear away.

"Off to the bar he goes staggering
Bring him back if you can,
A girl never knows her troubles
Until she marries a man."[73]

The ballad reflected how quickly reality dulled the romance of poor white marriages. Sex was a mystery for some, a challenge for others. But when sex so frequently resulted in the birth of a child, it posed serious problems regardless. Among twenty-three poor white families I surveyed, they averaged 8.41 children each.[74] During one year in the mid 1930s a survey team in a mountain community carefully recorded births. During that year, a child was born to every eighth landowning family, to one of every four white tenant families, and to one of every three white sharecropper families.[75] On farms where children's labor was essential, such large families could be an asset. But in mill villages and mines, children had to continue to work if the family was to survive. Children cost money to raise, whether to provide food, schoolbooks, or Christmas gifts. The costs may be seen in a single set of contrasting examples. Twelve Birmingham-area mining families without children estimated that they spent an average of $472.36 annually on living expenses; eight miners with one child estimated their expenditures at $598.58. Yet the average annual incomes of the miners with children was only $21.06 higher than the income of miners without children.[76] The average landowning Alabama farmer spent $54 to bring a child into the world in 1940; the average Alabama tenant spent $26 to reproduce his own.[77]

Few families could afford the services of physicians, so birthing children was largely a natural process attended by a neighbor woman or a midwife. When delivery time approached, Annie Flynt would sew newspapers between sheets made from feed and fertilizer sacks and gather old blankets and clean rags. Another sharecropper, Carlie Crocker, could not afford a doctor except in a life-or-death crisis: "We never did bother to call one. Most of my [twelve] children come along with no doctor nowhere about. It cost fifteen dollars to get a doctor out to our house and [we had] no money, so we just toughed it out."[78]

The initial source of such a problem was simple. Although many poor whites knew a great deal about sex, they understood little about human anatomy or birth control. Sex education came neither from parents nor preachers; as with most Americans in these times and later, they learned about sex from peers and experience. Lillie Mae Flynt Beason remembered that her parents "never told us about the birds and bees. . . . Never—there wasn't ever a word said about it." She and her two sisters and five brothers grew up innocently on their remote farms. Until the older children were about ten they swam together in a creek near their house without the luxury of bathing suits or any other clothes. But a neighbor lady ended their recreation by instructing their mother: "Now you shouldn't let the girls and boys go swimming together. They've been up too large." Lillie Mae resented the intrusion of someone else's child-rearing notions into the Flynt family:

Well we hadn't thought a thing about getting too large to swim. . . .
Well she told Mama, Mama told me, since being the oldest one . . .
I said, "what does Miss Ida know about letting the girls and boys play together in the water?" I couldn't see any harm in it, and Mama

didn't either, but Miss Ida did. . . . She was a dignified, little some-body without children of her own. . . . 'Course, she could help Mama, tell [her] how to raise 'em."[79]

Unlike most white tenant families, the Flynts summoned a doctor when Annie delivered. She usually farmed out the children to neighbors until the baby was born. But when the girls were a bit older, she let them stay home while she gave birth. Lillie Mae and Ora waited with keen anticipation while their mother prepared the sheets and bedding. When the time arrived, their faces were pasted to the window as a dignified-looking man with a black bag arrived, driving the first auto-mobile they had seen: "And when he got out of that [car] with that little black bag, we knew he was bringing the baby. . . . We just had it in our minds. . . . We had it all figured out. We hadn't been told anything."[80]

Coal miner John Gates prospered for a time, bought a house, and enrolled his son at Howard College. But a tornado destroyed his house, and the unplanned birth of a daughter interrupted his son's education. Julia Rhodes married at fifteen and had her first baby a year later. When interviewed in 1938 she had eight children ranging in age from a small baby to a nineteen-year-old son. Some poor whites, like farmer–coal miner Sam Cash who lived near Mentone, understood how to practice birth control but opposed it on religious grounds. He believed that large families, like hard times, were simply God's will. But most poor whites neglected birth control more out of custom and ignorance than because of religious scruples.[81]

Lack of knowledge about sex had tragic results for the son of an Alabama tenant farmer who became a labor organizer and jack-of-all-trades. He quit cotton mill work when he was seventeen and wound up working at Coney Island, where he met and married the Roman Catholic daughter of a Pennsylvania coal miner. Trouble began when he moved to California to take a job, leaving his bride behind. When she finally joined him, she insisted on separate beds. His interpretation of these events became a justification for his own violence:

> I didn't like that; I believe a man and his wife should sleep in the same bed. But she wouldn't have it, and she wouldn't have any sex either. The truth was she was afraid she'd get pregnant and it'd hurt her business [as a beautician]. She didn't want to spoil her figure either. She didn't know anything about birth control and I didn't either at the time. Well things got worse and worse and we was scrappin' all the time and finally we had a break-up.
>
> She moved downstairs in the same buildin'— . . . and I stayed upstairs. It was bad. Because of my religious trainin' I felt that I shouldn't step out on her. . . . Even if she wouldn't be a wife to me

I felt I couldn't go back on my vows I'd made in church. Well I couldn't satisfy myself and I'd nearly go crazy. Some nights I'd just go out of my head and I'd go downstairs and beat on her door beggin' her to let me in. One night I just had to break her door right in and we had a big fight. I don't mean I exactly beat her up—I was just wild—and you might say I raped my own wife, just took it away from her.

Unluckily, shortly after that night, she announced she was pregnant. Well there was nothin' for it but to have it out, so she took fifty dollars I gave her and went to a doctor and had—what do you call it?—yeah, an abortion. From that time things grew worse and worse and I finally decided we couldn't live together. So I divorced her and came back East.

He remarried, this time a nineteen-year-old Alabama tenant farmer's daughter "and our first baby . . . was born in the shortest period of time which could elapse between marriage and havin' a child." He went back into the cotton mills and they had a second daughter. But "this was three and a half years after the first one. I'd learned somethin' about birth control, y'see."[82]

Although often ignorant about birth control, poor whites were not entirely ignorant about sex. Sam Cash's oldest son disgraced his family by seducing a fifteen-year-old neighbor girl, then refusing to marry her when she became pregnant. The girl committed suicide and, according to the code of honor among mountain people, her relatives shot and killed the boy. Orrie Robinson received a varied education from a prostitute who got him drunk and took what little money he had. W. W. Jewell earned his own way in a textile mill when he was seventeen: "I went where I wanted to and done what I wanted to." His father let him keep five dollars a week from his earnings in the mill, but he did not use the money wisely: "I started drinking and running around with women when I was seventeen years old, and I spent all my five dollars after I had gotten me up a bunch of clothes on whiskey and women. I always said houses and lots [slang for whorehouses and lots of whiskey]." The textile town of Albany, Georgia, where he began his mill work, had a prostitution district of twenty-five houses with five to ten women in each. Located four or five miles from the mill village where he worked, it was surrounded by black housing. All the prostitutes were white and his favorite was a Jewish girl. The regular price for a girl was three dollars:

It was just according to how busy they was . . . that weekend. Now, if you had a regular one, if she wasn't busy, well you could just go over there anytime you liked. And you know, in all that time, now

*Avondale Mills, November 1910. " 'Hell's Half Acre,' a row of disreputable
houses at the edge of the mill settlement at Avondale. These houses harbor the
scum of the negroes and whites of the vicinity, and are separated from the
mill village by a shallow ditch, which gave Governor Comer, owner of the
mills, the excuse that they were not on the mill property when the question of
their removal was taken to him a while ago. A prominent social worker told
me that not only do the mill people patronize these resorts, but that the
broken down mill girls end up in these houses."—Lewis Hine. (Courtesy of
Lewis Hine Photographic Collection, Library of Congress)*

they had a country doctor that went over there and checked them
every . . . week, and all the times I went over there I never heard
tell of any gonorrhea or syphilis over there at all.

When Jewell moved to Opelika to begin mill work, he

liked to went nuts, I'm telling you: I missed everything over there
in Albany cause when I moved over here, they drug in the sidewalks
when the sun went down. And over there, seven days a week, night
or day, you could go find somebody to talk with. And over here they
just wasn't nothing, and I would have liked to blowed my mind,
but I toughed it out.

In fact, Jewell did more than tough it out. He courted and married a
woman with strong ethical standards, was "saved," became a devoted
Bible reader, and settled down.[83]

Mrs. W. W. Jewell was a religious woman like so many wives of poor whites. And like them, she had a mind of her own. Although weak and dependent women existed too, many poor white females defined their roles in surprising ways. Most seemed to reserve certain parts of their lives beyond the domain of their fathers or husbands, realms of religion or child rearing or housekeeping where they were sovereign and tolerated no interference. Occasionally southern poor white society produced its own variety of feminist.

Sex roles were not clearly defined in poor white society, but most families were surprisingly Victorian, at least in the theory of women's roles. The primary function of a female was to be a wife and mother. The more time she could spend in these roles, the better. Mary Wigley never remembered seeing her father cook, wash a dish or garment, sew a button, use a flat iron, or clean the house: "Things like that were out of his sphere, as with most other male heads of mountain homes." Conversely, her mother did not work in the fields unless absolutely necessary, although female children usually did so. Male heads of working-class families in Birmingham allowed or even encouraged their children to work, but they preferred that their wives stay home to take care of house and children. The *Labor Advocate*, unionism's official voice in Birmingham, editorialized at the turn of the century that female labor should be ended "so as not to injure the motherhood and family life of a nation." When asked if there were advocates of women's liberation in the textile community of Cordova, June Odom replied, "No, not back then. The women's place was considered to be in the home at that time, primarily and strictly." Her own mother cared for the house and the children until June was old enough for school, then worked in the mill, but only for several years in order to help the family through hard times.[84]

But few poor white families could afford division of responsibilities based on such perceptions of what was proper. Everyone had to work, and none worked harder than a farmer's wife on a tenant farm. Carlie Crocker spaced twelve children around house chores that included canning vegetables, sewing and knitting clothes, and a wash day without any conveniences:

you rubbed 'em on a rub board and boiled 'em in the pot. You'd build you a fire around that, the old metal pot, . . . we called it the black pot. You'd build your fire and heat your water, dip some out and put in the tub so it make good suds and you had a rub board, a wash board, you'd call it and . . . use that lye soap, rub it on them clothes and rub 'em and then put 'em in that pot and boil 'em and you had the purtiest white clothes and they smelled so good to hang 'em out in the sunshine.[85]

A heavy flat iron wielded with authority assured that country women had strong muscles in at least one arm. As if housework and child rearing were not demanding enough, most poor white women took their turn beside their man and children in the fields, especially when the fast-growing weeds required constant hoeing or when cotton had to be picked. Lillie Mae Beason marveled at her mother's ability to bear eight children and still work in the fields:

> She never missed a time. I don't know how she ever managed it with all of us with birthdays all the way through the year. But she was there [in the fields]. She taught us how to work. . . . And she'd have the pallet under the shadow of the tree . . . and she'd work until 10:00 in the morning . . . and then she'd go in to cook the meal. And . . . she had all the things to do, like water, the gathering of the food out of the field and out of the garden, and preparing it to use it. 'Cause she'd work the night before till it was dark. . . . It was just a full day every day. And we had cows that had to be milked . . . in the mornings, and she did that.[86]

When women tried to work in towns the major problem was child care. Few mills or factories provided either kindergartens or day-care nurseries. So mothers left babies with other children or with relatives who lived with them. Pauline Brewer separated from her husband just before her first daughter was born. She missed only a month of work at an Opelika textile mill before returning to work while her sister kept the baby. The House of Happiness staff in Jackson County decided the best service they could render poor working mothers was to establish a kindergarten and day-care center. In Birmingham, middle class reformers established the Committee for the Study and Prevention of Infant Mortality. The organization rented a seven-room cottage and hired a nurse to provide milk and child care to babies of mothers working in nearby cracker and biscuit factories.[87]

Despite whatever theoretical reservations they might have had about their wives working, many poor white males accepted all the help they could get. Mrs. Joseph Davis and Mrs. Issac Johnson used their educations to good advantage, teaching their illiterate husbands to read and write, then later earning the family income by teaching school when their husbands were out of work. Mrs. L. A. House's mother made more as a tailor than her father did as a farmer and saloon keeper. And

W. W. Jewell's sister brought in more income as a seamstress than her husband did as a welder.[88]

Of course doing more work in most jobs did not result in women's salaries equal to men's. Textile mills especially operated on a three-tiered structure. Men made most, women came next, and children earned least. Pauline Brewer explained that in the mill where she worked certain jobs were reserved for women and others for men. This arrangement made exact comparisons of salaries nearly impossible because men and women seldom performed the same jobs. But when asked if men were paid more than women, Brewer seemed astounded at the naiveté of the question: "Yeah, uh huh, naturally [laughter]."[89]

For Susie Wilson even inferior pay in a textile mill was a form of liberation. Born in the Hackneyville community in eastern Alabama, she married at age sixteen, the same year she graduated from high school. A bright woman who was twice double-promoted, she read many books that had belonged to her grandmother. After her marriage she gave birth to six children, five girls and one boy. Evaluating her family life, she commented: "Women didn't have rights. They had privileges. If they were good little wives their husbands might give them certain privileges . . . ; because I wanted to be recognized as a person, I had fewer privileges." But she was only partially a rebel against her culture. During the 1930s she worked in the fields beside her husband and children. She made clothes out of feed sacks, preserved foods, and surmounted hard times with a certain fatalism: "If you can't change something, find something to laugh about." And she protected her children as best she could from the reality of being poor. One daughter remembered: "I had grown up and moved to Atlanta before I realized we were poor." Susie also taught a Sunday school class at the Baptist church where her husband Bill served as a deacon.

But she also charted a life of her own. She smoked, unusual for a southern woman of her time, although the use of tobacco in other forms was more common. When an elderly aunt caught her smoking, she chided: "Susie, if you're gonna use tobacco can't you at least dip or chew?" Susie Wilson also left the farm to work as a seamstress at Russell Mill in nearby Alexander City, explaining simply that she "had rather work for Ben Russell's whistle [Russell owned the mill] than Bill Wilson's." For her, mill work was part of a personal emancipation.[90]

Mary Wigley's liberation was fully as complete. After perceiving clearly a woman's restricted role on Sand Mountain, she spent much of her life defining woman's sphere in other ways. She attended Auburn University, became a Home Demonstration agent, defied local political bosses in Cullman County while organizing small farmers into the Farm

Bureau Federation, voted as soon as she was old enough, and built a respected professional life.[91]

Not all poor white women were so independent as Susie Wilson and Mary Wigley. Mr. and Mrs. Tom Alsobrook worked at Cowikee Mill in Eufaula. Both described themselves as Democrats during the 1930s, but Tom voted and his wife did not. He did not think it appropriate for a woman to vote, and she acceded to his wishes.[92]

Perhaps such compromises were needed to keep their fragile social structure together in the face of so much stress from other sources. And keep it together they did, or at least most of them did.

One indication of stability was the persistence of the nuclear family: a male head of family, wife, and children, all living together. Even among the most rural impoverished sharecroppers, one rarely found a female head of family. And when such a case occurred she usually was a widow. Of course the arduous physical labor worked against such patterns. If a man died or deserted his wife, she usually moved into a nearby mill town where life was more predictable and where she experienced less loneliness and isolation. But even in industrial towns, where factory routine applied new pressures, most families remained cohesive. One study of Birmingham revealed that in 1900, 93 percent of the white working-class families surveyed contained male heads. Obviously the widely feared disruption of family life as farm people migrated to town did not occur.[93]

Neighborliness, a traditional southern value, was as evident in poor white families as in more affluent ones. They helped one another as much as was within their power. When children were injured or sick, they lent wagons or rattletrap cars to transport them for medical care. Joseph Davis, a tender-hearted coal miner who lived through hard times himself, believed that miners should take care of their own. He bought two food baskets for the widow of a miner at Sayreton Mines. He left the food at her back door so she would not know who brought it or feel embarrassed at his charity. When the Greenwood family moved into a deserted and dilapidated squatter's cabin on a farm near Ohatchee, Homer Flynt befriended them. Greenwood had lost his railroad job in the early 1930s and had no way to provide for his wife and six children. One morning near sunup he appeared in the fields as Flynt and two of his sons plowed. He related his tale of woe and told them he had no food for his family. Flynt, a hard-pressed sharecropper himself, realized that even among the poor there were descending levels of need. So he sent a son to the house to obtain a bushel of corn, a bucket of meal, some salted meat, and a gallon of syrup, sharing from their meager store with one even more desperate. Such acts of kindness made Flynt a respected member of the community even among small landowners who occupied higher social status.[94]

The predominant theme of most of the life histories recorded among Alabama poor whites is not degeneracy and social disintegration. It is concern for family, love for children, and pride in the work they did or in their ability to cope with adversity. Carlie Crocker typifies them. She was the wife of a sharecropper and mother of twelve children; her husband farmed and drove a pulpwood truck. She begged him to live off his pulpwood income and use his share of their cotton crop to buy a home. "Aw," he replied, "I'll never own a home." Months later he was injured while fixing a truck tire and died, leaving his widow with one dime after paying his hospital bills. Her brother tried to persuade her to go to the county offices in Centreville and apply for free lunches for the children. But her oldest son refused: " 'No, not as long as I can work, Mother's not going to do it.' We never got a penny of welfare or relief. We lived on what we had at home." She proved more daring than her husband, selling their cows and using income from a small life insurance policy to make the down payment on a house. It took three jobs—as cook at the high school and at Bibb County hospital and as a textile worker in a garment plant—but she finally paid for the house and realized her lifelong dream.[95]

Not all poor whites were as independent or resourceful as Carlie Crocker. Nor did the more affluent world always treat them as charitably as Carlie Crocker's banker, whose 5 percent loan well below the market rate made it possible for her to buy a house. Often the surrounding society stereotyped them in demeaning ways. In 1894 Mrs. Isaac B. Ulmer of Butler described to her son the plight of a local boy named Elijah, "a remarkably good boy from his birth," who was then residing in the local jail. Elijah admitted he was guilty of a crime, "and it came from his associating with poor white trash."[96]

Even acts of kindness between classes carried such overtones. Historian Glover Moore, Jr., described an episode just after the Civil War when his father, then a very young boy, became lost in the deep woods in southern Calhoun County. His anguished cries finally brought him the assistance of Dick Stone, son of a poor widow and recipient of the Moores' charity in the form of meal, meat, and old clothes. When young Glover misbehaved, his sister and aunt chided him by calling the boy just "another Dick Stone." To be rescued by a poor white was an ignominy, and the boy, already sensitive to the class feelings taking shape in his young world, first protested that he was not lost. When Dick Stone ignored his protestations and led him through the woods to a path he recognized, he then tried to break away; but there was no getting away from Stone, who realized he would be well rewarded when he arrived at the Moores' place with Glover in tow. And so he was. Stone related Glover's plight in humiliating detail to Mrs. Moore and carried away an entire basket of pies and cakes as a reward: "Glover saw Dick more often after that and they came to be very good friends, but always with a certain reservation on Glover's part."[97]

Like most stereotypes, the perceptions of degeneracy among poor whites did have some basis in fact. Under enormous economic and social pressure, cast about from farm to farm or from mill to mill, some people collapsed under the strain. The first and almost universal symptom of trouble was alcohol. Though many poor whites consumed homemade liquor in moderation, the incidence of alcohol abuse in poor white families was astonishingly high. For some it was a factor in their descent into poverty. Mrs. L. A. House remembered that her father made a fairly good living by operating a country store until he began to drink heavily. And that memory made a lasting impression: "Whiskey is a bad thing. I think now, even now, it causes more trouble than anything else ever causes." A man who lived twenty miles northeast of Birmingham owned a mountain rich in timber for logging and coal for digging. When he died he left each of his sons a home plus a dance hall pavilion by a creek where they could make a living. But none of the boys inherited their father's ambition and one by one they drank so heavily from the still they hid in a cave that they all became alcoholics. Within a decade they had lost their homes and property. One of the sons wound up in Hillman Charity Hospital as a volunteer in a 1930s pellagra experiment.[98]

The Smith Lipscomb family of Calhoun County proceeded through the full cycle of poverty over the course of a century. As dirt-poor settlers from South Carolina in 1845, they struggled to survive. During the ensuing cotton boom of the 1850s they prospered. The Civil War disrupted their lives and cost them the life of a son, but they remained prominent members of the Hebron Baptist Church and were respected in their community. Part of the family left for Texas in the 1860s, and another unit moved to Attala, near Gadsden, Alabama. In 1912 Edgar L. Lipscomb spent much time drinking with his cousins and had only a nickel to lend his family. He did day labor picking cotton and worked on the county roads for $1.25 a day. Edgar was unmarried, courting, but not very responsible: "if ever I marry it will Be a accident that Don't Happen every Day."[99]

Dr. Edward Palmer of the Smithsonian Institution visited Alabama in 1884 to conduct archaeological work at Fort Jackson near Wetumpka. County court was in session, and a large, raucous crowd of poorly dressed white males disturbed the peace with their drunkenness and "very bad language."[100]

Aubrey Williams, who would later help Alabama poor whites as head of the National Youth Administration, grew up in abject poverty in Birmingham. Like the Lipscombs, Williams descended from a sturdy middle class background of small farmers on his mother's side of the family and plantation owners on his father's side. But his father's family never recovered from the Civil War. His father, though too young to fight for the Confederacy, "never got over the feeling of having his roots cut from under him and being adrift." Although Mr. Williams became a skilled carpenter, blacksmith, and carriage builder, he never overcame his alcoholism. After moving to Birmingham the family lived in some twenty houses over time, all on the backside of the city. Young Aubrey was forced to drop out of school after only the first grade in order to help the family obtain food. He worked as a delivery boy on a laundry wagon, often going hungry. He began stealing change to buy food but was caught and fired. Later his first girl friend stopped dating him when she discovered his address, recognizing the location as the "wrong side" of Birmingham.[101] The memory of his father's alcoholism, and the economic and psychological damage it inflicted on his mother, brothers, and sisters, haunted Williams for a lifetime.

Williams's father was not unusual. Home brew circulated in the new industrial towns. W. W. Jewell remembered his drinking days in an Albany, Georgia, textile mill. Moonshine whiskey sold widely in the mill village, and he and other operatives became such compulsive drinkers that they would smuggle bottles into the mill, hide them behind machinery, and drink while they worked. Mrs. Champion, a weaver at Cowikee Mill in Eufaula, made an adequate living, thanks to her husband's job driving trucks. But then he began to drink heavily and their plight worsened. When interviewed in the late 1930s, she explained: "My ole man died 'bout three years ago. He was good, but he kilt hisself drinking liquor. 'Fore God, he drinked enough to float a creek."[102]

Not all women were as lucky as Mrs. Champion, whose husband drank silently and without violence. When Jim Lauderdale drank, he fought constantly with his deeply religious wife. Finally he "ran her off" along with their two children, who found work in Comer's Mill in Sylacauga. Poor white neighbors shunned him, and he served a prison term for making whiskey. But among the poor whites interviewed between the late 1930s and the 1980s, whiskey making was a popular source of income as well as a serious health problem.[103]

Whether out of preference for a life of subsistence living that allowed maximum independence from work, or because of alcoholism, wretched health, sexual promiscuity, or just plain laziness, some poor whites lived well outside traditional social values and structures. Within mainstream culture, poor white sexual mores became a subject of ridicule. One north Alabama joke defined an Appalachian virgin as a girl who could outrun her brothers. But one staff member at the House of Happiness discovered that incest was no laughing matter. She encountered a hungry, desperate mother and cluster of children outside a filthy log cabin in Coon Hollow. She learned from neighbors that the grandfather of all but one of the children, and the father-in-law of the woman, had driven his son away some years earlier and had appropriated his young wife, who had borne the old man one son. The staff also encountered battered wives and children.[104]

George Carter was a large man, six feet three inches tall and weighing 220 pounds. For forty-two years he worked as a logger. He had never known his mother and father, who had given him to a farmer to raise. The farmer had worked him so hard that at age fifteen he had run off. But the farmer caught him and beat him so badly that the blood seeped through his jacket. The next time he made good his escape and joined a circus as a laborer. He had to leave the circus suddenly when his boss kicked him. Carter exploded into violence, hit the man in the head with a sledgehammer, and ran. He moved to the Talladega forest, where he took up with a black man, Tom Green. They made whiskey, played poker, fished, and raised hell until Green tried to assault the wife of a black sawmill worker, who then killed him. Carter testified on behalf of the sawmill worker and the man's grateful boss gave him a job as a logger. He began to live with a poor white girl whose mother was dead and whose father "was too busy raisin' hell to mind after her. . . . I tuk her to my shack that night and she kotched on right off." She scrubbed the shack, planted flowers, and made a better wife than Carter deserved: "Her name was Texas sum'pn-er-other. Not pretty but a good woman. She woren't half my size—didn't weigh a hundert pound—but that suited me. . . . They don't give no trouble an' they don't eat much." His wife caught him with another woman and told his boss, who warned him if he continued the affair it would cost him his job. To mollify his boss, he attended a revival, feigned conversion, and became a regular churchgoer. He also beat his wife for reporting him. When he obtained a job at another sawmill in Shelby County, he began living with another woman who bore him three children. Not that he allowed fidelity to his new spouse to inhibit his sex life: "That was one place whar they was enough women to suit me, an' I runned after 'em 'til my tongue was rollin' out like a damned dog's." His wife died in childbirth, which allowed him to take up with a new woman. Carter failed as badly at parenting as he did at marriage. He lost count of how many children he had fathered either legitimately or illegitimately. When his children or stepchildren became older, they just "drifted away." One son made whiskey on Cohagie Creek and a daughter worked at a cotton mill where she was "runnin' after ev'ry pair of britches in sight." In his old age he was "saved" and regretted his indiscretions, but not enough to make any serious efforts to change his life. Having buried two wives, "you couldn't give me another'n. They's too many runnin' 'bout that you don't have to feed."[105]

Nor did decadence show partiality to males. Neeley Williams lived in a two-room pine shanty near the Coosa River. She had never seen a movie and had heard a radio only once. Neeley begged food and snuff from men who lived along the river, who also fathered her six children. Welfare workers took custody of her eldest daughter, and her twenty-year-old son refused to work. When a person from the Federal Writers' Project arrived to interview her in 1938, a nearly naked four-year-old with a speech impediment greeted him with a single phrase repeated over and over: "Dod-dammit-dod-dammit-dod-dammit."[106]

Such people were unusual and were ostracized even by poor whites. Orrie Robinson—who tried his hand at making a living by fishing, share-cropping, and moonshining—was no saint himself. Only his friendship with the county judge for whom he dug fishing bait kept him out of jail when his still was discovered. One reason for his indigence was that a prostitute had gotten him drunk and stolen all his money. Yet he compared his family favorably to his Ellison neighbors: "We ain't got nothin' but a shirt tail an' a prayer, but we ain't low-down. We ain't like them Ellisons over at the Kingdom. They ain't never tried to do nothin' but beat people outa ever' thing they could, an' they'd steal th' handles off'n a coffin."[107]

Decadence, like poverty, was a matter of degree.

NINE

"Out of the Dust"

Poor Folks' Culture

Strong nuclear families stood at the center of poor white society. But reinforcing that society was a culture that added strength and resonance. Culture provided resources that helped the poor make sense out of their economic predicament. It also provided them an aesthetic arena in which they could express their notions of beauty.

One central experience determined much of their cultural pattern: they were essentially powerless. Poor people lacked the financial resources to purchase adequate medical care. So they derived from the Indians and their own empirical experience extensive knowledge of herbs, barks, and roots that had curative powers. They lacked money to build warm, well-insulated houses. So they relied for warmth on quilts with their kaleidoscopic mingling of colors. They could not afford furniture or utensils. So they carved goblets and plates, made pottery and glazed it, built furniture from vines or wood, plaited baskets from white oak, pine straw, or honeysuckle, and designed toys from peach seeds, mountain laurel, or pine bark. They could not determine the weather. So they developed an elaborate folklore of weather signs. Many could not read or write. So they expressed profound ideas and emotions as well as bawdy humor and boundless wit in music and folklore. They did not feel comfortable in many mainline churches. So they formed their own congregations that did not restrict their mode of worship or inhibit ecstatic expression. In short, poor white culture was creative, flexible, clever, pragmatic, and satisfying.

A second factor determining culture was the nature of time in rural society. As discussions of the work cycle have already demonstrated, farmers worked extremely hard during certain seasons. During spring planting and fall harvesting there were never enough hours in a day. Some added occasional work during the winter by cutting logs for a sawmill, mining coal, or working in some other seasonal jobs. But even these people devoted segments of the year to fishing, hunting, crafts, and religion. Long winter evenings before a fire in houses without electricity or books provided ample time to spin yarns or make cotton baskets, quilts, furniture, or toys. "Lay-by" time in August afforded exhausted farmers time to attend camp-meeting revivals or visit relatives. Time was a gentle friend to rural people, not an adversary to be crowded with activities. They felt no guilt when they rested, because when they worked they exceeded other Americans in their exertions.

Above all else poor whites maintained a culture based on race. The color of their skin served a twofold purpose. It was the primary identification with those who inhabited the world above them, the world of prosperous small farmers and merchants, of bankers, and of lawyers. At first glance all whites looked the same. Conversely, it was the initial and most dramatic way of setting themselves apart from blacks beneath. Whites might borrow from black culture in their songs, rhythms, crafts, stories, and superstitions. But they disdained the people from whom they borrowed.

In a world where indigence should have bound poor people together across racial barriers, poor whites strove for spatial separation. They preferred not to work with blacks, live near blacks, worship with blacks, or associate with them in any way. Blacks often reciprocated these feelings, believing that paternalistic upper class whites would protect their precarious position in society. To poor whites the key issue in society was the level of threat posed by blacks. Negroes threatened poor whites' jobs and sense of self-worth. But once disfranchised and made politically impotent, blacks posed no such threat to Alabama's upper and middle classes.

As long as blacks "stayed in their place," poor whites seldom threatened them. In fact, the poverty common to both races sometimes created an uneasy familiarity. W. W. Jewell grew up in a rural area of northern Florida where his only playmates were black. Their mother fed him meals, and "they just weren't nothing like it is now. Everybody was friends." And in the world of Opelika's textile mills, where the only blacks were sweepers who cleaned the floors, race relations remained harmonious. Asked if black and white textile workers got along well, Jewell seemed incredulous: "All right. Plumb good. Never was no disturbance among them."[1]

But even "in their place" blacks could encounter trouble. June Odom remembered a different attitude among textile workers in Cordova. Asked about prejudice in her hometown, she responded: "There was never any prejudice that I can remember about anything other than colored people. There was a lot of that."[2] Jim Lauderdale, whose alcoholism led him in a long downward spiral that ended in wife abuse and prison, served briefly as a prison guard at a convict mine where he whipped Negro prisoners for entertainment.[3]

Such violence happened too frequently to ignore. And almost always opinion makers blamed the violence on poor whites. In 1894 racial violence erupted in Pike and Crenshaw counties. Members of an organization called "White Caps" whipped several blacks and ordered them out of the counties. They warned that they would deal harshly with any white man who sought to protect blacks. In that depression year, white farmers in danger of becoming tenants often reacted violently against wealthier neighbors who worked black labor or divided large land tracts among Negro tenants.[4] Governor Thomas G. Jones hired Pinkerton detectives to arrest the culprits and stop the turmoil.[5]

But it would take more than the Pinkerton Agency to stem the wave of violence. When poor whites became frustrated and dissatisfied, they often directed their anger at blacks. Usually a threat to poor white status was the catalyst to disorder. Black tenants replaced whites. Or black strikebreakers entered mines to assume jobs previously held by free black and white miners. Blacks ran for public office or in other ways became "uppity." Or most threatening of all, blacks infringed on the sexual realm.

Lurking only slightly beneath the psychological surface of white society was the belief that black males lusted after white women. Blacks would take their revenge for centuries of injustice by raping and ravishing. Such thoughts festered even among the best-educated whites whose lives seldom brought them into direct contact with any blacks other than trusted cooks or maids. But in the poor white world where notions of conspiracy, injustice, and persecution flourished, such notions took root in more fertile soil. Virtually every black attempt to move beyond a narrow and well-defined sphere was met with overwhelming and immediate force. The justice system put in place and administered by the upper classes was entirely too slow for those whose wives and daughters were the primary targets of black rapists. Most rumors and virtually every act of violence led to swift and violent reprisal.

During the summer of 1900 Elijah Clark allegedly raped "a poor factory girl" who worked at Dallas Mills in Huntsville. Mill officials attempted to maintain order. But owners, who could intimidate workers into rejecting unionism and maintain a full work force at near-starvation wages, were helpless to restrain white workers whose sexual inviolability had been challenged by Elijah Clark. Textile workers could accept much harsh reality; but they would not tolerate the excesses of the Elijah Clarks of this world. A mob of more than a thousand textile workers walked off their jobs, shut down the mill, marched to the jail, and seized Clark. Before a crowd of six thousand they lynched him. Dallas Mills acknowledged the makeup of the lynch mob by agreeing to pay for the damages its employees had done when they stormed the Huntsville jail.[6]

Lumber worker Cecil Spencer witnessed a similar lynching some fifteen years later near Milton in west Florida. Sawmill workers accused a black man of raping the wife of a white mill worker as she brought her husband's dinner to him. Officials took the prisoner to nearby Pensacola for safekeeping, but when mobs gathered there, the sheriff decided to move him out of the area. When the train moved north across the Alabama border, a T. R. Miller Lumber Company crew took the accused man off the train. While the sheriff's son watched from the limb of a tree, the white lumbermen chained the black man down, poured gasoline on him, and set him afire.[7]

Nearly two decades later, in the spring of 1933, assailants raped and killed Vaudine Maddox, the daughter of an itinerant sharecropper near Big Sandy Creek in Tuscaloosa County. Officials arrested and indicted three Negroes. The International Labor Defense Fund employed three lawyers to defend the blacks. The involvement of this organization, with its ties to the Communist party, infuriated white Alabamians. Unfortunately, the event occurred shortly after the Scottsboro trials, which involved a group of black boys accused of raping two white Huntsville textile workers aboard a freight train traveling through north Alabama. The two incidents, both involving blacks who allegedly assaulted poor white women, inflamed opinion across the state. Conflicting testimony, unreliable witnesses, aroused northern opinion, and a fair-minded Alabama judge saved the lives of the "Scottsboro boys." Dan Pippen, A. T. Harden, and Elmore "Honey" Clark, the three blacks accused of the Big Sandy Creek atrocity, were not so lucky. On Sunday night, August 13, Tuscaloosa officials sent the three black men by car through the hills toward Birmingham and a more secure jail. Near the Jefferson County line half a dozen masked men took the three from the automobile and lynched them. The "best people" decried the act, arguing that "hillbillies," "red necks," and "white trash" perpetrated the violence.[8]

Whether or not poor whites did indeed lynch Pippen, Harden, and Clark, the ability to blame the lynching on such people served a useful purpose. Such reasoning absolved the better classes of any real responsibility for the racial abuse and mindless violence that wracked Alabama. Even fiction gave poor whites no respite. When Alabama novelist Harper Lee crafted *To Kill a Mockingbird*, a compelling novel of racism, lynching, and moral courage, she relied on familiar stereotypes: an innocent, naive black man, Tom Robinson; a racially enlightened and sympathetic professional man, lawyer Atticus Finch; and the villains of the novel, Bob Ewell and his daughter Mayella, who accused Robinson of rape in order to disguise her own sexual flirtation and her father's drunken violence. As Lee depicted the Ewells, they were friendless "poor white trash," ne'er-do-wells who lived on a relief check, drank too much whiskey, seldom wore shoes, hauled water in buckets from a spring, infrequently bathed, suffered from chronic ground itch, and did not attend school. Indeed, Atticus Finch's primary strategy in his defense of Tom Robinson was to compromise Mayella's testimony by revealing her to be white trash and thus less believable to the white jury than even a Negro. Mayella played into his hands, taking offense immediately when Finch referred to her as "Miss Mayella" or "Ma'am." Because she had never been treated with such respect before, she interpreted the apparent good manners as just another "put down," a mocking charade. The final degradation came when Tom Robinson accused her of trying to seduce him.[9] No white jury could accept such a connection; but it was clearly Harper Lee's intent that her readers believe it. And it coincided with the assumptions about both blacks and poor whites that prevailed in the world of Monroeville, Alabama, in which Harper Lee grew up.

Even more sympathetic observers reached a similar conclusion. Aubrey Williams, himself a product of Birmingham's industrial poverty, did as much as any Alabamian to help the people from whom he came. As a New Dealer and director of the National Youth Administration, Williams sought earnestly to aid the poor of both races. As he lay dying in Washington, he tried to explain "the poor white Southerner" who was "worked to death on the land, worked to death in the mine or the mill or the factory," and who vented "his anger and his frustrations and fear and panic by taking after the Niggers." The poor white had not been understood: "he has been despised and insulted over and over, and he has been cheated and he has been gulled and he has been exploited. But the cause of the Negro cannot be won, the South cannot be saved until he too is saved."[10] It was a touching thought, as rare as it was eloquent.

Compounding the irony of poor whites who worked against their logical black allies was the reaction of Negroes. To them as to many affluent whites, it was poor whites who served up the witches' brew of violence in every city and crossroads in Alabama. Whatever the level of black degradation, poor whites rested even lower on the scales of humanity. During the particularly violent days of the early 1900s, an Auburn University student collected a song in Choctaw County sung by a "Negro guitar picker." He gave the song to his professor at Auburn, Newman

I. White, who was just beginning a career of collecting black folk songs. It contained rare insight into the troubled relationship between Alabama's bottom classes:

> "I went to the crap game the other night,
>   Which was against my will.
> I bet the last hundred that I had
>   On the whip-po-will,
> Every since then I've been wearing good clothes,
>   Living on chicken an' wine.
> I'd rather be a nigger than a poor white man—
>   Since I got mine."
>
>   Chorus
> "I got mine, boys, I got mine;
>   I grabbed that hundred-dollar bill
>   An' to the window I did climb.
> Every since then I've been wearing good clothes,
>   Living on chicken an' wine;
> I'd rather be a nigger than a poor white man—
>   Since I got mine."[11]

Although mutual hostility characterized the relationship between the poor of both races, exceptions existed. They worked together in labor unions, in the Populist party, and against the poll tax and literacy tests for voting. But nowhere did their spirits merge more fully than in their folk cultures. They did not attend the same churches—that would have violated the spatial separation so important to whites. But the same sense of fatalism sustained the poor of both races. The same simple theology of damnation, repentance, and salvation permeated their services. The same emotional preaching and faith healing attracted adherents from both races. The same ghosts and "haints" inhabited both worlds. The same music and crafts captured their deepest longings, hard times, and sense of aesthetics.

Mary Wigley grew up a sharecropper's daughter on Sand Mountain. She unfavorably compared beloved Baptist minister Peter Chitwood to a renowned black preacher whose voice contained a variety and eloquence unparalleled among his peers. The rhythm and cadence of the sermon, the participation of the audience, the shouting, rejoicing, crying, and above all the singing mesmerized her the first time she heard it: "I had never heard black people sing before and I was thrilled with the excellent but different kind of voices and in the way the audience took part in rounds." But the preaching, singing, and shouting were not entirely unfamiliar. In her childhood, her Methodist cohorts believed a revival had failed "if people did not get happy and shout for joy."[12]

In 1897 a black female preacher won quite a following among both poor blacks and poor whites on Sand Mountain, claiming that she was the Messiah and that she could heal diseases or call down lightning. She conducted a meeting where blacks and whites allegedly washed each other's feet and ended the service by exchanging a "holy kiss." Sister Sapp, so she was called, received a whipping from a Dr. Dozier as a result of an argument they had, and her outraged followers of both races talked of exterminating the "better element of white people."[13] Because a white Southern Baptist woman recounted this story while appealing for money to support mission work in Appalachian Alabama, she probably exaggerated the incident. But the suggestion that the poor of both races responded to the same emotional appeals, experienced the same sense of spiritual deprivation, and longed for the same sense of religious meaning and community is accurate.

On some occasions, the poor did relate to each other in such intimate ways. When white lumberman George Carter settled in Coosa County, he lodged with Tom Green, a Negro, whose whiskey making and hell raising so well fitted Carter's preferences. Aubrey Williams remembered the ostracism that greeted one of his father's friends when he married a black woman.[14] Although such breaches of the racial code occurred, they were probably no more frequent than among other classes. Indeed young Aubrey Williams, who worked in Loveman's Department Store at the time, puzzled over a society that could treat his father's poor white friend as black because he married a Negro woman, yet allow to go unnoticed mulatto mistresses of prominent Birmingham men who purchased finery with their white lovers' funds.

Racism was only a segment of poor white culture, a part that permeated upper class society as well. Nor was the violent expression of racial feeling unique to poor whites. Renowned for their hot tempers, southern whites had long settled petty disputes and family feuds with fist, gun, dagger, or club. But mayhem particularly permeated poor white culture. Possessing a pride swollen by the lack of tangible successes, poor whites flared at the least provocation. Rather than directing their aggression and violence into rational patterns such as political reform, labor unions, or toward the goal of economic change, they reacted in the traditional ways common to powerless peoples: blind and self-destructive rage, scapegoating that leveled the blame for their troubles on blacks, or fatalistic acceptance of whatever happened.

Violence seemed to represent a frenetic interlude in otherwise dull lives. Either actively or vicariously, poor whites could transcend their lives for a moment. A court case in Opelika demonstrated the point.

Five men became involved in a fist-swinging brawl on a front porch only six feet wide by eight feet long. When the case went before a jury, the attorney for the defense made a major issue of how long the fight had lasted. When questioning the woman at whose house the fight had occurred, he inquired about the length of the fight. She replied: "I don't own nary a watch. Ain't never owned nary a watch. And if I'd owned a watch, I wouldn't been alooking at the watch; I'd been awatching the fight."[15] The occasional violence that interrupted the monotony was not to be missed. Perhaps this same yearning for excitement explained pastimes as disparate as cockfighting and honky-tonk brawls as well as the everlasting appeal of demagogic, flamboyant politicians and preachers.

Pride of person and possessions, which often precipitated violence, was not determined by the extent of property. Cherokee County herb doctor Tommie Bass opposed gun control: "I wouldn't hurt anybody, never have in my whole life. But if I call on somebody breaking in my place and they keep on, buddy, there's going to be some sad singing and slow walking, and that ain't no joke."[16]

Indigence affected their folklore as powerfully as it did their racial notions. Folklore is a great deal more than a series of entertaining songs, rhymes, stories, and beliefs. It is a window that allows outsiders to peer into and glimpse what is valued by common people who seldom record these sentiments in any other form.[17]

Ancient folk traditions survived among poor whites. With little money for books, education, radios, or travel, poor whites experienced a high degree of cultural isolation. What endured in their culture was the wit and wisdom of ancestors who had transmitted their culture orally from one generation to the next. Often gifted storytellers uninhibited by the need to "get to the point," poor whites took sufficient time to embellish a story, develop a plot, and build the proper dramatic tension before driving home the point. Folklorist Ray Browne described a session of story telling in the Crane Hill community of Cullman County. Sitting in the home of Luther Freeman, whom he described as "an indigent farmer," on a hot summer night, Browne spent six hours recording stories.[18] Such sessions revealed the persistence of ancient European nursery rhymes, Mother Goose stories, and antiquated English wording ("swain" for boyfriend, "hoped" for helped) among Appalachian people.[19]

Alabama folk beliefs strikingly reveal the powerlessness of poor whites, although in this regard they were not different from farmers in general. Their dependence on agriculture and the capriciousness of nature conspired to produce a wealth of weather signs that governed every phase of farming. Thunder in February meant a frost in late spring. It was useless to try to wash the letters out of feed sacks unless it was done on the light of the moon. If meat would not lie flat in the pan, it must have been killed under the light of the moon. If the moon changed in the morning, the weather would change. To cause rain and end a drought, kill a cricket, bury a cricket on its back and spit on it, kill a frog, or hang a snake belly up on a fence or tree. If it rained the first day of a month, it would rain fifteen days that month. Thunder before seven, rain before eleven. Red sunrise, rain that day.[20]

Other themes in Alabama folklore fit poor whites more particularly. Nell Bruce of Jones, Alabama, told stories drawn from impoverished mountain people who seldom had sufficient food or medicine. In her short tales, she included traits valued by mountain people: generosity, neighborliness, pride, independence, and frankness.[21]

Lacking resources to purchase either medical care or drugs, poor whites compiled an elaborate store of folk remedies. Borrowing heavily from Indian lore, they became experts on the medicinal properties of herbs, roots, bark, and weeds. Powdered alum stopped bleeding. Black elderberries cured constipation, and the flowers and bark, when made into a salve using lard, healed scalds and burns. A tea made from rhubarb roots stopped diarrhea. A poultice made from sheep sorrel cured cancer. Alder-bark tea was good for chills. Wormwood tea cured cholera, red clover leaf took care of pimples, calamus root stopped cramps, papaw-root tea cured gonorrhea, pot liquor from collard stalks cured yellow jaundice, quinine from boiled bitterweed stopped malaria, and a tea made from yellowroot was good for pellagra sufferers.[22] A woman who could not afford a doctor to deliver her baby was told to put an ax on the floor under her bed with the blade up in order to cut the pain.[23]

Perhaps the most renowned herb doctor in Alabama was Tommie Bass. Born in 1908, Bass came to the Leesburg community in Cherokee County in 1918. He lived in a tin-roofed cabin and never owned a car or learned to drive. He learned about drugs by working in his father's fur-trading posts in north Alabama and north Georgia. Trappers supplemented their incomes by selling herbs, and the fur companies in turn sold them to pharmaceutical companies. Bass supplemented this education with cures gathered from Indians, books, his mother, and neighbors. Bass believed that the most important element of good health was "purified" and "thin" blood. Yellowroot was "queen of the herbs" and cured a multitude of ailments. He believed that manufactured and synthetic medicines were too harsh. In a sense, Bass practiced "holistic medicine." His cures were related to the fundamentalist theology of his humble, foot-washing, Freewill Baptist tradition:

"I feel there's only two ways to go—the good way and the bad way. And I go by the Bible. I take the whole book, not just a little bit because you got to go all the way to the end to find out what happens.

"The good Lord tells me in the Bible that he made us out of the dust out there. A lot of people don't think that. . . . I hadn't found too many that didn't, but some of them does, I understand.

"Anyway, we're made out of that earth out there and we've got to go back out there and get some of it to nurse this body. Each [plant] has something that we use in our body.

"Herbs work with nature. It don't work fast. That's the way I look at it. And I think the medical people should do more research on these common herbs. I think they would find a cure for everything out there, including cancer."[24]

Poverty dominates many other aspects of folklore. Maggie Lee Hayes of Vernon in Fayette County related a story based on the pride that poor whites maintained despite their illiteracy:

"One time there was an old woman who couldn't read a word, but she didn't like to admit that she couldn't read. So she kept up the pretense among her neighbors. One day she went to a neighbor's house and asked her to lend her a book to read. The woman knew that the other woman couldn't read a word, so she just picked up the first book she saw. It happened to be the Bible. When the old lady brought the book back in a few days, the owner asked her how she liked the book. 'Oh, it came out just like all the others. They got married in the end.' "[25]

Throughout their lore, poor people rejected what their betters considered fashionable and acceptable. Folk religion often censored practices thought to be typical of the upper class: ballroom dancing, horse racing, and gambling. "It's the Fashion," a folk song collected in the poor white bastion of Lamar County, contained a more sweeping indictment:

"When a poor man asks for bread or a place to lay
   his head,
He will get a kick in-stead. That's the fashion.
But a poo-dle dog they'll keep, in their arms
   they'll let him sleep;
When he dies oh how they'll weep. That's the
   fashion.

"Some think I'm very queer and some others often
   sneer,

But I hope that I stay clear of that fashion.
If you'll only wait a while I will someday be in
    style.
It will be my time to smile when it's fashion.

"If you curse and swear and sin . . . a man and
    don't look in,
Let the Savior take you in from that fashion.
For I'd rather know I'm right than wear diamonds
    every night,
For some day I'll dress in white when it's
    fashion."[26]

"The Old Miller," also collected in Lamar County, elaborated a classic theme of Alabama folklore: how the well-to-do cheated the poor. The song described a miller with three sons. The old man, growing old, decided to make his will, leaving his property to one of his sons. To decide which received his inheritance, the old man asked each boy how much toll he intended to charge. The first boy proposed to take a peck out of each bushel of corn he ground. "You're a fool," his father replied. Jeff, his second son, proposed to take half of all he milled, but this satisfied his father no better. The third son promised:

"Father, oh father, my name is Jack.
I'll take the whole turn and swear to the
    sack,
And if by this fortune I should make,
That is the toll I intend to take."
Foody inky dink dink, foody inka day.

"You're not a fool," the old man said.
"You've completely learned my way.
And this mill I intend for to will,
For any man can take that and live."[27]

The downward cycle that led small farmers into tenancy found expression in another ballad sung in Lamar County. The parody song "Down on the Farm" challenged nostalgic memories of farm life:

"I remember when a boy how my heart would leap
    with joy
When someone would speak of home and farms so
    dear,
Of Mother's old red shawl and mottoes on the wall,
All go far to make me feel sad and drear.

Chorus
"Then don't mention the farm to me where I climbed
　　the apple tree.
I'll take an ax and cut off my right arm.
　　For I'd rather go to jail and no one to go my
　　　　bail
Than to go and spend one hour on the farm.

"We had brickbats there for soap, wiped our faces
　　on a rope.
E'en my watch and chain, it lost its little charm.
Every hayseed that you'd pass would have whiskers
　　made of grass.
And I like to starved to death down on the
　　farm."[28]

The lore also reveals a good deal about women and their role in poor white families. Drucilla Hall of Lamar County used her memory and ingenuity to compensate for poverty and lack of opportunity. Among the numerous folk songs she sang was one entitled "A Single Life." No doubt it served as a warning to overly romantic adolescents contemplating early marriage:

"Some go courting on Saturday night,
Some go courting on Sunday.
And if you give them a chance to talk,
They won't go home till Monday.

Chorus
"A single life is a happy life,
A single life is lovely.
I'll live single and no man's wife,
And no man can control me.

"Some say there are nice young men.
Girls, where will you find them?
I've traveled this wide world over,
And never been able to find them.

"Some will court you for your love,
Some to deceive you.
When they find they have gained your love,
They'll run away and leave you."[29]

From Lawrence County in mountainous north-central Alabama came the legend of Aunt Jenny Brooks, collected from Frances Forney in 1925.

During the Civil War, Confederate recruiters invaded the Appalachian mountains to impress soldiers. Aunt Jenny's husband refused and was killed in the ensuing fight. Aunt Jenny swore eternal vengeance on the Confederates, and in the following years she and her sons killed every member of the raiding party. According to local legend, Aunt Jenny herself accounted for three notches on the hickory stick they used to record their murders. Local folk believed that just before she died, Aunt Jenny washed her hands in the skull of one of her victims, which she used as a washboard. People in Lawrence County were terrified of the small, shriveled woman with flashing blue eyes who reputedly could sway elections in the county simply by her endorsement.[30]

The supernatural qualities present in the folktale concerning Aunt Jenny Brooks found a place in Alabama folklore. Ghosts, witches, and "haints" inhabited the world of poor whites. Mary Wigley half-believed Sand Mountain lore that people received signs before tragedies struck.[31] "Fetch lights" would appear before a person died. Borrowed mainly from ancient Celtic lore, such apparitions and signs served as warnings and were widespread among poor whites.[32] Coal miners believed that hearing a cock crow at night was the harbinger of death in a mine. Many Appalachian hill people would not kill and eat doves, believing it a sin to shoot the bird that had been sent from the biblical ark to find land. Some believed that a hunter who shot a dove would find blood on his gun barrel.[33]

Trickster tales in which a weak or powerless creature got the better of a strong opponent proved enormously popular among both powerless blacks and poor whites. The Uncle Remus tales captured this theme best for blacks, but poor whites developed their own assortment. The symbolism of a powerful and prosperous person being brought low by a shrewd but illiterate poor white reveals a great deal about folk culture's capacity to build pride and a sense of self-worth. Lucy, an illiterate mountain girl, bore an illegitimate child. She persuaded a friend who could write to send a note blackmailing the father, a prosperous married merchant who had taken advantage of her. The one-sentence note warned: "Leave ten dollars in this stump, or I'll tell —and I'd a little ruther tell."[34]

Bud Medders, a lean, tall share-tenant living in Calhoun County, was a literary descendant of Johnson Hooper's famous poor white trickster Simon Suggs. Especially when under the influence of corn liquor, Medders became a rustic wit and skillful raconteur. During the Spanish-American War, Bud heard a rumor that the government might begin a draft. He also learned that a Spanish immigrant was working nearby turning wood into charcoal. So he asked the postmaster to write to Washington for permission to kill the local Spaniard as his contribution to winning the war. A "Hardshell" Primitive Baptist who had fallen from grace, Medders derived his humor from the clash between town and country, industry and provincial ruralism, with country and rural ways usually prevailing. A proud man, he liked to define his identity by the self-proclamation that he was "free-born, white, twenty-one and didn't give a goddam." Anyone of higher station who became "uppity" in the presence of Bud Medders was quickly put in his place.[35]

What others ridiculed—clothes, physical deformity, or personal eccentricity—poor whites often flaunted. Edgar L. Lipscomb, a hard-drinking downwardly mobile offspring of a Calhoun County yeoman family, made a living doing odd jobs. During cotton-picking season he hired out as a farm laborer to pick cotton. Sometimes he worked for $1.25 a day on the county roads. Other times he simply drank, attended movies, and fished. But his poorly written letters reflected no shame or anger at his plight. Recounting a successful fishing trip, he wrote that he set out two hooks, then "got up on the bank and was a Reading in a paper about some Democrats and I heard something on my hook. I thought id caught a Democrat But it Happened to be a Blue Cat it weighed 2 pounds."[36] Describing his girl friend to a relative, he wrote: "Oh Ben you just ought to see my girl I caught at Alabama City Her Head Looks Like a soap goard in hog killing time I sung Her a song about my Long Nose and she laughed so Hard she peeled Her lips over her Head and I had to call the undertakers." Proud of his composition, Lipscomb included the lyrics:

> "When I was a Little Boy, I was my Mamas joy.
> My Body was perfect my limbs fit up complete
> Except my Diroshus old nose and it stuck out a
>   foot.
>
> "I went to see my sweet Heart
> I ain't going to tell you where I went
> The girls all asked me
> What I come thare for and what in the Devil I
>   meant.
> "Thare was a chair by Misses side and in it I
>   taken a seat.
> The girls all sniggered Right out
> His Nose sticks out a feet.
>
> "I went to kiss my sweetheart
> Our Lips they would not meet
> My nose pushed Her bonnet off
> stuck over Her shoulder a feet.

> "I started out to traveling
> I could not Travel Right
> I travelled for Half a Day
>   and there put up for night
> Reckon what they Layed me on
>   nothing but a sheet
> It covered all my Body up
> My Nose stuck out a feet."[37]

James H. Flynt, a master storyteller, possessed an extensive collection of stories concerning coal miners in northern Jefferson County. One in particular, Curt Goodwin by name, was the subject of a cycle of stories:

Well he stuttered, he couldn't talk plain. He'd get to saying and so's and so's and so's and then he'd say what he wanted to say. They use to tell it on him, I don't know whether it's true or not, but him and his daddy was working one of these little ole wagon mines and you know they'd load a car of coal and they'd have to push it up the track far enough to where they could get the little ole mule to pull it on out. Him and his daddy was pushing on this car of coal just straining every nerve in their body, and old Curt said, "and so's and so's and so's some son of a bitch ain't pushing and it ain't me neither." Said his daddy picked up a two by four and like to have killed him.[38]

Folk crafts rivaled poor white lore for creativity and imagination. Working with whatever resources providence and nature provided them, poor whites crafted ingenious toys, furniture, clothes, bedding, and decorative objects. Quilting was the best-known and most utilitarian. Saving scraps of fabric from their sewing, housewives would pull down quilting frames normally tied to the ceiling and attach a simple piece of material firmly to the frames. Then they would cut the scraps into geometric designs and hand sew each piece to the fabric. Folk designs were elaborate, and the most skilled seamstress would use dozens of different stitches, making the sewing as intricate as the design. Family tradition required that a quilt be given to newlywed children and grand-children with which to begin housekeeping.[39]

The new couple then began building their house, furniture, cotton and egg baskets, and fishing traps. Cutting a small white oak tree with no limbs near the ground, they quartered the tree, then carefully pulled off thin splints, taking care to keep the width even. The best time for such work was spring when the trees had ample sap, but dry splints could be buried and then soaked before weaving them into intricately designed baskets.[40]

*Mr. and Mrs. Peacock and their children in front of their home in Coffee
County, Alabama, April 1939, airing quilts. Photo by Marion Post Wolcott.
(Courtesy of Farm Security Administration Photographs,
Library of Congress)*

When children came along, parents too poor to buy toys made "gee
haw whimmy diddles" out of mountain laurel. The ingenious toy consisted of a stick with notches cut in the side and with a propeller attached
to the end. By rubbing vigorously on the left side of the grooves the
propeller would spin to the right. Vigorous rubbing on the other side
produced the opposite effect (hence the name "gee" and "haw," com-
mands that farmers gave plow animals to turn them right or left). Carefully joined wooden creatures called "limber jacks" could buck dance
or jig to the finest fiddle tune. Well-rounded trees provided wooden
wheels for homemade wagons. Corn shucks were transformed into dolls.
Milk of magnesia bottles and other patent medicine bottles decorated
broken-off tree limbs. Poor boys carved flat pieces of pine bark to make
turtles and peach seeds to make monkeys holding their tails, which
could be used as watch fobs.[41]

Such crafts had their primary value to the family, as furniture or work
baskets to use, toys to entertain children, or as bedding on cold nights.
But in time they attained an important secondary function as a source
of income. By the 1920s large numbers of Americans had moved into

cities and rural folk crafts were slowly vanishing. Women, who often were the primary craftspeople in poor white families, had no time for such activity after a long shift in a textile mill. Also, America began to standardize manufacturing so that cottage industries and tedious crafts dependent on the availability of skilled craftsmen with large amounts of time began to disappear. As individual design and carefully crafted products disappeared, some Americans began to long for them. With more money available during that generally prosperous decade, a substantial market developed for folk crafts.

Auburn University's Home Demonstration agents recognized a possibility to help their poor white rural clients. Across Alabama they began to encourage women to gather and make handcrafts for sale. In 1926 the Clay County Basket Association, made up primarily of poor white rural women, began to sell pine-needle baskets. Using the traditional folk art of Clay County, the women did their first large-scale marketing in Birmingham two weeks before Christmas. Articles about the baskets appeared in Alabama newspapers as well as papers in Georgia, Tennessee, Kentucky, Illinois, Michigan, Ohio, Indiana, Montana, Utah, Pennsylvania, Massachusetts, and New York. Two Chicago women became interested in the baskets and became brokers, even obtaining space in department stores along Fifth Avenue, Broadway, and Savoy Plaza in New York City. In 1927 the association marketed $13,000 in pine-needle baskets, enough to significantly improve five hundred homes in Clay County. This activity immeasurably increased the confidence and self-respect of rural women who discovered they could earn as much as $20 a month by selling baskets, far more than their husbands could make farming. So impressed were Auburn Cooperative Extension agents that they hired a home industries specialist to extend the project to other counties.[42]

In Calhoun County the local specialty was tufted bedspreads. According to legend, an Appalachian woman repairing a torn spread, and lacking thread or yarn, used a candlewick instead. Repeating the procedure, she turned the tufts into patterns, then dyed the wicks. The result was "candlewick" spreads with tufts stitched into new spreads with various designs. The spreads became popular, employing entire families of women and children, who then sold the spreads from roadside stands or in country stores. The labor was arduous and the return meager. Women sometimes worked twelve- to fourteen-hour days in return for a quarter a day. But as with Clay County women, it was far more cash than they had earned before and a boost to pride as well. The cottage industry soon fell victim to technology. New machines standardized the work and allowed it to move into bedspread houses that employed full-time workers.[43]

The staff at the House of Happiness in Jackson County eagerly introduced the commercial crafts program to its indigent neighbors. Twice a week poor men and women came to the house to make tufted bedspreads, quilts, rag rugs, brooms from broom corn, leather purses and billfolds, and pillow tops. They worked on the front porch when weather permitted, swapping stories and enjoying the social aspects of the work. Older girls cared for younger children. With an inventory established, they borrowed a pickup truck, fashioned a cover for it to approximate a covered wagon, then drove off to sell their wares.[44]

A few miles away another mountain community also tried to earn income with folk crafts. In fact, half of the women in the community earned some income during the mid-1930s with their crafts. But 60 percent of the women reporting such income were wives of landowners, compared to only 27 percent who were sharecroppers' wives. For many individual poor white women, however, the crafts were a godsend. Textile worker Mrs. L. A. House sold twelve corduroy quilts in one year to a single neighbor.[45]

No aspect of poor white culture won a larger audience among middle class Americans than music. Like crafts, folk music at first served only a local interest. Emotions too deep to express in any other form found their way into song. Energetic fiddle tunes afforded them music to dance by and allowed a certain virtuosity for truly gifted musicians. Using folk instruments such as banjos and dulcimers, poor whites retained ancient tunes rapidly disappearing elsewhere. Mrs. Emory P. Morrow, who taught in a north Alabama mission school, recorded three separate versions of the haunting old English ballad "Barbara Allen." The shy mountain children in her school refused to sing the ballads for outsiders, so Mrs. Morrow collected them by listening to the children sing while bathing in the school's bathroom. She recorded the words while a friend, hiding in the same girl's bathroom, wrote the music. Among the ballads they recorded were "The Little Rosewood Casket," "My Last Gold Dollar Is Gone," "Nellie," and "The Blind Girl."[46]

As modernity slowly transformed Appalachia, the dulcimer gave way to the fiddle and guitar, and the ballads lost favor to faster tunes more appropriate for dancing.[47] New Yorker Carl Carmer, teaching for a brief stint at The University of Alabama during the early 1920s, visited a fiddle festival at Valleyhead in north Alabama. "Fatback" Shelton was speaking when he arrived: "I sure like to do the speakin' at meetin's like this 'un. It's about the only chance I git tuh say suthin 'though bein' broke in on. Not that my good wife talks any more than the next one. Why, I remember a fellow that didn't say nothin' for six years 'cause he was raised polite and didn't think he ought to interrupt." A fiddle contest followed the homespun humor. Chum Gizzard, a veteran of many contests, began the competition:

> "Devil's Hiccup," he said shortly, patted his right foot and was off. As the first notes raced from his fiddle, old man Ventress stepped up to him. In his left hand he bore what was apparently a broom straw. This he placed across the strings of the singing fiddle. Then with the straw between the second and third fingers of his right hand he began to bounce it up and down on the strings. He was drumming out an accompaniment on the same instrument that carried the melody. Chum was in full swing now; the notes flying from his fingers. But the swifter the pace, the swifter and merrier rose the jigging accompaniment. Loud whoops sounded from the audience. Everybody was getting warmed up. Then a tall man rose in the aisle and very solemnly did a shuffle, his big brogans banging on the wide-plank floor.[48]

The fiddle contest gave way to a spirited square dance with the musicians playing accompaniment.

On one of his tours of north Alabama, Carmer also attended a Sacred Harp singing. Based on a series of shaped notes taught at "singing schools," the Sacred Harp usually consisted of unaccompanied singing. The four parts—treble, alto, bass, and tenor—were sung by musicians sitting in a square facing each other. Though religious in lyric and setting, the singings served a social function much like the camp meeting. It brought isolated people together where they filled a Primitive Baptist church or some other edifice and spilled out onto the grounds. Oftentimes the occasion for a singing was a "decoration day" when the visitors also cleaned the cemetery, or a "homecoming" that brought former residents back to the church of their childhood. Variously called a Sacred Harp sing (for the name of the oblong songsters), a Fasola sing (because when singing the first verse only the names of the notes were sung), or a Shaped Note sing (because a different shaped note placed on the staff represented each of the four or seven notes), it was an important occasion, as depicted in the words of a popular Alabama mountain song:

> "Sacred Harp Singin'
> Dinner-on-the-grounds
> Whiskey in the woods
> An' the devil all around."[49]

Many strands of poor white Alabama music, religious and secular, converged during the 1930s in the unlikely community of Mt. Olive, Alabama. Elonzo Williams settled in Mt. Olive in 1923 after suffering psychological and physical injuries during the First World War. A sixth-grade dropout not well prepared to fend for himself, Williams worked as a water boy for the W. T. Smith Lumber Company, sawed logs, drove oxen, and finally ran a locomotive. He began a small store in a shed attached to his house and purchased a three-acre strawberry patch. Mrs. Williams operated a boardinghouse to supplement family income. There, on September 17, 1923, Hank Williams was born. Times were hard and became worse with the onset of the Great Depression. Of fourteen hundred people working for W. T. Smith Company in Butler County, one local man estimated that no more than a dozen owned their own homes. Wages were low and the Williams family had moved frequently, trying to better itself economically. In 1930 Elonzo Williams entered a Veterans Administration hospital, the beginning of a ten-year stay for his wartime wounds. Hank was only seven but immediately had to assume some responsibility for bringing in money. He sold peanuts at a logging camp, shined shoes, and did odd jobs. Mrs. Williams obtained a Works Progress Administration job at a cannery, making a dollar a day. One local woman remembered: "People were so poor then you can't imagine." Irene Williams, Hank's sister, tried to define the family's status to distinguish between the proud poor and the degenerate poor: "We were poor people but we weren't in poverty. No matter what anyone says, we never begged." She never liked the rags-to-riches legend that her brother inspired.[50]

Musical elements from many sources played a part in young Hank's life. His church-organist mother taught him gospel songs. On his eighth birthday she spent her meager resources on a guitar for him. By fourteen he had organized his own band, which played for hoedowns and square dances.[51] A black man in Georgiana taught him blues. The family moved to Montgomery late in the depression, and Mrs. Williams worked to obtain appearances for her son in the city's honky-tonks so he could return from Mobile's shipyards, where he worked during the Second World War.

After achieving local fame in Montgomery, Williams caught a bus for Nashville to sell himself and his songs. The Willis Brothers, then called the Oklahoma Wranglers, met him in those early days and were not impressed with his fundamentalist hymns or his country blues. His singing was unprofessional and his songs amateurish. They remembered him not as the legendary "hillbilly Shakespeare" he would become, but as a half-literate country rustic who knew few technical rudiments of music: "We hadn't been used to hearing a country singer who was as country as he was." When they agreed to sing a Williams song entitled "Wealth Won't Save Your Soul," they discovered that Williams could not pronounce "poor." No matter how much they coached him, the word always came out "purr." Finally they gave up on his elocution. Another Nashville friend from those (1940s) days, songwriter Vic McAlpin, described Williams in much the same way:

> "He was a country hick like me. The kind of hick that comes from so far back in the country you're like a damn whipped dog people kick around in this business. You don't make friends too easy because you got your own thing, and you don't trust nobody very much, and to hell with 'em. A backwoods cat, that's what I call 'em. That's kinda the way he was."[52]

Williams's first break came in 1947 when he signed with Acuff-Rose as a fifty-dollar-a-month songwriter. In 1949 he joined the Grand Ole Opry and was an immediate hit. As one Opry announcer remembered: "I never saw anybody have an affect [*sic*] on the Opry crowd the way he did when he was there. Nobody could touch Hank Williams and the only one who came close was [Red] Foley."[53] What made such a profound impression on his audience was the "white man's blues," a mixture of black and white elements from his childhood, rooted in family crises, frequent moves, hard times, economic uncertainty, and romantic failures. Songs such as "I'll Never Get Out of This World Alive" articulated the despair, resignation, and endurance of those who responded to his music:

> "Now you're looking at a man that's getting kind of mad,
> I had lots of luck but it's all been bad,
> No matter how I struggle and strive,
> I'll never get out of this world alive.

> "My fishing pole's broke, the creek is full of sand,
> My woman ran away with another man,
> No matter how I struggle and strive
> I'll never get out of this world alive.

> "My distant uncle passed away and left me quite a batch,
> And I was living high until the fatal day
> A lawyer proved I wasn't born, I was only hatched.
> "Everything's agin me and its got me down,
> If I jumped in the river I would probably drown,
> No matter how I struggle and strive,
> I'll never get out of this world alive.

"These shabby shoes I'm wearing all the time is
   full of holes and nails,
And brother if I stepped on a worn out dime,
I'll bet a nickel I could tell you if it was heads or tails.

"I'm not gonna worry wrinkles in my brow,
Cause nothing is ever going to be right no how,
No matter how I struggle and strive,
I'll never get out of this world alive."

Offstage, Hank Williams's life disintegrated. Alcoholism, drug abuse, infidelity, and divorce supplied lyrics that spilled from his brain. Merle Kilgore, a longtime friend and guitar player for Williams, remembered his heavy drinking and depression, times when he would confide: "Hell, this is a bad day. I'm gonna get me a bottle and tomorrow will be better." On occasion Kilgore remembered audiences booing Williams offstage because he was so hopelessly drunk: "People had paid to see him and he was sort of a God to them so they got angry."[54] The Grand Ole Opry fired him for his erratic behavior, but Williams moved to the Louisiana Hayride and continued his sensational rise. At the peak of his career, on New Year's Day 1953, he died at age twenty-nine of ailments related to alcohol and drug abuse. His funeral in Montgomery attracted twenty thousand people to the municipal auditorium, most of them rural people or textile workers from the city's mills. Williams went to his grave, but his songs, which blended sin, sex, and salvation, lived on. Perhaps folklorist D. K. Wilgus best captured the ambiguity of the Hank Williams legacy. He considered Williams the bridge by which country music entered urban America, a symbol to the millions of poor whites who moved into town between 1940 and 1960:

Hank Williams was as country-based as they come, or rather he was a typical product of the forces of urbanization on the southeastern poor white. He reeked of the parched fields of Alabama, the dirty streets and dives of Montgomery. He embodied drunken Saturday nights in the tavern and soul-saving Sundays in the country church. It was all there in him, and it was all there in his music. He had the gospel blues, and sentimental tradition from folk and professional sources. He had inhaled the postwar honky-tonk style with every breath. . . . He presented—in fact he was—the dichotomy, the polarization of the urban hillbilly.[55]

Rural religion, however corrupted by the world, contributed an important dimension to Hank Williams; it also served many of his fellows in diverse ways. In a land of open Bibles, small country churches, and resounding sermons and hymns, poor whites imbibed heavily of fun-

Baptism for Mignon Baptist Church, a textile mill church in Sylacauga.
(Author's Collection)

damental Christianity. Their religion was fundamental not in theological terms, though few of them would have doubted the inerrancy of scripture or the miracles described therein. But they were neither literate enough concerning theology nor did they have sufficient time and energy to argue about such matters. Their religion was fundamental in the more basic sense that they attributed what happened in their lives to the inscrutable will of God. They drew strength from a folk theology that proclaimed all persons equal in the sight of God, which repeatedly reminded them that the "ground at the foot of the cross was level." Their religion contended that all persons were creatures of personal concern to God, who required the same acts of repentance and salvation from all. Once they repented of their sins and were saved, they entered a sacred religious community, a family of God that offered fellowship, a sense of belonging, assistance during hard times, and not infrequently spiritual kinship with more affluent neighbors.

In the early days of the nineteenth century, poor whites worshiped mainly in Baptist or Methodist churches where free expression of emotion and fellowship across class barriers prevailed. Their pastor was probably bivocational, a farmer like themselves. Poorly educated, he was in most ways similar to the people he served. But by the 1830s and

Primitive Baptists and church on Sand Mountain. (Courtesy of Samford University Archives)

1840s, divisions both theological and along class lines had already appeared. Mountain whites and poorer people seemed to gravitate toward the Primitive or "Hardshell" Baptists, while better-to-do folk preferred missionary Baptists with their greater emphasis on an educated clergy and mission outreach.[56] When the missionary Baptists sent missionaries to the hill country, they often condemned mountain ways and were condescending toward Appalachian people. They seemed to discern little difference between darkest Africa and the remote hollows of Appalachia. Fierce verbal wars resulted in Alabama, with Primitive Baptists and missionary Baptists conducting their own varieties of inquisition. Although not precise, the final division of control tended to be both sectional and economic, with Primitive Baptists strongest in the north Alabama hills, the southeastern Wiregrass, and in rural areas generally, whereas missionary Baptists grew fastest in the wealthier Black Belt and in towns.

The second round in this intramural battle began after the Civil War. Like blacks, who felt uncomfortable in white-run churches and withdrew to establish their own congregations, evangelical Baptists and Methodists began dividing along class lines. Although many rural churches contained both tenants and landowners, the soaring rates of

tenancy left many former landowners ill at ease as their fortunes declined. Perhaps God was no respecter of persons, but his disciples here
on earth often were. As tenants began their wandering life, a journey
that often took them away from the church where they had grown up
and where they were known and respected despite their indigence, they
often dropped out of church. Ashamed of old clothes or lack of shoes,
they felt pride, which kept them from the house of God, though their
Christian beliefs might be as strong as ever. In textile towns the division
was even sharper, with the mill village developing its own churches,
which were attended exclusively by mill people.

The final phase of their religious pilgrimage often ended in Pentecostal
or Holiness churches. In the last decades of the nineteenth century a
sort of religious wildfire swept across the South, a form of religious
"come-outism," which caused thousands of poor whites to end former
religious commitments. They identified increasingly with the Holiness
sects newly emerging from the Methodists, or with the Church of God,
then expanding rapidly from its home base just northeast of Alabama,
in Cleveland, Tennessee, or with some charismatic evangelist who
might represent a more personal brand of Christianity.

Poverty contained religious implications. As rates of tenancy increased, rates of church attendance declined. In a 1922 survey of seventy southern counties, researchers found that fewer tenants than farm
owners belonged to churches. In only eight of seventy counties did the
percentage of tenant farmers who were members of churches equal or
exceed the percentage of tenant farmers in the total population. By the
mid-1930s, 59.5 percent of the South's farm owners belonged to
churches, compared to only 33.5 percent of tenants.[57] When tenants
moved into town, they were not likely to join a church. According to
one study of North Carolina textile workers, only one of five rural people
who began work in textile mills joined a church.[58] As tenancy grew,
the impact on southern churches could be seen in many places. By
1922, 34.5 percent of farmer-members of Southern Baptist churches
were tenant farmers.[59] As a consequence, rural ministers often shared
the poverty of their congregations. A 1913 survey of 5,400 quarter-time
Baptist churches revealed an average annual salary of only $378. That
was up from the 1906 average in rural congregations of only $334. By
comparison, rural Methodist churches that same year paid salaries that
averaged $681, and Presbyterians averaged $857.[60]

Testimony from life histories of Alabama's poor whites support these
generalizations. An overwhelming majority considered themselves de-
votedly Christian. Among twenty-seven biographies of tenants, textile
workers, and coal miners who identified either their denomination or
that of their relatives, Southern Baptists led with nine, including one

deacon and two Sunday school teachers. Methodists came in second place with six members, including one bivocational minister-miner, one Sunday school superintendent, and two stewards (deacons). Holiness sects claimed three, as did the Church of Christ. Primitive Baptist, Nazarenes, and the Church of God tied with two each.

Downward economic mobility found various religious expressions. When Mrs. L. A. House moved from a tenant farm and rural Methodist church into Comer's mill town at Sylacauga, she left her traditional church for Mignon Baptist. Both economic and theological causes led to the change. Most of the "big people" in the mill were Methodist, she explained, and she "just liked the people better over at the other church. They were more like I was, the labor." The Flynts left the Baptist church for the Church of Christ; the Jewells, the Methodist church for the Church of God; Sam Anderson's daughter, the Baptists for a Holiness church.[61]

Formerly active church members became infrequent attenders or dropped out altogether. The Isaac Johnsons considered themselves religious but not churchgoers. Bull Elliott had no time for church, and his wife was embarrassed to be seen in public because of their poverty. The M. B. Truitt family belonged to the Rock Springs Baptist Church in Chambers County but did not move their membership when Truitt became a sharecropper on a farm outside Opelika. Kathleen Knight attended a Baptist church with her sisters and brothers, but her parents seldom attended because they did not have suitable clothes. She remembered that most church officials were landowners.[62] The same was true in one carefully studied mountain community where two-thirds of the church officers owned land and the other third were tenants related to them.[63]

Another expression of hard-times religion was the growth of Pentecostal and Holiness sects in Alabama. In one mountain community tenants who were denied leadership roles in traditional churches found them in a new white sect called the Church of God's Children. The new congregation disparaged education, believed in divine healing, and drew the wrath of local church people as a church "steeped in ignorance and poverty and, being in that condition, they have become insane in their religion."[64]

Holiness congregations obviously met real needs of poor whites. A local historian in Jackson County dated the Holiness movement from 1910 and noted that it seemed "to prosper more among the poorer people on the mountains and in the coves." Coal miner Luther V. Smith commented that his coal camp at first contained only Baptist and Methodist churches; then suddenly a Holiness congregation appeared. The wife and daughter of alcoholic Jim Lauderdale became "holy rollers," objected to his whiskey making, and left him for a job in a textile mill when he became abusive. Textile worker Mrs. Sam Anderson worried when her daughter took up with "holy rollers": "It's about to kill me and her pa, us bein' Baptists and not believin' in nothing like that." Even worse, she had become a preacher, leading a Georgia congregation. The Andersons described "holy rollers" as ecstatic folks who sang, jumped up and down to the music, fell down, and spoke in tongues. Herman Nixon described an increasingly common occurrence in rural Calhoun County during the 1920s: Asbury Methodist Church closed and a "holy roller church" moved into the building.[65]

Herman Nixon also observed in the 1930s that the old-time evangelical fervor had passed to Holiness and Church of God congregations, which were growing rapidly among mill workers and tenant farmers. And even mainline churches produced demagogic evangelists who appealed especially to poor whites. Samuel Porter Jones, a converted drunk from northern Georgia who had turned Methodist evangelist, had gained a considerable following among poor whites. Nixon called Sam Jones the "Savonarola of the hillbillies," a man who took the frank language of the soil into the pulpit: "I photograph your ugliness, and you sit there and laugh at it; I would rather be in Heaven reading my ABC's than sitting in hell reading Greek; many a man imagines that he has got religion when it's only a liver complaint." Nixon's farm tenants relished, repeated, and expanded Jones's denunciations of "society women," who wore evening dresses with necklines that exposed so much nakedness at one dinner he attended that he dared not "look under the table."[66]

One reason poor people chose new churches was because better-educated Christians considered them religiously ignorant. In 1895 John C. Campbell recorded unfavorable impressions of the religious literacy on Sand Mountain in order to attract more contributions for his school and missionary efforts: "The ignorance of many is appalling. One little boy of ten, the son of a minister, didn't know who Christ was; and the extent of another's knowledge of Christ was given in her statement that Christ was a Baptist. Their religion is largely a matter of temporary feeling and of rigid adherence to what they believe is orthodox."[67]

Episcopal missionaries at the House of Happiness in Jackson County agreed. Only two of fifty-six children attending their school knew the Lord's Prayer, and forty-eight "had never said a prayer of any kind, nor heard the story of Christ, nor had seen an American flag."[68]

Even allowing for the hyperbole that accompanied fund-raising efforts to support their ministries, such accounts distorted the facts. John Campbell was one of a generation of activist ministers who sought to energize the church to social action and lead it toward interdenominational ministries. Mountain people who claimed Christ was a Baptist were not so much ignorant as they were fiercely sectarian and loyal to the teachings of J. R. Graves and other mid-nineteenth-century Baptist theologians who traced their denomination all the way back to the first century. And well-meaning Episcopalian missionaries failed to understand that unstructured worship in plain log churches supervised by untutored ministers had no place for memorized prayers and formal catechism. Religious ignorance, like cultural degeneracy, was often in the eye of the beholder.

More impressive than the ignorance was the realism of poor white religion. Long characterized as otherworldly and naive, such religion was in fact very much in touch with social reality. Talk of vindication and justice in heaven was hardly escapist in a world where striving came to nothing. When poor whites entered politics or formed unions, elections were stolen and strikes broken. They did not passively accept their fate. But once confined to it, they tried to make sense out of it. How could God be compassionate and fair and yet tolerate such injustice? Because someday the poor of this world would inherit a crown, and those who cheated and abused them would get their just reward.

Nor did their religion hold them aloof from society. Perhaps they took the prophetic message of scripture literally, but that message repeatedly urged justice toward the poor and help for the needy. Or perhaps poor whites compartmentalized their lives so completely that they saw no contradiction in loyal service to an evangelical church and equally fervent support of a labor union. Through the centuries Christian devotees have cited the Bible as a rationale for inquisition and crusade, murder and mayhem. Poor whites were certainly nearer the truth when they cited it as the basis for fair treatment.

They knew that landowners and mill owners often interpreted scripture toward different ends. They frequently observed that mills and mining companies paid the salaries of preachers or subsidized church budgets. Some of them cited ways that management tried to dictate to preachers. Coal miner Luther Smith particularly resented the company's cutting his pay without his consent when it was building or repairing a church.[69] But the larger detriment to their welfare seemed to be a doctrine of shared values and community that Christianity created among whites, a sense in which all the parties to the South's economic life supposedly worked for a common good. Such attitudes certainly inhibited the development of class grievances and kept workers unorganized. But racial animosity toward blacks seems to have played a far larger role than religion in dividing poor people along caste lines and blurring their common class problems. Furthermore, many devoted

Tent revival at Fairmont Baptist Church, Red Level (Covington County),
circa 1925. (Courtesy of Samford University Archives)

evangelicals became enthusiastic champions of unionism and class-based protest.

Adrian Northcutt saw no conflict between the worlds of the spirit and the flesh, a decision that cost him his life. In the fall of 1920 Northcutt pastored a Nazarene church and mined coal. Because he was a respected and articulate community leader, coal miners elected him president of their newly formed local of the United Mine Workers. When the UMW called a strike, Governor Thomas Kilby ordered the state militia into the coalfields. In one of several ensuing encounters, a militiaman shot and killed Mr. Northcutt.[70]

Sam Cash was also bivocational, tenant farming and mining coal near Mentone in northeast Alabama. An active member of the Church of God, he nonetheless ignored his church's admonition against membership in secret societies. As an active UMW member, he greatly admired union president John L. Lewis. Although fatalistic about hard times (they were "God's will"), he also believed that God and John L. Lewis would improve conditions: "things can't go on much longer like they is goin', cause they is too unjust in the sight of God." A complex man who urged mountain children to remain in the hills rather than take factory or mill jobs, he did not blame them for deserting Appalachia because mining and farming were such hard vocations: "Everybody else lives offen us farmers an' miners and all we gits for our labor is a grubstake, an' a po' one."[71]

William W. Sewell, called "Big Papa" by miners in mockery of his five-foot-six, 170-pound frame, was a round-faced, red-haired coal miner of Irish extraction who began mining in 1892. A deeply religious man who "wore out a dozen Bibles," he was also a tough union man. His grandson recalled waiting for him outside a cafe when suddenly a man with a guitar came crashing through the restaurant's plate-glass window. The elderly Sewell stepped through the hole, got in the car, bit off the end of a King Edward cigar, lit it, and began singing a favorite hymn:

> "Oh they tell me of a land where no storm clouds
>   rise,
> Oh they tell me of a home far away,
> Oh they tell me of a land where my friends have
>   gone,
> Oh they tell me of an unclouded day."

His grandson recounted Sewell's unswerving devotion to John L. Lewis: "If you wanted to say something bad about John L. Lewis around him you'd better say it and move."[72]

The Church of God of Cleveland, Tennessee, spread rapidly through the north Alabama hill counties during the years after 1880, and it too challenged traditional society. Women evangelists played prominent roles in the early history of the sect, sometimes crossing the race barrier to preach to congregations of the opposite color. In fact the black female preacher who created a furor on Sand Mountain and won a following among the poor of both races was probably a Pentecostal preacher. The church also contained a strong pacifist ethic, arguing that a literal interpretation of scripture taught members to suffer wrong rather than engage in violence. L. G. Rouse, a Church of God evangelist and coal miner near Anniston, refused to purchase a war savings stamp in 1918. Angry fellow miners challenged his loyalty to America because he did not support U.S. entry into the war. When he replied that the war "was of the devil and from the very pits of hell," the miners attacked him and only the timely arrival of the superintendent kept him from harm. The company fired Rouse, and two government officials arrested him. He remained in an Anniston jail for three months, abused by fellow inmates. Officials threatened to send his children to an orphanage. James B. Ellis, Church of God Overseer for Alabama, experienced similar indignities when he refused to buy war bonds. A Methodist preacher in the community called him "a traitor to his country and lower than a suck-egg hound." Vigilantes followed him to a revival he was preaching at Bradford Coal Mines, and government agents arrested him and charged him with spying for Germany.[73]

Many poor whites came to terms with reality in less combative ways. Fatalism served them well. The grave stones in Alabama cemeteries demonstrate how little control people had over their destiny until recent years. In the Hatchett Creek Presbyterian Church cemetery in rural Clay County, M. Y. and J. P. Swindall buried two infant sons. John Manly was born on September 1, 1884, and died on October 21, 1886. An unnamed son was born and died on April 9, 1887. G. J. and E. L. Berry lost two daughters, both age two. I. W. and M. E. Jones buried four children there, two daughters ages seventeen and twenty, another daughter age unknown, and a son age twenty-two. Such a world provided more questions than answers and required that people believe even when they did not understand. Poor white folklore contained the same fatalism. Writing a story of how an acquaintance died when a cocklebur stuck in his windpipe, master storyteller Weaver Sinyard explained simply: "now that's the Lord's work."[74]

But poor folks also treasured a large amount of lore that poked fun at preachers, or punctured religious hypocrisy, or tried to relate their own earthly lives to the divine. One tale collected from Isaac Rollins, a fiddler and local "character" in Wedowee, Randolph County, regarded a preacher and one of his deacons who were crossing a thick swamp on the way to a favorite fishing hole. The deacon was parting the canes with his fishing pole when he encountered a large snake. Temporarily forgetting his companion, the startled man shouted, "God damn what a snake," to which the preacher responded, "Yeah, that's what I say." Another tale by Chester Cunningham of Elmore County concerned a farmer-preacher who had piled his family in the wagon for the trip to church one Sunday morning. He asked his son if he had fed the calves. When the boy admitted he had forgotten, the farmer got off the wagon, filled his pail with milk, and reached over the fence to feed the calves. One eager yearling bumped the bucket with its nose and spilled milk all over the preacher's shirt and trousers. Slowly the preacher lowered the bucket, grabbed the calf's ears, stared intently into its eyes, and said gently: "Calf, if I wasn't on my way to do some preaching, and if I wasn't filled with the everlasting love of God, I'd shake the goddamned hell out of you."[75]

Logger George Carter experienced a genuine and life-changing conversion late in his life, but in his younger years he despised the hypocrisy of logging-camp preachers. When his common-law wife reported his adultery to the manager, Carter protected his job by attending a revival and "getting saved":

Ol' Reverent Sardis from over at the Valley was doin' th' hollerin', an' he was th' damndest hypocrite you ever seed. He run a little ol' store when he weren't preachin', an' when a gal'd come in th' store, he'd try to hug 'er. I 'member they tol' me that one gal come in fer a sack of sugar, an' that when he tried to love 'er up a little she busted that sack of sugar over his damned head. They said that he could comb his hair for a week an' get enough sugar to sweeten his coffee with.[76]

Such sentiments reflect the irreligious patterns of Carter's life, one renowned for violence, sexual promiscuity, and wife abuse. But his conversion later and the guilt he felt for neglecting his wife and children is more typical of poor white experiences. To the degree that poor whites maintained social cohesion and self-respect, religion must be given major credit. And like their crafts, folklore, and music, it allowed them to express themselves at a profound level of human experience. As for their racism, harmful as it was, it differed little from the pervasive white perception of blacks both North and South and among all classes.

"The Fight Is Not Social"

The Politics of Poverty

If political protest movements are born from economic and social unrest, Alabama poor whites should have spawned hundreds. Grievances abounded. Post-Reconstruction governments reduced expenditures for public services and education. Droughts, cyclical cotton prices, and other economic conditions threatened to drive small farmers into tenancy. The pressure of a market economy built on the commercial production of cotton replaced less-stressful subsistence agriculture and herding. The crop-lien system produced intense battles between merchants and landlords on one side and small yeomen farmers and tenants on the other. Large landowners favored fencing laws, which small livestock producers opposed. Rural values came under increasing assault from rapidly growing inland towns such as Birmingham, Anniston, Gadsden, Dothan, and Tuscaloosa. Social institutions important to rural life experienced constant challenge. The extended family groaned under the pressure of frequent moves and increasing debt. Illiteracy threatened both social standing and work performance. Rural churches weakened as the most competent preachers left for more affluent urban pastorates.

When the grievances of Alabama's industrial workers are added, the list grows even longer. Unaccustomed to the discipline of industrial labor, recently transplanted farm folks chafed under the close supervision, long hours, and cramped working conditions. Wages might be better than on tenant farms, but they still were low. Health problems bedeviled them, convict labor competed for their jobs, the poll tax effectively disfranchised them, industrial accidents imperiled their lives, and their children grew to adulthood illiterate.

That all these troubles failed to produce a successful protest movement, an overwhelming sense of common anger, a unified purpose, or a reform agenda demands explanation. Part of the answer rests in historic American distinctives such as a high level of social mobility, an egalitarianism based on achievement, individualism, and the supremacy of ethnicity and race over class. Another part of the answer can be found in historic loyalties to the Democratic party that were reinforced by what poor whites perceived as the excesses of Reconstruction. White men had to unite to prevent black rule. Caste considerations—that is, the identification with others of the same race—exceeded class concerns—or the identification with others of different races who also were poor.

Rather than developing a sustained, well-defined protest tradition, Alabamians reacted to immediate threats or altered conditions by forming poorly organized third parties (Grangers, the Agricultural Wheel, Greenback-Labor party, Knights of Labor, Farmers' Alliance, and Populist party) or by strikes that usually were doomed from the start. Animosity toward blacks ensured that many Negroes not only would reject these "reform" movements but would often vote for paternalistic Redeemer whites (so called because conservative white Democrats had "redeemed" the state from radical Republican rule).

The "radical" Republican constitution of 1868 contained many provisions that assisted poor whites. It raised property taxes and used the funds to improve public education. It also contained the first specific requirement that made the state general assembly responsible for "adequate provisions in each county for the maintenance of the poor."

When Redeemer Democrats took control of state government in the 1870s, they proceeded to dismantle the political, tax, and public welfare structures constructed by Reconstruction legislators. Democrats, or to be more precise, "Conservative Democrats" as they called themselves, changed the welfare provisions to place responsibility for indigents on county governments. Because counties funded such care in various inadequate ways, the almshouses became the standard last resort for indigents. The new Democratic government did establish a State Board of Health in 1875, the sixth state to do so. But it gave complete control to the Alabama Medical Association and allocated only three thousand dollars of state funds for its work. Conservative Democrats did not entirely destroy the structures that Republicans had erected, but they did reduce the tax rate, which in turn cut state services.[1]

Although agricultural problems surfaced early in the new era, the Redeemers did little to help. Landlords battled merchants over which set of crop liens would have priority before Alabama courts, and the landlords usually won. Legislators friendly to poor whites regularly attempted to repeal the lien laws at each legislative session before 1884, but they always failed. In fact, most agricultural legislation in the 1870s and 1880s was designed to improve the position of the large landowner and planter rather than address the problems of the yeoman farmer or tenant. In 1888 a proposal for a five-year tax exemption to farmers who owned fewer than eighty acres went down to defeat. Instead legislators revised the tax laws in such a way as to benefit large farmers. The legislature also sold valuable mineral lands for $1.25 per acre in an attempt to attract more industrial jobs.[2] Although Redeemers of planter origin sometimes clashed with industrialists, they often worked together for common goals.

Butler County on the edge of the Black Belt furnished a typical case study of the conflict brewing in Redeemer politics. Following Reconstruction, white voters overwhelmingly favored the Democratic party. The battle lines formed between black and white voters, the chief Democratic objective being the preservation of white supremacy. Fearing black majorities in many counties, political leaders adopted the convention system of nominating candidates for office rather than the direct primary. Some whites resented the convention process and argued correctly that it allowed county courthouse gangs to control the sheriff's office, the probate judge, tax assessor, and other minor county jobs. The controversy also divided white Democrats along rural/town lines, with country people often opposed to the convention system. Poor transportation and the constant labor required during the farming season, when the convention was usually held, prevented most farmers from attending. Country people increasingly attacked the "courthouse ring" that ran Butler from its base of power in the county seat, Greenville. They voted for independent candidates who tried to wrest power from the Greenville politicians. The independents lost, but they spread havoc within the Democratic party and constantly threatened to divide it and thereby allow united black Republicans to gain control of the county. Finally the Greenville politicians agreed to a direct primary during the 1880s as a way to preserve party unity.[3]

Although the Democratic strategy worked fairly well to contain insurgency in Butler County, it did not fare so well elsewhere in the state. One after another, independent movements articulated the grievances of poor whites and disrupted the unity of the Democratic party until they culminated in the Populist uprising of the 1890s.

Disgruntled farmers formed several farm organizations in order to express their complaints. They established the Alabama Grange in 1873. Within four years the organization boasted 678 Granges containing nearly fifteen thousand members. Most Grange leaders were substantial landowners and generally conservative in their political ideology. Although many small farmers joined, the organization did not exert much influence on state politics.

The Agricultural Wheel began in Arkansas in 1882 and arrived in Alabama sometime in the mid 1880s. The organization established an official paper, the *Alabama State Wheel*, and held a convention in 1887 that was attended by three hundred delegates. Lawrence County, a traditional center of political insurgency in north-central Alabama, contained forty chapters of the Wheel by 1887. Two years later the organization numbered seventy-five thousand members. Like the Grange, the Agricultural Wheel tried to relieve agrarian suffering. It sponsored cooperative stores, endorsed businessmen as "Wheel merchants," and appointed a state purchasing agent. The editor of the state paper in 1887, R. G. Malone, condemned landlords as "land-devils" and, according to one Democratic editor, tried to "array one class of our people against another class—to create unrest, dissatisfaction and hostility among our poor but now quiet and peaceable citizens."[4] Many members disagreed with Malone's radical pronouncements and stripped him of his editorship. But elements within the Wheel obviously favored political confrontation and worked to unite farmers and industrial laborers in a new alliance. Leaders of the Wheel met with representatives of the Greenback-Labor party and Knights of Labor in September 1887 in Birmingham to form a statewide Union Labor party. About one-third of the hundred delegates were Wheel members. They condemned national banks and the convict-lease system, earning the scorn of a Democratic editor who described the representatives as "the scum of creation . . . — anarchists, socialists and communists."[5]

By 1889 the Wheel had largely been absorbed by the Farmers' Alliance, but it served an important role in agrarian politics. It furthered the attempt of farmers to work with industrial workers, and its mavericks tended to be considerably more radical than the Alliance into which it merged. It made the formation of a viable third party a much simpler task.[6]

The 1887 Birmingham meeting also revealed the lingering influence of the Greenback-Labor party in Alabama. Officially called the "Independent-Greenback-Labor Party of Alabama," Redeemer Democrats christened it the "Independent-Greenback-Labor-Socialist-Radical-Sore-head-Party," or more simply, the "hyphenated crowd." Whatever its name, it combined farmers frustrated over currency questions and coal miners angry about working conditions.

Conditions in coal mines together with the rapid expansion of the industry during the last three decades of the nineteenth century combined to produce the new party. Earlier attempts by coal miners to organize in 1876 had failed. Despite these early failures, several Greenback Clubs existed in the Birmingham area by the autumn of 1877. The first clubs contained only white members, although clubs for blacks soon followed. In fact, a white club at Jefferson Mines financed an organizing tour by Willis Johnson Thomas, a black miner who was elected president of the blacks' club and whose popularity as a charismatic speaker transcended the color line. The clubs began to operate as collective bargaining agents, appointing biracial committees to negotiate and calling strikes when necessary. Utilizing the issue of convict labor, which threatened to displace many miners, the Greenback organizations entered politics. The party in 1878 laid the blame for the recent depression at the feet of both national parties. It advocated increased circulation of paper money, coinage of silver, and equal taxation of all property. Congress should guarantee full employment, establish a ten-hour workday, end the convict-lease system, and prohibit immigration. Wealth should be the property of the laborer who produced it, not "idlers" who lived off the sweat of others. But party leaders hastened to add that their organization was neither communistic nor agrarian.[7]

Although the Greenbackers did not vanquish their Democratic foes in 1878, they did elect William Manning Lowe U.S. congressman in the Eighth Congressional District of, north Alabama. The Huntsville resident was an ideal Greenback candidate. A Confederate veteran and formerly a prominent Democrat, he was an excellent speaker and popular with the common folk. The incumbent Democrat served Lowe a ready-made issue by advocating a property qualification for voting. In the mortgage-ridden district, with rising rates of tenancy, the mistake cost him dearly. Greenbackers portrayed Democrats as enemies of the common people and dedicated to their own narrow class interests. Lowe won the congressional seat by carrying five of eight counties.[8]

James P. Armstrong, described only as a "poor white" from Montgomery County, also ran well in the Second Congressional District. The *New York Times* observed that both blacks and whites were working for him, although state Democratic papers took less enthusiastic notice of that fact. The *Troy Messenger* dismissed the party as an assortment of "thieves and tramps" advocating "communism and . . . civil usurpation." Proving that a white candidate could appeal to black voters, Armstrong carried predominantly black Montgomery County, which also contained many white working-class people, by a margin of two to one. However, Democratic charges of radicalism (the "Greenback Party and the Communists are so closely allied in principle") and racial iconoclasm (electing Greenbackers meant "fastening upon the necks of Alabamians the degrading and intolerable yoke of negro domination") undercut his support among poor white farmers. In two predominantly poor white counties at the extreme southern end of the congressional district, Covington and Crenshaw, he lost badly enough to elect his Democratic opponent despite receiving 42 percent of the vote. In the fifth and sixth districts the Greenbackers carried only 29 and 30 percent of the vote. But independent candidates did win eleven seats in the lower house and two in the Alabama senate, a respectable showing given the Democratic record of racial demagoguery and electoral corruption. The Independent-Greenback-Labor party attracted considerable support among poor whites, especially in the north Alabama coalfields. But it also made inroads among black workers with a frank appeal for working-class solidarity.[9]

The party redoubled its efforts following the 1878 successes. It founded a newspaper, the *Montgomery Workingmen's Advocate,* to advance the cause of James P. Armstrong for mayor. The editor of the new paper minced no words. He immediately joined combat with the *Tuskegee News,* which had urged whites to refuse to sell small patches of land to blacks who, he alleged, would rather live on half rations than make more money as sharecroppers under white supervision. The *Workingmen's Advocate* wondered if this admonition referred just to blacks or if it constituted a conspiracy to keep white sharecroppers from obtaining land. The Alabama legislature, wrote the editor, consisted of "ex-slaveholding aristocrats" who had "no respect for poor men." Such plutocrats denounced poor people as "disorganizers," "Agrarians," "communist," or "Radical" when they refused "to be underlings and slaves." The editor then clearly enunciated the Greenback-Labor creed: "While we abhor all communistic theories and stand up boldly for law, order and the defense of property, we do not subscribe to the notion that men of property should control legislation and fill all the public offices. Men are of more consequence than property."[10]

Greenbackers organized in other areas of the state as well. They established the *Huntsville Advocate and Gazette* and the *Mobile Gazette.* In 1880 the party nominated a Baptist preacher from Lawrence County, the Reverend J. M. Pickens, as its gubernatorial nominee. He campaigned on a platform that denounced Democratic fraud and restrictions on suffrage and endorsed tax reform, better public schools, and abolition of the convict-lease system. The party was able to mount a strong challenge in thirty-five counties, including many predominantly poor white counties such as Colbert, Cullman, Jackson, and Winston in north Alabama. But the historic alliance between hill counties and the Wiregrass broke down again in 1880, with no significant Greenback challenge in Crenshaw, Covington, or Geneva counties. In fact, the party failed to mount a serious effort in half of Alabama's counties and carried only three—Colbert, Lawrence, and Winston. The party did receive 45,435 votes, 23.9 percent of all cast, and elected five state legislators as well as a probate judge, sheriff, and circuit clerk in Jackson County. Obviously Democratic race-baiting hurt the Greenbackers badly, though they did manage to return Lowe to Congress in a disputed election in the Eighth District.[11]

The party recouped some of its losses in 1882. Fielding a full state ticket and avoiding national issues, the Greenbackers fused with Republicans, attacked the convict-lease system and Democratic corruption, and championed public school reforms. The Greenback gubernatorial candidate doubled the 1880 successes, carrying six counties (Lawrence, Madison, Walker, and Winston in the north, Elmore in central Alabama, and Choctaw in the south). Although losing 100,000 to 46,000, he increased his percentage of the vote to 31.6, and the party elected twenty-two independents to the legislature, including one from Crenshaw County in the Wiregrass. Unfortunately for them, the death of Congressman Lowe in October 1882 deprived the party of its most respected leader, and many of his followers subsequently drifted back into the Democratic party. By the mid-1880s the party's strength had shrunk into a small fortress in north Alabama bounded by Walker and Shelby counties to the south and Jackson and Lawrence counties to the north. Certainly the party hurt itself by internal bickering among its Republican, Greenback, and Independent elements. But the Democratic charges of racial amalgamation probably played a larger role in denying the coalition its logical poor white constituency.[12]

One natural ally of the Greenback party was the Knights of Labor organization. Labor relations in Alabama had been relatively tranquil until the mid-1870s, when several strikes occurred during the national depression. But as the country emerged from hard times, Alabama industry made its long-awaited surge. Manufacturing jobs mushroomed from 10,019 in 1880 to 52,904 by 1900. Alabama's railroad mileage doubled, creating an enormous market for crossties and lumber. Iron, coal, and textile production kept pace or even exceeded timber production.[13] Despite their lack of experience with unionism and their poor bargaining position as unskilled laborers, many of these new industrial workers were attracted to the Knights of Labor.

The Knights organization was a unique experiment in American labor history. Unlike the American Federation of Labor, it accepted any applicant, skilled or unskilled, black or white, male or female, directly into the national movement. Workers joined a local assembly that often combined disparate trades. The Germania Assembly, L.A. 9331, in Birmingham included 50 members, all of German extraction, as diverse as nine common laborers, one cigar maker, two bakers, and six merchants. Birmingham's local 9348 was composed entirely of females. Most locals were more traditional, combining white or black males generally within the same occupation. By January 1879 the Mobile local contained 700 members; 1 local in Montgomery, 716; and 2 miners' locals in Helena, 945 and 949. By the end of 1879 the Knights had 12 locals in Alabama; by 1887, its 109 locals contained 10,000 members.[14] They even experimented with cooperative towns, forming Powderly and Travellick, where workers could buy their own homes and lots by paying ten dollars a month for four years. And the Knights established the Powderly Cooperative Cigar Works in which all workmen were shareholders.[15]

By the late 1880s the organization was sufficiently strong to flex its political muscles. In 1887 the Knights elected city officials in Mobile. A year later the union elected a mayor and seven councilmen in Anniston, a slate that included a carpenter, brickmaker, butcher, shoemaker, and two molders. The following year the union elected a member as mayor of Selma. Flushed with its initial successes, the Knights helped organize the Union Labor Party in March 1888. The initial meeting of the Knights, Agricultural Wheel, and Greenbackers in 1887 had not been successful. But the following year the coalition finalized plans for the Labor Party of the State of Alabama. It advocated better pay and working conditions, election reforms, elimination of convict leasing, and government ownership of communication and transportation systems.[16]

By 1894 the Knights had virtually disappeared from Alabama, a casualty both of the national depression and of the union's rapid decline after public abhorrence at its involvement in a bloody confrontation in Chicago.[17] Many of its mining members deserted for the newly formed United Mine Workers. But the Knights' cooperative experiments and political involvements helped prepare the way for the Populist party in Alabama, and industrial workers, trained by the Greenbackers and Knights, became loyal supporters of Populism.

The agricultural precursor of the Populist party was the Farmers' Alliance, which began in Lampassas County, Texas, in September 1877. As it spread, it enrolled a cross section of farmers from all classes, although its leadership came overwhelmingly from more prosperous farmers and from rural professionals such as teachers, ministers, and physicians. Local social and economic divisions played a role in the success of the Alliance, as did its cooperative stores and lecturer-organizers. It harnessed the evangelical language and culture of the rural South to the cause of agricultural reform. At its core, the Alliance functioned as an important institution that attempted to maintain the values and norms of rural America against the onslaught of industrial-urban society. Never before in American history had farmers felt themselves so much besieged. And the Alliance was their primary line of defense.[18]

Alliancemen celebrated ruralism and its values. The *Athens Alabama Farmer* editorialized in 1888: "It was the intention of the omnipotent, as well as omniscient God that man was to have been an agriculturist." Conversely, a minister in the small town of Livingston believed that "a filthy city always has been, and always will be, a wicked place." An editor in Anniston warned residents of bustling Birmingham to "remember the fate of Sodom and Gomorrah." To Alliancemen, people counted for more than money, and their dispute was with materialism and its minions: trusts, monopoly, the "money power," and Wall Street. Local Democratic courthouse rings and business elites who sought factories and mills cared nothing for farmers or their plight. Their new industries threatened traditional values and folkways and the warm human relationships contingent upon family, community, and home. One farmer, opposing local boosters who were planning a railroad, cautioned in 1888: "Well railroads and free Negroes are of but very little benefit to poor people."[19]

By the fall of 1889 membership in the three thousand Alliance lodges had reached 125,000. Separate black and white Alliances made sure that venerated racial traditions remained intact. Though the Knights of Labor made overtures toward political union, the Alliance represented farmers who believed that agrarian and industrial interests were antithetical. As one Alliance journal expressed it: "The worst elements of our population . . . are to be found in the ranks of the Knights of Labor," who advocated the destruction of landownership, whereas "farmers, as a class, are conservative, and are the strongest supporters of law and order."[20]

The Alliance placed less emphasis on social and educational programs than had the Grange and more emphasis upon cooperatives. It created a State Exchange in Montgomery to market seeds, implements, fertilizer, jute bagging, and other commodities at reduced prices. It organized boycotts of trusts that exploited farmers. Alliance warehouses reduced the price for storing cotton.

As its business ventures ran into economic trouble, the Alliance increasingly turned to politics. Unwilling to split the white vote and thus raise the specter of black rule, Alliancemen first contested control of the Democratic party. In 1890 the Alliance championed the candidacy of Reuben F. Kolb, Alabama's commissioner of agriculture. Although he seemed to have sufficient delegates to win the 1890 nomination for governor, the Democratic convention's credentials committee maneuvered anti-Kolb delegates into a number of contested seats and gave the nomination to Thomas G. Jones. Although disgruntled, Kolb and his Alliance allies supported the Democratic ticket in the 1890 elections, partly because their legislative ticket constituted a majority in the state legislature. Despite their control of the new legislature, however, Alliancemen proved incapable of enacting their program.

By 1892 economic conditions in Alabama had worsened substantially. In May of that year, representatives of the Alliance, Trades Council, colored Farmers' Alliance, Knights of Labor, and the Populist party met in Birmingham to decide a future course. Although the Alliance refused to merge with the Populist party, it did form a coalition called Jeffersonian Democrats as a vehicle for its political platform. Almost identical to the Populist statement, it demanded protection of Negro legal rights, a liberally funded public school system, equitable taxation, regulation of trusts, abolition of the convict-lease system and national banks, expansion of currency by the unlimited coinage of silver, direct statewide primaries to replace the Democratic state convention, a graduated income tax, and popular election of state railroad commissioners. Kolb again lost the nomination at the state convention, but he entered the general election as the candidate of a coalition consisting of Jeffersonian Democrats, Populists, and Republicans.

Despite fierce Democratic attacks on this "radical" amalgamation with its portent of race mixing and Negro rule, Kolb lost by only 11,000 votes, 127,000 to 116,000. Jones carried the Black Belt but won only eight counties north of there. Kolb carried thirty-seven counties, mainly in the north and Wiregrass, and beat Jones by 15,000 votes outside the Black Belt. The most careful student of this election believes that Kolb would have won a fair vote but was counted out by Democrats who manipulated Black Belt returns. Jeffersonians and Populists did well enough in legislative races to defeat a bill introduced in the legislature to disfranchise anyone who did not own at least forty acres of land worth a minimum of $250. Such a bill would have eliminated from Alabama politics all poor whites as well as many small farmers.[21]

The Jeffersonians, despairing of attempts to guarantee a fair black vote, sponsored disfranchisement of Negroes. Redeemer Democrats, who needed black votes to maintain their control of the nominating convention, joined Populists to defeat this proposal.

By 1894 the contest for political power had become more clearly defined and more frankly class based. Jeffersonians and Populists finally merged under the title of Jeffersonian Democrats. North Alabama coal miners, deeply involved in a bitter strike, endorsed the platform, which added planks for lien laws to protect miners, a state inspector of weights and measures to make sure miners were paid fairly, the election of mine inspectors, and a law prohibiting the use of children below age thirteen in mines. Some prosperous farmers who had supported the Alliance for years drifted back into the Democratic party. They were unable to accept a Populist party that seemed to have co-opted the Alliance and turned it into a movement aligned with poor white class grievances. The Populist party retained an overwhelmingly agrarian thrust elsewhere in the South, but it profited from a strong infusion of industrial workers in Alabama. Although Democrats again denied Kolb the governorship by manipulating Black Belt returns, the coalition won nine of thirty-three senate seats and thirty-three seats in the house. Milford W. Howard of Fort Payne also won as the Populist candidate for Congress from the Seventh Congressional District.[22]

By 1896 Alabama's agrarian protest movement had broadened to include economically dissatisfied groups such as miners, railroad workers, and city laborers. It also included politically alienated groups such as Republicans and anti–Redeemer Democrats unhappy about political corruption. Populists and Republicans fused and appealed openly for black votes by appointing a Negro to the Combined Executive Committee. Fusionists won eleven of thirty-three senate seats but lost badly in the house races and in the governor's contest. The agrarian reform movement collapsed in 1896 when William Jennings Bryan won the Democratic presidential nomination and stole much of the Populist platform.

In retrospect, the Populist movement in Alabama still defies complete explanation. Having initially sought black support, it soon deserted biracial politics. Elected as reformers, Populists serving in the 1894 legislature voted eleven to ten against abolishing the convict-lease system and hedged on raising taxes. They seemed to favor the working poor, believing that hard work would result in economic progress. A conspiracy had deprived them of their rightful economic place, of justice and equity and the brotherhood of man. But they could not sustain a long-term, class-oriented reform program nor even develop a clearly articulated ideology.[23]

But to dismiss or even underestimate the economic class origins of Populism in Alabama is a serious mistake.[24] If individual Populists disagreed on the preferable solution to their problems, they did not disagree on the basic economic inequity operating against their interests. Historians of Populism in Alabama trace its roots to declining economic conditions. The single most important factor determining the tendency of Alabama people to vote Populist was the rate at which tenancy increased in a county during the decade of the 1890s. The Populist vote increased in direct proportion to the decline in the percentage of owner-operated farms.[25]

Even stronger evidence of the class origins of Alabama Populism emerges from local sources. The *Sand Mountain Signal,* a Populist paper, reported instances of starvation, of people "restless and discontented." Bad crops had caused many Sand Mountain residents to emigrate to Texas. The average mortgage debt had risen from $2.14 per acre in 1880 to $3.95 in 1890, while the value of a farm that year had declined to only $5.58 per acre. Farm tenancy had increased during the decade of the 1880s from 30 to 37 percent. Social cleavages existed as well. Farmers in the town of Guntersville who sold produce door-to-door complained of housewives who called them "nigger lovers and nigger-huggers" because of the biracial economic appeal of the Populists.[26]

Elsewhere similar conditions prevailed. In Clay County, oftentimes called the "Cradle of Alabama Populism," the low price of cotton fueled the Populist party by making "the already miserable condition of the poor whites . . . almost unbearable."[27] A Democratic paper in Calhoun County criticized agrarians for arraying "class against class."[28]

But perhaps no single incident revealed the multiple dimensions of agrarian protest better than the Dothan cotton riot of 1899. The city council of the newly formed town of Dothan hired J. L. "Tobe" Domingus as marshal and instructed him to collect license fees from drays bringing cotton to the Farmers' Alliance warehouse located just outside the city limits. Farmers bitterly objected to the license and their anger mounted as several farmers were arrested for refusing to pay. Among those arrested was George Stringer, manager of the Alliance warehouse. The marshal and Stringer became engaged in a fight that left the Alliance-man severely injured and Domingus charged with assault. Farmers flocked in from miles around for the preliminary hearing on the assault charges on October 14. So charged was the atmosphere that the judge postponed the hearing. But the angry farmers refused to leave town, milling around city streets and denouncing Marshal Domingus. The mood turned violent when Domingus and Stringer met face-to-face on the street; they exchanged angry words, then each reached for his weapon. They exchanged a fusillade that killed Stringer and another man and critically wounded Domingus, Stringer's brother and father, and another bystander. Friends carried Domingus to a physician's office and posted a guard against further violence as the riot threatened to become a pitched battle between town and rural residents. Domingus recovered, was tried for second-degree murder, and was sentenced to ten years in prison, although the Alabama Supreme Court reversed the verdict and ordered a second trial, in which he was acquitted.[29] The elements in this episode—rural versus urban values, the economic frustration of hard-pressed small farmers, what were perceived as inequitable laws aimed at farmers by local business and political elites—all conspired to produce the Dothan cotton riot.

Beyond the vexatious problem of defining Populism is the challenge of determining who were the Populists. Virtually every attempt to answer that query has concluded that Populists came from all agricultural classes and in Alabama from industrial workers as well. Most historians have concluded that tenant farmers played a minor role in the movement. The tenants' lack of organization and financial resources prevented any effective political activity. However, Alabama had no poll tax in the 1890s and its traditional support of universal manhood suffrage together with vigorous Alliance and Populist opposition to property qualifications for voting allowed poor whites to express their political preferences freely. How they did so reflects again the complexity and independence of poor whites. Fortunately Alabama Congressman George P. Harrison made an extensive list of the political affiliation of his Geneva County constituents. The Wiregrass county was one of the earliest and most rabid of Alabama's Populist strongholds. Long populated by large numbers of poor whites, Geneva had supported a strong herding economy before the Civil War and had added timber and turpentine production to its large flocks of sheep after 1865. Tenancy increased rapidly between 1870 and 1900. Thanks to Congressman Harrison's careful notes, one can determine the occupation and political affiliation of each of the county's registered voters in 1897. Coded "R," "D," or "P," the list shows that the county contained a negligible number of Republicans. But Populists and Democrats battled fiercely for control.

The unpublished federal agricultural census of 1880 listed each farmer in Geneva County, whether landowner, tenant, or sharecropper, and provided information about the person's status. By comparing the 1897 voter list to the 1880 agricultural census, a clear profile of county voters emerges.

Census data do not support assumptions that white tenant farmers did not vote. Of 521 farm owners in the county in 1880, 17.9 percent appeared on Harrison's list as voters in 1897. They were almost equally divided between Democrats (49) and Populists (44). Of 112 sharecroppers and tenants listed in 1880, 11.6 percent were listed as voters seventeen years later. But they preferred the Populist party by a margin of more than two to one (9 voters to 4).

No obvious economic pattern exists among 1880 farm owners that might suggest why they chose one party over another in 1897. Most small farmers in Geneva County were little better off than sharecroppers. And the political divisions evident in 1897 do not translate into clear economic divisions seventeen years earlier.[30] Future Populist owners ran farms that were slightly larger and more productive, but their crops were less valuable and they had less money invested in livestock and implements. Future Populists owned more horses, oxen, and poultry but fewer mules, cattle, sheep, and swine. Their production of sweet potatoes, corn, and fruit trailed that of future Democratic owners, but they also employed farm labor because they harvested more cotton.

Whatever its constituency, the ultimate value of Populism was not in the victories it won but in the issues it raised. Almost every major political reform enacted after 1900 found its antecedent in the Populist manifesto. And by frightening the Democratic party in the 1892 and 1894 elections, Populists pushed Democrats to the left. When Populism collapsed in 1896 and sent its faithful streaming back into the Democratic party, they helped carry the party in new directions.

The Progressive era in Alabama that followed the demise of Populism never really amounted to much despite spirited rhetoric and much posturing. The first Progressive governor, B. B. Comer, narrowed his reform agenda to railroad regulation. He also employed more child labor in his textile mills than any other industrialist in Alabama. Progressive Governor Thomas Kilby used the state militia to crush a strike by coal miners. Bibb Graves, elected in 1926, was arguably the most progressive governor in the twentieth century and pushed through a sweeping reform program that included improvements for public schools, greater appropriations for public health, and abolition of the convict-lease system. Despite the inadequacies of the reformers, to dismiss Progressivism as an attempt by businessmen to restore order or by reformers to establish social control over the lower classes ignores a great many changes welcomed by poor whites and enacted by the legislature. Progressivism combined organized labor, socially activist club women and ministers, urban reformers, and others into an effective coalition that addressed issues of concern to poor whites.

Progressivism did not begin auspiciously. In 1901 Democrats decided to revise the state's constitution. The ensuing election of delegates to the convention brought together groups representing populistic factions and urban reformers, as well as conservative defenders of the status quo. The new constitution did not well serve poor white interests. It levied a poll tax that disfranchised an estimated 35 percent of native-white males between the ages of twenty-one and forty-four, most of them poor people who could not afford the luxury of paying a tax in order to vote. Literacy tests and good character clauses, though designed primarily to eliminate black voters, could be used by local registrars against poor whites as well. One wit, asked if the controversial requirements could be used to keep Christ and his disciples from registering, replied shrewdly, "that would depend entirely on which way he was going to vote."[31] Although the new constitution's disfranchisement of blacks won support among all white economic groups, poor whites understood only too well the implications of poll taxes and literacy tests. Alabama was one of the few states to submit a new constitution to a direct vote of the people, and poor whites from the traditional Populist counties joined blacks in unsuccessfully opposing ratification. Their opposition was well founded. In one mountain community in the late 1930s, eighty-five householders were qualified to vote. Of these, forty-seven were landowners, twenty-one were tenants related to them, and only thirteen were unrelated white tenants. Of thirty-five housewives registered, only three were unrelated tenants' wives. In the community's power structure, 81 percent of all voters were landowners, their wives, or tenants related to them. The biggest barrier to tenant voting was the annual $1.50 poll tax, which if not paid yearly, accumulated to $20 or $30, nearly half as much cash income as the average white sharecropper received in a year.[32]

As a sop to the masses, Alabama Democrats adopted a statewide direct Democratic primary in 1902 to nominate the governor and other officers. But conservatives suffered no loss of power. Conservative planters from the Black Belt allied with manufacturers from the cities to maintain effective control of the legislature on most matters.[33] By refusing to reapportion the legislature as required by the 1901 constitution, they were able to maintain power despite massive shifts in population that otherwise would have weakened their hold on the state. So, populistic-minded whites not infrequently elected a Lister Hill or a Hugo Black to the U.S. Senate, or even a Bibb Graves to the governorship. But they could not significantly shift the political balance away from the right, especially when they denied themselves the aid of black voters who were their natural allies.

Whereas farmers had played the central role in the Populist revolt, industrial workers took center stage in the Progressive insurgency. Despite political efforts by Greenback-Laborites and the Knights of Labor, workers had accomplished little in the nineteenth century. Their unions were short-lived and their occasional political victories of no lasting significance. But angry workers increasingly turned to other forms of protest. As mentioned earlier, labor unions operated both within an occupation to address specific work problems and within a wider political framework to influence public policy.

One promoter of Alabama's industrial resources proclaimed in 1892 that in "no other manufacturing region of the United States are relations between employer and employee so generally satisfactory."[34] The activities of the state's workers did not support his contention.

During the 1880s, coal miners formed at least five unions, but each floundered over the issues of strikes or allowing black miners to join. With a work force split almost evenly between black and white miners, no resolution of common problems was possible without racial accord. In 1890 several unions merged to form the United Mine Workers of

America and successfully lobbied the legislature to pass the Mine Inspection Act, Alabama's first attempt to regulate a business through legislative action.[35]

During the 1890s the crusade to organize miners briefly merged with the Populist rebellion. The newly formed United Mine Workers of Alabama, organized in 1893, launched an industry-wide strike the following year that effectively united its black and white members. The miners also entered politics, endorsing Jeffersonian Democratic–Populist spokesman Reuben F. Kolb for governor and nominating two UMW members for the legislature from Jefferson County. In all, miners waged twelve major strikes in the twelve years between 1882 and 1894 but won only two minor disputes. Most were called not to demand higher salaries but to protest wage reductions. Nearly half were spontaneous work stoppages by independent-minded miners and were not called by their unions.[36]

If anything, conditions were worse in 1894 than in the preceding years. A national depression wrecked the market for coal and caused widespread suffering among miners. Sloss-Sheffield Iron and Steel Company discharged 1,200 workers in 1893. In January 1894, Birmingham police arrested 22 "tramps," 20 of them white. At their trial it became obvious that they were not tramps at all. They knew trades but could find no work. When arrested they had been sleeping in freight cars without permission. Jurors ignored their defense, found them guilty, and sentenced them to jail. During 1893 the average Alabama miner made $318, while TCI paid a 4 percent semiannual dividend and rewarded its president with a salary of $25,000 a year and its vice-presidents with salaries ranging from $5,000 to $12,000.[37]

The new century brought the UMW better luck. It gradually reduced racial division within its ranks and won respect for its vigorous opposition to ratification of the 1901 constitution. Alabama became the best organized of any southern coal-producing state, and the UMW was clearly the strongest union, dominating the Alabama State Federation of Labor from its creation in 1900. It persuaded the legislature to limit leasing of convicts in 1903 and won an arbitration decision that same year. It was able to attract national leaders to Alabama to speak on its behalf, people such as Mary H. "Mother" Jones and Socialist presidential candidate Eugene V. Debs. It endorsed candidates in state political races, though its candidates seldom won. But a series of unsuccessful strikes, discussed earlier, crippled the union. In virtually all of them, Alabama's governor intervened on behalf of the companies, though ostensibly to preserve law and order. And in every case, the union lost. Although its crusades to end the use of convict and child labor in the mines were ultimately successful, these victories resulted more from broad support by middle class reformers than from pressure by the UMW.[38]

Poor whites joined the unions as an affirmation of personal dignity and independence. But membership was not without danger and sacrifice. William T. Minor joined the revived UMW in 1933 while working for the anti-union DeBardeleben company. The corporation organized a company union and tried to force Minor to join. He avoided joining or being fired by expressing reservations until the company provided literature explaining the union. The company never furnished the literature, so he joined the UMW instead.[39] Reuben Farr lost his TCI job when he tried to organize a union. Later in the 1930s he tried again as a CIO organizer for the Steel Workers Organizing Committee and finally won a contract in 1937.[40]

Forces driving workers to organize were broader than just work place issues. The conservative 1901 state constitution and the legislature continued Alabama's post-Reconstruction tradition of low property taxes. As a result, cities had to rely on license fees, school tuition, and other user fees for revenue. City services suffered accordingly. Birmingham's school tuition in the mid-1890s caused an estimated 25 percent of white and 38 percent of black school children to drop out of school during the first month of classes. The *Labor Advocate* led the drive to abolish school tuition and increase property taxes. Although unsuccessful at the state level, labor's crusade against school tuition and in favor of free textbooks won in Jefferson County. But labor failed to win its broader wage demands. Although public opinion sympathized with miners during the 1894 strike, it turned against them in the violent 1908 confrontation. Officials allowed companies to hire special deputies for two dollars a day plus a dollar to the Jefferson County sheriff for each man he deputized. The companies hired between six hundred and eight hundred special deputies during the 1908 strike. City officials believed government must protect property, that laborers had the right to organize, that employers had the right to hire and fire whomever they pleased, and that during a strike any employee had the right to quit but not the right to interfere with anyone who took his or her place. Despite years of political efforts by unions, Birmingham politics divided along social interest-group lines rather than along class lines.[41]

The political impotence of Birmingham-area labor began to change during the teens when unionists helped elect George Huddleston, Sr., to Congress. Huddleston became a consistent advocate of coal miners. Testifying in 1919 before a congressional committee investigating coal profiteering, he chided corporations for increasing coal prices 82 percent during the war while labor costs had increased by only 47 percent.[42]

Unionism would have made greater progress save for its unremitting racism. Of all the problems that poor white culture bequeathed its people, none crippled the struggle for economic and political justice more than belief in the racial superiority of whites over blacks.

On occasion, working-class people proved capable of surmounting racial barriers. In the years following Reconstruction, working-class neighborhoods tended to follow occupational rather than racial patterns. Blacks and whites lived together in uneasy fraternity. In the new industrial town of Anniston, black and white workers frequently boarded with people of the opposite race. The city contained eight interracial lodges, which housed six to fourteen men. In 1880 one housed three white, nine black, and two mulatto laborers.[43] Mine workers often practiced racial cooperation, especially during the 1894 strike.[44]

But such cooperation was an exception. More typical were incidents of racial conflict and even violence. Dr. Edward Palmer of the Smithsonian Institution spent Christmas of 1883 in Tuscaloosa. He described the city on Christmas Day, crowded with drunken men and boys of both races. As an ox-driven wagon passed full of factory workers with faces blackened and fancifully dressed, a Negro threw firecrackers at the wagon. The occupants jumped out of the wagon and beat the hapless black man before bystanders could break up the brawl.[45]

That same year poor white workingmen refused to allow blacks in several building trades. A black clergyman from Birmingham testified: "There seems to be disposition on the part of some laborers in some localities to shut our people out. . . . There are some labor organizations here which, while they have no definite rules forbidding colored men to enter, yet do practically exclude them."[46]

Skilled white workers particularly shunned blacks, refusing to allow them as apprentices or into unions. They did not support black strikers. In turn Alabama blacks distrusted white organizers, believing that they pocketed dues paid by black workers. Even the racially integrated Knights of Labor contained locals that refused to allow blacks into their union hall.[47]

Conditions worsened after 1900 as segregation became more rigid. Although the first convention of the Alabama State Federation of Labor in 1901 elected two black officers and the second conducted an integrated meeting the following year in Selma, racial lines hardened quickly. The worsening climate was part of a larger struggle, the desire of skilled white workers to exclude both blacks and unskilled whites from their unions and thus strengthen their bargaining position.[48]

Whatever the source of conflict, the result was the same. Labor organizer J. H. Leath reported a strike of electrical linemen who walked off their jobs because their employer hired blacks. A locomotive engineer wrote from Birmingham in 1897 that he refused to belong to a union "when I have to be on an equality with the negro."[49] When Samuel Gompers, president of the American Federation of Labor, inquired about the feasibility of appointing a black organizer, the Alabama State Federation opposed it.[50] The *Laborer's Banner*, a newspaper for the Alabama Knights of Labor, editorialized in 1902 that white members of District 15 would not agree to a black as district master workman (president). Although they had "never failed to give the negroes their share of recognition," including membership on the executive board, election as master workman was unthinkable. The master workman had to negotiate grievances between labor and management, "and it is well known that a negro, no matter how capable, cannot accomplish anything under the circumstances."[51] Organized labor in Birmingham, while fighting to democratize and improve public education for poor whites, opposed extending it to blacks.[52]

On those rare occasions when blacks and poor whites found common cause, especially during coal strikes, conservative whites used evidence of racial cooperation against them. During the 1908 strike, Alabama newspapers noted that most members of the UMW were black, which allegedly proved that the real objective of the union was Negro social equality. Shrewd exploitation of this issue contributed directly to the failure of the strike.[53]

Owners utilized the same weapon during the 1920 coal strike. Observing that the UMW oath contained a passage promising "never to discriminate against a fellow worker on account of creed, color, or nationality," operators claimed that the oath attempted to promote social equality for blacks. The *Labor Advocate* tried unsuccessfully to blunt the emotional issue in an October 1920 editorial:

> "The fight is not social—rather [it is] an industrial fight. The Negro miner is entitled to the same wage and working conditions as white miners. The Negro miners are a fine set of men for the coal operators as long as they are willing to work for starvation wages without complaining, but when they . . . attempt to raise the standards of living for the white miner and his family as well as themselves, then the coal operators attempt to prejudice the case . . . by taking up the race question."[54]

Despite such enlightenment, the newspaper failed to convince many white coal miners much less the larger white society.

The biracial organizing efforts of the CIO during the 1930s provided additional ammunition for conservative Alabama newspapers and politicians. Charges of communism, socialism, radicalism, and race mixing trumpeted from the Tennessee Valley to the Gulf of Mexico. Nor did the racial cooperation of coal miners and steelworkers spread. Members of the Mine, Mill and Smelter Workers experienced serious racial conflict during 1943. White iron-ore miners, angry at the leftist politics and black domination of the union, tried to withdraw and join the United Steel Workers. Fights broke out between black and white miners. Noel R. Beddow, regional director of the CIO, wrote President Philip Murray that the racial split "must be healed or we are faced with another Detroit massacre."[55]

That same year a race riot occurred among shipyard workers in Mobile. As thousands of poor white and black tenant farmers poured into the port city from rural Mississippi and Alabama, violence broke out at the Alabama Dry Dock and Shipbuilding Company. To resolve the conflict, mediators assigned four ways to black workers and the rest to whites.[56]

Racial differences among poor folk complicated their lives enough without additional problems. But often poor white farmers demonstrated little sympathy for poor white industrial workers. Appalachian subsistence farmers particularly criticized relatives and neighbors who moved to town in order to work in textile mills. Desperate sharecroppers could not understand why coal miners, who lived in relative ease compared to tenants, went on strike. The worst conflicts did not emerge until the Great Depression, with its bitter disputes over the disposition of relief funds. But Herman Nixon remembered the resentment white tenants who lived on his family's Calhoun County farm felt toward relatives who left for "good paying mill jobs," then went on strike. Nixon also recalled one reason for the failure of the United Textile Workers to organize Alabama's mills. A female mill hand, grateful for her owner's paternalism and the comfortable house he provided, told a frustrated labor organizer: "You are not a worker and still would not be a worker if you used your hands a hundred and fifty years."[57]

In the political battles that workers won, their unions were of less assistance than middle class reformers. When the issues were strictly class based, such as better wages or shorter hours, only the most advanced Alabama Progressives helped, and workers usually lost. But when an issue touched a deeper moral sensibility, it won them influential allies from among urban ministers, club women, physicians, social workers, teachers, lawyers, and even enlightened businessmen. Five issues of great importance to poor whites merged into the humanitarian impulse of Progressivism and serve as examples of both the promise and limitations of political reform.

The first was public health. We have seen already how malaria, tuberculosis, hookworm, and pellagra plagued the poor. Progressivism spawned a political campaign to eliminate them. Alabama appearances by Dr. Charles Stiles, who led the attack on hookworm, helped mobilize the state's medical community against the problem. Discovering hook-worm rates as high as 62 percent in one south Alabama county, the state in 1910 organized the Hookworm Commission under the State Board of Health. It treated as many as 455 people at a single dispensary in one day. Some patients walked ten to twelve miles for help. The Rockefeller Fund provided $56,000, the Board of Health appropriated $4,500 more, and fifty-seven counties raised nearly $8,000. Together these funds allowed 87,000 people to receive treatment in free clinics. Although the money did not solve the problem, it certainly helped. In 1908 reformers established the Alabama Tuberculosis Association and shortly thereafter built a hospital in Birmingham.[58]

State and county appropriations for public health were vital to a state with so many poor, and Alabama belatedly began to accept its respon-sibility. In 1907 the state established a public health laboratory, which monitored the quality of water and milk consumed in the state. Legis-lators increased public health appropriations from $25,000 in 1910 to $286,000 in 1928. By the late 1920s forty-eight of sixty-seven counties contained health units. But the onset of the depression reduced the state health budget from a high of $686,000 to $287,000 in 1933. The number of county health departments actually declined two from the 1928 level.[59]

But Alabama's commitment to public health was tardy and flagging. Not until 1914 did an Alabama county institute a comprehensive health program coordinated by a full-time county health officer and staff. In that year, Walker County appropriated $3,000 for such a system. As late as 1918, Alabama ranked eleventh of twelve southern states in appro-priations for its State Board of Health. Its appropriations for public health, though substantially higher than in 1900, were only one-fourth the southern average.[60]

Mine safety was a second issue that gained major attention. Although disasters were a routine part of life for coal miners and have been treated as such earlier, they also were an important element of political life. The issue of responsibility—whether of owner, foreman, miner, or mine inspector—frequently polarized politics and caused miners to organize, strike, or register to vote.

Alabama coal mines experienced major explosions almost every year from 1905 until 1911. Beginning with the Virginia Mine disaster in February 1905 that took 111 lives, and ending with the Banner Mine explosion in April 1911 that killed 132, this period was the most lethal in Alabama mining history. Between 1900 and 1910, 1,180 miners died in explosions. The UMW blamed the explosions on untrained, inex-perienced convicts, careless child laborers, and lax mine inspectors. Actually the issue was far more complex.

Thanks to an extensive investigation of the Virginia Mine disaster, we have a revealing account of the relationship between state officials, owners, supervisors, and poor white miners. The explosion at the mine operated by Alabama Steel and Wire Company and A. W. Reed Company occurred at 4:00 P.M. on February 20, 1905. State mine inspectors had last inspected the mine just over two months earlier, on December 12. Previous reports all the way back to 1903 indicated a cavalier attitude by the company regarding mine safety. Reports in November 1903 criticized the mine's poor ventilation and accumulation of dust. The mine foreman had no foreman's certificate and had not reported two accidents, both violations of state law. Also in the fall of 1903 mine inspectors warned that unless miners sprinkled water on the dust, an incorrect charge might set off an explosion. When three miners were burned in January 1904 because they used too much dynamite, associate mine inspector James Hillhouse urged miners to use picks or machines to undercut the coal, thus reducing the threat of explosions. But miners were paid by the ton, and pick and shovel work took longer and substantially reduced their pay. Dynamite charges reduced the soft coal to dust that was easily gathered into cars for the trip to the surface.[61]

Alabama's three mine inspectors regularly warned the mine superintendent and company officials about the danger of a "windy shot," miner jargon for a blowout. Miners in the Virginia Mine drilled a hole in the face of a coal seam. They put one charge of dynamite at the end of the hole and another toward the front. They attached a short fuse, lighted it, quickly sealed the hole with coal dust, then ran. If the charge fired properly, it broke the coal into fine particles, absorbing the blast. But on numerous occasions, something went wrong. The back charge did not ignite. Instead of demolishing the seam, the blast fired directly outward, leaving an enlarged funnel-shaped hole. Sometimes the blast blew a hole in the opposite side of the "room"; other times it burned or killed the miners who set the charge. Or worst of all, it ignited dry coal dust and blew up the shaft and everyone in it.

State mine inspectors suggested quite specific remedies. Miners should undercut the coal seam instead of blasting a solid face. This procedure would bring the upper part down and absorb the explosion. Men should use longer fuses and always seal or "tamp" the hole with rock or clay, never with slack coal or coal dust, which could contribute to an explosion. They should tamp the hole before lighting the fuse. Superintendents should limit powder or dynamite allowed in the mine to one day's supply to prevent secondary explosions. And the company should hire a "shot fixer," a skilled miner who would "shoot" the coal (set off the charges) at night when no one else was in the mine. Repeated violations of these instructions caused chief mine inspector J. M. Gray to write the superintendent on March 8, 1904:

> You have all the characteristics there that go to make up the disastrous dust explosions. You have gas in your mine, your mine is very dusty and you shoot the coal on the solid and use inexperienced labor to a certain extent, and it has been our observation of windy shots we have had in this State that they have been principally caused from misplacing and charging of shots.[62]

Owners, obviously concerned at reports of repeated violations, began to comply during the last months of 1904. The company ordered men to use longer fuses, tamp with wet material, and use picks to undercut the face. When miners ignored the rules, the company reprimanded them and laid them off. Miners complained that they had to buy their own fuses out of inadequate salaries, and therefore they bought the shortest fuses possible. In short, they gambled their lives in an attempt to stretch their wages. The superintendent also failed to communicate some rules to the miners. For instance, he did not tell the mine foreman to clean up or sprinkle piles of coal dust that had accumulated along the track in the shaft. When inspectors directly ordered him to do so, he had complied for several weeks, until May or June 1904, then stopped because he concluded that miners ignored his instructions. Mine superintendent F. H. Gafford testified at hearings into the explosion that he "did not undertake to mine this coal as [mine inspectors] suggested" because it would force miners to mine coal in a way they would not accept. He had posted the rules. Independent, fatalistic miners, trying to scrimp on costs to maximize earnings, ignored them.[63]

On the afternoon of February 20, 1905, the exact scenario that the three state mine inspectors had warned about for two years occurred. A "windy shot" blew out of a funnel-shaped hole. The fire ignited dry coal dust that had accumulated in the mine. The explosion set off secondary blasts among the dynamite stored in the shaft, and 111 men died.

Nor did the folly end after the Virginia Mine disaster. On February 27, 1906, Number Two mine at Piper blew up. The company had adopted safety rules, but independent, desperately poor miners had not followed them.[64]

In April 1907, chief mine inspector J. M. Gray wrote an angry letter to Governor B. B. Comer concerning the Flat Top Mine operated by convict labor for Sloss-Sheffield Company. At the urging of the state mine inspectors, the owners had employed free miners skilled as "shot firers" and had substantially reduced accidents. But Alabama's Convict

Board of Inspectors, perhaps as the result of political pressure from influential industrialists, complained because the company had to pay free miners to do work that convicts could do for nothing. As a result of this meddling, the company had replaced the free miners with convict shot firers. Gray, furious at company officials, informed the governor that he had also demanded that the powder magazine be removed from the mine and reminded Comer that recent explosions at Blocton, Coal City, Pratt City, Virginia Mine, and Piper Mines had all been caused by "windy shots" and inadequate handling of dynamite. Unless the Convict Board of Inspectors complied with his instructions within ten days, he requested permission to employ an attorney to enforce his instructions.[65]

Alabama's officials seemed to learn nothing from these disasters. The Banner Mine explosion in 1911 did result in a new forty-three-page mine safety law, but its strongest provisions died in a corporation-controlled legislature. The state not only refused to abolish the convict-lease system, but it also began to contract to operate Banner Mine itself and sell the coal to Pratt Consolidated. This effort earned the state sixteen thousand dollars a month in revenue and the enduring enmity of some mine owners who were furious not at the inhumanity of forced labor but at unfair competition from state-operated mines. To make matters worse, in 1913 officials embezzled state monies obtained from convict leases.

Hundreds of pages of correspondence and testimony demonstrate the frustrations of state mine inspectors as they fought a losing battle against the greed of mine owners and the independence, ignorance, and indigence of miners. Owners only reluctantly complied with orders that cost them additional money. And they refused altogether to enforce rules that miners seemed reluctant to obey. For their part, miners were caught between the need to be cautious, which reduced their already meager pay to subsistence levels or below, and their desire to stretch their luck in order to fatten paychecks. Imbued with a culture that fostered the rejection of rules set by outsiders and a fatalism that accepted certain risks as inevitable in life, they mined as they pleased, with little thought for the consequences.

Although the convict-lease system, the third reform issue, is often thought of as exclusively pertaining to mining, it actually operated in a broader range of occupations. But central to the system were its political origins and associations. The convict-lease system began as an attempt at economy by Democratic Redeemers who had to trim state expenditures as they reduced taxes. During antebellum days the plantation served as a penal institution for slaves, and small county jails sufficed for lawless whites. But Reconstruction governments had appropriated money for a state penitentiary. In order to reduce penal costs, the legislature allowed state and county convicts to be leased to private companies that paid the state a fee and assumed the cost of their care. With so many blacks and poor whites available, the system never had problems supplying a steady supply of prisoners, many of them guilty only of making illicit moonshine or stealing a pig for hungry families. Although plantations, textile mills, turpentine mills, sawmills, factories, and coal mines leased the convicts, mines employed the largest number. Because the supply of prisoners was steady, owners did not need to be concerned about their diet, clothing, or health. The diary of state convict inspector Reginal Dawson revealed the complex relationship between businessmen, convicts, and state politics.

Dawson was one of the first convict inspectors hired by the state, and his diaries between 1883 and 1893 reveal the problems inherent in the system. At the Thompson plantation in Macon County he found prisoners housed in cells "so low that a man cannot stand upright." On J. W. Comer's plantation in Barbour County he found a white convict with pneumonia because he had no fireplace in his cell. Everything was filthy, there was no provision for medical care, and many prisoners were bound in irons.

Even these conditions paled compared to conditions in coal mines. In March 1893, Dawson inspected Pratt Mines, which the company proclaimed to be the best convict operation in Alabama. Dawson disagreed, calling it filthy, crowded, and filled with men whose hair was full of lice. Convicts complained that they were kept beyond their sentences. In July 1883, he reported the illegal whipping of a female prisoner who had been stripped, held down, and given fifty-six lashes with a heavy strap for trying to escape. He came away from the incident convinced that "convicts should not be worked in mines." But in September the governor rejected his proposal to withdraw convicts from the coal industry. A month later, in October 1883, he found a prisoner working at Pratt Mines who had been sentenced to three years and nine months in May 1875, more than eight years earlier. Many others had served months beyond the end of their sentences. Despite repeated warnings, guards continued to beat convicts. In October, Dawson found prisoners at Pratt Mines ragged and dirty because their clothes had not been washed or changed in five weeks. In November he found convicts eating out of coal shovels because they had neither plates nor utensils. He appeared before a grand jury in November 1883, but the chief convict inspector begged him "as a personal favor that I should not report to the governor about things at the shaft [of Pratt Mines]." The inspectors met and agreed not to report conditions until the next inspection, when treatment of convicts had improved.[66]

Many poor whites confirmed Dawson's descriptions. Jim Lauderdale, a filthy, indigent alcoholic when interviewed during the 1930s, testified to beating Negro convicts for fun while serving as a guard at a Birmingham-area coal mine. E. H. Moore, who began working for the Jefferson County Convict Department in 1919, described punishment in detail. If he caught a convict loafing, he began with a diet of bread and water. Next, he administered a whipping. The third step was the "doghouse," a two-by-three-foot cubicle with ventilation holes. He gave the prisoner a dose of salts and warm water as a laxative then locked him in the cell overnight where he could not stand or sit down. His last resort was a three-foot length of hose pipe: "you can work a man over pretty good with a piece of hose pipe and never mark him. It doesn't break the hide. . . . And I've worked on a thousand of 'em."[67]

Miners began to agitate for abolition almost as soon as the convict system began. The practice was a major impetus for the creation of the Greenback-Labor party in the state, described earlier, and both the Knights of Labor and the Populists–Jeffersonian Democrats adopted the cause of abolition. Despite such pressure, the system continued and expanded. When TCI took over Pratt Coal and Coke Company in 1886, six hundred convicts worked in the mines. The new company, which dominated Birmingham's economic and political life, obtained a ten-year lease to all state convicts in 1888 and subsequent leases for 1898–1903, 1903–08, and 1908–11. By 1911 convict labor earned the state $404,000, a figure that grew to $2,115,000 by 1918 and involved four thousand convicts. Although black convicts outnumbered whites three to one, numbers of poor whites served also.[68] This powerful alliance between business leaders and politicians prolonged a system that Tennessee abolished in 1893 as a consequence of an armed uprising by free miners. Louisiana ended leasing in 1901 as a consequence of Progressive reforms. But a combination of more docile and fragmented labor and a timid and ineffective Progressive movement left the system intact in Alabama until Governor Bibb Graves finally ended it in 1927.

Opposition to the system began to build in the late 1890s. Dr. Russell M. Cunningham, a TCI physician, knew firsthand the high death rate and wretched treatment of convicts. He urged the legislature to appoint a joint committee to investigate the lease system. An 1897 legislative report found that the death rate for convict miners was four times higher than for free Negro miners and ten times higher than for free whites. The committee recommended abolition, but opponents in the house killed the bill. Revelations of corruption among convict inspectors in 1901 sparked another effort at reform that also came to nothing. Russell Cunningham tried again to abolish the system in 1906. After losing his job with TCI in 1902, partly because of his work on behalf of penal reform, he won election as Alabama's lieutenant governor. In 1906 he ran for governor against B. B. Comer, but his credentials on other reform issues were suspect and he lost. In 1907 the reform impetus finally reached the convict-lease system when the legislature passed a law overhauling leasing but allowing it to continue.[69]

When George Crawford became president of TCI in 1907, he began to seek different solutions for the company's labor shortage and in 1911 did not renew TCI's bid for convicts. Paradoxically, a reform-minded company physician and a corporate executive, aided by middle class sympathy and labor pressure, probably did more to abolish the state convict-lease system than decades of poor white efforts through their labor unions and political parties.

Middle class support also played the major role in limiting a fourth problem, child labor. The steady spread of the "family wage" concept, which required women and children to work in order for the family to survive, introduced large numbers of children into the state labor force. Though many poor white parents believed their children were better off working than living idle lives and getting into mischief, the chief impetus was still low wages for the head of family. And the claims of mill owners and superintendents that they would lose their work force unless they employed the children of their operatives was as much rationalization as reason.

In 1900, 59 percent of Alabama males and 31.3 percent of females between the ages of ten and fifteen held jobs. By 1910 the percentages had increased to 61.9 and 41.3.[70]

Two forces converged during the first two decades of the new century to restrict child labor. The historic opposition of labor unions continued and intensified. In 1900 AFL president Samuel Gompers commissioned Irene M. Ashby-Macfayden to publicize the abuses of child labor in Alabama in order to enact reform through the legislature. Ashby-Macfayden—a slender, vivacious woman with sparkling blue eyes and dimpled, rosy cheeks who came from England to study American manufacturing conditions—received a warm welcome from hospitable mill owners. Many of them expressed sympathy for her cause, though they complained that they would be put at a competitive disadvantage if Alabama limited child labor while surrounding states refused to do so.

She began immediately to research and publicize the problems, visiting twenty-four mills in sixteen towns and cities. She found operatives from "little isolated farms and cabins, very poor and very prolific." She also cultivated a wide circle of allies, including the Alabama Women's Christian Temperance Union, which voted in 1900 to lobby for child-labor restrictions. The Ministers Union of Montgomery led by the Reverend Edgar Gardner Murphy, the Society for the Propagation of Christian Knowledge of Mobile, and the Birmingham Women's Club joined the cause. The *Alabama Baptist* produced scathing editorials condemning child labor. James H. Leath, a labor organizer and legislator from Birmingham, introduced a bill in the 1901 legislature. It prohibited employment of children under age twelve, except when such a child was the sole support for a widowed mother or invalid father, and prohibited children under age sixteen from night labor or workweeks in excess of sixty hours. It also required functional literacy and three months of schooling for mill children under age fourteen and compulsory free education of sixty days annually for working children younger than twelve and for nonworking children younger than sixteen.[71]

Ashby-Macfayden soon found that research and publicity were easier than changing the minds of conservative, recalcitrant legislators. In fact, organized labor had tried repeatedly to enact reforms, all to no avail. Such bills had died in the 1892–93 and 1894–95 legislatures. In the 1897–98 session, Luther C. Jones, representative from Lee County and president of the Trades Council of Phenix City, introduced another child-labor bill in the house, and Populist Dr. J. A. Hurst sponsored it in the senate. The bill passed the senate but died in the house. Alabama had been the first state to regulate child labor in 1887 and the first to repeal restrictions in 1895 at the urging of Dwight mill officials from Chicopee, Massachusetts, who ran a large mill in Gadsden.

This fact furnished Ashby-Macfayden one of her most effective arguments. Noting that northern-owned mills employed more Alabama children than southern-run mills, she tried to appeal to the state's patriotism. She sought to blunt business opposition by citing eleven mill managers she interviewed as favoring abolition of child labor below age twelve.

But business opposition coalesced rapidly against the 1901 bill. Six of the fifteen managers Ashby-Macfayden interviewed opposed any restrictions on child labor as "irritating and harmful class legislation." Children were better off in mill villages than in miserable rural shanties. They would starve except for textile mills. State regulation would drive capital out of Alabama and halt industrial development. J. M. Faulkner, chief attorney for the powerful Louisville and Nashville Railroad, also testified against the bill, calling it "the most virulent form of paternalism that had ever been brought before the Alabama legislature." If the bill passed, it "would destroy the homes and the democracy of the State." Despite testimony by Mr. Murphy and several representatives of Birmingham Women's Clubs, the bill was killed after only five minutes of committee deliberations.[72]

The 1901 legislative battle did sow a seed that germinated quickly. Defeat of the reform mobilized the state press, both secular and religious. The Methodist *Alabama Christian Advocate* and the *Alabama Baptist* attacked the legislature for its lack of concern for the welfare of children, and papers in Mobile, Montgomery, and Birmingham joined the fray. Even more important were the new middle class allies, especially the Reverend Edgar G. Murphy.

An Episcopal priest at St. John's Church in Montgomery, Mr. Murphy was deeply imbued with Social Gospel ideas. He had played a major role in operating Montgomery Infirmary, the city's charity hospital that had opened in 1886. When the facility had to close for lack of funds in 1900, Murphy chided local citizens who spent more on music and bunting for the city's street fair than on medical care for the city's indigent. He began an annual "Free Dinner to the Children" on Thanksgiving and Christmas to feed youth from the city's cotton-mill district. He began a chapel to reach unchurched poor whites in the West End factories.[73]

By 1901 Mr. Murphy had turned his attention to child labor. Following his testimony to the legislature, he was maligned as a tool of New England industrialists who were eager to destroy southern competitors. Mr. Murphy, outraged by the defeat of the reform bill and the vilification of its advocates, organized the Alabama Child Labor Committee with local chapters scattered throughout the state. He launched letter-writing campaigns and tried to keep the AFL out of the battle for fear that association with it would taint reform. In 1903 he succeeded in piloting a compromise reform bill to passage, although it allowed children as young as ten to work if they had widowed mothers or dependent fathers. The new law allowed children over age ten to work as many as sixty-six hours a week and provided for no enforcement machinery. In 1907 Mr. Murphy, who by then had left Montgomery to organize and direct the National Child Labor Committee, orchestrated another effort in the Alabama legislature that substantially strengthened the 1903 law.[74] It raised the minimum age to twelve and provided for inspection. But the law authorized only one inspector who would be responsible for sixty-nine jails, seventy-one factories, and fifty-five almshouses.

During subsequent years, new allies joined the ranks of child-labor reformers. Julia Tutwiler and J. L. M. Curry, respected Alabama civic and religious leaders, endorsed child-labor reform. In 1908 Mrs. John Van Vorst wrote a muckraking book, *The Cry of the Children: A Study of Child Labor,* which contained dozens of stories concerning poor white mill children in Alabama. The National Child Labor Committee commissioned photographer Lewis Hine to photograph child laborers, and he produced an emotionally devastating series from Alabama that visually depicted the tragedy of child labor and rallied additional support.[75]

This enlarged base of humanitarian, religious, and middle class support brought new victories. Legislation in 1915 limited children below the age of fourteen to a sixty-hour workweek and prohibited their use in night work. Any child seeking work had to present certification of eligibility from a principal or school superintendent. The law also provided compulsory education for eighty days a year, though this requirement could be waived in cases of extreme poverty. A comprehensive survey in 1918 led to more sweeping legislation in the form of a maximum forty-eight-hour week, regulation of work certificates, and creation of a child welfare department to enforce existing state laws.

The new state welfare workers relentlessly pursued their duties. In their first annual report, they summarized inspections of 197 cotton mills and twenty coal mines where they discovered 530 boys and 694 girls under age sixteen working. They also discovered 14 children in Covington County living with their mothers in a house of prostitution. One girl of thirteen was pregnant and several had venereal disease. In another cotton mill community, they found 18 illegitimate and 4 crippled children receiving no medical attention and twenty-eight deserted families. Such investigations led to increased legislative funding, from $12,400 in 1919 to $50,000 in 1927. By the latter year eleven counties had begun child welfare boards, fifty-three counties had employed social workers, and sixty-six provided some form of child welfare service.[76]

A crusade begun by unions on behalf of workers and poor whites reached some of its goals only when it broadened its political boundaries. Paradoxically many of its middle class exponents only half understood the people they sought to help. The Reverend Edgar G. Murphy correctly attributed opposition to child-labor restriction partly to ignorant poor white parents who little appreciated the values of education; but his remedy imposed a highly regulated world. Despairing of effective state regulation, he increasingly favored uniform federal child-labor laws. His byword became "efficiency," and he sought for poor whites a world they did not necessarily seek for themselves.[77]

The same year as his appearance before the legislature on behalf of child-labor regulation, Mr. Murphy endorsed an educational test for voting in order to eliminate illiterate voters. His proposal, widely distributed in pamphlet form, earned a scathing denunciation from T. A. Street, who lived in the hill country of northeast Alabama. He blasted Mr. Murphy as "plutocratic":

> To white men of white counties not imbused [sic] with the political vices, frauds and corruptions of the Black Belt, this is the language of an oligarch and worse still, a deceiver. Among the plain white people of our state the plutocratic ideas . . . are not indigenous. . . .
> It is not to the interest of the Black Belt to goad the plain white people of the white counties on to desperation by disfranchising them. If the plutocratic tendencies of our times continue in our

Southland the time is not far distant when the plain white people in their desperate attempts to free themselves will bring desolation and ruin among us.[78]

Mr. Murphy must have puzzled over people who seemed so reluctant to be saved from their vices.

The fifth issue that energized Progressivism and affected the poor was literacy. Reformers increasingly tried to cure child labor and poverty by strengthening public schools, requiring attendance, and reducing illiteracy. But it was no easy task to reform in a decade educational problems that had accumulated for half a century.

The 1868 Reconstruction constitution had made the maintenance of a biracial free public school system a state responsibility. That year the first director of the Peabody Fund, created to promote education in the "more destitute portions" of the South, had found 1,300 Alabama students paying ten dollars each to attend school. Thanks to infusion of state tax funds and Peabody money, Montgomery, where no free public school had operated for white children, began one. A Peabody gift of two thousand dollars to Selma created a free public school for whites who had previously been charged seventy-five dollars a year. It was a good beginning.

Redeemers reversed this progress when they regained political control in the 1870s. By cutting property taxes, they eliminated a major source of school funding and left a small poll tax as the chief source of local funding. In 1878 the director of the Peabody Fund found few well-taught schools in Alabama: "the counties which have relied on the state funds . . . manifest no inclination to tax themselves. . . . The apathy of the people seems to be quite as great as their poverty."[79]

No one had better characterized the state's educational inadequacies. A combination of public apathy and conservative opposition to higher taxes condemned generations to illiteracy.

At the turn of the century, illiteracy rates remained high and education was in disarray. According to the 1910 census, Alabama had the sixth-highest native-white illiteracy of any state. A total of 84,768 native-born whites could neither read nor write (10.1 percent of the entire white population).[80] In Montgomery County during the mid-teens, the value of forty-seven white schools was only half the value of the county jail or one-fourth the value of the county courthouse. There were only sufficient desks for one-third of the county's 3,020 white school children. In twenty-eight of the schools teachers had no desks. Only two of forty-seven schools provided proper ventilation, and few had sanitation facilities or water.[81]

Reform began in 1907 when the legislature established county high schools. By 1918, fifty-seven of sixty-seven counties provided secondary schools for whites. In February 1915, the legislature established the Illiteracy Commission, designed to eliminate adult illiteracy. The Alabama Education Association, the Federated Women's Clubs, and other groups funded the work. The commission's first report was so shocking that it led to a rare victory for a local tax referendum in November 1916.

In the years that followed, commission reports regularly documented the extent of Alabama's educational crisis. The commission launched a special drive among draftees in 1918 that was funded by the Council of Defense and the Federated Women's Clubs. Of nearly 173,000 draft registration cards submitted in Alabama, approximately 10,000 indicated that the draft-age males were illiterate. Volunteer teachers started schools that usually began with patriotic rallies and speeches. At the courthouse in Andalusia, a fourteen-year-old seventh-grade boy taught two adult men. Minnie Belle Diamond taught her older brother, who had dropped out of school to work so his younger sister could obtain an education. At Camp Sheridan in Montgomery, local women taught 1,350 male illiterates.[82] In 1919 the state assumed the responsibilities and funding of the commission by entrusting its duties to the new Division of Exceptional Education within the State Department of Education. The legislature appropriated $12,500 to eliminate illiteracy.[83]

Such efforts made only a dent in the problem. In 1918 the state contained 455,000 white children of school age, but only 376,000 were enrolled in school. That same year a survey of twelve Alabama counties by the National Child Labor Committee revealed that, whereas the sons of farm owners missed school 29 percent of the time, the sons of tenants missed 39 percent. Tenants' children failed more grades because they simply could not attend. Investigators found four children in one school aged nine, ten, twelve, and thirteen, all in the first grade. None was being promoted and all had missed at least seventy days in order to work on farms.[84] By 1919, 60 percent of all white rural school children still attended one- or two-teacher schools, and 70 percent of rural teachers held the lowest grade certificate issued by the state. The crisis of local support remained a perennial problem. Alabama led the South in state appropriations but was forty-sixth among the forty-eight states in local tax revenue expended for education.[85]

Even so, the state did make progress. By 1927 it improved one rank from sixth to seventh among states with the highest white illiteracy. In 1914 rates of white illiteracy were highest in the hill counties and Wiregrass. But by 1920 rates in those areas had declined sharply. In the Wiregrass counties of Covington and Geneva, illiteracy among whites ten years of age and older stood at 13.4 and 17.4 percent in 1914. By 1920 the rates in those counties had declined to 9.1 and 11.5 percent.

In the east Alabama hill counties of Randolph and Cleburne, rates in 1914 were 21.3 and 14.6 percent; six years later they had dropped to 7.3 and 11.5 percent. Further north in Jackson County the 1914 rate was 13.6 percent, the 1920 equivalent only 11.9.[86]

Along with upgrading schools, reformers aimed at adult illiterates for whom school improvements had come too late. Their solution for the 57,208 adult whites who could not write in 1920 was the Opportunity Schools. The schools offered instruction to pupils age twenty-one and older, although they also enrolled teenagers between sixteen and twenty if they had not completed the fourth grade. The subjects were designed to be equivalent to a fourth-grade education. The schools were located in areas where at least fifteen people were eligible to enroll and promised to attend. Weekly attendance had to reach ten. In farming areas the schools ran four hours a session, twenty hours a week, for six weeks during idle seasons. In industrial centers the schools operated split shifts in the morning and at night for six weeks. A special curriculum taught basic reading and writing skills. But supplementary texts included the calendar, Sunday school literature, newspapers, and public signs. Special bulletins designed by Auburn University's Home Demonstration agents explained in simple language how to install a water system, make bread, or some other useful skill.[87]

Like most of the agricultural schools in the South, Auburn worked closest with conservative large farmers and property owners who organized into the Farm Bureau Federation. Membership dues required of Farm Bureau members effectively screened out the poorest white farmers and virtually all tenants. Gradually the bureau became a potent political force in Alabama, and one largely uninterested in the problems of poor whites.[88] Most members of Home Demonstration Clubs were wives or daughters of Farm Bureau members. In fact the County Home Demonstration Councils usually met at the county courthouse on the same day the directors of the Farm Bureau met.[89]

But in the years between 1924 and 1943 county agents and especially Home Demonstration representatives displayed increasing interest in the problems of their poorer white clients. In 1925 the Cooperative Extension Service employed a bright young home economics major at Auburn who was the daughter of a tenant farmer to accompany the state director when she visited Opportunity Schools. This woman worked closely with the State Welfare Department to locate children who were not attending school. And the Opportunity Schools attracted a new clientele to the work of Home Demonstration agents. An agent in Jackson County described her new clients as isolated mountain people, mill women, and farm laborers.[90]

The Opportunity Schools, patterned loosely after the popular Danish

Folk Schools, spread to fifty-seven counties and three cities by 1927 and enrolled 22,815 adult white illiterates in 836 schools. Teachers often reported touching stories. Two teachers in a Tuscaloosa County mining community could not conduct their first two sessions because they had only one lantern and a miner's carbide lamp. So one illiterate offered to buy additional lamps if the others would bring oil. The lamps rolled in and so did the people: 15 illiterates attended the second session, 26 enrolled by the end of the first week, and 42 at the end of the second. Discussions were lively, especially a geography lecture that resulted in "a very hot discussion . . . about the world's being flat." An illiterate white woman from Cleburne County attended the Opportunity School for two years, then became a school trustee. In 1926 she wrote the state director an imprecise but moving letter about the joy she had experienced in reading books and letters from her children: "I want another school this summer if we can have it. I can lay everything down and go I pray we can you may get tired of trying to read this if this school had not come about I would not learn to read those Books Some time I cry when I think how long I stayed in the old world and could not read or write." She was one of 321 enrolled in the Cleburne County school. Calhoun County educated 121, Jackson County 216, Covington County 198, and Birmingham 1,006.[91]

The legislature also created the Alabama School of Trades in 1925. The first trade school in the South, the Gadsden institution taught printing, electricity, cabinet making, and bricklaying to poor white boys from across the state. Later the curriculum expanded to include auto mechanics, drafting, and welding. Open to white males over the age of sixteen, poor boys often paid the ten-dollar tuition by supplying cords of wood or working on the school farm. Usually they arrived with nothing more than a quilt, sheets, and overalls.[92]

How all these reforms translated into enlarged opportunities for poor whites depended on individual circumstances. For those directly affected, Progressivism brought change for the good. But for most, the reforms were too late or too gradual or did not reach them at all. And worst of all, the poll tax greatly reduced their political participation. There is no evidence that increased literacy enlarged voter rolls. Many of the poor, such as lumber worker Cecil Spencer or sharecropper Homer Flynt, either were too busy earning a living to vote or too poor to pay the poll tax, although they both demonstrated keen political awareness. Many of them fell victim to the political corruption and manipulation of votes common to southern politics. Frank Uptain learned that to sell illegal moonshine all he had to do was bribe the sheriff. Textile worker W. W. Jewell first entered the political process as a recipient of free whiskey at the city jail on election day. For voting the proper way, the sheriff dispensed a quart of confiscated moonshine. Between elections the chief deputy gave whiskey to mill workers short on cash. County law officers also escorted prostitutes to the polls on election day. Later Jewell supported Georgia Governor Eugene Talmadge, a demagogic politician who talked much about helping poor whites, then betrayed their interests on almost every occasion.[93]

Most poor whites proved as independent and unpredictable in politics as in most other aspects of their lives. Because most of them were interviewed in the late 1930s or later, it is hard to evaluate their political preferences earlier. But their interviews supply surprising details that leave little doubt about the accuracy of their accounts. Textile worker Mrs. L. A. House termed her rural family "Shelby County Republicans" during the 1880s and 1890s. She recalled vividly how her father swung to the Fusion Populist ticket in 1894. The election split her school, with children whose parents supported Democrat William C. Oates wearing chains of oats and devotees of Populist Reuben Kolb trimming shuck hats with corn cobs.[94] Coal miner John Gates usually voted a straight Republican ticket, as did Cherokee County herb doctor Tommie Bass. Textile workers Mr. and Mrs. Sam Anderson and Mr. and Mrs. Tom Alsobrook were "straight voting Democrats," as were coal miner Sam Brakefield and miner's widow Ila Hendrix. The Great Depression and the New Deal were pivotal events in their political loyalties. Many miners expressed affection for Franklin D. Roosevelt, and Republican John Gates left the party of his father to vote for FDR As June Odom, a textile worker's daughter, explained, the mill people in Cordova "blamed all the hard times and Depression on the Republicans."[95]

If poor whites did not assert themselves politically as much as some wished, they often made herculean efforts against long odds. Leaving the Democratic party for Populism might seem easy enough a century later, but in the early 1890s it was considered to be racial and political treason that divided families, churches, and communities. Joining a union was no easy decision when it might cost a miner or mill hand a job or subject him to charges of communism or anarchism. And strikes were often desperate struggles with lives as well as jobs hanging in the balance.

PART FOUR

Disruption and Integration

ELEVEN

"We Didn't Know the Difference"

The Great Depression

The Great Depression is often remembered chronologically, etched in memory as one recalls a tornado, flood, or some other great calamity. Such recollection is entirely appropriate for upper and middle class folk or for skilled workers, whose comfortable lives were rudely interrupted and chaotically rearranged by the multiple shocks occurring between 1920 and 1940. But for the poor, these years presented a more complex panorama. Growing recognition of poverty, the creation of welfare-state capitalism and relief programs, federal assistance in unionization, and other changes often substantially improved their lives. Other poor people remember the depression as but another episode in lives filled with trouble, not as a sudden reversal of fortune.

Some who date their economic salvation to the New Deal perhaps attribute more credit to Franklin Roosevelt than rightly is due him. It was their dispossession from the land, migration to cities, and the opportunities generated by a wartime economy that changed the course of their lives. The historical basis of their affection for Roosevelt was not the long-term reforms of the New Deal, but the short-term relief it afforded. Unfortunately, historians who judge the past from many years' distance have dismissed this relief effort as largely inconsequential, which it most certainly was not. As a people whose vision seldom exceeded the problem of surviving a single day, the poor were grateful for help, however short its duration.

Some of the poor transcended that existential vision in search of a different kind of world. They wrote letters, organized, struck, sabotaged, fought, picketed, and sometimes killed with a fury born of desperation. Often they caused the middle class social workers and bureaucrats who sought to help them as much grief as the conservative businessmen and courthouse gangs who blocked their path to a better life.

Alabama's twilight of prosperity silhouetted a state of bounteous human and natural resources: moderate climate, perhaps the nation's best system of river drainage and clean water, the South's largest and most diverse industrial work force, seven major types of soil and some three hundred subtypes adaptive to almost any crop or livestock, and vast timber reserves despite the clear-cutting of the pine belt.

On the eve of the cataclysm, Alabama contained 206,835 cotton farms; 62,425 (30.2 percent) were operated by owners and 144,410 (69.8 percent) by tenants, of whom 58,143 were sharecroppers. In 1930 nearly 90,000 of the tenant farmers were white, a sharp increase from 74,000 in 1915. Of the 593,696 whites within the work force, nearly 30,000 labored in cotton mills, 15,000 in sawmills, 25,000 in iron and steel plants, and 17,500 in coal or iron-ore mines.

Low incomes resulted in dilapidated housing, unhealthful diet, shabby dress, poor health, and illiteracy. Some 61,000 native-born white Alabamians still could neither read nor write in 1930, 4.8 percent of the total population. Even that percentage was misleading. Some wealthy Black Belt counties registered rates of white illiteracy below 1 percent while scattered northern hill and southeastern Wiregrass counties topped 10 percent (Jackson County bordering Tennessee had a rate of 10.3 percent; Geneva County, in the southeastern Wiregrass, 11.3 percent). To cope with these manifold challenges, Alabama had a rural school system totally inadequate for either race, a State Board of Health with only fourteen clinics to serve indigents, and health departments that operated in only fifty-two of the state's sixty-seven counties.[1]

Reformers had long worried about Alabama's destitute people, but during the 1930s the number of poor increased dramatically. Employment rates declined for both races during the decade, by 5.6 percent for whites and by 13.6 percent for blacks. Only three southern states registered a total decline of white employment during the decade, and Alabama had the dubious distinction of leading the way. Total nonfarm employment in Alabama declined by 15 percent between 1930 and 1940, again outpacing other southern states. In 1932 more than 12,000 unemployed men registered for municipal jobs in Birmingham, and the Red Cross estimated that between 6,000 and 8,000 people lacked adequate food, fuel, and housing. The county almshouse, intended to house 220, held 500.[2]

Whatever affection one might have for the old order was immaterial in a world so jolted by social and economic shocks. The most prescient protectors of the world that once had been conceded a new reality even if they never came to terms with it. Grover Hall, award-winning editor of the conservative *Montgomery Advertiser,* wrote a journalist friend of his affection for the economic system of the 1920s that had been so profitable to their class. But that same system, he admitted, had been "disastrous to the great majority":

> However much we may love the days of Harding and Coolidge, they are gone forever—they will not be recaptured, no matter how much the newspapers of the land may rant and strain. Personally I fared much better under Pickle Coolidge than I have under any subsequent President—but I saw his world and mine *die.* Under Roosevelt I saw a new world born, even though much that Roosevelt has done annoys me and will not receive my approval. . . . But a new day, a new world, a new leadership, a new responsibility are here and you and I would be foolish to ignore the fact.[3]

To those desperately clinging to a job, a few acres of land, or even a piece of bread, the new world that Hall anticipated with such ambivalence emerged painfully slowly.

Relief

The initial response to the depression was a determined effort at emergency relief. Private charities such as the Red Cross and individual churches tried their best, but the magnitude of the financial collapse overwhelmed their well-intentioned efforts. The federal relief apparatus created by President Herbert Hoover, and greatly expanded by President Roosevelt, reached into every state. The Alabama Relief Administration was chaired by Montgomery real estate developer Algernon Blair and consisted of four prominent citizens: Birmingham textile tycoon Donald Comer, Montgomerian John H. Peach, Grover C. Hall, editor of the *Montgomery Advertiser,* and Gessner McCrovey of Mobile. Their choice as director was Thad Holt, who worked out of headquarters in Montgomery.

Luckily for Alabama, Aubrey Williams was named field representative of the Federal Emergency Relief Administration in 1933 to assist Holt in determining the extent of deprivation in the state. The choice could not have been better. After remedial education, he struggled through college and then turned his idealism from the Presbyterian ministry to social work. By 1934 Williams had become assistant administrator of FERA, a trusted lieutenant of that agency's chief, Harry L. Hopkins, and strategically located in a position that allowed him to provide vital assistance to his native state.[4] And Alabama needed all the help Williams and Holt could provide.

A study of transients conducted between January and July 1933 revealed one dimension of the crisis. The Louisville and Nashville Railroad kept accurate records of illegal riders ejected from L&N trains or property in Birmingham during the four months of January, February, June, and July 1933. Four detectives expelled 27,236 and believed they could have removed twice that number with more detectives. Two detectives riding a train from Birmingham to Montgomery on the night of July 1, 1933, removed 730 "hoboes" and 350 trespassers on railroad right-of-way. Perhaps hobo was the wrong term for the detectives to use. Between 25 and 30 percent were teenage boys without work, and another 10 to 15 percent were teenage girls; sometimes entire families were pulled off boxcars. Both races were found in the same cars and serious injuries were common. In 1932, 17 people were killed and 46 injured, with many of the injuries involving severed limbs when the victims jumped from trains. Other lines kept poorer records but confirmed the problem. The Central of Georgia crossed the Piedmont through a series of mill villages, and workers traveled illegally from town to town seeking work. Between July 11 and 17, 600 people were taken from trains that were arriving in Alabama's largest city.

What awaited transients in the Birmingham area was not appealing. Hobo jungles at Twenty-fourth Street Viaduct, Green Springs Bridge, Boyles, East Thomas, Pratt City, Jasper, and Carbon Hill provided a warm fire and fellowship but little else. Those successful at panhandling on the city's sidewalks stayed at one of the flophouses. Birmingham contained twenty-seven for whites, most with a capacity of ten to twenty-five people per day. They charged ten to fifteen cents a day with six to a dozen beds per room. Only three of the houses had clean sheets when inspected. Most had worn-out mattresses and none had bathing facilities other than a washbowl. Few had screens or heating in the wintertime. During winter months the houses were filled to capacity at night, but in other seasons transients slept in parks, under viaducts, in empty houses, boxcars, or wherever they could find six feet of space. Many of the transients were lured to Alabama in 1933 by hopes of a job with the newly established Tennessee Valley Authority. Discouraged when they found no job at Muscle Shoals, they hopped a southbound train. Their mood was often sullen. Railroad detectives who talked with them reported that "many said that the depression was still as bad as ever and that the newspapers were merely full of 'huey' so the working people would not start a revolution. Many expressed the hope that we would have a real revolution this winter and were expecting to take part in it."[5]

Nor was the transient problem confined to Birmingham. So serious had the crisis become by May 1933 that the Alabama Relief Committee was divided into three departments, one of them being the Alabama Transient Bureau. In some places, such as Muscle Shoals, the bureau provided relief through private boardinghouses. At other places it either created a transient camp or occupied an existing facility such as historic Fort Morgan across the bay from Mobile. By December 1934 there were four official transient camps in Alabama caring for more than 8,000 persons, including 424 family groups. When asked to explain their mobility, their reasons varied from "chronic hobo" (446) to "run away" (43) to "adventure" (150). But by far the most frequent responses from white transients were "unemployed" (2,245) or "looking for work" (1,911).[6]

Nor did the institutionalizing of transiency solve the problem. The chief of police of Flomaton, Alabama, a small community on the Florida border, petitioned in 1933 for location of a transient camp. The town of 915, located at the junction of two railroad lines and two highways, received 300 transients every twenty-four hours. During one seven-day survey, the chief and his four policemen counted 2,500.[7]

Transients could have saved themselves a lot of trouble by checking on conditions before traveling to the "Heart of Dixie." As relief funds were exhausted during the summer of 1933, weekly payments were slashed to between fifty cents and two dollars. In a number of counties, relief payments ended altogether in mid-July, and no new relief applications were accepted. The number of destitute families affected by the cuts was substantial, even staggering in counties such as Jefferson, containing Birmingham, which listed 20,000 indigent families. The director of the Social Service Division of the state Relief Administration terminated all relief families with "the slightest opportunity for the family to obtain food from relatives or other sources, even an inadequate amount of food." The shortage of food was complicated by chronic health problems, including mental stress generated by the depression. One state relief official described the challenge: "Pellagra, tuberculosis prevail to undreamed of extents; nervous breakdowns attributed to mental strains resulting from inadequate relief are discernable [sic] on every hand."[8]

As people were terminated from relief projects, they sent letters pouring into both state and federal offices. The letters came from desperate people seeking bread for the next meal and from middle class folk forced to live at a level lower than they had known. Writers complained that their relief payments for a ten-hour day one day a week amounted to only fifty cents, far too little to sustain life. Charges abounded of political appointments to relief jobs, favoritism, corruption, and insensitivity to the poor by middle class social workers.[9]

Most writers begged rather than complained. One man on relief had been reduced to only five hours of work per week, which provided insufficient income for his family of three. The family sometimes went for days without food. A man who ran a gristmill near Elba in south Alabama implored FDR to help those who came to him with crying children, begging for bread and grease. A correspondent who had been reduced to a relief payment of $1.20 per week compared his income to prevailing prices in the town of Ariton: flour, $1.10 for twenty-four pounds, pork 11 to 12¢ per pound, meal 30¢ a peck, sugar 6¢ a pound. E. M. Abercrombie wrote the president without emotion, almost matter-of-factly: "Mr. Roosevelt we are going to starve to death if you don't have something done at once for the relief of us poor distressed, oppressed people. . . . Mr. Roosevelt we are what you may say on starvation and without clothing and barefooted." A forty-five-year-old widow wrote Harry Hopkins a tale of woe in August 1933. Under the existing child-labor laws only one of her four children could work. He had been hurt in a sawmill accident but had obtained relief work on the county roads for $1.00 a day, working a three-day week. When relief funds ran out he was laid off. She had no relatives to ask for help, and farmers had plowed under their cotton, thus depriving her of seasonal employment as a picker. All her children contracted flu in the spring of 1933, leaving her with unpaid doctor's bills. Her cow had died in the spring, as had all but eighteen of her one hundred chickens. She was barefoot, without clothes or food, and had tasted no flour in five weeks or sugar in three months. She finally was compelled to write for help when her pig died. But even she was better off than A. A. Bonner of Choctaw County, who reported that neither state relief agencies nor the Red Cross had established work in his community and that people could get neither work nor bread.[10]

Careful investigations revealed that some of those who claimed to be destitute really were not. But the suffering was widespread despite occasional abuses.

Official state surveys listed 86,733 families on relief rolls on September 1, 1933. Relief administrators quietly acknowledged the inadequacy of payments by establishing a goal of $9.60 per person in net actual relief payments before accepting any appreciable number of new applications. Thad Holt conceded that funds allocated to counties for relief had been inadequate. A drought during the spring of 1933, loss of livestock, destroyed gardens, exhausted savings, landlords unable to furnish their tenants, all had combined to overwhelm the relief system: "The absolute facts in Alabama are that money was not available and, as a result, the county relief agencies were able to administer assistance only to those families where extreme starvation and emergencies of illness existed. As for the others, we somehow prolonged their misery." Unable to help the people he was intended to serve, he wrote bitterly: "I am weary unto death of prolonging the misery of good people."[11]

As seasonal jobs in lumbering and cotton picking ended in the fall of 1933, relief rolls began to increase again. By the end of September, 106,854 families plus 9,874 additional individuals received relief. Letters from the poor continued to be both pitiful and bitter. A resident of Fayette County in the northwest hill country, where relief was not yet well organized, reported that the boll weevil had destroyed what cotton had survived the drought. Children were barefoot, naked, and unable to attend school. He was paralyzed and crippled, and his wife and two children were in "serious condition." A Baldwin County woman from near Mobile reported that people in the upper part of the county had received only one consignment for the poor, averaging thirty yards of piece goods and three pounds of meat to a "white family of 6." When President Roosevelt in a fireside chat on October 22 asked people to contact him if they were losing their property to foreclosure, he was inundated with letters from Alabama. Particularly pathetic were letters from poor whites who were losing the furniture they had laboriously collected in more-prosperous years. E. W. Morgan, who rented Black Belt land near Selma, wrote the president that his mules had been taken from him in the spring before he could plant a crop. Without cotton, he could not pay the rent on the farm, and he would be evicted. His only possessions were a cow and a two-horse wagon with no animal to pull it. He asked the president who would pay his rent or buy him a pair of mules. Some letters minced no words and offered warnings instead of inquiries. A Birmingham resident warned the president that he intended to organize a welfare union to protest the inadequacy of the New Deal's relief system.[12]

A field report by Aubrey Williams admitted that relief in Alabama, "measured by any decent standard," was inadequate. Only by growing cabbage, turnip greens, and beans, which stretched their relief payments, could clients avoid starvation. Outside Birmingham, Mobile, and Montgomery, medical care and clothing were inadequate, especially for children. Destitute rural families, unable to obtain assistance, were moving into towns in some parts of the state; industrial workers, laid off their jobs, were moving onto the land in other places.[13]

A fifty-year-old man out of work traveled an estimated 38,000 miles from Georgia to the Texas panhandle to Michigan between 1930 and 1933. All his odd jobs produced no more than $1,000. Settled in Mobile, he was startled one night by a frantic knock. When he opened the door, a nearly hysterical Negro woman stood before him in the dark. She offered to do any kind of work to get milk for her baby. In her hand she held a paper sack with scraps given her from supper. He gave her change for milk then sat down to write Secretary of Labor Frances Perkins: Roosevelt must stop listening to welfare workers, chambers of commerce, and Democratic politicians, and become aware of the desperation of the poor.[14]

But many winters of privation and want lay ahead, and the poor were more patient than he imagined. As that first awful year of the New Deal came to an end, a field report from Alabama put the winter of discontent in a broader setting: "Centers of heavy industries show no sign of improvement. . . . Conditions in rural areas are discovered to be increasingly bad; [such] conditions revealed by attempts of tenant farmers and sharecroppers to secure C.W.A. employment. In all probability, these conditions are the accumulation of many years of dwindling income."[15]

As months turned into years, the relief effort became institutionalized, although not necessarily more effective. The Works Progress Administration divided Alabama into six districts with a headquarters in each. Farm families were cut from relief rolls and transferred to rural rehabilitation. But striking coal miners and textile workers took their places. Transient camps at Birmingham, Muscle Shoals, Montgomery, Mobile, and Fort Morgan received both larger numbers of displaced persons and a higher percentage of family groups. By summer 1934, the camps cared for more than five thousand people, 62 percent of them family groups. All were for whites only; not until fall 1934 was a camp organized for blacks. In the following months, short-lived camps were established in Calhoun and Bibb counties. Community work centers, created by the Works Division of the Alabama Relief Administration, provided more useful jobs by taking over and operating factories that had closed and by starting new shops. The Birmingham Iron and Wood Work Shop employed relief clients who made ten thousand wooden plow stocks for the Rural Rehabilitation Division. Another woodworking shop made one thousand steer yokes. Other facilities included a furniture factory at Montgomery, a brick plant and sawmill in Dale County, a Birmingham garage for reconditioning trucks, a sawmill in Barbour County, and a brick plant in Blount County.[16]

Relief primarily affected people living in urban areas. During most of the depression, at least 35 percent of Alabama's total relief load was located in three urban counties: Mobile, Montgomery, and Jefferson. Of 56,000 families on relief statewide in December 1934, 28,000 lived in Birmingham alone. Many of these were poor people who had long lived on the economic fringes of the city. In fact the unemployed that

Birmingham, Alabama, migrant camp. Photo by Arthur Rothstein.
(Courtesy of Farm Security Administration Photographs, Library of
Congress)

May included 30 percent "servant and allied workers," 16.8 percent unskilled, and 18.6 percent semiskilled, a total of more than 65 percent who had always clung to the precipice of Birmingham's volatile economy. And the temporary improvement in employment in the fall of 1934 did not last. By January 1935, Jefferson County listed 100,000 people on relief, causing Roosevelt to describe Birmingham as the "worst hit town in the country." Thad Holt explained that the fall reduction was due to the removal of the rural rehabilitation program and the ruthless exclusion of all but the most desperate from relief. The employment pattern in durable goods, Birmingham's lifeblood, followed the national cycle: 45,000 workers employed in 1929 and 25,000 in 1934.

The TCI operation at Docena declined from 1,000 employees to 78 by 1933. Mary Dolliver, a TCI social worker at Docena, publicly tried to maintain the morale of the village's miners. But privately she wrote her brother:

> "All I am doing now is taking care of clothing relief cases and flour lines, and all the people I deal with have been without work for months, and they are getting to the point where they are without hope. Like the fool that I am, I'd spend all my earthly goods on them, but it's just a drop in the bucket. . . . Tuesday is always a bad day, with a line of discouraging length to listen to one by one—a tale of woe, insufficient clothing and food, sickness. Pellagra is increasing and I wonder what the end will be. . . . If this thing continues, I will have forgotten how to play."[17]

On Christmas Eve 1934, Thad Holt telephoned Aubrey Williams to tell him that more than half of Birmingham's families would be without work after Christmas; Williams, a native of the city, replied with understatement: "that thing worries me in Birmingham."[18]

He had good reason to worry. The individual stories were more profoundly distressing than the cold statistics that Holt related to him in that Christmas tidings of bad cheer. Hattie Freeman had never experienced an easy life. In 1934 she was a white widow, unemployed, with a number of small children. She was two months behind in her rent, and her landlord, a black property owner, threatened to turn her case over to a lawyer and take her household goods in payment. She ended her plea to President Roosevelt with great urgency: "Please for God's sake send some one to help me in this distress."[19]

One of the major problems both statewide and in Birmingham was transiency. County relief agencies established minimum residency periods before a person was eligible for relief, and many poor people became casualties of bureaucratic regulations. Martha Albright, her husband, and three children moved from Shelby County to Bessemer, an industrial suburb of Birmingham, in order to care for an infirm eighty-year-old woman who had raised her. Stranded in Jefferson County, Mrs. Albright applied for help, only to be informed that she was not eligible in Jefferson and should move back to Shelby County, where she could be accepted on relief. Desperate, she wrote President Roosevelt: "I don't have a bit to eat except what my husband gets begin [sic] and bumming and that is very little and I live in a very small shack without any way to have a fire and I have 2 children to go to school without means to go on." Her family would gladly return to Shelby County "but we can't get something to eat much less moveing [sic] means. . . . its not so bad for me and my husband but the little children that cannot help themselves."[20]

The elderly suffered even more. When they were cut off relief, the only alternatives were to become a burden to already desperate families or to enter the county almshouse. The Jefferson County poorhouse at Ketona was bursting at the seams already. And as one elderly, desperate man wrote Harry Hopkins, "many old people had almost rather die than to go to the poor house."[21]

Mobile shared a fate common to Birmingham's, though the extent of deprivation was less. By 1935, 10.3 percent of the native-born white families were on relief; 21 percent of the white wage-earning families earned less than $500 a year and 51.7 percent less than $1,000. Relief payments in 1934, which averaged $10.08 per month in Jefferson County, amounted to only $8.36 in Mobile. Emmett Gale earned slightly above the county average for his family of three. But from his relief check of $2.15 per week he paid 9¢ for cooking oil, $2.06 for groceries, and $2.50 per week for room rent. When he begged relief officials for a pair of overalls for himself and a pair of shoes for his nearly blind and cancer-stricken wife, relief officials told him he would have to wait three more weeks to be eligible for clothes. Harassed relief officials stretched inadequate federal budgets as far as they could, but the state contributed little if anything for relief, and the poor unjustly blamed the relief officials for insensitivity and worse. But the human desperation remained, despite the good intentions of relief workers, and the publisher of the *Mobile Post* warned about the extent of suffering in the city: "In other words there are sparks of revolution in the air that may burst into flame at any moment."[22]

Although relief efforts were better organized and more extensive in Alabama's three largest cities, both the relief program and its inadequacies were obvious throughout the state. Problems such as transient ineligibility, loopholes in policies, and localized starvation appeared in all sections.

Three relief cases demonstrate the fate of marginal people who slipped through the "safety net" of New Deal programs. The first was Vassie Burney. In 1935 she lived on the line between Cullman and Morgan counties in a drought-stricken area where her family's crops had burned up and their horse had died. Her husband, desperate for food and too proud to beg, despite two strokes, a rupture, and kidney trouble, contracted to mine coal and moved his wife and five children to Warrior. The mine closed and they were stranded, ineligible for relief in their new location: "Time after time we go hungry. Sometimes our friends give us food. . . . I have tried every way to look on the sunny side of life and yet how can I. I don't want to be a beggar. I want work. I don't want things for nothing. Can you point me to a job?"[23]

Minnie Boatfield, a widow with four children, moved from Autauga

County into Montgomery during the depression. Shortly after arriving in the city, two of her children became gravely ill. She bitterly complained that relief workers first denied them medicine, then when both died, refused to lend her a truck to transport their bodies back to her home community for burial. Finally on relief, the $2.60 she received every two weeks did not provide adequate support.[24]

O. J. Perry of Odenville in St. Clair County recounted one elaborate saga of the depression. He and his wife and five children began the depression in their own home on one-half acre of land. He mined coal as his primary source of income until November 1931, when he was laid off. At first he worked a series of odd jobs, then purchased a mule and tried to grow his own food. But the first year his mule died and he had no money with which to purchase another. He obtained flour and clothing from the Red Cross, then in 1933 began working two days a week on a relief job. He was placed on a Civil Works Administration project in December 1933 but was transferred back to relief a week later when officials discovered that he was walking eight miles a day to his job. In January 1934, officials found a CWA job closer to his house, and he earned $4.50 per week until February, when his job ended. In March he reapplied for relief, but when he wrote begging for help, officials kept his case pending until the staff finished its routine investigation. He moved to Jefferson County, where he obtained work in a coal mine until it shut down. He then applied for relief, only to discover that he did not satisfy the residency requirement. Unable to feed the seven members of his family, he wrote Roosevelt a simple message in June 1936: "We are on starvation."[25]

The poor often turned their scorn on their benefactors, the relief workers who were almost always professional social workers or middle class people down on their luck. The field-workers, recruited primarily from the state child welfare association and from TCI social workers, functioned better than any other staff in the region. But that was not the way the poor perceived them. A TVA worker, laid off his job and off relief, lodged a common grievance that relief caseworkers drove fancy cars, dressed fine, and were crooks appropriating for themselves money intended for the poor. They also talked to poor people "like [we are] slaves when we ask for help."[26]

Such charges sometimes led to formal investigations, the most extensive coming in December 1934 in Jefferson County. Friction between the works division and the social service division of the Alabama Relief Administration became so great that administrators ordered a survey of relief operations. The survey revealed many problems and resulted in a conference of relief workers. Among disclosures was the fact that only 12,000 of 30,000 relief clients actually received jobs. Delays of one to six weeks between certification for relief and provision of a job were common. Some clients who were skilled laborers were allowed to work far in excess of the average budgeted relief time because so many of the jobs were construction projects. As a result, a minority of the clients received a majority of the funds. But many of the problems were intrinsic within the community. A militant labor movement precipitated a number of strikes, and management often retaliated with lockouts and layoffs. Labor unrest forced thousands of additional people onto relief rolls. Yet federal officials considered Alabama's relief effort and its director Thad Holt models of efficiency and often used them as examples for other states.[27]

Middle and upper class Alabamians criticized relief just as bitterly, though for quite different reasons. One Walker County resident complained to Senator John Bankhead that many people receiving relief had never worked and never would, and he urged that they not be given free commodities. A Sheffield man wanted transients sent back to the counties and states from which they came because they caused sharp increases in rent. Some Baldwin County citizens protested that the transient camp near their cottages at Fort Morgan had transferred "our little paradise" into "a living Hell" of burglaries and thefts; transients were a "race of shiftless nomadic barbarians." A petition opposing a transient camp in Perry County contained more than a hundred signatures of prominent citizens, including the presidents of both Marion Institute and Judson College. The petition against the "hobo camp" referred to transients as undesirables and criminals who "robbed and pillaged," and it warned that their wives, daughters, and the female students at Judson College would not be safe with such a facility in the county. The camp was located elsewhere.[28]

An extensive survey of prominent Birmingham citizens revealed the same attitudes toward the poor. The responses divided the poor into two broad categories: people of pride who were temporarily out of work and deserved assistance, and those chronically poor without pride who did not deserve relief. The Reverend Eugene L. Sands, a Catholic priest, separated relief clients into the chronically poor willing to live on charity and unemployed middle class industrious people anxious for work and ashamed of relief. Industrialist William H. Stockham observed that whites on relief were always complaining about the size of relief payments, unlike blacks who were grateful for anything. The long-term solution to poverty, he maintained, was to curb federal efforts to force "closed shop unionism on Industry" together with programs to locate the unemployed back on farms. One social worker also responded with a division into temporary and chronically poor. Into the latter category he placed large numbers of women and children who had been deserted

by husbands and fathers, the elderly and sick, alcoholics, and those
without job skills or training. But he also discussed a "certain integrity
of character" and "moral factor" that determined success or failure in
life. The chronically poor could be attributed to heredity and lack of
education as well as to economic circumstances. One angry Jewish labor
lawyer presented the other side, blaming the failures of the relief system
on the predominance of middle class college-educated relief workers
who were easily fooled by middle class whites who hid resources and
blacks who really did not want to work anyway. Hence truly deserving
poor whites received far too little. The Alabama Relief Administration
was "succeeding far better in making bolsheviks and radicals in the
State . . . than any group or groups of Russian envoys could do."[29]

Such tirades were unfair. Relief literally kept the social fabric of Birmingham stitched together during the 1930s. Senator John H. Bankhead saw the real issue of relief with much greater clarity. Informed in
1935 that the textile mills and coal mines of Walker County were operating at nearly 100 percent capacity and that several PWA projects
had employed several hundred more, Bankhead pondered how it could
be that the county still had 2,181 on work relief and 400 tenant farmers
on rural rehabilitation. In a letter to Harry Hopkins he wondered if this
contradictory evidence might not indicate that there must have been
many Walker County people without work even before the depression
began.[30]

Rural Poverty

Hopkins and Aubrey Williams knew only too well
the source of this paradox. Hidden from sight
down a hundred dirt roads were tens of thousands of small farmers,
yeoman and tenant, black and white, hardly visible to Bankhead in the
1920s but painfully obvious to the men and women reading government
reports in the 1930s. Urban relief did reach the chronically poor, but
mainly it served people temporarily down on their luck; rural rehabilitation struck at the most elemental and persistent problem of poverty
in Alabama, tenant farming.

Tenancy had increased with only brief interruptions since 1865. By
1935, Alabama contained 176,247 tenant families, 64.5 percent of all
farmers in the state. Some 68,000 of these families were sharecroppers,
the poorest of the poor; and white sharecrop families slightly outnumbered blacks, 34,717 to 33,257.[31] The age-old rural definition of the
good life—ownership of land—was still alive and well among such people. But history seemed to be moving in an opposite direction.

The initial contribution of the New Deal to the relief of tenant farmers was discovery. No solution, whether temporary or permanent, was possible until someone traveled those country roads, pausing before log cabins and unpainted board shacks to ask questions and record answers. Although James Agee's magisterial and tormented book, *Let Us Now Praise Famous Men*, resulted from research among white sharecroppers in west Alabama, it did not appear until 1941 and attracted few readers until the 1960s. Alabamians learned of the crisis in more pedestrian ways.

Social scientists, often funded with federal or state grants, began to investigate tenancy intensely when the federal government designated the South as the nation's number one economic problem. Two reports were particularly perceptive. Harold Hoffsommer, a specialist in rural sociology at Auburn University, undertook a study of landlord-tenant relations under sponsorship of FERA. As he conducted his investigation, his preconceived notions about rural poverty evaporated. How could one study the "employment" of cotton pickers and choppers? The labor was so highly seasonal, he wrote, that "I am personally coming to believe that the whole cropper system of cotton farming is nothing more than a certain species of unemployment."[32]

Hoffsommer's report was based on a survey of 1,022 rural families in ten Alabama counties who were receiving relief in December 1933. He discovered that 40 percent of the tenants owed debts to their landlords of more than a year's standing; for 80 percent of the years they had sharecropped, they broke even or went into debt. Rural relief families were relatively young: 63 percent of the heads of families were under age forty-five. One-third of the adult tenants were "essentially illiterate" and another third were not sufficiently literate to receive and follow simple written directions. Nor did they participate in the American dream of upward economic mobility; only 9 percent of those who began farming as croppers became owners. Tenants seldom knew how much they owed their landlord. They moved frequently, though not long distances; the average tenure for white croppers was 2.6 years, for blacks, 5.1 years. Of 719 white households in the survey, 15 percent combined families, usually adding the family of a son or daughter. Hoffsommer's extensive report was buried in a federal file, but he popularized his findings in a series of publications and speeches.[33]

Two University of Alabama professors selected the open country of north Alabama for their interviews. Providing the community a fictitious name, "Upland Bend," they focused on 196 families, almost all of them white, in the Appalachian foothills. Noting frequent kinship relationships between tenants and landlords, they focused on tenants who were not related to landowners. Tenants were not young people on the rise;

the median age was forty-two, far higher than in Hoffsommer's study. Livestock was another important gauge of wealth in rural society. All landowners had at least one mule. But only six sharecroppers (two whites and four blacks) owned a mule. Twenty percent of the sharecroppers owned no cows, 35 percent no chickens, and 45 percent no hogs. Women supplemented family income by renting out their labor, by quilting, and by selling crafts; 27 percent of the wives of sharecroppers reported such earnings. Few of the sharecroppers voted compared to owners, they were markedly sicker, and their birth rates were more than twice as high. Diet varied also, with 75 percent of landowners raising their own fruit trees compared to 40 percent of the sharecroppers. Few sharecroppers attended church except for a new congregation, the Church of God's Children, an emotional sect that frowned on education. This profile, though limited to one community, reflected the general condition of rural whites in the 1930s.[34]

Lack of stability characterized the lives of the poor, as it always had. Of the 158,382 white Alabama farm families in 1940, 29 percent had lived on their land for less than a year and 50 percent for fewer than three years.[35]

Despite the general economic deprivation, the internal structure of their lives varied from degenerate to stable and relatively happy. At one end of the scale were those who could find no assistance and literally faced starvation. In February 1931, Dr. Oliver C. Wenger, a physician employed by the Public Health Service, reported that he saw four white women in Macon County living on nothing but corn bread and sweet potatoes and trying to breast-feed babies. He reported an elderly man who had died after eating raw potatoes he found in a field. Dr. Wenger's trip through the county left him shaken. He was familiar with crop failures and hunger in the Philippines and China, he wrote, but "this is the first time I realized what is going on in the South."[36]

Rural poor whites coped with such conditions in different ways. A folk tale, probably apocryphal but full of meaning, recounted how a poor white boy went to school with only a collard green sandwich in a lard bucket for lunch. Tired of such humble fare, he snitched another boy's lunch and retired to the solitude of a stand of trees, only to discover when he opened his pilfered bucket that it contained nothing but six hickory nuts and a rock. One cropper's child still vividly remembers Christmases in the mid-1930s. The children would cut a cedar tree and string popcorn and cotton balls for decorations. Presents were simple; fruit and a peppermint stick were especially desirable because Christmas was the only time during the year when they were likely to have either. They received a single toy, usually handmade. His favorite was a tin monkey on a string; tighten the string and the monkey would climb, release the string and he would descend.[37] In such ways parents sheltered children as best they could from the harsh realities of being poor.

Into this somber world came the New Deal's rural rehabilitation program. Traditional relief and charity had failed completely by 1933. Of some three hundred rural people, mostly sharecroppers, near Red Bay who applied for relief in October 1933, only six or eight received cards entitling them to assistance.[38] Part of the problem stemmed from inadequate information, but there were less defensible explanations. The county courthouse rings that dominated state politics cared little about landless farmers who could barely afford the $1.50 annual poll tax, much less the accumulation of years of nonpayment that might equal a year's cash income. The spatial separation of rural poor people made them difficult to organize politically. Middle class farm leaders such as Ed O'Neal of the Alabama Farm Bureau Federation understood little about the state's rural poor and largely ignored them.

Alabama was one of three southern states to initiate rural rehabilitation operations in early 1934, and its program was the largest in the nation, with some 30,000 families enrolled by March. Social workers divided rural rehabilitation families into two groups. Group I families consisted of people who were judged capable of managing their own financial resources; by December 1934 this group included 13,438 families with 73,479 people. Group II consisted of farmers who needed intensive supervision to manage the resources provided them; by December 1934 it numbered 8,877 families containing 41,589 people. The average expenditure on Group I families was $108.55 per year compared to only $67.30 for Group II families. The federal agency contracted with Auburn University to provide supervision through its network of county agents. Male agents supervised farming and female Home Demonstration agents taught women homemaking skills.[39]

Harry Hopkins, head of FERA, decided early that he would rely heavily on the county extension agents and even required their endorsement of the state rural rehabilitation director. Robert K. Greene, a prominent planter and Auburn graduate, directed the program in Alabama. The local rehabilitation committee was also crucial because its committees played a major role in selecting rural poor people for the program. They also employed rehabilitation supervisors who should have the qualifications of "the more mature county agricultural agents." Because most land-grant colleges directed scientific research toward improving crops and technology, their agents worked most closely with progressive, relatively prosperous farmers. In contrast, relief officials were most often social workers who perceived their function as helping the poor. Clashes inevitably resulted.[40]

Under Greene's direction Alabama's rehabilitation program applied fairly rigid qualifications for transferring from the FERA program to rural rehabilitation. Tenants had to demonstrate that they had exhausted all sources of credit from landlords and the landlord had to sign an affidavit that he would not furnish his tenants. Owners also had to sign debt waivers, pledging not to take over equipment and goods provided by rural rehabilitation. A brochure furnished to clients listed rigorous guidelines. Rural rehabilitation clients had to find a farm and have the place approved by supervisors. They had a better chance of approval if they could obtain a pledge to rent for three years rather than one or two, preferably with an option to purchase the land later. Clients were expected to plant mostly food and feed crops rather than cotton. They were expected to buy seeds, groceries, fertilizer, and equipment from the Rehabilitation Corporation but were required to pay the full amount because "the Rehabilitation Corporation is not giving anybody anything. You will work for what you get and you will be expected to earn every cent. If you have an idea this is a 'set-up' and that you won't have much work to do, then don't come into the program because there is more work than anything else to it." For those without a work animal, Greene furnished a steer or ox, explaining that mules were inefficient. Mules would eat ten dollars' worth of corn and hay a month, almost as much as it cost to feed a family, while a steer ate only two dollars' worth of feed per month.[41] Such stringent guidelines reduced the number of clients from 30,000 in late March 1934 to 17,200 by April 22, 1934. For those clients who remained, FERA furnished loans for food, clothing, fuel, essential medical care, tools, livestock, feed, seed, and fertilizer.[42]

As in the cities, relations between relief officials, county agents, and clients were often stormy. Director Greene obviously had not spent many hours behind the rear end of a steer or ox. Cheap they might be, but effective plow animals they were not. When Harry Hopkins dispatched Lorena Hickok on a tour of Alabama to report on conditions in April 1934, she received an earful. Steers were hard to break to a plow and they would not work in the heat: "Let it get to be noon, and they just lay right down—or wander off to the swamp, draggin' the Nigger with 'em, if he ain't leadin' 'em." One landowner scowled: "Hell! This ain't no New Deal if we all gotto go back plowin' steers!" But Hickok found quite a different reaction among black sharecroppers who received the animals. They claimed the beasts were easy to train, and they were enormously pleased to have them. She also contrasted the confusion and ineptitude of the Tennessee program to the efficient organization and obvious success of Alabama's efforts.[43]

Hickok's estimation of the role of the county agent changed as she traveled the state. In an April 1934 letter from the Black Belt she reported that social workers in the relief agency had little respect for the county and Home Demonstration agents. In the past, Auburn agents had never been cooperative. Hickok's own contact with the extension agents caused her to agree. She had met few agents who really cared about people on relief. They were inclined to be "too silo-minded: They're interested only in better farming—more intensive cultivation. They like working with big, successful farmers." As for female Home Demonstration agents, they spent most of their time "fooling around with girls' clubs. They've got a kind of Chautauqua slant on life. They shudder at the idea of walking into a tenant farmer's shack and teaching the wife how to clean the place up." Relief workers also accused the Cooperative Extension Service of being too "political minded." If the choice of supervisors came down to a technically qualified agent, with "neither any understanding of these people nor any real desire to help them," or a practical individual "with a lot of common sense and understanding and sympathy—well, give me the latter." But in a later report from the Tennessee Valley she modified her conclusion. County agents were performing much better than the relief people had expected.[44]

The intransigence of rural poverty perplexed the county agents, who responded in a variety of ways. County agent F. C. Clapp, who worked mainly with black tenants in Barbour County, believed that only the education and inspiration provided by public schools, Future Farmers of America, and 4-H Clubs could break the cycle of rural poverty. Working with adults was useless because they lacked "desire, ambition and ability," and without these drives "people are better off as tenants and sharecroppers." County agent J. B. Mitchell of predominantly white Madison County agreed. He complained that the "high" wage scale paid by the WPA was denuding farms of labor. The typical tenant, cropper, or wage laborer "has become so indifferent . . . , his work . . . so unsatisfactory that many owners and landlords cannot put up with such a person's work." Some landlords did want "everything the tenant makes and then dispense with his services"; but most landlords "were as interested in the welfare of the tenant as anyone." The strife and discord inherent in such class arrangements could be ended only by each side's assuming its responsibilities. Some small yeoman farmers agreed. Mrs. Claude Harris, a self-sufficient farmer near Dadeville and president of the Eagle Creek Home Demonstration Club, wrote that "if more people worked like we did they would not be on relief."[45]

Poor people refused to participate in extension programs for many reasons. Mrs. H. G. Corbin, the Walker County agent, recorded the opinion of townswomen who complained that the extension workers did not reach those illiterates who most needed help; those who could read did not need the assistance of a county agent. In a carefully studied white hill county, only four of forty-nine women who belonged to the Home Demonstration Club were tenant farmers, and only one of the four was the wife of a sharecropper. One reason given was that meetings were held in homes of members, often a humiliating experience for tenant women.[46]

To infer from such evidence that state extension agents lacked either concern for the poor or determination to help them ignores massive evidence in the extension reports. Female Home Demonstration agents learned quickly from their contacts with the poor. Their attempts to form "Better Babies Clubs" and "Child Spacing" programs produced some perceptive reports. Mattie Joe Barber, working in mainly white Chilton County, attributed poverty to low income, not some flaw in character: "Families lack sufficient supply of milk, eggs, and year-round supply of vegetables which would lead to healthier babies." Josephine Mann wrote from Crenshaw County that health care for infants suffered due to illiteracy and nutritional diseases. Eliza Clark, describing conditions in overwhelmingly white Randolph County, noted high levels of anemia, dental decay, malnutrition, and poor health among both mothers and children. She added that "often times fathers do not appreciate and share responsibilities in the child's development and training." Home Demonstration agents expanded their research efforts to forty-nine families in thirty-eight counties to understand better the adequacy of food supplies. Not one of the families obtained adequate amounts of all twelve groups of foods, and only four families received adequate supplies of as many as seven categories.[47]

Nor did agents hesitate to move beyond research to public assistance. In rural Tallapoosa County, the board of county commissioners, the "Welfare Directress," social field-workers, and county agents met in 1932 to decide how they could better help the poor. Reports from across the state described the harmony in which extension agents and Resettlement Administration officials usually worked.[48]

Extension agents often filled their annual reports with praise for the relief efforts and social reforms attempted by the New Deal. They applauded the Farm Security Administration, which provided government loans to tenants. Because they provided supervision for the tenants who received such loans, they learned much about the lives of their clients, and one agent reported that "the living standards of the Farm Security tenants has been [sic] materially raised." A county agent in impoverished Franklin County deplored the growing tendency of landowners to replace sharecroppers with hired labor and cover crops. Only government assistance prevented a disaster, he wrote on Thanksgiving Day 1939: "This is a wonderful government of ours, to be able to protect its people in time of need."[49]

Even before the New Deal began, a Home Demonstration Club in Jefferson County supported the creation of a soup kitchen in the Patton's Chapel community. A county nurse visited the community and discovered that nearly one-half of the ninety children living there were dangerously undernourished. A preacher at Patton's Chapel described conditions to the women of his women's missionary society and suggested they provide meals. That society and the Home Demonstration Club established a soup kitchen at the school and served a warm lunch each day. Community families donated utensils, students collected Octagon soap coupons to buy dishes, a local dairyman donated milk, and the pastor bought groceries with donations. Female volunteers served an average of sixty free lunches a day during the desperate months of January, February, and March 1931. Often the initial contact with the poor came through a local church or the social chairman of rural churches, who introduced social workers and extension agents to the impoverished within a community.[50]

Such personal confrontations with poverty increased as the depression deepened. The Home Demonstration agent in Walker County confronted a perplexing case in 1933. Minnie and Maggie Abbott lived in the Oak Grove community with their widowed father. He was a proud but poor white man who knew nothing of housekeeping and resented the attempts of neighbors to change his methods of child rearing. The illiterate girls were so frightened of outsiders that they hid when strangers approached. When Red Cross representatives visited the cabin in the spring of 1933, they were so appalled at conditions that they sent food, clothing, and seeds for a garden. Pearl Rowe, the demonstration agent, visited the Abbott cabin later and found a set of bedsprings on the floor, bedding and walls covered with bedbugs, two filthy quilts, and two rags, one for washing dishes and the other for straining milk in the churn. Rowe, with help from Home Demonstration Club members, cleaned the house; washed the girls; gave them underclothes, dresses, and face powder; hung curtains; provided clean mattresses, sheets, towels, and dish rags. They persuaded Abbott to enroll one of his daughters in the Opportunity Literacy School in the summer, while the second daughter stayed home to work and tend her father. The girls learned how to can, whitewash walls, build simple furniture, wash clothes, and farm.[51]

Although county agents became involved in virtually every aspect of the lives of poor Alabamians, Home Demonstration agents made their largest contributions in four areas: the establishment of curb markets, canning, handicrafts, and mattress programs.

They had established the first curb market in Gadsden in the early 1920s when agricultural conditions had turned sour. By 1927 Alabama contained eighteen markets where farmers sold more than $313,000 in commodities. The network of markets expanded during the 1930s. WPA labor constructed sheds, and county agents urged their clients to produce fresh vegetables for local consumption. Only farmers who grew their own products were allowed to sell. By 1937 the Gadsden market provided booths for five hundred farmers who sold between $75,000 and $150,000 annually in commodities. Mrs. A. P. Satterfield was one seller. She had begun in the 1920s and earned enough to buy a farm, which she lost during the depression. During 1937 she earned $500 from the sale of plants and flowers and another $800 from vegetables, enough to enable her to pay cash rent for her farm and prevent descent into sharecropping. Joe Igou supported fourteen people on the $790 he earned selling produce during 1934.[52]

Such testimonies came from across the state. A woman who sold at the Montgomery market remembered that she and her unemployed husband were losing their home when she began selling. After nine months she had managed to stabilize their declining finances. Lillie Morrow of Cordova wrote a demonstration agent: "I just cannot express the thanks you are due for helping we poor old farmers get customers to buy at the curb market." The social outlet that the markets provided rural women was also significant. Mrs. Morrow remembered the names of most of her customers and enjoyed conversations with them. A Shelby County farm woman managed "to get a world of recreation out of contact with our fellow saleswomen."[53]

Many of the Home Demonstration agents spent the majority of their time on the state canning program. Following a disastrous drought in 1931, the Community Chest in Anniston inaugurated a canning drive that August. As Calhoun County's demonstration agent remembered the times: "Poor people were poorer, many were hungry, all were rather hopeless, and cotton was down to five cents a pound. Banks were closing. No credit was being extended to farmers." The campaign was organized through the churches, with two congregations assigned each day to dig trenches, build charcoal and log fires, and fill huge iron wash pots with surplus vegetables. From 7:00 in the morning until 11:00 at night, for 2½ weeks, volunteers of both races cooked, canned with a Burpee steam pressure cooker and hand sealer, and distributed the vegetable soup to the poor for use during the winter. By September they had filled 5,546 quart jars.[54]

By 1933 the canning effort had become a statewide effort to prevent starvation. The state relief agency purchased 583 pressure cookers and placed them in 1,091 canning centers under the supervision of demonstration agents. Pauline Holland supervised the 16 sealers and 2 pressure cookers purchased by Blount County. She established 35 canning centers in the mountains surrounding Oneonta. Local men constructed vats and furnaces, and farmers transported their food in wagons or walked to the centers. Some poor whites walked five or six miles, carrying large sacks of beans and tomatoes. More than 1,000 people filled 112,538 cans in 1933. The demonstration women in Walker County made sure they established canning centers within three miles of all the county's population, but even then many women rolled wheelbarrows full of vegetables three miles over mountain trails to reach one of the 255 demonstrations. More than 6,900 poor people filled 19,900 cans and 1,220 jars provided by relief agencies. In Lawrence County 9 white men, some of them barefoot, walked ten miles to the canning center to obtain jars. The county demonstration agent drove her car as far as she could into the mountains, then took wagons into the more remote hamlets, reaching 1,200 people in 1933. So popular did the canning centers become that Alabama mine owners sometimes asked agents to visit their camps to teach miners' wives how to can.[55]

Training rural women to sew, whittle, and build was a major task of the Home Demonstration agents in order to provide families alternative sources of income. The women's and girls' clubs, scorned by Lorena Hickok as examples of the "Chautauqua mentality" of female agents, actually performed more practical functions. The female agent in Calhoun County called her effort "Live at Home" and designed it to make rural people self-sufficient. After extensive sewing and craft lessons, she organized a rally for June 30, 1932. She gave prizes to the woman with the best dress made from a fertilizer, flour, or feed sack and another for the best quilt. Mrs. Alex Rogers won the dress contest with a creation sewn from a Jazz feed sack dyed rose color that cost twenty cents to make. Ironically, the prize was a twenty-five-pound sack of flour. That same year forty-five Calhoun County girls dropped out of the girls' club because they were unable to obtain materials for sewing. Others remained but had to switch from store-bought cloth to flour sacks. During 1933, Home Demonstration Clubs made nearly forty thousand garments for relief families.[56]

Handicrafts, long a staple of poor families, became an important source of income during the 1930s. Demonstration agents had begun exploring the commercial possibilities of traditional crafts in the 1920s. By 1929 four women in Perry and Pickens counties were making and selling baskets that earned them $74. In another community three farm women earned $60 from baskets made of honeysuckle vines. A woman in Autauga County made thirty-seven pine-needle baskets and sold them for $35.60; she also won a first prize at the state fair of $3. A woman living at Wadley had been making and giving away white-oak and honeysuckle baskets when a demonstration agent suggested that people were willing to buy them; during 1931 she earned $167.85 in purchases and $21.40 in fair prizes with which she fed and clothed her family and bought a new stove.[57]

Clay County, one of Alabama's poorest white counties, had become a major center for basket making during the 1920s involving more than five hundred women. They formed a cooperative in 1926, the Clay County Basket Association, and hired a full-time manager. During 1929 members of the collective earned more than $6,000. One of the women who made pine-needle baskets, Essie Thomas, earned enough to purchase clothing for her family, one milk cow, three pigs, and groceries plus enough to pay her father's debts.[58]

During 1935, 4,806 Alabama families participated in the handicraft program. They made nearly twenty-five thousand baskets, bedspreads, and rugs and earned $9,438 in extra income. As the depression abated, the number of families involved dropped but their earnings increased.[59]

The mattress program was designed to teach low-income families to utilize cotton from their own farms in order to make better mattresses for family use. Initially only families with annual incomes below $400 were eligible to participate, although the figure was soon raised to $500 and the number of mattresses allowed per family was increased. Many female tenant farmers joined the county mattress clubs. Mattress material was given to the family with training in constructing the mattress. Programs began in all sixty-seven counties, though Dale County led the way with seventy-one centers staffed by 375 leaders; six of the centers were for whites, thirteen for blacks, and fifty-two served both races. Some 3,000 people requested mattresses and nearly nine thousand were made. By 1942 when the program was terminated in Alabama, the centers were producing sixty thousand mattresses per year; the program furnished mattresses to more than 200,000 poor Alabama farmers during its lifetime. One craftswoman, Mrs. O. W. Reaves of Perry County, made twenty-two mattresses to sell during 1939. Together with slipcovers and upholstery, she earned nearly $125. Although the amount might seem modest, she wrote that she did not know how her family "could have kept going without this additional income." A white woman from Dale County testified that the mattress program "has given beds and covers to numbers of families that were in dire need of them. They actually could not buy ticking and percale to better their beds and cover."[60]

These activities by no means exhausted the range of activities designed to help the poor. In local communities where no specific state or federal program addressed critical needs, extension agents often discovered other ways to direct a ray of light into the rural darkness. An agent in Fayette County, a desperately poor white hill county north of

Tuscaloosa, organized a Christmas celebration in the tiny community of Possum Trot. Many residents had never before seen a decorated Christmas tree. Farmers came in rattletrap cars, in buggies, and by foot from the hollows to see a local citizen dressed as Santa Claus. The agent also organized community picnics and took pictures of families too poor to own a camera.[61]

Such efforts did not go unrewarded. Membership in Home Demonstration Clubs climbed steadily during the 1930s, from 11,551 white women in 1930 to 31,761 in 1940. Although no data are available on the class background of these new members, many of them obviously were poor white women. A 1937 survey of DeKalb County, a predominantly rural, white county in north Alabama, revealed an average per-family income of $920; but the average per-family income for women in the Home Demonstration Clubs was only $620. Among female club members, 14.5 percent owned no cows, 25 percent no hogs, and only 50 percent produced sufficient meat for their own needs. When the clubs sponsored a DeKalb County Achievement Day in November, Mrs. J. R. Burgess, a white tenant farmer's wife, won first prize in the canning competition. The social symbolism of her participation and victory was perhaps as great a reward as the monetary value of her prize.[62]

As laudable as relief might be, even when sensitively administered by officials concerned about the poor, it offered little more than a way of coping temporarily with poverty that seemed intractable. The New Deal did set in motion more daring experiments. The first was the resettlement concept designed to create subsistence homesteads. Drawing inspiration from the historic American hunger for land, administrators reasoned that poor people would prosper if provided a home, a plot of land, and equipment. Symbolically connecting Alabama's resettlement efforts to an earlier epoch of homesteading, officials even experimented with low-cost sod houses at Mount Olive north of Birmingham, patterning them after the legendary "soddies" built on the prairies of Kansas and Nebraska during the 1870s and 1880s. Seven houses built of packed earth with walls eighteen inches thick and costing only a few thousand dollars proved resistant to temperature changes and were surprisingly attractive.

The Mount Olive experiment recognized a fundamental fact of life in depression-wracked Alabama, the problem of inadequate housing. A 1934 federal survey of Birmingham disclosed that of 82,704 houses inspected, 43,524 needed ordinary repairs, 20,398 needed structural repairs, 3,244 were unfit for habitation, and 9,316 extra families shared occupancy with another family; 15,000 of the houses lacked running water, 39,000 had no indoor toilets, 53,000 had neither bathtubs nor showers. The city had an extreme housing shortage for low-income families. Birmingham's cyclical economy had collapsed, and a local witticism about pollution and depression was never more accurate: "When Birmingham is not black it is blue." Nor did affluent residents sacrifice very much for their impoverished neighbors. Of sixty-eight American cities with more than 120,000 residents, Birmingham ranked next to last in per capita expenditures on vital city services during 1933. With nearly 100,000 people on relief, coal mines in adjacent counties idle, and welfare rolls groaning, the Birmingham district begged for help. U.S. Senator John H. Bankhead responded with an amendment to the NIRA in June 1933, allocating $25 million for subsistence homesteads. Some $6 million, nearly one-fourth the total appropriation, was expended on five projects in Jefferson and Walker counties, more than was spent anywhere else in the nation. The five low-cost public housing projects were located at Palmerdale, Gardendale (Mount Olive), Trussville (called Cahaba Farms and also "Slagheap Village" because it was built on the site of an old mine), Bessemer (called Greenwood), and Jasper (called Jasper Subsistence Farms or Bankhead Farms). Each was organized as a democratic cooperative association. Unemployed workers on relief performed the construction, sometimes using the actual settlers for unskilled labor. The average cost of the houses was $6,500, but they were financed at less than that. Because the basic resettlement philosophy combined part-time wage work and subsistence gardening, each plot contained some four or five acres, with sufficient space for small gardens and pastures. The communities created small industries (hosiery mills were a favorite) to provide reliable cash income.[63]

Although noble in conception and sometimes successful in execution, the resettlement communities merely skimmed the top off the bottom class. The process of selecting the lucky folks to be resettled was arduous. Social workers visited applicants, interviewed them, required letters of reference, observed their living quarters, inquired of neighbors about their habits and backgrounds, checked the employment record of the head of the family, and conducted credit checks. Although the combined family income for applicants the year before they applied was below $1,800 for 82 percent of those who obtained homesteads, some projects set a minimum annual income of $1,200. As a consequence, homestead families contained a large number of machinists, skilled artisans, and unemployed professional people and those from service occupations. Poor people were not common in the five projects adjacent to Birmingham.[64]

An exception to this pattern occurred in mountainous Jackson County on the Tennessee River. The county, almost entirely white, contained large numbers of farm tenants and a few factory workers in scattered textile mills. By 1933 the county enrolled 4,500 families on work relief, and as late as 1935 rural rehabilitation officials listed 224 Group I and 460 Group II families. An additional 111 families were still on direct relief. In 1934 Alabama's Rural Rehabilitation Administration began Cumberland Farms on a high plateau fourteen miles from Scottsboro. More than 700 farmers applied, and 238 were selected, all of them from Group II rehabilitation clients. Virtually all were Anglo-Saxon in origin and worked as sharecroppers or farm laborers, although a few had also worked in textile mills. They produced large families (the average was seven) and 80 percent of the adults were illiterate. By religious preference they were Methodists, Baptists, Seventh Day Adventists, or Pentecostals. They came from isolated communities where the only social organization was a rural church. Women were shy and reticent. In their homes the women usually did not sit at the table with men; they served the males first and ate later. They also held strong racial prejudice against blacks. Optimistic social workers initially praised them as "sturdy mountain people" of high native intelligence, ability, and morality, "lacking only education and opportunity."[65]

The first group of twenty-five homesteaders was scheduled to gather on December 10, 1934, but only eleven braved the snow, sleet, and rain that fell that day. The project director explained all the problems and possibilities, then asked those who wanted to proceed to step to the right and those no longer interested to step to the left. Eight sharecroppers moved right in search of a new life and three stepped left (later the three who declined membership in Cumberland Farms Cooperative tried to enroll but were rejected). One of the eight who enrolled did so with grave reservations, remembering years later: "We were all skeptical of such crazy doings, but anything was worth trying then." The eight were transported fourteen miles up the mountain and spent the rest of the day gathering sandstone to build the foundation for a kitchen. Unaccustomed to this kind of labor, they wore the skin off their fingers and mixed their blood with the snow and concrete on that initial day of their new lives. At first they had no place to live, so some of them awakened at 3:00 A.M., walked four or five miles to trucks that transported them to the site, worked ten hours until dark, climbed aboard the trucks for the return trip, then walked four or five miles back home, arriving about 9:00 P. M. With such incentives to spur them, they quickly finished a kitchen and bunkhouse so they could remain at the site. Next they built shacks so they could bring their families to the mountain. By spring 1935, they had finished a sawmill and could employ the steers used in hauling logs to plow their fields. In the early days they had little supervision, selected their own foremen and timekeepers, and often practiced shabby craftsmanship. They kept careful work records because houses were assigned as they were completed on the basis of which person had the most hours to his credit. In 1935 the Resettlement Administration took over the project, reduced the workweek from fifty-five to forty hours, established a wage scale of fifteen to forty cents per hour based on level of skill, and built a medical center staffed by a resident nurse. By October, the men had finished the school, and by January 1936 they had completed twenty-five houses.[66]

By March of that year nearly 100 families had moved into permanent homes, though only nineteen were complete. The school began vocational classes to teach practical skills to two hundred high school–age children, many with only three or four years of education. Auburn extension agents summoned to provide technical assistance were optimistic that the project was both sound and self-sustaining: "The families . . . have the old pioneer spirit, are willing to work and have the best community spirit we have yet seen on any project." Upon the recommendation of federal experts, the 215 families living on the mountain in the spring of 1936 incorporated as Cumberland Farms Cooperative Association, applied for a loan to the Resettlement Administration, and purchased ten thousand more acres to add to the eight thousand bought initially. Members of the cooperative held regular meetings, elected directors and officers, and enacted their own policies. They even established their own paper, the *Cumberland Farms News*.[67]

In 1936, the Reverend W. Frank Moore, pastor of the Cumberland Farms Baptist Church, surveyed the changes that two years had wrought in the lives of his parishioners, and decided to write Franklin Roosevelt. Mr. Moore had given up an established congregation to cast his lot with these people to "accomplish something not religiously but in all community welfare." In his letter he praised Cumberland Farms and projects like it. They represented a better future for millions of poor people who otherwise had no hope. Combining evangelical religious rhetoric to social conscience, Mr. Moore concluded: "Future generations will rise up to call you blessed for your great leadership in work that is fundamental to rebuilding millions of the people, and I believe the final saving of America itself."[68]

But not all went so smoothly on the mountain. The experiment created both class and cultural conflict. Within this one social experiment in the salvation of Alabama's poor whites, all the strengths, hopes, foibles, and inadequacies of the New Deal could be found. Chief among the problems was the cultural pattern of fierce individualism, pride, and general cantankerousness of the "clients." By 1935, residents were already complaining about the inadequate shacks that kept them neither dry nor warm. Relief pay of fifteen cents an hour for ten hours per day provided nothing more than food, water, and clothes. Settlers who refused to work overtime were laid off. Women working in the cannery spread contagious diseases. The physician obtained to provide health care stayed out of his office half the time. At first the cooperative idea seemed logical, but as time passed ambitious members demanded the right to open stores, blacksmith shops, syrup mills, and barber shops to compete with those of the cooperative. As the winter of 1937 approached, two hundred angry men gathered to discuss the allocation of houses. Newer members demanded a change in the method of assigning homes, insisting that all names be placed in a hat and the residences given to those whose names were drawn. Older members furiously rejected any change from allocation by work seniority. The community newspaper criticized families who refused to send their children to school. Internal strife crippled the supervisory staff, and half the families who had been brought to the mountain with such high hopes in 1934 still lived in shacks. Some homeless settlers accused administrators of mismanagement and financial irregularities. Administrators, embarrassed by the sheds of "Bluff City" on the edge of the project, threatened to rip off the roofs if the impoverished squatters refused to move. Many of the squatters were not members of the cooperative, having moved in later; but others were original settlers who still had no houses. "Radicals" in Bluff City allegedly stirred up the trouble. Cumberland Farms became a magnet, drawing desperately poor farmers from the countryside who were allowed to move into deserted shacks and watch others build new lives for themselves.[69]

Federal officials also discovered thorns in the pastoral paradise. Project expenses outstripped estimates, partly because unskilled sharecroppers had to be taught construction skills, which increased costs and lowered standards. So bad had conditions become by January 1936 that the Resettlement Administration sent an expert to reorganize the cooperative. He recommended that the surplus squatter families be removed and that others be prevented from settling. Payments to homesteaders of twenty-five dollars per month to help them purchase their forty-acre units must be eliminated as quickly as possible in order to make them self-supporting. "The whole philosophy of the project," he wrote, "must be to get out from under Government subsidy in the way of wages at the earliest possible moment."[70]

Much of the land proved to be infertile and some agricultural experts argued that forty-acre farms were too small to be practical. Supervision was inadequate and one expert warned RA director Rexford Tugwell in October 1936 that "the whole future of the project is doubtful in the extreme."[71] Wells were too shallow and had to be redrilled in 1939. Minutes of cooperative meetings either were not kept at all or were inaccurate. Members began to withdraw from the cooperative. A prominent judge in Scottsboro complained to Senator John J. Sparkman about the settlers' alleged drinking and carousing.[72]

At the root of much of the community's troubles was conflict between the class and cultures of federal officials, local administrators, and co-op members. Some "experts" brought to "educate" the folk romanticized them and fantasized a Marxist class structure; others were patronizing; and still others accepted folk culture on its own terms as rich and satisfying.

Some of the class conflict was internal between the homesteaders and the fifty or so salaried employees who administered the community. One recreation director wrote his supervisor about bickering between the two classes: "They speak of our group and the other group. The homesteaders are called subscribers, flat heads, homesteaders, colonists and a number of other funny things." Another federal expert had been told that all was "honey and sugar" in the cooperative; but it was not true. Upon meeting people, he was immediately told whether they were salaried or settler. The two groups even had separate parties. When he staged a minstrel show, salaried people tried to take all the parts. In a report, he summarized the problem: "The majority of the homesteaders . . . are former tenant farmers or share croppers and considered by 'the' people as pretty poor material." Cumberland Farms was the only resettlement community where he had found a "quite definite class division." His supervisor thought such conflicts had more to do with musical and theatrical performances and attendant ego problems than with class conflict and urged his representative to keep such discussions out of his reports.[73]

Federal experts sent by the RA and later by the Farm Security Administration attributed the problems to internal class division, but their own presumptions about poor white culture contributed to the problem. Baptist preacher W. Frank Moore, who had been so ecstatic in praise of federal assistance in 1936, was not so sure three years later. He criticized administrators for seeking to centralize all religious activities in a Sunday interdenominational "union meeting" at the public school. The settlers preferred to worship in their own churches, but Farm Security administrators who visited the cooperative opposed denominational work. Mr. Moore protested this unconstitutional meddling with religion, but he raised the wrong issue.

Cultural paternalism was as much a problem as class conflict. Margaret Valiant was one of several recreation specialists working for the Special Skills Division of the Resettlement Administration. So devoted to the homesteaders that she contributed part of her own salary to fund their projects, she nonetheless revealed precisely the sort of biases that Mr. Moore protested. In February 1937, she praised a female Episcopalian missionary from the House of Happiness, a Social Gospel–type settlement house a few miles away, because she was "a very *practical* Christian missionary and joins with us heartily in all secular functions." After local administrators clashed with Valiant over the content of her programs, she promised to lean over backwards to be conservative, especially with the Easter program: "It will be such as I experienced, at the age of eight, in the Bible Belt of Mississippi." Not surprisingly the community liked her conventional Easter hymn sing. After attending a "Holy Roller" meeting she offered a backhanded compliment: "I regret to say, the best adult singing I have heard on the mountain; it was a good show, if you care for the Frankenstein horror element." In fact, Cumberland Farms contained "the most backward group of people" she had encountered; "this mountain is a tough nut to crack but I still believe the effort, from our angle, will be well justified . . . if we keep hammering at it constantly."[74]

Charles Seeger, technical assistant in music for the RA's Special Skills Division, tried to educate his activist staff to the values of Appalachian poor white culture, but it was no easy task. A Mr. Van Dyke, sent to provide musical instruction to the settlers, was an excellent musician but insisted on educating "the people" to "real music." He played Franz Liszt and Czechoslovakian folk songs. To involve the settlers, he asked self-conscious young boys to imitate instruments, which they understandably declined to do. He persisted with another participation song that required the children to "flutter their fingers over their heads and bring them to rest, clasped, next to the cheek while the lullaby was 'cooed.' " This was too much even for Margaret Valiant. She wrote Seeger: "Picture stalwart mountaineers and farmer boys over 15 doing this. Well they wouldn't—and he reproved them for giggling." The only songs they enjoyed were ones familiar from their own culture like "Down in the Paw-Paw Patch." Seeger admonished musicians not to impose their own ideas but instead to encourage the settlers and help them organize so they could administer their own programs without outside assistance.[75]

When the federal experts realized they had as much to learn as they did to teach, relations improved. The community nurse found it difficult to persuade women to attend meetings to discuss nursing, hygiene, and prenatal care because of the traditional isolation, reticence, and secondary status of mountain women. But she gradually overcame their reluctance by involving them in the planning and organization of the meetings.[76]

The most successful adviser to work on the mountain was Bascom L. Lunsford, who, though differing from the tenants in class, shared their culture. A renowned expert in Appalachian folk music, he had contributed already to the folk music revival of the 1930s by organizing a traditional music festival in Asheville, North Carolina. Seeger sent him to the mountain in early February 1937 to work under the supervision of Margaret Valiant. His supervisors assigned him five tasks: to play and sing traditional music; to teach traditional songs and singing games to children; to conduct square dances; to assist dance bands in both their technique and their repertoire; and to organize fiddle and dance contests. All five were consistent with Appalachian customs, and that made his job easier. He attended a movie at the school the night he arrived and announced at the conclusion of the film that he wanted to collect ballads the people knew.

The next day musician-settlers began playing for him. He collected from shy residents by visiting their homes and offering boxes of candy to the homesteader who provided the best collection of ballads. During the winter of 1937 when the weather was too severe for outside work, Lunsford took the community's string band into Scottsboro for a performance. The musicians performed for a sparse audience, which Miss Valiant attributed to a "local snobbish attitude toward 'mountain music' " and the cooperative; Lunsford, who was less ideological and more realistic, attributed the attendance to poor weather and the reluctance of small-town people to come out to see performers from their own county whom they already knew. He began a precision square dance team and staged festivals to which he invited traditional musicians from surrounding communities. He discovered fine musicians such as the Dawson Brothers String Band from Mud Creek and Walter Patterson, a ninety-two-year-old fiddler from Scottsboro who also danced a graceful step called "the wild cow." At the musicals, he encouraged story telling, musical skits, and teenagers who played dulcimers, guitars, and banjos.

Many settlers possessed both talent and desire but few of them had money for instruments. Mary McLean was a fine traditional fiddler but her instrument was broken. In his field report, Lunsford noted that one hundred dollars "would work wonders" and "would bring more contentment than anything I know of." When the Scottsboro Business Men's Association received the cooperative's string band with enthusiastic applause, Lunsford persuaded them to translate their gratitude into cash; they contributed twenty dollars to the band fund for instruments. Obviously more comfortable with folk religion than Miss Valiant was, he also led singing at Sunday school and church services.[77]

So successful was Lunsford in ballad collecting that he asked his supervisor to extend his stay and send him recording machines. Many tunes were variations of the Child Ballads collected in England, but he found some lyrics so unusual that he sent them to Robert Van Hyning,

Fiddler Mary McLean, Skyline Farms, Alabama, 1937. Photo by Ben Shahn. (Courtesy of Farm Security Administration Photographs, Library of Congress)

assistant director of the RA's Special Skills Division. Van Hyning was so impressed by the musical treasure located at the cooperative that he urged Lunsford to send copies of all lyrics that were in Cecil Sharp's famous Appalachian collection and to keep the tunes in his head until he returned to Washington where he could record them. By the end of his service, Lunsford had collected thirty folk songs, photographed the ballad singers and contributors, organized a superb string band and square dance group, taught dozens of children traditional music and ballads, and proven that excellent traditional music could be obtained from Alabama's poor whites.[78]

By the late 1930s the Cumberland Farms Cooperative, now renamed Skyline Farms, had become the subject of numerous articles in journals and newspapers, many of which focused on its music. As word spread within the federal bureaucracy, someone suggested that a group of musicians from the resettlement communities be invited to the White House to perform. Eleanor Roosevelt, who had inspired the resettlement program, apparently initiated the invitation. Groups from four resettlement communities were selected, but the band from north Alabama was regarded as the best and was asked to play for all. On May 10, 1938, twenty-eight musicians left the mountain bound for a capital none of them had seen before. People once divided by class found a common identity in culture: eleven of the musicians were former sharecroppers who had been original homesteaders; two lived as squatters in the Bluff City shacks and were considered "radicals"; the rest were salaried administrators. The organizer was warned to select no "foreign folk tune which was not indigenous to the mountain people." On their journey they acted like tourists, visiting historic sites, attending a session of Congress, and meeting Senator John J. Sparkman and Speaker of the House William B. Bankhead. Mrs. Roosevelt met them at the White House and escorted them to the president's private office, where Franklin Roosevelt received them warmly. When the dinner guests had eaten at tables set up on the White House lawn, the fiddlers struck up "Fox Chase" and the musicians sang "Going Across the Mountain," "John Henry," and "On Top of Old Smokey." Afterwards, the musicians dined with the Alabama congressional delegation and ended the day with a moonlight cruise on the Potomac. Perhaps it was little more than a political gesture by a shrewd president's wife, though one suspects more honorable motives. But no matter. To the once-impoverished folks who were treated as "honored guests" at the White House, it was a symbolic integration into mainstream American society, an acknowledgment that what had once distinguished them as "quaint" or even bizarre was accepted as authentic and meaningful culture.[79]

Gradually, Skyline Farms solved its economic problems. In 1939 the co-op farmers experimented with potatoes grown from seeds, the first such effort in Alabama. The yield of one hundred bushels contained some potatoes so fine that they sold for $2.50 a bushel. Whereas the community had no social life in the early years because the settlers would not assemble together, by 1940 pride in their culture and confidence in their organizing skills had produced a community that planned its own recreation and entertainment without need for federal

Dance team and band from Skyline Farms performing on the White House lawn at Mrs. Roosevelt's entertainment. (Courtesy of the National Archives)

advisors. At first, families suspicious of education had kept their children at home to work the fields; now they encouraged them to attend school. A hosiery mill built in 1941 provided supplemental employment, especially for young people. Vocational training produced carpenters and other skilled craftsmen. The agricultural economy had been diversified from cotton to include potatoes, tomatoes, 4,000 baby chicks, and milk cows. Although the average 1940 family income was only slightly above $200 when the project began in 1934, this figure did not reflect improvements in housing, diet, and general living conditions; and completion of the new hosiery mill and livestock program substantially increased family income in the early 1940s. By then the community boasted 225 neatly painted farmhouses together with barns, garages, smokehouses, a modern stone school with gymnasium, a movie house, stone commissary, office, and vocational units.[80] Problems remained, but Skyline Farms became a testimony to the cultural richness and tenacity of poor whites as well as to the ability of the government to help even with its bureaucratic bungling and ideological condescension.

Perhaps the noblest and most imaginative federal attempt to expand the resettlement concept and thus to improve the lives of Alabama's poor was the Farm Security Administration. By 1936, New Deal agricultural and relief programs clearly had not eliminated Alabama's rural poverty. The Agricultural Adjustment Act had decreased the land under cultivation at the expense of tenant farmers who were even less secure than they had been before. Landowners increasingly preferred seasonal day laborers to tenants whom they had to furnish with supplies during the year. Often they used federal subsidies given for land reduction to buy tractors and through mechanization displaced even more tenants. In 1935 Alabama's conservative Senator John H. Bankhead, whose home county of Walker was one of the state's poorest, introduced a sweeping bill to provide more than a billion dollars in federal loans to tenants for land, equipment, and livestock. When the bill attracted fire from congressional conservatives, Alabama's liberal Senator Hugo Black, perhaps remembering his impoverished neighbors in rural Clay County, praised the effort to assist "the forgotten tenant farmers and sharecroppers, those little men, a few of whom vote . . . who live upon the fringe and the border line of subsistence."[81] The bill passed the Senate but died in the House.

An emasculated version of the Bankhead-Jones bill was passed in 1937, providing only $10 million dollars for the purchase of land. Because funds were so inadequate the new Farm Security Administration gave preference to tenants who had some equipment and livestock or who could make a small down payment. By 1944 the FSA had granted 200,000 emergency subsistence grants of $20 to $30 each and 44,300 land-purchase loans. Although seven-tenths of the purchase loans were made to southern tenants, only a small percentage of those requesting help received it. In its best year, 1941, the FSA was able to assist only one of every twenty-two southern applicants; and in Region V, which included Alabama, only about 35 to 40 percent of those requesting emergency rural rehabilitation loans received them. Those who received aid were the best of the worst, the most responsible, hardworking, vigorous, and prosperous poor whites.[82]

Yet the FSA, inadequate as it was, helped. Alabamians who received the small rehabilitation grants during the 1939 crop year had the lowest average net incomes of anyone in any state involved in the program, $180 compared to a high of $654 dollars in Kentucky. And the $180 average was *up* from $155 dollars in the mid-1930s. As the FSA became more selective, poorer tenants had less chance of being chosen. The average net worth of clients when selected the first year was $106; by 1938 the net worth at time of selection was $405. Even these higher average incomes were inadequate, however; one expert in 1939 estimated that a family of five needed a yearly income of $705 to live above the poverty line.[83]

The gap between needs and resources was most evident within Alabama's poorest regions. In Pike County, 74 percent of the farmers were tenants in 1939, 2,183 of them sharecroppers; the FSA made crop loans to 194 clients and land-purchase loans to 13. Tallapoosa County in east central Alabama contained 1,500 white tenants and 1,000 blacks in 1939; the FSA made 366 loans totaling $109,588. In adjacent Chambers County, 3,016 tenants operated 74 percent of the farms and received 277 FSA loans. In 1939 the FSA enrolled 308 of Chilton County's 2,240 tenant families, in St. Clair County 218 of 2,141, and in Coffee County 200 of 3,170 tenants. During 1939 the FSA bought eight farms for tenants in DeKalb County, raising the total to sixteen. The agency also provided emergency rehabilitation and medical care loans to 157 families, bought pressure cookers for 57 clients, and sponsored six livestock and four pasture projects; but DeKalb contained 3,523 tenant families.[84]

For the lucky few who received FSA assistance, life took a turn for the better. In 1937 Wallace Gowens was a sharecropper on J. D. Thornton's place in the Ball Play community; but he was not a typical tenant. His share of the vegetable, cotton, and livestock sales amounted to $1,200, and he owned two horses. He was an ideal, "safe" candidate for a loan. The FSA provided him enough money to buy 120 acres, where he constructed terraces, seeded perennial hay crops and winter legumes, repaired buildings, and produced fine crops. By 1939 his farm was so productive that Sears, Roebuck and Company selected him to attend a four-week short course at the land-grant university.[85]

Nor was the relief sexist. Irene Davis was a widow living in Greenville, Alabama. Her husband's death in 1924 left the college-educated woman destitute with three children to raise. She obtained work as a stenographer until the depression, then lived with her parents. When they died in 1934 she was left without home, money, or job. She sought help from Alabama's Rural Rehabilitation Administration, but it turned her down, explaining that an inexperienced woman could not make a living by farming. But she persisted and the administrators finally relented, lending her one hundred dollars. With that she rented an eight-acre farm containing a shack without windows, a leaky roof, and wide cracks between the wall boards; but "it was my home." She borrowed a mule from her neighbor and put her fourteen-year-old son Lawrence behind the plow. For each day's use of the mule, she and her eleven-year-old daughter Lois hoed her neighbor's field. Before full light she weeded her own land. Despite drought, insects, and rain at the wrong time, she harvested a crop sufficient to repay her loan and to can enough food for winter. The following year she planned to buy an ox. A nervous middle class, anxious to discover persistence of the American Dream, named her "Alabama's Most Courageous Woman of 1934."[86] People such as Irene Davis were ideal candidates for FSA sponsorship because they already had proven themselves to be good risks.

Of course the FSA and Rural Rehabilitation Administration cannot be isolated from the entire assortment of federal programs that funneled relief to the poor. Thad Holt, director of the Alabama Relief Administration, long after the depression reminisced about the extent of federal assistance. The Civil Works Administration had been announced on November 8, 1933, and the next morning people had been put to work. Before the CWA was demobilized in 1934, it had expended fifteen million dollars in Alabama, employing 129,000 people at its peak. Rural Rehabilitation had helped 25,000 families. The Civilian Conservation Corps had provided jobs to 66,837 needy Alabama youths. The enrollees had sent more than sixteen million dollars to dependent relatives, and the agency spent more than fifty-five million dollars in the state on parks, forests, and erosion-control projects. Resettlement communities had opened, though Holt considered only Skyline Farms a success. The FSA had furnished loans to thousands.[87]

Given such herculean efforts, what is astounding is how many people were neglected. Beginning in 1929 and continuing through 1940, letters poured into Montgomery and Washington from desperate people somehow ignored. How could so many fall through the cracks in the relief network? Oftentimes tenant farmers were unable to obtain releases from landlords who declared that they were not willing to furnish their tenants. Without such releases, tenants could not qualify for relief. Even when FERA relief was forthcoming, it was pitifully inadequate. Sometimes the deficiency resulted from shortages of funds, as in July 1933, when relief clients were "ruthlessly cut." But even in good times, relief in Alabama was "far from adequate measured by any decent standards." The statewide average of eight or nine dollars per month was inflated by twenty thousand Birmingham families who received seventeen or eighteen dollars; in rural counties relief was sometimes half the state average.[88]

In 1935, Alabama created the Department of Public Welfare with a $250,000 grant from FERA. One purpose of the new agency was to close the wretched almshouses, the solution of last resort for the poor. Alabama contained in that year sixty-five poorhouses in sixty-one counties. The houses contained 1,413 patients, 67.5 percent of them white. The majority were located in rural areas. Most patients were indigent, feeble, old, and illiterate. The Department of Public Welfare also tried to assist dependent children but with less success. When employees gave physical examinations to 1,581 indigent children, they discovered that 67.1 percent had a physical defect or disease, including malnutrition, tuberculosis, venereal disease, and hookworm. But of 9,527 applications for aid that flooded the new department, only 4,744 were approved.[89]

When Franklin Roosevelt asked ministers in the fall of 1935 to describe conditions within their communities, little did he realize that many Alabama recipients of his letter were uneducated, rural, bivocational preachers who were poor themselves. From simple, barely literate preachers he received replies that told him more than he wanted to know in the third year of the new order. A minister from Bayou La Batre described a long bar-shaped building where thirty-two families lived. Conditions in the New Market community were worse in 1935 than in 1934. Public works had disappeared and families could not send their children to school. In Double Springs, Winston County, fifty men who headed families had no work. The Reverend Mark L. Hargraves had given up his church to help a much older minister. Now "my family is hungry today, almost naked, house rent due. No coal. Nothing but bread. No milk for the baby. No coats for school children. Only a 50 cent dress change for the school girls; many are sick, weak, hungry and become radicals that were once good church going and God loving people." A minister for fifty years in Walker County had never seen such suffering; people went hungry and children lacked clothes. A pastor of four rural quarter-time churches, whose membership consisted mainly of tenant farmers, proposed a biblical solution: the president should declare a "Jubilee Year" as in the time of Moses and abolish all debts. A sixty-five-year-old minister from Winston County urged that money be divided according to need: "I am imbariest to say iny thing about our condition for I have allways wanted to mak my own support but we are very poor and have no one to look to for a support and in debt to Doctors and cannot pay the Bills."[90]

For chronically poor whites fortunate enough to get on relief, life was better than ever before. Their standard of living, diet, and security all improved. One federal official noted that Alabama sharecroppers crowded onto relief rolls because of "conditions [that] are the accumulation of many years of dwindling income." One survey of 1,022 families, most of them tenants, discovered that 90 percent believed they were better off on relief than they had been in the years before welfare. One farmer-minister in the Easonville community was on rural rehabilitation. He praised President Roosevelt for the program because agency officials told him he had a chance to own a home, "which is my hearts Desire as I've never had that opportunity in my 35 years of life."

He described the poverty of his community, begged Roosevelt to help enact Senator Bankhead's farm tenancy bill, and closed with praise and a promise:

> In other words we are just a crowd of old hard working farmers who could hardly live until . . . the last few years. But I wish to extend to you my sincere thanks Honorable Sir for these great things your noble brain being guided by unseen power has done and if I possibly can get my 14 years back poll tax paid up you will certainly get my vote and influence in the next election.[91]

A less-enthusiastic response came from a sharecropper's daughter who grew up in northeast Alabama and in the Mississippi Delta during the 1930s. Asked how the Great Depression affected her life, she replied simply: "Well we didn't know the difference in a depression, except . . . what we would hear. It just increased the fear a little bit of maybe not being able to get any food at all. We was just living on the bare necessities anyhow." Lillie Mae Beason remembered the same experience. She did not recall that the depression affected her sharecropper parents very much: "because they had never had very much, and they still didn't have very much." Or as blues musician Lonnie Johnson put it in a song contrasting the depression to conditions before 1919: "Hard times don't worry me, I was broke when it first started out."[92]

But pride died hard among the poor. Many sharecroppers wanted work, not welfare. One tenant, asked to list the "greatest needs" of his community, proposed that the government "buy up a lot of small farms, put the relief people on these and make 'em work." Another young tenant thought the government ought to make large landowners divide their farms and sell small tracts to their tenants. Even the poorest folk strove mightily to retain some autonomy over their lives. A rural rehabilitation client in Limestone County presented his grocery order to be filled exactly as designated by his welfare supervisor except for one substitution. Instead of twenty-five cents in rice he asked for ten cents in rice and fifteen cents change in cash with which he intended to buy one guitar string.[93] Poor people did not live by bread alone.

Totaling successes and failures for Alabama's rural poor is not easy. By 1940 the number of white Alabama tenant farmers had declined from 100,705 families in 1935 to 78,573. White tenancy dropped 11.3 percent between 1930 and 1940. Sharply higher incomes in the 1940s allowed many tenants to improve their homes and diets. The State Welfare Department virtually eliminated almshouses by 1945.[94] But many rural poor people disappeared into the cities, where they experienced trauma nearly as painful as the Great Depression.

Organized Labor

The history of the 1930s inevitably focuses on efforts of the emerging welfare state to aid indigents, but that perspective distorts the poor white experience. It makes the history of poor people seem passive, as if they were mere recipients of federal largesse. Many of them were angry and determined to control their own fate. I have already discussed unionism in individual industries and as a political force statewide before 1930. But the years between 1880 and 1932 were generally years of frustration and failure. Not until the 1930s did labor succeed in organizing a significant portion of Alabama's poor and in establishing an enduring bifactionalism in state politics.

Although Alabama's most persistent and extensive poverty was in rural areas, the state contained the largest industrial population of any southern state. Concentrated mainly in the northern region in densely populated pockets, this poorly paid work force awaited a spirited drive for unionization. Such efforts had occurred before, especially among coal miners, and had won temporary victories. But tenacious business opposition, supported from the governor's office, had always broken the unions. When John L. Lewis began an organizing campaign in 1933, only 225 of Alabama's 17,500 miners belonged to the United Mine Workers of America.

Between 1933 and 1938 the New Deal installed a legislative framework for unionization. First came Section 7(a) of the National Industrial Recovery Act (June 1933), which gave employees the right to organize and bargain collectively. The National Labor Relations Board enforced the act. In July 1935, Congress replaced 7(a) with the National Labor Relations Act, usually called by its sponsor's name, the Wagner Act. The legislation remedied some of the defects of earlier measures by forbidding a number of unfair practices used by employers. The third change came in 1936 when the Walsh-Healy Act established minimum labor standards for firms receiving government contracts. Finally, the Fair Labor Standards Act in 1938 fixed minimum wage and maximum hours for companies engaged in interstate commerce. Of 690,000 workers earning less than 30¢ an hour in the spring of 1939, 54 percent lived in the South. The 32½-¢ law, which went into effect in October 1939, affected 44 percent of southern textile workers but only 6 percent in the North. In lumber and timber, half the southern laborers in 1939 –40 earned exactly the national minimum wage of 30¢ per hour. Partly as a result of this legislation as well as economic changes since 1914, the South was no longer an isolated labor market.[95] Furthermore, Congress, the NLRB, and federal courts became less tolerant of vigilantism,

*Birmingham barber shop window, February 1937. Photo by Arthur
Rothstein. (Courtesy of Farm Security Administration Photographs,
Library of Congress)*

violence, intimidation, and other violations of the civil liberties of union
organizers. Divisions within the labor movement, especially creation of
the CIO, also focused new attention on southern workers.

These initiatives were balanced by powerful southern conservatives
in Congress who waged effective warfare against labor reforms. They
lobbied Roosevelt successfully for wage differentials that allowed lower
wages for southern workers. They effectively branded CIO organizers
as communists and integrationists, and they ignored well organized
extralegal campaigns to prevent unionism.

The first major victory of poor white industrial workers occurred in
mining. Alabama coal miners averaged $12.75 for a three-day week in
1930. By comparison, truck drivers earned $20 to $25 per week.

Because the narrow coal seams of the Warrior and Cahaba fields were expensive to mine, Alabama operators felt entirely justified in rejecting the NIRA's uniform hourly pay scale. When the UMW sent William Mitch and William Dalrymple to Birmingham to resurrect District 20 of the UMW, the stage was set for confrontation. Miners angrily demanded that the companies adhere to the NIRA coal codes and joined the UMW in droves. Many owners, needing fewer laborers anyway in the depressed industry, fired miners and evicted them from company housing. They often blacklisted discharged miners, making it difficult for them to acquire jobs elsewhere.[96]

Henry DeBardeleben, president of the DeBardeleben Coal Corporation, and Charles D. DeBardeleben, who headed the Alabama Fuel and Iron Company, led the anti-union effort. In October 1933, miners at the Hull Mine near Dora wrote President Roosevelt that the company was denying them the right to organize, as guaranteed by Section 7(a). A Labor Department investigation confirmed the allegation but did nothing for miners who lost their jobs. Henry DeBardeleben organized a company union and paid women to circulate petitions that denounced the UMW. When the *Birmingham Post* editorialized that the De-Bardeleben Coal Corporation "had systematically intimidated its men against joining the United Mine Workers," the influential businessmen threatened to sue the paper.[97]

Alabama miners established the validity of New Deal policies in their own way through a series of bitter strikes in 1933–34. Violence was common. The governor sent the National Guard to the Piper and Coleanor mines when pickets clashed with strikebreakers and company guards. This strike finally idled seven thousand miners and threatened to close down all the mines in the state unless the coal board approved the checkoff of union dues. The decision of New Deal officials to allow striking miners to apply for relief tilted the balance of power in favor of the union, and on March 14, 1934, thirty-eight companies representing 90 percent of Alabama's mines signed an agreement with the UMW. Wages rose from $3.40 a day to $3.60, and companies agreed to collect union dues.[98]

The notable exception to the March agreement was the DeBardeleben empire. A federal investigator managed to negotiate an understanding between Mitch and the DeBardelebens in April 1934, but the owners quickly broke it by planting dynamite on a road that led to their coal camps and by mounting machine guns at mine entrances. The De-Bardelebens coerced their employees to reject the UMW and warned of impending violence. The prophecy was fulfilled in October 1934, when fifteen hundred striking miners engaged company guards in a gun battle that left one man dead and ten wounded. Despite the best efforts of federal mediators and the UMW, the DeBardeleben mines remained unorganized, the major exception to the UMW triumph in the South. Although Alabama operators continued to pay the lowest wage in the industry, the differential declined, thanks to NIRA codes and UMW contracts.[99]

For those who retained jobs, the benefits of New Deal and union policies accrued steadily. For those unemployed, such victories were Pyrrhic. A fifty-nine-year-old crippled miner-preacher, W. N. Kizziah, lived at Vance, Alabama. He pastored four churches in Tuscaloosa County and two in Fayette, but none of the poor parishes could afford to pay him. He praised Roosevelt in 1935, announced that he had voted for labor-endorsed candidates, then added that he had never seen conditions so bad. The Reverend Jirden Frye was a Baptist preacher-miner who lived in a nearby abandoned mining camp in Walker County with thirty-seven families, thirty of them white and seven black; twenty were on relief and two lived off old-age pensions. A loyal union man, he had belonged to the UMW local before it died from mismanagement and he had lost his job. Undaunted by his fate, he remained a union man: "Union means onesty [sic] friendship love and truth—everything else beside these is ununion ungodly inhuman and unconstitutional."[100]

Textile workers ranked with miners and timber workers as the poorest-paid industrial workers in the state. The average Alabama mill hand made thirteen dollars a week in 1930 for a ten- to twelve-hour day, but sweepers earned as little as three dollars. By comparison, a stenographer in that same year made between twenty and twenty-five dollars per week.[101]

In many ways the industry was both the most important and complicated in Alabama. It employed more people than any other industry, made different kinds of products, and was dispersed in large and small communities throughout the state. Despite the depression, textile mills continued to move South during the 1930s, primarily to the Carolinas, Georgia, and Alabama. Conditions that caused northern firms to come to the South also made the work of labor organizers more difficult: the North-South wage differential; the proximity of raw materials; extensive agricultural poverty, which provided a cheap, tractable labor force; weak labor union tradition; individualism; aggressive community support for the mills; and state policies that favored management and were hostile to labor. The southern industry also relied more heavily on female operatives whose labor was largely unregulated. Whereas New England states limited the hours females could work (varying from a maximum of forty-eight in Massachusetts to fifty-six in Vermont), the variation in the South ranged from South Carolina, which limited women to fifty-five hours per week, to Alabama, which had no statutory limitation at all.[102]

The industry experienced hard times in the 1930s complicating an already volatile labor-management relationship. Seeking to improve efficiency and reduce costs, mills laid off some workers and stretched out the hours worked by others, thus allowing a reduction in the labor force. Historic grievances over low wages and paternalistic control of mill villages combined with economic insecurity to spawn a bitter series of strikes.

Even a book inspired by the industry detected trouble on the eve of the depression. At the suggestion of industry spokesmen, author Harry I. Shumway attempted to refute a barrage of negative articles in national magazines. He selected the Chattahoochee Valley of Alabama, which contained dozens of mills along the river between Fairfax and Phenix City. His report emphasized the pride of the people—"I may be poor— but I'm just as good as anybody"—their good wages, bank accounts, neatly appointed homes, and healthful entertainment and schools. He deplored child labor, noting that one worker he interviewed had entered the mills at age eleven and that others had started at six or seven when they were so small they had to stand on boxes to reach their work. This outrage, however, he blamed on parents. One man put his children to work in the mills so he could hunt and fish, relenting only when someone sent him a crude drawing of a coffin with a note warning "Git to work or git this!" He got to work. Textile workers were generally religious and men of "spirit when aroused." They were contented with their work despite the desire of some "Bolshevik or communistic labor leaders" to turn the Chattahoochee Valley into "a branch of Soviet Russia."[103]

The "contentment" quickly disappeared after 1930 as unrest spread across central and north Alabama. An AFL organizer trying to recruit members at the Davis Alcock Hosiery Mill in Gadsden succeeded only in getting twenty-six workers fired and the mill closed. The furious organizer ceased his efforts and wrote the Department of Labor "that he would not be a party to taking these people into deep water and then leave them to drown. When they are discharged at one mill they can't get a job at any other which shows they are black-listed." If the Department of Labor allowed such practices, he would refuse to organize textile workers. Thirty miles south, in Anniston, six hundred workers struck Utica Knitting Company after the manager cut women's salaries by 30 to 40 percent and then told the angry women they could seek work elsewhere if they were not satisfied. Three women, the president of Anniston's Central Labor Union, and a plumber-contractor "who was a Holy Roller" led the strikers. The strike spread to the American Net and Twine Mill, where the manager believed that "some communists had gotten in with" workers, and local police were inadequate to "handle the agitators." Conservative governor B. M. Miller sent guardsmen to Anniston in May 1933.[104]

The strike spread to Huntsville on July 16, 1934, where it escalated into a new phase. Thugs, allegedly led by a former state commander of the American Legion, kidnapped John Deal, the textile union leader. To make matters worse, the Alabama State Federation of Labor granted only the most grudging strike support. W. C. Hare, secretary of the federation, which was already reeling from unionbusting and lost jobs, issued a statement that "the American Federation of Labor was and is against the general textile strike." Angry workers swept AFL leaders aside and the strike spread by August to 23,000 Alabama textile workers in twenty-eight mills. South and central Alabama mills were still unorganized and generally continued to operate; but in Huntsville, Birmingham, Florence, Guntersville, Albertville, Gordo, and Winfield mills closed. "Flying squads" of workers began in July to visit mills still operating to try to persuade workers to join the strike. At Haleyville in northwestern Alabama, armed company guards met a truckload of strikers from Huntsville at the railroad tracks, refused to allow them to enter town, and threatened mill workers who crossed the tracks to talk with them.[105]

The strike polarized towns such as Winfield in Marion County. Businessmen opposed the union and refused to extend credit to strikers. The mayor and a county commissioner sought to prevent them from obtaining relief. As their children went hungry, strikers became more desperate, and their union president wrote Harry Hopkins: "Naturally when they are forced into this disorderly mood they are likely to do unlowful [sic] things." A year later conditions were no better, and a local minister implored President Roosevelt to intervene. The city council had closed streets near the mill, arrested violators for trespassing, and searched former employees walking near the mill. Local relief administrators refused jobs to strikers, trying "to crush labor and make slaves of men and women. . . . Is this fair, is this American, is this justice?" Why was it, he concluded, that capitalists and men who did not need it received all the relief money?[106]

At Opelika in east-central Alabama, mill officials mounted a machine gun on a small building and turned back a "flying squad" from Phenix City. In Lanett, thirty miles to the east, where labor had been so satisfied according to Shumway, the West Point Manufacturing Company piled bales of cotton on the highway that bisected the mill town. Company guards behind the bales stopped cars and searched occupants. They shot holes in the tires of a Dr. O'Neil, who did not stop quickly enough, and assaulted a man who was rushing his injured daughter to a doctor.

"Machine gun" men patrolled roads in the Chattahoochee Valley. A striking worker at Pepperell Mill in Opelika was dispossessed from his home by a local realtor who was also a stockholder in the mill. He moved to Phenix City where the United Textile Workers union helped him for several weeks before closing its relief station. When he wrote Franklin Roosevelt in October, he was unable to qualify for relief in Russell County because he had not lived there for six months. He was "completely out of something to eat" and had "no means by which to get anything." In fact, the county's relief rolls groaned under the weight of striking mill workers; by October they constituted 75 percent of all clients.[107]

Downstate at the Mobile Cotton Mill on the northern fringe of the city, Annie Crabtree Hudson participated in the 1934 strike. She had been born into a mill family, went to work in the mill when she was fifteen, married a fellow worker at age nineteen, and bore three children. Their mill house had neither water nor electricity in the 1930s. Her work as a spinner and her husband's in the boiler room earned them a total of twelve to sixteen dollars for sixty-five-hour weeks. To make ends meet she took in washing, padded holes in her shoes with cotton, and bought the children's clothes at rummage sales at the Methodist mission they attended. During the strike her husband was charged with carrying a gun, which he claimed was for self-protection. Two striking female friends were arrested and refused to post bond, saying they preferred jail where they at least could enjoy food, electric lights, and hot running water. Neither of the Hudsons could read or write nor did they vote, though in 1940 they praised FDR to whom they gave credit for the forty-hour week, higher wages, Social Security, unemployment insurance, and a better life generally.[108]

Seven months after the July 1934 general strike, John Goins, president of the Alabama State Textile Council, was not so sure workers had gained anything. Without sufficient money even to buy stationery, he begged the Alabama State Labor Council for legal assistance to aid textile pickets who were being prosecuted in Florence. Addressing W. C. Hare, who had opposed the strike, he inquired: "My God, what on earth is the matter that we are left alone in a time when we need help as we do now."[109] His fate was not uncommon. The 1934 national textile strike, largest in American history, was defeated. Many workers lost their jobs and houses.

The labor movement also expanded to include agriculture. Alabama had perhaps the longest history of agrarian unionism of any state in the cotton belt due to divisions in types of farming, regional conflict within the state, and the presence of a strong labor movement in Birmingham. During the 1930s the Farmers Union organized farm laborers, sharecroppers, and small independent farmers in counties adjacent to Birmingham. At their 1936 state convention, the Farmers Union endorsed the urban union agenda and sought its help in organizing tenants and day laborers. But the effort was short-lived. By 1937, communists, operating from their southern headquarters in Birmingham, organized a rival Sharecroppers Union. Although the communists sought to organize whites and blacks, their major successes occurred among black sharecroppers in east-central Alabama and led to violence. Clashes between the two unions weakened both and played into the hands of opponents of rural unionism. Despite a 1937 decision of Farmers Union locals in Bibb, Winston, Fayette, Franklin, Marion, Tuscaloosa, and Shelby counties to affiliate with the CIO, the union declined rapidly. By 1940 it survived only in strong union counties.[110]

At the heart of all union efforts in Alabama during the 1930s was a single critical issue recognized by both proponents and opponents of unionism: were strikers eligible for New Deal relief programs? If so, they had little to lose in a strike because relief payments were only slightly less than their depressed wages. But if denied relief, they faced the specter of eviction and starvation. Eligibility for relief became a central issue for New Deal administrators in Alabama.

State relief administrator Thad Holt contacted Harry Hopkins to request guidelines almost as soon as Roosevelt took office. Hopkins instructed Holt to use his own judgment about providing relief to strikers until the administration could formulate policy. Months later, in March 1934, striking coal miners in St. Clair County explained to relief workers that the president had told them to organize; but when they had done so they had lost their jobs. Now they expected the president to put them on relief. Opinions differed as to whether Roosevelt conveyed this notion in his fireside chats on radio or whether UMW organizers promised it as part of overzealous promotion. Whatever the source, relief officials often refused to certify miners who owned small plots of land, although the miners complained that they earned their livelihood in the mines, not on their infertile farms. One relief official wrote Holt that local people opposed putting striking miners on relief, contending that these men had good jobs "and of their own free will did something which caused them to lose their jobs." But this official was less than objective. She was the sister of the purchasing agent for the Margaret Coal Mine, a fact that led miners to claim that she was helping her brother break the union. UMW District 20 director William Mitch demanded that Holt investigate discrimination against unionists by such relief officials.[111]

Union members often complained that middle class relief officials discriminated against them. A petition from Russellville in northwest Alabama alleged that the local relief official warned that anyone joining a labor union would be dropped from the relief roll. When eight thousand iron-ore miners struck TCI, Republic, and Sloss-Sheffield Steel companies in May 1934, the miners believed the woman in charge of relief for Bessemer, who was the wife of TCI's employment agent, purposely delayed relief for the strikers. In February 1936, the Birmingham Building Trades Council sent Holt a diatribe against W. D. Twing, WPA director for Jefferson County. With men such as Twing directing relief, the country need not worry about "a Musulini [sic] or a Hitler"; the United States had its own dictator in Birmingham: "Slavery was abolished years ago, but according to . . . Twing and his henchmen it is just started. We are revolting against such tyrany [sic], especially by persons who live on charity themselves." A similar warning came from Bibb County, where officials of UMW Local 5797 called the county commissioners who supervised relief work "God forsaken dirty low down crooks" and warned: "we are trying to settle it [low pay for relief work] in peace. if [sic] we fail—well nature will take her course."[112]

Other relief officials drew union fire also, the most controversial being Milton H. Fies. Harry Hopkins appointed Fies chairman of the state relief administration at the recommendation of both Senators John Bankhead and Hugo Black. Hopkins made the appointment in the hectic first hundred days of the New Deal, without consulting state labor leaders, who were furious when they learned of the appointment. Fies was vice-president of DeBardeleben Coal Corporation and had personally discharged miners for joining the UMW.[113]

Any attempt to accommodate labor subjected Holt to similar attacks by Alabama business leaders and lawyers. A Birmingham attorney, Oliver Henderson, complained to Senator Bankhead that Roosevelt's policy of providing relief to strikers prolonged strikes by encouraging "insubordination on the part of the working man both white and black." As evidence, Henderson cited one of his tenant farmers who was on strike and whose "attitude is that he would just as soon . . . remain on a strike and let the Government feed him and his family as to work." Scott Roberts, president of the Alabama Cotton Manufacturers Association, blasted the New Deal for putting striking textile workers on relief during July–September 1934. Alabama's Associated Industries condemned Hopkins for feeding striking coal miners. And lumber company officials chided Roosevelt for prolonging a lumber workers' strike by providing federal relief.[114]

Caught in such cross fire, Holt raged in frustration. To Hopkins's unofficial envoy, Lorena Hickok, he complained about the "union labor crowd" who were trying to run the New Deal. When UMW organizers tried to boss Hickok, however, they met their match. She wrote Harry Hopkins that they sought to get all they could from the government with little concern for the nation's welfare or even that of the rank and file: "My assumption is that they are NOT running the Federal Government—at least not YET—and I have a hard time to keep from getting a bit hot under the collar at their attitude. They are certainly 'feeling their oats.' " After enlisting Hickok's assistance, Holt angrily called Aubrey Williams, Hopkins's lieutenant, several days later. He urged Hopkins to contact William Mitch and explain federal relief procedures. Mitch and the UMW were losing public support by insisting on immediate, direct relief for striking miners when such relief meant that others would have to be dropped from the rolls. Holt reasoned, "If you tell a farmer, I have not enough money to give you rural rehabilitation, because I have to feed the miners, Mitch has got to see that there is public ill will against his group." Williams advised him to continue Roosevelt's policy of administering relief without regard to whether the indigents were strikers or not. That is precisely what Holt did, announcing in July 1934 that striking workers would receive neither discriminatory nor preferential treatment. But by September, he was on the phone again to Hopkins, complaining that strikers had drained the state's relief funds. Nearly 8,200 of the 20,000 textile strikers were on relief, costing an extra $120,000. As a result Holt had to cut agricultural relief by one-half. Hopkins again came to the rescue, authorizing an additional $250,000 in federal relief funds for Alabama. But even Hopkins was losing patience. When Holt expressed fear that textile union leaders might tell strikers to refuse work required for relief payments, Hopkins replied: if they did, "tell them to go to hell."[115]

Despite such pique in Washington, labor won its battle. By the spring of 1935, Noel R. Beddow, regional director of the Steel Workers Organizing Committee (CIO), had been appointed Alabama director of the NRA and could write that his office was "keeping in as close touch as is permissible in any of the State NRA officers . . . with labor conditions." He added that if business had adhered to NIRA codes, there would have been no labor troubles. Of 18,395 striking textile workers in eleven counties in mid-September 1934, 6,589 received relief. Of 18,000 coal miners in the state, 13,000 were on relief in October 1935, 6,000 in Birmingham alone.[116]

Organized labor shrewdly utilized its political power. Despite the debilitating effect of the poll tax on poor whites, industrial unions steadily raised the political consciousness of workers. Although class politics may be too strong a term for the emergence of the new political order, it certainly contained obvious elements of such division. The state AFL campaigned actively for New Dealer Bibb Graves in his 1934 gubernatorial race. William Mitch and Noel Beddow endorsed and actively supported Lister Hill for U.S. senator in 1937. And organized labor helped elect one of the most liberal congressional delegations from any southern state.[117]

Despite gains among poor white workers, not all of labor's campaigns were triumphs during the 1930s. Birmingham police, backed by some of the city's most powerful corporations, harassed political radicals and union organizers. Vigilantes flogged alleged communists, often with the connivance of city officials.[118]

Sixty miles to the northeast, Gadsden proved to be one of the most impenetrable anti-union towns in the South. The city's economy rested on a tripod of three industries: Gulf States Steel, with three thousand employees; Dwight Manufacturing Company, employing two thousand textile workers; and Goodyear Tire and Rubber Company, which employed fifteen hundred. Goodyear had located its plant in Gadsden in 1929 because of the large number of poor white farmers in the vicinity. Prospective employees were asked to pledge not to join a union and were reminded, "there's a barefoot boy waiting at the gate for your job." Aided by a community eager to attract industry and keep out unions, these three companies made Gadsden a major battleground.

Labor tried repeatedly and unsuccessfully to break through the barriers. The first attempt to unionize Gadsden occurred in 1933 when the AFL tried to organize Gulf States Steel. Gulf States formed a company union, shut down briefly, fired two hundred unionists, then reopened. The United Textile Workers of America tried next in 1934, but Dwight Manufacturing obtained an injunction against the union and broke the strike. In June 1936, the United Rubber Workers dispatched Sherman H. Dalrymple to organize Goodyear, but he was beaten by a gang of thugs led by a former Auburn University football player and was run out of town. Not until 1941 did labor crack the town, when Noel Beddow obtained an NLRB ruling against Republic Steel (formerly Gulf States Steel) that allowed a representational election, which was won by labor. Two years later, in 1943, federal pressure finally forced Goodyear to recognize the URW, and Gadsden subsequently became a union stronghold.[119]

Following a decade of strife and trauma, most Alabama whites ended the 1930s just as they had begun: poor. New Deal urban strategies were at best stopgap measures. Relief was too little and too localized. It never reached some rural areas at all, and in others it was subject to political manipulation. New Deal efforts to uplift tenant farmers were halting, and the AAA actually displaced poor whites. Rural rehabilitation, resettlement, and the Farm Security Administration enjoyed some successes but did not reach the majority of rural poor people.

The primary changes in the quality of life of poor whites came in three areas. First, the federal government became more responsive to the problems of the poor. Changes in policy between 1930 and 1940 consistently improved opportunities and slowly restored hope. Second, New Deal relief programs provided a floor beneath which the poor were not allowed to sink. So completely did charity, state relief, and the private sector break down, that the federal government became an employer of last resort. Without such help, tens of thousands of Alabamians would quite simply have starved and frozen. Finally, organized labor allowed the poor to seek their own salvation. By organizing individualistic people, labor transferred power from well-meaning bureaucrats to the poor themselves. Whether because of union power or New Deal sympathies, federal officials provided support to labor, though sometimes grudgingly. And that support, especially the controversial decision to allow strikers to receive relief, literally saved the union movement in Alabama.

To argue that the New Deal transformed the lives of poor whites is to claim too much. To dismiss the New Deal as a chimera is to ignore the perils of the time and place. Somewhere between those claims of historians lies the truth of history. Down a hundred dirt roads, up endless hollows, in dark mines and sweltering textile mills, the poor continued much as they had, though with a ray of hope for the future, a bit less fear of their bosses, a little more control of their own lives, and a bit more pride in themselves. They had survived the Great Depression.

TWELVE

"The Poor You Have with You Always"

The Enduring Legacy

The years of the Great Depression and the Second World War constituted a second great watershed in the experience of Alabama's poor. The Civil War had precipitated a disastrous decline. The New Deal and the struggle against totalitarianism marked a turning point in the battle against white poverty. Although the poor remained, their numbers declined markedly, thanks both to growth in the private sector and to federal spending.

As events in Europe and Asia raced toward climax during the late 1930s, America geared for battle. The cheap TVA electricity and huge manpower reserves of the Tennessee Valley beckoned new civilian industry and defense plants. Strong national unions, supported by favorable rulings from the National Labor Relations Board and federal courts, won organizing battles that substantially raised manufacturing salaries. Nonunion industries such as textiles had to increase wages because of steady increases in minimum-wage laws. Improvements in the state's school system and later the GI Bill broadened educational opportunities. Poor whites entered both the economic and the cultural mainstream, affecting and altering each.

As America prepared for war in 1940, the general economic upturn reached into Alabama. Military bases, ordnance plants, and other facilities opened or expanded. In the tier of east Alabama counties stretching from Madison (Huntsville) to Talladega, wartime federal spending was particularly significant. The government built large ordnance facilities in Huntsville, Anniston, and Childersburg and expanded Fort McClellan in Calhoun County.

Construction both displaced the poor and afforded them new opportunities. The Farm Security Administration established offices in Anniston and Childersburg to assist people displaced by defense projects. The agency provided advice, grants, and loans to those who requested them. Whereas passage from poverty to prosperity had once been symbolized by landownership, it now came to mean salaries. Tens of thousands of poor whites who had been forced off tenant farms by New Deal agricultural policies moved to cities where they found blue-collar industrial jobs.

Upheaval was inevitable. Childersburg, formerly a town of five hundred in 1940, had to absorb fourteen thousand construction workers who came to build a power plant for DuPont Chemical. The project required the condemnation of thirty-two thousand acres of land, which uprooted three hundred farm families. The FSA had difficulty relocating them because many marginal landowners had so small an equity that they received little or no cash for their property. Sharecroppers received nothing at all. Furthermore, the order for removal came so late that farmers would have difficulty making a crop in a new location during the 1941 season.

This dislocation often resulted in a better life for the persons involved. When Fort McClellan expanded its artillery range, one of the farms it bought from the Anniston National Bank was the "Bell place," home to elderly tenant farmers Mr. and Mrs. Homer Flynt. Their children, who had left the farm in the 1930s for industrial jobs at the Goodyear Plant in Cedartown, Georgia, or Birmingham's steel mills, found their parents a small house on Buttermilk Road. Claude Flynt, oldest of the boys, began to prosper when he obtained a used truck and moved families to and from the booming town of Childersburg. Before the Flynts were displaced from the farm, Mae Ellis Moore Flynt got a job at the Anniston Ordnance Depot while her husband recovered from severe surgery for osteomyelitis.[1]

A debt-ridden farmer some forty miles away on the border with Georgia obtained work at Fort McClellan as an unskilled carpenter, building barracks for the princely sum of seven dollars a day. Previously he had earned fewer than three hundred dollars a year by farming. Although he had to leave home at 3:30 in the morning and did not return until 7:30 at night, he rejoiced in a job that allowed him to build his savings and reduce his indebtedness.[2]

Edward Imirie traveled a longer distance over a different route in order to better his life. Born in Mobile in 1906, he finished only seven grades of school. The aunt and uncle who raised him could afford no more than that. He worked briefly in a paint shop until it went out of business, then he tried to live with his parents, who were too poor to support him. Unable to find a job, he left Mobile for Houston, Texas, where wartime expansion allowed him to find work as a merchant seaman.[3]

A second major source of new opportunities came from women who augmented family income with jobs in the better-paying war industry. One important source of labor during the war years was the state's married women. Although most were middle class, many poor white women responded enthusiastically to the opportunity for job training and steady income.

A number of the new defense industries relied heavily on female labor. The Mobile Air Service Command at Brookley Field in Mobile employed women as almost half its labor force. Birmingham's Betchel-McCone-Parsons plant to recondition aircraft employed 40 percent females. Alabama Ordnance Works at Childersburg hired 48 percent women, Redstone Arsenal in Huntsville 25 to 35 percent females, and the Mobile shipyards about 10 percent.

Government recruitment publicity emphasized that women did not have to possess specialized occupational skills to obtain jobs. The Mobile Air Command recruited women to repair airplane instruments with the appeal: "If you can operate a sewing machine, open a can of tomatoes, take a vacuum cleaner half apart or make emergency repairs on the refrigerator, you can help defeat the Axis."[4] Although the list clearly applied to middle class women, literate poor white females had approximately the same skills as any other Alabama women, and many were more accustomed to hard regular work. No doubt many female textile workers in Huntsville, Mobile, Birmingham, and Anniston gave up mill work for higher-paying defense jobs. And the war placed the textile industry on overtime as workers frantically labored to supply clothing and fabric for the military.

Many women who needed additional skills acquired them at the Alabama School of Trades in Gadsden. The facility had long been an avenue by which poor white males had escaped poverty. But in the early 1940s it served women equally well. Shortly after it opened its doors to women, they made up most of the student body. The school began operating three shifts a day, training women and draft-ineligible males in tin sheet metalwork and welding. The school taught them how to make airplane parts, including wings, a skill they applied immediately upon graduation at the Mobile Air Command at Brookley Field. The school constructed three women's dorms during the 1940s, added a program in nursing, and remained coed after the war.[5]

Despite such advances among the poor, progress remained uneven. Illiteracy often disqualified poor whites from better opportunities, and the displacement of tenant farmers could as often lead down the economic ladder as up. Fortunately, the advent of the mechanical cotton picker and other technological innovations occurred at about the same time as the upsurge in wartime manpower requirements. Thus in the long run, America's industrial expansion absorbed most displaced tenant farmers. Unfortunately people do not eat, clothe, or care for themselves in the long run. Food, medicine, housing, and clothing were immediate and critical needs that often went unmet. In July 1942, Alabama farm laborers earned an average of $1.35 per day without board. Common laborers in Alabama industry that same month earned 43¢ an hour, or an average of $3.44 for an eight-hour day. Farm laborers, then, earned only 39 percent as much as common industrial workers. And even this comparison is misleading because the average farm laborer worked much longer than eight hours per day.[6]

One family whose fortunes did not improve was the Roberts family of Perry County. Seth Roberts, fifty-three years old when his plight drew national attention in 1941, was a white sharecropper who had finished only four years of school. His mother had been an orphan and was illiterate. Roberts had moved frequently, tending cotton farms or contracting timber to sawmills in eight different counties. He contracted malaria while sharecropping bottomland along a river and entered a hospital in 1940. His six children remained behind in Lowndes County. Their landlord, when he discovered that Roberts was hospitalized, refused to honor an oral contract to allow the family to tenant farm. He hired the boys as farm laborers, paying the oldest ten dollars a month plus three pounds of salt pork and a peck of meal a month, and paying the others eight dollars and the same allotment of food. The oldest boy, then fifteen, did not serve out the year. The landowner killed his puppy, cursed the boy when he tried to prevent it, and ordered the teenager off the farm. He let the rest of the family stay until the end of the year but warned them they would all have to leave then. Roberts had no idea where he would take his family when he got out of the hospital or how he would earn a living.[7]

Seth Roberts becomes nothing more than a cipher on government census data after 1940. But it is unlikely that he long remained a tenant farmer. More likely he was caught up in a maelstrom that swept across agriculture and transformed it more radically than at any other time in American history. The historic assumption that the good life depended on landownership died slowly but surely. Federal agricultural policies encouraged farmers to mechanize and many of them did so, using government loans or crop-reduction payments to purchase equipment. As they did so, they no longer needed tenants to perform the arduous labor that machines could do cheaper, faster, and better.

In 1948 International Harvester built a new plant in Memphis, Tennessee, to manufacture cotton pickers. Mississippi Delta plantations began using them in large numbers and they slowly invaded Alabama's cotton fields. One machine could harvest a thousand pounds of cotton per hour, compared to fifteen or twenty pounds produced by a human cotton picker. Tractors had an even wider effect, especially in counties containing the largest number of poor whites. By 1963, machines harvested 37 percent of Alabama's cotton crop.

Mechanization encouraged consolidation. Tractors required forty acres or more and cotton pickers at least one hundred acres for efficient operation. As a consequence, the average farm size increased steadily, as more prosperous farmers bought out less-fortunate neighbors. This process displaced thousands.

Farmers also diversified. Montgomery County, a traditional cotton center, derived more income from cattle than from cotton by the 1940s. Broilers, eggs, cattle, soybeans, peanuts, and dairy products eclipsed cotton in many counties as a source of cash income. The 1956 Soil Bank Act encouraged farmers to remove land from production and convert it to pasture, timber, dairying, or poultry use. None of these were as labor intensive as cotton had been, and diversification had the same effect as mechanization: displacement of the poorest people at the bottom of the agricultural ladder. Ironically, the same process would in time displace the small family farmer, who despite his plight, had enormously more educational and financial resources than the state's tenants had possessed. Between 1940 and 1970 the number of southern farmers declined from nearly fourteen million to fewer than three million.

The wartime boom and military draft absorbed the rural population surplus, and the South's farm population dropped 22 percent between 1940 and 1945. The average family size on Alabama farms dropped from 5.8 to 4.5 persons during those five war years.[8] In later years, industrial cities North and South continued this process of absorption.

The Farm Security Administration and its successor, the Farmers Home Administration, played little role in the transition. Their efforts to transform tenants into landowners were never popular with Congress or the land-grant colleges.[9] Many middle and upper class Alabamians considered the FSA a radical organization that threatened venerated economic, social, and racial patterns. Congress underfunded the FSA from its inception, and appropriations declined even more as wartime needs assumed greater priority. Its underfunded record of helping tenants become landowners was no better in the 1940s than in the late 1930s.

Nevertheless, the decline in white tenancy was inexorable. From 55.3 percent of all farmers in 1935, Alabama's percentage declined to 49.6 in 1940, 32.2 in 1950, and 18.4 in 1959. By 1969 the state contained only 4,605 white tenants, compared to more than 100,000 in 1935.[10]

The change constituted perhaps the most significant social and economic transformation in Alabama's history.

Counties that had contained the largest numbers of white tenants experienced the most dramatic declines. By 1969 Calhoun County had only 41 white tenant farmers, Cleburne 17, Clay 11, Randolph 17, Winston 20, Jackson 245, Cherokee 113, Covington 82, and Crenshaw 69.[11]

During the 1980s three journalists revisited the sharecroppers who had been the subject of Walker Evans's and James Agee's classic work *Let Us Now Praise Famous Men*. Perhaps the interest of the *New York Times* and the *Sacramento Bee* in Alabama's white poor reflected a long tradition of outsiders both caring more and understanding less about the nature of Alabama's poverty than the state's own people. Although none of the former sharecroppers were wealthy, they were no longer impoverished either. (One drove a tractor on a plantation and thus technically was a farm laborer, but he earned thirty-five dollars a day.) They had survived hard times in the 1940s and 1950s and lived fairly well in mobile homes or low-rent housing by the 1980s.[12] They deeply resented Walker Evans's photographs, which depicted them as more destitute than they remembered, and for good measure they sued the *New York Times* and author Howell Raines when one of the articles appeared. The British Broadcasting Corporation came calling also, and the families achieved a notoriety in the 1970s and 1980s far exceeding the fame generated by Evans's and Agee's book.

Mechanization took its toll in other occupations as well. New machinery made coal mining safer and more efficient, but it also displaced thousands of miners. In 1940 nearly 17,000 Alabama whites mined coal and iron ore. By 1950, employment had risen to 17,500. But ten years later, in 1960, white employment in mining had plummeted to 8,876.[13]

Thanks to the United Mine Workers of America, coal miners could no longer be listed among the white poor. Although poverty spawned their culture and dominated their life histories, those who lived into the postwar era experienced unprecedented prosperity. And sons and daughters who entered the mines knew poverty only through the memory of their parents. In terms both of hourly earnings and of total income, mining wages ranked third among more than 155 American industries. In May 1949, coal miners averaged $1.95 an hour, including overtime, compared with an average of $1.37 in all U.S. manufacturing.[14]

Not only did Alabama miners make a great deal more, they also labored in a much safer work place. During the period between 1920 and 1935, Alabama ranked third from the bottom among Appalachian coal-producing states with one fatality per 300,300 tons of coal produced. During a similar time span between 1963 and 1978, Alabama had risen two places to the third-safest state with one fatality for every 2,033,000 tons of coal produced in underground mines. Strip-mining, which displaced underground miners, rapidly reduced fatalities.[15]

None of this increased safety eliminated individual suffering. Coal mining remained a dangerous, cyclical occupation. Thousands of miners were injured or killed by slate falls and explosions. Employment was irregular, tied closely to general American economic patterns. The work gyrated wildly between periods of intense labor with considerable overtime and periods of extended layoffs. Inflation and large families combined to strain budgets, even those augmented by fat UMW contracts.

Herbert South, an uneducated bivocational Methodist minister–coal miner from Marion County, kept his pay slips. From them he reconstructed his salary, which averaged $39.93 per week in 1958, $35.46 in 1959, $41.36 in 1960, and $49.98 in 1961. Recalling the struggle to feed his wife and eight children, he commented: "it was a hard go to feed a large family on $40 a week." In March 1961 he quit the Taylor Coal Company because of severe black lung problems and moved his family to Arkansas, where he sharecropped, raising cotton and soybeans.[16]

But the South's problems were those of an earlier and different age surviving into a new era. By the 1980s, Alabama coal miners worried mainly about a new set of problems, such as imported coal and job security. Traditional ways were disappearing. Folk beliefs and superstitions died slowly but surely. Male miners who had believed that women in a mine brought bad luck had to learn to work beside females. In 1940, fifty-five white women mined coal in Alabama. By 1950 that figure had more than doubled.[17]

By 1986 unskilled Alabama coal miners started work making $110 a day. As Susan Ellis, a miner at Jim Walter's Bessie Mine, phrased it: "The only reason we do this crazy thing is for the money. The money is great. We're not trying to prove a point, we just want to do the best we can with the skills we've got." Instead of puzzling over starvation wages, payment in scrip at the company store, convict labor, or drives to unionize, Ellis had helped organize the Alabama Women Coal Miners Support Group. Its goals included parental leave for parents who had to stay with a sick child, or for a man whose wife had just had a baby, or for couples who had adopted a child: "People in those situations need to be able to feel they can take off for a short time without fear of losing their jobs."[18]

Such an agenda reveals how dramatically coal mining had changed in the half century since the Great Depression. And such issues were a world removed from the concerns of Ms. Ellis's impoverished occupational ancestors.

Although unionism played little role in the transition, Alabama's textile industry also changed rapidly. The industry remained the South's least organized, defying one wave of unionism after another. Wages remained lower than those of coal miners, and international competition cost jobs.

In 1940, textile mills constituted the largest industrial employer of Alabama whites, affording jobs to nearly 46,000. Employment grew to more than 51,000 in 1950, divided nearly evenly between male and female. By 1960 the textile products, apparel, and fabricated textile industries provided work for nearly 65,000 Alabama whites, but that number fell rapidly during the ensuing twenty-five years.[19]

Huntsville furnishes an excellent case study of industrial change. Considered one of the South's largest textile centers since 1900, the depression and Second World War completely altered the city's economy and history. Redstone Arsenal became the base of a new high technology center for NASA, and soon engineers with Ph.D.'s outnumbered textile workers. Once a town whose eight major textile mills rivaled the Piedmont centers of the Carolinas and Virginia, by the 1980s city leaders proudly compared their community to North Carolina's "research triangle" or to California's "Silicon Valley." They hardly mentioned the town's mills and for good reason.

Of the eight mills that once towered above the city's fringes, only one continued to operate. Erwin Mills and Lowe Manufacturing were casualties of the depression, closing in 1936. Dallas Mills, the first weaving operation to locate in Huntsville and for many years its largest employer, survived the depression only to succumb in the postwar years. A 1947 strike crippled the company. It employed seven hundred when the strike began but only three hundred when it closed permanently in 1949. Only Merrimack Mill continued to operate into the mid-1980s. Having long since sold its company houses to their occupants and having dissolved its mill village, it underwent several reorganizations. M. Lowenstein and Company of New York bought Merrimack in January 1946 and renamed it Huntsville Manufacturing Company.[20] Wages increased even as employment declined, and by the 1980s foreign imports troubled employees far more than low wages or racial problems.

In 1986 Walton Monroe Mills of Monroe, Georgia, purchased Avondale Mills. The merger was a powerful symbol of the new world in which Alabama textile workers lived. The Comer family of Barbour County, Sylacauga, and Birmingham had kept the company in the family for eighty-nine years. Its paternalism had been a legend. The family had produced one Alabama governor and had built the largest textile empire in the state, with mills stretching at one time or another from Eufaula to the Tennessee Valley.

The new company planned significant changes for the 3,700 remaining Avondale employees. Their company pension plan would end, as would inexpensive vacations at Camp Helen, a popular company-owned Florida beach resort. The company would discontinue contributions to the employee stock-ownership plan and amend the profit-sharing plan.[21] Ownership would also pass beyond the state's borders. Even then most Avondale workers were grateful to still have jobs in an industry buffeted by imports from the Orient.

Sawmilling flourished even as coal mining and textiles fell on hard times. Logging and sawmilling furnished jobs for more than 18,000 Alabama whites in 1940, a figure that increased to nearly 26,000 ten years later. By the mid-1940s, timber companies were experiencing trouble obtaining enough labor because of low wages, undesirable working conditions, long travel distances to work, and the reputation of many small operations for cheating employees.[22] Technology helped resolve the labor shortage. Narrow-gauge railroad tracks and "pecker-wood" portable sawmills gave way to the "wood dealer system" with its contracts to poor whites who could borrow or buy a secondhand truck and contract to supply pulpwood.

Alabama's forests were a natural ally both of gigantic pulpwood mills and of impoverished farmers who desired to remain on the land. The high humidity, hot summers, and high rates of rainfall furnished an ideal climate for the hardy species of pine trees that flourished in the region.

Although census data record the rise and fall of employment in the industry, they obscure the profound changes occurring in the southern forest industry. In 1900 lumber was the principal forest product harvested in the South. It was a migratory industry with little concern for conservation or replacement. By the 1980s, pulp and paper products had become the dominant wood industry, more than doubling lumber production in many southern states. Companies began to put down roots, aware that pine trees could be planted and harvested like any other crop, even if the harvest seemed unusually delayed. Alabama had four pulp and paper mills in 1950 and thirteen in 1970.

Many factors produced the southern paper industry, including new technology, changes in packaging, especially the use of strong brown paper bags, and promotion of the South's splendid natural environment for growing pine trees. Alabama's water resources, transportation facilities, and surplus rural labor equipped it well for expansion. The depressed agricultural economy of the 1930s created thousands of unemployed rural poor who were looking desperately for alternative employment.

As the pulp and paper industry moved to the South, it owned little timberland of its own. Instead, companies relied on thousands of rural landowners to sell their timber. They had to deal with each landowner individually, a time-consuming and frustrating business when a single day's supply of pulpwood at a mill might require negotiations with many different landowners.

Cultural patterns complicated this problem. Landowners were often suspicious of outsiders. Racial barriers hindered efficient negotiations. A heritage of independence, violence, resistance to authority, and cultural isolation made labor unreliable and difficult to manage. Contracts and schedules counted for very little in southern folk culture.

So companies began enlisting the help of local businessmen, politicians, and sheriffs, the small-town southern elite that could both purchase timber and coordinate harvesting and hauling. These men, imbued with entrepreneurial skills and community authority, became wood dealers. They contracted with local producers, who hired labor from among the rural poor who cut and hauled the wood. The dealers delivered a specified amount of wood to railroad cars, which were then pulled to a pulp mill. Dealers worked independently of the company and were not its employees.

Because of the intense localism of the system, what appears at first glance to be an informal, unpredictable, chaotic arrangement actually functioned smoothly and efficiently. It delivered a reliable supply of wood at lower costs than wood-supply arrangements in other sections of the country. Community dealers often furnished loans to allow their suppliers to purchase a truck and saws. A poor white paid his loan with a share of the profits from his cutting and hauling. In one typical situation, a dealer paid his producers $5.00 per cord of wood, $1.00 of which was deducted to pay the loan on his truck, $2.50 to the crew of two men who did the actual cutting, and 50¢ to the landowner whose trees they cut, leaving about $1.00 for the producer.

Dealers knew local customs as well as the county's rural poor. They knew whom they could count on to deliver according to a contract. And if necessary they could fall back upon the authority of the county sheriff when coercion became necessary. Both poor whites and blacks from deserted turpentine and logging camps and those forced from sharecropping found a new existence as pulpwood producers. But as debts for trucks and equipment mounted, the rural power structure sometimes forced them into a condition of semipeonage not unlike what they had known before.

Because the pulp companies did not directly employ the dealers or producers, they were able to ignore minimum wage and fair labor standard laws. Producers were generally ignorant of such laws and incapable or unwilling to fill out forms or pay taxes. Tax authorities could not monitor the thousands of small producers delivering wood indirectly to dealers, so much of the pulpwood supplied to mills was technically produced illegally. Everyone along the complex line—landowners, producers, dealers, pulp and paper companies, and consumers—profited from the lack of taxes paid and of accompanying accounting costs. Companies avoided paying Social Security and other fringe benefits. Many of the rural poor found employment sufficient to allow them to stay on the land, even if what they earned kept them in a state not much above the poverty line.[23]

The iron and steel industry followed more traditional ways, though the advent of unionism, new technology, and foreign competition changed that industry also. In 1940, Alabama's iron and steel mills employed 21,428 whites. The total increased to 25,359 in 1950 and to 33,578 in 1960.[24] Like coal and textiles, the number of white iron- and steelworkers declined sharply in the 1970s and 1980s. Birmingham, whose night skies once glowed as giant caldrons spilled their loads of molten iron into molds, went the way of Huntsville. Retail and educational jobs replaced industrial work.

The shifts in occupation and population became more stark when applied to the entire state instead of to individual industries. Technically, thirty-five of Alabama's sixty-seven counties were defined as Appalachian. Most of the state's poor whites lived within those counties. Between 1950 and 1960, twenty-one of the thirty-five counties lost population. Although hill counties containing cities or major industries—such as Madison, Jefferson, Etowah, or Calhoun—grew, rural Appalachian Alabama declined. Every one of the thirty-five counties experienced declines in agricultural employment between 1960 and 1966. Although north Alabama's factories absorbed many of these displaced rural whites, others left for Dayton, Detroit, Chicago, Cincinnati, or some less-familiar haven.

Appalachian economic patterns particularly affected the state's poor whites. Between 1950 and 1960, agricultural employment, which was mostly white, declined from 133,117 to 51,615, or by 61 percent. Whereas farm labor had accounted for 21.5 percent of the jobs in these thirty-five counties in 1950, it supplied only 8 percent in 1960. During the same decade, mining jobs in the area declined by 59 percent. But manufacturing jobs rose 28 percent, construction jobs by more than 34 percent, and trades and services employment by nearly 27 percent. The Neighborhood Youth Corps enrolled 9,430 in the thirty-five counties during 1966–67, providing a transition from a rural/agricultural to an urban/industrial way of life.[25]

The critical determinant of whether rural poor whites stayed on the land and improved their lot or joined the migration to cities was location.

If they lived close enough to a city to commute, or if an industry located in a rural area nearby, their prospects of remaining and improving their lives were excellent. If they were not so fortunate, they joined the trek to the city. Mobile's population nearly doubled between 1940 and 1944, and most of the newcomers were poor whites attracted from the countryside by high-wage war industry.

Between 1940 and 1970 state leaders desperately tried to persuade new industry to locate in Alabama. Offering numerous incentives—state bonds for factory construction, postponement of state taxes, and state-funded job training programs—Alabama was partly successful. Industries often located in rural areas of Appalachian Alabama, attracted by inexpensive land, cheap TVA power, and large pools of low-skilled non-union labor willing to work long hours for minimum wages. By 1970 nearly 40 percent of the South's industry was in rural areas or small towns.

But like so many earlier panaceas, this one also failed. By the 1980s cheap foreign imports had closed or imperiled many of these plants. Already crippled by declining farm income, rural areas of Alabama faced a second shock of plant closings. So urgent was the crisis that the Federal Reserve Bank in Atlanta held an unusual day-long session in Birmingham in March 1985 to counsel Alabama communities on economic development.[26] The long cycle of boom and bust, with its shattering effects upon the lives of Alabama's poor whites, seemed about to begin a new chapter.

One example of the change that rolled over the mountain region was the transformation of Sauta Bottom, the valley in Jackson County where missionaries had established the House of Happiness in the 1920s. During the Great Depression some sharecroppers from the valley were among the lucky ones who moved up Sand Mountain to the Skyline Farms resettlement community.

Those who remained behind changed too. Well-built and well-equipped schools replaced poorly lighted and inadequately heated one-room shacks. Primitive trails gave way to paved roads. A school session of seven months replaced a sixty-day term. County services improved markedly. A men's club began meeting weekly, featuring speeches by physicians, lawyers, or extension agents. Four-H Clubs were formed in the schools. The state Division of Exceptional Education and Auburn University's extension service conducted regular programs. Jackson County began a health clinic and child welfare office. An adult literacy school opened.

Such progress did not come without a price. The clashing cultural values of middle and upper class female Episcopalian missionaries and poor white religious fundamentalists never had made for easy relations.

Commenting upon the community, one missionary warned that "change from isolation and introspection, with its attendant stagnation, cannot be wrought quickly."[27] The same kind of cultural battles that had raged at Skyline Farms in the late 1930s came to Sauta Bottom.

But it is easy to glamorize folk life, to celebrate its independence, freedom, and imaginativeness. Whereas middle class Alabamians deplored the life of the poor, historians have tended to romanticize it. To them, middle class reformers became nosy meddlers. Teachers were agents of mainstream values indoctrinating the poor in order to change them. Parents content to allow their children to grow to adulthood illiterate became the heroes of the story, reformers who tried to bend them to mainstream values were the villains.

It is curious, however, how few poor whites saw the issue in those terms when looking back retrospectively. Those who received decent medical care for the first time quickly forsook folk medicine and midwives for physicians and clinics. Children of illiterate parents graduated from high school and a few went on to college. At the end of their educational journey lay opportunities undreamed of by their parents. They became nurses, teachers, even college professors. TVA dammed their rivers and altered their society. But it also introduced the miracle of electricity, which eased the physical burdens of their lives and afforded new job opportunities. All social and cultural change involves trade-offs. The loss of some independence was a price most were willing to pay, though perhaps Americans should ponder a society that demands such a sacrifice as the price of a better life. Whatever the conclusion, only those who never lived the lives of poor whites in Sauta Bottom can easily wish for the good old days.

Labor unions were one agent of alien America. Organizers from beyond their borders and with different values came to organize them and to raise their class consciousness as well as their salaries. Unionism failed as often as it succeeded, a tribute perhaps as much to the tenacity of poor white culture as to the opposition of entrenched special interests. But where unions succeeded, conditions usually improved.

Although the American Federation of Labor continued its organizing efforts, the primary champion of poor, unskilled workers was the Congress of Industrial Organizations. Organized in 1935, the CIO operated as an industrial rather than as a craft union. It recruited all workers within a single industry—rubber, steel, autos, coal, or textiles—without regard to whether they were skilled or unskilled, male or female, black or white. This strategy gave the CIO unprecedented bargaining power to paralyze an industry by striking, because it did not have to beg cooperation from a series of competing craft unions. But its membership policies also opened it to charges of political and racial radicalism.

Whereas the AFL had shown little interest in organizing poor people of either race, the CIO almost immediately tackled some of the nation's most powerful unorganized industries. Many of these companies in Alabama worked large numbers of unskilled poor whites; coal mining, textiles, steel, and iron were notable examples.[28]

Following the initial triumphs in coal and steel in the 1930s, victories came hard. Not until the mid-1940s did CIO unions finally organize Goodyear Tire and Rubber Company and Republic Steel in Gadsden. And its drive to organize the state's textile mills largely failed, as had the earlier effort in 1934.

Although some historians have attributed this failure partly to "outside organizers" who little understood the people they sought to recruit, there were less culturally based problems. Some Jewish, communist, or northern organizers did seek to penetrate poor white culture, resulting in conflicts perhaps best depicted in an award-winning 1970s movie, *Norma Rae*, which was appropriately filmed in an Opelika textile village.

But many organizers were homegrown, and they fared little better. As society moved further from the historical events, it was easier to forget how bitterly middle and upper class Alabamians resisted unionism.

Aubrey Lee Osborne remembered well. A native of poverty-stricken east-central Alabama, Osborne began his union career by trying to organize the third shift at the Hog Mountain gold mine where he worked in 1934. When the mine closed in 1937, he began mining near Bessemer for Republic Steel Corporation. He joined the International Union of Mine, Mill and Smelter Workers in 1939 and began a lifelong union career. In 1944 he went to Alexander City, only a few miles from his birthplace, as an agent of the United Textile Workers. His first sojourn there was interrupted by wartime service in the merchant marine, but he returned in 1946. He found his earlier organization in shambles. Most textile workers he had recruited in 1944 had lost their jobs. Those who remained would have nothing to do with him for fear of dismissal.

But that was the least of his problems. As he left a clothing store in downtown Alexander City and walked toward his car, two men asked him his name, then beat him senseless. When he regained consciousness the chief of police told him the best protection for him would be to leave town. When he refused to leave, policemen locked him up in the city jail.

Upon his release, he filed charges against Russell Manufacturing Company with the National Labor Relations Board. But when two NLRB investigators came to town, police threatened to arrest them and warned that law enforcement officials could not protect them. Following its investigation, the union lodged formal charges against both Russell

Manufacturing and Alexander City's political and law enforcement officials.

Attempts were made to ruin Osborne's reputation. Rumors spread that he was living with a woman at the Russell Hotel and was taking her across the state line for immoral purposes. A church delegation came calling to investigate the charge and found to its embarrassment that the woman was his wife. In fact, the Osbornes also had their small son with them. On another occasion he furtively received a delegation of textile workers in his hotel room. Fearful of losing their jobs, they came up the hotel's back stairs at night. After the delegation left, Osborne and another union official heard a knock on the door. Two attractive women asked if they could come inside to provide important information. Appropriately suspicious, Osborne refused them entry. Later that evening he saw them in the lobby chatting with a policeman and several other men, one of whom had a camera. As Osborne passed through the lobby, one of the women tried to put her arm around his neck, but the labor organizer pushed her away, aware that such a photograph would destroy his work among textile employees.

After a six-week hearing, the NLRB issued an order restraining both the company and city from interfering with Osborne's work and advising workers of their right to join a union. The company also had to reinstate and pay back wages to all employees dismissed for union activity.

Most of Osborne's efforts in Alexander City, Sylacauga, Opelika, and Tallassee failed. And in 1948 Osborne left his home region to work for Progressive party presidential candidate Henry Wallace.[29]

The more conservative AFL had similar problems. When the CIO launched "Operation Dixie" in the late 1940s, the campaign began a bitter dispute between the two labor giants that crippled both and led to their eventual merger in the 1950s. But it also spurred AFL unions in Alabama to unaccustomed interest in poorer workers. In 1945 the Hatters, Cap, and Millinery Workers International began organizing employees of the Merrimack Hat Manufacturing Company in Greenville. Butler County did not prove a hospitable host for the union, anxious as local leaders were to attract new industry to their declining, mostly rural county. Two textile organizers were beaten in downtown Greenville in 1945, an attack allegedly witnessed by policemen who made no effort to stop it. The NLRB forced an election after years of litigation, a referendum that unionists won. In 1949 the company signed a contract.

But the trouble continued. In December 1949, Carmen Lucia, vice-president of the Millinery Workers, was stopped by four men who were armed with shotguns and who told her to stay out of Greenville. The following February, Cora Valentine, an AFL organizer, was attacked in her hotel room by four women who stripped and beat her and threatened to throw her from the second-story window of her room. When she called the state AFL president in Birmingham, he could hear in the background an angry mob on the streets outside her hotel room. They contemplated filing charges until they learned that one of the county's circuit judges was related to the manager of the hat company. Furthermore, they discovered that the four women who assaulted Valentine were themselves employees of Little Manufacturing Company and feared for their jobs should the union organize the company.[30] The curious spectacle of one group of poor whites joining a union to advance their welfare while another group resisted the union for the same reason was not unusual.

Herbert South felt no ambivalence about the United Mine Workers. He just could not afford membership. Among the salary slips paid by Taylor Coal Company during the 1950s and early 1960s were no records of union dues collected. South tried to explain the omission to former U.S. Congressman Carl Elliott: "No. There wouldn't be any. There probably should have been, but brother Carl, times was so hard. The coal business was pretty well 'shot,' and men who had been good union men, UMWA members for years, had had to come out of the union in order to get a job and make a living for their families." During the coal decline of 1960, South averaged mining only two days a week, not enough to feed eight children and continue paying UMW dues.[31]

Iva Goodwin of Ensley made whatever sacrifices she had to in order to pay her dues. To her, the union had been the avenue that led to a better life. The retired secretary of an Ensley Steelworkers' local reminisced in 1982: "My daddy was a coal miner and we were looked on as poor people. We never had money, only clacker to buy groceries at the commissary. The union gets blamed for what's happening now, but people forget what the union has done—the union brought them up. We're really the middle class people now."[32]

Buddie Watson King of Wylam attended The University of Alabama on money her father earned after he joined the union. As a child she remembered his saying: "That coke plant will be my memorial. But I don't want you to break your back at that plant." Instead, she went to college, became a nurse, and provided an education for her own daughter.[33] So it went for the new generation, the one that benefited from unionism without fighting its battles.

Some Birmingham businessmen conceded that unions had substantially raised per capita income to rates higher than in other Alabama or southeastern cities. Even with the decline of manufacturing and unionism, the likelihood of a company's being unionized in the city in 1982 was fifty-fifty, the highest in the Southeast. In 1970, 20.3 percent of Alabama's nonagricultural workers belonged to unions. In 1983 the figure remained almost exactly the same at 21 percent, only slightly below the national average of 23 percent and well above neighboring states such as Georgia (17 percent) and Florida (14.8 percent).[34] In 1983 Alabama trailed only Kentucky among southern states in union membership. Those who belonged to unions earned wages that raised them above the poverty level.

As in earlier years, unions never quite reached the poorest of the poor. During the 1930s H. L. Mitchell tried to organize Alabama's rural poor. Having served an apprenticeship as a sharecropper in the early 1920s, "Mitch" knew whereof he spoke. From the unlikely forum of a small laundry in Tyronza, Arkansas, Mitchell and friends launched the Southern Tenant Farmers' Union in the mid-1930s. Although it reached into north Alabama, its primary base was further west.[35]

In the 1940s the Farmers Union sought to reach the same audience but with no better results. An old organization, it had begun in Alabama about 1902. At its peak it had enrolled 50,000 members, its major attraction being the age-old desire of farmers for their own cooperatives that would provide low-cost fertilizer, seed, equipment, and provisions. But Alabama membership had dropped to only 1,445 in 1947. Its strongholds were Butler County (208 members), Cherokee (183), Chilton (359), Covington (307), and Etowah (165). Skyline Farms also had a prosperous local.

Aubrey Williams was elected state president of the Farmers Union and tried to breathe life back into it. After holding influential jobs in New Deal agencies during the 1930s, Williams returned to Alabama full of idealism and determined to save his people.

Allied to Gould Beech, Clifford and Virginia Durr, Charles Dobbins, Lister Hill, and other Alabama liberals, Williams tried to forge poor people of both races and all occupations into a powerful political alliance. He worked with Orville H. Mastin, a labor organizer in Gadsden who served as secretary of the state Farmers Union, and urged that farmers and factory workers labor for common goals. The president of Farmers Union Local 586 at Skyline Farms was John Lewis, a former textile worker at Huntsville's Lincoln Mills and one of the first to join the United Textile Workers of America in 1933.[36]

Williams emphasized the union's interest in Alabama's family farmer, and many of its economic programs were relatively noncontroversial. In March 1947, Williams conducted a meeting at Muscle Shoals for the purpose of creating a fertilizer cooperative. The cooperative's board of directors decided to locate it in south Alabama, where it could serve an area encompassing Covington, Conecuh, and Butler counties. Local farmers invested much labor and forty thousand dollars in the enterprise and soon had recruited eight hundred members of the cooperative. The union expanded its cooperative program to include better seeds, farm chemicals, and livestock, and it opened a large cooperative mill at Decatur. Union officials also conducted training schools to educate farmers. By 1949 the south Alabama fertilizer cooperative had sold farm machinery worth eight thousand dollars, and Williams announced a major recruiting drive for the Farmers Union in the South, centered on six pivotal areas. Three of them were in Alabama (Andalusia and Georgiana in the Covington-Conecuh-Butler counties region, Clanton in Chilton County, and Centre–Hokes Bluff–Agricola–Coates Bend in Cherokee and Etowah counties.[37]

Williams's extravagant plan hardly left the drawing boards. Problems mounted by the day, some of them of his own making. Accepting help wherever he could find it, he welcomed the assistance of Myles Horton, who headed the Highlander Folk School in Tennessee. Although the school performed yeomanly work in training the southern poor as labor organizers and community leaders, it also offered a congenial home for a variety of what in those years were considered radical people and ideas. Whites and blacks met together on what seemed to be socially equal terms. Radical ideas on everything from race and politics to the rights of women received an open if sometimes negative hearing. The CIO and other widely criticized liberal groups funded the Highlander School, a fact that was not lost on Alabama's business and political leaders.

During 1947–49 Highlander gave increasing attention to agricultural problems. The state's Farmers Union sent many of its leaders to Highlander for training and requested the services of a Highlander staffer, Tom Ludwig, to work as an organizer in south Alabama. Ludwig came and led a successful union drive, forming twenty locals.[38]

But this progress came at a price. During the 1947 convention of the Alabama Farm Bureau, state representative Walter C. Givhan claimed that the Farmers Union was based on "Russian ideologies." At a 1949 meeting of the Farmers Union in Springhill, one of the "county leaders" told the assembled farmers that Aubrey Williams, the organization's president, had been educated at a Protestant college but had then renounced God and was "one of the biggest communist[s] in the country." A local organizer wrote Williams asking for a rebuttal. Williams replied that the Farm Bureau was merely a part of the chamber of commerce and that such charges were "part of the smear the Big Monopoly interest of Alabama . . . have carried on." He was not a communist, and his accuser had picked up these allegations from people who sought to destroy all American liberalism, including such institutions as TVA, rural electrification, and labor unions.[39]

But even the agenda that Williams openly advocated was radical enough for Alabamians. At the 1946 state Farmers Union meeting in

Clanton, the organization endorsed abolition of the poll tax, reapportionment of the legislature, expansion of rural health care and hospitals, an old-age pension of forty dollars per month, a farm program to include homestead exemption, low-interest loans to tenant farmers, cooperatives to process and market farm produce, and fair wages and collective bargaining rights for labor. At its 1948 meeting in Centre, the union endorsed adequate education for all children, white and black. In his 1949 presidential address Williams demanded educational reforms, reminding his audience that farm children had only one-seventh the chance of city children to attend college.[40]

Throughout his years with the Farmers Union, Williams blasted the state Cooperative Extension Service, which operated from its headquarters at Auburn University. Its agents in each county had become powerful allies of the Alabama Farm Bureau, which used this alliance to oppose increased property taxes for schools, reapportionment of the state legislature, and other reforms. Increasingly and overtly political, the extension service network helped the Farm Bureau oppose the renomination of U.S. Senator Lister Hill in 1944 and sought to block the election of agrarian reformer James Folsom in the 1946 gubernatorial campaign. Gould Beech, Aubrey Williams, most of their friends, and the Farmers Union backed Jim Folsom. After his election, Folsom tried to depoliticize the extension service by packing Auburn's board of trustees with friends who would ensure at least the service's political neutrality. But the attempt failed when the legislature blocked his trustee appointments.[41]

Williams made his opposition to the extension service clear in a variety of ways. In his 1949 presidential address, he argued that small farmers received little help from the service, which "in recent years devoted the major part of its time to servicing the Farm Bureau." "Few farmers," he continued, "even see a county agent, much less have a service visit from one."[42]

Privately Williams was even more critical. In letters to friends in 1949 he blasted the "Land Grant College/Extension Service/Farm Bureau triumvirate" who directed most of their policies toward big agriculture and "do less and less for the little guy."[43] He used the *Southern Farmer*, which he published in Montgomery, to work for federal legislation that would restrict the extension service's political activities. The Farmers Union lobbyist in Washington sought Williams's testimony before a congressional committee inquiring into the political involvements of extension service employees. He particularly wanted Williams to testify concerning the activities of Alabama's extension director, P. O. Davis, and his subordinates.[44]

All such issues were minor irritants compared to the Farmers Union's racial policies. Looking back after the union died, Williams wrote in 1952 that its major accomplishment was to treat black and white farmers the same. He made his racial views clear when members proposed him as state president in 1949. He repudiated Jim Crow laws that required segregation. When segregationists within the union opposed his re-election, other members went house to house, defending him and plead-ing for his reelection. County leaders who supported him also stood "unequivocal . . . in behalf of Civil Rights."[45]

The dissension within their ranks continued and increased. The 1950 Covington County Farmers Union picnic was racially integrated as usual. Although some members complained about Negroes attending, the president reported that more of them griped about mismanagement of the fertilizer cooperative. In fact, local south Alabama leaders claimed later that the failure of the fertilizer cooperative did more to cripple the union than its liberal racial policies. But criticism of Williams's civil rights views intensified throughout the late 1940s and early 1950s.[46]

The extent to which white unionists wrestled with their racial culture is illustrated in an exchange of correspondence concerning H. D. Cobb of Red Level, a black member and officer of the Friendship Local in Covington County. In June 1949, Cobb visited the board of registrars and registered to vote "as slick as a whistle." Tom Ludwig wrote Williams:

> Aubrey, you cannot imagine how proud this man is of his new status. [I] haven't seen a better glow on a man's face since the old days when people got "converted."
>
> Mr. Cobb mentions that you first brought this matter up some time ago, and finally, when he heard that we have a prominent member on the board, who also sent out word to get Negroes before the board, he went down and got registered. He's now telling the other Negro members of the community [to] do likewise.[47]

Williams rushed a letter of congratulations to Cobb.

It is well that Farmers Union leaders savored some small victories, for they lost the larger struggle to forge an alliance of poor white and black farmers. Defections by white segregationists and the failure of the fertilizer cooperative resulted in continuing membership losses. In March 1951, the National Farmers Union revoked Alabama's charter, ostensibly because its membership dropped below one thousand. But Williams believed the real reason was his close identification with the peace movement and opposition to the Cold War. About the same time, in fact, Williams's close friend Clifford Durr was fired as NFU attorney because of his wife's association with the peace movement and un-founded allegations of her communist affiliation.[48]

The increasing political activism of the CIO and Farmers Union demonstrated a major change in Alabama politics. Whereas conservatives had dominated political life for six decades, the Great Depression had begun the development of enduring political division along conservative-liberal lines. Though offically united in the Democratic party, Alabama Democrats actually divided into two equally hostile camps. One contained Birmingham industrialists, Black Belt planters, and Farm Bureau members. The other relied on support from organized labor and small farmers, especially in the hill counties.

Poor whites, largely ignored by Alabama politicians, suddenly found themselves courted with great passion by a variety of suitors. Perhaps the fall 1937 campaign to fill Senator Hugo Black's seat when he won appointment to the Supreme Court best depicted the choices. Thomas Heflin, though in poor health due to his heavy drinking and politically disgraced by his endorsement of Republican presidential candidate Herbert Hoover in 1928, offered for the job. A demagogue with little to show for his twenty-six years in Congress, he appealed to impoverished white farmers, calling his opponent, Lister Hill, "this great Ajax of the Hill dynasty, Lord Lister of the Aristocracy of the Dollar."

But where such demagoguery had won sympathetic votes among poor white textile workers for Cole Blease and Eugene Talmadge in South Carolina and Georgia, the increasingly class-based politics of the 1930s did not serve Heflin so well. Alabama industrialists, timber owners, and businessmen quietly endorsed Heflin, less out of support for him than opposition to his opponent.

Lister Hill, descendant of a prominent Montgomery family, won his first congressional campaign in 1923, campaigning in a district that stretched from Montgomery to the Gulf of Mexico and that was filled with destitute white farmers. As a congressman he had consistently supported FDR and New Deal legislation. This support won him a 1937 coalition of organized labor and hill farmers across TVA territory. He ran best in areas populated by poor whites and took his place in the U.S. Senate.[49]

Other Alabama politicians mirrored Hill's concerns. Senator John Sparkman was the offspring of sharecropper parents. Congressman Carl Elliott worked for the Works Progress Administration while attending The University of Alabama and lived in an area of Tuscaloosa called "Poverty Ridge." Although "Big Jim" Folsom was not from a poor family, he identified as closely with poor people as any other Alabama politician of his time. Opponents frequently accused him of stirring class hatreds by his attacks on "Big Mules" and special interests. His legislative program of improved farm-to-market roads, expansion of education, old-age pensions, repeal of the state right-to-work law, and constitutional revision and reapportionment set a standard for Alabama liberalism. It also largely failed at the hands of a conservative state legislature.[50]

Most liberal candidates owed at least part of their success to the CIO's Political Action Committee, established in 1943, and to the Committee on Political Education, formed when the AFL and CIO merged in 1955. These political arms of labor raised money for sympathetic candidates and helped educate unionists. Among successful Alabama candidates endorsed by the two committees were Senators Lister Hill and John Sparkman, Congressmen Albert Raines and Carl Elliott, and gubernatorial candidate James E. Folsom. In 1960 Daniel A. Powell helped the Alabama Labor Council formulate a "Program of Progress." It was a long-range political action–public relations program, designed to enact labor's legislative program in Alabama and funded by a one-dollar assessment on each union member in the state.[51]

Although labor enjoyed more success in Alabama than in other southern states, most victories came before racial polarization in the mid-1950s. The New Deal had defined liberalism primarily in economic terms. The hope of politicians such as Jim Folsom was to build a liberal coalition based on north Alabama's white farmers and augmented by black and white working-class people. Such a coalition won victories for Senators Lister Hill, John Sparkman, and Hugo Black, Congressmen Luther Patrick, Bob Jones, Albert Raines, Carl Elliott, and Kenneth Roberts, and Governors Bibb Graves and Jim Folsom. But the budding class-based liberalism of the 1930s and 1940s gradually gave way to a new kind of liberal politics. Both southern conservatives and northern liberals, for quite different reasons, increasingly focused on the issue of race. By doing so they divided working-class whites and blacks, the whites opting for racial politics. As poor whites increasingly moved into the middle class, politics that aligned them with blacks became repugnant. Politicians such as Governor George Wallace and Senator James Allen, both with traditional ties to labor and economic liberalism, made their transition easier by endorsing some economic reforms while denouncing racial integration.

Among Alabama's liberal politicians who fell casualty to racial politics were Luther Patrick (1946), Ryan DeGraffenried (in the 1962 governor's race), and Carl Elliott (in the 1966 governor's race). Folsom's demise in the 1960s owed something to racial polarization, and even Lister Hill and John Sparkman had close calls in the 1960s and 1970s. Lieutenant Governor Bill Baxley tried to reconstruct the historic liberal coalition in 1986 by putting together an alliance of blacks, north Alabama's rural whites, and organized labor. His initial loss in the Democratic primary and his subsequent loss in the general election probably owed as much to alleged personal indiscretions as to his economic and racial liberalism. Prosperity and racism did not well serve the cause of Alabama liberalism.

Perhaps poor whites bore too much of the blame for Alabama's racial troubles. Though many newly enfranchised whites did descend from a culture of poverty that was racist in tone, they differed from prosperous whites more in style than substance. Virginia Durr, a courageous Montgomery liberal and sister-in-law to Hugo Black, blamed the state's racial violence largely on "poor white rednecks" who were so "ignorant, pitiful, stupid and dangerous"; yet "I feel so akin to them. I feel so sorry for them for I know the long background of poverty, disease, ignorance, oppression and lack of any cultural enrichment in their lives."[52]

Actually, many upwardly mobile poor whites were not so hopeless. Textile worker Carter Priest, who had lost jobs because of his own union efforts, praised blacks for their solidarity. Although in many ways a captive of his racial culture (he believed blacks would not work as hard as whites), he admired the way they worked together to unionize and improve their economic condition. And when blacks obtained jobs in her textile mill in Opelika, Pauline Brewer could not remember any trouble between the races.[53]

In small personal ways, the upwardly mobile poor of both races made uneasy peace with each other. Perhaps had the rate of economic progress been more even, Alabama would have been spared a great deal of racial violence. When most blacks and whites were impoverished they seemed capable of some level of cooperation, as in the 1890s. When both became successful, their differences seemed less urgent. But as poor whites began to improve their status, they feared any threat to their mobility. The most obvious danger came from the thousands of indigent blacks who desperately sought better jobs.

Just as poor whites finally entered the mainstream of Alabama politics, their culture penetrated America's consciousness. In a multitude of ways, cultural patterns generally associated with poor whites attracted a wider audience. Pentecostal religion moved into America's middle class and crossed racial boundaries. Blacks deserted Baptist and Methodist churches in large numbers for Pentecostalism, and some Pentecostal sects managed to transcend race for a Christian equality not found in mainstream denominations.[54]

Athletics offered a socially acceptable outlet for the children of textile workers, coal miners, and tenant farmers. It afforded ways to channel frustration and even violence into constructive purposes. Robert Victor Sullivan, better known to football trivia experts as Coach Bob "Bull Cyclone" Sullivan, once commented that there were two reasons people played football: "One is love of the game. The other is out of fear. I like the second reason a helluva lot better."[55] The fear that initially drove Sullivan was poverty. His family were the poorest whites in a poor community. His mother supported the six Sullivan children by working at the cotton mill in Aliceville, near the Mississippi border. His father, "Wild Bill" Sullivan, died while fishing a creek for the family's dinner. When Mrs. Sullivan moved to Mobile to search for a better job, she left sixteen-year-old Bob behind to play football at Aliceville High School. He got a room in back of a store near the cotton mill and paid for it by keeping the store clean. Embarrassed by his clothes, he determined that as a football coach he would never allow a player to be embarrassed even if he had to buy the boy clothes with money out of his own pocket.

After graduating from Aliceville in 1937, Cyclone Sullivan manipulated his football prowess into an opportunity few poor whites had. He won a football scholarship to a small Baptist school in Jackson, Tennessee. At Union University he played well enough to earn an offer from the Detroit Lions, but in 1942 he joined the Marine Corps instead. Following wartime service in the South Pacific, Sullivan completed his college work and football eligibility at the University of Nevada, then began a long coaching career. He made his greatest mark at East Mississippi Junior College at Scooba, Mississippi, just across the border from Aliceville. There he recruited poor white boys from Alabama and Mississippi and drove them like the Marine drill sergeant he had been. Although he compiled an outstanding record during his sixteen years, he was most famous for his brutal discipline. Long before Mississippi's four-year colleges played black athletes, Sullivan brought them to Scooba for the same reason he had recruited poor whites: they were "hungry," and football and military service were the best ways to escape poverty.

Sullivan was an independent, ornery, cussed man who recognized few conventions and sometimes flaunted his poor white origins. One Sunday Sullivan took his family to Scooba's finest restaurant. A leader of the town's social elite was dining there and kept casting sideway glances at Sullivan. Bull Cyclone stared back, muttering to his family not to laugh. Then smiling at his antagonist, he reached over, picked up a daffodil from the table decoration, and ate it stem and all.[56]

Paul "Bear" Bryant also descended from humble origins in Moro Bottom, near Fordyce, Arkansas. He often related the story of how he obtained his nickname. A traveling circus came to town and advertised that it would pay anyone willing to wrestle its trained bear. Bryant agreed because it was so much easier to wrestle a bear than to earn fifty cents a day chopping cotton in depression-wracked Arkansas. As longtime coach at The University of Alabama, he attributed his legendary success partly to a culture of poverty that produced poor boys, white and black, whose best prospect for advancement seemed to be on a gridiron, a basketball court, or a baseball diamond.[57]

The social mannerisms that apparently betrayed Bob Sullivan in Scooba's best restaurant posed a constant hazard to mobility. Social class might be obscure for a white person until he talked, but even his language was often an unmistakable clue to his origins. Although poor whites and poor blacks had language differences, even greater ones existed between upper and lower class whites. In one revealing study conducted among schoolchildren in east-central Alabama, upper class white children used only seven nonstandard verb forms. Upper class Negro children used only eighteen. But a study of lower class white children produced sixty-four.[58] Language often betrayed class origins as readily as table manners.

The music they enjoyed and played also set poor whites apart. But unlike bad grammar or slovenly manners, the middle class gradually accepted their music.

Country music attracted a commercial and scholarly audience early in the twentieth century. The A. P. Carter family collected and recorded mountain music and Olive Dame Campbell, John C. Campbell's second wife, helped English folklorist Cecil Sharp recover ancient English ballads in Appalachia. Fiddling John Carson of Georgia sold several thousand copies of a recording entitled "The Old Hen Cackled and the Rooster's Going to Crow." Carl Carmer filled his depression-era book, *Stars Fell on Alabama*, with tales of fiddling festivals and Sacred Harp singings. Jimmie Rodgers broadened the audience for country music in the 1920s. But it remained for Hank Williams to carry country music to a new urban audience. During his brief career, Williams gave a voice to poor whites who were experiencing the trauma of leaving the land and oftentimes the region, caught as they were between two cultures. In 1949 five of the top ten country songs belonged to Williams. He won gold records for four more in 1950: "I Just Don't Like This Kind of Livin'," "Long Gone Lonesome Blues," "Moaning the Blues," and "Why Don't You Love Me?" In 1951 he topped the music charts with seven hits. The list continued—"Cold, Cold, Heart," "Dear John," "Hey, Good Lookin'," "Honkey Tonk Blues," "Jambalaya"—until his death at age twenty-nine in January 1953. Even the year following his death, three of his songs dominated the country charts: "Kawliga," "I Won't Be Home No More," and "Your Cheatin' Heart."[59]

The next three decades brought further integration of country music into mainstream American culture. Johnny Cash, Kris Kristofferson, Willie Nelson, and Waylon Jennings provided a counterculture audience for country music. "Southern rock" from Charlie Daniels and the Marshall Tucker Band added to the "outlaw" imagery of scraggly beards and rebellious lyrics. The musical group "Alabama" from Fort Payne dominated country music awards. And popular singers from other regions—Joan Baez, Linda Rondstadt, and others—further broadened the audience. Country music's unattractive estimate of human nature, its increasingly seamy description of infidelity and materialism that corrupted the honest though impoverished relationships of simpler times found a receptive audience. In 1961 the United States had only eighty all-country radio stations. By the mid-1970s it had more than one thousand, including station WHN, in the heart of New York City, which adopted a country format and doubled its audience in a single year.[60]

Economic mobility, religious respect, musical adulation: what more could a people desire? All seemed well among Alabama's formerly poor whites. Yet in a sense the success of those who went on to a better life further obscured the ones they left behind. The prosperity of the 1940s and 1950s seemed uniform and pervasive. It was, in fact, limited and sporadic.

In 1960 America contained 9.6 million poor rural families and 6.3 million unattached individuals. Of these the greatest number lived in the South. The region contained only 30 percent of all families and 27 percent of all unattached individuals; but it included within its boundaries 46 percent of all poor families and 32 percent of indigent single persons. Of these poor southerners, two-thirds were white.[61]

Statistics for Alabama were particularly grim. In 1960, 14.9 percent of Alabama whites aged fourteen and older earned between $1 and $499 per year. Another 14.6 percent earned between $500 and $999. A total of 37.7 percent of all white Alabamians in 1960 had per capita incomes of fewer than $1,500 per year.[62] Such deprivation led to the war on poverty launched by the John F. Kennedy and Lyndon B. Johnson administrations.[63]

Improvements came slowly. By 1979 the South, containing 25 percent of the nation's people, counted 38 percent of its poor. Most lived in rural areas and most were white.[64]

Alabama's poverty rate among whites was 13.6 percent, fourth highest of eleven southern states, ahead of only Arkansas, Mississippi, and Tennessee.[65] According to the Federal Interagency definition of poverty in 1970, 25 percent of Alabama's individuals and 20 percent of its families were poor. And more whites (93,614) than blacks (86,821) lacked the basic necessities. Among poor whites, 59 percent of the heads of families had completed only some elementary education; the median number of school years completed was only 8.2.[66] White poor families earned average incomes of only $2,147 in the mid-1970s.[67]

Indigence did decline during the years. Poverty rates for the eleven southern states dropped from 37 percent in 1959 to 22 percent ten years later and to a low of 15.6 in 1979. But in that year the rate began a steady increase that reached 18.2 percent by 1983.[68]

Definitions of poverty followed a sliding scale based on what a family of four needed in cash income to meet its basic needs. In 1983 the figure was $10,178. The fact that more and more Alabamians fell below this level reflected a general downturn in the nation's economy. In 1977, Alabama's unemployment rate had been below the national average for six consecutive years and its gross state product and per capita income were growing faster than the national average. But then came the depression of 1981–82 and a sharp decline in the nation's manufacturing sector. By November 1982, Alabama had the dubious distinction of leading the nation in unemployment with a figure of 15 percent. Alabama's 1981 per capita income of $8,219 was third lowest in a twelve-state region, ahead of only South Carolina and Mississippi. Its growth of jobs between 1970 and 1980 had fallen to the lowest rate within the region and its growth of per capita income trailed the national average.[69]

The causes of this decline were complex. Alabama's economy depended heavily on metals, automotive parts, and textiles, all hard hit by the slump in manufacturing. Poor political leadership, lack of vision by the legislature and business communities, racial upheaval, a regressive tax system, and poor educational opportunities contributed to the decline.

But whatever the cause, Alabama found itself in serious trouble during the 1980s. It had become the third poorest state in America, slipping one notch from fourth in 1970. In Jefferson County, 19 percent of the population lived below the poverty line in 1980. Although 31 percent of all blacks who lived there were poor, 8 percent of the county's whites were also indigent.[70] Birmingham's newspapers featured articles in 1983 on men and women who had lost their jobs at Pullman-Standard or U.S. Steel and who stood in line to receive surplus government food. In Mobile a 1984 survey estimated that more than one-third of the population of the city lived in poverty.[71] A 1984 investigation by the Physician Task Force on Hunger in America estimated that 720,000 Alabamians lived below the poverty level and that more than 25 percent of the state's people qualified for food stamps (although only 15 percent were receiving them).[72] In rural areas where most poor whites lived, social services were hard to procure and the poor faded from view.

Health care for the poor remained a serious problem. Six of Alabama's counties in 1985 had more than five thousand residents per physician. Severe shortages of general practitioners, pediatricians, internists, and obstetrician-gynecologists existed in twenty-one of the state's sixty-seven counties. Several of the worst shortages were in counties with large numbers of rural poor whites (notably Bibb and Coosa counties). Other heavily poor white counties—Winston, Blount, and St. Clair—provided only slightly better care. As a result, the infant mortality rate increased with rising unemployment. Dr. Robert Goldenberg, associate professor of obstetrics and gynecology at The University of Alabama in Birmingham, noted in 1983: "We are getting stories all through the state about people falling through the cracks. Two-thirds of women receiving care in public clinics are getting no prenatal care until the second trimester. Ten counties have no public clinic at all for prenatal care." And for every infant death, two or three babies developed physical or mental handicaps: "We are talking about preventable deaths and preventable physical and mental handicaps." A 55 percent reduction in Medicaid funds deepened the crisis in 1983 and left the Bureau of Maternal and Child Health with a deficit of $1.3 million. Children's Hospital in Birmingham lost nearly $1.5 million that year caring for poor children, and regional prenatal centers lost an equal amount.[73]

Across the state poor whites continued to cope in the ways they always had. In Opelika a poor white family shopped one Sunday afternoon in January 1983. The man wore a well-worn suit with trousers six inches too long, the cuffs turned up. Half a dozen children, stair step in size, quickly gathered groceries from their lists. The eldest daughter, who appeared to be about sixteen, was dressed in corduroy pants with dirty feet beneath her flip-flops, and she wore a message T-shirt. She urged her family to hurry or she would be late for her own wedding. They purchased a small wedding cake and a handful of plastic flowers for a wedding bouquet. Hurrying from the store, they pulled kids, cake, and flowers into a 1960s vintage Pontiac, which had not aged well, and raced off amid cries of "don't mash the cake back there."[74]

A hundred miles north in Anniston, Arthur Couch became fed up with youthful harassment. Couch and his family were classic ne'er-do-wells: illiterate, unwashed, and unemployed. He had driven a taxi for a while but his sons, all in their thirties, refused to work during the summer of 1986 because it was too hot. Couch, age sixty-five, crippled by a shotgun blast from his son-in-law, lived in a filthy three-room house on Christine Avenue on the wrong side of town. His yard contained an old refrigerator, a washing machine, an old tire, a bunch of used car batteries and ramshackle automobiles. His bathroom sink was stuffed with newspapers and there was no bathtub, which was just as well, inasmuch as the house had no running water and Couch saw no particular value in bathing. The one luxury he afforded himself was cable television with Home Box Office. He plugged the television set into the house's single electrical outlet. Couch lived off Social Security and other benefits, though he refused to take food stamps, arguing "there's too many people that needs it worse than I do." When mail had to be read, he carried it to a next-door neighbor who read it to him.

It was not a life satisfying to most Alabamians, but it suited Arthur Couch until the drought-plagued summer of 1986. Trouble began in June when truckloads of bored teenagers from affluent Anniston suburbs began driving by at night, sometimes just taunting Couch, but at other times throwing beer or soft-drink bottles, rocks, firecrackers, or eggs. They knocked out the windshield on his car and peppered his tarpaper house with air-rifle holes. On particularly disquieting nights, Couch dispatched one of his sons to the nearest pay phone to call the police. They investigated but refused to stake out the house; instead, they ridiculed Couch and his way of living. Finally on the night of July 19 Couch had suffered enough. Seventeen-year-old Pam Turner from the Indian Oaks suburb came by in her father's pickup truck, which was filled with a dozen teenagers. This night Couch was waiting for them with a twelve-gauge shotgun. He fired into the group, hitting Pam Turner in the head and nearly costing her an eye.

Subsequent news coverage by the *Birmingham Post-Herald* polarized its readers just as the case had divided Anniston. Some Alabamians directed furious letters to the newspaper that condemned teenagers who had nothing better to do than terrorize an illiterate old man. Sympathetic Annistonians bought groceries by his house, an outpouring of sympathy that moved him to tears. Others agreed with the Turner family, which condemned Couch's hot temper and willingness to resolve differences with a shotgun. The proud old man responded to the police charges by explaining simply: "My mama taught me better than that [throwing objects at a person's house and ridiculing him]. If she was livin', she'd tell you I don't bother nobody if they don't bother me."[75] It was an eloquent enough defense to convince a grand jury not to indict him, although he did determine to leave Anniston for the solitude of rural Alabama.

The Couch incident raised troubling questions about the people left behind. No doubt many of the children from homes in Indian Oaks were only a generation removed from a life similar to Arthur Couch's. Many of their grandparents during the depression must have worked in Blue Mountain's textile mill or as sharecroppers on the farms surrounding Anniston.

But not everyone had forgotten, at least not those who had lived through poverty and survived long enough to prosper. The experience had left its mark, though a surprisingly large number of people expressed no great regrets about their lives. Some believed that poverty had made them stronger. Many said that even if they could change their lives they would not do so.

Most great historical sagas are filled with irony. The poor white experience in Alabama is no exception. The American Dream of landownership often ended in failure and deprivation. Forced into industrial jobs they did not seek, poor whites frequently found a better life. Then, just as these occupations allowed them access to the middle class, America's manufacturing sector entered the postindustrial age of declining markets, increased foreign competition, layoffs, and unemployment. Government programs designed by well-meaning bureaucrats to help the poor actually displaced them from the land and drove them into distant cities away from the nourishment of the soil. Desperately needing help, they often rejected it because it offended their sense of pride or ridiculed their culture. When reformers tried to force conformity to mainstream educational values, the poor rejected them as meddlesome do-gooders. So individualistic by nature that they resisted organization, they made difficult two recourses that could have made their lives better, unionism and political activism. Locked into a common struggle for survival with poor blacks, they frequently rejected biracial activity and scorned Negroes. Crippled by negative stereotypes of their culture, they watched in wonder as their betters harnessed their violence into sports, their fundamentalist, pentecostal, or charismatic religion into mainstream denominations, and their soulful poetry into country music. Despite all the stress and irony, they generally retained their folkways, social order, and cultural richness.

But it seems appropriate that the last word belongs to the people who led such prideful, independent, and unpredictable lives. Lillie Mae Beason rose from a sharecrop farm but carried some psychic baggage with her:

> I . . . know that the life that we had to live, the hardships that we had to endure, and the nothingness that we had to work with helped to strengthen those feelings that we have even now, of being conservative with every little thing. I throw nothing away nor destroy anything that's edible nor allow, even when I was teaching, . . . the children to be wasteful . . . with food, or with materials that we worked with, or anything. And it's just something that's so ingrained that . . . it's hurtful to see things wasted. It hurts me to see other people throw food and things away. . . . But I know that without having a background of that type. . . . You wouldn't know these things and wouldn't know how to manage or how to make ends

meet. . . . I think experience is the best teacher in the world. And as I grew up, it was strictly hard.[76]

An interviewer recalled the circumstances that had caused Andrew McClain to leave a small farm for work in a textile mill forty-five years earlier. He asked McClain whether he would make the same choice if he had it to do over again. Insisting on answering the question according to the circumstances of the times, McClain replied: "Well, it's quite a bit of difference in coming off a job making fifty cent a day plowing a mule than it would be making nine dollars a week working in a cotton mill. That was back in the early 1930s and if a man could get fifty cents a day working on a farm he was lucky."[77]

Textile worker Pauline Brewer was even more positive. Asked whether she would change her life if she had the opportunity she replied: "No, not a bit (laughter)."

Question: Were you happy while you worked in the mill?
Answer: Yeah, I was happy.
Question: Even knowing what you know now, having some
                 of the problems [brown lung] you have, you
                 wouldn't have changed anything?
Answer: I wouldn't have changed anything.[78]

Sharecropper's daughter Kathleen Knight disagreed:

Question: You don't think you would have a hankering to
                 have that type of life again?
Answer: No part of it—no way! Memory of it, if I can't
                 express it too well, it's still real vivid in my
                 mind. . . . 'Cause there wasn't any good thing
                 about it as far as I am concerned.[79]

Appendixes

██████████████████████

White Tenancy in
Ten Selected Alabama
Counties in 1880

My procedure for gathering data was uncomplicated. I studied white sharecroppers in ten Alabama counties in great detail. The counties were chosen at random, the only consideration being geographical representation and a majority white population. One county chosen, Winston, is in northwestern Alabama. Jackson County is located in the northeastern corner of the state. Cherokee is also a northeastern county, touching the Georgia border. Calhoun, Cleburne, Randolph, and Clay are contiguous east-central counties. Geneva and Covington are contiguous counties in the southeastern Wiregrass bordering Florida, and Crenshaw borders Covington to the north. Six of the ten counties existed in 1860, three were created in 1866, and one in 1868.

To obtain the sharecroppers for this analysis, I selected names at random from the 1880 manuscript county agricultural census. In nine counties I chose a selected list. In Winston County I studied every sharecropper listed, a total of 112. Then I used the manuscript county 1880 population census to determine age, sex, and race. Black sharecroppers were eliminated, leaving a total of 372 white heads of families. For these 372, I tabulated complete data from the 1880 agricultural census. Unfortunately, some census enumerators were less faithful than others in recording data. Where they obviously omitted categories, I tabulated the totals using fewer counties. Nonetheless, the data are sufficiently complete to provide an accurate picture of the life of Alabama's white sharecroppers in 1880. In the text I have summarized data. In this appendix I have provided a much more extensive summary for those who may be interested. The value of these data is not only the detail they furnish but also their scope. Previous studies tended to examine only a few closely bunched counties, causing some doubt about how representative they were. By examining ten counties in four separate sections of the state and noting the consistency of findings in each, I hope to provide more revealing patterns. I used the categories in the agricultural census rather than county-by-county summaries, although I coded data both ways to be sure that no single county presented an erratic pattern.

None did, although Wiregrass counties with poor soil for growing cotton and a tradition of livestock raising predictably produced sharecroppers who grew less cotton and grazed larger herds and flocks. But the obvious conclusion of the data is the consistency with which the sharecropper system operated among white tenants across the state.

Of the total 372 white sharecroppers I studied, I found ages for 365 in the county population census. The ages fell into the following pattern:

6 in their teens,
149 in their twenties,
102 in their thirties,
57 in their forties,
32 in their fifties,
14 in their sixties,
4 in their seventies, and
1 in his eighties.

In seven counties, I examined the names adjacent to the sharecroppers I selected for possible kinship relationships. If the last name of a cropper was the same as an adjacent landowner's, I assumed they were related. Of the 228 croppers' names I examined, 47 (20.61 percent) were listed next to a landowner with the same last name. By checking ages in the population census, I could infer that most of these croppers were the sons of landowning farmers. As a matter of fact, 32 of the 47 related sharecroppers were in their teens or twenties. Because I could find no way to correlate for sons-in-law who farmed next to relatives, I will not speculate on the extent of kinship except to note it was probably at least one-quarter of my sample group.

I examined five counties for female sharecropper heads of families and found 10 of 239 (4.18 percent). The 10 were significantly older than the average male sharecropper (1 in her twenties, 2 in their thirties, 3 in their forties, 3 in their fifties, 1 in her seventies), suggesting perhaps that most were widows. But this is merely conjecture.

After compiling lists from the 1880 census, I selected all sharecroppers who were age thirty-eight or older. I tried to locate these names in the same counties in the 1860 agricultural and population censuses. I located 22 of them (they would have been eighteen or older in 1860). From the 14 listed in the agricultural census I was able to make some comparisons. For the other 8, I was able to obtain only brief biographical information and some listing of property and real estate holdings. This information allows some conclusions about downward economic mobility between 1860 and 1880.

AVERAGE IMPROVED ACRES

County	No. Persons	Acres	Average No. Acres per Person
Geneva	29	651	22.45
Crenshaw	32	745	23.28
Covington	29	697	24.03
Winston	111	2,125	19.14
Cherokee	5	152	30.40
Clay	27	601	22.26
Cleburne	25	480	19.20
Randolph	31	770	24.84
Calhoun	16	451	28.19
Jackson	35	619	17.69
Total/10 counties	340	7,291	= 21.44*

*acres average per sharecropper

VALUE OF FARM (LAND, FENCES, BUILDINGS)

County	No. Persons	Dollars	Averages
Geneva	11	1,625	$147.73
Crenshaw	Not	Listed	——
Covington	16	4,740	296.25
Winston	111	32,762	295.15
Cherokee	5	1,054	210.80
Clay	26	8,067	310.27
Cleburne	25	7,350	294.00
Randolph	Not	Listed	——
Calhoun	13	4,650	357.69
Jackson	16	7,289	455.56
Total/8 counties	223	67,537	$302.86*
	(220**	62,537	= $284.26)

*average value per farm
**excluding 3 farms that were valued at $1,200, $1,800, $2,000

VALUE OF FARM PRODUCTS

County	No. Persons	Dollars	Averages
Geneva	28	4,169	$148.89
Crenshaw	29	7,060	243.45
Covington	26	7,639	293.81
Winston	111	13,993	126.06
Cherokee	16	3,470	216.88
Clay	47	9,597	204.19
Cleburne	25	5,740	229.60
Randolph	31	5,765	185.97
Calhoun	17	5,025	295.59
Jackson	35	7,210	206.00
Total/10 counties	365	69,668	$190.87

HORSES/MULES

175 had horses
 95 had mules
115 had neither (30.9% of 372)
181 had 1 horse/mule (48.7% of 372)
 56 had 2 horses/mules
  8 had 3 horses/mules
  2 had 5 horses/mules
  1 had 7 horses/mules

COWS, CATTLE, OXEN

County	No. of Persons	Cattle	Average	No. with 1 or 2	Total No. of Persons in County Sample
Geneva	22	154	7.00	4	29
Crenshaw	25	82	3.28	10	32
Covington	22	196	8.91	5	29
Winston	107	593	5.54	13	111
Cherokee	14	55	3.93	4	16
Clay	45	190	4.22	13	47
Cleburne	24	101	4.21	11	25
Randolph	30	120	4.00	12	31
Calhoun	16	71	4.44	3	17
Jackson	30	139	4.63	13	35
Total 10 counties	335	1,701	5.08	88	372

SWINE

County	No. of Persons	Swine	Average	No. with 1 or 2	Total No. of Persons in County Sample
Geneva	24	318	13.25	4	29
Crenshaw	26	246	9.46	4	32
Covington	27	355	13.15	1	29
Winston	98	852	8.69	25	111
Cherokee	14	101	7.21	9	16
Clay	31	240	7.74	12	47
Cleburne	21	165	7.86	9	25
Randolph	20	150	7.50	8	31
Calhoun	13	107	8.23	4	17
Jackson	21	317	15.10	7	35
Total 10 counties	295	2,851	9.66	83	372

POULTRY

County	No. of Persons	No. of Chickens	Average Chickens	No. with 20 or more	Total No. of Persons in County Sample
Geneva	19	249	13.11	2	29
Crenshaw	27	1,058	39.19	21	32
Covington	25	767	30.68	17	29
Winston	84	968	11.52	11	111
Cherokee	16	249	15.56	5	16
Clay	40	474	11.85	6	47
Cleburne	24	357	14.88	6	25
Randolph	23	224	9.74	2	31
Calhoun	15	399	26.60	10	17
Jackson	27	336	12.44	4	35
Total 10 counties	300	5,081	16.94	84	372

COTTON

County	No. of Persons	No. of Acres	No. of Bales	Average Bales/ Farmer	Average Acres/ Bale	No. with 5 bales or fewer	Total No. of Persons in County Sample
Geneva	20	226	31.76	1.59	7.12	19	29
Crenshaw	30	349	99.00	3.30	3.53	26	32
Covington	17	—	50.00	2.94	—	16	29
Winston	75	366	103.50	1.38	3.54	75	111
Cherokee	15	168	52.00	3.47	3.23	11	16
Clay	37	222	69.00	1.86	3.21	36	47
Cleburne	21	88	39.25	1.86	2.24	21	25
Randolph	28	206	69.00	2.46	2.99	26	31
Calhoun	16	158	64.00	4.00	2.47	13	17
Jackson	23	229	72.50	3.15	3.16	22	35
Total 10 counties	282	2,012*	650.01	2.30	3.35*	265	372

*9 counties

CORN

County	No. of Persons	Bushels	Acres	Average Bushels/Farmer	Total No. of Persons in County Sample
Geneva	25	1,718	351	68.72	29
Crenshaw	30	3,423	——	114.10	32
Covington	29	3,612	——	124.55	29
Winston	110	12,307	1,171	111.88	111
Cherokee	16	2,640	217	165.00	16
Clay	47	4,805	440	102.23	47
Cleburne	25	6,030	273	241.20	25
Randolph	31	3,255	343	105.00	31
Calhoun	17	3,050	221	179.41	17
Jackson	35	9,685	417	276.71	35
Total					
10 counties	365	50,525	3,433*	138.42	372

*8 counties

WHEAT

County	No. of Persons	Bushels	Acres	Average Bushels/Farmers	Total No. of Persons in County Sample
Geneva	—	—	—	——	29
Crenshaw	—	—	—	——	32
Covington	—	—	—	——	29
Winston	23	527	133	22.91	111
Cherokee	4	41	41	10.25	16
Clay	23	658	133	28.60	47
Cleburne	20	771	106	38.55	25
Randolph	17	478	88	28.12	31
Calhoun	5	78	—	15.60	17
Jackson	4	75	—	18.75	35
Total					
7 counties	96	2,628	501*	27.38	372**

*5 counties

**10 counties

SHEEP

County	No. of Persons	No. of Sheep	Average Sheep/Farmer	Total No. of Persons in County Sample
Geneva	5	197	39.40	29
Crenshaw	—	—	——	32
Covington	5	259	51.80	29
Winston	—	—	——	111
Cherokee	2	24	12.00	16
Clay	—	—	——	47
Cleburne	10	138	13.80	25
Randolph	2	10	5.00	31
Calhoun	—	—	——	17
Jackson	8	121	15.13	35
Total 6 counties	32	749	23.41	372*

*10 counties

IRISH POTATOES

County	No. of Persons	No. of Bushels	Average Bushels/Farmer	Total No. of Persons in County Sample
Geneva	—	—	——	29
Crenshaw	2	110	55.00	32
Covington	—	—	——	29
Winston	—	—	——	111
Cherokee	1	25	25.00	16
Clay	—	—	——	47
Cleburne	4	118	29.50	25
Randolph	—	—	——	31
Calhoun	3	45	15.00	17
Jackson	3	38	12.67	35
Total 5 counties	13	336	25.85	372*

*10 counties

SWEET POTATOES

County	No. of Persons	Bushels	Average Bushels/Farmer	Total No. of Persons in County Sample
Geneva	16	840	52.50	29
Crenshaw	21	827	39.38	32
Covington	—	——	——	29
Winston	36	1,402	38.94	111
Cherokee	3	140	46.67	16
Clay	10	283	28.30	47
Cleburne	13	480	36.92	25
Randolph	2	62	31.00	31
Calhoun	4	155	38.75	17
Jackson	5	130	26.00	35
Total 9 counties	110	4,319	39.26	372*

*10 counties

APPLE TREES

County	No. of Persons	Trees	Average Trees/Farmer	Total No. of Persons in County Sample
Geneva	4	46	11.50	29
Crenshaw	4	146	36.50	32
Covington	—	—	——	29
Winston	3	36	12.00	111
Cherokee	—	—	——	16
Clay	4	190	47.50	47
Cleburne	8	92	11.50	25
Randolph	7	695	99.29	31
Calhoun	1	100	100.00	17
Jackson	5	290	58.00	35
Total 8 counties	36	1,595	44.31	372*

*10 counties

PEACH TREES

County	No. of Persons	Trees	Average Trees/Farmer	Total No. of Persons in County Sample
Geneva	4	115	28.75	29
Crenshaw	2	60	30.00	32
Covington	—	—	——	29
Winston	14	1,039	74.21	111
Cherokee	—	—	——	16
Clay	4	190	47.50	47
Cleburne	8	390	48.75	25
Randolph	6	202	33.67	31
Calhoun	2	200	100.00	17
Jackson	2	120	60.00	35
Total 8 counties	42	2,316	55.14	372*

*10 counties

Comparison of Status of 1880 Sharecroppers
Listed in 1860 Agricultural Census

Average farm value:	1860 $ 815.38 (14 names)
	1880 $ 389.00 (8 names)
Average improved acres farmed:	1860 38.61 acres (13 names)
	1880 30.40 acres (22 names)
Average horses and mules owned:	1860 1.78 horses, 0.28 mules (14 names)
	1880 .90 horses, 0.31 mules (22 names)
Average swine owned:	1860 20.78 (14 names)
	1880 11.13 (22 names)
Average cattle, cows, oxen:	1860 18.35 (14 names)
	1880 6.13 (22 names)
Average bushels of corn grown:	1860 287.14 bushels (14 names)
	1880 69.25 bushels (22 names)

Only 6 of 14 in 1860 produced an average of 33.16 bushels of wheat. None of 22 was listed as wheat producers in 1880.

Cotton: 10 of 14 produced an average of 2.5 bales in 1860
   3 of 22 produced an average of 1.6 bales in 1880

*Sample of Thirteen Farm Owners in Geneva County Selected
at Random from 1880 Agricultural Census*

Average improved acres (13 names):	17.53 acres
Average value of farms (13 names):	$207.30
Average value of farm products (13 names):	$153.23

Horses/Mules: 10 of 13 had horses   6 of 13 had 1 horse
                0 of 13 had mules   3 of 13 had 2 horses
                3 of 13 had neither 1 of 13 had 3 horses

Cows/cattle/oxen (12 names):	average of 20.25
Swine (13 names):	average of 23.38 each
Poultry (12 names):	average of 15.58 each
Sheep (7 names):	average of 72.28 each
Corn (13 names):	average of 76.76 bushels each
Wheat (none listed)	
Cotton (8 names):	total of 9.5 bales

1 bale averaged per 4.10 acres
farmers averaged 1.18 bales each

Sweet potatoes (13 names):	average of 76.53 bushels each
Apple trees (8 names):	average of 7.37 trees
Peach trees (11 names):	average of 21.09 trees

*Sample of Twelve Farm Owners in Winston County Selected
at Random from 1880 Agricultural Census*

Average improved acres (12 names):	9.08 acres
Average value of farms (12 names):	$198.25
Average value of farm products (11 names):	$24.54
Horses (10 names):	average of 2.5 horses each
Cows/cattle/oxen (11 names):	average of 4.36 each
Swine (10 names):	average of 7.4 swine each

APPENDIX 2

1897 Populist Voting Patterns and Agricultural Indigence in 1880

My voting analysis is based upon two sources. Congressman George P. Harrison of Alabama's Third Congressional District compiled a list of 1897 voters in Geneva County with a code that listed their occupations and political affiliations (coded "R" for Republican, "D" for Democrat, and "P" for Populist). This information, listed as "Voters and Party Affiliations Record, 1897," is located in the Auburn University Archives, Auburn, Alabama, and supplied a list of names, which I alphabetized and placed on single cards. I then compared each name with the farmers listed in the unpublished 1880 agricultural census of Geneva County. When two persons with the same name appeared in the census, I omitted them in order to avoid confusion. But when the name of an 1897 voter clearly corresponded to an 1880 farmer, I recorded all pertinent agricultural data. I examined a total of 521 landowning farmers (38 of them women), 3 renters, and 109 sharecroppers (2 of them women). Among the owners, 49 were listed as Democrats in 1897 and 44 as Populists. Of the 112 sharecroppers and renters, 13 appeared on the 1897 voting list, 9 as Populists and 4 as Democrats. Obviously the time lag of seventeen years allows for a major change in agricultural status; but the 1890 agricultural census was lost in a warehouse fire in Washington and the 1900 census did not elaborate so fully. Therefore the 1880 census is the nearest complete listing. Many tenants were related to landowners and thus were more highly mobile economically than unrelated tenants. By 1897 some of the 1880 sharecroppers were landowners. On the other hand, tenancy rates increased sharply in Geneva County between 1880 and 1900, so many persons listed as landowners in the former year were doubtless sharecroppers by 1897.

The following table provides data for 49 1880 owners who were listed as Democrats in 1897 and 44 owners who became Populists by 1897.

	49 Democratic Owners	44 Populist Owners
Average improved acres	32.06	34.32
Average value farm	$ 378.50	$ 340.80
Average value farm implements	$ 15.80	$ 11.80
Average value livestock	$ 332.30	$ 299.00
Average estimated farm products on hand, sold, consumed	$ 271.50	$ 344.30
Average no. horses	1.00	1.48
Average no. mules	.24	.20
Average no. oxen	1.31	1.77
Average no. cows, cattle	13.59	10.18
Average no. sheep	62.27	43.68
Average no. swine	25.10	22.82
Average no. poultry	10.12	11.61
Average no. bushels of sweet potatoes	76.49	71.36
Average no. fruit-bearing trees	15.53	14.77
Average no. bushels of corn	120.73	107.86
Average amount paid for farm labor	$ 18.33	$ 29.57
Average no. cotton bales and average acres planted in cotton	1.76 bales 7.76 acres	2.48 bales 11.07 acres

NOTES

1. "UNKNOWN AND FORGOTTEN ANCESTORS"

1. Donald B. Dodd and Wynelle S. Dodd, *Historical Statistics of the South, 1790–1970* (University: University of Alabama Press, 1973), p. 2.

2. See James F. Doster, "Land Titles and Public Land Sales in Early Alabama," *Alabama Review* 16 (April 1963): 108–24; Leah Rawls Atkins, "Southern Congressmen and the Homestead Bill" (Ph.D. diss., Auburn University, 1974), p. 28.

3. Thomas P. Abernethy, *The Formative Period in Alabama, 1815–1828* (University: University of Alabama Press, 1965), p. 37.

4. Quoted in Richard T. Goodwin, Jr., "A History of the Public Lands in Alabama to 1830" (M.A. thesis, Auburn University, 1969), p. 35. For brief background on the politics of public land sales, see Frances C. Roberts, "Politics and Public Land Disposal in Alabama's Formative Period," *Alabama Review* 22 (July 1969): 163–74.

5. Ibid., pp. 39, 41.

6. J. Mills Thornton III, *Politics and Power in a Slave Society: Alabama, 1800–1860* (Baton Rouge: Louisiana State University Press, 1978), p. 7.

7. Goodwin, "A History of the Public Lands," p. 92.

8. U.S., Annual Report, *Commissioner of the General Land Office, 1841* (N.p., n.d.), pp. 32–33.

9. Thornton, *Politics and Power*, p. 17.

10. For a convincing argument on this ideology, see ibid., pp. 87–101.

11. Gordon B. Cleveland, "Social Conditions in Alabama as Seen by Travellers, 1840–1850," pt. 1, *Alabama Review* 2 (January 1949): 18.

12. Margaret M. Cowart, *Old Land Records of Jackson County, Alabama* (Huntsville, Ala.: N.p., 1980), p. iii.

13. U.S., Annual Report, *Commissioner of the General Land Office, 1837* (N.p., n.d.), p. 930.

14. U.S., Annual Report, *Commissioner of the General Land Office, 1845*, (N.p., n.d.), p. 9.

15. Leah Rawls Atkins, "Felix Grundy McConnell: Old South Demagogue," *Alabama Review* 30 (April 1977): 83–100.

16. Quoted in Atkins, "Southern Congressmen and The Homestead Bill," p. 98.

17. Ibid., pp. 77–86.

18. Ibid., pp. 100–104, and Leah Rawls Atkins, "Williamson R. W. Cobb and the Graduation Act of 1854," *Alabama Review* 28 (January 1975): 16–31.

19. Atkins, "Southern Congressmen and the Homestead Bill," p. 104.

20. Ibid., p. 173.

21. Dodd and Dodd, *Historical Statistics*, p. 2, and U.S., Annual Report, *Commissioner of the General Land Office, 1850* (N.p., n.d.), p. 2.

22. J. Crawford King, Jr., "The Closing of the Southern Range: An Exploratory Study," *Journal of Southern History* 48 (February 1982): 53–70.

23. Three excellent recent studies emphasize this ambivalence over class. All three describe the issues and elements necessary for a full-fledged class struggle in Alabama, yet each historian properly concludes that despite all their differences, whites struggled in only the preliminary stages of class conflict. The most wide-ranging study is Thornton, *Politics and Power.* The most comprehensive study of the land controversy is Atkins, "Southern Congressmen and the Homestead Bill." And although his essay concerns north Georgia, Steven Hahn's conclusions generally are applicable to Alabama as well: Steven Hahn, "The Yeomanry of the Nonplantation South: Upper Piedmont Georgia, 1850–1860," in Orville V. Burton and Robert C. McMath, Jr., eds., *Class, Conflict, and Consensus: Antebellum Southern Community Studies* (Westport, Conn.: Greenwood Press, 1982), pp. 30–47.

24. Virginia Van der Veer Hamilton, *Alabama: A Bicentennial History* (New York: W. W. Norton and Co., 1977), p. 12.

25. Thornton, *Politics and Power*, pp. 280–81, 285, 292, 413, 449.

26. William L. Barney, "Towards The Civil War: The Dynamics of Change in a Black Belt County," in Burton and McMath, *Class, Conflict, and Consensus*, pp. 150–57.

27. U.S., Manuscript Census, Population, 1860, Winston County; manuscript census on microfilm, Alabama Department of Archives and History, Montgomery. All mss. of county censuses cited are located at the state archives.

28. Smith Lipscomb to "Brother," June 11, 1846, Lipscomb Family Papers, in the Southern History Collection, University of North Carolina, Chapel Hill.

29. "List," September 1851, Lipscomb Papers.

30. The descriptions of Benton County are taken from Augustine D. Edwards, "Economic and Social History of Benton County, Alabama" (M.A. thesis, University of Alabama, 1941).

31. This profile was developed from U.S., Manuscript Census, Population, 1860, Calhoun County. The total figure for landless whites was obtained by omitting farm laborers who lived with relatives, then adding propertyless urban workers and landless farm laborers. Families were assigned an average size of six (husband, wife, and four children).

32. One of my graduate students carefully studied Russell County, using a methodology developed by Frederick A. Bode and Donald E. Ginter for Georgia. He estimates that the Alabama county contained a white tenancy rate of at least 16 percent in 1860. See Bode and Ginter, *Farm Tenancy and*

the Census in Antebellum Georgia (Athens: University of Georgia Press, 1986); and Don McIlwain, "Land Ownership and Tenancy: Russell County in 1860," seminar paper, May 1987, copy in author's possession.

33. Dollie Wiginton, "Some Social and Economic Factors in Southeastern Alabama in 1860" (M.A. thesis, University of Alabama, 1941), p. 10.

34. Ibid., p. 16. New counties were created after 1865. The Wiregrass includes all of present-day Covington, Coffee, Geneva, Houston, Henry, and Dale counties, and part of Crenshaw.

35. I am indebted to Ann Patton Malone, Alberto Meloni, and Jerry Devine for sharing with me their work on the Georgia Wiregrass. Their studies of local records and reconstruction of the region will eventuate in an important book. But in the meantime, the best summary of their work is one prepared for the National Endowment for the Humanities, "The Georgia Wiregrass Rural History Project: Class and Society in an Industrializing Pine Belt Region, 1870–1900," November 30, 1983. A preliminary portion of their study covers the antebellum era, and the information compares favorably to Wiginton's 1941 thesis on the Alabama Wiregrass, cited in n. 33. See also Ann Patton Malone, "Piney Woods Farmers of South Georgia, 1850–1900: Jeffersonian Yeomen in an Age of Expanding Commercialism," *Agricultural History* 60 (Fall 1986): 51–84, especially pp. 59, 71–72.

36. Comparable 1860 averages for all Calhoun County families and for 1,128 Wiregrass families support these conclusions:

	Calhoun	*Wiregrass*
Cotton:	7.06 bales	4.67 bales
Corn:	352 bushels	194 bushels
Land Value:	$ 1,458	$ 936
Milk Cows:	2–3	2–3
Sheep:	4–5	3–4
Swine:	19–20	18–19

Comparisons are made from Edwards, "Economic and Social History of Benton County," pp. 31–33, and Wiginton, "Some Social and Economic Factors," pp. 21–23.

37. Wyley D. Ward, *Early History of Covington County, Alabama, 1821–1871* (Huntsville, Ala.: N.p., 1976), pp. 85–89, 143–44, 161.

38. Minnie C. Boyd, *Alabama in the Fifties: A Social Study* (New York: Columbia University Press, 1931), p. 63.

39. Ibid.

40. Richard W. Griffin, "Poor White Laborers in Southern Cotton Factories, 1789–1865," *South Carolina Historical Magazine* 61 (January 1960): 36.

41. Randall M. Miller, "The Cotton Mill Movement in Antebellum Alabama" (Ph.D. diss., Ohio State University, 1971), p. 33.

42. Daniel R. Hundley, *Social Relations in Our Southern States* (New York: Henry B. Price, 1860), p. 258.

43. Miller, "Cotton Mill Movement," p. 33.

44. Quoted in ibid., p. 53.

45. Quoted in ibid., p. 62.

46. Quoted in ibid., p. 93.

47. Randall M. Miller, "Love of Labor: A Note on Daniel Pratt's Employment Practices," *Alabama Historical Quarterly* 37 (Summer 1975): 146–50.

48. Quoted in Miller, "Cotton Mill Movement," p. 217.

49. Quoted in ibid., p. 204.

50. The Fish Pond Factory in Tallapoosa County returned no less than 25 percent profit on the original investment between 1845 and 1849; ibid., p. 90.

51. Harriet E. Amos, "Social Life in an Antebellum Cotton Port: Mobile, Alabama, 1820–1860" (Ph.D. diss., Emory University, 1976), pp. 45–47; Barbara J. Davis, "A Comparative Analysis of the Economic Structure of Mobile County, Alabama, Before and After the Civil War, 1860 and 1870" (M.A. thesis, University of Alabama, 1963), pp. 14–16.

52. Harriet E. Amos, " 'City Belles': Images and Realities of the Lives of White Women in Antebellum Mobile," *Alabama Review* 34 (January 1981): 11–12.

53. This discussion of poor whites in Mobile comes from two sources, both by Harriet Amos: her thorough dissertation, cited in n. 51 (pp. 92–310), and a revised copy of the dissertation published by The University of Alabama Press. Two chapters of her book contain the cited information: "Working People," and "Social Services"; Harriet E. Amos, *Cotton City: Urban Development in Antebellum Mobile* (University: University of Alabama Press, 1985), pp. 80–113, 168–92.

54. See Knox G. Jennings, "Almshouses in Alabama" (M.A. thesis, Florida State University, 1964).

55. Gordon B. Cleveland, "Social Conditions in Alabama as Seen by Travellers, 1840–1850," pt. 2, *Alabama Review* 2 (April 1949): 127.

56. *Cherokee County Heritage* 1 (January 1972): 29.

57. U.S., Census Office, *The Statistics of the Population of the United States, Ninth Census, 1870, Vol. I* (Washington, D.C.: Government Printing Office, 1872), pp. 396–97.

58. Boyd, *Alabama in the Fifties*, pp. 129, 131.

59. Quoted in Ulrich B. Phillips, *Life and Labor in the Old South* (Boston: Little, Brown and Co., 1929), pp. 340–41.

60. Gary B. Mills, "Miscegenation and the Free Negro in Antebellum 'Anglo' Alabama: A Reexamination of Southern Race Relations," *Journal of American History* 68 (June 1981): 23–25.

61. In his seminal work, *The Making of the English Working Class* (New York: Pantheon Books, 1964), E. P. Thompson argued that class experience was determined primarily by the productive relations into which men are born or enter voluntarily. But he adds that one cannot understand class without comprehending the distinctive social and cultural formations arising from class differences and extending over a considerable historical period. Indeed, Thompson concludes that class is as much cultural as it is economic in origin and that Scottish and English working classes, though

economically similar, were culturally quite distinctive (pp. 10–14). In the same way, the southern bottom class, with its rural, Anglo-Saxon, and Celtic roots, was culturally dissimilar to the northern urban immigrant working class.

62. For a lengthy discussion and the quotations cited in this section, see Wayne Flynt, "Alabama," in *Religion in the Southern States*, ed. by Samuel S. Hill (Macon, Ga.: Mercer University Press, 1983), pp. 5–15.

63. Quoted in Walter B. Posey, *Alabama in the 1830's as Recorded by British Travellers* (Birmingham: Birmingham-Southern College, 1938), p. 28.

64. Quoted in Bobby L. Lindsey, *"The Reason for the Tears": A History of Chambers County, Alabama, 1832–1900* (West Point, Ga.: Hester Printing Co., 1971), p. 75.

65. Sir Charles Lyell, *A Second Visit to the United States of North America*, 2 vols. (New York: Harper and Brothers, 1850), 2:49.

66. Frederick L. Olmsted, *A Journey in the Back Country* (New York: Mason Brothers, 1860), pp. 205–20.

67. Frederick L. Olmsted, *A Journey in the Seaboard Slave States, with Remarks on Their Economy* (New York: Dix and Edwards, 1856), pp. 550–55.

68. Lyell, *Second Visit*, 2:62–64.

69. G. Ward Hubbs, collector, *Rowdy Tales from Early Alabama: The Humor of John Gorman Barr* (University: University of Alabama Press, 1981), p. 9.

70. W. Stanley Hoole, *Alias Simon Suggs: The Life and Times of Johnson Jones Hooper* (University: University of Alabama Press, 1952), pp. 25–35.

71. Johnson J. Hooper, *Adventures of Captain Simon Suggs Late of the Tallapoosa Volunteers Together with "Taking the Census" and Other Alabama Sketches* (Philadelphia: T. B. Peterson and Brothers, 1846), pp. 151–53.

72. Ibid., pp. 12, 88–89.

73. Johnson J. Hooper, *A Ride with Old Kit Kuncker and Other Sketches and Scenes of Alabama* (N.p., n.d.); copy in special collections, Auburn University Library.

74. Hundley, *Social Relations*, pp. 254–83.

75. Boyd, *Alabama in the Fifties*, p. 64

2. "A POOR MAN'S FIGHT"

1. Tax receipts; Elizabeth Lipscomb to Smith and Sally Lipscomb, June 19, 1874; Denson and Disque to Smith Lipscomb, 1880; Ellis T. Martin to Smith Lipscomb, March 12, 1880; Bowling and Co. to Smith Lipscomb, March 10, 1880; Green and Whatley to Smith Lipscomb, January 15, 1881; R. W. Draper to Smith Lipscomb, April 18, 1880; all in Lipscomb Papers.

2. Bessie Martin, *Desertion of Alabama Troops from the Confederate Army: A Study in Sectionalism* (New York: AMS Press, 1966), p. 103. This excellent study actually should be subtitled "A Study in Class and Sectionalism"

because the author believes class differences were a major factor in desertions.

3. Albert B. Moore, *History of Alabama* (Tuscaloosa: Alabama Book Store, 1951), pp. 416–17. Moore denied that class was a factor in the secession vote. He attributed the division to long-standing sectional differences between north and south Alabama and the linkage of mountain counties to Tennessee's economy and folkways, together with the belief that Tennessee would not secede.

4. Phyllis LaRue LeGrand, "Destitution and Relief of the Indigent Soldiers' Families of Alabama During the Civil War" (M.A. thesis, Auburn University, 1964), pp. 15–16, 19.

5. S. K. Rayburn to Gov. John Gill Shorter, July 10, 1862; Charles Gibson to Gov. Shorter, September 30, 1862; H. J. Marley to Gov. Shorter, July 20, 1862; Lucreesy Simmons to Gov. Shorter, July 17, 1862; W. D. Roberts to Gov. Shorter, September 12, 1862; in Gov. John Gill Shorter Papers, Alabama State Archives.

6. LeGrand, "Destitution and Relief," pp. 63–65.

7. Martin, *Desertion of Alabama Troops*, pp. 135–40.

8. Ibid., p. 141.

9. Wesley S. Thompson, *"The Free State of Winston": A History of Winston County, Alabama* (Winfield, Ala.: Pareil Press, 1968), pp. 132–33.

10. For examples, see Peter Wallenstein, "Rich Man's War, Poor Man's Fight: Civil War and the Transformation of Public Finance in Georgia," *Journal of Southern History* 50 (February 1984): 15–42.

11. The information on destitution is found in LeGrand, "Destitution and Relief," pp. 73, 109–19, 121–22, 143, 160–62, 199, 219, 224, 237, 255–61. See also Donald B. Dodd, "Unionism in Northwest Alabama Through 1865" (M.A. thesis, Auburn University, 1966), pp. 2, 58.

12. LeGrand, "Destitution and Relief," pp. 74–84.

13. Quoted in ibid., p. 71.

14. E.g., see John H. Chapman to Gov. Thomas H. Watts, May 14, 1864, Gov. Thomas H. Watts Papers, Alabama State Archives.

15. Francis Mitchell Grace, "From the Unpublished Autobiography of Francis Mitchell Grace, D.D., 1832–1904," pp. 20–22, Birmingham Public Library.

16. Ibid., pp. 22–24.

17. Martin, *Desertion of Alabama Troops*, pp. 128, 130.

18. Quoted in LeGrand, "Destitution and Relief," pp. 51–52.

19. Quoted in Martin, *Desertion of Alabama Troops*, p. 134.

20. See Malcolm C. McMillan, *The Disintegration of a Confederate State: Three Governors and Alabama's Wartime Home Front, 1861–1865* (Macon, Ga.: Mercer University Press, 1986).

21. J. L. Sheffield to Gov. Thomas H. Watts, April 22, 1864, Watts Papers.

22. Ellen E. Eddins to Gov. Thomas H. Watts, May 13, 1864, Watts Papers.

23. Sarah R. Espy Diary, Alabama State Archives; oral history with Essie Holdridge, November 27, 1975, in Samford University Oral History Collection, Samford University Library Archives, Birmingham, Alabama.

24. LeGrand, "Destitution and Relief," pp. 257, 261; Martin, *Desertion of Alabama Troops*, pp. 128, 130.

25. These generalizations apply both to Alabama and to other states. See Wallenstein, "Rich Man's War," and Clarence L. Mohr, "Slavery and Class Tensions in Confederate Georgia," ms. presented at the 1984 Southern Historical Convention at Louisville, Kentucky. I am grateful to Professor Mohr for sharing a copy of his paper.

26. Martin, *Desertion of Alabama Troops*, p. 64.

27. Quoted in LeGrand, "Destitution and Relief," p. 252.

28. Ward, *Early History of Covington County*, pp. 181–82. For estimates of deserters, see Martin, *Desertion of Alabama Troops*, pp. 31–39.

29. Both LeGrand and Martin conclude that economic factors contributed most to desertion. Historians Hugh C. Bailey and Donald B. Dodd agree in their studies of Unionist sentiment in the hill counties and Wiregrass. See Hugh C. Bailey, "Disaffection in the Alabama Hill Country, 1861," *Civil War History* 4 (June 1958): 183–93; Dodd, "Unionism in Northwest Alabama."

30. Quoted in Martin, *Desertion of Alabama Troops*, p. 122.

31. Quoted in ibid., p. 101.

32. Ibid., pp. 115–16.

33. See McMillan, *Disintegration of a Confederate State*.

34. Executive Letter of Gov. Thomas H. Watts, April 25, 1864, Watts Papers.

35. W. B. Cooper to Gov. Lewis E. Parsons, August 8, 1865, in "Destitution" file, Gov. Lewis E. Parsons Official Files, Alabama State Archives.

36. Report by Probate Judge Jackson Gardner of Bibb County, November 18, 1865; Moses M. Guise to Gov. Robert M. Patton, February 1866; Louis Wyeth to Gov. Patton, April 2, 1866; Rev. J. J. Grace to Gov. Patton, April 20, 1866; J. L. Sheffield to Gov. Patton, September 17, 1866; Benjamin F. Porter to Gov. Patton, October 2, 1866; S. S. Anderson to Gov. Patton, June 13, 1867; all in "Destitution" file in Gov. Robert M. Patton Official Files, Alabama State Archives. There are dozens of such letters from every part of the state from spring 1865 through 1867.

37. John R. Kennamer, *History of Jackson County* (Winchester, Tenn.: Southern Printing Co., 1935), p. 65.

38. L. M. Stiff et al. to Gov. Lewis E. Parsons, August 6, 1865, "Destitution" file, Parsons Official Files.

39. Resolution, March 19, 1866, in "Destitution" file, Parsons Official Files.

40. S. K. McSpadden to Gov. Robert M. Patton, September 21 and October 19, 1866; both in "Destitution" file, Patton Official Files.

41. Quoted in Robert A. Gilmour, "The Other Emancipation: Studies in the Society and Economy of Alabama Whites During Reconstruction" (Ph.D. diss., Johns Hopkins University, 1972), p. 69.

42. Ibid., p. 128; for many such accounts, see John L. Rumph, "A History of Bullock County, Alabama, 1865–1906" (M.A. thesis, Auburn University, 1955).

43. Gene L. Howard, *Death at Cross Plains: An Alabama Reconstruction Tragedy* (University: University of Alabama Press, 1984), pp. 38, 62.

44. Gilmour, "Other Emancipation," pp. 193–94.

45. Ibid., p. 211.

46. Mollie Wright to Cousin [Frankie], March 22, 1887, Lewis-Plant Papers, Auburn University Archives, Auburn, Alabama.

47. Sarah R. Espy Diary, entry for March 28, 1866.

48. Randolph B. Campbell, "Population Persistence and Social Change in Nineteenth-Century Texas: Harrison County, 1850–1880," *Journal of Southern History* 48 (May 1982): 183–204. Campbell argues that persistence in the county was influenced most by property ownership and occupation. See also Peter Kolchin, *First Freedom: The Responses of Alabama's Blacks to Emancipation and Reconstruction* (Westport, Conn.: Greenwood Press, 1972). Kolchin demonstrates the same rapid emigration patterns for blacks just after the war.

49. Gilmour, "Other Emancipation," pp. 42–53, 124, 129–33.

50. Ibid., pp. 58–60.

51. Ibid., pp. 73–106.

52. Ibid., pp. 120–23; Ward, *Early History of Covington County*, p. 89; Mrs. Frank Ross Stewart, *Alabama's Cleburne County* (Centre, Ala.: Stewart University Press, 1982), p. 8.

53. Louis Wyeth to Gov. Robert M. Patton, April 2, 21, and 24, 1866; telegram, William Chrichton to Gov. Robert M. Patton, May 14, 1866; both in "Destitution" file, Patton Official Files; S. Draper et al. to Lewis E. Parsons, November 9, 1865, Parsons Official Files.

54. Horace M. Holderfield, "The Freedmen's Bureau in Alabama in 1865 and 1866" (M.A. thesis, Auburn University, 1970), pp. 32–37.

55. M. H. Cruikshank to Judge Probate of Winston County, copy in M. H. Cruikshank to Gov. Robert M. Patton, January 16, 1866, "Destitution" file, Patton Official Files.

56. Ibid., and A. Stikes to Gov. Robert M. Patton, August 11, 1866, "Destitution" file, Patton Official Files.

57. Holderfield, "Freedmen's Bureau in Alabama," pp. 38–41.

58. Jennings, "Almshouses in Alabama," pp. 8–11.

59. Rumph, "History of Bullock County," pp. 101–03.

60. S. K. McSpadden to Gov. Robert M. Patton, October 19, 1866, "Destitution" file, Patton Official Files.

61. Dodd and Dodd, *Historical Statistics*, pp. 4–5.

62. Davis, "Comparative Analysis," p. 16.

63. Sarah A. E. Bynerson to Gov. Robert M. Patton, undated, but probably sometime in August 1866, "Destitution" file, Patton Official Files.

3. "LOOKING FOR SOMETHING BETTER": ALABAMA'S FARM TENANTS

1. U.S., Manuscript Censuses, Agriculture and Population, 1880, Geneva County, Alabama.

2. Arthur M. Ford, *The Political Economics of Rural Poverty in the South* (Cambridge, Mass.: Ballinger Publishing Co., 1973), pp. 20–21.

3. U.S., Bureau of the Census, *Agriculture, 1910, Vol. V* (Washington, D.C.: Government Printing Office, 1914), pp. 126, 213; idem, *Agriculture, 1920, Vol. VI, Part 2* (1922), p. 480; idem, *Agriculture, 1930, Vol. II, Part 2* (1932), pp. 30–35.

4. The first chapter contains an extensive sample from the 1860 census rolls of Calhoun County. A recent study of Georgia emphasizes with more extensive data that farm tenancy was not a product of emancipation and Reconstruction. Tenancy was already firmly established by 1860. See Bode and Ginter, *Farm Tenancy.*

5. Grady McWhiney, "The Revolution in Nineteenth-Century Alabama Agriculture," *Alabama Review* 31 (January 1978): 21–23.

6. Forrest McDonald and Grady McWhiney, "The South from Self-Sufficiency to Peonage: An Interpretation," *American Historical Review* 85 (December 1980): 1095–1118; idem, "Celtic Origins of Southern Herding Practices," *Journal of Southern History* 51 (May 1985): 165–82.

7. J. Mills Thornton III, "Fiscal Policy and the Failure of Radical Reconstruction in the Lower South," in *Region, Race, and Reconstruction: Essays in Honor of C. Vann Woodward,* ed. J. Morgan Kousser and James M. McPherson (Oxford: Oxford University Press, 1982), pp. 351, 370, 381–87.

8. See Rumph, "History of Bullock County."

9. J. [T.?] P. Camp to L. S. Camp, August 3, 1871, Iron Station, North Carolina Papers, Southern History Collection.

10. Mrs. Isaac B. Ulmer to Isaac B. Ulmer, July 20, 1892, Isaac B. Ulmer Papers, Southern History Collection.

11. Oral history with Mrs. L. A. House, July 10, 1974, Samford University Oral History Collection; life history of Nancy Nolan, Federal Writers' Life History Project (hereafter referred to as Life History Project), microfilm copy in Southern History Collection.

12. James C. Cobb, *Industrialization and Southern Society, 1877–1984* (Lexington: University Press of Kentucky, 1984), pp. 10–11.

13. A number of books and articles have examined late-nineteenth-century southern agriculture. Particularly notable are Gilbert C. Fite, *Cotton Fields No More: Southern Agriculture, 1865–1980* (Lexington: University Press of Kentucky, 1984), and Pete Daniel, *Breaking the Land: The Transformation of Cotton, Tobacco, and Rice Cultures Since 1880* (Urbana and Chicago: University of Illinois Press, 1985). Both emphasize the relatively small change in methods of growing and harvesting cotton until well into the twentieth century. The most useful studies for changing market conditions and the forces that caused them are Gavin Wright, *Old South, New South: Revolutions in the Southern Economy Since the Civil War* (New York: Basic Books, 1986), especially pp. 17–112, and Steven Hahn, *The Roots of Southern Populism: Yeoman Farmers and the Transformation of the Georgia Upcountry, 1850–1890* (Oxford: Oxford University Press, 1983), especially pp. 139–200. See also Lacy K. Ford, "Rednecks and Merchants: Economic

Development and Social Tensions in the South Carolina Upcountry, 1865–1900," *Journal of American History* 71 (September 1984): 294–318.

14. William W. Rogers, *The One-Gallused Rebellion: Agrarianism in Alabama, 1865–1896* (Baton Rouge: Louisiana State University Press, 1970), p. 14.

15. For an excellent discussion of the crop-lien system and the animosity between merchants and planters, see Jonathan Wiener, *Social Origins of the New South: Alabama, 1860–1885* (Baton Rouge: Louisiana State University Press, 1978). Professor Wiener's thesis is argued on the basis of his careful study of five Alabama Black Belt counties and is less convincing for the hill counties, where his argument is strongly ideological: "White farmers in the hills were forced into tenancy by the merchant elite's monopoly on credit and increasing ownership of land" (p. 93). Both Steven Hahn and Lacy Ford found the same tension between upland farmers and merchants in Georgia and South Carolina. See Hahn, *Roots of Southern Populism*, and Ford, "Rednecks and Merchants." Another recent study touching on this issue is Thavolia Glymph and John J. Kushma, eds., *Essays on the Postbellum Southern Economy* (College Station: Texas A&M University Press for the University of Texas at Arlington, 1985).

16. Melodee Joy French, "Farming in the New South: Agricultural Periodicals of Alabama, 1865–1880" (M.A. thesis, Auburn University, 1985), pp. 26, 77.

17. Ibid., pp. 123–24.

18. Hiram Hawkins, "Achievements of the Grange in the South," in A. E. Allen, *Labor and Capital* (Cincinnati: Central Publishing House, 1891), p. 488.

19. Quoted in Daniel, *Breaking the Land*, p. 162.

20. Quoted in McWhiney, "Revolution in Nineteenth-Century Alabama Agriculture," p. 30.

21. French, "Farming in the New South," p. 52.

22. King, "Closing the Southern Range," pp. 54, 57–59, 63.

23. Dodd and Dodd, *Historical Statistics*, pp. 4–5.

24. Jonathan Kaledin, "The Economic Consequences of the Civil War in Clarke County, Alabama," *Alabama Historian* 2 (Fall 1980): 11–13.

25. Rumph, "History of Bullock County," pp. 49, 52–56, 129.

26. Historian Gilbert Fite advanced the thesis of an "inadequate resource base" in a paper presented at the November 1985 annual meeting of the Southern Historical Association. For a brief summary, see David A. Shannon, "The Fifty-First Annual Meeting," *Journal of Southern History* 52 (May 1986): 218. Also see Fite, *Cotton Fields No More*, p. 22.

27. Many historians have agreed with planters, viewing tenancy as a logical response to market conditions; see Joseph D. Reid, Jr., "Sharecropping as an Understandable Market Response: The Post-Bellum South," *Journal of Economic History* 33 (March 1973): 106–30. For notable rebuttals, see Edward C. Royce, "Social Change and the Constriction of Possibilities: The Rise of Southern Sharecropping" (Ph.D. diss., State University of New York at Stony Brook, 1983), and Harold D. Woodman, "Sequel to

Slavery: The New History Views the Postbellum South," *Journal of Southern History* 43 (November 1977): 523–54. The literature on this subject is quite extensive. In addition to sources that I used in this chapter, the interested reader might wish to read: Robert Higgs, *Competition and Coercion: Blacks in the American Economy, 1865–1914* (Cambridge: Cambridge University Press, 1977); Joseph D. Reid, Jr., "Sharecropping in History and Theory," *Agricultural History* 49 (April 1975): 426–40; Stephen DeCanio, *Agriculture in the Postbellum South* (New Haven, Conn.: Yale University Press, 1975); Michael Schwartz, *Radical Protest and Social Structure: The Southern Farmers' Alliance and Cotton Tenancy, 1880–1890* (New York: Academic Press, 1976); Jay R. Mandle, *The Roots of Black Poverty: The Southern Plantation Economy After the Civil War* (Durham: Duke University Press, 1978); Gavin Wright and Howard C. Kunreuther, "Cotton, Corn and Risk in the Nineteenth Century," *Journal of Economic History* 35 (September 1975): 526–51; Robert McGuire and Robert Higgs, "Cotton, Corn and Risk in the Nineteenth Century: Another View," *Explorations in Economic History* 14 (April 1977): 167–82; Susan A. Mann, "Sharecropping in the Cotton South: A Case of Uneven Development in Agriculture," *Rural Sociology* 49 (Fall 1984): 412–29; Donghyu Yang, "Notes on the Wealth Distribution of Farm Households in the United States, 1860: A New Look at Two Manuscript Census Samples," *Explorations in Economic History* 21 (January 1984), 88–102; John B. Boles, *Black Southerners, 1619–1869* (Lexington: University Press of Kentucky, 1983), pp. 208–09; Harold D. Woodman. *King Cotton and His Retainers: Financing and Marketing the South's Cotton, 1800–1925* (Lexington: University Press of Kentucky, 1968).

28. French, "Farming in the New South," pp. 25–26, 50, 81.

29. Charles L. Flynn, Jr., *White Land, Black Labor: Caste and Class in Late Nineteenth-Century Georgia* (Baton Rouge: Louisiana State University Press, 1983), pp. 150–59. Although this study deals with Georgia, most of its conclusions are applicable to Alabama.

30. U.S., Manuscript Censuses, Agriculture and Population, 1880, Winston, Jackson, Cherokee, Calhoun, Cleburne, Randolph, Clay, Geneva, Crenshaw, and Covington counties. See Appendix 1.

31. Stewart, *Alabama's Cleburne County*, p. 8.

32. Wendell M. Adamson, *Income in Counties of Alabama, 1929* and *1935* (Tuscaloosa: Bureau of Business Research, University of Alabama, 1939), p. 6.

33. Stewart, *Alabama's Cleburne County*, p. 8.

34. King, "Closing the Southern Range," p. 67.

35. U.S., Census Office, *Agriculture, 1900, Part I* (Washington, D.C.: U.S. Census Office, 1902), pp. 58–59; idem, *Agriculture, 1910*, pp. 44–45; idem, *Agriculture, 1920*, pp. 488–94; Alabama Farm Tenancy Committee, *Farm Tenancy in Alabama* (Wetumpka, Ala.: Wetumpka Printing Co., 1944), pp. 36–37.

36. Fite, *Cotton Fields No More*, p. 48.

37. Roger L. Ransom and Richard Sutch, *One Kind of Freedom: The Eco-*

nomic Consequences of Emancipation (Cambridge: Cambridge University Press, 1977), p. 100

38. Oral history with Lillie Mae Beason, January 3, 1976, Samford University Oral History Collection.

39. Mary Wigley Harper, "The Wind is From the East," pp. 88–101, Auburn University Archives. This rather disorganized ms. is one of the most searing descriptions of Alabama tenancy yet written.

40. Herman C. Nixon, *Forty Acres and Steel Mules* (Chapel Hill: University of North Carolina Press, 1938), p. 26.

41. Oral history with Mrs. Carlie H. Crocker, January 27, 1975, Samford University Oral History Collection.

42. Oral history with Carl Forrester, January 27, 1975, Samford University Oral History Collection.

43. Harper, "The Wind is From the East," pp. 95, 185, 205. For a general summary of the country store, see Lewis E. Atherton, *The Southern Country Store, 1800–1860* (Baton Rouge: Louisiana State University Press, 1949). For a wonderfully evocative essay on tenants, risks, and country stores in Calhoun County, see Herman C. Nixon, "Small Farms and Country Stores," in *Lower Piedmont Country: The Uplands of the Deep South* (University: University of Alabama Press, 1984 edition), pp. 54–68.

44. Oral history with Mrs. Kathleen Knight, January 23, 1975, Samford University Oral History Collection.

45. Herman C. Nixon, *Possum Trot: Rural Community, South* (Norman: University of Oklahoma Press, 1941), pp. 53–54.

46. Oral history with Lillie Mae Beason.

47. Ibid.

48. Both the Crockers and Flynts recall vivid memories of the "rolling stores." Oral histories with Carlie Crocker and Lillie Mae Beason.

49. Oral histories with Kathleen Knight and Lillie Mae Beason.

50. Oral history with Carlie Crocker.

51. Oral history with Carl Forrester.

52. Oral history with Frank Uptain, November 23, 1975, Samford University Oral History Collection; Harper, "The Wind is From the East," pp. 114–15.

53. Oral history with Lillie Mae Beason.

54. Oral history with Kathleen Knight.

55. Harper, "The Wind is From the East," p. 99.

56. Ibid., p. 97.

57. Fite, *Cotton Fields No More*, pp. 70–71.

58. Oral history with Carl Forrester.

59. Harper, "The Wind is From the East," p. 101.

60. Ibid., p. 114.

61. Oral history with Kathleen Knight.

62. Oral histories with Carlie Crocker, Lillie Mae Beason, Carl Forrester, and Kathleen Knight.

63. Fite, *Cotton Fields No More*, pp. 13, 831.

64. Ibid., p. 26.

65. I derived these figures by multiplying the average pounds of cotton raised per acre by the 265 sharecroppers in my sample ten counties (149 pounds) by the prevailing price (ten cents in 1879, five cents in 1895), and then dividing that figure by 102 hours.

66. Fite, *Cotton Fields No More*, p. 104.

67. Life history of E. J. Alexander, Life History Project.

68. Alabama Farm Tenancy Committee, *Farm Tenancy in Alabama*, p. 8.

69. Mitchell B. Garrett, *Horse and Buggy Days on Hatchet Creek* (University: University of Alabama Press, 1957), p. 90.

70. Alabama Farm Tenancy Committee, *Farm Tenancy in Alabama*, p. 8; Paul W. Terry and Verner M. Sims, *They Live on the Land: Life in an Open-Country Southern Community* (University: University of Alabama, Bureau of Educational Research, Studies in Education no. 1, 1940), p. 36; Nixon, *Forty Acres*, pp. 24–25.

71. Life history of E. J. Alexander.

72. Terry and Sims, *They Live on the Land*, pp. 42–43, 60.

73. Harper, "The Wind is From the East," p. 107; oral history with Lillie Mae Beason.

74. Peggy G. Walls, "Folklore and Folk Life in Southern Literature" (M.A. thesis, Auburn University, 1985), p. 80.

75. Oral histories with Lillie Mae Beason and Carl Forrester; Walls, "Folklore and Folk Life," pp. 77–79.

76. Alabama Farm Tenancy Committee, *Farm Tenancy in Alabama*, pp. 16–17.

77. Oral histories with Carlie Crocker and Lillie Mae Beason.

78. Life history of E. J. Alexander.

79. Terry and Sims, *They Live on the Land*, pp. 29, 208–09.

80. Life history of M. B. Truitt, Life History Project; oral history with Lillie Mae Beason; Walls, "Folklore and Folk Life," p. 77.

81. Oral history with Lillie Mae Beason; Harper, "The Wind is From the East," p. 119.

82. Alabama Farm Tenancy Committee, *Farm Tenancy in Alabama*, p. 11.

83. Terry and Sims, *They Live on the Land*, pp. 133, 215.

84. Home Demonstration Annual State Report, 1926, Cooperative Extension Service Papers, Auburn University Archives.

85. Oral histories with Kathleen Knight and Lillie Mae Beason; life history of "Bull" Elliott, Life History Project.

86. Oral history with Kathleen Knight.

87. Ibid.

88. Harper, "The Wind is From the East," p. 143; Terry and Sims, *They Live on the Land*, p. 33.

89. Oral history with Lillie Mae Beason.

90. Ibid., and with Kathleen Knight; life history of Orrie Robinson, Life History Project; Harper, "The Wind is From the East," p. 101; Garrett, *Horse and Buggy Days*, p. 90.

91. Garrett, *Horse and Buggy Days*, pp. 90, 101; quoted in Sarah Newman

Shouse, "Herman Clarence Nixon: A Biography" (Ph.D. diss., Auburn University, 1984), p. 9.

92. Terry and Sims, *They Live on the Land*, pp. 43, 75.

93. Oral history with Lillie Mae Beason.

4. "A SIGHT TO GRATIFY ANY PHILANTHROPIST":
ALABAMA'S TEXTILE WORKERS

1. Dwight M. Wilhelm, *A History of the Cotton Textile Industry of Alabama, 1809–1950* (Montgomery: N.p., 1950), pp. 11–13, 74–75. For the way market factors affected southern textile workers, see Wright, *Old South, New South*.

2. Wendell M. Adamson, *Industrial Activity in Alabama, 1913–1932* (Tuscaloosa: Bureau of Business Research, University of Alabama, 1933), p. 76.

3. These figures are taken from a variety of sources: U.S., Census Office, *Report on Population of the United States, Eleventh Census, 1890, Part II* (Washington, D.C.: Government Printing Office, 1897), 530–31; idem, *Population, 1900, Part II* (1902), pp. 510–18; idem, *Population, 1910, Vol. IV* (1914), pp. 434–35; idem, *Population, 1920, Vol. IV* (1923), pp. 874–76; "Workers in Southern Manufactures," *American Federationist* 36 (May 1929), 588.

4. Burton R. Morley, *Characteristics of the Labor Market in Alabama Related to the Administration of Unemployment Compensation* (Tuscaloosa: Bureau of Business Research, University of Alabama, 1937), p. 24.

5. Patricia Ryan, *Northern Dollars for Huntsville Spindles* (Huntsville, Ala.: Huntsville Planning Department, Special Report no. 4, 1983), p. 13; Wilhelm, *History of the Cotton Textile Industry*, p. 54.

6. Will Mickle, "Huntsville, Alabama: Cotton Textile Center of the New South," *Cotton History Review* 2 (1961): 92–102; B. B. Comer to Mrs. D. L. McDonald, January 24, 1917, B. B. Comer Papers, Southern History Collection.

7. G. T. Schwenning, "Prospects of Southern Textile Unionism," *Journal of Political Economy* 39 (December 1931): 795; Matthew W. Clinton, "Economic Conditions in Tuscaloosa City and County, 1865–1880" (M.A. thesis, University of Alabama, 1942), p. 90.

8. Life history of Julia Rhodes, Life History Project.

9. Life history of Nancy Nolan; oral history with Mrs. L. A. House.

10. Edward N. Akin, " 'Mr. Donald's Help': The Birmingham Village of Avondale Mills During the Great Depression," April 1978, ms. copy in author's possession; oral history with Andrew McClain, March 10, 1982, Auburn University Archives.

11. Census Office, *Report on Population, 1890*, pp. 530–31; idem, *Population, 1900*, pp. 510–18; idem, *Population, 1910, Vol. IV*, p. 102; Harry Boyte, "The Textile Industry, Keel of Southern Industrialization," *Radical America* 6 (March–April, 1972): 9.

12. Census Office, *Population, 1910, Vol. IV*, pp. 434–35; idem, *Population, 1920, Vol. IV*, p. 519.

13. Life histories of Nancy Nolan and Mrs. Tom Alsobrook and Mrs. Lee Snipes, Life History Project; oral histories with W. W. Jewell, February 18, 1982, Pauline Brewer, March 9, 1982, and Carter Priest, February 25, 1982; all in Auburn University Archives; oral history with S. L. Hardy, November 18, 1974, Sylacauga High School Oral History Program, copy in Samford University Library.

14. Saffold Berney, *Hand-Book of Alabama* (Birmingham: Roberts and Son, 1892), pp. 482–83.

15. *Huntsville Mercury Centennial*, July 23, 1916.

16. Donald Comer, *Braxton Bragg Comer: An Alabamian Whose Avondale Mills Opened New Paths for Southern Progress* (New York: Newcomen Society of England, American Branch, 1947), p. 16.

17. T. C. Acree to Donald Comer, July 9, 1923, Donald Comer Papers, Department of Archives, Birmingham Public Library, Birmingham, Alabama.

18. B. B. Comer to Mrs. D. L. McDonald, January 24, 1917, B. B. Comer Papers.

19. Comer, *Braxton Bragg Comer*, p. 18.

20. Hastings H. Hart, *Social Problems of Alabama: A Study of the Social Institutions and Agencies of the State of Alabama as Related to Its War Activities* (Montgomery: State of Alabama, 1918), p. 86.

21. Oral history with Mrs. L. A. House.

22. See Jacquelyn Dowd Hall, Robert Korstad, and James Leloudis, "Cotton Mill People: Work, Community, and Protest in the Textile South, 1880–1940," *American Historical Review* 91 (April 1986): 245–86.

23. Life history of Susie R. O'Brien, Life History Project.

24. Mickle, "Huntsville," pp. 92–102.

25. "Birmingham: Smelting Iron Ore and Civics," *Survey* 27 (January 6, 1912): 1467, 1479, 1525.

26. Oral histories with W. W. Jewell, Pauline Brewer, and Mrs. L. A. House.

27. Oral history with Annie and Houston Burrow, March 2, 1982, Auburn University Archives.

28. Life history of Tom Alsobrook, Life History Project; oral history with Pauline Brewer.

29. Oral history with Mrs. L. A. House.

30. Ibid.

31. Mickle, "Huntsville," pp. 92–102.

32. Broadus Mitchell, "Why Cheap Labor Down South?" *Virginia Quarterly Review* 5 (October 1929): 481–91.

33. Life history of Mrs. Sam Anderson, Life History Project, and of Mrs. Lee Snipes, and Tom Alsobrook; oral histories with Mrs. L. A. House, Carter Priest, Pauline Brewer, and Andrew McClain.

34. For comparative data on Alabama textile wages, see: Boyte, "Textile

Industry," p. 9; Elizabeth L. Otey, "Women and Children in Southern Industry," *Annals of the American Academy of Political and Social Science* 153 (January 1931): 164; Louis Stark, "The Meaning of the Textile Strike," *New Republic* 58 (May 8, 1929): 324; James A. Hodges, "The New Deal Labor Policy and the Southern Cotton Textile Industry, 1933–1941" (Ph.D. diss., Vanderbilt University, 1963), p. 107.

35. Dexter M. Keezer, "Low Wages in the South," *Survey* 57 (November 15, 1926): 227.

36. Life histories of Nancy Nolan, Tom Alsobrook, and Susie O'Brien; oral histories with W. W. Jewell, S. L. Hardy, Carter Priest, Andrew McClain, Pauline Brewer, and Mrs. L. A. House.

37. Oral histories with Carter Priest, Annie Burrow, W. W. Jewell, S. L. Hardy, and Mrs. L. A. House.

38. Oral history with W. W. Jewell; life history of Mrs. Sam Anderson.

39. Oral history with Carter Priest.

40. Life histories of Mrs. Lee Snipes, Tom Alsobrook, Nancy Nolan, and of Mrs. Champion, Life History Project.

41. Oral history with Mrs. L. A. House.

42. Oral histories with Carter Priest and W. W. Jewell.

43. Historians of textile life have noted the development of uptown and milltown subcultures. For two examples, see Liston Pope, *Millhands and Preachers: A Study of Gastonia* (New Haven, Conn.: Yale University Press, 1942), and David L. Carlton, *Mill and Town in South Carolina, 1880–1920* (Baton Rouge: Louisiana State University Press, 1982).

44. Oral histories with Mrs. L. A. House, Pauline Brewer, and with June W. Odom, November 23, 1974, Samford University Oral History Collection.

45. Clarence Cason, *90° in the Shade* (University: University of Alabama Press, 1983 reprint), p. 153.

46. Schwenning, "Prospects of Southern Textile Unionism," p. 798.

47. See Carlton, *Mill and Town*, especially pp. 157–65.

48. Irene M. Ashby-Macfayden, "The Fight Against Child Labor in Alabama," *American Federationist* 8 (May 1901): 150–57; Verna P. Curtis and Stanley Mallach, *Photography and Reform: Lewis Hine and the National Child Labor Committee* (Milwaukee: Milwaukee Art Museum, 1984). Hine's photographs in the Library of Congress constitute one of the finest collections of early "documentary photography."

49. Mrs. John Van Vorst, *The Cry of the Children: A Study of Child Labor* (New York: Moffat, Yard, and Co., 1908), pp. 20–21.

50. Ibid., p. 37.

51. Ibid., pp. 43–96.

52. "Birmingham," *Survey*, pp. 1524–25.

53. Ibid., p. 1523; W. D. Adams to Donald Comer, January 29, 1923; Comer to Adams, February 1, 1923, Donald Comer Papers.

54. *Huntsville Mercury Centennial*, May 1, 1912.

55. Oral history with Susie Wilson, in possession of Peggy Walls, Hackneyville, Alabama; oral histories with Pauline Brewer, Mrs. L. A. House,

Carter Priest, W. W. Jewell, and Houston Burrow; life histories of Nancy Nolan, Mrs. Sam Anderson, Tom Alsobrook, Julia Rhodes, and Mrs. Champion.

56. *Huntsville Telegram*, March 9 and 14, 1921.

57. Melton A. McLaurin, *Paternalism and Protest: Southern Cotton Mill Workers and Organized Labor, 1875–1905* (Westport, Conn.: Greenwood Press, 1971), p. 113.

58. Holman Head, "The Development of the Labor Movement in Alabama Prior to 1900" (M.A. thesis, University of Alabama, 1955), p. 163.

59. The 1930s strike will be discussed fully later.

60. Oral histories with Carter Priest, June Odom, Pauline Brewer, Annie and Houston Burrow, and Andrew McClain.

61. Oral history with Carter Priest.

62. Oral histories with Mrs. L. A. House, W. W. Jewell, S. L. Hardy; life history of Mrs. Lee Snipes.

63. Life history of Mrs. Lee Snipes.

5. "DARK AS A DUNGEON, DAMP AS A DEW": ALABAMA'S COAL MINERS

1. William B. Phillips, *Iron Making in Alabama* (University: Geological Survey of Alabama, 1912), p. 151; Alabama, Mine Inspector, *Coal Mine Statistics of State of Alabama for 1910* (Birmingham: Grant and Pow, 1911), p. 40; O. E. Kiessling, "Coal Mining in the South," *Annals of the American Academy of Political and Social Science* 153 (January 1931): 84.

2. Alabama, Mine Inspector, *Coal Mine Statistics for 1910*, pp. 1–36; Morley, *Characteristics of the Labor Market*, p. 9; U.S., Census Office, *Fifteenth Census of the United States, 1930, Population, Vol. IV, Occupations by States* (Washington, D.C.: Government Printing Office, 1933), p. 118.

3. Census Office, *Report on Population, 1890*, pp. 530–31; idem, *Population, 1910, Vol. IV*, pp. 1198, 1205; Kiessling, "Coal Mining in the South," p. 84.

4. Robert D. Ward and William W. Rogers, *Labor Revolt in Alabama: The Great Strike of 1894* (University: University of Alabama Press, 1965), pp. 20–21; United States, *Report of the United States Coal Commission, Part III* (Washington, D.C.: Government Printing Office, 1925), pp. 1412, 1415, 1421.

5. Marjorie L. White, *The Birmingham District: An Industrial History and Guide* (Birmingham: Birmingham Historical Society, the First National Bank of Birmingham, and the Junior League of Birmingham, 1981), p. 272.

6. Marlene Hunt Rikard, "An Experiment in Welfare Capitalism: The Health Care Services of the Tennessee Coal, Iron, and Railroad Company"

(Ph.D. diss., University of Alabama, 1983), p. 17; R. D. Currie, *Coal-Mine Safety Organizations in Alabama*, Technical Paper 489, Bureau of Mines, U.S. Department of Commerce (Washington, D.C.: Government Printing Office, 1931), pp. 5, 12, 14, 16–17, 33; United States, *Report of the Coal Commission*, pp. 1263–64.

7. Carl Elliott, Sr., and Susan Crittenden, *Alabama Coal Miners*, vol. 7, *Woodie Roberts* (Jasper, Ala.: Northwest Alabama Publishing Co., 1979); idem, vol. 6, *Alfred J. Renshaw* (1979).

8. "Birmingham," *Survey*, pp. 1538–39.

9. Quoted in Rikard, "Experiment in Welfare Capitalism," p. 48.

10. *American Federationist* 6 (September 1899), in Philip Taft Research Notes, Archives, Birmingham Public Library; oral history with Elmer Burton, December 3, 1974, Samford University Oral History Collection.

11. Oral history with Luther V. Smith, November 27, 1974, Samford University Oral History Collection.

12. "Birmingham," *Survey*, p. 1486.

13. United States, *Report of the Coal Commission*, pp. 1436–37, 1467, 1471, 1473.

14. Ibid., pp. 1181, 1458.

15. Oral histories with Ila Hendrix, May 1, 1976, and Mrs. John Sokira, August 7, 1975, Samford University Oral History Collection; life histories of John Gates and Sam Brakefield, Life History Project; oral histories with Luther V. Smith and Elmer Burton.

16. United States, *Report of the Coal Commission*, pp. 1460, 1566.

17. Life history of Sam Brakefield. Other life histories reveal how common clacker was to the mining economy: see life history of John Gates, oral histories with Ila Hendrix and Luther V. Smith.

18. Elliott and Crittenden, *Woodie Roberts*, p. 14.

19. Oral histories with Ila Hendrix, Luther V. Smith, and with James H. Phillips, March 11, 1982, Auburn University Archives.

20. This wonderful description is found in the life history of Mr. and Mrs. Joseph Davis, Life History Project.

21. Oral histories with James H. Phillips and Luther V. Smith.

22. U.S., Census Office, *Twelfth Census of the United States, 1900, Special Report, Occupations* (Washington, D.C.: Government Printing Office, 1904), pp. 222–23; idem, *Fifteenth Census, 1930, Occupations by States*, pp. 109, 118.

23. Oral history with John Gioiello, August 14, 1975, Samford University Oral History Collection.

24. Oral histories with John Sokira and Mrs. John Sokira, August 7, 1975, Samford University Oral History Collection.

25. Quoted in James Seay Brown, Jr., ed., *Up Before Daylight: Life Histories from the Alabama Writers' Project, 1938–1939* (University: University of Alabama Press, 1982), p. 82.

26. Life history of Sam Brakefield; oral history with Ellis Self, July 28, 1975, Samford University Oral History Collection.

27. Carl Elliott, Sr., and Susan Crittenden, *Alabama Coal Miners*, vol. 4, *Lester D. Williams* (Jasper, Ala.: Northwest Alabama Publishing Co., 1978); oral histories with Ellis Self and Elmer Burton; Elliott and Crittenden, *Woodie Roberts*; life history of John Gates.

28. Oral history with Elmer Burton; life history of Sam Cash, Life History Project.

29. Carl Elliott, Sr., and Susan Crittenden, *Alabama Coal Miners*, vol. 1, *William T. Minor* (Jasper, Ala.: Northwest Alabama Publishing Co., 1977); idem, *Woodie Roberts*; life history of Mr. and Mrs. Joseph Davis.

30. Census Office, *Report on Population, 1890*, pp. 530–31; United States, *Report of the Coal Commission*, p. 1424.

31. "Birmingham," *Survey*, p. 1540.

32. Oral history with Elmer Burton.

33. United States, *Report of the Coal Commission*, pp. 1421, 1567.

34. Carl Elliott, Sr., and Susan Crittenden, *Alabama Coal Miners*, vol. 5, *William M. Warren* (Jasper, Ala.: Northwest Alabama Publishing Co., 1979); idem, *Woodie Roberts* and *Alfred J. Renshaw*; *Birmingham News*, October 27, 1985; oral histories with Elmer Burton, James Phillips, and John Sokira.

35. Elliott and Crittenden, *William M. Warren, Alfred J. Renshaw, William T. Minor*, and *Woodie Roberts*; oral histories with Elmer Burton, John Sokira, and Ellis Self; life histories of Mr. and Mrs. Joseph Davis and Sam Brakefield; *Birmingham News*, February 14, 1982, and October 27, 1985.

36. Census Office, *Population, 1920, Vol. IV*, p. 519.

37. For this pattern, see Elliott and Crittenden, *Woodie Roberts* and *Alfred J. Renshaw*.

38. *Birmingham News*, October 27, 1985.

39. Elliott and Crittenden, *Alfred J. Renshaw*; oral history with John Sokira.

40. For the lore of mules in the mine, see oral history with C. D. Patterson, April 28, 1975, Samford University Oral History Collection; Elliott and Crittenden, *Alfred J. Renshaw* and *William T. Minor*; *Birmingham News*, February 14, 1982; Rikard, "Experiment in Welfare Capitalism," p. 49.

41. For excellent technical descriptions, see Elliott and Crittenden, *Alfred J. Renshaw*; and life history of Sam Brakefield.

42. *Birmingham News*, February 14, 1982; life history of John Gates; oral history with C. D. Patterson.

43. Elliott and Crittenden, *Alfred J. Renshaw*; idem, vol. 2, *Herbert South* (Jasper, Ala.: Northwest Alabama Publishing Co., 1978). A majority of the twenty miners surveyed for this study claimed to have contracted black lung, though the medical diagnosis is complicated by the similarity of symptoms to emphysema and tuberculosis. Many of them coughed heavily during tape sessions.

44. Rikard, "Experiment in Welfare Capitalism," quoted on p. 49.

45. *United Mine Workers' Journal*, May 21, 1891; oral history with Luther V. Smith.

46. Alabama, Mine Inspector, *Report of Inspector of Alabama Coal Mines for the Year 1909* (Birmingham: Freret and Grant, 1910), pp. 35–36; idem,

Third Biennial Report of the Inspectors of Mines, 1900 (Birmingham: Dispatch Printing Co., 1900), pp. 71–76; idem, *Report of Inspector of Alabama Mines for the Year 1914* (Birmingham: Dispatch Printing Co., 1914), pp. 34–36.

47. Alabama, Mine Inspector, *Report for the Year 1909*, pp. 41–46.

48. Currie, *Coal-Mine Safety Organizations*, p. 1; Charles S. Perry and Christian Ritter, *Dying to Dig Coal: Fatalities in Deep and Surface Coal Mining in Appalachian States, 1930–1978* (Lexington: Department of Sociology, College of Agriculture, Agricultural Experiment Station, University of Kentucky, 1981), p. 6.

49. Currie, *Coal-Mine Safety Organizations*, pp. 9–10, 14; oral history with Luther V. Smith.

50. Carlton Jackson, *The Dreadful Month* (Bowling Green, Ohio: Bowling Green University Popular Press, 1982), pp. 2, 98–99.

51. Ibid., pp. 77–78.

52. Life history of Bennie Amerson, Life History Project; Elliott and Crittenden, *Alfred J. Renshaw*.

53. Life histories of Bennie Amerson and Sam Brakefield.

54. *Birmingham News*, February 14, 1982; life histories of Sam Brakefield and Mr. and Mrs. Joseph Davis; oral history with Elmer Burton.

55. Oral histories with James H. Phillips, Luther V. Smith, Ellis Self, and John Sokira.

56. Life histories of Sam Brakefield and Mr. and Mrs. Joseph Davis; United States, *Report of the Coal Commission*, pp. 1180–81.

57. Morley, *Characteristics of the Labor Market*, p. 29; Kiessling, "Coal Mining in the South," 84.

58. Oral histories with Mrs. John Sokira, Ila Hendrix, and C. D. Patterson; life history of Mr. and Mrs. Joseph Davis.

59. Elliott and Crittenden, *William T. Minor*; life history of Mr. and Mrs. Joseph Davis. Philip Taft, *Organizing Dixie: Alabama Workers in the Industrial Era*, ed. Gary M. Fink (Westport, Conn.: Greenwood Press, 1981), provides a general survey of Alabama unionism.

60. Currie, *Coal-Mine Safety Organizations*, pp. 5, 12, 14, 16–17, 33.

61. United States, *Report of the Coal Commission*, p. 1052; F. Ray Marshall, *Labor in the South* (Cambridge, Mass.: Harvard University Press, 1967), p. 143.

62. "Birmingham," *Survey*, pp. 1541–42.

63. *Birmingham News*, January 2, 1983

64. I am indebted to John M. Dollar for his insights on the early history of the Greenback-Labor party. This information comes from his essay, "The Greenback-Labor Party in Alabama," a paper read to the Southern/Southwestern Labor History Conference at Arlington, Texas, March 29–31, 1984.

65. Ibid.

66. Ibid.

67. Ward and Rogers, *Labor Revolt in Alabama*, pp. 23–25; Frank M. Duke, "The United Mine Workers of America in Alabama: Industrial Union-

ism and Reform Legislation, 1890–1911" (M.A. thesis, Auburn University, 1979), p. 6.

68. Duke, "United Mine Workers of America in Alabama," pp. 5–6, 53.

69. Ward and Rogers, *Labor Revolt in Alabama*, p. 22; *United Mine Workers Journal*, April 30, 1891.

70. *Birmingham News*, February 14, 1982.

71. Duke, "United Mine Workers of America in Alabama."

72. Ward and Rogers, *Labor Revolt in Alabama*, pp. 71–72, 89.

73. W. A. Pinkerton to Gov. Jones, June 18, 1894, copy in Taft Research Notes; Ward and Rogers, *Labor Revolt in Alabama*, p. 127. For a perceptive essay on black union solidarity and the use of black strikebreakers, see Ronald L. Lewis, "Job Control and Race Relations in Coal Fields, 1870–1920," *Journal of Ethnic Studies* 12 (Winter 1985): 35–64.

74. Duke, "United Mine Workers of America in Alabama," pp. 78–81.

75. Richard A. Straw, "Soldiers and Miners in a Strike Zone: Birmingham, 1908," *Alabama Review* 38 (October 1985): 303; idem, "The Collapse of Biracial Unionism, The Alabama Coal Strike of 1908," *Alabama Historical Quarterly* 37 (Summer 1975): 103; oral history with John Sokira.

76. Straw, "Soldiers and Miners," pp. 295, 300–302.

77. Duke, "United Mine Workers of America in Alabama," pp. 84–86; "Birmingham," *Survey*, p. 1536; Nancy R. Elmore, "The Birmingham Coal Strike of 1908" (M.A. thesis, University of Alabama, 1966), pp. 57–60.

78. Duke, "United Mine Workers of America in Alabama," p. 86; Richard A. Straw, "The United Mine Workers of America and the 1920 Coal Strike in Alabama," *Alabama Review* 28 (April 1975): 105.

79. "Birmingham," *Survey*, pp. 1538–40; oral history with James H. Phillips.

80. *Birmingham News*, February 14, 1982.

81. J. R. Kennamer to John L. Lewis, August 5, 1918, copy in Taft Research Notes; Straw, "United Mine Workers and the 1920 Coal Strike," pp. 105–13; Jimmie F. Gross, "Strikes in the Coal, Steel, and Railroad Industries in Birmingham from 1918 to 1922" (M. A. thesis, Auburn University, 1962), pp. 62–77, 105, 116.

82. Straw, "United Mine Workers and the 1920 Coal Strike," pp. 117–19; *Birmingham News*, October 27, 1985.

83. Quoted in Gross, "Strikes," p. 116.

84. Ibid., pp. 119–26.

85. Straw, "United Mine Workers and the 1920 Coal Strike," pp. 121–22.

86. *Birmingham News*, October 27, 1985; Elliott and Crittenden, *William T. Minor*.

87. Straw, "United Mine Workers and the 1920 Coal Strike," pp. 127–28; life history of Bennie Amerson; Marshall, *Labor in the South*, p. 143.

88. Oral history with Elmer Burton; *Birmingham News*, February 14, 1982.

89. Oral histories with Luther V. Smith, James H. Phillips, and Ila Hendrix.

6. "A MAN THAT'S LUMBERING AS LONG AS ME KNOWS A FEW THINGS": ALABAMA'S TIMBER WORKERS

1. Rev. J. J. Grace to Gov. Robert M. Patton, April 20, 1866, "Destitution" file, Patton Official Files.

2. Wyley D. Ward, *The Folks From Pea Ridge in Covington and Conecuh Counties, Alabama* (Huntsville, Ala.: N.p., 1973), pp. 155, 167–68.

3. Richard W. Massey, Jr., "A History of the Lumber Industry in Alabama and West Florida, 1880–1914" (Ph.D. diss., Vanderbilt University, 1960), p. 37; Ward, *Early History of Covington County*, p. 89.

4. Massey, "History of the Lumber Industry," p. 55. The following discussion of changing technology comes from this excellent Massey work, pp. 55–167.

5. U.S., Census Office, *Special Reports of the Census Office, Manufactures, Part II, States and Territories, 1905* (Washington, D.C.: Government Printing Office, 1907), p. 6; idem, *Fifteenth Census, 1930, Occupations by States*, p. 118.

6. Taft, *Organizing Dixie*, pp. 4, 6.

7. Morley, *Characteristics of the Labor Market*, pp. 13, 26.

8. Census Office, *Report on Population, 1890*, pp. 530–31; idem, *Population, 1910, Vol. IV*, p. 434.

9. Census Office, *Report on Population, 1890*, pp. 530–31; idem, *Population, 1910, Vol. IV*, p. 434; idem, *Population, 1920, Vol. IV*, p. 519.

10. Quoted in Pete Daniel, *The Shadow of Slavery: Peonage in the South, 1901–1969* (London: Oxford University Press, 1973), p. 66.

11. Sara E. O. Stoddard, "An Experiment in Progressivism: Alabama's Crusade Against Peonage, 1900–1915" (M.A. thesis, Auburn University, 1979), p. 16; Daniel, *Shadow of Slavery*, p. 67.

12. Stoddard, "Experiment in Progressivism," pp. 15, 26, 51.

13. Ibid., especially pp. 53–68.

14. Massey, "History of the Lumber Industry," pp. 144–48.

15. Ibid., pp. 130–37.

16. Ibid., pp. 140–42.

17. Ibid., p. 127; *Laborer's Banner* (Brewton, Alabama), September 15, 1900, and May 18, 1901, copies in Taft Research Notes.

18. Life history of George Carter, Life History Project.

19. Oral history with Cecil Spencer, December 20, 1977, in possession of author.

20. Life history of Isaac Johnson, Life History Project.

7. "BAREFOOT MAN AT THE GATE": IRON WORKERS AND APPALACHIAN FARMERS

1. *Birmingham News*, June 20, 1982.

2. U.S., Census Office, *The Statistics of the Population of the United States*,

Tenth Census, 1880 (Washington, D.C.: Government Printing Office, 1883), p. 808; "Workers in Southern Manufactures," *American Federationist*, p. 588; Morley, *Characteristics of the Labor Market*, pp. 26–27.

3. Wright, *Old South, New South*, pp. 172–73.

4. For technical discussions of iron- and steelmaking, see Phillips, *Iron Making in Alabama*, especially pp. 213–23, and White, *Birmingham District*, pp. 49–59.

5. Adamson, *Industrial Activity in Alabama*, pp. 59, 66, 69.

6. Massey, "History of the Lumber Industry," pp. 131, 144; Melton A. McLaurin, *The Knights of Labor in the South* (Westport, Conn.: Greenwood Press, 1978), pp. 26–27.

7. Rikard, "Experiment in Welfare Capitalism," p. 17.

8. "Birmingham," *Survey*, pp. 1528–29.

9. Ibid., p. 1532.

10. Rikard, "Experiment in Welfare Capitalism," pp. 17, 66, 161–64.

11. Eleanor De La Vergne Risley, *The Road to Wildcat: A Tale of Southern Mountaineering* (Boston: Little, Brown, and Co., 1930), p. 40.

12. Oral history with Lillie Mae Beason.

13. Harper, "The Wind is From the East," pp. 116–40, 211.

14. Olive Dame Campbell, "First Mountain Teaching, Joppa, Alabama, 1815–1898," in *The Life and Work of John Charles Campbell, September 15, 1868–May 2, 1919* (Madison, Wis.: N.p., 1968), pp. 51–53, 60–61, 71, 76.

15. Copy of speech ms., "Series of Writings, Joppa, Ala. [1895–98]," File 128, John C. Campbell Papers, Southern History Collection.

16. Campbell Long, *The House of Happiness* (Selma: Selma Printing Co., 1973), pp. 84, 86.

17. Ibid., pp. 1–2, 11, 14–16.

18. Ibid., pp. 19–20.

19. "Moonshining as a Fine Art," in *The Foxfire Book*, ed. Eliot Wigginton (Garden City, N.Y.: Doubleday, 1972), pp. 301–45.

20. William F. Holmes, "Moonshining and Law Enforcement in Turn of the Century Alabama," in *Perspectives on the American South: An Annual Review of Society, Politics and Culture*, vol. 1, ed. Merle Black and John Shelton Reed (New York: Gordon and Breach Science Publishers, 1981), pp. 71–72.

21. Ibid., p. 73.

22. Ibid., p. 77.

23. William F. Holmes, "Moonshiners and Whitecaps in Alabama, 1893," *Alabama Review* 34 (January 1981): 32–38.

24. Oral history with Frank Uptain.

25. Life history of Charley Ryland, Life History Project.

26. Life history of Jim Lauderdale, Life History Project.

27. Life history of Orrie Robinson.

28. Long, *House of Happiness*, p. 80.

29. Risley, *Road to Wildcat*, p. 40; Harper, "The Wind is From the East," pp. 118–19.

8. "WE AIN'T LOW-DOWN": POOR WHITE SOCIETY

1. Charles M. Wilson, *The Landscape of Rural Poverty: Corn Bread and Creek Water* (New York: Henry Holt and Co., 1940), p. 186.

2. Garrett, *Horse and Buggy Days*, p. 91.

3. Life history of M. B. Truitt; oral histories with James H. Phillips and Kathleen Knight; Harper, "The Wind is From the East," p. 211.

4. Elizabeth W. Etheridge, *The Butterfly Caste: A Social History of Pellagra in the South* (Westport, Conn.: Greenwood Press, 1972), pp. 7–8.

5. Ibid., pp. 70–72, 116, 121–28, 131, 138.

6. Ibid., pp. 115–16, 133, 135, 143–45, 192.

7. Ibid., pp. 207–10, 216–17.

8. George A. Denison, "The History of Public Health in Alabama," ms., 1951, p. 20, Alabama State Archives.

9. J. H. McCormick, "Public Health," in Edward N. Clopper, ed., *Child Welfare in Alabama: An Inquiry by the National Child Labor Committee Under the Auspices and with the Cooperation of the University of Alabama* (New York: National Child Labor Committee, 1918), pp. 46, 57.

10. Oral history with Kathleen Knight; life history of Orrie Robinson.

11. Long, *House of Happiness*, pp. 8, 77; Harper, "The Wind is From the East," p. 239; Home Demonstration Annual State Report, 1926, p. 180.

12. John Ettling, *The Germ of Laziness: Rockefeller Philanthropy and Public Health in the New South* (Cambridge, Mass.: Harvard University Press, 1981), pp. 3–5. Other useful insights can be found in the work of Charles W. Stiles, who was the pioneer in finding the cause and cure of hookworm. For samples of his work, much of which is applicable to Alabama, see: "Early History, in Part Esoteric, of the Hookworm (Uncinariasis) Campaign in Our Southern United States," *Journal of Parasitology* 25 (August 1939): 283–308; *Hookworm Disease (or Ground-Itch Anemia): Its Nature, Treatment, and Prevention* (Washington, D.C.: Government Printing Office, 1910); *Report on the Prevalence and Geographic Distribution of Hookworm in the United States*, Hygienic Laboratory Bulletin no. 10 (Washington, D.C.: U.S. Public Health and Marine Hospital Service, 1903); *Soil Pollution as a Cause of Ground Itch, Hookworm Disease, and Dirt Eating*, R.S.C. Publication no. 1 (Washington, D.C.: R.S.C., 1910); and "Some Recent Investigations into the Prevalence of Hookworm Among Children," in *Child Conference for Research and Welfare, Proceedings, Volume II* (New York: G. E. Stechert and Co., 1910).

13. Robert W. Twyman, "The Clay Eater: A New Look at an Old Southern Enigma," *Journal of Southern History* 37 (August 1971): 439–48. Perhaps the most notable example of the continuing fascination of Americans in clay eating as an aspect of southern folk culture is revealed in the major attention given the 1986 Philadelphia symposium by the *New York Times* (see the *New York Times*, July 22, 1986).

14. Denison, "History of Public Health in Alabama," pp. 17, 20–21.

15. Ettling, *Germ of Laziness*, pp. 143, 215–16; McCormick, "Public Health," p. 11.

16. Ettling, *Germ of Laziness*, pp. 209–10.

17. Denison, "History of Public Health in Alabama," p. 21; McCormick, "Public Health," p. 20.

18. Terry and Sims, *They Live on the Land*, p. 121.

19. Oral history with Lillie Mae Beason.

20. Long, *House of Happiness*, pp. 20, 38.

21. Ibid., p. 19; Home Demonstration Annual State Report, 1926, p. 180.

22. Terry and Sims, *They Live on the Land*, p. 120; Denison, "History of Public Health in Alabama," p. 22.

23. Denison, "History of Public Health in Alabama," p. 22; Rikard, "Experiment in Welfare Capitalism," p. 181.

24. Denison, "History of Public Health in Alabama," p. 20; McCormick, "Public Health," p. 44; Long, *House of Happiness*, p. 77.

25. McCormick, "Public Health," p. 12; oral histories with Carlie Crocker and with James H. Flynt, December 27, 1981, in possession of author.

26. See earlier chapters dealing with textile workers and coal miners. The following oral histories with textile workers contain references to brown lung: Andrew McClain, Annie Burrow, Pauline Brewer, and Carter Priest. For black lung, see oral history with Frank Uptain, and see Elliott and Crittenden, *Herbert South* and *Alfred J. Renshaw*.

27. Oral histories with Frank Uptain, Lillie Mae Beason, and Carlie Crocker; life histories of Mrs. Sam Anderson and Orrie Robinson; Harper, "The Wind is From the East," p. 103. For a more detailed description of Alabama folk medicine, see Jack Solomon and Olivia Solomon, *Cracklin' Bread and Asfidity* (University: University of Alabama Press, 1979).

28. Oral history with Carter Priest.

29. Oral histories with Ila Hendrix and Lillie Mae Beason; Nixon, *Possum Trot*, p. 49; Terry and Sims, *They Live on the Land*, pp. 124–25.

30. Denison, "History of Public Health in Alabama," p. 10.

31. Rikard, "Experiment in Welfare Capitalism," pp. 183, 225.

32. Glenn Sisk, "The Poor in Provincial Alabama," *Alabama Historical Quarterly* 22 (Spring and Summer 1960): 101–02.

33. "Birmingham," *Survey*, pp. 1503–04.

34. Jennings, "Almshouses in Alabama," p. 16.

35. Ibid., pp. 15–22.

36. Elizabeth Rowe, "Alabama's Disappearing Almshouses" (M. A. thesis, Tulane University, 1946), p. 11.

37. Jennings, "Almshouses in Alabama," pp. 26, 30, 34, 38.

38. U.S., Manuscript Census, Population, 1880, Calhoun County; transcript of interview with Lillian Ward Duncan, by Myra W. Crenshaw, May 1982, in "Butler County, People–Personalities" file, Alabama State Archives.

39. "Records of Inmates of Poor Farm, 1910," ms. in Birmingham Public Library Archives.

40. "Inmates of Asylum for the Poor, Mobile County, Alabama," log kept

by John Simmons, superintendent of Mobile Almshouse, approximately 1897–1914; in possession of Mrs. Helen Wilson, Mobile, Alabama.

41. Rowe, "Alabama's Disappearing Almshouses," pp. 14–27.

42. "Birmingham," *Survey,* p. 1502.

43. Alabama, *Laws for the Relief of Needy Confederate Soldiers and Sailors, 1911* (Montgomery: Brown Printing Co., 1911), pp. 16–17.

44. For a more complete discussion of dogtrots, single-pen, double-pen, and saddlebag houses, see Eugene M. Wilson, *Alabama Folk Houses* (Montgomery: Alabama Historical Commission, 1975).

45. Harper, "The Wind is From the East," p. 239; Long, *House of Happiness,* p. 82. For romantic descriptions of the dogtrot and saddlebag houses that sheltered sharecroppers, see James Agee and Walker Evans, *Let Us Now Praise Famous Men* (New York: Ballantine Books, 1973), pp. 129–30, and Carl Carmer, *Stars Fell on Alabama* (University: University of Alabama Press, reprint edition, 1985), p. 38.

46. Long, *House of Happiness,* p. 77; Elliott and Crittenden, *William M. Warren,* p. 43; life histories of Isaac Johnson and "Bull" Elliott and of Henry Kelly, Life History Project; oral histories with Kathleen Knight and W. W. Jewell.

47. Mel McKiven, "The Household Composition of Working Class Families in the Birmingham District, 1900," December 19, 1983, ms. in possession of author. I am grateful to Mr. McKiven for sharing this excellent essay. Oral history with W. W. Jewell.

48. Quoted in McKiven, "Household Composition," pp. 3–4.

49. Oral history with June W. Odom.

50. Ibid., and oral histories with Frank Uptain, Lillie Mae Beason, Ila Hendrix, and Carl Forrester.

51. Oral histories with June W. Odom and Lillie Mae Beason.

52. Long, *House of Happiness,* p. 83; oral history with Carl Forrester; Carmer, *Stars Fell on Alabama,* pp. 35–48.

53. Oral history with Lillie Mae Beason.

54. Oral histories with James H. Phillips and Luther V. Smith.

55. Oral history with Carlie Crocker.

56. Oral history with Carl Forrester.

57. Ibid.

58. Oral histories with Lillie Mae Beason, W. W. Jewell and Kathleen Knight.

59. For instances of children's becoming coal miners at the urging of fathers, see Elliott and Crittenden, *William T. Minor, William M. Warren, Alfred J. Renshaw,* and *Woodie Roberts.*

60. Van Vorst, *Cry of the Children,* pp. 46, 55, 64, 67–68, 84–86.

61. Unidentified clipping, February 7, 1901, in vol. 1 of Edgar Gardner Murphy Papers, Southern History Collection; J. Howard Nichols to Editor, the (Boston) *Evening Transcript,* October 30, 1901, clipping in vol. 1 in Murphy Papers.

62. Irene M. Ashby-Macfayden, *Child Labor in Alabama,* Document no. 1, Report of the Executive Committee of the State on the History of Child

Labor Legislation in Alabama (Montgomery: July 1901), p. 10; pamphlet in Edgar Gardner Murphy Scrapbooks, vol. 1, in Murphy Papers.

63. McKiven, "Household Composition," pp. 9–10.

64. Census Office, *Statistics of the Population, 1880,* p. 920; idem, *Report on Population, 1890,* p. xxxix; idem, *Population, 1900,* p. ciii; idem, *Population, 1920, Vol. II,* p. 1175; Alabama, State Department of Education, *Literacy and Illiteracy in Alabama: Biennial Census, 1914* (Montgomery: State Department of Education, 1914), pp. 26–27. Rates of illiteracy in 1920 for the ten sample counties used for my analysis were: Calhoun, 7.9; Cleburne, 11.5; Clay, 7.4; Randolph, 7.3; Winston, 9.5; Jackson, 11.9; Cherokee, 12.1; Covington, 9.1; Crenshaw, 7.9; and Geneva, 11.5. By comparison the rates in the Black Belt counties were: Dallas, 1.7; Lowndes, 2.4; and Montgomery, 1.1. See Census Office, *Population, 1920, Vol. III,* pp. 59–65.

65. Alabama, State Department of Education, *Annual Report, 1913* (Montgomery: Brown Printing Co., 1913), p. 34.

66. Head, "Development of the Labor Movement," p. 64.

67. Oral history with Lillie Mae Beason.

68. Oral history with June W. Odom.

69. Oral history with W. W. Jewell.

70. Interview with Mrs. W. Albert Smith, May 16, 1982, Auburn, Alabama.

71. Life history with Mr. and Mrs. Joseph Davis.

72. Oral histories with Pauline Brewer, Carlie Crocker, and Mrs. L. A. House; life history of Julia Rhodes; Elliott and Crittenden, *William M. Warren*; *Birmingham News,* February 14, 1982; Walls, "Folklore and Folk Life," p. 70.

73. Long, *House of Happiness,* p. 28.

74. The twenty-three families I surveyed represented a cross section of tenant, mining, textile, and lumbering families. In some cases, the life histories/oral histories listed brothers and sisters, and at other times they listed the number of children. I tabulated both sets of figures where it was clear that both sets were poor. The histories used in this analysis were: Alexander, Beason, Brakefield, Cash, Crocker, Davis, Elliott, Hendrix, Johnson, Knight, Minor, Renshaw, Rhodes, Roberts, South, Truitt, Uptain, Warren, Williams (two families), and Wilson. In two cases, I tabulated both brothers/sisters and children, providing the total of twenty-three. The largest family had twenty-two children, the smallest had two.

75. Terry and Sims, *They Live on the Land,* p. 123.

76. McKiven, "Household Composition," pp. 11–12.

77. Alabama Farm Tenancy Committee, *Farm Tenancy in Alabama,* p. 13.

78. Oral histories with Lillie Mae Beason and Carlie Crocker.

79. Oral history with Lillie Mae Beason.

80. Ibid.

81. Life histories of John Gates, Julia Rhodes, and Sam Cash.

82. Federal Writers' Project, *These Are Our Lives* (Chapel Hill: University of North Carolina Press, 1939), pp. 399–403.

83. Life histories of Sam Cash and Orrie Robinson; oral history with W. W. Jewell.

84. Harper, "The Wind is From the East," p. 150; McKiven, "Household Composition," p. 8; oral history with June W. Odom.

85. Oral history with Carlie Crocker.

86. Oral history with Lillie Mae Beason.

87. Oral history with Pauline Brewer; Long, *House of Happiness,* p. 2; "Birmingham," *Survey,* p. 1521.

88. Life histories of Mr. and Mrs. Joseph Davis and Isaac Johnson; oral histories with Mrs. L. A. House and W. W. Jewell.

89. Oral history with Pauline Brewer.

90. Walls, "Folklore and Folk Life," p. 70.

91. Harper, "The Wind is From the East," pp. 191–92, 194, 205–06, 233.

92. Life history of Mr. and Mrs. Tom Alsobrook.

93. McKiven, "Household Composition," p. 4.

94. Life history of Joseph Davis; oral histories with Lillie Mae Beason and James H. Flynt.

95. Oral history with Carlie Crocker.

96. Mrs. Isaac B. Ulmer to Isaac B. Ulmer, November 24, 1894, Ulmer Papers.

97. Glover Moore, Jr., *A Calhoun County, Alabama, Boy in the 1860s* (Jackson: University Press of Mississippi, 1978), p. 27.

98. Oral history with Mrs. L. A. House; Nelwyn H. Dill, "Monument to Willie," *Atlanta Weekly,* November 27, 1983, pp. 75–81—a greatly exaggerated, though useful, article.

99. Edgar L. Lipscomb to Ben Lipscomb, October 2, 1912; Edgar L. Lipscomb to Ben Lipscomb, 1912; Lipscomb Papers.

100. Notes from March 1884, Dr. Edward Palmer, "Alabama Notes," Alabama State Archives.

101. John A. Salmond, *A Southern Rebel: The Life and Times of Aubrey Willis Williams, 1890–1965* (Chapel Hill: University of North Carolina Press, 1983), pp. 3–11.

102. Oral history with W. W. Jewell; life history of Mrs. Champion.

103. Life history of Jim Lauderdale. Other accounts of whiskey making can be found in the life histories of Henry Kelly, Bennie Amerson, Sam Cash, and George Carter, as well as in the oral histories with Frank Uptain and James H. Flynt.

104. Long, *House of Happiness,* pp. 1–2, 72.

105. Life history of George Carter.

106. Life history of Neeley Williams, Life History Project.

107. Life history of Orrie Robinson.

9. "OUT OF THE DUST": POOR FOLKS' CULTURE

1. Oral history with W. W. Jewell.

2. Oral history with June W. Odom.

3. Life history of Jim Lauderdale.

4. For an essay exploring the class origins of "whitecapping," see William F. Holmes, "Whitecapping: Agrarian Violence in Mississippi, 1902–1906," *Journal of Southern History* 35 (May 1969): 165–85.

5. W. A. Pinkerton to Gov. Thomas G. Jones, March 29, 1894; copy in Taft Research Notes.

6. *Huntsville Mercury*, July 25, 1900.

7. Oral history with Cecil Spencer.

8. See Dan Carter, *Scottsboro: A Tragedy of the American South* (Baton Rouge: Louisiana State University Press, 1969); and Cason, *90° in the Shade*, p. 120.

9. Harper Lee, *To Kill a Mockingbird* (Philadelphia: J. B. Lippincott Co., 1960), especially pp. 90–211.

10. Quoted in Salmond, *Southern Rebel*, pp. 279–80.

11. Newman I. White, *American Negro Folk-Songs* (Hatboro, Pa.: Folklore Associates, 1965), p. 197.

12. Harper, "The Wind is From the East," p. 162.

13. *Alabama Baptist*, September 9, 1897.

14. Life history of George Carter; Salmond, *Southern Rebel*, pp. 5–6.

15. I am grateful to my colleague, Professor Ward Allen, for sharing this incident with me from his experience on jury duty in February 1983.

16. *Birmingham Post-Herald*, February 23, 1983.

17. Robert Darnton, *The Great Cat Massacre and Other Episodes in French Cultural History* (New York: Vintage Books, 1985), is an excellent example of the intelligent use of folklore to reconstruct peasant culture.

18. Ray B. Browne, *"A Night with the Hants" and Other Alabama Folk Experiences* (Bowling Green, Ohio: Popular Press, n.d.), pp. 1–4. A number of Browne's storytellers are identified as uneducated, poor, or indigent (see pp. 232–38). Of some sixty informants, all but four were white.

19. Long, *House of Happiness, pp. 28–29*.

20. Harper, "The Wind is From the East," p. 164; Long, *House of Happiness*, p. 73; Ray B. Browne, *Popular Beliefs and Practices from Alabama*, Folklore Studies no. 9 (Berkeley and Los Angeles: University of California Press, 1958); pp. 205–23 deal entirely with weather signs. Only six of the more than one hundred informants to this volume were black. However, the weather lore seems to be common to all farmers, black and white, because no matter their financial resources, they could not control the weather.

21. Browne, *"A Night with the Hants,"* p. 108.

22. Browne, *Popular Beliefs and Practices*, pp. 32–129.

23. Ibid., p. 9; Mrs. Mary Tutwiler, "Mountain People," *Tennessee Folklore Society Bulletin* 26 (December 1960); 87.

24. *Birmingham Post-Herald*, February 23, 1983.

25. Browne, *"A Night with the Hants,"* pp. 113–14.

26. Ray B. Browne, *The Alabama Folk Lyric: A Study in Origins and Media of Dissemination* (Bowling Green, Ohio: Bowling Green University Popular

Press, 1979), pp. 338–39.

27. Ibid., pp. 371–73.

28. Ibid., pp. 384–85.

29. Ibid., pp. 152–53.

30. S. M. Taylor, "A Preliminary Survey of Folk-Lore in Alabama" (M.A. thesis, University of Alabama, 1925), p. 54.

31. Harper, "The Wind is From the East," p. 164.

32. For dozens of examples, see Browne, *"A Night with the Hants,"* especially pp. 86–87; and idem, *Popular Beliefs and Practices,* pp. 184–201. See also Jack Solomon and Olivia Solomon, *Ghosts and Goosebumps: Ghost Stories, Tall Tales, and Superstitions from Alabama* (University: University of Alabama Press, 1981).

33. Long, *House of Happiness,* p. 29.

34. Tutwiler, "Mountain People," p. 88.

35. Nixon, *Lower Piedmont Country,* pp. 109–10.

36. Edgar L. Lipscomb to Ben Lipscomb, October 2, 1912, Lipscomb Papers.

37. Edgar L. Lipscomb to Ben Lipscomb, 1912; Lipscomb Papers.

38. Oral history with James H. Flynt.

39. Oral histories with Ila Hendrix, Lillie Mae Beason, and Mrs. L. A. House.

40. Oral history with Lillie Mae Beason.

41. Ibid. For an excellent example of folk toys that circulated widely in Alabama, see Florence H. Pettit, *How To Make Whirligigs and Whimmy Diddles and Other American Folkcraft Objects* (New York: Thomas Y. Crowell Co., 1972). James H. Flynt, in addition to his skill as a storyteller, makes excellent peach-seed monkeys.

42. Home Demonstration Annual State Report, 1927.

43. Nixon, *Lower Piedmont Country,* pp. 135–37.

44. Long, *House of Happiness,* pp. 70, 73, 84.

45. Terry and Sims, *They Live on the Land,* p. 47; oral history with Mrs. L. A. House.

46. Taylor, "Preliminary Survey of Folk-Lore," pp. 63–67. The issue of middle class teachers hiding in the bathroom to record Appalachian ballads raises issues of conflicting cultural values, even cultural colonialism. For the implications of such cultural clashes, see David E. Whisnant, *All That Is Native and Fine: The Politics of Culture in an American Region* (Chapel Hill: University of North Carolina Press, 1983).

47. The leading authority on southern folk music and musicians is Bill Malone, whose books fully develop the various transitions in folk music: *Country Music, U.S.A.* (Austin: University of Texas Press, 1968); *Southern Music/American Music* (Lexington: University Press of Kentucky, 1979); and *Stars of Country Music: Uncle Dave Macon to Johnny Rodriguez* (Urbana: University of Illinois Press, 1975).

48. Carmer, *Stars Fell on Alabama,* pp. 43–44.

49. Ibid., pp. 49–57. For a fuller discussion, see the classic work on the

subject by George P. Jackson, *White Spirituals in the Southern Uplands: The Story of the Fasola Folk, Their Songs, Singings, and "Buckwheat Notes"* (Chapel Hill: University of North Carolina Press, 1933). For a wonderful account by two longtime Fasola singers, see oral history with Walter and Nora Parker, April 22, 1976, Samford University Oral History Collection. Additional accounts of the importance of dances and singings in poor white culture can be found in: Harper, "The Wind is From the East," pp. 110–11; Long, *House of Happiness*, p. 83; oral histories with Lillie Mae Beason and June W. Odom.

50. Roger M. Williams, *Sing a Sad Song: The Life of Hank Williams* (New York: Ballantine Books, 1970), pp. 8–13.

51. Irwin Stambler and Grenlun Landon, "Hank Williams," *Encyclopedia of Folk, Country and Western Music* (New York: St. Martin's Press, 1969), p. 333.

52. Jack Hurst, *Nashville's Grand Ole Opry* (New York: Harry N. Abrams, 1975), pp. 175–77.

53. Ibid., p. 177.

54. *Birmingham Post-Herald*, June 12, 1981.

55. D. K. Wilgus, "Country-Western Music and the Urban Hillbilly," *Journal of American Folklore* 83 (April–June 1970); 172–73.

56. For the class issues in the Primitive Baptist–Missionary Baptist conflict, see two articles by Bertram Wyatt-Brown: "The Antimission Movement in the Jacksonian South: A Study in Regional Folk Culture," *Journal of Southern History* 36 (November 1970): 501–29, and "Religion and the Formation of Folk Culture: Poor Whites of the Old South," in *The Americanization of the Gulf Coast, 1803–1850*, ed. Lucius F. Ellsworth (Pensacola, Fla.: Historic Preservation Board, 1972), pp. 20–33.

57. Edmund des. Brunner, *Church Life in the Rural South* (New York: George H. Doran Co., 1923), pp. 22, 48; Charles M. McConnell, "Farm Tenants and Sharecroppers," *Missionary Review of the World* 60 (June 1937): 288.

58. L. G. Wilson et al., "The Church and Landless Men," *University of North Carolina Extension Bulletin* 1 (March 1, 1922): 8–10.

59. J. W. Jent, *The Challenge of the Country Church* (Nashville: Sunday School Board, 1924), p. 85.

60. Victor I. Masters, *Country Church in the South* (Atlanta: Publicity Department of the Home Mission Board of the Southern Baptist Convention, 1916), p. 143.

61. See oral histories with Mrs. L. A. House, Lillie Mae Beason, and W. W. Jewell; life history of Sam Anderson, Life History Project.

62. Life histories of "Bull" Elliott, M. B. Truitt, and Isaac Johnson; oral history with Kathleen Knight.

63. Terry and Sims, *They Live on the Land*, p. 149.

64. Ibid., pp. 180, 187.

65. Kennamer, *History of Jackson County*, p. 83; life histories of Sam Anderson and Jim Lauderdale; Nixon, *Possum Trot*, p. 55.

66. Nixon, *Lower Piedmont Country*, pp. 84–85, 89.

67. Campbell, *Life and Work of John Charles Campbell*, pp. 54–55.

68. Long, *House of Happiness*, p. 11.

69. A number of Alabama poor whites cited company support of pastor's salaries and church budgets; oral histories with Cecil Spencer, Pauline Brewer, W. W. Jewell, Mrs. L. A. House, and Luther V. Smith.

70. *Birmingham News*, October 27, 1985.

71. Life history of Sam Cash.

72. *Birmingham News*, February 14, 1982.

73. Elmer M. Crews, Jr., "Pentecostal Religion: The Social Origins of the Church of God" (M.A. thesis, Auburn University, 1983), pp. 73–112.

74. Browne, *"A Night with the Hants,"* pp. 6–7.

75. Ibid., pp. 101–02, 114.

76. Life history of George Carter.

10. "THE FIGHT IS NOT SOCIAL": THE POLITICS OF POVERTY

1. Allen J. Going, *Bourbon Democracy in Alabama, 1874–1890* (University: University of Alabama Press, 1951), pp. 191–210.

2. Ibid., pp. 93, 99, 118–20. Wiener, *Social Origins of the New South*. The major debate concerning the Redeemers was whether they were new leaders inclined toward industrialism or the older planter elite battling against manufacturing. See Wiener, *Social Origins of the New South*, and James T. Moore, "Redeemers Reconsidered: Change and Continuity in the Democratic South, 1870–1900," *Journal of Southern History* 44 (August 1978): 357–78.

3. See Michael J. Daniel, "Red Hills and Piney Woods: A Political History of Butler County, Alabama, in the Nineteenth Century" (Ph.D. diss., University of Alabama, 1985).

4. Quoted in Rogers, *One-Gallused Rebellion*, p. 125. For an excellent discussion of the Alabama Grange, Wheel, and Farmers' Alliance in the state, see ibid., pp. 56–79, 121–46.

5. Quoted in ibid., p. 127.

6. Ibid., pp. 128–31.

7. Dollar, "Greenback-Labor Party."

8. See Frances C. Roberts, "William Manning Lowe and the Greenback Party in Alabama," *Alabama Review* 5 (April 1952): 100–121.

9. See Gerald L. Roush, "Aftermath of Reconstruction: Race, Violence, and Politics in Alabama, 1874–1884" (M.A. thesis, Auburn University, 1973), pp. 200–224.

10. *Montgomery Workingmen's Advocate*, March 2, 1879.

11. Roush, "Aftermath of Reconstruction," pp. 242–89.

12. Ibid., pp. 295–356.

13. John H. Abernathy, Jr., "The Knights of Labor in Alabama" (M.A.

thesis, University of Alabama, 1960), pp. 24–26; McLaurin, *Knights of Labor,* pp. 21–27.

14. Head, "Development of the Labor Movement," pp. 46–52.

15. Ibid., p. 75.

16. Ibid., pp. 69–70; Rogers, *One-Gallused Rebellion,* pp. 165–66.

17. Abernathy, "Knights of Labor," pp. 85—86.

18. For the Farmers' Alliance and its evangelical roots in southern rural culture, see Robert C. McMath, Jr., *Populist Vanguard: A History of the Southern Farmers' Alliance* (Chapel Hill: University of North Carolina Press, 1975).

19. Quoted in Karl Rodabaugh, "Agrarian Ideology and the Farmers' Revolt in Alabama," *Alabama Review* 36 (July 1983): 196–212.

20. Quoted in Rogers, *One-Gallused Rebellion,* pp. 138–39.

21. Ibid., pp. 213–26, 242.

22. Ibid., pp. 243, 271–90; See also Ward and Rogers, *Labor Revolt in Alabama.*

23. Sheldon Hackney, *Populism to Progressivism in Alabama* (Princeton: Princeton University Press, 1969), pp. 71–81.

24. The debate over the nature of Populism is even more complicated than the movement itself, proving that historians can obfuscate history more thoroughly than its actual participants. Lawrence C. Goodwyn, *Democratic Promise: The Populist Movement in America* (New York: Oxford University Press, 1976); Schwartz, *Radical Protest;* Bruce Palmer, *"Man Over Money": The Southern Populist Critique of American Capitalism* (Chapel Hill: University of North Carolina Press, 1980); and C. Vann Woodward, *Origins of the New South, 1877–1913* (Baton Rouge: Louisiana State University Press, 1951), attribute the source of agrarian unrest to class cohesion and class conflict. Hahn, *Roots of Southern Populism,* and idem, "Common Right and Commonwealth: The Stock-Law Struggle and the Roots of Southern Populism," in Kousser and McPherson, *Region, Race, and Reconstruction;* Barton C. Shaw, *The Wool Hat Boys: Georgia's Populist Party* (Baton Rouge: Louisiana State University Press, 1984); and James Turner, "Understanding the Populists," *Journal of American History* 67 (September 1980): 353–73, all contend that Populism was not so much the product of economic hard times as of rural isolation. Whatever its applicability to individual counties in Texas and Georgia, their model does not fit Alabama, where economic issues fueled the Populist rebellion. Rogers (*One-Gallused Rebellion*) attributes Populism to sharecropping, the crop lien, and spiraling labor unrest among miners. Hackney, *Populism to Progressivism,* attributes it to increasing rates of farm tenancy.

25. Rogers, *One-Gallused Rebellion,* pp. 3–30; Hackney, *Populism to Progressivism,* pp. 25–26.

26. Thomas K. Hearn, "The Populist Movement in Marshall County" (M.A. thesis, University of Alabama, 1935), pp. 16, 19–21, 60.

27. Henry P. Martin, "A History of Politics in Clay County During the Period of Populism from 1888 to 1896" (M. A. thesis, University of Alabama, 1936), pp. 42, 47.

28. Grace Hooten Gates, *The Model City of the New South: Anniston, Alabama, 1872–1900* (Huntsville, Ala.: Strode Publishers, 1978), p. 249.

29. *Dothan Eagle Centennial*, November 11, 1985. Although not based precisely on this incident, Dothan novelist Douglas F. Bailey wrote an excellent novel that centers on the exploitation of poor whites by town merchants: *Devil Make a Third* (New York: E. P. Dutton and Co., 1948).

30. The second appendix explains these data more completely. My data for this summary come from two sources: George P. Harrison, "Voters and Political Affiliations Record, 1897," ms. in Auburn University Archives; and U.S. Manuscript Census, Agriculture, 1880, Geneva County. Harrison was the congressman representing Alabama's Third Congressional District in the 54th Congress (1895–97) and apparently compiled this list of party affiliations in anticipation of the 1898 congressional elections.

31. Hackney, *Populism to Progressivism*, pp. 206–08; J. Morgan Kousser, *The Shaping of Southern Politics: Suffrage Restriction and the Establishment of the One-Party South, 1880–1910* (New Haven, Conn.: Yale University Press, 1974), pp. 48–65, 133–35, 166–67.

32. Terry and Sims, *They Live on the Land*, p. 75.

33. Allen W. Jones, "Political Reforms of the Progressive Era," *Alabama Review* 21 (July 1968): 179–80; J. Mills Thornton III, "Alabama Politics, J. Thomas Heflin, and the Expulsion Movement of 1929," *Alabama Review* 21 (April 1968): 83, 112.

34. Berney, *Hand-Book of Alabama*, p. 464.

35. Duke, "United Mine Workers of America in Alabama," pp. 8–23.

36. Ibid., pp. 28–36; for a complete history, see Ward and Rogers, *Labor Revolt in Alabama*; Harold J. Goldstein, "Labor Unrest in the Birmingham District, 1871–1894" (M.A. thesis, University of Alabama, 1951), pp. 72–73; Head, "Development of the Labor Movement," p. 161.

37. Goldstein, "Labor Unrest," pp. 75–87.

38. Duke, "United Mine Workers of America in Alabama," pp. 59–93; Taft, *Organizing Dixie*, pp. 31–32, 45–55.

39. Elliott and Crittenden, *William T. Minor*, p. 30.

40. *Birmingham News*, June 20, 1982.

41. Carl Harris, *Political Power in Birmingham, 1871–1921* (Knoxville: University of Tennessee Press, 1977), pp. 63, 124, 172–73, 217–27.

42. Gross, "Strikes," p. 22.

43. Gates, *Model City*, p. 154.

44. Herbert G. Gutman, "Black Coal Miners and the Greenback-Labor Party in Redeemer Alabama, 1878–1879," *Labor History* 10 (Summer 1969): 506–35; Taft, *Organizing Dixie*, pp. 54–55; Ward and Rogers, *Labor Revolt in Alabama*.

45. Dr. Edward Palmer, "Alabama Notes," Alabama State Archives.

46. Quoted in Head, "Development of the Labor Movement," p. 30.

47. McLaurin, *Knights of Labor*, pp. 60, 138, 146.

48. See Paul B. Worthman, "Black Workers and Labor Unions in Birmingham, Alabama, 1897–1904," *Labor History* 10 (Summer 1969): 375–407.

49. *American Federationist* 8 (May 1901): 181; *Locomotive Firemen's Magazine* (February 1897): 125.

50. Samuel Gompers to David U. Williams, February 16, 1903; Gompers to H. E. Sandle, March 19, 1903; copies in Taft Research Notes.

51. *Laborer's Banner,* February 1, 1902, copy in Taft Research Notes.

52. Harris, *Political Power in Birmingham,* pp. 172–73.

53. Duke, "United Mine Workers of America in Alabama," p. 86.

54. Quoted in Gross, "Strikes," p. 116.

55. Noel R. Beddow to Philip Murray, July 14, 1943; copy in Taft Research Notes.

56. Francis J. Haas to J. N. Gruser, June 2, 1943; Haas to Malcolm Ross, March 6, 1944; copies in Taft Research Notes.

57. Nixon, *Lower Piedmont Country,* p. 77.

58. Shirley Garrett Schoonover, "Alabama's Quest for Social Justice During the Progressive Era" (M. A. thesis, Auburn University, 1970), pp. 105–06, 111.

59. Denison, "History of Public Health in Alabama," pp. 19, 26–30.

60. Schoonover, "Alabama's Quest for Social Justice," p. 109; Hart, *Social Problems of Alabama,* p. 330.

61. Mine Reports, October 13, November 18, November 23, 1903; January 26, 1904; J. M. Gray to F. H. Gafford, January 30, 1904; all in State Mine Inspector Reports, 1904–1906, AAR 3, Box 4, Alabama State Archives.

62. J. M. Gray to F. H. Gafford, March 8, 1904, State Mine Inspector, Reports, 1904–1906.

63. Interrogations of Joseph Hoskins, P. R. Jordan, A. W. Reed, and F. H. Gafford, Report to R. M. Cunningham, Acting Governor, March 16, 1905, State Mine Inspector Reports, 1904–1906.

64. M. M. Kuffner to J. M. Gray, March 1906, State Mine Inspector Reports, 1904–1906.

65. J. M. Gray to Gov. B. B. Comer, April 8 and June 18, 1907, State Mine Inspector Reports, 1904–1906. For another excellent case study, see Robert D. Ward and William W. Rogers, *Convicts, Coal, and the Banner Mine Tragedy* (Tuscaloosa: University of Alabama Press, 1987).

66. "Reginal Dawson Diaries, 1883–1897," Alabama State Archives.

67. Life history of Jim Lauderdale; oral histories with Kathleen Knight and with E. H. Moore, November 26, 1975, Samford University Oral History Collection.

68. Schoonover, "Alabama's Quest for Social Justice," pp. 22–23.

69. Hackney, *Populism to Progressivism,* pp. 144–45, 264–65, 270–72, 302.

70. Census Office, *Population, 1910, Vol. IV,* 75.

71. Ashby-Macfayden, "Fight Against Child Labor," pp. 150–57; also see *American Federationist* 8 (November 1901).

72. See Ashby-Macfayden, *Child Labor in Alabama.*

73. Edgar Gardner Murphy to Editor, *Montgomery Advertiser,* October 11, February 17, and December 2, 1900, clippings in vol. 1 of Murphy Papers.

74. Hugh C. Bailey, "Edgar Gardner Murphy and the Child Labor Movement," *Alabama Review* 18 (January 1965): 47, 54. For a more complete account, see Bailey, *Edgar Gardner Murphy: Gentle Progressive* (Coral Gables: University of Miami Press, 1968). Also see ms. of speech to Alabama legislature, July 8, 1907, in vol. 2 of Murphy Papers.

75. Van Vorst, *Cry of the Children*, pp. 21–96. See also David A. Harris, "Racists and Reformers: A Study of Progressivism in Alabama, 1896–1911" (Ph.D. diss., University of North Carolina, 1967).

76. Alabama, State Child Welfare Department, *First Annual Report. State Child Welfare Department of Alabama for Year Ending September 30, 1920* (N.p., n.d.); idem, *Annual Report for the Fiscal Year Ending September 30, 1930* (N.p., n.d.).

77. Clipping from 1901 in Vol. 1 in Murphy Papers.

78. Clipping from April 1901; T. A. Street to Editor, *Montgomery Journal,* May 20, 1901; in Murphy Scrapbooks, vol. 1, in Murphy Papers.

79. Kenneth R. Johnson, "The Peabody Fund: Its Role and Influence in Alabama," *Alabama Review* 27 (April 1974): 102–10.

80. Census Office, *Population, 1910, Vol. I,* p. 1205.

81. Schoonover, "Alabama's Quest for Social Justice," p. 87.

82. Alabama, State Department of Education, *Report of Special Drive Against Illiteracy Among Men of Draft Age, 1918* (Montgomery: Brown Printing Co., 1918), pp. 5–31.

83. Hart, *Social Problems of Alabama,* p. 39.

84. Eva Joffee, "Rural School Attendance," in Clopper, *Child Welfare in Alabama,* pp. 101–23.

85. Schoonover, "Alabama's Quest for Social Justice," p. 91.

86. Alabama Department of Education, *Literacy and Illiteracy in Alabama,* pp. 26–27; Census Office, *Population, 1920, Vol. III,* pp. 59–65.

87. Alabama, State Department of Education, *Opportunity Schools for White Adults: Course of Study and Suggestions to Teachers* (Birmingham: Birmingham Printing Co., 1929), pp. 1–25.

88. For an excellent survey of the political power of the Farm Bureau, see Daniel, *Breaking the Land.*

89. Home Demonstration Annual State Report, 1924.

90. Home Demonstration Annual State Reports 1926 and 1927.

91. Alabama, State Department of Education, *Report on Illiteracy by Division of Exceptional Education, 1927* (Birmingham: Birmingham Printing Co., 1927), pp. 14–20.

92. Interview with E. L. Darden, May 7, 1986; *Bulletin of the Alabama School of Trades, Gadsden, Alabama* 3 (July 1932), Alabama School of Trades.

93. Oral histories with W. W. Jewell and Frank Uptain.

94. Oral history with Mrs. L. A. House.

95. Life histories of Mr. and Mrs. Sam Anderson, Mr. and Mrs. Tom Alsobrook, Sam Brakefield, and John Gates; oral histories with Ila Hendrix, June W. Odom, Mrs. L. A. House, and Lillie Mae Beason; and *Birmingham Post-Herald,* February 23, 1983.

11. "WE DIDN'T KNOW THE DIFFERENCE": THE GREAT DEPRESSION

1. For general conditions, see U.S., National Emergency Council, *Report on Economic Conditions of the South* (Washington, D.C.: Government Printing Office, 1938), pp. 6–41; Census Office, *Agriculture, 1930, Vol. III,* p. 705; idem, *Agriculture, 1930, Vol. II, Part II,* pp. 978–83; idem, *Population, 1930, Vol. III, Part I* (Washington, D.C.: Government Printing Office, 1932), pp. 91, 99–103; D. S. Gill, "How Alabama Meets Her Social Hygiene Problems," *Journal of Social Hygiene* 16 (1930): 530–31.

2. Joseph B. Gittler and Roscoe R. Giffin, "Changing Patterns of Employment in Five Southeastern States, 1930–1940," *Southern Economic Journal 11* (October 1944): 174; and Edward S. LaMonte, "Politics and Welfare in Birmingham, 1900–1974" (Ph.D. diss., University of Chicago, 1976), pp. 164–65.

3. Grover Hall to Major Howell, November 29, 1936, Grover Hall Papers, Alabama State Archives.

4. See Salmond, *Southern Rebel.*

5. Kenneth E. Barnhart, "Supplement to a Study of the Transient and Homeless in Birmingham, Alabama, January–July, 1933," copy in FERA State Series, Alabama, Box 3, Record Group 69, National Archives, Washington, D.C. (hereafter cited as RG 69).

6. "Statement of Wm. J. Plunkert, Director, Alabama Transient Bureau"; "Alabama Relief Administration, Montgomery, Alabama, Report of the Central Registration Department of the Alabama Transient Bureau, September, 1933"; Aubrey Williams to Mr. Hopkins, January 20, 1934; and "Alabama Transient Bureau Monthly Statistical Report"; all in FERA State Series, Alabama, Box 3, RG 69.

7. "Resolution" by Flomaton Town Council to William J. Plunkert, September 29, 1933, FERA State Series, Alabama, Box 3, RG 69.

8. L. B. Tunstall to Thad Holt, July 28, 1933, FERA State Series, Alabama, Box 1, RG 69.

9. For complaints about the administration of welfare in Alabama, see FERA State Series, Alabama, Box 7, RG 69. For specific examples, see "Digest of Report on DeKalb County, Alabama," 1933, in ibid., Box 8, RG 69; J. F. Hazelwood to Harry L. Hopkins, October 9, 1933, ibid., Box 7, RG 69.

10. E. Shipp to Franklin D. Roosevelt, August 10, 1933; Curry Taylor to President Roosevelt, August 19, 1933, ibid., Box 8; E. M. Abercrombie to Franklin D. Roosevelt, August 14, 1933, ibid., Box 7; Georgia Sinclair to Harry L. Hopkins, August 24, 1933, ibid., Box 8; A. A. Bonner to "Our President," August 29, 1933, ibid., Box 7; all in RG 69.

11. Thad Holt to Harry L. Hopkins, September 23, 1933; L. B. Tunstall to Thad Holt, September 23, 1933; ibid., Box 1, RG 69.

12. Cooper Norris to Harry L. Hopkins, October 30, 1933, ibid., Box 8; Mrs. R. H. Hall to Harry L. Hopkins, November 25, 1933, ibid., Box 7; Will Hill to President Franklin D. Roosevelt, November 15, 1933, ibid., Box 8;

Mrs. Daisy Fuller to Franklin D. Roosevelt, November 13, 1933, ibid., Box 8; E. W. Morgan to Franklin D. Roosevelt, November 21, 1933, ibid., Box 8; Alex E. Vaughn to F. D. Roosevelt, August 11, 1933, ibid., Box 8; all in RG 69.

13. "Field Report" by Aubrey Williams, September 13, [1933], ibid., Box 3; Harold Hoffsommer to Dr. E. D. Tetreau, December 15, 1933, ibid., Box 8; both in RG 69.

14. Mort L. Bixler to Frances Perkins, July 26, 1933, ibid., Box 7, RG 69.

15. "Field Report" by Edith Foster, January 9–14, 1934, ibid., Box 3, RG 69.

16. LaMonte, "Politics and Welfare in Birmingham," pp. 212–21; F. F. Newcomb to William J. Plunkert, July 19, 1934, FERA State Series, Alabama, Box 4, RG 69; "Alabama Field Reports, October 15, 1934, Box 56, Harry L. Hopkins Papers, Franklin D. Roosevelt Library, Hyde Park, New York.

17. "Summary Data Regarding Unemployment Relief," FERA State Series, Alabama, Box 2, RG 69; Harry L. Hopkins to Senator John H. Bankhead, March 14, 1935, ibid., Box 3, RG 69; Thad Holt to Harry L. Hopkins, December 21, 1934, ibid., Box 1, RG 69; "Slagheap Village Project, May 15, 1936," FSA Project Records, Alabama, Box 2, Record Group 96, National Archives (hereafter cited as RG 96). Rikard, "Experiment in Welfare Capitalism," pp. 268–69, 276, 284.

18. Notes of telephone call, Thad Holt to Aubrey Williams, December 24, 1934, FSA Project Records, Alabama, Box 4, RG 96.

19. Hattie Freeman to President Franklin D. Roosevelt, June 2, 1934, FERA State Series, Alabama, Box 8, RG 69.

20. Martha Albright to Charles H. Alspach, July 17, 1936, and Albright to Franklin D. Roosevelt, June 10, 1936, FERA State Series, Alabama, Box 5, RG 69.

21. Joseph G. Kohlenberg to Harry L. Hopkins, December 18, 1934, FERA State Series, Alabama, Box 7, RG 69.

22. A. D. H. Kaplan et al., *Family Income and Expenditures in the Southeastern Region, 1935–36*, U.S. Department of Labor Bulletin no. 647, 1940; Aubrey Williams to George Huddleston, June 13, 1934, FERA State Series, Alabama, Box 7, RG 69; Emmett Gale to Elizabeth Wickendon, May 9, 1935, ibid., Box 5, RG 69; quoted in S. Berrey to Senator Pat Harrison, May 5, 1934, ibid., Box 8, RG 69.

23. Vassie Burney to Franklin D. Roosevelt, January 19, 1936, FERA State Series, Alabama, Box 5, RG 69.

24. Minnie Boatfield to Mrs. Franklin D. Roosevelt, April 29, 1936, ibid., Box 5, RG 69.

25. Margaret Purnam to Lavinia Keys, April 6, 1934, ibid., Box 1; O. J. Perry to Franklin D. Roosevelt, June 2, 1936, ibid., Box 5; both in RG 69.

26. Salmond, *Southern Rebel*, pp. 48–49; O. V. McCutchen to Harry L. Hopkins, December 1934, FERA State Series, Alabama, Box 4, RG 69.

27. "Alabama Field Report," December 22, 1934; "Alabama Field Reports," October 15, 1934; both in Box 56, Hopkins Papers.

28. Henry Sudduth to John H. Bankhead, March 24, 1935; Bankhead to Harry L. Hopkins, March 27, 1935; both in FERA State Series, Alabama, Box 8; Robert W. Pawley to Harry L. Hopkins, December 12, 1934, ibid., Box 4; Carl Martin et al. to William J. Plunkert, January 10, 1935, ibid., Box 5; L. B. Sprott to Congressman W. B. Oliver, December 31, 1934, ibid., Box 4; all in RG 69.

29. For dozens of individual letters, see "Confidential Report on Birmingham, Ala." (1934), Box 68, Hopkins Papers.

30. One careful historian goes so far as to claim that the FERA literally saved the city of Birmingham (LaMonte, "Politics and Welfare in Birmingham," p. 233); John H. Bankhead to Harry L. Hopkins, March 27, 1935, FERA State Series, Alabama, Box 8, RG 69.

31. W. G. Poindexter, Jr., "Sharecroppers in the South," *Southern Workman* 65 (April 1937): 120. For a regional summary of the 1930s farm crisis, see Pete Daniel, "The Transformation of the Rural South, 1930 to the Present," *Agricultural History* 55 (July 1981): 231–48.

32. Harold Hoffsommer to Dr. E. D. Tetreau, January 10, 1934, FERA State Series, Alabama, Box 8, RG 69.

33. Harold Hoffsommer, *Landlord-Tenant Relations and Relief in Alabama,* Research Bulletin, series 2, no. 9, Division of Research, Statistics and Finance, November 14, 1935; copy in FERA State Series, Alabama, Box 8, RG 69. For an example of Hoffsommer's work, see "The AAA and the Cropper," *Social Forces* 13 (May 1935): 494–502.

34. Terry and Sims, *They Live on the Land.*

35. Annual Report, "Home Management," State Home Demonstration Work, 1941, p. 16, Cooperative Extension Service Papers.

36. Quoted in James H. Jones, *Bad Blood . . .* (New York: Free Press, 1981), pp. 62–63.

37. Interviews with James H. Flynt, January 30, 1983, and January 3, 1984.

38. S. L. Chestnutt to Harry L. Hopkins, October 27, 1933, FERA State Series, Alabama, Box 7, RG 69.

39. Viola Suttles, "Development of Rural Rehabilitation Program in Alabama," ms. in ibid., Box 2, RG 69; "Alabama Field Report," December 3, 1934, Box 56, Hopkins Papers.

40. Paul E. Mertz, *New Deal Policy and Southern Rural Poverty* (Baton Rouge: Louisiana State University Press, 1978), pp. 74–80.

41. "Instructions to Rehabilitation Subscribers in Group I, Alabama Relief Administration," Box 56, Hopkins Papers.

42. Mertz, *New Deal Policy,* pp. 83–89.

43. Lorena Hickok to Harry L. Hopkins, April 7, 1934, "FERA Hickok Reports, March–April, 1934," Box 11, Lorena Hickok Papers, FDR Library. Hickok to Hopkins, June 7, 1934, "May–August, 1934," Box 11, Hickok Papers.

44. Ibid, June 7, 1934, Box 11, Hickok Papers. Hickok's negative estimate of county extension agents also dominates Mertz, *New Deal Policy,* see p. 63, for instance.

45. Annual Reports, County Agents, Barbour and Madison counties, 1939, Tallapoosa County, 1934–35, Cooperative Extension Service Papers.

46. Annual Report, County Agent, Walker County, 1934–35; Terry and Sims, *They Live on the Land,* p. 215.

47. Home Demonstration Annual State Report, 1940, p. 19; Annual Report, "Child Care and Family Life," State Home Demonstration Work, 1942, Cooperative Extension Service Papers.

48. Home Demonstration Annual Report, Tallapoosa County, 1932–33; Etowah County, 1937; Annual Report, County Agent, Cullman County, 1939.

49. Annual Report, County Agent, Dallas and Franklin counties, 1939.

50. Home Demonstration Annual State Report, 1930, p. 78; ibid., 1931, pp. 57–58; Home Demonstration Annual Report, Walker County, 1932.

51. Home Demonstration Annual Report, Walker County, 1931, pp. 16–18.

52. Home Demonstration Annual State Report, 1937, pp. 21–23; ibid., 1934, p. 62.

53. Ibid., 1932, p. 65; Home Demonstration Annual Report, Walker County, 1934–35.

54. Home Demonstration Annual Report, Calhoun County, 1931 and 1932.

55. Home Demonstration Annual State Report, 1933, p. 17; Home Demonstration Annual Reports Blount, Walker, Lawrence, and Jackson counties, 1933, and Tuscaloosa County, 1932.

56. Home Demonstration Annual Report, Calhoun County, 1932; Home Demonstration Annual State Report, 1933, p. 19.

57. Home Demonstration Annual State Report, 1929; Home Demonstration Annual Report, Autauga County, 1929, and Tallapoosa County, 1931.

58. Home Demonstration Annual State Report, 1929, pp. 77, 126.

59. Ibid., 1935, p. 7, and 1940, p. 14.

60. Home Demonstration Annual State Report, 1939, p. 29; ibid., 1941, pp. 43–49; ibid., 1942, p. 38.

61. Annual Report, "Child Care and Family Life," State Home Demonstration Work, 1942, pp. 18–19.

62. Home Demonstration Annual Report, DeKalb County, 1937, p. 9.

63. "Slagheap Village Project, May 15, 1936," FSA Project Records, Alabama, Box 2, Record Group 96; U. S., Department of Commerce, *Statistical Abstract of the United States* (Washington, D.C.: Government Printing Office, 1935), pp. 220–21.

64. For excellent summaries of the Birmingham-area projects, see: Ray Rutledge, "The Development of the Bankhead Farmsteads Community" (M.S. thesis, Auburn University, 1951); and Paul W. Wager, *One Foot on the Soil: A Study of Subsistence Homesteads in Alabama* (Tuscaloosa: Bureau of Public Administration, University of Alabama, 1945).

65. "Cumberland Mountain Rural Industrial Community, Jackson County, Alabama," FSA Project Records, Alabama, Box 45; ibid., Alabama, Box 44; Katharine F. Deitz, "Factors to be Considered in the Plan Book for

Cumberland Mountain Project, Jackson County, Alabama," June 1936, ibid., Box 44; all in RG 96.

66. For an excellent description of the early days of the Cumberland Farms Cooperative, see Coburn H. Thomas, "An Economic and Social History of Jackson County" (M.A. thesis, Auburn University, 1938), pp. 123–29.

67. Robert W. Hudgens to R. G. Tugwell, July 14, 1936, FSA Project Records, Alabama, Box 49; and Hudgens to Tugwell, December 1936, ibid., Box 42; see copy of the *Cumberland Farm News,* January 4, 1937, in ibid., Box 51; all in RG 96.

68. The Reverend W. Frank Moore to President Franklin D. Roosevelt, January 14, 1936, ibid., Box 49, RG 96.

69. Lloyd Smith to Franklin D. Roosevelt, August 9, 1935, ibid., Box 41; Cletus B. Zeigler, September 15, 1936, ibid., Box 43; T. J. Cauley to Frate Bull, August 18, 1936, ibid., Box 44; "Cumberland Mountain Farms," October 2, 1936, ibid., Box 41; *Cumberland Farm News,* December 14 and November 30, 1936, copies in ibid., Box 51; Robert W. Hudgens to W. W. Alexander, December 16, 1936, ibid., Box 43; William H. Dent to John Fischer, June 5, 1939, ibid., Box 42; "Plans for Skyline Farms Project, RF-AL 16," ibid., Box 42; all in RG 96.

70. "Statement of Status, Cumberland Mountain Farms," December 31, 1936, ibid., Box 44; ERH to F. H. Robinson, January 9, 1936, ibid., Box 41; both in RG 96.

71. Notes of telephone conversation between a Mr. Woods and E. R. Henson, June 6, 1936, ibid., Box 50; and Robert W. Hudgens to R. G. Tugwell, October 23, 1936, ibid., Box 42; both in RG 96.

72. E. S. Morgan to C. B. Baldwin, November 30, 1940, ibid., Box 41; C. B. Baldwin to Robert W. Hudgens, January 23, 1939, ibid., Box 41; both in RG 96.

73. Leonard Kirk to Charles Seeger, September 19, 1936; R. W. Hampton to Charles Seeger, September 17, 1936; Hampton to Seeger, September 18, 1936; Seeger to Hampton, September 24, 1936; all in ibid., Box 48, RG 96.

74. W. Frank Moore to W. W. Alexander, June 12, 1939, ibid., Box 42; Margaret Valiant to Robert Van Hyning, February 16, 1937, ibid., Box 49; Margaret Valiant to Charles Seeger, February 10, 1937, ibid., Box 49; Valiant to Van Hyning, February 2, 1937, ibid., Box 49; Valiant to Miss Franke, March 8 and 25, 1937, ibid., Box 49; all in RG 96.

75. Margaret Valiant, "Field Report," December 5, 1936, ibid., Box 49; Charles Seeger to Rupert W. Hampton, September 24, 1936, ibid., Box 48; both in RG 96.

76. Katharine F. Deitz, "Factors to be Considered in the Plan Book for Cumberland Mountain Project, Jackson County, Alabama," ibid., Box 44, RG 96.

77. Loyal Jones, *Minstrel of the Appalachians: The Story of Bascom Lamar Lunsford* (N.p.: Appalachian Consortium Press, 1984), pp. 67–75; Bascom L. Lunsford, "Field Reports," January 29, February 3, 6, 17, 27, and March 4, 1937, all in FSA Project Records, Alabama, Box 49, RG 96; Robert Van

Hyning to Bascom L. Lunsford, February 2, 1937, ibid., Box 49, RG 96; Margaret Valiant to Robert Van Hyning, January 30 and February 16, 1937, ibid., Box 49, RG 96.

78. Bascom L. Lunsford, "Field Reports," February 17 and 23, and March 6, 1937, FSA Project Records, Alabama, Box 49; Robert Van Hyning, February 20, 1937, ibid., Box 49; Bascom L. Lunsford to Adrian J. Dornbush, March 12, 1937, ibid., Box 46; all in RG 96. These "Field Reports" contain titles of ballads Lunsford collected.

79. Newspaper clipping in ibid., Box 48; Harry N. Ross et al. to J. H. Wood, May 19, 1938, ibid., Box 51; Margaret Valiant to John O. Walker, April 14, 1938, ibid., Box 51; Nicholas Ray to Adrian J. Dornbush, [1938?], ibid., Box 48; all in RG 96.

80. William H. Dent to John Fischer, July 17, 1939, ibid., Box 51; Harry N. Ross to W. W. Alexander, January 27, 1939, ibid., Box 44; "Report of Activities, Skyline Farms," ibid., Box 41; J. O. Walker to Harry N. Ross, January 3, 1939, ibid., Box 44; E. S. Morgan to C. B. Baldwin, August 10, 1940, and March 27, 1941, ibid., Box 49; all in RG 96; Thomas, "Economic and Social History of Jackson County," p. 129.

81. Quoted in Mertz, *New Deal Policy, p.* 134.

82. Ibid., pp. 181–204.

83. Ibid., pp. 219–20.

84. Annual Reports, County Agents, 1939, for Pike, Tallapoosa, Chambers, Chilton, St. Clair, Coffee, and DeKalb counties.

85. Annual Report, County Agent, Etowah County, 1939.

86. *Birmingham Post,* February 22, 1935, copy in Box 1921, Eleanor Roosevelt Papers, FDR Library.

87. Thad Holt, "Establishment of Unemployment Relief Agencies in the Hoover-Roosevelt Era," ms. in Thad Holt Papers, Alabama State Archives. For the CCC in Alabama I relied on an excellent seminar paper: Robert D. Gunnels, "Forest Army: The Civilian Conservation Corps in Alabama, 1933–1942," May 1987, copy in author's possession.

88. George Huddleston to Thad Holt, June 2, 1934, FERA State Series, Box 7, RG 69; Mertz, *New Deal Policy,* pp. 52–53.

89. Rowe, "Alabama's Disappearing Almshouses," pp. 3–51; Odelle Carmichael, "A Decade of Aid to Dependent Children in Alabama" (M.A. thesis, Tulane University, 1946), pp. 1–2, 23, 65, 75.

90. Rev. M. R. Evans to FDR, October 3, 1935; Rev. Joe Jones to FDR, October 5, 1935; Rev. E. B. Welborn to FDR, October 17, 1935; Rev. Mark L. Hargraves to FDR, October 17, 1935; Rev. J. W. Poston to FDR, October 14, 1935; Rev. L. G. Nunnally to FDR, November 2, 1935; Rev. W. W. Vines to FDR, November 12, 1935; all in President's Personal Files 21-A, Clergy Letters, Alabama, Box 3, FDR Library.

91. Quoted in Mertz, *New Deal Policy,* p. 59; Hoffsommer, *Landlord-Tenant Relations,* p. i; Rev. E. H. Murphy to FDR, September 30, 1935, Clergy Letters, Box 4.

92. Oral histories with Kathleen Knight and Lillie Mae Beason.

93. Terry and Sims, *They Live on the Land,* p. 264; Suttles, "Development of Rural Rehabilitation Program."

94. U. S., Bureau of the Census, *Agriculture, 1940, Vol. III, Part 4* (Washington, D.C.: Government Printing Office, 1942), p. 184; Annual Report, "Home Management," State Home Demonstration Work, 1943; Rowe, "Alabama's Disappearing Almshouses," p. 69.

95. Wright, *Old South, New South,* pp. 219–20.

96. William Green, "Southern Labor at the Crossroads," *American Federationist* 37 (January 1930): 23–40; Rev. G. E. Lint to FDR, October 7, 1935, Clergy Letters, Box 4; Foster, "Field Report." For an overview, see Taft, *Organizing Dixie;* J. M. Brown to Harry W. Hopkins, October 30, 1933, FERA State Series, Alabama, Box 7, RG 69; Will Roberts to FDR, October 7, 1933, ibid., Box 8, RG 69.

97. President, UMW, Hull Coal Mining Camp, to FDR, October 7, 1933; William Mitch to Hugh L. Kerwin, August 8, 1933; Charles Edmundson to H. L. Kerwin, March 21, 1934; copies in "Correspondence File, 1930–35," Taft Research Notes.

98. Marshall, *Labor in the South,* pp. 143–44.

99. William Mitch to Frances Perkins, August 3, 1934; Mitch to H. L. Kerwin, September 30, 1935; both in "Correspondence File, 1930–35," Taft Research Notes; Marshall, *Labor in the South,* p. 141.

100. Rev. W. N. Kizziah to FDR, September 30, 1935, Clergy Letters, Box 4; Rev. Jirden Frye to FDR, March 8, 1936, Clergy Letters, Box 3.

101. Green, "Southern Labor at the Crossroads," 28.

102. Irving Bernstein, *Turbulent Years: A History of the American Worker, 1933–1941* (Boston: Houghton Mifflin Co., 1970), pp. 616–17; see Hodges, "New Deal Labor Policy," especially pp. 25–104.

103. Harry I. Shumway, *I Go South: An Unprejudiced Visit to a Group of Cotton Mills* (Boston: Houghton Mifflin Co., 1930), pp. 44–88.

104. George H. Van Fleet to H. L. Kerwin, April 10, 1930; C. L. Richardson to H. L. Kerwin, June 8, 1933; copies in "Correspondence File, 1930–35," Taft Research Notes.

105. Alexander Kendrick, "Alabama Goes on Strike," *Nation* 139 (August 29, 1934): 233–34.

106. M. F. Herren to Harry Hopkins, August 4, 1934, FERA State Series, Alabama, Box 8, RG 69; Rev. Tom Jones to FDR, October 18, 1935, Clergy Letters, Box 3.

107. Billy H. Wyche, "Southern Attitudes Toward Industrial Unions, 1933–1941" (Ph.D. diss., University of Georgia, 1970), pp. 8–9; J. C. Bradley to FDR, October 15, 1934, Box 7, and M. J. Miller to Aubrey Williams, October 15, 1934, Box 3; both in FERA State Series, Alabama, RG 69.

108. Bernadette K. Lofton, "A Social History of the Mid-Gulf South (Panama City–Mobile), 1930–1950" (Ph.D. diss., University of Southern Mississippi, 1971), pp. 245–49.

109. John B. Goins to W. C. Hare, January 19, 1935, copy in "Correspondence File, 1930–35," Taft Research Notes.

110. United States, *Labor Unionism in American Agriculture,* Department of Labor Bulletin no. 836, 1945, pp. 289–92. For a survey of biracial radicalism in Alabama, see Robert P. Ingalls, "Antiradical Violence in Birmingham During the 1930s," *Journal of Southern History* 47 (November 1981): 521–44; Langston Hughes, "An Open Letter to the South," *Southern Worker,* February 10, 1934; Noel R. Beddow to Miss Mercedes Daugherty, July 27, 1943, "Correspondence File, 1943," Taft Research Notes.

111. Harry L. Hopkins to Thad Holt, June 28, 1933; Margaret Purnam to Lavinia Keys, March 14, 1934; William Mitch to Thad Holt, April 6, 1934; all in FERA State Series, Alabama, Box 1, RG 69.

112. W. I. Davison to FDR, April 30, 1935, Box 7; C. L. Pegues to Harry L. Hopkins, May 23, 1934, Box 1; both in ibid., RG 69; Birmingham Building Trades Council to Thad Holt, February 29, 1936, "Correspondence Files, 1936–1940," Taft Research Notes; Ed O'Brien to Harry L. Hopkins, January 18, 1935, FERA State Series, Alabama, Box 7, RG 69.

113. C. L. Richardson to H. L. Kerwin, August 21, 1933; UMW Local 5734 to FDR, October 7, 1933; copies in "Correspondence File, 1930–35," Taft Research Notes.

114. Oliver Henderson to John Bankhead, May 16, 1934, Box 8; Scott Roberts to Harry L. Hopkins, September 10, 1934, Box 7; telegram from Ashton B. Collins to Harry L. Hopkins, October 4, 1935, Box 8; T. R. Simmons to FDR, May 13, 1935, Box 7; all in FERA State Series, Alabama, RG 69.

115. Lorena Hickok to Harry L. Hopkins, April 8, 1934, Box 11, Hickok Papers; notes of telephone call, Thad Holt to Aubrey Williams, April 10, 1934, FERA State Papers, Alabama, Box 1, RG 69; Loula Dunn to Directors of Relief, July 26, 1934, ibid., Box 7, RG 69; notes of telephone call, Thad Holt to Harry L. Hopkins, September 11, 1934, Box 73, Hopkins Papers.

116. Noel R. Beddow to Donald Richberg, April 15, 1935, notes in "Correspondence File, 1930–35," Taft Research Notes; Thad Holt to Carrington Gill, October 17, 1934, FERA State Series, Alabama, Box 1, RG 69; notes on telephone conversation, Aubrey Williams to Thad Holt, October 29, 1935, ibid., Box 2, RG 69; telegram, William Mitch to Aubrey Williams, October 6, 1935, ibid.

117. Robert R. Moore to William O. Hare, June 5, 1934; William Mitch and Noel R. Beddow to Secretaries, Officials, and Members of Local Unions of Steel Workers Organizing Committee, December 21, 1937; Noel R. Beddow to Honorable Joe Starnes, January 14, 1939; all in Taft Research Notes.

118. See Ingalls, "Antiradical Violence," pp. 521–44.

119. Charles H. Martin, "Southern Labor Relations in Transition: Gadsden, Alabama, 1930–1943," *Journal of Southern History* 47 (November 1981): 545–68; Daniel Nelson, "A CIO Organizer in Alabama, 1941," *Labor History* 18 (Fall 1977): 579; and John D. House, "Report on Violations of Civil Liberties in Gadsden, Alabama," in URW Records, Local No. 12, Gadsden, Alabama, Southern Labor Archives, Georgia State University, Atlanta, Georgia.

12. "THE POOR YOU HAVE WITH YOU ALWAYS":
THE ENDURING LEGACY

1. Oral histories with James H. Flynt and with Mae Ellis Moore Flynt, May 14, 1983, in possession of author.

2. Henry H. Collins, *America's Own Refugees: Our 4,000,000 Homeless Migrants* (Princeton: Princeton University Press, 1941), pp. 220–21.

3. Ibid., pp. 89–93.

4. Mary Martha Thomas, "Rosie the Alabama Riveter," ms. copy in author's possession.

5. Interviews with Horace Porter and Elizabeth Thompson, both June 27, 1985, Gadsden, Alabama.

6. Herman J. Braunhut, "Farm Labor Wage Rates in the South, 1909–1948," *Southern Economic Journal* 16 (October 1949): 190.

7. Collins, *America's Own Refugees*, pp. 29–30.

8. For these agricultural patterns, I have relied heavily upon Fite, *Cotton Fields No More*, especially pp. 167–70, 180–205, 208.

9. Sidney Baldwin, *Poverty and Politics: The Rise and Decline of the Farm Security Administration* (Chapel Hill: University of North Carolina Press, 1968), pp. 290–91, 414.

10. U. S., Bureau of the Census, *Agriculture, 1950, Vol. I, Part 21* (Washington, D.C.: Government Printing Office, 1952), pp. 4, 68–70; idem, *Agriculture, 1969, Alabama, Vol. I, Part 32* (1972), p. 3; idem, *Agriculture, 1978, Vol. I, Part 1* (1982), p. 2.

11. Census Office, *Agriculture, 1969, Alabama*, pp. 65–537.

12. Howell Raines, "Let Us Now Revisit Famous Folk," *New York Times Magazine*, May 25, 1980, 31–46; Dale Maharidge and Michael Williamson, "The Same Road Taken," *Sacramento Bee Magazine*, September 28, 1986, pp. 6–14.

13. U. S., Census Office, *Population, 1940, Vol. II, Part I* (Washington, D.C.: Government Printing Office,1943), pp. 230–32; idem, *Population, 1950, Vol. II, Part II: Alabama* (1952), pp. 2–234; idem, *Population, 1960, Vol. I, Part 2* (1963), pp. 2–137.

14. Jules Backman, *Bituminous Coal Wages, Profits, and Productivity* (Prepared for Southern Coal Producers Association, February 1950), pp. 18, 34.

15. Perry and Ritter, *Dying to Dig Coal*, p. 6.

16. Elliott and Crittenden, *Herbert South*, pp. 10, 23, 29.

17. Census Office, *Population, 1940*, pp. 230–32; idem, *Population, 1950, Alabama*, pp. 2–234.

18. *Birmingham News*, June 22, 1986.

19. Census Office, *Population, 1940*, pp. 230–32; idem, *Population, 1950, Alabama*, pp. 2–234; idem, *Population, 1960, Vol. I, Part 2*, pp. 2–137.

20. See Mickle, "Huntsville."

21. *Birmingham News*, June 22, 1986.

22. Census Office, *Population, 1940*, pp. 230–32; idem, *Population, 1950, Alabama*, pp. 2–234; letter dated January 14, 1944, in Taft Research Notes.

23. I am indebted to my Auburn University colleague, Warren Flick of the Forestry School, for his extensive thought and research on the wood dealer system: "The Wood Dealer System," Crosby Lecture, February 28, 1985, ms. copy in author's possession.

24. Census Office, *Population, 1940*, pp. 230–32; idem, *Population, 1950, Alabama*, pp. 2–234; idem, *Population, 1960, Vol. I, Part 2*, pp. 2–137.

25. United States, *Manpower Study of Appalachian Alabama* (Auburn, Ala.: Auburn University, 1968), pp. 10, 12, 13, 20–27, 209.

26. *New York Times*, March 21, 1985.

27. Long, *House of Happiness*, p. 82.

28. For an overview, see Wayne Flynt, "The New Deal and Southern Labor," in *The New Deal and the South*, ed. James C. Cobb and Michael V. Namorato (Jackson: University Press of Mississippi, 1984), pp. 63–96.

29. Walls, "Folklore and Folk Life," pp. 95–100.

30. Sam S. Douglas to William Green, February 13, 1950, copy in Taft Research Notes.

31. Elliott and Crittenden, *Herbert South*, p. 30.

32. *Birmingham News*, June 20, 1982.

33. Ibid.

34. *Opelika-Auburn News*, September 6, 1983.

35. See H. L. Mitchell, *Mean Things Happening in This Land: The Life and Times of H. L. Mitchell, Cofounder of the Southern Tenant Farmers Union* (Montclair, N. J.: Allanheld, Osmun, 1979).

36. John Lewis to Aubrey Williams, Williams to Lewis, October 19, 1948; W. T. Adcock to Aubrey Williams, February 1, 1947; Orville H. Mastin to Aubrey Williams, April 7, 1948; all in Box 33, Aubrey Williams Papers, FDR Library. Also see "Address by Aubrey Williams," 1949, ibid.

37. "Operating Guide for the Southern Area, National Farmers' Union, March 1, 1949," ibid.

38. Ibid.

39. Orville H. Mastin to Editor, *Birmingham Post*, October 29, 1947; G. K. Williams to Aubrey Williams, January 16, 1949; A. Williams to G. K. Williams, January 18, 1949; all in Box 33, Williams Papers.

40. "Annual Convention of Alabama Farmers' Union, Clanton, Alabama, Dec. 1, 2, 3, 1949, Address by Aubrey Williams, State President," Box 33, Williams Papers.

41. For discussions, see William D. Barnard, *Dixiecrats and Democrats: Alabama Politics, 1942–1950* (University: University of Alabama Press, 1974), and George Sims, *The Little Man's Big Friend: James E. Folsom in Alabama Politics, 1946–1958* (University: University of Alabama Press, 1985).

42. Address by Aubrey Williams, State President, Box 33, Williams Papers.

43. Aubrey Williams to James G. Patton, February 10, 1949, ibid.

44. Benton J. Strong to Aubrey Williams, March 5, 1949; Williams to Strong, March 11, 1949; both in ibid.

45. Aubrey Williams to James G. Patton, February 14, 1952; Williams to William Rose, February 23, 1949; both in ibid.

46. J. D. Mott to Aubrey Williams, July 3, 1950; Williams to Orville Mastin, October 27, 1948; both in ibid.

47. Tom Ludwig to Aubrey Williams, June 18, 1949; Williams to Mr. H. D. Cobb, June 23, 1949; both in ibid.

48. "Alabama Farmers' Union Meeting," April 12, 1951, ibid.

49. Virginia Van der Veer Hamilton, *Lister Hill: Statesman from the South* (Chapel Hill: University of North Carolina Press, 1987), pp. 78–84.

50. See Sims, *Little Man's Big Friend*.

51. Daniel Powell, "PAC to COPE: Thirty-Two Years of Southern Labor in Politics," in *Essays in Southern Labor History: Selected Papers, Southern Labor History Conference, 1976*, ed. Gary M. Fink and Merl E. Reed (Westport, Conn.: Greenwood Press, 1977), pp. 244–57.

52. Virginia Durr to Clark and Mairi Jemison, September 1959. I am grateful to Mairi Jemison for supplying a copy of this letter.

53. Oral histories with Pauline Brewer and Carter Priest.

54. See David E. Harrell, Jr., *White Sects and Black Men in the Recent South* (Nashville: Vanderbilt University Press, 1971).

55. Frank Deford, "The Toughest Coach There Ever Was," *Sports Illustrated* 58 (April 30, 1984): 46.

56. Ibid., pp. 46–61.

57. See Frank Deford, "I Do Love the Football," *Sports Illustrated* 55 (November 23, 1981): 96–108.

58. Richard L. Graves, "Language Differences Among Upper- and Lower-Class Negro and White Eighth Graders in East Central Alabama" (Ph.D. diss., Florida State University, 1967), especially pp. 9, 118–19.

59. Stambler and Landon, *Encyclopedia of Folk, Country and Western Music*, p. 333.

60. James C. Cobb, "From Muskogee to Luckenbach: Country Music and the 'Southernization' of America," *Journal of Popular Culture* 16 (Winter 1983): 81–91. For additional insights, see: Malone, *Country Music*, and *Southern Music/American Music*; and a series of provocative essays by Richard A. Peterson: "The Production of Cultural Change: The Case of Contemporary Country Music," *Social Research* 45 (Summer 1978): 292–314; "Has Country Lost Its Homespun Charm?" *Chronicle Review*, May 29, 1979, pp. 22–24; "Single-Industry Firm to Conglomerate Synergistics: Alternative Strategies for Selling Insurance and Country Music," in *Growing Metropolis: Aspects of Development in Nashville* (Nashville: Vanderbilt University Press, 1975), pp. 341–57.

61. Ford, *Political Economics of Rural Poverty*, p. 3.

62. Census Office, *Population, 1960, Vol. I, Part 1*, pp. 1–230; *Part 2*, pp. 2–145.

63. Carl M. Brauer, "Kennedy, Johnson, and the War on Poverty," *Journal of American History* 69 (June 1982): 98–119.

64. Gretchen Maclachlan, *The Other Twenty Percent: A Statistical Analy-*

sis of Poverty in the South (Atlanta: Southern Regional Council, December 1974), p. 5.

65. Ibid., p. 13.

66. Mary Lee Rice Shannon, *Poverty in Alabama: A Barrier to Post-Secondary Education* (Tuscaloosa: Institute of Higher Education Research and Services, 1976), pp. 8, 14–18.

67. Alabama Migrant and Seasonal Farmworkers Council, "Funding Request" (Montgomery: N.p., 1977), p. 27.

68. Steve Suitts, *Patterns of Poverty: A Special Report of the Southern Regional Council, Inc.* (Atlanta: Southern Regional Council, 1984), p. 4.

69. *Birmingham Post-Herald,* November 29, 1982.

70. Ibid., January 1, 1983. During this depression, I spent the summer of 1982 in Hong Kong and the People's Republic of China. The *South China Morning Post* (Hong Kong) featured a front-page article on August 20, 1982, describing American poverty. When I returned to rural Calhoun County for a visit in April 1983, I saw an elderly white couple going through a dumpster, looking for food and clothes.

71. *Birmingham Post-Herald,* April 13, 1983; *Opelika-Auburn News,* September 11, 1984.

72. *Birmingham Post-Herald,* November 7, 1984.

73. Ibid., March 3, 1983, September 27, 1985.

74. I am grateful to my colleague Don Olliff for this graphic account.

75. *Birmingham Post-Herald,* August 4 and 13, 1986.

76. Oral history with Lillie Mae Beason.

77. Oral history with Andrew McClain.

78. Oral history with Pauline Brewer.

79. Oral history with Kathleen Knight.

BIBLIOGRAPHY

ARCHIVAL MATERIALS

Alabama School of Trades. Gadsden, Alabama.
   Bulletin of the Alabama School of Trades, Gadsden, Alabama. Vol 3 (July
      1932).
Alabama State Archives. Montgomery, Alabama.
   "Reginal Dawson Diaries, 1883–1897."
   Lillian Ward Duncan Interview by Myra W. Crenshaw, May 1982. In
      "Butler County, People–Personalities" file.
   Sarah R. Espy Diary.
   Grover Hall Papers.
   Thad Holt Papers.
   Dr. Edward Palmer. "Alabama Notes."
   Gov. Lewis E. Parsons Official Files.
   Gov. Robert M. Patton Official Files.
   Gov. John Gill Shorter Papers.
   State Mine Inspector Reports, 1904–1906.
   Gov. Thomas H. Watts Papers.
Auburn University Archives. Auburn, Alabama.
   Alabama Cooperative Extension Service Papers.
      County Agent Reports, 1934, 1935, and 1939, for all sixty-seven
         counties.
      Home Demonstration Annual Reports by counties:
         Autauga, 1929
         Blount, 1933, 1937, 1939
         Calhoun, 1931–33, 1939
         Cherokee, 1932–33, 1937
         DeKalb, 1933, 1937
         Etowah, 1933, 1937, 1939
         Jackson, 1933
         Lamar, 1933–35, 1937
         Lawrence, 1931, 1933, 1937
         St. Clair, 1933, 1937, 1939
         Tallapoosa, 1931–35, 1937, 1939
         Tuscaloosa, 1932
         Walker, 1931–35, 1939
      Home Demonstration Annual State Reports, 1914.–49.

Harper, Mary Wigley. "The Wind is From the East."
Lewis-Plant Papers.
"Voters and Party Affiliations Record, 1897."
Birmingham Public Library and Archives. Birmingham, Alabama.
  Donald Comer Papers.
  Grace, Francis Mitchell. "From the Unpublished Autobiography of
    Francis Mitchell Grace, D.D., 1832–1904."
  "Records of Inmates of Poor Farm, 1910."
  Philip Taft Research Notes.
Franklin D. Roosevelt Library. Hyde Park, New York.
  Clergy Letters, Alabama.
  Lorena Hickok Papers.
  Harry L. Hopkins Papers.
  Eleanor Roosevelt Papers.
  Aubrey Williams Papers.
National Archives. Washington, D.C.
  Farm Security Administration, Project Records, Record Group 96.
  Federal Emergency Relief Administration, State Series, Alabama,
    Record Group 69.
Southern History Collection. University of North Carolina,
    Chapel Hill, North Carolina.
  John C. Campbell Papers.
  B. B. Comer Papers.
  Iron Station, North Carolina Papers.
  Lipscomb Family Papers.
  Edgar Gardner Murphy Papers.
  Isaac B. Ulmer Papers.
Southern Labor Archives. Georgia State University, Atlanta, Georgia.
  Stetson Kennedy Papers.
  United Rubber Workers Records, Local No. 12, Gadsden, Alabama.
  United Textile Workers of America Papers.
Mrs. Helen Wilson. Mobile, Alabama.
  "Inmates of Asylum for the Poor, Mobile County, Alabama."

LIFE HISTORIES

Federal Writers' Project, Life Histories, Folders 110–84.
  On microfilm. Originals in Southern History
  Collection, University of North Carolina Library,
  Chapel Hill, North Carolina.
  E. J. Alexander   George Carter
  Mr. and Mrs. Tom Alsobrook   Sam Cash
  Bennie Amerson   Mrs. Champion
  Mr. and Mrs. Sam Anderson   Mr. and Mrs. Joseph Davis
  Sam Brakefield   "Bull" Elliott

John Gates
Isaac Johnson
Henry Kelly
Jim Lauderdale
Nancy Nolan
Susie R. O'Brien

Julia Rhodes
Orrie Robinson
Charley Ryland
Mrs. Lee Snipes
M. B. Truitt
Neeley Williams

ORAL HISTORIES

Oral Histories in Samford University Oral History
Collection, Archives, Birmingham, Alabama.
Lillie Mae Beason by Wayne Flynt, Steele, Alabama, January 3, 1976.
Elmer Burton by Sybil Burton, Jasper, Alabama, December 3, 1974.
Mrs. Carlie H. Crocker by Peggy Burnett, Centreville, Alabama,
January 27, 1975.
Carl and Ted Forrester by Dru Flowers, Houston County, Alabama,
January 27, 1975.
John Gioiello by Selena Cason, Birmingham, Alabama, August 14,
1975.
S. L. Hardy by Doug Sawyer, Sylacauga, Alabama, November 18, 1974.
Ila Hendrix by Ben Hendrix, Sumiton, Alabama, May 1, 1976.
Essie Holdridge by Michael Brownfield, Fort Payne, Alabama,
November 27, 1975.
Mrs. L. A. House by Wayne Flynt, Sylacauga, Alabama, July 10, 1974.
Mrs. Kathleen Knight by Daniel Knight, Guin, Alabama, January 23,
1975.
E. H. Moore by John Earnest, McCalla, Alabama, November 26, 1975.
June W. Odom by Pamela Sterne, Pleasant Grove, Alabama, November
23, 1974.
Walter and Nora Parker by Cathy Hanby, Centerpoint, Alabama, April
22, 1976.
C. D. Patterson by Curtis W. Jones, Parish, Alabama, April 28, 1975.
Ellis Self by Selena Cason, Birmingham, Alabama, July 28, 1975.
Luther V. Smith by Benny Hendrix, Quinton, Alabama, November 27,
1974.
John Sokira by Selena Cason, Brookside, Alabama, August 7, 1975.
Mrs. John Sokira by Selena Cason, Brookside, Alabama, August 7,
1975.
Frank Uptain by Caroline Roberts, Jasper, Alabama, November 23,
1975.
Oral Histories in Author's Collection.
James H. Flynt by Wayne Flynt, Pinson, Alabama, December 27, 1981.
Mae Ellis Moore Flynt by Wayne Flynt, Pinson, Alabama, May 14,
1983.

Cecil Spencer by Wayne Flynt and Everett Smith, Tuscaloosa,
Alabama, December 20, 1977.
Oral Histories in Auburn University Archives, Auburn, Alabama.
Pauline Brewer by Lynne Anderson, Opelika, Alabama, March 9, 1982.
Annie and Houston Burrow by Angie Chandler, Salem, Alabama,
March 2, 1982.
W. W. Jewell by Kevin Price, Opelika, Alabama, February 18, 1982.
Andrew McClain by James M. Pietkiewicz, Opelika, Alabama, March
10, 1982.
James H. Phillips by Barry Hocutt, Opelika, Alabama, March 11, 1982.
Carter Priest by Virginia McGee, Opelika, Alabama, February 25, 1982.
Oral History in Peggy Walls Collection, Hackneyville, Alabama.
Oral History with Susie Wilson by Peggy G. Walls, Hackneyville,
Alabama.

INTERVIEWS

Interview with E. L. Darden, May 7, 1986, Auburn, Alabama.
Interviews with James H. Flynt, January 30, 1983, and January 3, 1984,
Auburn, Alabama.
Interview with Horace Porter, June 27, 1985, Gadsden, Alabama.
Interview with Mrs. W. Albert Smith, May 16, 1982, Auburn, Alabama.
Interview with Elizabeth Thompson, June 27, 1985, Gadsden, Alabama.

MANUSCRIPTS

Akin, Edward N. " 'Mr. Donald's Help': The Birmingham Village of
Avondale Mills During the Great Depression," April 1978. Copy in
author's possession.
Denison, George A. "The History of Public Health in Alabama." Bound
but unpublished ms., 1951. Copy in Alabama State Archives.
Dollar, John M. "The Greenback-Labor Party in Alabama." Ms. of paper
presented to Southern/Southwestern Labor History Conference at
Arlington, Texas, March 29–31, 1984. Copy in author's possession.
Flick, Warren. "The Wood Dealer System." Ms. of Crosby Lecture,
February 28, 1985. Copy in author's possession.
Gunnels, Robert D. "Forest Army: The Civilian Conservation Corps in
Alabama, 1933–1942." Seminar paper, May 1987. Copy in author's
possession.
Holt, Thad. "Establishment of Unemployment Relief Agencies in the
Hoover-Roosevelt Era." Typed ms. in Thad Holt Papers, Alabama State
Archives, Montgomery.

McIlwain, Don. "Land Ownership and Tenancy: Russell County in
1860." Seminar paper, May 1987. Copy in author's possession.

McKiven, Mel. "The Household Composition of Working Class Families
in the Birmingham District, 1900." December 19, 1983. Copy in
author's possession.

Malone, Ann Patton, Alberto Meloni, and Jerry Devine. "The Georgia
Wiregrass Rural History Project: Class and Society in an Industrializing
Pine Belt Region, 1870–1900." November 30, 1973. Report for
National Endowment for the Humanities. Copy in author's possession.

Mohr, Clarence L. "Slavery and Class Tensions in Confederate Georgia."
Ms. presented at 1984 Southern Historical Convention, Louisville,
Kentucky. Copy in author's possession.

Thomas, Mary Martha. "Rosie the Alabama Riveter." Copy in author's
possession.

GOVERNMENT DOCUMENTS, ALABAMA

Alabama. *Laws for the Relief of Needy Confederate Soldiers and Sailors,*
1911. Montgomery: Brown Printing Co., 1911.

Alabama Migrant and Seasonal Farmworkers Council. "Funding
Request." Montgomery: N.p., 1977.

Alabama. Mine Inspector. *Coal Mine Statistics of State of Alabama for*
1910. Birmingham: Grant and Pow, 1911.

———. *Report of Inspector of Alabama Coal Mines for the Year 1909.*
Birmingham: Freret and Grant, 1910.

———. *Report of Inspector of Alabama Coal Mines for the Year 1914.*
Birmingham: Dispatch Printing Co., 1914.

———. *Third Biennial Report of the Inspectors of Mines, 1900.*
Birmingham: Dispatch Printing Co., 1900.

Alabama. State Child Welfare Department. *Annual Report for the Fiscal*
Year Ending September 30, 1930. N.p., n.d.

———. *First Annual Report. State Child Welfare Department of Alabama.*
For the Fiscal Year Ending September 30, 1920. N.p., n.d.

Alabama. State Department of Education. *Annual Report, 1913.*
Montgomery: Brown Printing Co., 1913.

———. *Literacy and Illiteracy in Alabama: Biennial Census, 1914.*
Montgomery: State Department of Education, 1914.

———. *Opportunity Schools for White Adults: Course of Study and*
Suggestions to Teachers. Birmingham: Birmingham Printing Co.,
1929.

———. *Report of Special Drive Against Illiteracy Among Men of Draft Age,*
1918. Montgomery: Brown Printing Co., 1918.

———. *Report on Illiteracy by Division of Exceptional Education, 1927.*
Birmingham: Birmingham Printing Co., 1927.

GOVERNMENT DOCUMENTS, U.S.

United States. *Labor Unionism in American Agriculture.* Department of Labor Bulletin no. 836, 1945.
————. *Manpower Study of Appalachian Alabama.* Auburn, Ala.: Auburn University, 1968.
————. *Report of the United States Coal Commission, Part III.* Washington, D.C.: Government Printing Office, 1925.
U.S. Annual Report. *Commissioner of the General Land Office, 1837.* N.p., n.d.
————. *Commissioner of the General Land Office, 1841.* N.p., n.d.
————. *Commissioner of the General Land Office, 1845.* N.p., n.d.
————. *Commissioner of the General Land Office, 1850.* N.p., n.d.
U.S. Bureau of the Census. *Agriculture, 1910, Vol. V.* Washington, D.C.: Government Printing Office, 1914.
————. *Agriculture, 1920, Vol. VI, Part 2.* Washington, D.C.: Government Printing Office, 1922.
————. *Agriculture, 1930, Vols. II & III, Part 2.* Washington, D.C.: Government Printing Office, 1932.
————. *Agriculture, 1940, Vols. I & III, Part 4.* Washington, D.C.: Government Printing Office, 1942.
————. *Agriculture, 1950, Vol. I, Part 21.* Washington, D.C.: Government Printing Office, 1952.
————. *Agriculture, 1959, Alabama, Vol. I, Part 32.* Washington, D.C.: Government Printing Office, 1961.
————. *Agriculture, 1969, Alabama, Vol. I, Part 32.* Washington, D.C.: Government Printing Office, 1972.
————. *Agriculture, 1978, Alabama, Vol. I, Parts 1 and 2.* Washington, D.C.: Government Printing Office, 1982.
————. *Manufactures, 1929, Vol. III.* Washington, D.C.: Government Printing Office, 1933.
————. *Population, 1910, Vols. I & IV.* Washington, D.C.: Government Printing Office, 1913, 1914.
————. *Population, 1950, Vol. II, Part II: Alabama.* Washington, D.C.: Government Printing Office, 1952.
————. *Population, 1960, Vol. I, Parts 1 and 2.* Washington, D.C.: Government Printing Office, 1963.
U.S. Census Office. *Agriculture, 1900, Parts I & II.* Washington, D.C.: U.S. Census Office, 1902.
————. *Fifteenth Census of the United States, 1930, Population, Vol. IV, Occupations by States.* Washington, D.C.: Government Printing Office, 1933.
————. *Population, 1920, Vols. II, III, and IV.* Washington, D.C.: Government Printing Office, 1922, 1923.

————. *Population, 1930, Vol. III, Part I.* Washington, D.C.: Government Printing Office, 1932.

————. *Population, 1940, Vol. II, Part I.* Washington, D.C.: Government Printing Office, 1943.

————. *Report on Cotton Production in the United States, 1880, Part II.* Washington, D.C.: Government Printing Office, 1884.

————. *Report on Manufacturing Industries in the United States, Eleventh Census, 1890, Part I.* Washington, D.C.: Government Printing Office, 1895.

————. *Report on Population of the United States, Eleventh Census, 1890, Part II.* Washington, D.C.: Government Printing Office, 1897.

————. *Report on the Manufactures of the United States, Tenth Census, 1880.* Washington, D.C.: Government Printing Office, 1883.

————. *Report on the Production of Agriculture, Tenth Census, 1880.* Washington, D.C.: Government Printing Office, 1883.

————. *Report on the Statistics of Agriculture, Eleventh Census, 1890.* Washington, D.C.: Government Printing Office, 1895.

————. *Report on the Statistics of Agriculture of the United States, Eleventh Census, 1890.* Washington, D.C.: Government Printing Office, 1895.

————. *Special Reports of the Census Office, Manufactures, Part II, States and Territories, 1905.* Washington, D.C.: Government Printing Office, 1907.

————. *The Statistics of the Population of the United States, Ninth Census, 1870, Vol. I.* Washington, D.C.: Government Printing Office, 1872.

————. *The Statistics of the Population of the United States, Tenth Census, 1880.* Washington, D.C.: Government Printing Office, 1883.

————. *Twelfth Census of the United States, 1900, Special Report, Occupations.* Washington, D.C.: Government Printing Office, 1904.

U.S. Department of Commerce. *Statistical Abstract of the United States.* Washington, D.C.: Government Printing Office, 1935.

U.S. Manuscript Census, Agriculture, 1860, for the following counties:

Calhoun	Jackson
Cherokee	Randolph
Covington	Winston

U.S. Manuscript Census, Agriculture, 1880, for the following counties:

Calhoun	Crenshaw
Cherokee	Geneva
Clay	Jackson
Cleburne	Randolph
Covington	Winston

U.S. Manuscript Census, Population, 1860, for the following counties:

Calhoun	Jackson
Cherokee	Randolph
Covington	Winston

U.S. Manuscript Census, Population, 1880, for the following counties:

Calhoun	Crenshaw

Cherokee   Geneva
Clay   Jackson
Cleburne   Randolph
Covington   Winston

U.S. National Emergency Council. *Report on Economic Conditions of the South.* Washington, D.C.: Government Printing Office, 1938.

NEWSPAPERS

Alabama Baptist, September 9, 1897.
Birmingham News, 1980–86.
Birmingham Post-Herald, 1980–86.
Dothan Eagle Centennial, November 11, 1985.
Huntsville Mercury, July 25, 1900.
Huntsville Mercury Centennial, May 1, 1912, and July 23, 1916.
Huntsville Telegram, March 1921.
Montgomery Workingmen's Advocate, March 2, 1879.
New York Times, 1981–86.
Opelika-Auburn News, 1980–86.
United Mine Worker's Journal, 1891.
Dill, Nelwyn H. "Monument to Willie." *Atlanta Weekly,* November 27, 1983.
Hughes, Langston. "An Open Letter to the South." *Southern Worker,* February 10, 1934.
Maharidge, Dale, and Michael Williamson. "The Same Road Taken." *Sacramento Bee Magazine,* September 28, 1986.
Raines, Howell. "Let Us Now Revisit Famous Folk." *New York Times Magazine,* May 25, 1980.

THESES AND DISSERTATIONS

Theses

Abernathy, John H., Jr. "The Knights of Labor in Alabama." M.A. thesis, University of Alabama, 1960.
Carmichael, Odelle. "A Decade of Aid to Dependent Children in Alabama." M.A. thesis, Tulane University, 1946.
Clinton, Matthew W. "Economic Conditions in Tuscaloosa City and County, 1865–1880." M.A. thesis, University of Alabama, 1942.
Crews, Elmer M., Jr. "Pentecostal Religion: The Social Origins of the Church of God." M.A. thesis, Auburn University, 1983.
Davis, Barbara J. "A Comparative Analysis of the Economic Structure of Mobile County, Alabama, Before and After the Civil War, 1860 and 1870." M.A. thesis, University of Alabama, 1963.

Dodd, Donald B. "Unionism in Northwest Alabama Through 1865." M.A. thesis, Auburn University, 1966.

Duke, Frank M. "The United Mine Workers of America in Alabama: Industrial Unionism and Reform Legislation, 1890–1911." M.A. thesis, Auburn University, 1979.

Edwards, Augustine D. "Economic and Social History of Benton County, Alabama." M.A. thesis, University of Alabama, 1941.

Elmore, Nancy R. "The Birmingham Coal Strike of 1908." M.A. thesis, University of Alabama, 1966.

French, Melodee Joy. "Farming in the New South: Agricultural Periodicals of Alabama, 1865–1880." M.A. thesis, Auburn University, 1985.

Goldstein, Harold J. "Labor Unrest in the Birmingham District, 1871–1894." M.A. thesis, University of Alabama, 1951.

Goodwin, Richard T., Jr. "A History of the Public Lands in Alabama to 1830." M.A. thesis, Auburn University, 1969.

Gross, Jimmie F. "Strikes in the Coal, Steel, and Railroad Industries in Birmingham from 1918 to 1922." M.A. thesis, Auburn University, 1962.

Head, Holman. "The Development of the Labor Movement in Alabama Prior to 1900." M.A. thesis, University of Alabama, 1955.

Hearn, Thomas K. "The Populist Movement in Marshall County." M.A. thesis, University of Alabama, 1935.

Holderfield, Horace M. "The Freedmen's Bureau in Alabama in 1865 and 1866." M.A. thesis, Auburn University, 1970.

Isbell, Frances A. "A Social and Economic History of Mobile, 1865–1875." M.A. thesis, University of Alabama, 1951.

Jennings, Knox G. "Almshouses in Alabama." M.A. thesis, Florida State University, 1964.

LeGrand, Phyllis LaRue. "Destitution and Relief of the Indigent Soldiers' Families of Alabama During the Civil War." M.A. thesis, Auburn University, 1964.

Martin, Henry P. "A History of Politics in Clay County During the Period of Populism from 1888 to 1896." M.A. thesis, University of Alabama, 1936.

Roush, Gerald L. "Aftermath of Reconstruction: Race, Violence, and Politics in Alabama, 1874–1884." M.A. thesis, Auburn University, 1973.

Rowe, Elizabeth. "Alabama's Disappearing Almshouses." M.A. thesis, Tulane University, 1946.

Rumph, John L. "A History of Bullock County, Alabama, 1865–1906." M.A. thesis, Auburn University, 1955.

Rutledge, Ray. "The Development of the Bankhead Farmsteads Community." M.S. thesis, Auburn University, 1951.

Schoonover, Shirley Garrett. "Alabama's Quest for Social Justice During the Progressive Era." M.A. thesis, Auburn University, 1970.

Stoddard, Sara E. O. "An Experiment in Progressivism: Alabama's

Crusade Against Peonage, 1900–1915." M.A. thesis, Auburn
University, 1979.
Taylor, S. M. "A Preliminary Survey of Folk-Lore in Alabama." M.A.
thesis, University of Alabama, 1925.
Thomas, Coburn H. "An Economic and Social History of Jackson
County." M.A. thesis, Auburn University, 1938.
Walls, Peggy G. "Folklore and Folk Life in Southern Literature." M.A.
thesis, Auburn University, 1985.
Wiginton, Dollie. "Some Social and Economic Factors in Southeastern
Alabama in 1860." M.A. thesis, University of Alabama, 1941.

Dissertations

Amos, Harriet E. "Social Life in an Antebellum Cotton Port: Mobile,
Alabama, 1820–1860." Ph.D. diss., Emory University, 1976.
Atkins, Leah Rawls. "Southern Congressmen and the Homestead Bill."
Ph.D. diss., Auburn University, 1974.
Daniel, Michael J. "Red Hills and Piney Woods: A Political History of
Butler County, Alabama, in the Nineteenth Century." Ph.D. diss.,
University of Alabama, 1985.
Gilmour, Robert A. "The Other Emancipation: Studies in the Society and
Economy of Alabama Whites During Reconstruction." Ph.D. diss.,
Johns Hopkins University, 1972.
Graves, Richard L. "Language Differences Among Upper- and Lower-
Class Negro and White Eighth Graders in East Central Alabama."
Ph.D. diss., Florida State University, 1967.
Harris, David A. "Racists and Reformers: A Study of Progressivism in
Alabama, 1896–1911." Ph.D. diss., University of North Carolina, 1967.
Hodges, James A. "The New Deal Labor Policy and the Southern Cotton
Textile Industry, 1933–1941." Ph.D. diss., Vanderbilt University, 1963.
LaMonte, Edward S. "Politics and Welfare in Birmingham, 1900–1974."
Ph.D. diss., University of Chicago, 1976.
Lofton, Bernadette K. "A Social History of the Mid-Gulf South (Panama
City–Mobile), 1930–1950." Ph.D. diss., University of Southern
Mississippi, 1971.
Massey, Richard W., Jr. "A History of the Lumber Industry in Alabama
and West Florida, 1880–1914." Ph.D. diss., Vanderbilt University,
1960.
Miller, Randall M. "The Cotton Mill Movement in Antebellum Alabama."
Ph.D. diss., Ohio State University, 1971.
Rikard, Marlene Hunt. "An Experiment in Welfare Capitalism: The
Health Care Services of the Tennessee Coal, Iron, and Railroad
Company." Ph.D. diss., University of Alabama, 1983.
Royce, Edward C. "Social Change and the Constriction of Possibilities:
The Rise of Southern Sharecropping." Ph.D. diss., State University of
New York at Stony Brook, 1983.

Shouse, Sarah Newman. "Herman Clarence Nixon: A Biography." Ph.D. diss., Auburn University, 1984.

Wyche, Billy H. "Southern Attitudes Toward Industrial Unions, 1933–1941." Ph.D. diss., University of Georgia, 1970.

BOOKS

Abernethy, Thomas P. *The Formative Period in Alabama, 1815–1828.* University: University of Alabama Press, 1965 reprint.

Adamson, Wendell M. *Income in Counties of Alabama, 1929 and 1935.* Tuscaloosa: Bureau of Business Research, School of Commerce and Business Administration, University of Alabama, 1939.

———. *Industrial Activity in Alabama, 1913–1932.* Tuscaloosa: Bureau of Business Research, University of Alabama, 1933.

Agee, James, and Walker Evans. *Let Us Now Praise Famous Men.* New York: Ballantine Books, 1973.

Alabama Farm Tenancy Committee. *Farm Tenancy in Alabama.* Wetumpka, Ala.: Wetumpka Printing Co., 1944.

Amos, Harriet E. *Cotton City: Urban Development in Antebellum Mobile.* University: University of Alabama Press, 1985.

Ashby-Macfayden, Irene M. *Child Labor in Alabama.* Document no. 1, Report of the Executive Committee of the State on the History of Child Labor Legislation in Alabama. Montgomery, July 1901.

Atherton, Lewis E. *The Southern Country Store, 1800–1860.* Baton Rouge: Louisiana State University Press, 1949.

Backman, Jules. *Bituminous Coal Wages, Profits, and Productivity.* Prepared for Southern Coal Producers Association, February 1950.

Bailey, Douglas F. *Devil Make a Third.* New York: E. P. Dutton and Co., 1948.

Bailey, Hugh C. *Edgar Gardner Murphy: Gentle Progressive.* Coral Gables: University of Miami Press, 1968.

Baldwin, Sidney. *Poverty and Politics: The Rise and Decline of the Farm Security Administration.* Chapel Hill: University of North Carolina Press, 1968.

Barnard, William D. *Dixiecrats and Democrats: Alabama Politics, 1942–1950.* University: University of Alabama Press, 1974.

Berney, Saffold. *Hand-Book of Alabama.* Birmingham: Roberts and Son, 1892.

Bernstein, Irving. *Turbulent Years: A History of the American Worker, 1933–1941.* Boston: Houghton Mifflin Co., 1970.

Bode, Frederick A., and Donald E. Ginter. *Farm Tenancy and the Census in Antebellum Georgia.* Athens: University of Georgia Press, 1986.

Boles, John B. *Black Southerners, 1619–1869.* Lexington: University Press of Kentucky, 1983.

Boyd, Minnie C. *Alabama in the Fifties: A Social History.* New York: Columbia University Press, 1931.

Brown, James Seay, Jr., editor. *Up Before Daylight: Life Histories from the Alabama Writers' Project, 1938–1939.* University: University of Alabama Press, 1982.

Browne, Ray B. *The Alabama Folk Lyric: A Study in Origins and Media of Dissemination.* Bowling Green, Ohio: Bowling Green University Popular Press, 1979.

――――. *"A Night with the Hants" and Other Alabama Folk Experiences.* Bowling Green, Ohio: Popular Press, n.d.

――――. *Popular Beliefs and Practices from Alabama.* Folklore Studies no. 9. Berkeley and Los Angeles: University of California Press, 1958.

Brunner, Edmund des. *Church Life in the Rural South.* New York: George H. Doran Co., 1923.

Burton, Orville V., and Robert C. McMath, Jr., eds. *Class, Conflict, and Consensus: Antebellum Southern Community Studies.* Westport, Conn.: Greenwood Press, 1982.

Campbell, Olive Dame. *The Life and Work of John Charles Campbell, September 15, 1868–May 2, 1919.* Madison, Wis.: N.p., 1968.

Carlton, David L. *Mill and Town in South Carolina, 1880–1920.* Baton Rouge: Louisiana State University Press, 1982.

Carmer, Carl. *Stars Fell on Alabama.* University: University of Alabama Press, 1985 reprint.

Carter, Dan. *Scottsboro: A Tragedy of the American South.* Baton Rouge: Louisiana State University Press, 1969.

Cason, Clarence. *90° in the Shade.* University: University of Alabama Press, 1983 reprint.

Clopper, Edward N., ed. *Child Welfare in Alabama: An Inquiry by the National Child Labor Committee Under the Auspices and with the Cooperation of the University of Alabama.* New York: National Child Labor Committee, 1918.

Cobb, James C. *Industrialization and Southern Society, 1877–1984.* Lexington: University Press of Kentucky, 1984.

Cobb, James C., and Michael V. Namorato, eds. *The New Deal and the South.* Jackson: University Press of Mississippi, 1984.

Collins, Bruce. *White Society in the Antebellum South.* New York: Longman Group, 1985.

Collins, Henry H. *America's Own Refugees: Our 4,000,000 Homeless Migrants.* Princeton: Princeton University Press, 1941.

Comer, Donald. *Braxton Bragg Comer: An Alabamian Whose Avondale Mills Opened New Paths for Southern Progress.* New York: Newcomen Society of England, American Branch, 1947.

Conrad, David E. *The Forgotten Farmers: The Story of Sharecroppers in the New Deal.* Urbana: University of Illinois Press, 1965.

Cowart, Margaret M. *Old Land Records of Jackson County, Alabama.* Huntsville, Ala.: N.p., 1980.

Currie, R. D. *Coal-Mine Safety Organizations in Alabama.* Technical Paper 489, Bureau of Mines, U.S. Department of Commerce (Washington, D.C.: Government Printing Office, 1931).

Curtis, Verna P., and Stanley Mallach. *Photography and Reform: Lewis Hine and the National Child Labor Committee.* Milwaukee: Milwaukee Art Museum, 1984.

Daniel, Pete. *Breaking the Land: The Transformation of Cotton, Tobacco, and Rice Cultures Since 1880.* Urbana and Chicago: University of Illinois Press, 1985.

————. *The Shadow of Slavery: Peonage in the South, 1901–1969.* London: Oxford University Press, 1973.

Darnton, Robert. *The Great Cat Massacre and Other Episodes in French Cultural History.* New York: Vintage Books, 1985.

DeCanio, Stephen. *Agriculture in the Postbellum South.* New Haven: Yale University Press, 1975.

Dodd, Donald B., and Wynelle S. Dodd. *Historical Statistics of the South, 1790–1970.* University: University of Alabama Press, 1973.

Elliott, Carl, Sr., and Susan Crittenden. *Alabama Coal Miners.* Vol. 1, *William T. Minor.* Jasper, Ala.: Northwest Alabama Publishing Co., 1977.

————. *Alabama Coal Miners.* Vol. 2, *Herbert South.* Jasper, Ala.: Northwest Alabama Publishing Co., 1978.

————. *Alabama Coal Miners.* Vol. 4, *Lester D. Williams.* Jasper, Ala.: Northwest Alabama Publishing Co., 1978.

————. *Alabama Coal Miners.* Vol. 5, *William M. Warren.* Jasper, Ala.: Northwest Alabama Publishing Co., 1979.

————. *Alabama Coal Miners.* Vol. 6, *Alfred J. Renshaw.* Jasper, Ala.: Northwest Alabama Publishing Co., 1979.

————. *Alabama Coal Miners.* Vol. 7, *Woodie Roberts.* Jasper, Ala.: Northwest Alabama Publishing Co., 1979.

Etheridge, Elizabeth W. *The Butterfly Caste: A Social History of Pellagra in the South.* Westport, Conn.: Greenwood Press, 1972.

Ettling, John. *The Germ of Laziness: Rockefeller Philanthropy and Public Health in the New South.* Cambridge, Mass.: Harvard University Press, 1981.

Federal Writers' Project. *These Are Our Lives.* Chapel Hill: University of North Carolina Press, 1939.

Fink, Gary M., and Merl E. Reed, eds. *Essays in Southern Labor History: Selected Papers, Southern Labor History Conference, 1976.* Westport, Conn.: Greenwood Press, 1977.

Fite, Gilbert C. *Cotton Fields No More: Southern Agriculture, 1865–1980.* Lexington: University Press of Kentucky, 1984.

Flynn, Charles L., Jr. *White Land, Black Labor: Caste and Class in Late Nineteenth-Century Georgia.* Baton Rouge: Louisiana State University Press, 1983.

Ford, Arthur M. *The Political Economics of Rural Poverty in the South.* Cambridge, Mass.: Ballinger Publishing Co., 1973.

Garrett, Mitchell B. *Horse and Buggy Days on Hatchet Creek.* University: University of Alabama Press, 1957.

Gates, Grace Hooten. *The Model City of the New South: Anniston, Alabama, 1872–1900*. Huntsville, Ala.: Strode Publishers, 1978.

Glymph, Thavolia, and John J. Kushma, eds. *Essays on the Postbellum Southern Economy*. College Station: Texas A&M University Press for the University of Texas at Arlington, 1985.

Going, Allen J. *Bourbon Democracy in Alabama, 1874–1890*. University: University of Alabama Press, 1951.

Goodwyn, Lawrence C. *Democratic Promise: The Populist Movement in America*. New York: Oxford University Press, 1976.

Hackney, Sheldon. *Populism to Progressivism in Alabama*. Princeton: Princeton University Press, 1969.

Hahn, Steven. *The Roots of Southern Populism: Yeoman Farmers and the Transformation of the Georgia Upcountry, 1850–1890*. Oxford: Oxford University Press, 1983.

Hamilton, Virginia Van der Veer. *Alabama: A Bicentennial History*. New York: W. W. Norton and Co., 1977.

———. *Lister Hill: Statesman from the South*. Chapel Hill: University of North Carolina Press, 1987.

Harrell, David E., Jr. *White Sects and Black Men in the Recent South*. Nashville: Vanderbilt University Press, 1971.

Harris, Carl. *Political Power in Birmingham, 1871–1921*. Knoxville: University of Tennessee Press, 1977.

Hart, Hastings H. *Social Problems of Alabama: A Study of the Social Institutions and Agencies of the State of Alabama as Related to Its War Activities*. Montgomery: State of Alabama, 1918.

Hawkins, Hiram. "Achievements of the Grange in the South." In A. E. Allen, *Labor and Capital*. Cincinnati: Central Publishing House, 1891.

Higgs, Robert. *Competition and Coercion: Blacks in the American Economy, 1865–1914*. Cambridge: Cambridge University Press, 1977.

Hill, Samuel S., ed. *Religion in the Southern States*. Macon, Ga.: Mercer University Press, 1983.

Hoffsommer, Harold. *Landlord-Tenant Relations and Relief in Alabama*. Research Bulletin, series 2, no. 9, Division of Research, Statistics and Finance, November 14, 1935.

Holmes, William F. "Moonshining and Law Enforcement in Turn of the Century Alabama." In *Perspectives on the American South: An Annual Review of Society, Politics and Culture*. Vol. 1. Edited by Merle Black and John Shelton Reed. New York: Gordon and Breach Science Publishers, 1981.

Hoole, W. Stanley. *Alias Simon Suggs: The Life and Times of Johnson Jones Hooper*. University: University of Alabama Press, 1952.

Hooper, Johnson J. *Adventures of Captain Simon Suggs Late of the Tallapoosa Volunteers Together with "Taking the Census" and Other Alabama Sketches*. Philadelphia: T. B. Peterson and Brothers, 1846.

———. *A Ride with Old Kit Kuncker and Other Sketches and Scenes of Alabama*. N.p., n.d.

Howard, Gene L. *Death at Cross Plains: An Alabama Reconstruction Tragedy.* University: University of Alabama Press, 1984.

Hubbs, G. Ward, collector. *Rowdy Tales from Early Alabama: The Humor of John Gorman Barr.* University: University of Alabama Press, 1981.

Hundley, Daniel R. *Social Relations in Our Southern States.* New York: Henry B. Price, 1860.

Hurst, Jack. *Nashville's Grand Ole Opry.* New York: Harry N. Abrams, 1975.

Jackson, Carlton. *The Dreadful Month.* Bowling Green, Ohio: Bowling Green University Popular Press, 1982.

Jackson, George P. *White Spirituals in the Southern Uplands: The Story of the Fasola Folk, Their Songs, Singings, and "Buckwheat Notes."* Chapel Hill: University of North Carolina Press, 1933.

Jent, J. W. *The Challenge of the Country Church.* Nashville: Sunday School Board, 1924.

Johnson, Charles S. *Statistical Atlas of Southern Counties.* Chapel Hill: University of North Carolina Press, 1941.

Johnson, Charles S., Edwin R. Embree, and W. W. Alexander. *The Collapse of Cotton Tenancy: Summary of Field Studies and Statistical Surveys, 1933–35.* Chapel Hill: University of North Carolina Press, 1935.

Jones, James H. *Bad Blood: The Tuskegee Syphilis Experiment—A Tragedy of Race and Medicine.* New York: Free Press, 1981.

Jones, Loyal. *Minstrel of the Appalachians: The Story of Bascom Lamar Lunsford.* N.p.: Appalachian Consortium Press, 1984.

Kaplan, A. D. H., et al. *Family Income and Expenditures in the Southeastern Region, 1935–36.* U.S. Department of Labor Bulletin no. 647, 1940.

Kennamer, John R. *History of Jackson County.* Winchester, Tenn.: Southern Printing Co., 1935.

Kolchin, Peter. *First Freedom: The Responses of Alabama's Blacks to Emancipation and Reconstruction.* Westport, Conn.: Greenwood Press, 1972.

Kousser, J. Morgan. *The Shaping of Southern Politics: Suffrage Restriction and the Establishment of the One-Party South, 1880–1910.* New Haven, Conn.: Yale University Press, 1974.

Kousser, J. Morgan, and James M. McPherson, eds. *Region, Race, and Reconstruction: Essays in Honor of C. Vann Woodward.* Oxford: Oxford University Press, 1982.

Lee, Harper. *To Kill a Mockingbird.* Philadelphia: J. B. Lippincott Co., 1960.

Lindsey, Bobby L. *"The Reason for the Tears": A History of Chambers County, Alabama, 1832–1900.* West Point, Ga.: Hester Printing Co., 1971.

Long, Campbell. *The House of Happiness.* Selma: Selma Printing Company, 1973.

Lyell, Sir Charles. *A Second Visit to the United States of North America.* 2 vols. New York: Harper and Brothers, 1850.

Maclachlan, Gretchen. *The Other Twenty Percent: A Statistical Analysis of Poverty in the South.* Atlanta: Southern Regional Council, December 1974.

McLaurin, Melton A. *The Knights of Labor in the South.* Westport, Conn.: Greenwood Press, 1978.

————. *Paternalism and Protest: Southern Cotton Mill Workers and Organized Labor, 1875–1905.* Westport, Conn.: Greenwood Press, 1971.

McMath, Robert C., Jr. *Populist Vanguard: A History of the Southern Farmers' Alliance.* Chapel Hill: University of North Carolina Press, 1975.

McMillan, Malcolm C. *The Disintegration of a Confederate State: Three Governors and Alabama's Wartime Home Front, 1861–1865.* Macon, Ga.: Mercer University Press, 1986.

Malone, Bill. *Country Music, U.S.A.* Austin: University of Texas Press, 1968.

————. *Southern Music/American Music.* Lexington: University of Kentucky Press, 1979.

————. *Stars of Country Music: Uncle Dave Macon to Johnny Rodriguez.* Urbana: University of Illinois Press, 1975.

Mandle, Jay R. *The Roots of Black Poverty: The Southern Plantation Economy After the Civil War.* Durham: Duke University Press, 1978.

Marshall, F. Ray. *Labor in the South.* Cambridge, Mass.: Harvard University Press, 1967.

Martin, Bessie. *Desertion of Alabama Troops from the Confederate Army: A Study in Sectionalism.* New York: AMS Press, 1966.

Masters, Victor I. *Country Church in the South.* Atlanta: Publicity Department of the Home Mission Board of the Southern Baptist Convention, 1916.

Mertz, Paul E. *New Deal Policy and Southern Rural Poverty.* Baton Rouge: Louisiana State University Press, 1978.

Mitchell, H. L. *Mean Things Happening in This Land: The Life and Times of H. L. Mitchell, Cofounder of the Southern Tenant Farmers Union.* Montclair, N.J.: Allanheld, Osmun, 1979.

Moore, Albert B. *History of Alabama.* Tuscaloosa: Alabama Book Store, 1951.

Moore, Glover, Jr. *A Calhoun County, Alabama, Boy in the 1860s.* Jackson: University Press of Mississippi, 1978.

Morley, Burton R. *Characteristics of the Labor Market in Alabama Related to the Administration of Unemployment Compensation.* University: Bureau of Business Research, University of Alabama, 1937.

Nesbitt, C. H. *Annual Reports of Coal Mines: State of Alabama, 1914.* Birmingham: State of Alabama, 1914.

Nixon, Herman C. *Forty Acres and Steel Mules.* Chapel Hill: University of North Carolina Press, 1938.

———. *Lower Piedmont Country: The Uplands of the Deep South.* University: University of Alabama Press, 1984 edition.

———. *Possum Trot: Rural Community, South.* Norman: University of Oklahoma Press, 1941.

Odum, Howard W. *Southern Regions of the United States.* Chapel Hill: University of North Carolina Press, 1936.

Olmsted, Frederick L. *A Journey in the Back Country.* New York: Mason Brothers, 1860.

———. *A Journey in the Seaboard Slave States, with Remarks on Their Economy.* New York: Dix and Edwards, 1856.

Palmer, Bruce. *"Man over Money": The Southern Populist Critique of American Capitalism.* Chapel Hill: University of North Carolina Press, 1980.

Perry, Charles S., and Christian Ritter. *Dying to Dig Coal: Fatalities in Deep and Surface Coal Mining in Appalachian States, 1930–1978.* Lexington: Department of Sociology, College of Agriculture, Agricultural Experiment Station, University of Kentucky, 1981.

Peterson, Richard A. "Single-Industry Firm to Conglomerate Synergistics: Alternative Strategies for Selling Insurance and Country Music." In *Growing Metropolis: Aspects of Development in Nashville.* Nashville: Vanderbilt University Press, 1975.

Pettit, Florence H. *How to Make Whirligigs and Whimmy Diddles and Other American Folkcraft Objects.* New York: Thomas Y. Crowell Co., 1972.

Phillips, Ulrich B. *Life and Labor in the Old South.* Boston: Little, Brown, and Co., 1929.

Phillips, William B. *Iron Making in Alabama.* University, Ala.: Geological Survey of Alabama, 1912.

Pope, Liston. *Millhands and Preachers: A Study of Gastonia.* New Haven, Conn.: Yale University Press, 1942.

Posey, Walter B. *Alabama in the 1830's as Recorded by British Travellers.* Birmingham: Birmingham-Southern College, 1938.

Preston, Dennis R. *Bituminous Coal Mining Vocabulary of the Eastern United States.* Publication of the American Dialect Society, no. 59, April 1973.

Ransom, Roger L., and Richard Sutch. *One Kind of Freedom: The Economic Consequences of Emancipation.* Cambridge: Cambridge University Press, 1977.

Risley, Eleanor De La Vergne. *The Road to Wildcat: A Tale of Southern Mountaineering.* Boston: Little, Brown, and Co., 1930.

Rogers, William W. *The One-Gallused Rebellion: Agrarianism in Alabama, 1865–1896.* Baton Rouge: Louisiana State University Press, 1970.

Ryan, Patricia. *Northern Dollars for Huntsville Spindles.* Huntsville, Ala: Huntsville Planning Department, Special Report no. 4, 1983.

Salmond, John A. *A Southern Rebel: The Life and Times of Aubrey Willis Williams, 1890–1965.* Chapel Hill: University of North Carolina Press, 1983.

Schwartz, Michael. *Radical Protest and Social Structure: The Southern*

Farmers' Alliance and Cotton Tenancy, 1880–1890. New York: Academic Press, 1976.

Shannon, Mary Lee Rice. *Poverty in Alabama: A Barrier to Post-Secondary Education.* Tuscaloosa: Institute of Higher Education Research and Services, 1976.

Shaw, Barton C. *The Wool Hat Boys: Georgia's Populist Party.* Baton Rouge: Louisiana State University Press, 1984.

Shumway, Harry I. *I Go South: An Unprejudiced Visit to a Group of Cotton Mills.* Boston: Houghton Mifflin Co., 1930.

Sims, George. *The Little Man's Big Friend: James E. Folsom in Alabama Politics, 1946–1958.* University: University of Alabama Press, 1985.

Solomon, Jack, and Olivia Solomon. *Cracklin' Bread and Asfidity.* University: University of Alabama Press, 1979.

———. *Ghosts and Goosebumps: Ghost Stories, Tall Tales, and Superstitions from Alabama.* University: University of Alabama Press, 1981.

Stambler, Irwin, and Grenlun Landon. "Hank Williams." In *Encyclopedia of Folk, Country and Western Music.* New York: St. Martin's Press, 1969.

Stewart, Mrs. Frank Ross. *Alabama's Cleburne County.* Centre, Ala.: Stewart University Press, 1982.

———. *Cherokee County History, 1836–1956.* Vols. 1 and 2. Birmingham: Birmingham Printing Co., 1958.

Stiles, Charles W. *Hookworm Disease (or Ground-Itch Anemia): Its Nature, Treatment and Prevention.* Washington, D.C.: Government Printing Office, 1910.

———. *Report on the Prevalence and Geographic Distribution of Hookworm in the United States.* Hygienic Laboratory Bulletin no. 10. Washington, D.C.: U.S. Public Health and Marine Hospital Service, 1903.

———. *Soil Pollution as a Cause of Ground Itch, Hookworm Disease, and Dirt Eating.* R.S.C. Publication no. 1. Washington, D.C.: R.S.C., 1910.

———. "Some Recent Investigations into the Prevalence of Hookworm Among Children." In *Child Conference for Research and Welfare, Proceedings, Volume II.* New York: G. E. Stechert and Co., 1910.

Suitts, Steve. *Patterns of Poverty: A Special Report of the Southern Regional Council, Inc.* Atlanta: Southern Regional Council, 1984.

Taft, Philip. *Organizing Dixie: Alabama Workers in the Industrial Era.* Edited by Gary M. Fink. Westport, Conn.: Greenwood Press, 1981.

Terry, Paul W., and Verner M. Sims. *They Live on the Land: Life in an Open-Country Southern Community.* University: University of Alabama, Bureau of Educational Research, Studies in Education no. 1, 1940.

Thompson, E. P. *The Making of the English Working Class.* New York: Pantheon Books, 1964.

Thompson, Wesley S. *"The Free State of Winston": A History of Winston County, Alabama.* Winfield, Ala.: Pareil Press, 1968.

Thornton, J. Mills, III. *Politics and Power in a Slave Society: Alabama, 1800–1860.* Baton Rouge: Louisiana State University Press, 1978.

Van Vorst, Mrs. John. *The Cry of the Children: A Study of Child Labor.* New York: Moffat, Yard and Co., 1908.

Wager, Paul W. *One Foot on the Soil: A Study of Subsistence Homesteads in Alabama.* Tuscaloosa: Bureau of Public Administration, University of Alabama, 1945.

Ward, Robert D., and William W. Rogers. *Convicts, Coal, and the Banner Mine Tragedy.* Tuscaloosa: University of Alabama Press, 1987.

———. *Labor Revolt in Alabama: The Great Strike of 1894.* University: University of Alabama Press, 1965.

Ward, Wyley D. *Early History of Covington County, Alabama: 1821–1871.* Huntsville, Ala.: N.p., 1976.

———. *The Folks from Pea Ridge in Covington and Conecuh Counties, Alabama.* Huntsville, Ala.: N.p., 1973.

Whisnant, David E. *All That Is Native and Fine: The Politics of Culture in an American Region.* Chapel Hill: University of North Carolina Press, 1983.

White, Marjorie L. *The Birmingham District: An Industrial History and Guide.* Birmingham: Birmingham Historical Society, the First National Bank of Birmingham, and the Junior League of Birmingham, 1981.

White, Newman I. *American Negro Folk-Songs.* Hatboro, Pa.: Folklore Associates, 1965.

Wiener, Jonathan. *Social Origins of the New South: Alabama, 1860–1885.* Baton Rouge: Louisiana State University Press, 1978.

Wigginton, Eliot, ed. *The Foxfire Book.* Garden City, N.Y.: Doubleday, 1972.

Wilhelm, Dwight M. *A History of the Cotton Textile Industry of Alabama, 1809–1950.* Montgomery: N.p., 1950.

Williams, Roger M. *Sing a Sad Song: The Life of Hank Williams.* New York: Ballantine Books, 1970.

Wilson, Charles M. *The Landscape of Rural Poverty: Corn Bread and Creek Water.* New York: Henry Holt and Co., 1940.

Wilson, Eugene M. *Alabama Folk Houses.* Montgomery: Alabama Historical Commission, 1975.

Woodman, Harold D. *King Cotton and His Retainers: Financing and Marketing the South's Cotton, 1800–1925.* Lexington: University Press of Kentucky, 1968.

Woodward, C. Vann. *Origins of the New South, 1877–1913.* Baton Rouge: Louisiana State University Press, 1951.

Wright, Gavin. *Old South, New South: Revolutions in the Southern Economy Since the Civil War.* New York: Basic Books, 1986.

———. *The Political Economy of the Cotton South: Households, Markets, and Wealth in the Nineteenth Century.* New York: Norton, 1978.

Wyatt-Brown, Bertram. "Religion and the Formation of Folk Culture: Poor Whites of the Old South." In *The Americanization of the Gulf Coast, 1803–1850,* edited by Lucius F. Ellsworth. Pensacola, Fla.: Historic Preservation Board, 1972.

PUBLISHED ARTICLES

Amos, Harriet E. " 'City Belles': Images and Realities of the Lives of White Women in Antebellum Mobile." *Alabama Review* 34 (January 1981): 3–19.

Anderson, Mary T. "Mountain People." *Tennessee Folklore Society Bulletin* 26 (December 1960): 87–91.

Ashby-Macfayden, Irene M. "The Fight Against Child Labor in Alabama." *American Federationist* 8 (May 1901): 150–57.

Atkins, Leah Rawls. "Felix Grundy McConnell: Old South Demagogue." *Alabama Review* 30 (April 1977): 83–100.

———. "Williamson R. W. Cobb and the Graduation Act of 1854." *Alabama Review* 28 (January 1975): 16–31.

Bailey, Hugh C. "Disaffection in the Alabama Hill Country, 1861." *Civil War History* 4 (June 1958): 183–93.

———. "Edgar Gardner Murphy and the Child Labor Movement." *Alabama Review* 18 (January 1965): 47–59.

"Birmingham: Smelting Iron Ore and Civics." *Survey* 27 (January 6, 1912).

Boyte, Harry. "The Textile Industry, Keel of Southern Industrialization." *Radical America* 6 (March–April 1972): 4–49.

Brauer, Carl M. "Kennedy, Johnson, and the War on Poverty." *Journal of American History* 69 (June 1982): 98–119.

Braunhut, Herman J. "Farm Labor Wage Rates in the South, 1909–1948." *Southern Economic Journal* 16 (October 1949): 189–99.

Campbell, Randolph B. "Population Persistence and Social Change in Nineteenth-Century Texas: Harrison County, 1850–1880." *Journal of Southern History* 48 (May 1982): 183–204.

"Census Records for Cherokee County, Alabama." *Cherokee County Heritage* 1 (January 1972): 28–32.

Cleveland, Gordon B. "Social Conditions in Alabama as Seen by Travellers, 1840–1850." Part 1, *Alabama Review* 2 (January 1949); 3–23; Part 2 (April 1949): 122–38.

Cobb, James C. "Muskogee to Luckenback: Country Music and the 'Southernization' of America." *Journal of Popular Culture* 16 (Winter 1983): 81–91.

Daniel, Pete. "The Transformation of the Rural South, 1930 to the Present." *Agricultural History* 55 (July 1981): 231–48.

Deford, Frank. "I Do Love the Football." *Sports Illustrated* 55 (November 23, 1981): 96–108.

———. "The Toughest Coach There Ever Was." *Sports Illustrated* 58 (April 30, 1984): 46–61.

Doster, James F. "Land Titles and Public Land Sales in Early Alabama." *Alabama Review* 16 (April 1963): 108–24.

Ford, Lacy K. "Rednecks and Merchants: Economic Development and

Social Tensions in the South Carolina Upcountry, 1865–1900."
Journal of American History 71 (September 1984): 294–318.

Gill, D. S. "How Alabama Meets Her Social Hygiene Problems." *Journal of Social Hygiene* 16 (1930): 530–31.

Gittler, Joseph B., and Roscoe R. Giffin. "Changing Patterns of Employment in Five Southeastern States, 1930–1940." *Southern Economic Journal* 11 (October 1944): 169–82.

Green, William. "Southern Labor at the Crossroads." *American Federationist* 37 (January 1930): 23–40.

Griffin, Richard W. "Poor White Laborers in Southern Cotton Factories, 1789–1865." *South Carolina Historical Magazine* 61 (January 1960): 26–40.

Gutman, Herbert G. "Black Coal Miners and the Greenback-Labor Party in Redeemer Alabama, 1878–1879." *Labor History* 10 (Summer 1969): 506–35.

Hall, Jacquelyn Dowd, Robert Korstad, and James Leloudis. "Cotton Mill People: Work, Community, and Protest in the Textile South, 1880–1940." *American Historical Review* 91 (April 1986): 245–86.

Hoffsommer, Harold. "The AAA and the Cropper." *Social Forces* 13 (May 1935): 494–502.

Holmes, William F. "Moonshiners and Whitecaps in Alabama, 1893." *Alabama Review* 34 (January 1981): 31–49.

———. "Whitecapping: Agrarian Violence in Mississippi, 1902–1906." *Journal of Southern History* 35 (May 1969): 165–85.

Hooper, William R. "The Freedmen's Bureau." *Lippincott's Magazine of Popular Literature and Science* 7 (June 1871): 609–16.

Ingalls, Robert P. "Antiradical Violence in Birmingham During the 1930s." *Journal of Southern History* 47 (November 1981): 521–44.

Johnson, Kenneth R. "The Peabody Fund: Its Role and Influence in Alabama." *Alabama Review* 27 (April 1974): 101–26.

Jones, Allen W. "Political Reforms of the Progressive Era." *Alabama Review* 21 (July 1968): 173–94.

Kaledin, Jonathan. "The Economic Consequences of the Civil War in Clarke County, Alabama." *Alabama Historian* 2 (Fall 1980): 11–13.

Keezer, Dexter M. "Low Wages in the South." *Survey* 57 (November 15, 1926): 226–28.

Kendrick, Alexander. "Alabama Goes on Strike." *Nation* 139 (August 29, 1934): 233–34.

Kiessling, O. E. "Coal Mining in the South." *Annals of the American Academy of Political and Social Science* 153 (January 1931): 84–93.

King, J. Crawford, Jr. "The Closing of the Southern Range: An Exploratory Study." *Journal of Southern History* 48 (February 1982): 53–70.

Lewis, Ronald L. "Job Control and Race Relations in Coal Fields, 1870–1920." *Journal of Ethnic Studies* 12 (Winter 1985): 35–64.

Locomotive Firemen's Magazine (February 1897): 125.

McConnell, Charles M. "Farm Tenants and Sharecroppers." *Missionary Review of the World* 60 (June 1937): 287–93.

McDonald, Forrest, and Grady McWhiney. "Celtic Origins of Southern Herding Practices." *Journal of Southern History* 51 (May 1985): 165–82.

———. The South from Self-Sufficiency to Peonage: An Interpretation." *American Historical Review* 85 (December 1980): 1095–1118.

McGuire, Robert, and Robert Higgs. "Cotton, Corn and Risk in the Nineteenth Century: Another View." *Explorations in Economic History* 14 (April 1977): 167–82.

McWhiney, Grady. "The Revolution in Nineteenth-Century Alabama Agriculture." *Alabama Review* 31 (January 1978): 3–32.

Malone, Ann Patton. "Piney Woods Farmers of South Georgia, 1850–1900: Jeffersonian Yeomen in an Age of Expanding Commercialism." *Agricultural History* 60 (Fall 1986): 51–84.

Mann, Susan A. "Sharecropping in the Cotton South: A Case of Uneven Development in Agriculture." *Rural Sociology* 49 (Fall 1984), 412–29.

Martin, Charles H. "Southern Labor Relations in Transition: Gadsden, Alabama, 1930–1943." *Journal of Southern History* 47 (November 1981), 545–68.

Mickle, Will. "Huntsville, Alabama: Cotton Textile Center of the New South." *Cotton History Review* 2 (1961): 92–102.

Miller, Randall M. "Love of Labor: A Note on Daniel Pratt's Employment Practices." *Alabama Historical Quarterly* 37 (Summer 1975): 146–50.

Mills, Gary B. "Miscegenation and the Free Negro in Antebellum 'Anglo' Alabama: A Reexamination of Southern Race Relations." *Journal of American History* 68 (June 1981): 16–34.

Mitchell, Broadus. "Why Cheap Labor Down South?" *Virginia Quarterly Review* 5 (October 1929): 481–91.

Moore, James T. "Redeemers Reconsidered: Change and Continuity in the Democratic South, 1870–1900." *Journal of Southern History* 44 (August 1978): 357–78.

Nelson, Daniel. "A CIO Organizer in Alabama, 1941." *Labor History* 18 (Fall 1977): 570–84.

Nixon, Herman C. "Changing Background of Southern Politics." *Social Forces* 11 (October 1932): 14–18.

Otey, Elizabeth L. "Women and Children in Southern Industry." *Annals of the American Academy of Political and Social Science* 153 (January 1931): 163–69.

Peterson, Richard A. "Has Country Lost Its Homespun Charm?" *Chronicle Review* (May 29, 1979): 22–24.

———. "The Production of Cultural Change: The Case of Contemporary Country Music." *Social Research* 45 (Summer 1978): 292–314.

"Pioneer Feast Time or Hog Killing in Cherokee." *Cherokee County Heritage* 2 (January 1973): 15–19.

Poindexter, W. G., Jr. "Sharecroppers in the South." *Southern Workman* 65 (April 1937): 118–26.

Reid, Joseph D., Jr. "Sharecropping as an Understandable Market
Response: The Post-Bellum South." *Journal of Economic History* 33
(March 1973): 106–30.

———. "Sharecropping in History and Theory." *Agricultural History* 49
(April 1975): 426–40.

Roberts, Frances C. "Politics and Public Land Disposal in Alabama's
Formative Period." *Alabama Review* 22 (July 1969): 163–74.

———. "William Manning Lowe and the Greenback Party in Alabama."
Alabama Review 5 (April 1952): 100–121.

Rodabaugh, Karl. "Agrarian Ideology and the Farmers' Revolt in
Alabama." *Alabama Review* 36 (July 1983): 195–217.

Schwenning, G. T. "Prospects of Southern Textile Unionism." *Journal of
Political Economy* 39 (December 1931): 738–810.

Shannon, David A. "The Fifty-First Annual Meeting." *Journal of Southern
History* 52 (May 1986): 218.

Sisk, Glenn. "The Poor in Provincial Alabama." *Alabama Historical
Quarterly* 22 (Spring and Summer 1960): 101–02.

"Soap Making Time." *Cherokee County Heritage* 1 (April 1972): 76.

Stark, Louis, "The Meaning of the Textile Strike." *New Republic* 58 (May
8, 1929): 323–25.

Stiles, Charles W. "Early History, in Part Esoteric, of the Hookworm
(Uncinariasis) Campaign in Our Southern United States." *Journal of
Parasitology* 25 (August 1939): 283–308.

Straw, Richard A. "The Collapse of Biracial Unionism: The Alabama Coal
Strike of 1908." *Alabama Historical Quarterly* 37 (Summer 1975): 92–
114.

———. "Soldiers and Miners in a Strike Zone: Birmingham, 1908."
Alabama Review 38 (October 1985): 289–308.

———. "The United Mine Workers of America and the 1920 Coal Strike
in Alabama." *Alabama Review* 28 (April 1975): 104–28.

Thornton, J. Mills III. "Alabama Politics, J. Thomas Heflin, and the
Expulsion Movement of 1929." *Alabama Review* 21 (April 1968): 83–
112.

Turner, James. "Understanding the Populists." *Journal of American
History* 67 (September 1980): 353–73.

Tutwiler, Mrs. Mary. "Mountain People." *Tennessee Folklore Society
Bulletin* 26 (December 1960): 86–88.

Twyman, Robert W. "The Clay Eater: A New Look at an Old Southern
Enigma." *Journal of Southern History* 37 (August 1971): 439–48.

Wallenstein, Peter. "Rich Man's War, Poor Man's Fight: Civil War and
the Transformation of Public Finance in Georgia." *Journal of Southern
History* 50 (February 1984): 15–42.

Wilgus, D. K. "Country-Western Music and the Urban Hillbilly." *Journal
of American Folklore* 83 (April–June 1970), 157–79.

Wilson, L. G., et al. "The Church and Landless Men." *University of
North Carolina Extension Bulletin* 1 (March 1, 1922): 8–10.

Woodman, Harold D. "Sequel to Slavery: The New History Views the

Postbellum South." *Journal of Southern History* 43 (November 1977), 523–54.

"Workers in Southern Manufactures." *American Federationist* 36 (May 1929): 588.

Worthman, Paul B. "Black Workers and Labor Unions in Birmingham, Alabama, 1897–1904." *Labor History* 10 (Summer 1969), 375–407.

Wyatt-Brown, Bertram. "The Antimission Movement in the Jacksonian South: A Study in Regional Folk Culture." *Journal of Southern History* 36 (November 1970), 501–29.

Yang, Donghyu. "Notes on the Wealth Distribution of Farm Households in the United States, 1860: A New Look at Two Manuscript Census Samples." *Explorations in Economic History* 21 (January 1984): 88–102.

INDEX

ABOUT THE AUTHOR

Wayne Flynt is Hollifield Professor of Southern History, Auburn University. He received his A.B. from Howard College (now Samford University) in Birmingham, Alabama, and his M.S. and Ph.D. from Florida State University, Tallahassee. From 1977 to 1985 he served as chairman of the Department of History, Auburn University. Among his publications are *Duncan Upshaw Fletcher: Dixie's Reluctant Progressive* (1971), *Cracker Messiah: Governor Sidney J. Catts of Florida* (1977), *Dixie's Forgotten People: The South's Poor Whites* (1979), *Montgomery: An Illustrated History* (1980), *Southern Poor Whites: A Selected Annotated Bibliography* (1981), and *Mine, Mill and Microchip: A Chronicle of Alabama Enterprise* (1987).